A Ben Jonson Companion

A Ben Jonson Companion

D. HEYWARD BROCK

INDIANA UNIVERSITY PRESS
BLOOMINGTON

THE HARVESTER PRESS
SUSSEX

This edition first published in the United States in 1983 by
INDIANA UNIVERSITY PRESS
Tenth and Morton Streets, Bloomington, Indiana
and in Great Britain by
THE HARVESTER PRESS LIMITED
Publisher: John Spiers
16 Ship Street, Brighton, Sussex

Manufactured in the United States of America

Library of Congress Cataloging in Publication Data

Brock, D. Heyward (Dewey Heyward), 1941-
  A Ben Jonson companion.

  Bibliography: p.
  1. Jonson, Ben, 1573?–1637—Dictionaries, indexes, etc.
I. Title.
PR2630.B7   1983   822'.3   81-48383
1 2 3 4 5 87 86 85 84 83

ISBN 0-253-31159-4

British Library Cataloguing in Publication Data

Brock, D. Heyward
  A Ben Jonson companion.
  1. Jonson, Ben—Criticism and interpretation
I. Title
822 .3   PR2638

ISBN 0-7108-0438-5

Contents

Preface

This book makes no pretense to be exhaustive on all matters relating to Jonson. Its primary purpose is to provide a convenient central reference and critical resource for important and useful information and criticism on Jonson's life, works, times, and critics. Modeled on F. E. Halliday's *A Shakespeare Companion,* this companion should fulfill a critical need for Jonsonian students and scholars. Since there is no Jonson handbook or companion now available and since Jonson is a seminal literary figure in the English Renaissance, the work should also appeal to all those interested in Renaissance studies in general. Unlike Halliday's book, this one does not include general entries on literary terms and history unless they are relevant to Jonson in some way—"War of the Theatres," for example. Since Jonson's canon is so diverse—plays, poems, masques, entertainments, inscriptions, a commonplace book, an English grammar—and his acquaintances, friends, and enemies so varied, the scope of the book is quite broad and far-ranging. Essentially, it has become a Jonson dictionary or encyclopedia, with entries listed alphabetically.

The entries for characters from the plays are fairly complete, but I have not included those who play no significant part in the action, who are used mainly to fill a scene. Characters from the masques and entertainments, who are usually symbolic anyway, are only included when they contribute in some way to the action or to the working out of ideas represented. I have included individual entries for the actors known to have played in the first performance of each play. I have, however, made no effort to identify the multitude of actors who have performed in Jonson's plays over the years. The stage history given for the individual plays is for the initial performance only, in so far as it can be ascertained or documented. A summary of the action is provided for each play, masque, and entertainment.

The entries for *Timber* and Drummond's *Conversations* essentially constitute a subject index to the most important topics dealt with in these works, with each subject entry providing a brief summary of Jonson's opinions, comments, or observations on the particular topic under consideration. There are entries under the title of the collection for each of Jonson's three collections of poems, and entries for his UNCOLLECTED VERSE, and POEMS ASCRIBED TO JONSON. Poems Jonson wrote to commemorate (or denigrate) others or their works and poems written by others to commemorate (or attack) Jonson or his works are discussed in the general entry COMMENDATORY POEMS. The major mythological and classical figures and places Jonson used are briefly identified, but for additional information on Jonson's uses of them one should consult C.F. Wheeler's *Classical Mythology in the Plays, Masques and Poems of Jonson* (Princeton, 1938) and Allan H. Gilbert's *The Symbolic Persons in the Masques of Ben Jonson* (Durham, N.C.: Duke University Press, 1948). The original participants in the masques and entertainments who are not elsewhere identified are listed in the entry MASQUERS AND TILTERS.

Many of the major allusions in Jonson's works are identified, but I have of necessity been very selective and highly subjective about entries of this kind. My guiding principle has been to include entries for those allusions that show us something about Jonson's opinions, sources, or influences or that reflect his awareness of contemporary affairs and attitudes. For example, I have made no effort to cite every one of Jonson's allusions to Homer, but I have summarized Jonson's observations on Homer recorded in *Timber* and Drummond's *Conversations* and identified most of his references to the ancient poet.

Critics included are primarily, although not exclusively, those twentieth-century scholars who, in my judgment, have made the most important contributions to Jonsonian scholarship. For those readers who wish to explore the scholarship itself, I have provided a selected bibliography at the end of the book.

Unless otherwise noted, references to and quotations from Jonson's works cited throughout this book are keyed to the Herford and Simpson edition of Jonson's complete works, to which edition I am heavily indebted.

In the preparation of this book I have also become indebted to many other scholars too numerous to cite although certainly not unappreciated. I am particularly grateful to Susan Davis, who served as my research assistant for two years and contributed substantially to the preliminary stages of the work, and to Deborah Lyall and Rita Beasley I owe eternal thanks for innumerable hours of expert typing from my inscrutable notes and tapes. Whatever deficiencies or imperfections this book has are the result of my own difficulties in performing the task I undertook and can in no way be attributed to all those who have so graciously assisted me along the way.

I am also indebted to my wife, Patricia, and my children, Michelle, Paul, and David, who patiently endured the task with me although my youngest never did fully understand why it took Daddy so long to make a book when he could easily put one together on a rainy afternoon with some scissors, a little paste, and a few magazine pictures.

D. H. B.

A Ben Jonson Companion

Abbreviations and shortened titles frequently used in the text are:

Conversations	William Drummond's memoranda of his conversations with Ben Jonson
Epig.	*Epigrams*
Every Man in	*Every Man in His Humour*
Every Man out	*Every Man out of His Humour*
For.	*The Forest*
Timber	*Timber, or Discoveries*
Und.	*The Underwood*

A

Accidence. A character in *The King's Entertainment at Welbeck* whose daughter Alphabet serves as one of the six bridal attendants for Pem.

Accius, Lucius (170–86 B.C.). Roman tragic poet and prose writer. He was greatly esteemed for his adaptations of Greek play cycles and his treatment of Roman subjects. In *Poetaster,* Ovid says that "Accius high-reard straine, / A fresh applause in everie age shall gaine" (i). Accius is also alluded to in Jonson's tribute to Shakespeare (i. 35) prefaced to the First Folio.

Achates. In mythology, a faithful companion of Aeneas'.

Achelous. A mythological river god who, in the form of a horned bull, fought with Hercules for the love of Deianira.

Acheron. A river of Thesprotia reputed to lead to Hades.

Achilles (Achilleus), son of the sea nymph Thetis and Peleus, king of Phthia, was educated by Phoenix and Chiron and was noted for both his valor and his fury.

aconite. Substance that sprang from the foam spilled from Cerberus' mouth during his strife with Hercules.

Acrisius. In Greek mythology, the king of Argos, Danaë's father, who locked Danaë up in a tower in order to keep her from bearing a son, who would, according to an oracle, kill Acrisius. In *Volpone* (v) Mosca says that Volpone's gold would have been powerful enough to get through Acrisius' guard.

Actaeon, son of Aristaeus and Autonoë. While hunting, he chanced upon Artemis bathing naked. The goddess turned him into a stag and he was killed by his own hounds.

acting, Jonson's. Although we do not know for certain how Jonson became involved in the acting profession, we do know that by 1597 he was playing in a strolling company of actors in London. Satirical allusions to Jonson's acting ability in Dekker's *Satiro-mastix* suggest that Jonson probably had a reputation for playing the hero's part in Kyd's *Spanish Tragedy*. It seems probable that he also played Zulziman in a lost play on an Eastern theme which was performed at Paris Garden, a bear-baiting pit refurbished as a theater and owned by Philip Henslowe. By July 1597 Jonson was identified not only as an actor but also as a playwright in Henslowe's employ. Although he was never a good actor, Jonson had several qualities which probably appealed to the audience of Paris Garden: a muscular, broad-shouldered figure; a loud voice; and, probably, great energy in action. By 1598 Jonson's reputation seems to have rested primarily upon his ability as a playwright, not as an actor.

acting companies. The London acting companies with which Jonson was associated were the Admiral's, the Chamberlain's, the King's, Lady Elizabeth's, Queen Henrietta Maria's, and a children's company, known successively as the Children of Her Majesty's (or Queen Elizabeth's) Chapel, the Children of the Queen's Revels, the Children of the Blackfriars, and the Children of the Whitefriars.

None of Jonson's extant plays was performed by the Admiral's Men although Jonson did apparently collaborate with Dekker and others on two lost tragedies played by that company—*Page of Plymouth* and *Robert II King of Scots.*

The Chamberlain's Men, the most important London company, performed *Every Man in,* with Shakespeare playing a leading role, and *Every Man out.* After 1603 the Chamberlain's Men were taken into the service of James I and became known as the King's Men. The King's Men performed more of Jonson's plays than any other company. They played the following: *Sejanus, Volpone, The Alchemist, Catiline, The Devil Is an Ass, The Staple of News, The New Inn,* and *The Magnetic Lady.*

Lady Elizabeth's Men were patronized by the daughter of James I, later Elizabeth of Bohemia. Her company performed *Bartholomew Fair* at the Hope Theatre in 1614. In 1625 the company was replaced by Queen Henrietta Maria's Men, who acted *A Tale of a Tub* in 1633.

The Children of the Chapel, who were part of the royal household, played *The Case Is Altered, Cynthia's Revels,* and *Poetaster.* After 1603 they were known as the Children of the Revels and performed *Eastward Ho* and *Epicoene.*

Adam de Alde-legh. Ancestor of Lady Digby's alluded to in "Eupheme" (*Und.* LXXXIV).

Adams, John. Clown who was a member of the Queen's Company with Richard Tarlton. In the Induction to *Bartholomew*

Fair, the stagehelper says he wishes that Tarlton were still alive, so he could caper with Adams in the play.

adaptations (plays). Three of Jonson's plays have been adapted, translated, or abridged. As might be expected, *Volpone* has proved to be the most popular work for adaptation and translation, although *Epicoene* too has been translated.

In 1793 Ludwig Tieck introduced his version of the play which was entitled *Herr von Fuchs. Ein Lustspiel in drei Aufzügen, nach dem Volpone des Ben-Jonson*. Émile Zola's adaptation, *Les Héritiers Rabourdin*, was a farce and a burlesque on *Volpone*. The play was performed unsuccessfully at the Théâtre Cluny in Paris in 1874, and an English version performed at the Independent Theatre in 1894 met the same fate. The adaptation by Stefan Zweig and Jules Romains was successfully played in 1928 at the Théâtre d'Atelier in Paris. In 1939 Zweig and Romains wrote the screenplay for the feature-length film of *Volpone*, directed by Maurice Tourneur, and starring Harry Baur and Louis Jouvet. *Sly Fox*, a 1976 film scripted by Larry Gelbart, directed by Arthur Penn, and starring George C. Scott and Trish Van Devere, was loosely based upon Zweig and Romains' adaptation.

Jean-Baptiste Rousseau's adaptation of *Epicoene*, entitled *L'Hypocondre, ou la femme qui ne parle point*, was published in 1751. In 1769 a Portuguese translation of the play was published and performed in Lisbon. Francis Gentleman's version, *The Coxcombs*, was published in 1771. In 1800 Ludwig Tieck published a close translation entitled *Epicoene oder Das stille Frauenzimmer. Ein Lustspiel in fünf Akten von Ben Jonson*. In 1921 E. and R. Blokh published a Russian translation at Petrograd, and Marcel Achard's adaptation called *La Femme Silencieuse de Ben Jonson* was acted at the Théâtre d'Atelier in Paris in 1926. An adaptation, *Lord Spleen*, by Hugo F. Köningsgarten was published in Berlin in 1930. Stefan Zweig's libretto for Richard Strauss's opera *Die schweigsame Frau: Komische Oper in 3 Aufzügen* was published in 1935 in Berlin.

Francis Kirkman's abridgment of *The Alchemist* was published in 1672, and from 1770 to 1815 Francis Gentleman's low-farce adaptation entitled *The Tobacconist* ran side by side with Garrick's performances of Jonson's original.

Addison, Joseph (1672–1719). Essayist, playwright, poet, and statesman, who is best known for his contributions to the *Spectator*. In the *Spectator*, No. 70, Addison wrote that Ben Jonson had said he would rather have been the author of Southwell's "Burning Babe" than of all his works, probably a distorted reflection of a comment about Southwell that Drummond of Hawthornden recorded in the *Conversations*.

Adonis. Son of Cinyras, king of Cyprus, by an incestuous union with his daughter Myrrha or Smyrna. Noted for his beauty, Adonis was beloved by Aphrodite.

Aeacus. Son of Zeus and Aegina, noted for his piety. Sometimes referred to as Eacus.

Aeglamour. "The sad" shepherd in Jonson's unfinished play *The Sad Shepherd*. He mourns for his love Earine, who he believes has drowned. He plans vengeance on the river in which she drowned and refuses to be comforted. Karolin is sent to watch out for him. Aeglamour believes that Douce, who wears Earine's clothes and (in F. G. Waldron's continuation of the play) uses Earine's voice when she sings through the tree, is Earine's ghost.

Aelianus, Claudius. Author of a *Tactica* (in Greek), probably in Trajan's reign. Jonson's library contained a heavily annotated seventeenth-century edition of the *Tactica* (Leyden, 1613). Aelianus is alluded to in *Und.* XLIV (1. 35).

Aeneas. In classical legend, in the *Iliad*, and in the *Aeneid*, Aeneas is a Trojan leader, the son of Anchises and Aphrodite. After the fall of Troy, he leaves Troy and wanders, finally reaching Italy and founding the city of Lavinium. In *Poetaster*, Ovid writes that the story of Aeneas will be read while Rome is master of the world (1.i). In *Timber* (11. 2359–62) Jonson cites Aeneas's inscription upon the hanging of the Arms of Abas as an example of a perfect poem.

Aenobarbus. A name meaning "red-beard." In *Poetaster* (III. iv) Tucca invites Histrio to dinner but cautions him not to bring his fellow player Aenobarbus, a fiddler who plays "villanous / ly / out-of-tune." Aenobarbus has been tentatively identified as a satirical portrayal of Cowley, a musician contemporary with Jonson.

Aeolus. The ruler of the winds who ties up the winds in a sack to keep them from blowing.

Aesculapius. Latinized name for Asclepius, hero and god of healing. In *Poetaster* (v. iii) Caesar tells Horace to be

Aesculapius for Crispinus and purge him of all the affected words he uses in his poetry. Later in the play, when Crispinus vomits up the outlandish words he favors, Horace says "thanks to . . . Aesculapius" (v. iii). In *Sejanus* (I. iii) Sejanus calls Eudemus "my Aesculapius."

Aeson. In mythology, Jason's father. His youth was renewed by Medea's magic. In *Volpone* (I) Volpone says that Corbaccio, like Aeson, seeks to have his youth restored.

Aesop. A sixth-century B.C. Greek compiler of animal fables. In *Poetaster,* Tucca invites Histrio to dinner, but cautions him not to bring his talkative, smelly friend Aesop (III. iv). In this play Aesop has been identified as a satirical portrait of either John Heminge or Shakespeare. Later in the play, Tucca mocks Equites, calling him "Master Aesope" (v. iii). Aesop's *Fables* are alluded to in *The Devil Is an Ass* (v. iv) and *The Staple of News* (I. ii).

Aethalides, Mercury's son and the herald of the Argonauts, had the gift of remembering everything. In *Volpone,* during their fooling, Nano, Androgyno, and Castrone claim him as the second owner of the soul of Pythagoras which passed through many transmigrations until it lodged happily in Androgyno (I. ii).

Aethiopia. A character in *The Masque of Blackness* who appears as the moon and helps beautify the daughters of Niger.

Aetna. Europe's highest active volcano.

Afer, Domitius. Crafty orator in *Sejanus,* who follows Sejanus in hope of getting power for himself. He speaks against Silius and Cordus and is mocked by the noble Romans although the others are impressed by his words. His name is not mentioned again in the play, although he may be present in the second Senate meeting.

affairs. In *Timber* (11. 28–32), Jonson begins his observations on this subject by noting that "In great *affaires* it is a worke of difficulty to please all." Later in *Timber* (11. 959–66), drawing on Seneca (*Epist.* CX. 3), he writes: "If wee would consider, what our affaires are indeed; not what they are call'd; wee should find more evils belong to us, then happen to us."

Affections. Four symbolic characters who appear in *Hymenaei* and attempt to disrupt the wedding ceremony.

affliction. In *Timber* (11. 182–83) Jonson includes a random note that affliction teaches a wicked person to pray, but prosperity never does.

Agamemnon. In Greek mythology, son of Atreus and brother of Menelaus and leader of the Greek forces against Troy. Agamemnon was murdered by his wife Clytemnestra.

Agape. A symbolic personage representing loving affection who appears in Jonson's part of the *King's Coronation Entertainment*.

Aglaia. A character symbolic of pleasant conversation who appears as one of the Graces and an attendant of Venus in *The Haddington Masque*.

Agrippa, Cornelius (1486–1535), of Nettesheim, was a soldier, physician, and reputed magician who served the emperor Maximilian. In *News from the New World*, Jonson alludes to Agrippa's *De occulta Philosophia* (1531), and much of the satire on lawyers and doctors in *Volpone* is borrowed from Agrippa's *De incertitudine et uanitate scientiarum* (1540?) and his *De Vanitate*.

Agrippa, M. Vipsanius (63–12 B.C.). Roman statesman and general, who commanded the Roman fleet at Actium in 31 B.C. In *Poetaster* (I. ii) Tucca fails to get money from Agrippa.

Agrippina. The noble, courageous widow of Germanicus in *Sejanus,* mother to Drusus junior, Nero, and Caligula. She is the center of opposition to the corrupt Tiberius and Sejanus, since her sons stand in line for the throne; Tiberius, Sejanus, and their followers fear and hate her. Noble Romans praise her throughout the play; Sejanus plots to make it look as though she is embroiled in treasonous plots. She expresses her proud disdain of Sejanus' spies to Silius and is amazed at Drusus senior's death. After Silius and Cordus are taken, she rages against the corrupt government and warns her friends to leave her for their own safety. She entreats her sons to be brave in the face of Sejanus' power. Late in the play, the news comes that she has been taken prisoner and confined at Pandataria.

Agrypnia. A symbolic personage representing vigilance who appears in Jonson's part of the *King's Coronation Entertainment*.

Aikenhead, David. Dean of Guild of the City of Edinburgh, whose accounts for 1618 show that Jonson was made a guild brother and issued a burgess-ticket.

Aiton, Sir Robert (1570–1638), secretary to Anne of Denmark, wife of James I, was an elegant poet. He is buried in Westminster Abbey. In the *Conversations* (1. 163), Jonson claimed Aiton loved him dearly.

Ajax, son of Telamon, was one of the bravest Greek warriors in the *Iliad.*

Albion. Ancient name for Great Britain.

Albius. A foolish jeweller in *Poetaster;* one of Jonson's typical foolish commoners, like the "citizen" in *Every Man in His Humour.* He is very excited when the courtiers come to visit Cytheris at his house; his fussing and over-concern with appearances angers Chloe, his wife, who despises him. He is easily bossed by her and does not notice that she is openly flirting with Crispinus. Against Chloe's wishes, he is brought to Ovid's masquerade as Vulcan, where he acts foolishly. Caesar upbraids him along with the others when he bursts into the masquerade.

Albricus. Author of *De Imaginibus Deorum* (1490) to which Jonson alludes in the *King's Entertainment in Passing to his Coronation* (Temple barre).

Alcaeus (fl. about 600 B.C.). Greek lyric poet who, according to Jonson's comments in *Timber* (11. 2475–82), was imitated by Horace. See HORACE.

Alcestis. See EURIPIDES.

Alchemist, The.

Acted: 1610 at the Globe by the King's Men.

Published: 1612 in quarto by Walter Burre.

Printer: Thomas Snodham.

Prologue: Jonson says that he will set his play in London, since his country is foremost in chicanery, and his play will be about tricksters and their vices. He laments that in England people allow corruption to thrive without attempting to check it, but says that he hopes his audience will be uncorrupted enough to enjoy seeing vice corrected in the play. Anyone who is guilty of the manners portrayed will be able to watch his play and not be embarrassed because of his method of presentation.

ACT I. Face, dressed in a captain's uniform, and Subtle argue, and from their argument the audience learns that Face, a butler, has taken Subtle into the house of his master, Lovewit, while Lovewit is away and that together they are tricking and cheating many people, posing as an alchemist and his assistant. Dol, their accomplice, settles the quarrel. Dapper, a lawyer's clerk, enters and, assuring Face that he comes in all sincerity, petitions Subtle for a familiar to aid him in gam-

bling. Subtle tells Dapper that he is a favorite of the Queen of Fairy and must bathe and perform various rituals before he may see her. Drugger, a tobacconist, enters and asks Subtle for advice in setting up his shop. Using much jargon, Subtle gives him advice and tells him to return later for more. Dol re-enters and says that Sir Epicure Mammon is coming; Subtle announces that this is the day he promised Mammon the philosopher's stone and mockingly lists all the deeds that Mammon has said he will do with it.

ACT II. Mammon enters, speaking to Surly, a gamester, of his impending good fortune. Surly is very skeptical and speaks mockingly to Mammon, who is thoroughly convinced of Subtle's authenticity. Face, now in the role of the servant, Lungs, meets them and tells Mammon that the stone will be ready by evening. Mammon gives a sensuous description of all the corrupt pleasures he will win for himself with the stone. Surly questions him, saying that he thought that only a pure man could obtain the stone. Mammon tells him that he is buying it from Subtle, whom he believes to be a very pious man. Subtle enters and cautions Mammon about being overly eager and corrupt. Subtle and Face speak in jargon about the stone's formation, with Surly breaking in with questions and comments. Mammon gives Subtle money. Surly launches into an extensive criticism of alchemy and its terminology, saying that it is only trickery. Dol appears, and Face explains her presence by saying that she is a lord's sister who falls into a fit at any discussion of theology and that she has been sent to him to be cured of her madness. Surly insists to Mammon that Subtle's house is a place of cheating and corruption and says that he plans to expose it as such. Surly leaves, and Mammon lingers to encourage Face to recommend him to Dol. After Mammon leaves, Subtle, Face, and Dol meet and discuss their plan to further entrap Mammon. The Anabaptist Ananias comes, and Subtle and Face greet him with a barrage of obscure terms. Ananias says that the Brethren will give him no more money until they see results in his research on the philosopher's stone. Subtle drives him out by abusing him verbally and bidding him send one of his superiors to apologize for his rashness. Drugger comes back, and Subtle makes a comic anagram of his name. Drugger then mentions that Pliant, a rich young widow, and her brother Kastril have vowed that she will not marry anyone of lower rank than a knight. He mentions that Kastril wishes to

4

learn to quarrel fashionably; Face encourages him to bring Kastril and Pliant to Subtle, who he says is an expert in such things.

ACT III. Tribulation, one of the Brethren, tells Ananias that they must bear with Subtle's corruption in order to employ his knowledge to do good works. They go to Subtle to make peace. Subtle at first acts angry, then is pacified by Tribulation's apology for Ananias and his offer of more money. Ananias continues to inveigh against Subtle, so Subtle again has to be calmed by Tribulation. Subtle tells them that the stone will soon be done and that if they need money, they can obtain it by counterfeiting Dutch dollars.

There is a difference of opinion between the two Brethren as to whether such coining—even of foreign currency—is lawful, and they depart to lay the question before the Brethren. Meanwhile, although Face has been unable to find Surly, he has met a noble count, a don of Spain, who is coming to the house under the pretext of taking Subtle's curative baths but actually to visit Dol.

Soon other clients arrive. The angry boy (Kastril) goes with Drugger to get his sister, but when Kastril learns how successful Subtle has been in making matches all over England the way seems momentarily clear for Dapper, who is now ready to meet the Queen of Fairy (alias Dol). Dapper is blindfolded, bound, and pinched by the fairies while they pick his pockets. Before Dapper can meet the Queen, Mammon knocks at the door. Dapper is told not to speak for two hours, is gagged with a piece of gingerbread, and is locked in the privy.

ACT IV. Cautioning Mammon that Subtle cannot tolerate the least act of sin and that the scholarly lady can discourse on any subject provided that no word of theological controversy is introduced to bring on her madness, Face, now in the role of Lungs, introduces Mammon to Dol. Changing roles again, Face joins Subtle in receiving Dame Pliant and Kastril, but they are all shortly interrupted by the arrival of the solemn Spaniard—Surly in disguise. Since the Spaniard doesn't speak English, Face and Subtle insult him in various ways and assure him that he shall be milked before he leaves. Since Dol is already busy, the don is introduced to Dame Pliant, and the two are left in the garden while Subtle gives Kastril a lesson in quarreling.

Meanwile, the rendezvous between Mammon and the learned lady has gone awry because Mammon has inadvertently alluded to the philosopher's stone, and the learned lady has lapsed into violent madness. Face, as Lungs, tries to quiet the couple, and Subtle discovers their "deeds of darkness" and proclaims that work on the philosopher's stone will be retarded for a month. Suddenly, the alchemical apparatus explodes: all has been ruined because of Mammon's voluptuous mind. Concurrently, Surly has revealed the sham to Dame Pliant and seriously proposed marriage to her. Denouncing Face and Subtle, Surly throws off his disguise and exposes their scheme while Face tells Kastril that here is his chance to quarrel, that Subtle and Dame Pliant, expecting a real Spanish Count, have been deceived by an impostor employed by a competitor. Kastril, however, will neither fight nor be convinced by Surly that Face and Subtle are rascals. Drugger arrives, as does Ananias with word that the Brethren have concluded that coining money is lawful. Offended by the Spaniard's ostentatious dress, the Anabaptist, with the aid of Face, is able to turn Surly out of the house, but this triumph is short-lived. Dol announces that Lovewit has come home.

ACT V. Talking to his neighbors, Lovewit hears reports about the various sorts of men and women who have flocked to his house the past few weeks, and he is about to break down the door when Jeremy (Face), the butler, appears. Jeremy tries to face down the neighbors and nearly succeeds, but Surly and Mammon return, calling for the rogues and cheaters. Kastril demands his sister, and Ananias and Tribulation beat on the door. All leave in search of officers of the law, as the neighbors recognize some of the people as the ones they have seen at the house in the past few days. Inside, the gingerbread having melted, Dapper calls for the Queen of Fairy. Jeremy realizes he is trapped. Lovewit promises to be indulgent if Jeremy will make a clean breast of everything and help his master to gain a rich widow as Jeremy has said he can do if the master will allow him to work things out in his own way.

Accordingly, Dapper finally is allowed to meet the Queen of Fairy and is satisfied. Hopeful of marrying the widow, Drugger brings a Spanish costume and is sent out to get a parson. In preparation for flight, Subtle and Dol quickly pack the booty, but Face, who holds the keys, claims everything for his master, and with officers pounding on the door, the two are glad just to escape, even though empty-handed. Meanwhile, Lovewit has assumed Drugger's Spanish dress and married Dame Pliant, thus triumphing over both Drugger and Surly. Lovewit permits the officers brought by the angry Mammon, Ananias, and Tribulation to search the house, but the rogues have fled. Lovewit demands a certificate of how the gulls were taken before he will return any goods they claim, and they all depart empty-handed, leaving only Kastril, who does not wish to fight since he is happy with the fine match his widowed sister has made with Lovewit, who compliments him. Face, having outwitted all with whom he traded and pleased his master in the process, throws himself upon the mercy of the audience for their approval.

Alchindus. Abu Yūsuf Al Kindi, often called "the philosopher of the Arabs" (fl. 9th Century A.D.). He was one of the first Arabs to study the Greek philosophers and may have written as many as two hundred books covering the range of the sciences. Jonson alludes to his work on palmistry in *The Gypsies Metamorphosed.* The palmistry work was much read during the Renaissance.

Alchorne, Thomas. Bookseller in London from 1627 to 1639 who in 1631 published in octavo *The New Inn.*

Alcibiades (450–404 B.C.). Athenian general and statesman, known for his brilliance and egotism. In *Poetaster* (I. ii) Tucca calls Ovid "my pretty Alcibiades."

Alcides. Another name for Heracles, the most popular and widely worshipped of Greek heroes. His wife, Deianira, unwittingly sent him a poisoned robe. In *Poetaster* (III. ii) Horace refers to this incident when he says that Crispinus "cleaves to [him] like Alcides shirt." In *Sejanus* (IV. vii) Arruntius calls Sejanus Alcides when entreating him to send his club to halt the injustices in contemporary Rome.

Alcyone. One of the seven Pleiades, the daughters of Atlas.

Alecto. One of the Furies.

Alençon, Francis, Duke of (afterwards Duke of Anjou). One of Queen Elizabeth's suitors. In 1572 he sent the queen a love letter and subsequently paid three visits to England to court her. His last visit, in 1579, was often referred to as if the date marked the end of an era. Jonson alludes to this visit in the *Conversations* (1. 344), *Mercury Vindicated,* and the Induction to *Cynthia's Revels.* The duke came to be known in England by the nickname "Mon-

sieur," from the queen's habit of calling him that.

Alewife, Lady. A brewery worker from St. Katharine's who appears in *The Masque of Augurs* and, together with her cohorts, wants to present a masque before the court.

Alexander the Great (356–323 B.C.), became king of Macedon when he was twenty. Tutored by Aristotle, he showed great intellectual prowess. After he became king, he emerged as a great military leader and tried to create and rule a world empire. He ended forever the autonomy of the Greek city-states and spread Greek culture throughout the East. In *Timber* (11. 1259–61), Jonson, in the course of discussing the responsibilities of the prince, notes that Alexander was said to have commented that he hated the gardener who pulled his herbs or flowers up by the roots. Later in *Timber* (11. 1579–80) Jonson mentions that the ancient painters Zeuxis and Parrhasius were contemporaries during the time of Philip, the father of Alexander. (Actually, Zeuxis was not a contemporary of Philip's; Jonson is in error.) See also CESTIUS.

Alexander, Walter. Gentleman usher to Prince Charles who was responsible on at least three occasions between 1617 and 1620 for conveying messages from the Prince to Jonson.

Alexander, Sir William, Earl of Stirling. Author of four *Monarchick Tragedies* on classical themes, Alexander was created Earl of Stirling by Charles I. In the *Conversations* (11. 161–62), Drummond records that Jonson said that Alexander was not kind to him because Alexander was Drayton's friend.

Alice. A prostitute who appears once in *Bartholomew Fair.* She rushes in to beat up Mrs. Overdo, whom she mistakes for a rich prostitute who is stealing her trade.

Alken. "The Sage" shepherd in *The Sad Shepherd.* He is learned in lore about witches and comments on the ominous raven met by Marion's hunting party. He describes himself as a "feeble eld." Both when Maudlin appears as Marion and when she comes as herself to curse the cook, he is present and comments on her powers of deception. He is one of the witchhunters and gives much learned advice to the party about catching Maudlin.

allegory. See STYLE.

Allestree, Richard, of Derby, A maker of almanacs from 1624 to 1643, is alluded to in *The Magnetic Lady* (IV. ii).

6

Alleyn, Edward (1566–1626), a famous actor. In 1583 he was a member of a provincial company of actors of the Earl of Worcester, but soon after he joined the Admiral's Company, of which his brother John was already a member. In 1592 he married Joan Woodward, who was Henslowe's stepdaughter, and Alleyn and Henslowe formed a partnership that lasted until Henslowe's death in 1616. From 1594 to 1597 Alleyn was with the Admiral's Men at Henslowe's Rose; then he left acting for a brief period but returned in 1600 to the Fortune, which he and Henslowe had built. In 1603 the Admiral's became Prince Henry's Men, and Alleyn, as their leader, delivered an address to James I apostrophizing him the Genius of the City. By 1604 Alleyn was a wealthy man; he retired and in 1605 bought the manor of Dulwich upon which he built a college that was opened in 1619. When Alleyn's wife died in 1623, he married Constance, the daughter of John Donne.

There are numerous records of Alleyn's genius as an actor, and we know that he played Tamburlaine, Faustus, and Barabbas in Marlowe's plays and numerous other roles. He apparently also encouraged writers of promise, and in 1602 Henslowe recorded in his diary lending Ben Jonson money to write additions to plays, with Alleyn being mentioned as one of those who would guarantee that the works would be completed by the playwright. In *Epig.* LXXXIX, "To Edward Allen," Jonson praised Alleyn for bringing the work of so many poets to life in his acting.

Allin, John. According to Jonson, a tenor in the service of Queen Anne who sang some of the songs in *The Masque of Queens.*

Allin (Allen or Alleyn), Richard. An actor who was one of the Children of the Queen's Revels when he played in *Epicoene* in 1609. In 1613 he joined the Lady Elizabeth's Men.

Allobroges. In *Catiline,* foreign ambassadors who help Cicero gather documentary evidence of Catiline's conspiracy for the Senate.

Allot, Mary, widow of Robert Allot, was a bookseller in London from 1635 until 1637, when she transferred her copyrights to John Legatt and Andrew Crooke. Included in this transaction were the copyrights to *Bartholomew Fair, The Devil Is an Ass,* and *The Staple of News.*

Allot, Robert. Bookseller in London from 1625 to 1635, who in 1631 published *Bartholomew Fair, The Devil Is an Ass,* and *The Staple of News.*

Almanac. In *The Staple of News,* a doctor of physic who is one of the suitors to Lady Pecunia.

Alphabet. A character in *The King's Entertainment at Welbeck* who is the daughter of Accidence and serves as one of the bridal attendants for Pem.

Alpheus. Largest river of the Peloponnesus, whose waters were fabled to pass unmixed through the sea and to rise in the fountain Arethusa at Syracuse.

Amadis de Gaule. The most important of the old romances of chivalry, the first edition of which was printed at Saragossa in 1508. A translation by Anthony Munday was published in 1590. Jonson had only contempt for the work, as can be seen in *Epicoene* (IV. i), *The Alchemist* (IV. vii), *The New Inn* (I. vi), and *Und.* XLIII.

Amalasunta. According to Jonson, Queen of the Ostrogoths and daughter of Theodoric. She appears as one of the virtuous queens in *The Masque of Queens.*

Amaltei, Girolamo. Minor poet from whose *Horologium Pulverum* Jonson borrowed for his "Hour-glasse" (*Und.* VIII).

Amazons. Mythical tribe of female warriors who fought on the Trojans' side in the Trojan War.

Ambler. 1. A groom who appears in *The Staple of News.*

2. The gentleman-usher to Lady Tailbush in *The Devil Is an Ass.*

Amboyna. A Dutch castle in the Moluccas, where ten Englishmen were tortured and executed in 1623 for allegedly plotting to seize the castle. The news of this massacre reached England in 1624. In 1625 the Dutch government promised to bring the perpetrators to trial but did not; the promise was renewed in 1628 after some Dutch ships had been seized and restored. This episode is referred to in *The Staple of News* (III. ii).

Ambrose, Saint (c. 340–397). The son of a prefect of Gaul, Ambrose became Bishop of Milan. He combined a Stoic background with Christian faith and eventually developed into one of Christendom's most famous bishops, administrators, and preachers. He also wrote hymns. He converted many to Christianity, his most famous convert being Augustine. Jonson quotes briefly from Ambrose's *Epistles* at the end of *Poetaster* and alludes to his *De Officiis* in *Volpone* (II. i).

ambrosia and nectar. The food and drink of the gods.

Ambry (Ambree), Mary. An unhistorical character in Percy's popular ballad *The valorous acts performed at Gaunt by the brave bonnie lass Marye Aumbree.* Her name became associated with "Amazon" or "virago." She is alluded to in *Epicoene* (IV. ii) and *Tale of a Tub* (I. iv). She appears as a character in the antimasque for *The Fortunate Isles.*

Amie. "The Gentle" shepherdess in *The Sad Shepherd,* sister to Lionel. She mourns Earine's death and Aeglamour's mourning with the rest of the company. Aeglamour forces her to kiss Karolin after Karolin sings, and she falls ill of lovesickness for Karolin. She is oblivious to the comfort Marion and Mellifleur try to give her.

Amorphus. A foolish traveling courtier in *Cynthia's Revels.* He drinks from the fountain of self-love and praises himself after Echo runs away from him. Crites mocks him and introduces Asotus to him; he worries about how to make the best superficial impression on Asotus. He and Asotus become friends; he speaks about his travels in fantastic stories, and Asotus vows to be tutored in the "science" of courtiership by him. He mocks all kinds of men, especially serious scholars, when teaching Asotus what expression to keep on his face. Mercury mocks his shallow concern with being fashionable to Cupid. He teaches Asotus the proper way to accost a lady. He plays the games of wit with the other courtiers. Phantaste praises him, but the other ladies mock him; he brings water from the fountain of self-love to the other courtiers and tells them an unbelievable story of how he was feasted by many important nobles and how a king's daughter died of lovesickness for him. He sings a courtly song and invents the idea for the courtship contest so that his pupil, Asotus, can show off his skill. He is challenged during the contest instead, is defeated, and is disgraced by Mercury. He takes part in the second masque; Cynthia realizes that he is corrupt and sentences him to be punished at Crites' discretion. He marches, weeps, and sings the palinode with the other courtiers.

Amphion, one of the twin sons of Zeus and Antiope, was so great a harper that his music could draw stones into place.

Amphitrite, the wife of Neptune (although Jonson incorrectly calls her the wife of Oceanus), appears leading the triumph in *Love's Triumph Through Callipolis.*

Amphitryo. According to the *Conversations* (11. 420–23), a play Jonson intended to write modeled on Plautus, but he abandoned the project.

Anabaptists. The name applied scornfully to certain Christian sects that believed in adult baptism and the baptism of believers only. Prominent in Europe in the sixteenth century, the Anabaptists were persecuted everywhere. They believed in the separation of church and state, stressed individual conscience and inspiration, and held the church to be a voluntary association of believers. Martin Luther considered them enemies of the Reformation. About 1533 some Anabaptists established a theocracy in Münster, first under the direction of the preacher Bernard Rothmann, then under the fanatical Dutch banker Jan Matthys and Bernhard Knipperdollinck. In 1534 John of Leiden proclaimed himself King David and ruled this theocracy in which communal ownership and polygamy were practiced, but this radical form of Anabaptism ended in 1535 when the leaders were executed. The Mennonites and the Hutterites are later descendants of other branches of the Anabaptists. Ananias in *The Alchemist* (II. iv) is an Anabaptist, and they are referred to in *Eastward Ho* (v. ii) and *Epicoene* (III. ii).

Anacreon (born c. 570 B.C.). Greek lyric poet. He traveled widely, founding and fighting for the colony of Abdera in Thrace, serving the tyrant Polycrates at Samos as a music tutor and court poet, writing poems for Thessalian royalty, and visiting Athens. His poetry deals mostly with pleasure and is characterized by his use of the Ionic vernacular and his good-natured use of wit and fancy. Daw dismisses Anacreon as worthless along with many other ancient authors in *Epicoene* (II). Jonson alludes to him in "Ode to Himself" written after the failure of *The New Inn,* in *The Fortunate Isles,* in *Cynthia's Revels* (v. iv), and in *Volpone* (II. iv). In *Timber* (11. 2414–15), Jonson alludes to Seneca's comment that, according to Anacreon, it is pleasant to be frenzied at times—meaning filled with poetical rapture. The most skillful imitator of Anacreon was the seventeenth-century poet Robert Herrick.

anagram. Rearrangement of letters or words to make other letters or words. According to Drummond in the *Conversations* (11. 437–39), Jonson scorned anagrams, but he used them in *Hymenaei* and *Prince Henry's Barriers*.

Anaides. A foolish gallant in *Cynthia's Revels* who was supposedly intended to represent Thomas Dekker. Mercury calls him "impudent" and mocks him for his slavish attachment to fashion and for his shallow interest in only material things. Anaides mocks Crites and is angry when Crites is not insulted by his snub. Moria favors Anaides, who flirts with the ladies. He plays the games of wit and drinks from the fountain of self-love with the others. He is present at the courtship contest and is mocked and made to leave in disgrace by Crites at the end of it. He takes part in the second masque, but Cynthia discovers him and allows Crites to decide his punishment. He marches, weeps, and sings the palinode with the other courtiers.

Ananias. In *The Alchemist,* a deacon of the Brethren of Amsterdam, an Anabaptist sect. He is sent to Subtle to ask for some proof that the Brethren's investment is going to pay off before they invest more money. Subtle flies into a rage and drives him out; Ananias returns with Tribulation to ask pardon but gives continual evidence of his blind zeal and his foolishness. He is drawn into a plot to counterfeit Dutch money and is later convinced by Face to abuse Surly. When Lovewit returns, Ananias comes to take back his money but is driven away, raving about the lost wealth and Subtle's corruption.

ancients. See AUTHORITY.

Androgyno. In *Volpone,* Volpone's hermaphrodite.

Andromeda. Daughter of Cepheus, king of the Ethiopians, who was saved by Perseus from a sea monster.

Aneau, Barthélemi. Born at Bruges, Aneau was a professor of rhetoric at Trinity College, Lyons, in 1530 and principal in 1542. Aneau translated More's *Utopia* in 1549 and published *Picta Poësis* in 1552, from which Jonson adapted *For.* VII.

Angel. A symbolic character who appears in the Barriers for *Hymenaei* and announces the arrival of Truth.

Angelo. A young man, friend to Paulo in *The Case Is Altered.* Paulo confides his love for Rachel to Angelo and asks him to be Rachel's guardian in Paulo's absence. Angelo has a reputation for being a rake; he flirts with the spirited Aurelia, daughter of Count Ferneze, and the count warns his daughters away from him. Angelo decides to betray Paulo's trust and woo Rachel for himself but is twice frightened off by her father. Learning of of Christophero's love for Rachel, he plots with Christophero to lure Jaques away from his daughter with a trail of gold, then double-crosses Christophero by tricking Rachel into going to an isolated spot with him. He assaults her but is beaten away by Paulo, who passes by just in time on his return from captivity. Angelo is forgiven and accompanies Paulo to the count's, where he is only a little disappointed when, after her true identity is revealed, Rachel is betrothed to Paulo.

Anna Parenna. A Roman goddess of uncertain attributes whose festival was on March 15, the first full moon of the year by the old reckoning.

Annandale. Region in the Scottish lowlands. Jonson told Drummond in the *Conversations* (11. 234–35) that he thought his grandfather originally came from Annandale but moved to Carlisle.

Anne of Denmark (1574–1619), queen of James I of England, was the daughter of Frederick II of Denmark and Norway. She married James in 1589 and was crowned with him in 1603. Although not openly Catholic, she attended mass privately and refused communion in the Church of England. Of her six children, the only three to survive infancy were Henry, prince of Wales (d. 1612); Charles (later Charles I); and Elizabeth (later Electress Palatine and Queen of Bohemia). During her reign Anne was more interested in the embellishment of buildings and court entertainments than affairs of state.

Jonson was called upon to provide entertainments for the King and Queen at Althorp (1603), at Highgate (1604), and at Theobalds (1607). The queen is also mentioned in the *King's Coronation Entertainment* (1603). *The Masque of Blackness* (1605), *The Masque of Beauty* (1608), and *The Masque of Queens* (1609) were all written at Anne's request, and she performed as the leading masquer in each one. She also danced in *Love Freed.* In 1608 Jonson presented the Queen a gift copy of the *Masques of Blackness and Beauty* with a Latin dedication. Jonson alludes to Anne in his "An Expostulation with Inigo Jones." In an extant letter of 1619 to William Drummond he mentions his part in the funeral preparations for the queen and that he wrote an elegy for her, but either he never finished the work or it has been lost.

Antaeus. A giant, son of Poseidon and Earth, who compelled strangers to wrestle with him and then killed them when they were overthrown. Antaeus was eventually defeated and killed by Hercules.

Anteros. 1. A character in *Love's Welcome at Bolsover* who is the son of Venus and the brother of Eros.

2. Cupid's double, who was created when Themis advised Venus that Cupid would not prosper without a companion. See also Cupid.

antimasque. A grotesque and often humorous dance, one or more of which were sometimes interspersed with the serious actions and dances of the masque proper. The antimasque was usually performed by professional actors and dancers whereas the masque proper was often performed by courtly amateurs. Although masque writers before Jonson had used the antimasque, Jonson is usually credited with developing the antimasque as a meaningful element in the masque itself. Jonson first formally introduced the antimasque in his shows in the *Masque of Queens*. As he explained in the preface to the work, his idea was to create a foil to the real masque, a foil that would delay the actual masque and thus by suspense contribute to the wondrous effect of the masque and at the same time, because of the grotesqueness or strangeness of the antimasque, enhance the beauty and appeal of the main masque by contrast.

Whether Jonson developed the idea himself or borrowed it entirely from previous masques on the continent is not known, but one point is clear: Jonson developed the poetic possibilities of this technique further than any writer before or since his day. It is also clear that he intended the antimasque to serve not merely as a variety show, but as an integral part of the whole. At the outset his antimasques were either combinations of a dialogue and a dance or simply dance by itself. In some of his later shows, such as *The Irish Masque,* however, the antimasque took the form of a comedy of manners instead of a dance, but as Jonson originally conceived it, the antimasque was employed as an element of disorder as opposed to the order and harmony of the masque proper. These opposites were usually represented through the contrast of antic with graceful dancing or the juxtaposition of physical ugliness and beauty or the unnatural and the natural. In either case the technique is fundamentally the same: by dramatizing what is not natural or harmonious that which is natural or ordered or harmonious is thereby made more cogent, as in *Hymenaei,* where the antimasque of the disordered and contentious Humors and Affections only makes the harmony and order of the real masque of men and women more strikingly apparent.

Jonson probably did not fully realize the potentially dangerous implications of this invention. His antimasque was immediately a success, and presently other masque writers began to imitate his technique, but they misunderstood the function of the device—a misunderstanding reflected in the terminology they used in referring to the antimasque. Some writers called it "antemasque" and thus indicated that it was merely an element which preceded the main masque. To Jonson it was much more. Other writers referred to it as the "anticmasque" and thereby suggested that it was only an antic show. Jonson indicated his distaste for this idea by satirizing the "antickmasque" in *The Masque of Augurs*. Again in *Neptune's Triumph* he satirically criticized the way in which the antimasque had been exploited by his fellow writers.

By 1624 it was clear to him that the antimasque was actually destroying the masque, for the spectators enjoyed it more than the actual masque, and thus writers tended to include more and more of the antimasques in their shows. Originally Jonson himself employed only one antimasque, but in his later shows he used more, probably because of pressure from Inigo Jones to do so. Thus Jonson's only recourse was to satirically remind his spectators that the antimasque was not the main element in the masque. Jonson's attack on his contemporaries' overuse of the antimasque was probably justified, for only two years after Jonson's death Davenant included twenty antimasques in his *Salmacida Spolia* (1639).

Antinoüs. Emperor Hadrian's favorite, famous for his youthful beauty. In *Volpone* (II) Volpone tells Celia that he received much acclaim from the ladies present when he acted this part.

Anton, Robert. Author of *The Philosopher's Satyrs* (1616) and the possible writer of verses ("Each like an Indian ship or Hull appears") on Jonson's *Works* (1640).

Antoninus Pius (A.D.86–161). Roman emperor 138–161. During his reign, Italy was embellished with fine buildings, and the Wall of Antoninus was built in England. Jonson alludes to Antoninus in his

Conversations (11. 548–49) with Drummond.

Antonius, Caius. In *Catiline*, co-consul with Cicero who gives his full support to Cicero when Cicero offers him a province.

Antony, Abbot. Probably an unidentified fencer, who is alluded to in *The New Inn* (II. v).

Antony, Marc (82?–30 B.C.) Roman general and member of triumvirate. He served in Palestine and Egypt and became a close follower of Caesar's. He fled Rome after Caesar's death, and joined with Octavian (later Augustus) and Lepidus in the second triumvirate in 43 B.C. They defeated Brutus and Cassius in 42 B.C.; soon after, Marc Antony went to live in Alexandria with Cleopatra, abandoning his wife Octavia. He conducted an unsuccessful expedition against Parthia in 36 B.C. and committed suicide in Egypt after losing the battle of Actium to Octavian in 31 B.C. In *Poetaster*, Tucca claims to have served in Caesar's war against Marc Antony (v. iii).

Antony of Correggio. See CORREGGIO.

Apelles. A painter who lived in the fourth century B.C. Alexander the Great was said to have forbidden any painter other than Apelles, the most celebrated Greek painter of antiquity, to represent him.

Apicius, Marcus Gavius, lived under Augustus and Tiberius and wrote a scientific treatise on his interest and expertise as a gourmet. Supposedly he squandered the equivalent of 800,000 pounds sterling on luxury and then, on discovering that he only had 80,000 pounds left, committed suicide. In *Sejanus* (I. ii) Arruntius says that Sejanus was once a serving boy and "pathick" to "that great gourmond, fat Apicius." He is also alluded to in *The Alchemist* (II. ii) and *The Staple of News* (IV. iv).

Apollo. Mythological god of many attributes who was regarded among the Greeks as the son of Zeus and Leto and the brother of Artemis. Apollo was the god of light, prophecy, healing, music, and archery, and protector of the herds.

Apollo appears in *The Masque of Augurs* as the god of light (Phoebus), the founder of the College of Augury, and the interpreter of augury for the king and his court.

In *Neptune's Triumph for the Return of Albion,* Apollo appears on a floating island with other gods and announces the return of Albion. In *The Fortunate Isles, and Their*

Union, he appears in a similar role but has no speaking part.

Apuleius, Lucius, born c. A.D. 123 at Madauros in Africa, is best known for his *Metamorphoses,* the only Latin novel to survive in its entirety—later novelists were very much influenced by it. Apuleius was frequently associated with the knowledge of black magic, a subject in several of his works. Jonson quotes from Apuleius in the *Masque of Queens,* and two sections in *Timber* (11. 1323–49; 1358–72) are taken from Apuleius' *De Magia.*

Arachne. In Greek mythology, a young maiden from Maeonia who was so skilled in weaving that she challenged Athene to a competition in which the jealous Athene destroyed Arachne's web and struck her, causing the shamed Arachne to attempt suicide by hanging. Declaring that Arachne should hang and weave forever, Athene changed her into a spider.

Aratus. Greek didactic poet who was born at Soli in Cilicia in 314 B.C. and died in Macedonia in 240 B.C. He wrote *Phenomena,* a poem that contains information on astronomy and weather signs, and an invocation to Zeus quoted by St. Paul. In *Poetaster* (I. i) Ovid writes a poem which claims that Aratus' fame will last as long as the "sunne, to moone."

Arcadia. An area in the central Peloponnesus whose inhabitants led a pastoral existence and claimed to be the oldest inhabitants of Greece. Many myths and cults were associated with the region.

Arcadians. The masquers who appear in *Pan's Anniversary* and celebrate the shepherds' holiday.

Arcas, ruler of the Arcadians, was the son of Zeus and Callisto.

Archilochus. Greek lyric poet, active around 700–650 B.C. He was very intelligent and sensitive, but was embittered by poverty and wrote biting satires and lampoons. He lived as a soldier of fortune, often getting into trouble because of his wit. He was innovative in language, meter, and subject matter, and was considered one of the greatest poets by the ancient world. In *Poetaster,* Jonson refers to an episode in Archilochus' life when his verses reportedly caused the suicide of a girl he had courted and that of her father, who had broken the engagement, when he says in the Apologetical Dialogue that he wishes he could punish the inferior poets who are satirizing him by writing "Iambicks . . .

arm't with Archilochus' fury . . . should make the lashers hang themselves." See also HORACE.

Architecture. A symbolic character who appears in *Chloridia* and supports the efforts of Fame to immortalize great actions.

Arden, Kate. An unidentified person mentioned in "On the Famous Voyage" (*Epig.* CXXXIII) and "An Execration Upon Vulcan" (*Und.* XLIII).

Arete. 1. Wife of King Alcinous of the Phaeacians. She induced her husband to aid the shipwrecked Odysseus, and she saved Medea from the Colchians. Her name came to personify virtuous womanly character.
2. A noble, high-minded, beautiful nymph in Cynthia's court in *Cynthia's Revels.* She is friendly with Crites and praises him for his honorable nature. After she tells the shallow courtiers that they are free for the night but should work up "solemne revels" to please Cynthia instead of the merry dances they were planning, they mock her for being overly solemn. She encourages Crites to write a masque that will honor Cynthia and expose the corruption of the courtiers, and she praises Crites to Cynthia. She is Cynthia's favorite, gracefully praising Cynthia when she appears. Cynthia gives Arete and Crites the power to punish the courtiers, but Arete graciously delegates her power to Crites.

Aretino, Pietro (1492–1556). Italian satirist who wrote abusive works for hire. Titian, who painted his portrait, was one of his friends. His comedies and letters are known for their coarseness and verve. Jonson mentions Aretino in *Volpone* (III) and *The Alchemist* (II. ii.).

Argenis. A Latin romance by John Barclay that was very popular in Jonson's day. In 1622 the king commissioned Jonson to translate it. The translation was entered on the Stationers' Register on October 2, 1623, but the work was consumed in the fire that destroyed Jonson's library later in the year.

Argive Queen. Helen of Troy.

Argo. The name of the ship Jason built to procure the golden fleece in Colchis.

Argurion. A foolish courtier in *Cynthia's Revels.* Cupid describes her as being like money, very fickle, and whimsically preferring shallow men. She gossips about the male courtiers with the other ladies, tells how Moria mockingly told her to flirt with Crites, and says that she prefers Asotus.

She is very taken with Asotus and gives him many rich presents. She plays the games of wit with the other courtiers. When Asotus gives away her presents to the others, she faints; presumably she becomes very sick or even dies, since she is not present during the courtship contest and is not even mentioned by Cynthia when the other courtiers are punished.

Argus. A herdsman with a hundred eyes sent by Hera to guard the cow Io. After Argus was killed by Hermes, Hera put his eyes in the tail of the peacock.

Ariadne, daughter of Minos and Pasiphaë, fell in love with Theseus and gave him a clew of thread so that he could find his way out of the Labyrinth after he had killed the Minotaur. When Theseus fled Crete, he took Ariadne with him but later abandoned her on Dia.

Arion. Greek lyric poet, legendary inventor of the dithyramb. According to Herodotus, legend states that Arion was rescued from drowning by a dolphin who was moved by the poet's beautiful song.

Ariosto, Ludovico (1474–1533). Italian poet. His *Orlando Furioso,* an epic on the subject of Roland and Angelica, daughter of the king of Cathay, was translated into English by Sir John Harrington in 1591. In the *Conversations* (ll. 35–36) Jonson told Drummond that Harrington's translation of Ariosto was the worst of all possible translations (probably he objected to Harrington's freedom in translation and his defense in the Preface of polysyllabic meter). In *Volpone* (III. iv), Lady Politic Would-be refers to Ariosto as one of the poets she has read.

Aristarchus of Samothrace (c. 217–c. 145 B.C.). Famous Greek scholar, an innovator of scientific scholarship noted for his painstaking recension of the text of Homer. He wrote numerous commentaries on such writers as Alcaeus, Anacreon, Pindar, Hesiod, and the tragedians. Jonson mentions Aristarchus in *Every Man out* (Ind.), in *Cynthia's Revels* (II. iii), and in his translation of Horace's *Art of Poetry.*

Aristius, Fus. A minor character in *Poetaster,* friend to Horace, who meets Horace while he is being bothered by Crispinus, and teases him by stranding him with the foolish Poetaster. Unlike several other characters in *Poetaster,* he is not a caricature of one of Jonson's contemporaries.

Aristophanes (c. 448–c. 388 B.C.). Athenian comic poet, the greatest of the ancient writers of comedy. His plays mix political, social, and literary satire. Eleven of his more than 40 plays are extant; they are the only whole plays from the Greek Old Comedy to have survived. Aristophanes' direct attacks on persons, the severity of his invective, and his burlesque extravagances had great appeal for Jonson, who had a copy of Aristophanes in his personal library. Several of Jonson's works show Aristophanic influence, notably *Cynthia's Revels* and *The Staple of News.* Jonson discusses Aristophanes in *Timber* (ll. 2654ff.) in connection with Old Comedy and in *Every Man out.* Aristophanes is also alluded to in Jonson's eulogy on Shakespeare prefaced to the First Folio, in *Sejanus* (III), in *Poetaster* (Apol. Dia.), and in *Epig.* CXXXIII.

Aristotle (Aristoteles). Greek philosopher. Born in 384 B.C. at Stagira in Macedonia, he was often referred to as the Stagirite. At seventeen he went to Athens and became a pupil of Plato at the Academy. In 342 B.C. he was appointed tutor to Alexander the Great, and in 335 B.C. he founded the Lyceum where he spent twelve years teaching and writing. He died in Chalcis in 322 B.C.

Over four hundred works were attributed to Aristotle, of which only two hundred are known. After the decline of Rome, Aristotle's works were lost in the West, but they were introduced to Islam by Arab scholars in the ninth century. Through Arab and Jewish scholars his works were eventually reintroduced in the West and became the basis for medieval scholasticism.

The writings of Aristotle that we have today are largely notes made on his lectures by his students and edited in the first century B.C. Chief among the works are: the *Organon,* six treatises dealing with the methods of reasoning and establishing proof; *Physics; Metaphysics; On the Soul; Nicomachean Ethics* and *Eudemian Ethics; Politics; Rhetoric; Poetics;* and a series of works on biology and physics. The influence of Aristotle on science, theology, literature, and philosophy has been pervasive over the centuries in many cultures, and every age has attempted a reinterpretation of his thought. The *Poetics* in particular greatly influenced Renaissance and neoclassical poets and critics.

Jonson had a copy of Aristotle's *Works* in his personal library, and the general influence of the *Poetics* can be detected in Jonson's thought. In *Magnetic Lady* (I. i), there is a discussion of Aristotle's theory of universals. The Stagirite is mentioned in

"An Execration upon Vulcan" (*Und.* XLIII), and the *Ethics* is alluded to in *Epicoene* (IV. iv). In *Timber* (ll. 2350–51), Jonson notes that, according to Aristotle (*Poetics,* i), the word *poet* comes from a Greek word meaning to make or to feign; and later, when discussing the need for the poet to have natural wit, Jonson alludes to Aristotle's comment that no great genius exists without some madness and that it is not possible to say a noble thing unless the spirit is moved (*Timber,* ll. 2416–19).

When discussing the need for the poet to study the masters, Jonson cites Horace and Aristotle as those most worthy of study, and he further notes that Aristotle was the greatest philosopher the world ever had (*Timber,* ll. 2510–17).

Armin, Robert (d. 1615). Comic actor and author who was apparently a member of the Chamberlain's Company in 1599. In 1610 as a member of the King's Men he acted in *The Alchemist.* He performed in a number of Shakespeare's plays, and some believe that Shakespeare wrote the parts of Touchstone, Feste, and the fool in *Lear* specifically for Armin. He wrote several books, including *Fool Upon Fool* (1599 and 1605), *A Nest of Ninnies* (1608), *Quips Upon Questions* (1600), and *Phantasma, the Italian Tailor and His Boy* (1609). He also wrote a play entitled *Two Maids of Moreclacke* (1609), which was performed by the King's Men.

Armstrong, Archibald. Court jester mentioned in *The Staple of News* (III. ii) and *Neptune's Triumph.*

Arnold of Villanova. (c. 1235–1314) A French physician, theologian, astrologer, and alchemist. Jonson quotes from Arnold's *Rosarium Philosophorum* in *The Alchemist* (II. i; iii) and mentions the alchemist in *Mercury Vindicated.*

Arruntius, Lucius. A noble, high-minded Roman senator in *Sejanus.* He is one of the most vocal critics of, and opponents to, Sejanus and Tiberius, lamenting that the Roman race has fallen from its former glory. He praises Germanicus and mourns his death. He rails at Sejanus' followers, refusing to remain expediently silent, and mocks Tiberius' craftily written speeches. He admires Drusus once he sees his courage in opposing Sejanus and mocks the followers of Tiberius and Sejanus. As Sejanus' power grows, Lucius Arruntius calls on the gods for vengeance, speaks with Lepidus on the corruption of the age, and rails against Tiberius' corruption and lust. With Lepidus, he mocks the senators who rush to acclaim Sejanus and sits unmoved by most of the other senators' jostlings for favor in the Senate. He gives a mocking commentary of asides on Tiberius' letter denouncing Sejanus and comments on the fickleness of fortune. He predicts that Macro will grow as bad as Sejanus and expresses great disgust for the impulsive, inhuman actions of the mob against Sejanus.

Art of Poetry, The. Jonson's translation of Horace's *Ars Poetica*, first published in the duodecimo edition of the *Poems* (1640) and revised and printed in the second folio (1640–41). The first version was probably completed in 1604 when Jonson was living at Lord D'Aubigny's, and it was announced as ready for publication in the address to the readers prefixed to the quarto of *Sejanus* in 1605. The 1623 fire that destroyed most of Jonson's library consumed a preface he had written for the translation, but somehow the translation itself survived. The composition date of the revised version is uncertain, but it certainly followed Daniel Heinsius' critical reconstruction of Horace's text (which no scholar has ever completely accepted), first published by the Plantin press in 1610. Perhaps the publication of Heinsius' reconstruction explains why Jonson did not carry out his original plan to publish his translation soon after the appearance of *Sejanus*.

Horace's *Ars Poetica* (first so called by Quintilian) is not really a systematic treatise on poetics, but rather a desultory, witty hexameter epistle that propounds various critical maxims and historical statements with specific reference to the circumstances of Horace's own time. The epistle is addressed to Piso and his sons. The Pisos were friends of Horace's, and the letter is informal in tone, but it does generally follow the traditional Hellenistic structure for a treatise on literary criticism, which required discussion of *poiesis* (poetic subject matter), *poema* (poetic form), and *poeta* (the nature of the poet himself). Within this overall framework, the chief topics covered are: artistic unity, style and vocabulary, meter and genres, originality and imitation, the proper end of poetry, genius and art, and the uselessness of mediocrity.

Since Jonson was primarily concerned with literal translation, his translations of the *Ars Poetica* are competent but pedestrian, failing to reflect the wit and vitality of the original. In both his versions he expanded the verse epistle from Horace's original 476 lines to 680. Like many of his contemporaries, Jonson tended to view Horace's *Ars Poetica* as a key to Aristotle's *Poetics*, and Jonson's lost preface apparently interpreted Horace's work in this light.

In the *Conversations* (ll. 82–88; 416–17), Drummond reports that Jonson read him the preface to *The Art of Poetry*, which contained an apology for *Bartholomew Fair* and a character named Criticus who stood for John Donne. The work had a prefatory epigram by Sir Edward Herbert, and the translation of Horace's *Art of Poetry* Jonson said he had done in Lord Aubigny's house.

Artemidorus. A Greek physician of Hadrian's reign who believed that dreams revealed the future. He wrote five books on the subject. In *Epicoene* (III), Mrs. Otter says that Lady Haughty interpreted one of her dreams according to Artemidorus and it came true.

Artemisia. According to Jonson, Queen of Caria who lived during the time of Xerxes. She appears as one of the virtuous queens in *The Masque of Queens*.

Arthur, King. Mythological king who appears as a constellation in *The Speeches at Prince Henry's Barriers* and presents a symbolic shield to the young knight Meliadus.

Arthurian legend. The collection of legends popular in medieval lore centering on King Arthur of Britain and the Knights of the Round Table. Although Jonson told Drummond in the *Conversations* (ll. 148–50) that no fiction was better for a heroic poem than Arthurian legend and that Sir Philip Sidney had considered transforming all of his *Arcadia* into stories of Arthur, Jonson made use of Arthurian materials only in *Prince Henry's Barriers*. The rest of Jonson's references to Arthurian lore are generally contemptuous: *Every Man out* (II. iii), *The New Inn* (I. vi), and *Und.* XLIII and XLIV.

Arthur of Bradley. The hero of an old song entitled "The Ballad on the Wedding of Arthur of Bradley." Although it was first printed in *Wits Merriment* (1656), it dates from the reign of Edward VI. Mooncalf alludes to Arthur in *Bartholomew Fair* (II. ii).

Ashley (or Astley), Sir John (d. 1639). Ashley was a gentleman pensioner knighted by King James in 1603. He later became Master of the Revels to James and served in this office and as a gentleman of the Privy Chamber to King Charles. He danced in Jonson's *Hymenaei*. In 1621 Jonson received a grant of reversion that would have given him the office of Master of Revels upon Ashley's death, but Ashley survived Jonson.

Ashmore, John. Translator who published in 1621 *Certain Selected Odes of Horace, Englished,* which includes a paraphrase of Horace's ode II. iii that is attributed to Jonson. Because the paraphrase is at variance with Jonson's theory and practice of translation, the attribution is doubtful. This collection also included a Latin epigram on Jonson by Ashmore.

Asotus. A foolish gallant in *Cynthia's Revels,* newly come to court and eager to learn how to act like a courtier. Crites introduces him to Amorphus; Asotus is very much taken with Amorphus, and resolves to imitate his every move. He is taught how to compose his features, how to eat, how to dance, and, at the greatest length, how to properly accost and flirt with a lady. The first time he meets the courtiers he makes a fool of himself, but the second time he has great success, making Argurion fall in love with him and give him presents. He inadvertently makes himself appear foolish during one of the games of wit played by the courtiers. In Argurion's presence, he gives her gifts to the other courtiers in order to gain their favors; she faints. He drinks the water from the fountain of self-love with the others, and laments when he realizes that he will not be called upon to dance before Cynthia. Amorphus devises the courtship contest so that Asotus can show off his newly acquired skills, but he plays only a minor role in the scene after Mercury challenges Amorphus instead. Asotus takes part in the second masque, is discovered by Cynthia, and sentenced to punishment by Crites. He weeps, marches, and sings the palinode with the other courtiers.

Aspasia (5th century B.C.). Pericles' mistress, famous for her wit, erudition, and beauty. During their fooling in *Volpone* (I), Nano, Androgyno, and Castrone include her as one of the high points in the transmigrations of the soul which has happily lodged in Androgyno.

Asper. The presenter in *Every Man out of His Humour,* a character of "ingenious and free spirit, eager and constant in reproof."

Aspley, William. Bookseller in London from 1598 to 1640 who published three quartos of *Eastward Ho* in 1605.

Asterope. One of the Pleiades, the wife of Oenomaus and the daughter of Cepheus, king of Tegea.

Astraea. A goddess who appears in *The Golden Age Restored* and represents the return to earth of law and justice in the new golden age.

Ate. The goddess personifying man's blind impulses in Greek mythology. She was associated with punishment for crimes. In *Catiline* (IV) Cicero says that Catiline is as innocent of leading people astray as Ate.

Athenaeus. Greek writer of the late 2nd and early 3rd centuries A.D. whose anthological work *Banquet of the Sophists* is useful because of the great amount of information it contains on Greek manners and customs. *Volpone* (I. i; III. i), *The Staple of News* (III. ii; IV. ii), and *The Masque of Queens* all show the influence of Athenaeus' work.

Atlas. The Greek mythological character who was punished for taking part in the rebellion of the Titans by being forced to support the heavens with his head and his hands. Perseus, the son of Zeus and Danaë, transformed him into a mountain, and he appears as such in *Pleasure Reconciled to Virtue.*

Atreus, the son of Pelops, was king of Mycenae and the father of Agamemnon and Menelaus. His brother Thyestes seduced Atreus' wife and stole a marvelous golden ram given to Atreus by the gods that was the pledge of sovereignty over Mycenae. In revenge Atreus invited Thyestes to a banquet and served him a dish made of the flesh of Thyestes' children. The horror of it caused the sun to turn back in its course.

Atropos. One of the Fates. She is often portrayed holding shears.

Attwell (Attawel), Hugh (d. 1621). An actor who played in *Epicoene* as one of the children of the Queen's Revels in 1609. In 1613 he joined the Lady Elizabeth's Men.

Atys, son of Croesus, was loved by Rhea, mother of the gods.

Aubigny, Esmé Stuart, 8th Seigneur of (afterwards Duke of Lennox) (1579–1624), was the younger brother of the 2nd Duke of Lennox whom he succeeded in February 1624. Jonson had a long and intimate relationship with Aubigny. Jonson told Drummond (*Conversations,* ll. 254–5) that he lived with Aubigny for five years (probably 1602–1607) and that he did his translation of Horace's *Art of Poetry* while staying with Aubigny (*Conversations,* ll. 82–88). Aubigny was apparently instrumental in helping secure Jonson's release from prison for his part in the offensive satire of *Eastward Ho,* and there is extant a 1605 letter Jonson probably wrote to Aubigny from jail. Jonson dedicated *Sejanus* to Aubigny and wrote *Epig.* CXXVII as a tribute to him and *For.* XIII in honor of his wife. *Und.* LXXV is an epithalamium on the marriage of Aubigny's sister to Hierome Weston. Aubigny danced in the *Haddington Masque* and is mentioned in Lord Falkland's "An Eclogue on the Death of Ben Jonson" in *Jonsonus Virbius.*

Aubigny, Katherine, Lady (d. 1627), daughter of Sir Gervase Clifton of Leighton Bromswold, married Esmé, Seigneur d'Aubigny, in 1609. Her son James became the 4th Duke of Lennox in 1624. She had four daughters and six sons, three of whom died in the Civil War fighting for the king. When her husband died, she married the 2nd Earl of Abercorn. Jonson's *For.* XIII was written in tribute to her.

Aubrey, John (1626–1697). English antiquary and writer. Educated at Trinity College, Oxford. Aubrey knew most of the famous people of his day, and he left copious letters and memoranda, including notes on Jonson's life. *Lives of Eminent Men* was his most celebrated work, although it did not appear in print until 1813. Only *Miscellanies* (1696), a collection of stories and folklore, was published during Aubrey's lifetime.

augurs. Carrying augurs' staves, the augurs appear as the noble masquers in *The Masque of Augurs* and perform the dances of augury which are interpreted by Apollo and his sons.

Augusta. See LIVIA Drusilla.

Augustus (63 B.C.–A.D. 14). Grandnephew of Julius Caesar. As the first Roman emperor he was called Imperator Caesar Augustus, but his name, after his adoption by Caesar, was Caius Julius Caesar Octavianus. Augustus was a strong supporter of arts and letters and a close friend and patron of Virgil, Ovid, Livy, and Horace. Augustus strengthened his imperial government by establishing the concept of the Pax Romana.

Augustus appears as a character playing himself in *Poetaster,* and he is referred to in *Sejanus* (I; III).

Aurelia. Daughter to Count Ferneze in *The Case Is Altered.* She mourns the death of her mother but chides her sister for continuing to be melancholy long after their mother's death merely because fash-

ion says she should be. Aurelia is apparently beautiful and spirited, being wooed by Maximilian and Angelo. She is very much taken with the prisoner called Gasper. When she learns, after he is released in exchange for her brother, that he is really an important French lord, Lord Chamont, she is anxious for his return. After he returns, bringing her brother, her father gratefully betroths her to Chamont.

Aurora. Roman goddess of the dawn who appears in *The Vision of Delight.*

Ausonius, Decimus Magnus, was born in Bordeaux at the beginning of the fourth century. He taught grammar and rhetoric in Bordeaux for thirty years, then was called to Trèves by Valentinian to be a tutor to Gratian. He later became governor of Gaul and other provinces and consul. He wrote many poems about a wide variety of subjects, but his best known is *Mosella,* a description of his journey on the Moselle River. In *Epicoene* Daw dismisses him as worthless along with many other ancient writers (II). He is also alluded to in *Sejanus* (II).

authority. In *Timber* (ll. 129–59), Jonson, largely paraphrasing Juan Luis Vives (*In Libros de Disciplinis Praefatio* [*Opera,* i. 324–25]), observes that the ancients should be viewed as "Guides, not Commanders" so that to their observations we should add that of our own experience, but, above all, one should always stand for the authority of truth wherever it may be found: "Stand for *Truth,* and 'tis enough."

Autronius. In *Catiline,* one of the conspirators who supports Catiline's abortive attempt to seize power in Rome.

avarice. In *Timber* (ll. 1373–1414), Jonson, paraphrasing Seneca (*Epist.* CXIX; CX), states that "*Money* never made any man rich, but his mind. He that can order him selfe to the Law of nature, is not onely without the sense, but the feare of poverty." Continuing, he argues that "Wee serve our avarice, and not content with the good of the Earth, that is offer'd us; wee search, and digge for the evil that is hidden." He lists a number of superfluous things that we covet and concludes that "wee make our selves slaves to our pleasures; and wee serve *Fame,* and ambition, which is an equall slavery." He especially deplores the pomp and lavishness of kings and their entertainment of each other.

Avernus. Deep lake near Cumae, often used as a name for the Underworld because of a nearby cave through which Aeneas reputedly descended into Hades.

Averroës (1126–1198). Spanish-Arabian philosopher and physician, best known for his commentaries on Aristotle, which were influential long after his death. He declared philosophy the highest form of inquiry and attempted to delimit the domains of faith and reason. His doctrines on personal immortality and the eternity of matter were condemned by the Catholic church. Averroës is mentioned in *The Magnetic Lady* (III. iii).

Avicenna (980–1037). Arabian physician and philosopher. From 1100 to 1500 he was the greatest name in medicine, *Canon of Medicine* being his masterpiece. His interpretation of Aristotle was very much influenced by the Neoplatonists. He established the classification of the sciences used in the medieval schools of Europe. Avicenna is mentioned in *The Magnetic Lady* (III. iii).

Avocatori. The judges in *Volpone* who distribute justice at the end of the play.

Aytoun, Sir Robert. See AITON, SIR ROBERT.

B

Babie-Cake. A character dressed like a boy in a long fine coat who appears as one of the children of Christmas in *Christmas, His Masque.*

Bacchus. Greek god of wine who was a fertility spirit often identified with Dionysus.

Bacon, Francis (1561–1626). English philosopher, essayist, and statesman. Born in London, educated at Trinity College, Cambridge, and at Gray's Inn. His father was Sir Nicholas Bacon, Lord Keeper to Queen Elizabeth. When he was a member of Parliament in 1584, he opposed Elizabeth's tax reform program, but through the efforts of the Earl of Essex on his behalf, Elizabeth accepted Bacon as an unofficial member of her Learned Council. When Essex was tried in 1601, Bacon took an active part in the prosecution, an act for which many later condemned Bacon. Bacon was knighted in 1603 by James I. He was made Attorney General in 1613 and Lord Keeper in 1617; in 1618 he was made Lord Chancellor and the title Baron Verulam was conferred on him. In 1621 he

was created Viscount St. Albans. In the same year he was accused of accepting bribes while in office. He pleaded guilty. The sentence called for him to be fined £ 40,000, barred from holding public office, banished from court, and imprisoned in the Tower. The fine, banishment, and imprisonment were remitted, but his public career was terminated, and he spent the rest of his life writing in retirement. He planned a long philosophical work (the *Instauratio Magna*), but completed only two parts—*The Advancement of Learning* (1605) and the *Novum Organum* (1620). Attacking the authority of Aristotle, Bacon attempted to apply the inductive method of modern science and urged full investigation in all matters. Although he has been widely criticized for not following his own investigations to their logical ends, today he is widely respected. In 1627 he published *The New Atlantis*, which described a scientific utopia that was partially realized in the founding of the Royal Society in 1660. His best known writings are the *Essays* (1597–1625), aphoristic observations on life written in an engaging and lively style.

Jonson had great respect for Bacon and seemed to know a great deal about him. He lauded Bacon highly in *Timber* (ll. 938–47) and in *Und.* LI praised him on his sixtieth birthday (January 26, 1621). Jonson had a copy of the *Novum Organum* in his personal library, and in *Timber* (ll. 2090–2124) he paraphrased a long passage from *The Advancement of Learning* (Bk. I, chap. 4) on the distemper of learning. In the *Conversations* (ll. 333–35), Jonson said that Bacon told him that he did not like to see poetry go on any feet but dactyls or spondees, and later (ll. 361–63) Jonson told Drummond that Bacon wrung his speeches from the strings of his band (Seventeenth-century barristers wore a collar with long linen strips hanging from it) while other chancellors did so from the pickings of their teeth.

Bacon, Roger (1214?–1294). Franciscan monk of English birth who was a philosopher and scientist. He studied at Oxford and the University of Paris and became one of the most celebrated teachers at Oxford, stressing the value of knowing the original languages in the study of Aristotle and the Bible. Holding an interest in natural science far in advance of his times, he believed in controlled experiments and in the accurate observation of phenomena, and he thought mathematics was the gateway to science. He also taught that experience as a guide to the outer world was not divorced from theology, for wisdom and faith to him were one. His writings were numerous. His deep interest in alchemy may account for many of his contemporaries' crediting him with great learning in magical practices. He may have been the first man to observe spiral nebulae through a telescope. He was long given credit for the invention of gunpowder, but this too seems to be doubtful. He is the subject of Greene's play *Friar Bacon* (1589).

Roger Bacon is mentioned or alluded to in *A Tale of a Tub* (IV. vi) and *Every Man in* (1616 folio version, I. iv).

Bacon, Sir Nicholas (1509–1579). English statesman who by his second wife Ann Cooke was the father of Francis Bacon. Probably because Ann was the sister of the wife of William Cecil, later Lord Burghley, Sir Nicholas was appointed keeper of the great seal in 1558 under Elizabeth. Jonson mentions Sir Nicholas in *Und.* LI and in *Timber* (ll. 905–7).

ballad. Although Jonson told Drummond in the *Conversations* (l. 475) that a poet should detest a ballad maker, and although Jonson condemned balladry in *Neptune's Triumph* (ll. 163–65) and in *Und.* XXIII (ll. 19–22), he quoted, mentioned, or alluded to several ballads in his works:

"A Caveat Against Cutpurses" in *Bartholomew Fair* (III. v), "A Dozen of Divine Points" in *Bartholomew Fair* (II. iv), "The Ferret and the Coney" in *Bartholomew Fair* (II. iv), "Good Counsel" in *Bartholomew Fair* (II. iv), "Goosegreen Starch and the Devil" in *Bartholomew Fair* (II. iv), "Jane Shore" in *The New Inn* (v. ii), "John Urson" in *The Masque of Augurs*, "Paggington's Pound" in *Bartholomew Fair* (III. v), "Saint George" in Bartholomew Fair (II. iv), "Sampson" in *Eastward Ho* (II. ii), "Tom Long the Carrier" in *A Tale of a Tub* (IV. i), "Whoop Barnaby" in *The New Inn* (v. i) and *The Gypsies Metamorphosed*, and "The Windmill Blown Down by the Witch's Fart" in *Bartholomew Fair* (II. iv).

Balladino, Antonio. The "pageant poet to the City of Milan" in *The Case Is Altered*. He is introduced into the play merely as a satire of Anthony Munday, and his only appearance comes early in the play, when he promises Onion that he will make him a song to help him woo Rachel.

Ballard, Thomas. Bookseller and book auctioneer in London from 1698 to 1725

who was one of the publishers of the so-called Booksellers' Edition of Jonson's *Works* in 1716–17.

Balthasar. Servant to Count Ferneze in *The Case Is Altered*. He has a minor role in the play, first appearing to greet Valentine with the other servants. He is one of the servants whose inability to find Paulo exasperates Count Ferneze. His only other appearances are during the fencing bout between Onion and Martino, possibly (although he is not named) as one of the servants who bring in Camillo at the end of the play, and when he comes in with the other servants to mock Onion and Juniper's new wealth.

Banck. A usurer satirized in *Epig.* XXXI and XLIV.

Band. In *The Staple of News*, the second woman to Lady Pecunia.

Bankes. A juggler who became a vintner in Cheapside and is mentioned in *Every Man out* (IV. vi) and *Epig.* CXXXIII.

Barber. A craftsman called to take part in the courtship contest in *Cynthia's Revels*, who grooms Mercury's mustache during his staged primping and is abused by him.

Barclay, John. (1582–1621). Born in Lorraine, Barclay went to England about 1603 and shortly thereafter published a politico-satirical romance chiefly directed at the Jesuits. In 1616 he went to Rome, where he died a good Catholic in 1621, the same year his *Argenis* appeared. Written in Latin, *Argenis* was a political romance resembling the *Arcadia* in its romantic adventures and the *Utopia* in its discussion of political problems. It was a roman à clef, reviewing under disguised names and circumstances the people and events of European history during the latter half of the sixteenth century. King James was very fond of the work, and he commissioned Jonson to translate it for him. Although he entered the translation on the Stationers' Register on October 2, 1623, Jonson never published the work—the fire which destroyed his library later that year also consumed the manuscript.

Bard. A singer who appears in *The Irish Masque at Court* and offers two songs in praise of the monarch's transforming power.

Barish, Jonas (1922–   ). American scholar educated at Harvard University. He has taught at Yale University and since 1966 has been Professor of English at the University of California, Berkeley. He has published extensively on Elizabethan drama and is the author of the influential *Ben Jonson and the Language of Prose Comedy* (1960) and other essays and books on Jonson.

Barksted (Backsted), William. Actor and author who published *Myrrha* in 1607 and *Hiren* in 1611. He was also co-author of Marston's *Insatiate Countess* (1613). In 1609 as a member of the Children of The Queen's Revels, he played in *Epicoene*. He joined the Lady Elizabeth's company in 1611 and the Prince's Men in 1616.

Barlow, William. Archdeacon of Salisbury when he died in 1625, Barlow published *Magnetical Advertisements* in 1616, which provoked a reply from Mark Ridley entitled *Magnetical Animadversions* in 1617. Barlow responded in 1618 with *A Brief Discovery of the Idle Animadversions of Mark Ridley.* Barlow, who helped improve the hanging of ships' compasses, is mentioned in *The Magnetic Lady* (1. iv).

Barnaby. In *The New Inn,* a hired coachman.

Barnfield, Richard (1574–1627). English poet. His canon consists of three works: *The Affectionate Shepherd* (1594), *Cynthia* (1595), and *The Encomion of Lady Pecunia* (1598). The last work probably influenced the characterization of Jonson's Lady Pecunia in *The Staple of News.*

Barrenger, William. Bookseller in London from 1600 to 1622 who in 1609 published with Bartholomew Sutton *The Case Is Altered* in quarto.

barriers. The palisades or fences enclosing the lists of a medieval tournament. By Jonson's day the term had come to be used to refer to the jousting or tilting tournaments themselves. Jonson wrote the speeches for Prince Henry's Barriers of 1610.

Bartholomew Fair.

Acted: October 31, 1614, at the Hope Theatre on the Bankside by the Lady Elizabeth's Men.

Published: 1631 by Robert Allot.

Printer: John Beale.

Induction: The Stage-keeper comes out and tells the audience to patiently await the opening of the play. He "confides" that he thinks that the play is not an accurate representation of the fair, and that there are other playwrights who could do a better job. He says that Jonson would not listen to his criticism and kicked

him and laments that this sort of disrespect is shown to a man with as much experience in the theater as he. He reminisces about former actors. The Bookholder comes on and reprimands him, then tells the Scrivener to read the "agreement" Jonson makes with his audience. The Scrivener reads the document, which is formally worded and says that the audience should stay in their seats, quietly watch the play, only criticize in proportion to the admission charge they have paid, and make their own honest, firm critical decisions about the play. The document answers the Stage-keeper's charges that many sights of the fair are left out by telling what other sights will be included; it also says that Jonson does not want his audience to spend a great deal of time figuring out exactly who is being satirized in each of the characters.

Act I. At his house John Littlewit, a proctor, takes great delight in his own punning. He remarks on the coincidence that Bartholomew Cokes, an esquire of Harrow, is coming for a marriage license on Bartholomew's Day, and he tells his wife, Win, how pretty she looks. Winwife, a gentleman, enters and compliments Win; Littlewit advises Winwife that if he wants to win Dame Purecraft (who is Win's widowed mother), he must act mad, since a fortune teller told her recently that she could only be happy with a "gentleman mad-man." He says that Zeal-of-the-Land Busy has come courting Purecraft. Quarlous, a gamester and a companion of Winwife's, comes running in, behaving foolishly; the men joke together about their drinking the night before. Quarlous remembers that Littlewit promised that he could kiss Win, and at Littlewit's urging, he does, calling Littlewit a fool. Quarlous teases Winwife about all the old rich widows he has courted, especially the Puritan Dame Purecraft. Winwife laments that Busy seems to be winning her hand, and they talk about how foolish Busy is. Waspe comes in for Cokes's marriage license; Win and Solomon, Littlewit's servant, are sent to fetch it, and while waiting, Waspe abuses and insults the three men for no reason. Waspe tells of the foolishness and childishness of Cokes, and how he is to marry Grace Wellborn, Justice Overdo's ward. Cokes, Mrs. Overdo, and Grace enter, and when Waspe abuses them, Mrs. Overdo preaches to him about curbing his passions. Winwife and Quarlous notice Grace and her attitude of scorn toward Cokes, who prattles on about his desire to see the fair. John tells Win that he wants her to see his puppet show at the fair; she fears that her mother will forbid her to go, but they decide that since Win is pregnant, she will pretend that she has a craving to go to the fair. This device fools Purecraft and Busy, who appears willing to rationalize and compromise his principles for a taste of roast pig.

Act II. Justice Overdo enters and tells of his plan to disguise himself and spy out corruption in the fair, thus avoiding the mistakes in judgment most magistrates make. Ursula and some other rogues enter, teasing each other about the shoddiness of their wares. Overdo listens with rapt attention and makes mental notes as he hears them speak about exploiting their customers. He acts like a madman to come in closer and drink with them. Knockem, a horse courser, comes in and jokes with Ursula, speaking of Edgworth, a cutpurse, who enters with Nightingale, a ballad singer. Overdo thinks that Edgworth is a misguided young man in bad company and decides to help him. They drink together, then Winwife and Quarlous enter, quarrel with them, and insult Ursula and Knockem. They fight and leave after Ursula falls and scalds herself on a pan she meant for them. When their companions check to see if she is hurt, they find skin diseases on her leg. Cokes and Waspe enter with Mrs. Overdo and Grace; Edgworth picks Cokes's pocket. Waspe accuses Overdo of being a pickpocket and beats him.

Act III. Captain Whit enters and puns with the watchmen Bristle and Haggise about watchmen. He accosts Quarlous and Winwife, asking to pimp for them, and they can only get rid of him by paying him off. Busy steers Purecraft, Littlewit, and Win through the fair, warning them of its profanity. When he smells roast pig, he forgets his admonitions and leads them into Ursula's booth. Overdo soliloquizes about how that night he will take off his disguise and tell his friends who he was that day. Until then, he will nobly continue to seek out the truth, even though it may result in personal discomfort. Cokes comes on with his party, and quarrels with Waspe, insisting on buying more knicknacks. He buys both Leatherhead's and Trash's shops, giving them forty shillings and telling them to take care of the wares for him until after the fair. Nightingale sings a ballad about cutpurses, and Cokes mocks them until his purse is stolen again by Edgworth. Waspe greatly insults him because of his foolishness, and Quarlous asks Edgworth to steal Cokes's marriage license out of the box in Waspe's pocket. Quarlous and Winwife meet Grace, and speak sym-

pathetically with her. His stomach full, Busy rails against the fair and meets Leatherhead and Trash, who are trying to resell the goods Cokes bought from them earlier. Busy wrecks their stalls in a fit of rage, and the watch carries him away. Embarrassed but desperate, Win whispers to her husband that she has to relieve herself; John takes her back to Ursula's.

Act IV. Trouble-All, a madman, enters and asks the watch for a "warrant." Trouble-All and the watchmen speak of Overdo (who is listening in disguise in the stocks); then officers bring in Busy. They decide to take Busy and Overdo before Justice Overdo rather than keeping them both in the stocks. Edgworth, Nightingale and the costardmonger hatch a plot against Cokes: Edgworth and Nightingale will trip the costardmonger and while Cokes is scrambling for the the spilled pears, they will steal from Cokes. They carry out their plan, running away with Cokes's cloak and hat. Grace tells Quarlous and Winwife that she would much rather marry either of them than Cokes but does not know enough about them to choose one or the other. She has them each write a word on a paper; they agree to ask the next person to come by to choose which word he prefers—the writer of the chosen word will get Grace. The next person is Trouble-All, who picks a word. According to their agreement, Grace waits to tell them which was chosen. The scene switches to Ursula's booth where Knockem, Whit, Edgworth, Waspe, Mrs. Overdo, and others are drinking. They are all very drunk, and the men are playing vapours, a game in which they all disagree. Quarlous comes in and quarrels with Cutting; they all fight. Members of the watch come in and carry Waspe away when he insults them. Whit becomes friendly with Mrs. Overdo, and she goes back into Ursula's shop to relieve herself. Littlewit leaves Win with them while he goes to ready his puppet show, and Knockem and Whit persuade Win that she would be wise to act like a prostitute. Alice rushes in and attacks Mrs. Overdo, believing her to be a rich prostitute who is stealing her trade. She is driven away, and Win and Mrs. Overdo are outfitted to look like prostitutes.

Edgworth enters with Quarlous. He has stolen Cokes's marriage license from Waspe; he asks Quarlous if he wants to go to Ursula's and meet some loose women, but Quarlous dismisses him. Some of the watchmen enter and fix Waspe in the stocks. Quarlous mocks him. The rest of the watch bring in Busy, but while they are putting him in the stocks Trouble-All accosts them; they fight with him, and the prisoners escape.

Act V. Lanthorn, a toy seller, stands before Littlewit's puppet show and reminisces about all the shows of which he has been master. He tells the gatekeepers to ask unequal prices of the customers, according to what they can pay. Quarlous enters another part of the fair dressed like Trouble-All. Purecraft comes in and says that she is in love with him, since she has been looking for a gentleman madman. He looks at Grace's paper and discovers that Winwife's word was chosen. Purecraft tells him that Busy is corrupt, she is rich, and she would gladly marry him. He decides to marry Purecraft, since he has no hope of marrying Grace. Overdo comes on and, believing him to be Trouble-All, is anxious to make amends for his madness which, since he fired Trouble-All, Overdo believes to be his fault. He signs a paper that Quarlous later uses to give Grace permission to marry Winwife. In another part of the fair, Cokes goes into the puppet show to see the greatly altered and vulgarized version of the stories of Hero and Leander and Damon and Pithias that Littlewit is presenting. Cokes greatly overpays admission and speaks about the puppets as if they were real people. Littlewit goes to fetch Win and Grace, Winwife, Knockem, Whit, Edgworth, Win, and Mrs. Overdo enter the puppet show. Mrs. Overdo is very drunk, and she and Win are dressed like prostitutes. Overdo is shocked by their presence and does not recognize his wife. Waspe comes in and grumbles at Cokes. The puppet show is played, with Hero, Leander, Damon, and Pithias being low, vulgar commoners in London. The play is coarse and vulgar, but Cokes thinks it excellent and loudly comments during it. Busy comes in, preaching about the abomination of a puppet show. He loses a debate with a puppet and stays to quietly watch the play. Quarlous enters with Purecraft, whom he has recently married. Overdo throws off his disguise and threatens the others with the law. They are frightened until Quarlous reveals how foolishly Overdo has been acting, and Overdo discovers that the disguised Mrs. Overdo is his wife. He is chagrined and invites the company to dinner at his house, saying that they will be in no danger of arrest there.

Epilogue. Jonson says that the King can best judge if he has overstepped his bounds of satire in the play and hopes that the play has pleased him, for he would rather please the King than all the other men there.

See also John DRYDEN; John SELDEN.

Basse, William. Author of some verses published in *Annalia Dubrensia* (1636) and the author of an unpublished but well-known elegy on the death of Shakespeare to which Jonson alluded in the opening lines of his elegy on Shakespeare which was prefaced to the First Folio of 1623.

Bassett, Thomas. Bookseller who was one of the publishers of the third folio of Jonson's *Works* (1692).

Bathurst, Ralph (1620–1704). President of Trinity College, Oxford, and Dean of Wells. According to John Aubrey's notes on Jonson's life, Bathurst told Aubrey in 1646 when he was a student at Trinity that Ben Jonson was a Warwickshire man.

Baxter, Robert. An actor who performed in *Cynthia's Revels* in 1601 as a member of the Children of the Chapel.

Bayard. Bayard was the magic horse given to Charlemagne by Rinaldo; the name came to stand for any horse. Chaucer wrote of a blind Bayard who traveled everywhere, having no fear or caution. Subtle refers to Drugger as a Bayard when, in *The Alchemist* (II), he blunders in on Subtle's work.

Bayly, Lewes (1565–1631), chaplain to James I and Bishop of Bangor. He was the author of a famous work entitled *The Practice of Piety: Directing a Christian How to Walk That He May Please God,* which was first licensed for publication in 1612 and went through over seventy editions, the last one appearing in 1842. The book was often ridiculed by writers. Jonson mentions it in *The Gypsies Metamorphosed* and in *The Magnetic Lady* (IV. iv).

Beale, John. A printer who in 1631 printed for Robert Allot *Bartholomew Fair, The Devil Is an Ass,* and *The Staple of News.*

Beater. In *Love's Welcome at Bolsover,* a mortar mixer who appears in Colonel Vitruvius' dance of the mechanics.

Beaufort, Lord. In *The New Inn* the old Lord Beaufort is a former companion of Lovel's. His son, young Lord Beaufort, is Lovel's ward and in the play eventually marries Laetitia, daughter of Lord Frampul.

Beaumont, Francis (1584–1616), was the third son of Francis Beaumont, Justice of

Common Pleas. In 1597 Beaumont entered Broadgates Hall, Oxford, and in 1600 the Inner Temple. In London he made the acquaintance of Michael Drayton and Jonson, and about 1606 he wrote *The Woman Hater,* a comedy showing the influence of Jonson's humor theory. The next year Beaumont's *Knight of the Burning Pestle* was produced. In about 1608 Beaumont began collaborating on plays with John Fletcher; their collaboration produced more than thirty plays and lasted until Beaumont's marriage to Ursula Isley in 1613. The first folio of their plays was published in 1647, the second in 1679.

Beaumont was considered a master in the construction of plots, and John Dryden claimed that Jonson submitted all his plays to Beaumont for his advice on plotting. Whether or not this claim is true, there apparently existed an affectionate relationship between Beaumont and Jonson although Jonson reportedly told Drummond of Hawthornden in the *Conversations* (l. 454) that Beaumont loved himself and his own verses too much. Beaumont contributed a prefatory poem to the quarto of *Volpone,* one to the quarto of *Catiline,* and a poem on *Epicoene* to the folio of 1616. The Beaumont and Fletcher folios contain a famous verse epistle ("The sun which doth the greatest comfort bring") on Jonson, to which Jonson's *Epig.* LV is an answer. Another verse epistle by Beaumont ("Neither to follow fashion nor to show") addressed to Jonson and written about 1615 was first published in 1930 in E. K. Chambers's *William Shakespeare* (Vol. 2, pp. 222–25). Beaumont was buried in Westminster Abbey, near Chaucer and Spenser.

Beaumont, Sir John (1583–1627). Brother of Francis Beaumont. Buckingham was his patron. *Bosworth-Field,* to which Jonson affixed a commendatory poem ("On the Honored Poems of his Honored Friend, Sir John Beaumont, Baronet") was published posthumously in 1629. Beaumont apparently composed verses for Buckingham to welcome the king to the performance of Jonson's *The Gypsies Metamorphosed* at Burley. Beaumont's son, who edited *Bosworth-Field,* also contributed an elegy ("Had this been for some meaner poet's hearse") to *Jonsonus Virbius.*

Beaurline, L. A. (1927–   ). American scholar specializing in English drama and Renaissance literature, educated at the University of Missouri and the University of Chicago. Professor Beaurline has taught at several American colleges and since 1969 has been Professor of English at the University of Virginia. He has published several influential essays on Jonson and is the author of the provocative *Jonson and Elizabethan Comedy: Essays in Dramatic Rhetoric* (1978).

Beaw (Bew), William (1615–1705), a fellow of New College in 1637, took his B.A. in 1639, his M.A. in 1644, and his D.D. in 1666. He contributed a Latin elegy ("Epitaphium in Ben: Ionson") to *Jonsonus Virbius.* He became vicar of Adderbury in 1661 and Bishop of Llandaff in 1679.

Becon, Thomas. Author of *The Sick Man's Salve* (first published 1561), a work that taught Christians how to live and die. Becon's work is mentioned by Wolf in *Eastward Ho* (v. ii) and discussed by Haughty and Trusty in *Epicoene* (IV. iv).

Bedford, Lucy Harington, Countess of (1581–1627), married Edward, 3rd Earl of Bedford, in 1594. She was a great patroness of literary men, befriending Jonson, Donne, Daniel, Drayton, and Florio. In an extant 1605 letter which he wrote from prison, Jonson probably requested her help in securing his release, and in a grace most likely delivered at her house Jonson asked that the Countess be blessed. A brilliant figure at court for both her beauty and talent, she was often prominent in court masques. She danced in the *Masques of Blackness and Beauty, Hymenaei,* and *The Masque of Queens.* In 1617 she organized *Lovers Made Men* for Lord Hay. Jonson celebrated her in *Epig.* LXXVI, LXXXIV, and XCIV. He also printed a special dedication to her in a gift-copy of *Cynthia's Revels.* According to the *Conversations* (ll. 394–95), Jonson told Drummond that Lucy was Ethra in his lost pastoral *The May Lord.*

Beeston, Christopher. An actor who performed in *Every Man in his Humour* in 1598 as a member of the Chamberlain's Men. In 1602 he joined Worcester's Men and passed with them to the Queen's Men in 1603. He eventually became a leading actor and owner of the Cockpit Theatre, where he was joined by Queen Anne's in 1617, Prince Charles's in 1619, Lady Elizabeth's in 1622, Queen Henrietta's from 1625 to 1637, and the King's and Queen's young company (Beeston's Boys) in 1637. He died about 1639.

Behn, Aphra. (1649–1689), became the first female professional English writer. She is considered a forerunner of the feminist movement. She denied woman's subservience to man and led a bohemian life. After the death of her husband, she served as a spy during the Dutch Wars from 1665 to 1667, adopting the code name Astraea, under which she later published much of her verse. She was unsuccessful as a spy and turned to writing. By 1670 her first play had been performed, and in 1677 she gained considerable fame with her successful play *The Rover*. She wrote quickly, industriously, and prolifically. Her best literary efforts can be found in her numerous novels, the most notable being *Oroonoko* (1688), a heroic love story in which the noble savage first appears in literature. Her reputation declined rapidly in the eighteenth century, but there has been a revival of interest in her work during the twentieth century.

In her Epistle to the Reader in *The Dutch Lover* (1673), Behn, in explaining why women with equal education to men were not as capable of knowledge, argued that plays have no room for the advantage which men generally have over women, that is, specifically learning, and to defend her position alluded to Shakespeare and Jonson as follows: "We all well know that the immoral Shakespeare's plays (who was not guilty of much more of this than often falls to women's share) have better pleased the world than Jonson's works, though by the way 'tis said that Benjamin was no such Rabbi neither, for I am informed his learning was but grammar high; (sufficient indeed to rob poor Salust of his best orations) and it hath been observed, that they are apt to admire him most confoundedly, who had just such a scantling of it as he had; and I have seen a man the most severe of Jonson's sect, sit with his hat removed less than a hair's breadth from one sullen posture for almost three hours at *The Alchemist;* who at that excellent play of Harry the Fourth . . . hath very hardly kept his doublet whole; but affectation hath always had a greater share both in the actions and discourse of men than truth and judgment have."

Bel-Anna. According to Jonson, the royal Queen of the Ocean. A symbolic character representing Queen Anne, who appears as one of the virtuous queens in *The Masque of Queens.*

Bellerophon. In the *Iliad,* a young man of great virtue and valor who was beloved by Anteia, wife of Proteus, king of Argos. Bellerophon killed the Chimaera with the help of Pegasus, conquered the Solynis, and defeated the Amazons. In his later years Bellerophon was hated by the gods.

Bembo, Pietro, Cardinal (1470–1547). A great humanist. In *Volpone* (II), Volpone says in the mountebank scene that his rival and enemy has been spreading the lie that he has been in prison for poisoning a member of Bembo's household.

Benn, Sir Anthony, Recorder of London, was knighted in 1617 and died the following year. Jonson's *Und.* XXXIII is addressed to him.

Bennet, Sir Thomas. Lord Mayor of London who is alluded to with respect by Genius in *The King's Entertainment in Passing to his Coronation.*

Benson, John. Bookseller in London, 1635–67, who published the 1640 duodecimo of Jonson's *Poems,* which included the translation of *Ars Poetica* and *The Gypsies Metamorphosed.* He also published the *Poems* in quarto (1640).

Bentley, Gerald Eades (1901–   ). American scholar, educated at DePauw University, University of Illinois, and University of London. Since 1950 Professor of English at Princeton University. Professor Bentley has published numerous essays and books on English drama, including *Shakespeare and Jonson: Their Reputations in the Seventeenth Century Compared* (1945)— the standard reference work on the subject.

Berenice. Mythical woman who sacrificed her hair to Venus for the safe return of her husband from an expedition.

Beronice. Also known as Berenice. According to Jonson, the daughter of Ptolomaeus Philadelphus. She appears as one of the virtuous queens in *The Masque of Queens.*

Bertie, Robert. See Robert Bertie, Lord WILLOUGHBY.

Bestia, Lucius. In *Catiline,* one of the conspirators who supports Catiline's abortive attempt to seize power in Rome.

Bettrice. A waiting woman to Gertrude in *Eastward Ho.*

Bew, William. See William BEAW (BEW).

Biancha (Dame Kitely). Character in *Every Man in His Humour,* of which there are two versions, that of the 1601 quarto and that of the 1616 folio. (Differing names and courses of action in the 1616 folio version are given here in parentheses.) Biancha (Dame Kitely) is sister to Giuliano (Downright), Prospero (Wellbred), and Hesperida (Bridget) and wife to

Thorello (Kitely). She protests to Giuliano (Downright) that she cannot prevent Prospero (Wellbred) and his companions from entering her house; although she listens to Matheo's (Matthew's) foolishness and poetry with her sister, she is not unfaithful, as her husband fears. She acts impetuously and a little foolishly when Prospero (Wellbred) tells her that Thorello (Kitely) is being unfaithful to her with Cob's wife, and rushes to Cob's house, where she meets her husband, who suspects her of going there to be unfaithful to him. Dr. Clement (Justice Clement) unravels the complications Musca (Brainworm) has woven, and she and her husband are reconciled.

Bias. In *The Magnetic Lady,* a sub-secretary who is one of the suitors to Lady Loadstone's niece.

Bible. We know that Jonson's library contained the following scriptures: (1) *Biblia Sacra Vulgatae Editionis Sixti V.P.M. jussu recognita.* Antwerp, 1599. (2) *The Whole Psalter Translated in English Metre.* (Archbishop Parker's version printed by John Day about 1567). (3) *The Gospels of the Fower Evangelistes translated in the olde Saxons tyme out of Latin into the vulgare toung of the Saxons.* Preface by John Foxe. London, 1571. (Bishops' version in parallel columns).

He may have owned others that were destroyed in the fire of 1623 along with his treatise on divinity. No record of his owning a copy of the King James Version (1611) has been found although he certainly knew the work. No doubt he was also well versed in the Geneva Bible, The Bishops' Bible, and the Rheims-Douay.

The majority of Jonson's scriptural allusions are to books of the Old Testament with Psalms being the most popular. New Testament books referred to include Matthew, Luke, Romans, and Revelations, which is the New Testament book most frequently alluded to.

The following is a list of Jonson's obvious scriptural allusions (Biblical citations refer to the King James Version).

Genesis 2:11–14 (*Und.* LXXXIV. 3, ll. 21–24)
35:18 (*Epig.* XLV)
42:16 (*Every Man in* [Q 1601], I. iii. 75)
Exodus 28:17, 39:10 (*Ungathered Verse* (I, ll. 13–16)
Judges 14:14 (*Love's Welcome at Bolsover,* ll. 181–2)
I Samuel 15:22 (*Und.* I, ll. 11–13)

Psalms 7:9 (*For.* XV, ll. 5–6)
45:7 (*Und.* IX, ll. 100–102)
51:17 (*Und.* I, l. 10)
104:15 (*The New Inn,* I. ii. 24–27)
Proverbs 8:15 (*King's Entertainment in Passing to His Coronation,* l. 63)
Matthew 10:16 (*King's Entertainment in Passing to His Coronation,* ll. 60–61)
Luke 1:28 (*Und.* LXVI, ll. 1–3)
Romans 7:24 (*For.* XV, ll. 23–24.
Revelation 7:8 (*Und.* XLVII, ll. 11–15; 77–78)
8:3–4 (*Und.* LXXXIV, 9, ll. 187–88)
12:14 (*The Staple of News,* III. ii. 128–29)

Bill, John. King's printer and important bookseller in London from 1604 to 1630 who often traveled abroad to buy books for the Bodleian Library on commission. Jonson mentions him in *Epig.* XCII.

Bingham, John. Translator of *The Tactics of Aelian* (1616) alluded to by Jonson in *Und.* XLIV.

Bishop, Richard. Printer and publisher who in 1640 published the first volume of the second folio of Jonson's works.

Bitterness. The name of one of the witches making up the antimasque in *The Masque of Queens.*

Blaney, John. An actor who played in *Epicoene* in 1609 when he was a member of the Children of the Queen's Revels. He was one of the Queen's Men from 1616 to 1619.

Blinkinsop, John. Fencer admitted to the Association of the Masters of the Noble Science of Defense in 1579 and mentioned by Jonson in *The New Inn* (II. v).

Bloody Brother, The. A play of uncertain date and authorship that may have been written by John Fletcher, Francis Beaumont, and Philip Massinger. Some scholars think that Jonson may also have had a hand in the play, but there seems to be very little evidence that Jonson wrote any of the play although there are some passages which may have been borrowed from him.

Blount, Edward. Bookseller in London from 1594 to 1632, one of the publishers of the First Folio of Shakespeare in 1623. In 1604 he entered *Sejanus* on the Stationers' Register but transferred the play to Thomas Thorp in 1605. Later in 1604 he published in quarto Jonson's part of the

King's Entertainment through the City of London, together with the *Entertainment of the Queen and Prince at Althorp* and *A Panegyre.*

Blount, Mountjoy. See Mountjoy Blount, Earl of NEWPORT.

Blyenberch, Abraham. See PORTRAITS.

Bobadilla, Captain. In *Every Man in His Humour,* a very foolish gallant. (The version of the play in the folio of 1616 differs from that in the quarto of 1601—many of the characters have different names. Names used in the folio version are in parentheses here.) Captain Bobadilla fancies himself very fashionable and brave. His name connotes braggart and is derived from Boabdil, the name of the last king of the Moors in Spain. (He is described as "Paulesman," or lounger in the middle aisle of St. Paul's, which was a popular meeting place in the early seventeenth century.) He is first seen rising after a night of drinking; he is happy in his lodgings at Cob's, but a little ashamed because they are not quite fashionable. He claims to know a great deal about fencing, often using technical terms, and he teaches Matheo (Matthew) a thrust to use when he is threatened by Giuliano (Downright). Lorenzo junior (Edward) and Prospero (Wellbred) mock him for his foolishness; he swears colorfully and in excess. He claims to have been at great battles and to be a skillful soldier, and makes a long speech on the virtues of tobacco. He offers to fight Giuliano (Downright) when surrounded by his friends but is afraid to draw later, when Giuliano (Downright) actually fights with him, and covers his shame by bragging to Matheo (Matthew). He tells of a plan to rid Italy (England) of his "forty thousand" enemies by, with the help of nineteen other men, killing them all in combat. He and Matheo (Matthew) "arrest" Giuliano (Downright) and go with him to Dr. Clement's (Justice Clement's) where Clement, realizing what a fool Bobadilla is, sentences him to spend the night in jail and stand bound the whole next day in the town square, then to sing for repentance (sentences him to stand in his courtyard and fast and wait with Matthew while the others feast).

Boccaccio, Giovanni (1313–1375). Italian poet and novelist, best known as the author of the *Decameron,* a hundred tales supposed to have been told by seven young ladies and three young men who withdrew from Florence into the country during the plague of 1348. A number of incidents in Shakespeare's plays are indebted to Boc-

caccio. Jonson's indebtedness seems to be somewhat limited. In *The Devil Is an Ass,* Fitzdottrel is apparently inspired by Boccaccio's Francesco from the *Decameron,* and Mrs. Fitzdottrel is apparently modeled on Francesco's wife. In the same play, Wittipol seems to be modeled upon Boccaccio's Il Zima. The episode of the cloak is also apparently derived from the *Decameron.* In *The Alchemist* (II. i. 103) Boccaccio's Demogorgon, a character said to have existed from eternity, is referred to as an abstract riddle of a philosopher's stone. Jonson most likely also borrowed the phrase "Tale of a Tub" from Boccaccio's *Decameron.* Boccaccio died less than a year after the death of his dearest friend, Petrarch.

Bodin, Jean (1530–1596). French social and political philosopher who studied at Toulouse and developed a successful legal career. Because he was tolerant of various religious views, he was accused of being a free thinker. His *Les Six Livres de la république* (1576; English trans. 1606) is often considered the first attempt at formulating a modern philosophy of history. Replacing the idea of a golden age with that of progress, he foreshadowed Hobbes by arguing for the necessity of absolute monarchic sovereignty, and he anticipated Montesquieu by stressing the influence of environment in shaping laws, customs, and events. Although he held many mercantilist views about economic theory, he believed that the rise of prices was a function not only of the debasement of the coinage but also of the amount of currency in circulation. Bodin is mentioned by Sir Politic in *Volpone* (IV. i) in order to impress Peregrine, and Jonson used Bodin's *De Magorum daemonomania* (1581) in *The Masque of Queens.*

Bolton, Edmund (c. 1575–1633?). Historian and poet who secured the patronage of Buckingham and James I and was a friend of Jonson's. In 1617 he nominated Jonson as a candidate for an academy of letters which he proposed to James I, but the proposed academy was never realized. In his critical account of contemporary authors entitled *Hypercritica* (c. 1616) Bolton praised Jonson for his poetic language, and he wrote prefatory verses for *Volpone* ("Ad Utramque Academiam De Beniamin Ionsonio") and probably for *Sejanus* ("To the Most Understanding Poet"). In *The Staple of News* (II. ii), Jonson alludes to Bolton's book *The Elements of Armories* (1610).

Bonario. Corbaccio's son in *Volpone.* Disinherited by his foolish, scheming father in favor of Volpone, young Bonario comes to Volpone's house in anger, overhears the plot to prostitute Celia, and saves her. He is later viciously slandered in court, but when his father is punished he inherits his estate.

Bonion, Richard. Bookseller in London from 1607 to 1611 who, together with Henry Walley, published in 1609 the first quarto of Shakespeare's *Troilus and Cressida* and in the same year the quarto of Jonson's *Masque of Queens*.

Bonefonius (Bonnefons), Jean (c. 1550–1614), born at Clermont in Auvergne, cultivated Latin poetry with success and wrote imitations of Catullus. In the *Conversations* (l. 68), Drummond reports that Jonson considered Bonnefons excellent.

Book-holder. A man who comes onto the stage before *Bartholomew Fair*, reprimands the Stage-helper for speaking freely, and tells the Scrivener to read the text of an "agreement" between Jonson and his audience.

Boreas. 1. A character in *The Masque of Beauty* who appears as a messenger.
2. The north wind in Greek mythology.

Boughner, Daniel C. (1909–1974). American scholar educated at West Virginia University, Tufts University, and Princeton. He taught at a number of American institutions and from 1964 served as Professor of English at Brooklyn College. In 1968 he published his controversial book on Jonson's debt to Machiavelli.

Bouleutes. A symbolic personage appearing in Jonson's part of the *King's Coronation Entertainment* who represents the council of the city.

Boulstred, Cecilia. See Cecilia BULSTRODE.

Bowl-Bearer. An unnamed character who appears in *Pleasure Reconciled to Virtue* as the bowl bearer for Hercules and recites a long speech in praise of the pleasures of the belly.

Bradamante. An Amazon in Ariosto's *Orlando Furioso*. In Fletcher's *Love's Cure,* one of his characters, Clara, is addressed by this name. In *The Alchemist* (II), Mammon calls Dol by this name after he sees her, and Face tells him that she is a lord's sister, sent there to be cured of her madness.

Bradock, Richard. Printer in London from 1581 to 1615 who probably printed in quarto in 1600 *Every Man out of His Humour* for William Holme.

Brainworm. See MUSCO.

Bramble. 1. In *Eastward Ho* a lawyer who prepares a legal document for Security giving him Gertrude's land in exchange for a loan to Sir Petronel Flash. The lawyer later visits Security when he is in prison but is unable to help him.
2. See Justice PREAMBLE.

Branchus. A character who appears in *The Masque of Augurs* as one of the sons of Apollo and assists in the interpretation of the augury.

Bretnor, Thomas. Noted almanac-maker and student of astrology whose almanacs and predictions for 1605–1618 have survived. In Jonson's *The Devil Is an Ass* (I. ii), Fitzdottrel alludes to Bretnor as one who is unable to show man the devil.

Breton, Nicholas (1551?–?1623). Prolific English writer of both verse and prose. Jonson wrote a commendatory sonnet ("In Authorem") for Breton's *Melancholike Humors* (1600). In *No Whipping, nor Tripping, but a Kind, Friendly Snipping* (1601), Breton replied to *The Whipping of the Satyre* (1601), in which Jonson had been attacked. Jonson's only direct reference to Breton occurs in *Und.* XLIII, in which Breton's Pasquil pamphlets are referred to contemptuously.

Brewster, Edward. Bookseller who in 1692 was one of the publishers of the third folio of Jonson's *Works.*

Briareus. A hundred-handed monster brought by Thetis to protect Zeus against Hera, Poseidon, and Athena.

Brideoake, Ralph (1613–1678). M.A. New College, Oxford, in 1636, D.D. in 1660, Dean of Salisbury in 1667, and finally Bishop of Chichester in 1675. He contributed an elegy ("Tis not secure to be too learn'd, or good") to *Jonsonus Virbius.*

Bridget, Mistress. See HESPERIDA (Bridget).

Briggs, Richard, from 1602 to 1630 was headmaster of Norfolk School. He was probably the brother of the mathematician Henry Briggs. In 1623 Jonson wrote Richard a letter in Latin in the margin of Jonson's own copy of Thomas Farnaby's edition of *Martial* (1615).

Brisk, Fastidious. In *Every Man out of His Humour,* a finicking courtier who eventually ends up in prison because of his excessive debts.

Bristle. A watchman at the fair in *Bartholomew Fair.* He puts Waspe and Zeal-of-the-Land Busy in the stocks, but Trouble-all attacks him and Haggise, and the prisoners escape.

Brisson, Barnabé. Author of *De Formulis et Sollemnibus Populi Romani Verbis* (1592), one of Jonson's archaeological authorities for *Sejanus*. Brisson also wrote *De Ritu Nuptiarum* (1564), which Jonson used in *Hymenaei*.

Broker. In *The Staple of News*, the secretary and gentleman usher to Lady Pecunia.

Brome, Alexander. The editor of Richard Brome's *Five New Plays* (1659) in which the prefatory comments allude favorably to Richard Brome's relationship with Jonson. Alexander Brome claims that no one could find a better master than Jonson to teach him how to write a good play. Alexander Brome translated and published Jonson's *Leges Convivales* in his *Songs and Other Poems* (1661), and he edited *The Poems of Horace . . . Rendered into English Verse By Several Persons* 1666; 1671; 1680), in which Jonson's translation of *The Art of Poetry* was reprinted from the folio.

Brome, Richard (1590–1652). Friend, servant, and disciple of Jonson's. He became a successful dramatist, primarily writing realistic satirical comedies in the Jonsonian vein but also several less successful tragicomedies. The majority of his comedies, characterized by humor figures, complicated comic intrigue, and an abundance of action, were produced between 1629 and 1642. The most successful of them were *The Northern Lass*, for which Jonson wrote a commendatory poem ("To My Old Faithful Servant"), *The City Wit*, and *The Jovial Crew*. Brome is alluded to as Jonson's servant in the Induction to *Bartholomew Fair*. See also Alexander BROME.

Brontes. One of the Cyclopes who assisted Vulcan at his forge on Mount Aetna.

Brooke, Christopher. (d. 1628) A bencher of Lincoln's Inn. Donne and William Browne were among his friends. Brooke was the author of *The Ghost of Richard the Third* (1614), for which Jonson wrote a commendatory poem ("When these, and such, their voices have employed").

Brooke, Ralph. York herald who published *A Catalogue of the Nobility* (1619), which was attacked by Augustine Vincent in 1622 and resulted in a well-known quarrel between Brooke and Vincent alluded to by Jonson in *The New Inn* (II. vi).

Brooke, Sir Robert. Chief Justice of the Court of Common Pleas and Speaker of the House of Commons and author of *La Graunde Abridgement* (1568). Brooke is mentioned by Fungoso in *Every Man out* (II. iii).

Broughton, Bess. A London prostitute well-known for her beauty and wit, who died of the pox. She was remembered in song. Jonson mentions her in *Und.* XLIII.

Broughton, Hugh (1549–1612). A divine and rabbinical scholar who became a strong Puritan. He wrote a number of learned monographs and controversial pamphlets, and in 1590 he published *A Concent of Scripture*, an effort to settle Biblical chronology. Broughton's collected works were published by John Lightfoot in 1662.

In *Volpone* (II. ii), during the mountebank scene, Peregrine remarks that the only chicanery he has seen equal to Volpone's is alchemy and Broughton's writings. In *The Alchemist* (II. iii), Face tells Mammon that Dol has gone crazy studying Broughton's books, and Mammon is later (IV. v) convinced when he sees her wildly quoting from Broughton's *A Concent of Scripture*.

Browne, John. Bookseller and bookbinder in London from 1598 to 1622 who, together with John Busby, Jr., entered *Epicoene* on the Stationers' Register in 1610 but transferred his rights to Walter Burre in 1612.

Browne, Robert. An actor who in 1599 when he may have been a member of Lord Derby's company brought suit against Jonson for a bad debt. Browne won the suit, and Jonson was imprisoned in the Marshalsea in Southwark and ordered to pay.

Browne, William, of Tavistock. Author of *Britannia's Pastorals. The Second Book* (1616), for which Jonson wrote a commendatory poem ("Some men, of books or friends not speaking right"), one of his uncollected poems. The work was dedicated to Jonson's patron William, Earl of Pembroke, and in the second song in the book Browne paid a tribute to contemporary poets, including Jonson. "On the Countess Dowager of Pembroke," usually ascribed to Jonson, was probably written by Browne.

Browning, Elizabeth Barrett (1806–1861). English poet and wife of Robert Browning. She spent much of her early life in semi-invalidism, but in 1838 the family moved to London, where she met Robert Browning. They carried on an ardent love affair and were married in 1846 over the objections of Elizabeth's tyrannical father.

They eloped to Italy, where they lived most of their married life and their only child, a son, was born. In Italy Elizabeth's health improved, and she devoted herself to the cause of Italian liberation and to her poetry, the best of which is *Sonnets from the Portuguese* (1850).

In a letter to H. S. Boyd, Mrs. Browning expressed her great admiration for Jonson's *Epig.* XXXII and proclaimed, "you will acknowledge it to be very superior in force of expression and elevation of sentiment. I scarcely ever read anything which seemed to me at once so simple and so noble."

Brutus, Marcus Junius (85 B.C.–42 B.C.), was renowned for his high moral character, independence of spirit, and contemplative nature. He fought with Pompey in the civil war but was pardoned by Caesar; he conspired against Caesar, apparently for high partriotic motives. He quarreled with Antony and campaigned in the East; he committed suicide after Antony and Octavian defeated him and Cassius at the second battle of Philippi. In *Sejanus* (I. i) he is praised by Arruntius, who laments that, in his age, there is no "constant Brutus, that (being proofe / Against all charme of benefits) did strike / So brave a blow into a monsters heart / That sought unkindly to captive his countrie." Later in the play Sabinus praises Germanicus by saying that he had "wise Brutus temperance," and Cordus is accused of slandering Caesar by writing in praise of Brutus (III. iv). Cordus attempts to defend himself by telling how well-regarded writers of the past also honored Brutus.

Bryant, Joseph A., Jr. (1919–). American scholar educated at Western Kentucky State University, Vanderbilt University, and Yale University. Since 1971 Professor of English at the University of Kentucky. Author of books on Shakespeare and Eudora Welty and the highly acclaimed study *The Compassionate Satirist: Ben Jonson and His Imperfect World* (1973).

Buchanan, George (1506–1582). Scottish humanist. Driven into exile because of his Protestant views, he held academic posts on the Continent, where he was regarded as a good Latin poet. In 1560 he returned to Scotland to tutor Queen Mary and later James VI (later James I of England). His most influential work was the *De Jure regni apud Scotos* (1579), which declares that the king rules by popular will and for the general good.

In the *Conversations* (ll. 561–63) Jonson claimed that he told James that Buchanan had corrupted the king's ear when he was young because the tutor taught him to sing verses when he should have read them.

Buckhurst, Baron. See Richard SACKVILLE.

Buckingham, George Villiers, Duke of (1592–1628), arrived at the English court in 1614 when James I was becoming disenchanted with his favorite, Robert Carr, Earl of Somerset. After Somerset's disgrace, Villiers was made a gentleman of the bedchamber in 1615, Earl of Buckingham in 1617, Marquess of Buckingham in 1618, and Lord High Admiral in 1619. The following year he married the daughter of the Earl of Rutland, Lady Katharine Manners, who favored Catholicism. As the king's new favorite, Buckingham received considerable privileges. In 1621 he was censored by Parliament for the abuses of his monopolies by his brothers and dependents. He himself escaped punishment, but he was unable to help his friend Sir Francis Bacon on his bribery charges. In 1623 Buckingham went to Spain incognito with Prince Charles in an effort to effect the Prince's proposed marriage to the Infanta Maria. When they found Spanish demands impossible to meet, they returned to England and Buckingham, now a Duke, was considered a hero for having prevented the unpopular marriage. Shrewdly, he promoted war with Spain and urged James to disregard his promise to Parliament concerning religious restrictions on the proposed match of Charles with Henrietta Maria, sister of Louis XIII of France.

During the Thirty Years War, he unsuccessfully supported Frederick the Winter King against the emperor in the Palatinate. After Charles's accession, Buckingham was still the favorite, and he was essentially the dictator of English affairs, for which he was resented by Parliament, who suspected him of being interested only in personal gain. After the failure in 1625 of an expedition against Cádiz, Buckingham was impeached in 1626, and only Charles's dissolving of Parliament saved him from a trial. Following the failure of his attempted relief of the Huguenots on the Isle of Ré off La Rochelle, Parliament again censured Buckingham. In 1628 while preparing another expedition for La Rochelle, he was murdered by John Felton, a discontented naval officer.

Jonson seems to have been not close to

Buckingham but circumspect about him. In his extemporaneous grace before James, he blessed Buckingham as "the fortunate," and he alluded to him with official respect in *For the Honor of Wales* and *Neptune's Triumph*. Buckingham commissioned the Burley performance of *The Gypsies Metamorphosed*, and he danced in *The Golden Age Restored, The Vision of Delight, Pleasure Reconciled,* and *For the Honor of Wales*. He also appeared in *News From the New World in the Moon, Time Vindicated,* and *The Fortunate Isles;* and he played the first gypsy in *The Gypsies Metamorphosed,* telling the king's fortune.

On October 26, 1629, Jonson was questioned by the Attorney General, Sir Robert Heath, about his knowledge of the authorship of an anonymous poem praising John Felton, Buckingham's assassin. Jonson told Heath that he had heard that the verses were written by Zouch Townley.

Budé, Guillaume (1467–1540). One of the greatest humanists and French scholars of all time. He was secretary to Francis I and persuaded the king to found the Collége de France. Budé made scholarly contributions in the study of Roman law, language, Greek literature, politics, and economics. His *De Asse et Partibus Eius* (1522) served as one of Jonson's authorities for *Sejanus.*

Buffone, Carlo. In *Every Man out of His Humour,* a scurrilous and profane jester.

Bullokar, William. Author of *Amendment of Orthographie* (1580) and *Bref Grammar for English* (1586), both of which were used by Jonson as authorities for his *English Grammar.*

Bulmer, Sir Bevis. A famous mining engineer and speculator who was knighted in 1604, Bulmer mined lead and silver in Scotland, and in 1606 he was given a grant for five years of all the gold and silver mined in the kingdom provided he paid rent of one-sixth of the produce. In 1608 he was appointed master of the mines for life, but in spite of his success he died in debt in 1615. Jonson mentions him under the pseudonym of Sir Bevis Bullion in *The Staple of News* (I. iii).

Bulstrode, Cecilia, Lady, died in 1609 after an agonizing illness, and Jonson wrote a very sympathetic epitaph for her, "Stay, view this stone: And if thou beest not such," one of his uncollected poems. The epitaph is something of an enigma since *Und.* XLIX is a satirical attack on Lady Bulstrode, which Jonson read to Drum-

mond, according to the *Conversations* (ll. 103–4). Jonson also told Drummond (ll. 646–48) that a man had gotten him drunk, stolen the verses on Cecilia as the court pucelle and given them to her, bringing the poet "great displeasure."

Burbage, Richard (1568?–1619). The son of James Burbage, who was the builder of the Blackfriars Theatre, Richard joined the Chamberlain's men in 1594, quickly established himself as a prominent member, and continued as one of the King's Men until his death. He acted in *Every Man in His Humour, Every Man out of His Humour, Sejanus, Volpone, The Alchemist,* and *Catiline,* probably playing the roles, respectively, of Brainworm, Brisk, Sejanus, Mosca, Face, and Cicero. He also played the leading roles in many of Shakespeare's plays, including *Hamlet, Lear,* and *Othello.* Burbage and Shakespeare were apparently good friends, and Shakespeare left money to Burbage in his will. Jonson lauded Burbage in *Bartholomew Fair* (v. iii. 86–8). An epigram on Burbage ("Tell me who can when a player dies") has sometimes been attributed to Jonson.

Burby, Cuthbert. Bookseller in London from 1592 to 1607 who, together with Walter Burre, entered *Every Man in His Humour* in the Stationers' Register in 1600. The play appeared in quarto in 1601 under Burre's imprint.

Burges, John. Friend of Jonson's and a clerk of the Exchequer whom Jonson appointed in 1621 to see that a debt to John Hull was satisfied by funds from Jonson's pension. In *Und.* LV Jonson thanked Burges for a gift and in LVII asked that he remind the Exchequer to pay his pension. In a portrait of Jonson attributed to Rubens, but probably by an English painter influenced by the Flemish school, Jonson is shown holding a scroll on which *Und.* LVII is written. The portrait may have been painted for the Burges family.

Burghley, William Cecil, Lord (1520–1598). English statesman who first rose to power in 1548 when Edward Seymour was Protector. From 1550 to 1553 he served as secretary of state. Although he was not in the favor of Mary I, he was reappointed to office by Elizabeth I and served her faithfully for forty years. He was created Baron Burghley of Burghley (sometimes Burleigh) and knight of the Garter in 1571, was appointed Lord High Treasurer in 1572, and became the Queen's principal adviser. Clever, bold, and diplomatic, he contributed greatly to the development of

England as a leading European power. Burghley took responsibility for the execution of Mary, Queen of Scots, and he worked constantly for the peaceful establishment and consolidation of English Protestantism. Even though his advice was not always followed, Burghley's hand can be detected in most of the major policies of Elizabeth's reign.

Although Burghley did not encourage poets, choosing instead to patronize historical and political writers, Jonson wrote a laudatory poem about him (*Und.* XXX) which was presented on a plate of gold to Burghley's son, Robert, Earl of Salisbury, when he, like his father before him, was Lord High Treasurer.

Burlase, Sir William (also Borlase, Borlace, or Burlacy) (d. 1629). The son of John Borlase of Little Marlow, Sir William entered Gray's Inn in 1594, served as Sheriff of Buckinghamshire in 1601, and was knighted in 1603. In 1624 he founded a school at Great Marlow. Jonson's *Und.* LII is in part a response to a poem that Burlase sent him. The other part of Jonson's poem commemorates a portrait of Jonson painted by Burlase. Where the portrait is, if it still exists, is not known.

Burratines. Either puppets or grotesque, lean young men in ruffs and masks. They were stock characters in the Italian *Commedia dell'arte*. In *The Vision of Delight* they dance with six Pantalones in the first antimasque.

Burre, Walter. Bookseller in London from 1597 to 1622 who published several of Jonson's plays in quarto: *Every Man in His Humor* in 1601; *Cynthia's Revels* in 1601; *Catiline* in 1611; and *The Alchemist* in 1612. Burre also entered in the Stationers' Register *Volpone* in 1610 and *Epicoene* in 1612. After Burre's death, his widow assigned to John Spencer, in 1630, her rights to *Cynthia's Revels, The Alchemist, Epicoene,* and *Catiline.*

Burst, Bat. In *The New Inn,* an unhappy citizen who becomes a companion of Colonel Tipto's.

Burton, Henry (1578–1648). Burton was the Puritanical rector of St. Matthew's who published in 1627 *The Baiting of the Pope's Bull,* which is alluded to in *The Magnetic Lady* (I. v.).

Burton, Robert. (1577–1640). English clergyman and scholar born in Leicestershire and educated at Oxford. Burton's famous work *The Anatomy of Melancholy* originally appeared in 1621 under the pseudonym of Democritus Junior; it was revised and enlarged several times before his death in 1640. Originally intended as a treatise on the causes and effects of melancholy, *The Anatomy* eventually covered a wide range of subjects, including science, history, and political and social reform. In the fourth edition (1632) Burton defines humor; in the 1621 edition he refers to Fastidious Brisk (pp. 205; 677–78) and Sir Petronel Flask (p. 205), and in the 1624 version he cites Deliro (pp. 468–69) and Juniper (p. 222) in his examples. Burton owned a copy of the 1606 quarto of *Hymenaei* and the 1624–25 quarto of *The Fortunate Isles.*

Busby, John, Jr. Bookseller in London from 1607 to 1631 who, together with John Browne, entered *Epicoene* in the Stationers' Register in 1610.

Busy, Zeal-of-the-Land. A zealous Puritan in *Bartholomew Fair.* He is a suitor to Dame Purecraft and preaches to her and her family about the corruption of the fair. He is put in the stocks for his railing and finally loses a debate with a puppet. In a speech to Quarlous, Purecraft reveals that he is actually selfish and materialistic.

Butler, Charles. Grammarian who published in 1633 *The English Grammar, Or the Institution of Letters, Syllables, and Words, in the English Tongue,* a work which served as one of Jonson's authorities for his own *English Grammar.*

Butler, Nathaniel. Bookseller in London from 1605 to 1664. Often considered the founder of English journalism because of his publication of one of the first periodical news sheets. Nathaniel, the clerk of the Staple, in *The Staple of News* is thought to be modeled after him, and he is alluded to in *The Magnetic Lady* (III. vii) and *Und.* XLIII. In 1622 Butler issued his first newspaper *News from most Parts of Christendom* in cooperation with William Shefford. Together with Inigo Jones, Butler attended the opening of *The Magnetic Lady,* and their reactions were humorously satirized in a poem on the play by Alexander Gill.

Butler, William (1535–1618), was born at Ipswich and educated at Clare Hall, Cambridge, which in 1572 granted Butler a license to practice physic. He was usually styled Doctor although he never took the M.D. He acquired an extraordinary reputation in his profession and was considered the first Englishman "to quicken Galenic physic with a touch of Paracelsus" and to deal successfully in chemical treatments for illnesses. In October 1612 he was summoned to attend Prince Henry, Prince of Wales, in his last illness, and in November 1614 he treated James I at Newmarket for an injury received while hunting. The Latin epitaph on his tomb in Great St. Mary's, Cambridge, reflects his reputation: "Easily the leader of all the doctors the present age has seen" (my translation). In the *Conversations* (ll. 459–60), Jonson said that Butler excommunicated from his table all readers of long poems, disputers, and tedious discoursers.

Buttone, Alessandro. A mountebank. In *Volpone* (II), in the mountebank scene Volpone claims him as an enemy, calling him a "shame to our profession" and accusing him of spreading damaging lies.

Buz. In *The Staple of News,* a groom.

Buz, Froy Hans. See Matthew DeQuester.

C

Cadmus. Son of Agenor, king of Tyre, who founded the city of Thebes and married Harmonia, daughter of Ares and Aphrodite. Cadmus had four daughters and a son, Polydorus, who was the grandfather of Laius, the father of Oedipus.

Caduceus. The herald's rod carried by Mercury. Two snakes entwine the rod and it is topped by a pair of wings.

Caesar, Augustus. The ruling emperor in *Poetaster*, father to Julia. He is wise and just, but he flies into a rage at the "impious sight" of Ovid's masquerade. In anger, he banishes Ovid from court and locks Julia up. He makes it clear, however, that his objection is not to "true poetry," and he reinstates Gallus, Horace, and Mecaenas in his favor. He welcomes Virgil, seats him in his chair, and listens eagerly to the *Aeneid*. He expresses impatience with Lupus when he comes to "inform" on Horace and punishes both Lupus and Historio. He sets up the trial and punishment of Demetrius and Crispinus by the true poets and gives Horace freedom to administer his punishment. Realizing that Tucca is foolish, he orders him to wear "a case of vizards." He approves of Crispinus' and Demetrius' disgrace and praises the true poets.

Caesar, Caius Julius. In *Catiline,* a conspirator who shrewdly operates behind the scenes and escapes punishment when the conspiracy is put down by Cicero.

Caesar, Julius. Roman statesman and general who became dictator for life of Rome in 44 B.C., the same year he was murdered by a conspiracy of his former friends and protégés. Caesar excelled in war, statesmanship, and oratory, and his literary works have always been highly regarded, especially his commentaries on the Gallic Wars. Caesar has always been one of the most controversial figures in world history, some considering him a defender of the people's rights against an oligarchy, others an ambitious demagogue who destroyed the republic. Jonson quotes Caesar twice in *Timber* (ll. 1891, 2012).

Caesarean, Madam. A brothel keeper. In *The Alchemist* (V), Face mockingly tells Dol, when the officers are coming for her, that if she escapes he will help her get a place with Madam Caesarean.

Caligula. In *Sejanus,* Caligula, the youngest son of Germanicus and Agrippina, is seen by Sejanus as an obstacle to his ascent to absolute power, since Caligula is fourth in the line of succession to the emperor. At Macro's insistence, he goes and begs Caesar's mercy after his brothers are indicted and so survives.

Callimachus. Greek grammarian, poet, and critic, who was born in North Africa at Cyrene in the early part of the third century B.C. and died in 240 B.C. at Alexandria. He is best known for his contributions in cataloguing the Library at Alexandria and for his short polished poems, one of which served as one of the sources for Jonson's portrait of Berenice in *The Masque of Queens*. In *Poetaster* (V. iii), Virgil includes Callimachus in the list of the best Greeks Crispinus should read after he is purged.

Callisto. A nymph who followed Artemis and by Zeus became the mother of Arcas, the legendary founder of the Arcadians. Out of jealousy, Hera transformed Callisto into a bear, and Zeus turned Callisto and her son into the constellations Ursa Major and Ursa Minor.

Calypso. A nymph, the daughter of Atlas, who entertained Odysseus for eight years on her island of Ogygie when he was shipwrecked after leaving Circe's island.

Camden, William (1551–1623). English antiquary and historian. Educated at Christ's Hospital, St. Paul's, Magdalen, and

Christ Church, Oxford. In 1593 he became Headmaster at Westminster, where, according to the *Conversations* (l. 240), he was Jonson's schoolmaster. Camden was a conscientious scholar who edited manuscripts, collected materials of antiquarian interest, and helped to revive the study of Anglo-Saxon. In 1586 he published the first edition of his *Britannia,* and in 1615 the first part of his *Annales,* a history in Latin of Elizabeth's reign. The second part was published posthumously in 1625. Philemon Holland translated and published in 1610 the *Britannia,* a description in Latin of England, Scotland, and Ireland which is full of archaeological and historical information. In 1605 the *Remains* appeared. It was a selection of information from *Britannia* with the only clue to authorship being an "M. N." signed to the dedication. According to Jonson in the *Conversations* (l. 608), Camden was also the author of the *Remains.* Camden founded a Chair of History at Oxford; and the Camden Society, organized in 1838 for the publication of historical documents, was established in his honor.

As is evident from his praise of Camden in *Epig.* XIV, Jonson was greatly indebted to Camden and considered him not only his teacher but also his dear friend. In the *Conversations* (ll. 377–78) Jonson told Drummond that he always wrote his verses out first in prose, as his master Camden had taught him, and when Jonson and Chapman were released from prison for their part in the *Eastward Ho* affair Camden was one of Jonson's friends at the banquet celebrating their freedom (l. 278). According to a late tradition, Camden was the one who recommended Jonson as a tutor for the son of Sir Walter Raleigh in 1612. Jonson wrote an inscription in Latin for Camden's gift copy of the 1601 quarto of *Cynthia's Revels,* and he used *Britannia* as one of his sources for *The Haddington Masque.* Jonson dedicated the opening play (*Every Man in*) in the 1616 folio to Camden, and in *The King's Coronation Entertainment* he described Camden as "the glorie and light of our kingdome." Camden's *Remains* contained an "Epitaph on Prince Henry," which W. R. Chetwood ascribed to Jonson, but this attribution seems doubtful since the lines are a translation of Giles Fletcher's Latin epitaph published in *Epicedium Cantabrigiense* (1612).

Camilla. According to Jonson, Queen of the Volscians, who was celebrated by Virgil in the *Aeneid.* She appears as one of the virtuous queens in *The Masque of Queens.*

Campion, Thomas (1567–1620). English lyricist, masque writer, lutenist, composer, physician, and literary critic. His *Observations in the Art of English Poesie* (1602) attempted to demonstrate that "the English tongue will receive eight several kinds" of rhymeless verse. He was answered by Daniel in a *Defense of Ryme* (1608), which argues that "ryme is the fittest harmony of words that comports with our language." According to the *Conversations* (ll. 5–11), Jonson wrote a discourse of poetry against both Campion and Daniel. The discourse is apparently lost. Campion was also the author of a famous epigram on Barnaby Barnes alluded to in the *Conversations* (ll. 627–29). Campion's graceful lute songs were published in five books of airs (1601–17), and he introduced an "antic" masque into his masque for the wedding of Lord Hay in 1607, some time before Jonson formally introduced his antimasque in *The Masque of Queens.*

Campis, Julian de (Julius Sperber) (d. 1616). Julian de Campis was the pseudonym of Julius Sperber, a councillor of Dessau in the duchy of Anhalt and the author of several well-known works on mystical theology. He is mentioned in *The Fortunate Isles.*

Candace. According to Jonson, an Ethiopian queen who governed in Neroë. She appears as one of the virtuous queens in *The Masque of Queens.*

Canidia. A Neapolitan courtesan, who lived in the second half of the first century A.D. She was loved by Horace, but he called her a witch and reviled her after he deserted him. In *Poetaster* (III. v), Horace cites the corruption of "the witch, Canidia" as an example of the present corruption of Rome. Later in the play (IV. iii), Gallus asks if Horace has written a poem "to his bright mistress, Canidia."

Capaneus. One of the Seven against Thebes who was slain as he stood on the walls by a bolt of lightning hurled by Zeus.

Capella, Martianus. Also known as Felix Capella. A Latin writer who lived in either the fourth or fifth century whose most famous work, *The Marriage of Mercury and Philology,* was a long allegory about the seven branches of medieval learning. Jonson relied heavily upon Capella in the fourth chapter of his *English Grammar.*

Captain. The leader of the gypsies in *The Gypsies Metamorphosed* who tells the fortune of the king.

Caranza, Jeronimo de. Author of *De la Filosofia de las Armas* (1569), the first of a series of Spanish treatises on fencing. Caranza's work is mentioned in *Every Man in* (1616 folio, I. v) and *The New Inn* (II. v; IV. iv).

Cardano, Girolamo (1501–1576). A great Milanese physician who visited London in 1552 and was consulted about the health of Edward VI. In the *Conversations* (ll. 541–43), Drummond records that Jonson scorned Cardano, who, according to Jonson, believed that by keeping a stone of Dover between one's teeth he would prevent illness. Cardano was also the author of a famous work on natural history which Jonson cites as one of his sources in *The Masque of Beauty.*

Carew, Richard (1555–1620). English poet and antiquary. Two of his better known works are *Survey of Cornwall* (1602) and *Epistle on the Excellency of the English Tongue* (1605). According to *Und.* XLIII, Carew lent Jonson books.

Carew, Thomas (1595?–?1639). English author, educated at Merton College, Oxford, who became a disciple of Jonson's and one of the so-called Cavalier poets. He had a short diplomatic career, returned to England, became a favorite of Charles I's, and was made a court official. Best known for his courtly, amorous lyrics, he also wrote "Elegy on the Death of Dr. Donne," the highly erotic "A Rapture," and the masque *Coelum Britannicum* (1634). In his use of metaphysical and classical material, Carew reveals the influence of both Jonson and Donne.

Considered one of the Sons of Ben, Carew seems to have been close to Jonson, but he also seems to have been capable of criticizing Jonson dispassionately, as can be seen in Carew's poem on the failure of Jonson's *The New Inn* ("To Ben Jonson Upon Occasion of his Ode to Himself").

Carie (Cary), Giles. An actor who performed in *Epicoene* in 1609 as a member of the Children of the Queen's Revels and later joined the Lady Elizabeth's Men.

Carleton, Sir Dudley (afterwards Viscount Dorchester) (1573–1632). English diplomatist educated at Westminster and Christ Church, Oxford. In 1603 he was elected to Parliament, and he was knighted in 1610 when he succeeded Sir Henry Wotton as ambassador at Venice. From 1616 to 1621 he served as ambassador at the Hague. He was created Lord Carleton of Imbercourt in 1626 and Viscount of Dorchester in

1628, after which he became chief Secretary of State to Charles I. An able diplomat, Carleton was also a voluminous writer of despatches and letters, many of which give us insight into the events, personalities, and cultures of his day. In a June 14, 1616, letter from Gerrard to Carleton, we find some evidence that various London companies had apparently asked Jonson for help or formulas of language for addressing royalty: "Dyers, cloth dressers with their shuttles, and Hamburgians were presented to the King, and spake such language as Ben Jonson put in their mouths."

Carlyle, Thomas (1795–1881). Scottish historian and essayist. He abandoned the ministry, law, and mathematics to study German literature. He was strongly influenced by Goethe and the transcendental philosophers. In 1826 he married Jane Baillie Welsh, who did much to further his career; they moved to Craigenputtock in 1828. There Carlyle wrote *Sartor Resartus,* and there Ralph Waldo Emerson visited him in 1832, beginning a famous friendship. In 1834 the Carlyles moved to London so that he could complete his *French Revolution* (1837). In subsequent works Carlyle attacked laissez-faire theory and parliamentary government and developed his theory of the heroes who have shaped history and have been the spiritual leaders of the world. Carlyle was one of the most important social critics of his day, and his views influenced many younger men like Matthew Arnold and Ruskin. Carlyle has always attracted attention too because of his distinctive style.

In the section on the knighting of Prince Henry in his *Historical Sketches of Notable Persons and Events in the Reigns of James I and Charles I* (1898), Carlyle expressed his admiration for Jonson's masques and what they stood for: "Ben made many masques; worked in that craft for thirty years and more, the world applauding him. . . . Certainly it is a circumstance worth noticing that surly Ben. a real poet, could employ himself in such business, with the applause of all the world; it indicates an age very different from ours. An age full of pageantry of grotesque symbolising, —yet not without something in it to symbolise."

Caroll. A character dressed in a long tawny coat and a red cap who appears as one of the children of Christmas in *Christmas, His Masque.*

Cartari, Vicenzo. Author of *Le Imagini dei Dei degli Antichi* (1556), one of Jonson's

33

principal sources for *The Haddington Masque.*

Cartwright, William (1611–1651). Noted dramatist and divine educated at Westminster and Christ Church. An ardent royalist and a disciple of Jonson's, he contributed an elegy ("Father of Poets, though thine own great day") to *Jonsonus Virbius.* His comedies and poems were collected and published in 1651 under the title *Comedies, Tragedies and Other Poems.* See also Humphrey MOSELEY.

Cary, Sir Henry (1575?–1633), the son of Sir Edward Cary of Aldenham, Hertfordshire, was created Viscount of Falkland in the peerage of Scotland in 1620, served as Comptroller of the Household from 1618 to 1622, and as Lord Deputy of Ireland from 1622 to 1629. In 1605 in a battle near the confluence of the Ruhr and Rhine, an army of Dutch and English troops fled in panic from a smaller Italian band, and when Sir Henry tried to stem the rout he was captured. *Epig.* LXVI lauds Cary's valor on this occasion. He jousted in 1614 at the wedding of Robert, Earl of Somerset, to Frances Howard.

Cary, Sir Lucius (1610?–1643), the eldest son of Sir Henry Cary, was reared in Ireland and took his B.A. at Trinity College, Dublin. He was knighted in 1626 and succeeded his father as Viscount Falkland in 1633. He was made Secretary of State in 1642. He died fighting for Charles at the battle of Newbury. Sir Lucius and Sir Henry Morison, to whose sister Cary was married, are the subjects of Jonson's *Und.* LXX, the first Pindaric ode in English. Sir Lucius referred to Jonson in his elegy on the anniversary of Morison's death ("This is poëtique furie! When the pen"), and he addressed a verse epistle to Jonson as his noble father. Cary's "An Eclogue on the Death of Ben" is the first poem in *Jonsonus Virbius.*

Casaubon, Isaac (1559–1614). Classical scholar and theologian born in Geneva. He became professor of Greek at Geneva and at Montpellier. His learning attracted the attention of Henri IV, who made Casaubon his royal librarian. Both Protestants and Catholics attempted to gain his support, and both denounced him when he joined the Church of England. In 1610 James I made Casaubon prebendary at Canterbury and Westminster; he spent the rest of his life in England and was buried in Westminster Abbey. Casaubon's great works are his editions of the classics, especially Athenaeus and the *Characters* of Theophrastus.

Jonson gave his friend Sir John Roe a valued edition of Casaubon's *Persius,* and Casaubon probably introduced Jonson to Cardinal Duperron in 1612. There is an erroneous allusion to Casaubon in the *Conversations* (l. 517), and Jonson used Casaubon's *De Satyrica Graecorum Poesi* as one of his sources for *Oberon.*

Case Is Altered, The.

Acted: The play was probably first acted sometime in 1598; it is mentioned in Nashe's *Lenten Stuffe,* which was entered in the Stationers' Register in January of 1599.

Published: 1609 in quarto by Bartholomew Sutton.

Printer: unknown.

Title: Taken from a corrupt legal practice of a famous lawyer, Edmund Plowden (1518–85), which became a proverb. Plowden would reputedly plead for his client in an uninspired way until offered a better fee, then would pretend that "the case [was] altered" by new evidence, which would make him plead more enthusiastically.

Act I. The setting is the shop of Juniper, a cobbler. He tries to speak a short prologue of introduction to the play but is interrupted by Peter Onion, a groom, who urges him to hurry and serve Count Ferneze. Juniper and Onion urge Antonio Balladino, pageant poet to the city of Milan, to write Onion a song to aid him in his courtship of Rachel de Prie. (Jonson satirizes popular verse and plays in Antonio's speeches.) Valentine, servant to Francisco Colonnia, enters and is warmly greeted by Onion, who tells him of the recent death of Countess Ferneze; Valentine is saddened. Juniper greets him and listens with interest to his talk of the distant lands he has recently visited with his master. Other servants enter and greet Valentine. Paulo Ferneze and his servant enter. Paulo sends the boy to fetch Angelo away from the count. Paulo confesses his love for Rachel de Prie, the daughter of a beggar, to his friend Angelo, who professes his loyalty. The count is angry when his servants cannot locate his son, flies into a rage, and dismisses Onion. On Juniper's plea, Onion is reinstated. The count tells Maximilian, general of the Milanese army, to take good care of Paulo when he takes him to war against the French, and tells the sad story of his older son, lost when he was a baby during a battle with the French. Maximilian and his men march off to war; Paulo lingers behind for a few minutes to say goodbye to Rachel and tell her that she is in Angelo's care. They pledge their love.

Act II. The setting is the house of Jaques de Prie. In a long soliloquy Jaques reveals that he is not the poor beggar he pretends to be but the former steward of Lord Chamont and that after stealing his master's gold and his infant daughter, he fled to Milan to live under an assumed name. He makes it clear that he stole Rachel because she loved him and hints at his intimacy with Chamont's wife. He expresses both his love of the gold and his fear that Paulo and Angelo somehow know about it and are trying to get it for themselves.

At Count Ferneze's house, Onion confesses his love of Rachel to the steward, Christophero, and urges him to advance Onion's suit; Christophero decides to court Rachel himself. Aurelia, Count Ferneze's daughter, spiritedly tells her sister Phoenixella that they should not continue to mourn for their mother merely because fashion says they should. Angelo flirts with Aurelia, who pertly answers him; Francisco Colonnia tells Phoenixella to forget her grief but is gently rebuffed by her protestations of real sadness and her dislike of the "ceremony" of courtship. The count enters and embarrasses Angelo by speaking of Angelo's many amorous conquests. After Angelo leaves, the count warns his daughters to avoid Angelo, whom he rightly calls a "wild youth." Christophero asks the count's permission to court Rachel; the count gives it but then decides to court Rachel himself. The servants joke together, and Valentine tells of the behavior of people toward the theater in "Utopia" (a thinly disguised satire of England). To amuse themselves Onion and Martino stage a mock fight with cudgels; Martino cuts Onion's head, and against Onion's will, the fight is stopped.

Act III. Angelo, in a soliloquy, reveals that his promise to Paulo to take care of Rachel means little to him and that he wants her for himself. He goes to see her but is frightened off when Jaques arrives on the scene. Christophero goes to ask Jaques's permission to marry Rachel, but Jaques believes him to be a fortune hunter and refuses to speak to him. The count comes to court Rachel and gets the same reception from Jaques. A messenger tells the count that Paulo has been taken prisoner by the French; the count rails at Maximilian and regrets that he thought of anything except his son during his absence. Jaques buries his gold under horse dung to keep it safe from the hordes of thieves he imagines are plotting to steal it.

Act IV. Maximilian returns to Milan,

bringing two prisoners: Lord Chamont (son of the Lord Chamont from whom Jaques stole the gold) and another Frenchman named Gasper, who, unbeknownst to anyone, including himself, is actually Camillo, the long-lost older son of Count Ferneze. In private the two prisoners reveal that they have exchanged names to fool their captors and regret that an untrustworthy servant named Pacue knows of the switch. Maximilian arranges with the French the exchange of the prisoner he believes to be Gasper for Paulo. Aurelia is much taken with the man who is really Chamont; she teases her sister for being much taken with the other prisoner. Onion mocks Pacue and Finio (Camillo's page), and they joke with him. Chamont leaves France and, after saying goodbye to his friend, tells of his friend's noble character and their close friendship, and reveals how Gasper was found during a battle with the Milanese, thus giving the audience a clue to his real identity. Lovesick Onion persuades Juniper to accompany him to Rachel's; he is angry at Valentine for not writing him a love song, as he promised. Angelo entreats Rachel to forget her grief over Paulo's capture and woos her, but Jaques frightens him off. Onion and Juniper stand outside Rachel's house and call to her; Jaques finds them there, calls them thieves, and threatens to set his vicious dog on them. Onion climbs a tree. Jaques seizes Juniper, who tears free and runs away. Jaques, forgetting about Onion, uncovers his gold to see if it is safe; Onion catches sight of it. Jaques leaves, Juniper returns, and Onion and Juniper take the money. Pacue inadvertently reveals the prisoners' exchange of identities to one of the count's daughters, who tells her father. The count flies into a rage, reasoning that once the French have their valuable nobleman back, they will not return his son. Maximilian assures him that the trade will be honored, but the count decides to torture the prisoner, who is willing to "suffer for a friend." Phoenixella speaks of her love for the prisoner; Aurelia of her love for Chamont.

Act. V. Angelo and Christophero plot together to lure Jaques away from his home with a trail of gold, supposedly to give Christophero an opportunity to marry Rachel. But Angelo really intends to double-cross Christophero and lure Rachel away to an isolated spot for himself. Jaques follows the gold, and Angelo easily persuades Rachel to accompany him by telling her that he is taking her to meet the newly released Paulo. Jaques returns, discovers

35

the theft of his gold, and nearly goes mad with anger. Onion and Juniper enter, richly dressed because of their new-found wealth. Juniper, who is drunk, "hires" Finio to import a French servant for Juniper. Pacue is brought in to satisfy him. Angelo tries to assault Rachel in a remote spot; she is saved just in time by Paulo, who chances to pass that way on his return from captivity. Paulo pardons Angelo after harshly scolding him. The count decides to kill the prisoner but hesitates at the moment of execution; meanwhile, Christophero comes in lamenting Rachel's disappearance, and Jaques arrives, lamenting the loss of his gold. In the nick of time, Chamont enters with Paulo; the count apologizes for his harsh treatment of the prisoner but says that it was because of his grief over losing both his sons and tells of the loss of his older son. Chamont realizes that his friend is the count's lost son and reunites him with his father. All rejoice except Phoenixella, who is dismayed to realize that the man she loves is her brother. Jaques complains of his lost gold, inadvertently putting himself in a position where he must reveal who he is and who Rachel really is. The count has Onion and Juniper found and returns Chamont's gold to Lord Chamont. Rachel is betrothed to Paulo, Aurelia to Chamont. Maximilian hints that he may court Phoenixella and ends the play on a happy order to march.

Cash, Thomas. See PIZO.

Cassandra. Daughter of Priam, king of Troy, who was given the gift of prophecy by Apollo because of his love for her. When she spurned him, Apollo turned his gift into a source of torment by decreeing that no one should ever believe Cassandra's prophecies.

Cassiopeia, wife of Cephus, king of the Ethiopians, boasted that she and her daughter Andromeda were more beautiful than the Nereids. Poseidon punished her by causing Andromeda to be chained to a rock by the seashore and Cassiopeia to be turned into a star.

Cassius (d. 42 B.C.). Gaius Cassius Longinus, soldier and conspirator against Julius Caesar. He was active in the eastern campaigns in his career, winning influence by his victories. After the murder of Caesar, Cassius was forced to leave Rome. He was hated and feared because of his ruthlessness and violent temper. Brutus and Cassius, who was the more practical of the two, campaigned against Antony and Octavian. Cassius committed suicide at Philippi, believing the battle to be lost. In *Sejanus,* Arruntius agrees with Cordus' writing that present day Romans are not "good, / Gallant, or great," since "Brave Cassius was the last of all that race" (I. i). Later in the play (III. iv), Cordus is accused of treason because of this statement. Cordus attempts to defend himself by countering that well-regarded writers of the past also honored Cassius.

Castiglione, Baldassare (1478–1529). Italian statesman who was attached to the court of the Duke of Milan and later to that of the Duke of Urbino. Castiglione's *Libro del Cortegiano* (1516; English trans. by Hoby, *The Courtier,* 1561) is one of the most famous books of the Renaissance. Jonson mentions the work in *Timber* (l. 2282) and in *Every Man out of His Humour* adapts Sordido's attempted suicide (III. vii) and the trick played on Saviolina (v. ii) from it.

Castor. In Greek mythology, Castor and Polydeuces (Latin: Pollux) are the twin sons of either Zeus and Leda or Leda and her husband Tyndareus. Known as the Dioscuri, the twins were regarded both as courageous mortals and gods and as protectors of sailors.

Castrone. In *Volpone,* Volpone's eunuch.

Cat. A character who danced in the second antimasque in *Time Vindicated to Himself and His Honors.*

Catiline, His Conspiracy.
    Acted: 1611 by the King's Men.
    Published: 1611 in quarto by Walter Burre.
    Printer: unknown.

Act I. In Catiline's house in Rome, Sylla's ghost appears, recounts Catiline's past crimes, and invokes terror on the city comparable to what Sylla himself brought in the past. In his study, Catiline announces that he has decided to become the head of Rome by whatever means necessary. His wife, Aurelia Orestilla, enters and he greets her warmly. Reminding her that he murdered his former wife and his son in order to marry her, Catiline reassures Aurelia of his love for her, explains how he plans to use men like Lentulus and Cethegus to help him gain power and asks her to assist him by organizing a meeting of the feminine auxiliary of the conspiracy. When they hear someone approaching, Aurelia leaves the room. Lentulus and Cethegus arrive, discussing the business of their meeting; Autronius, Vargunteius, Longinus, Curius, Lecca, Bestia, Fulvius, and Gabinius arrive soon after. As they begin their meeting, darkness comes over the place, the groaning of many people is heard, and a fiery image of a bloody arm holding a lighted pine appears above the Capitol, but Catiline rallies his supporters with a stirring speech calling for the pursuit of liberty and dignity to overthrow those currently in power. They begin to outline strategies: one is to get Catiline elected consul; the other is to start a military insurrection. They discuss how they will divide the spoils after their victory. To seal their conspiracy they all partake of a perverted communion in which they drink a mixture of wine and the blood of a slave Catiline has sacrificed for the occasion.

The act ends with a chorus questioning whether anything great can remain so without being destroyed by its own weight and bemoans the vices that have made Rome "both her own spoiler and own prey."

Act II. At her home, Fulvia, an extravagant courtesan, instructs her servant Galla not to admit Quintus Curius, a former senator ejected from the senate for infamous behavior, should he come to see her. As they talk, Galla expresses her admiration for Sempronia, the wife of Decius Brutus, a witty intellectual stateswoman past her prime who remains active politically and still craves masculine attention for which she pays lavishly. Presently, Sempronia herself arrives to invite Fulvia to accompany her to a meeting called by Orestilla, but Fulvia politely declines. As they discuss their recent activities, Fulvia learns that Sempronia, Caesar, and Crassus have been working behind the scenes to get Catiline elected consul. When Fulvia suggests that the virtuous Cicero seems a likely candidate for a consulship, Sempronia retorts that since he has no aristocratic blood his virtue is only "sauciness." As they discuss her current clients, Fulvia informs Sempronia that she only gives her favors to the most extravagant spenders, and she reiterates her dislike for the disgraced Curius, whom Sempronia describes as Fulvia's idolator. Curius arrives at the house, and Fulvia reminds Galla not to let him in, but Sempronia admits Curius as she departs, much to Fulvia's displeasure. The insistent Curius quickly begins to disrobe, and when Fulvia strongly resists his passion and advances, he tries to force her, but she draws a knife. Curius reluctantly leaves, proclaiming that she will soon be sorry she rejected a man of such eminent power and wealth. On second thought, Fulvia suspects some major plot is afoot

and allows Curius to reenter so she can wheedle his secret from him. By flattering him, she learns of the conspiracy to elevate Catiline to power.

On the eve of the election the chorus desperately calls for consuls who will embody the virtues of the consuls of old and who will be the "sinews of the public good."

Act III. In the Field of Mars Cicero makes a victory speech after being elected consul along with Antonius, who defers to the popular orator now styled the "New Man" by the people. Although Cato, who is considered the voice of Rome, lauds Cicero, Caesar and Crassus try to play down Cicero's virtues and popularity. After Cicero departs, the defeated Catiline and his supporters arrive on the scene. Scorned by Cato and spurred by Lentulus and Cethegus, Catiline tries to be a conciliatory leader, but finally proclaims to his cohorts that "our objects must be sought with wounds not words."

At Cicero's house, Fulvia reports her knowledge of the conspiracy to Cicero, and he praises what he takes to be her patriotism and enlists her help in trying to persuade Curius to spy on the conspirators. Although Curius is reluctant at first, when Fulvia tells him privately that she has not elected to join the conspirators as he had suggested because she doesn't want to be second to Sempronia and that he and she both may be able to profit by cooperating with the consul, Curius agrees to Cicero's offer. After Curius and Fulvia leave, Cicero bemoans the depths to which powerful Rome has sunk when its salvation depends upon a common strumpet. He also decides that he must gain Antonius' support by giving him a province and that he must make sure his family and friends are all completely loyal and trustworthy.

Meanwhile, at Catiline's house, Caesar urges Catiline to put his plot into action quickly. Under Aurelia's leadership the women, now including Sempronia and Fulvia, plan their part in the plot, and Catiline gives instructions and assignments to all of his conspirators, who are to act at the appropriate time. Longinus and Statilius are to set fire to the city, Cethegus is to murder Cicero, and Vargunteius and Cornelius are to assist Cethegus if he needs help. At the discreet suggestion of Curius, Fulvia excuses herself because of ill health. When all have gone, Catiline exclaims: "What ministers men must for practice use, / The rash, the ambitious, needy desperate, / Foolish and wretched, and e'en the dregs of mankind, / To whores and women!" After leaving Catiline's, Fulvia goes to Cicero and reports the murder plot, and with the aid of his brother Quintus, Cicero plans his defense. When Vargunteius and Cornelius arrive at Cicero's house to carry out the deed, they are easily captured, and Cicero lectures them about the folly of their cause. Cato becomes impatient with the consul's leniency as a violent storm breaks out, showing, according to Cato, the gods' anger with Cicero's patience.

The chorus proclaims that the tumult and horror in their minds is greater than the tumult of the storm.

Act IV. As the storm continues, the Allobrogian ambassadors meet Cicero on the street before the foot of the Capitol. They are all very much impressed with the consul's courteous manner when he asks that they delay their meeting with him until the next day and that they send their communications through Fabius Sanga. Cicero proceeds to the temple of Jupiter Stator, where he meets with the senators and reports the abortive attempt on his life and that a conspiracy is afoot. Presently, Catiline arrives, and Cicero eloquently accuses him of conspiracy before the assembly and suggests that he banish himself from the republic, but Catiline argues that Cicero's charges are empty rhetoric. When he senses that the senators agree with Cicero, Catiline leaves in anger, warning them of the mistake they are making in putting their trust in a new man like Cicero. After Catiline has left, it is agreed that Curius and Fulvia must be somehow rewarded and that the powerful Caesar and Crassus, who have seemed to support Catiline in debate, must be carefully watched. Catiline returns to his house and with his supporters decides that the conspiracy must be put into action immediately. Catiline will go to his army, and he instructs his followers to spread the word about the city that he, an innocent man, has gone into exile in order to keep peace in the republic. Lentulus announces that he has attempted to gain the support of the Allobroges, who feel oppressed by the tribute they must currently pay and who tend to be a warlike people.

Afterwards, Sanga reports to Cicero that the conspirators have solicited the aid of the Allobroges, and Cicero is able to convince the Allobroges to seem to play along with the conspirators but actually to help the commonwealth entrap them. When the Allobrogian ambassadors later meet the conspirators at Sempronia's house, they follow Cicero's instructions.

Through Sanga, Cicero learns that the Allobrogians, accompanied by the conspirator Volturtius, will be travelling over the Milvian bridge, and they are easily captured there by Flaccus and Pomtinius. Meanwhile, Cicero sends for the unsuspecting Lentulus, Gabinius, Cethegus, and Statilius. When captured, Volturtius promises to talk in exchange for leniency.

The chorus expresses some relief but exclaims:

> What age is this, where honest men,
> Placed at the helm,
> A sea of some foul mouth or pen
> Shall overwhelm?
>
> And call their diligence, deceit;
> Their virtue, vice;
> Their watchfulness, but lying in wait;
> And blood, the price?
>
> O, let us pluck this evil seed
> Out of our spirits:
> And give to every noble deed
> The name it merits.

Act V. At Etruria in the country near Fesulae, Petreius, taking the place of the ailing Antonius, prepares to lead his troops to battle against Sylla's old army, who support Catiline. Back in Rome, Caesar and Crassus decide that they must take a more active role in the plot and try to help their fellow conspirators. At Cicero's, Quintus and Cato try to persuade the consul to take action against Caesar, but Cicero refuses to do so because of lack of evidence against him. At the Temple of Concord, Cicero presents overwhelming evidence of treason and conspiracy against Cethegus, Statilius, Gabinius, and Lentulus; with the testimony of Volturtius and the Allobrogian ambassadors, it is clear that they are guilty, but it is decided that they will be held in custody until the Senate can decide what to do with them. Volturtius and the Allobrogians are rewarded, and Cicero is lauded for saving the state without bloodshed. When both Crassus and Caesar are accused of being part of the conspiracy, Cicero assures the two that he does not believe the charges.

In the country near Fesulae, Catiline attempts to rally his now desperate army, while in Rome at the Temple of Jupiter Stator, the Senate debates the fate of the arrested conspirators. Syllanus argues for instant execution, but Caesar calls for confiscation of their property and imprisonment in free towns distant from Rome while Cato pleads: "Let them not live an hour, / If you mean Rome should live a day." Before a decision is reached, a messenger brings letters from the conspirators to Caesar. Cato demands that they be read in public, and the praetors attempt to seize Caesar, but Cicero calls for no violence and declares Caesar to be safe. The public executioners are sent for, and Lentulus, Cethegus, Gabinius, and Statilius are ordered to be strangled. Petreius enters and reports the defeat of the rebellious army and the valiant death of the desperate Catiline. Cicero proclaims that his labors are now rewarded, thanks Rome for all the praises, triumphs, and honors bestowed upon him and exclaims:

> . . . only the memory
> Of this glad day, if I may know it lives,
> Within your thoughts, shall much affect my conscience,
> Which I must always study before fame.
> Though both be good, the latter yet is worse,
> And ever is ill got, without the first.

Catiline, Lucius Sergius. In *Catiline*, a patrician traitor who, failing to win a consulship by election, leads an abortive revolution that is quelled by Cicero.

Cato, Marcus Porcius. In *Catiline*, a staunch, loyal citizen who is a strong supporter of Cicero and who is considered by many to be the voice of Rome.

Cato the Younger. Marcus Porcius Cato. (95–46 B.C.) Famous for his upright character, which combined stoicism and traditional Roman morality. He opposed Caesar and supported Pompey in the civil war, during which he tried to prevent the killing of citizens. He governed Utica wisely during the war. After Caesar's triumph, he committed suicide. His noble death has been the subject of many tragedies. In *Sejanus* (I. i) Arruntius laments that "the soule / Of god-like Cato . . . he, that durst be good, / When Caesar durst be evill" is not present in his age. Later in the play, Sabinus praises Germanicus by saying that he had "the innocence of Cato" (I. i), and Cordus attempts to defend himself by saying that Caesar did not accuse Cicero of treason, even though he openly praised Cato (III. iv). Cato's integrity is also alluded to in Jonson's dedication of the *Epigrams* to the Earl of Pembroke.

Cato, Valerius. Roman poet, teacher, critic, and grammarian who became head of the neoteric school of poets to which Catullus belonged. He is referred to in *Timber* (l. 2597).

Catullus, Gaius Valerius (84?–54 B.C.). Roman poet born in Verona into a wealthy family. About 62 B.C. he went to Rome. There with other young writers he formed a cult of youth. He fell in love with, and wrote poems to, his beloved Clodia whom he addressed in the poems as Lesbia. Over a hundred poems have been attributed to Catullus; these include poems to his young friend Juventius, epigrams, elegies, an epithalamium, and various short pieces. Influenced by the Alexandrians, he drew heavily upon Greek forms and meters, but his poetic genius outdid his models. He is now considered one of the greatest lyric poets of all time. Many echoes from Catullus can be heard throughout Jonson's works, although in *Epicoene* (II. iii) Daw dismissed him as a worthless ancient. Catullus is specifically alluded to in *Bartholomew Fair* (V. vi), quoted in *The Masque of Queens,* and drawn upon in *Hymenaei.* In *Catiline,* the character Catullus is a strong supporter of Cicero in his efforts to quell Catiline's conspiracy against Rome.

Caucasus. Scene of the punishment of Prometheus recorded in Aeschylus.

Cavendish, Charles. 1. A Charles Cavendish is buried at Bolsover. On his monument is an epitaph written by Jonson in 1619 ("Sonnes, seek not me among these ancient stones").
2. Charles Cavendish, the second son of William, 2nd Earl of Devonshire, was born in 1620, and Jonson's *An Entertainment at the Blackfriars* celebrated his christening. Charles was a royalist general in the Civil War and was killed at Gainsborough in 1643.

Cavendish, William, Earl (afterwards Duke) of Newcastle. See William Cavendish, Earl (afterwards Duke) of NEWCASTLE.

Cecil, Lady Diana. See Diana Cecil, Countess of OXFORD.

Celaeno. One of the Harpies or supernatural winged beings who carry off various persons and things.

Celia. In *Volpone*, Celia is Corvino's beautiful wife, of whom he is very jealous. When Corvino tries to prostitute her to Volpone in order to become Volpone's heir, she refuses to listen to her husband's threats or Volpone's song and is saved by Bonario. Vicious lies are told about her in court, but when her husband's corruption is revealed she wins back her spotless reputation.

Censure. A gossip who appears in the induction and the intermeans to *The Staple of News.*

Centaure, Lady. A lady collegiate and friend of Lady Haughty in *Epicoene.* She is proud and independent and professes loyalty to her friends until, in competition for Dauphine Eugenie, she criticizes them behind their backs.

Centaurs. In Greek mythology, a tribe of wild beings the top half of whose bodies are human, the bottom half equine. Centaurs are depicted by the Greeks as wild, sensual, lustful, and very fond of wine. In *Epicoene* (IV), Truewit tells Daw, during the mock quarrel between Daw and La Foole, that Epicoene and Morose's wedding feast will not involve fighting and bloodshed, as did Peirithous' wedding, when the Centaurs fought with the Lapiths. In *Catiline* (II), Fulvia and Sempronia speak of the impetuous men of their time, calling them "rude and as boistrous as Centaures."

Ceparius. In *Catiline,* one of the conspirators who supports Catiline's abortive attempt to seize power in Rome.

Cephalus. In Greek mythology, the husband of Procris, whom Cephalus accidentally killed while hunting, thinking his wife was a wild beast hiding in the bushes.

Cerberus. Monstrous dog who guarded the entrance to Hades.

Cercopes. Ape-like creatures who had once been human but had suffered deformity because of their impiety.

Ceres. Roman goddess of agriculture who wandered the world in search of her daughter Proserpina, who had been raped and taken to the underworld by Pluto, until Jove promised that Proserpina should spend half of each year in heaven.

Cervantes Saavedra, Miguel de (1547–1616). Spanish novelist, dramatist, and poet. A failure as a soldier and a businessman, Cervantes wrote more than twenty plays between 1582 and 1587, but only two have survived. In 1605 he published the first part of his masterpiece, *Don Quixote de la Mancha* (Part II, 1615); it was an immediate success and eventually had a major effect upon the development of the European novel. In his later years Cervantes wrote other works of fiction; today he is considered one of the world's great literary masters. Jonson, however, was always hostile to *Don Quixote* and referred unfavorably to it in *Epicoene* (IV. i), *The Alchemist* (IV. vii), and *Und.* XLIII.

Cestius. A rhetorician of Smyrna noted for his declaiming against Cicero. In *Timber* (ll. 2002–4), Jonson notes that Cestius' remark that the ocean roars because of Alexander's leaving the land is ridiculous. According to Jonson, Cestius in his day was preferred to Cicero (ll. 605–6).

Cethegus, Caius. In *Catiline,* a savage, indiscreet, and tactless conspirator who is executed with the rest of the rebels who remain in Rome when Catiline leaves.

Chair. In *The Magnetic Lady,* a midwife who delivers the illegitimate child of Placentia and devises a plot to try to convince everyone that the child is her daughter's son.

Challenge at Tilt, A.
   Performed: December 27, 1613, and January 1, 1614.
   Published: 1616 in folio by William Stansby.
   Printer: William Stansby.
   As with *Hymenaei,* Jonson suppressed any reference in the folio to the occasion of this work. The tilt was in honor of the marriage of the Earl of Somerset and Lady Frances Howard, which took place on December 26, 1613, and was one act in what became a great scandal. See SOMERSET.

   The day after the marriage two Cupids, pages of the bride and bridegroom, entered, arguing over which one of them was the real Cupid and was the cause of the love between the new bride and bridegroom. Unable to resolve their differences, the second Cupid, page of the bride, challenged the first Cupid to settle the quarrel by tilting on New Year's Day with ten knights on each side. The first Cupid accepted the challenge and agreed that the winner would be declared the real Cupid.
   On the appointed day, the second Cupid arrived with ten knights attired in the bride's colors and proclaimed himself to be a true champion, and the other Cupid entered with his knights and made the same claim. The tilting followed, but neither side could prevail, and finally Hymen appeared and announced that they both would have to yield because there was another kind of tilting more appropriate for love. Hymen presented the Cupids with a palm, proclaimed that the one who won the bough would be declared the real Cupid, and promised to tell something about themselves that they did not know. Hymen explained that, in fact, both were true Cupids, both the offspring of Venus and Mars. According to Hymen, Venus' firstborn was called Eros, and his mother noticed that as he matured his growth did

not match his form. Concerned, Venus consulted the oracle, who informed her that Eros merely needed companionship, and so she bore a second son whom she called Anteros who, with reciprocal affection, might provide the exchange of love needed. Hence the nature of the two sons was such that they prosper and flourish by mutual respect and affection. This, Hymen noted, is the love that is required, the love without which no marriage is happy. The real contention is not whose is the true love, both being true, but who loves the most, as in clearing the bough and dividing the palm. In such strife, both parties win, and they create a concord worthy of the emulation of all married couples. Likewise, Hymen proclaimed, the knights on both sides should imitate such peace and friendship forever more, and to Hymen's suggestion the two loves mutually assented.

Chaloner, Thomas (1521–1565). English diplomatist who translated *An Homily of St. John Chrysostom* (1544) and Erasmus' *Praise of Folly* (1549). He is mentioned in *Timber* (l. 903) as a man admirable for his time.

Chamberlain, John (1553–1627), was educated at Trinity, Cambridge. He led a quiet, scholarly life and wrote voluminous letters, becoming a newsmonger for his day. One of his correspondents was Sir Dudley Carleton, whom Chamberlain accompanied on his Venetian embassy. Chamberlain's letters give us a vivid insight into the culture of his day. In a letter to Sir Dudley Carleton at the Hague in 1621 he states that since Donne has recently been named Dean of St. Paul's it would be very pleasant and poetical if Jonson were to be made Dean of Westminster.

Chamont, Lord. An important character in *The Case Is Altered.* Many years before the action of the play, Lord Chamont's father and Count Ferneze headed opposing armies. In the battle in which Lord Chamont's father took Vicenza, Count Ferneze lost his older son Camillo, who is presumed dead. Young Chamont is taken prisoner with his friend Gasper (really Camillo, lost son of the Count, although no one realizes it); they vow to trade identities to deceive their captors into letting the more influential Chamont go free. Gasper, who is pretending to be Chamont, stays a prisoner in Milan while Chamont, who is pretending to be Gasper, is sent home in exchange for Count Ferneze's son Paulo. Chamont brings Paulo back to Milan just in time to save Camillo from being tortured by Count Ferneze, who has dis-

covered the exchange of identities and fears that Paulo will never be returned now that the more important Frenchman is free. From evidence in the count's story and in his own memory, Chamont realizes that Gasper is Camillo, the count's lost son and, to great rejoicing, reunites him with his father. The count restores the gold stolen from Chamont's father by Jaques. Chamont betroths his sister Rachel (Isabel) to Paulo, and is himself betrothed to Aurelia, who earlier fell in love with him.

chaos. According to classical writers, the first thing that came into being, or the potentialities of matter.

Chapman, George (1559?–1634). English dramatist, translator, and poet. He went to either Oxford or Cambridge in 1574, and in 1594 he published his philosophical poem "The Shadow of Night." His first extant play, *The Blind Beggar of Alexandria,* was produced in 1596, followed the next year by *An Humourous Day's Mirth,* which preceded Jonson's humor plays but is quite different from them, although Chapman may have given Jonson some hints in the play for his humor theory. By 1598 Chapman had apparently finished two acts of an unidentified or lost tragedy based upon a plot probably given to him the previous year by Jonson. In 1598 Meres mentioned Chapman as one of the best dramatists for both comedy and tragedy. Chapman was a classical scholar, and his works often reveal the influence of the Stoics Epictetus and Seneca. In his best known tragedies, *Bussy D'Ambois* (1607) and *The Conspiracy and Tragedy of Byron* (1608), the hero is destroyed by his inability to control his passions and to resist temptations. Chapman collaborated on or wrote about a dozen comedies, two of the most notable being *All Fools* (1605) and *Eastward Ho* (1605), which was written in collaboration with John Marston and Jonson. Because this play was considered offensive, Chapman and Jonson were imprisoned, and between May 4 and September 4, 1605, they both wrote numerous letters from prison to various powerful people seeking help in gaining their freedom, which was finally granted. Chapman's greatest contributions to literature are his translations of the *Iliad* (1612) and the *Odyssey* (1614–15). Among his other works are several metaphysical poems, a completed version of Marlowe's *Hero and Leander* (1598), and translations of Petrarch and Hesiod. Jonson and Chapman were close friends most of their lives; in the *Conversations* Jonson said he loved Chapman and Fletcher (l. 169) and knew a piece of Chapman's translation of the *Iliad* by heart (ll. 124–25). However, because of Jonson's treatment of Inigo Jones, Chapman wrote a deathbed invective against Jonson and another unpleasant poem ("Epicure's Frugality") about him, both of which remained in manuscript. Chapman was buried at St. Giles in the Fields, where Inigo Jones erected a monument to his memory.

Virgil in *Poetaster* is probably meant to represent Chapman, and Chapman may have helped Jonson in the writing of *Sejanus,* for which he wrote a long commendatory poem ("In Seianum Ben. Ionsoni"). Chapman also wrote a prefatory poem ("Come, yet, more forth, Volpone, and thy chase") for *Volpone.* In his sonnet on Susan Vere ("To the Great and Virtuous, the Countess of Montgomery") inserted in his *Iliad* (Bks. I-XII, 1609), Chapman refers to Jonson's praise of the Countess in *Epig.* CIV. Jonson wrote a commendatory poem ("Whose work could this be Chapman, to refine") affixed to Chapman's *Georgics of Hesiod* (1618), and in the *Conversations* he told Drummond that next to himself only Chapman and Fletcher could make a masque (ll. 55–56) and that Chapman had translated *Musaeus* (1616) like his Homer. Jonson's copy of Chapman's edition of Homer's *Works* (1616) has survived. It is clearly annotated in Latin, and Jonson is severely critical of Chapman's scholarship. See also Ben JONSON; John FLETCHER; Sir Henry WOTTON.

Charis. In the *Iliad,* the wife of Hephaestus.

Charles I (1600–1649). King of England 1625–1649. Second son of James VI of Scotland (James I of England) and Anne of Denmark. Born at Dunfermline. Charles was made Duke of Albany, became heir to the throne after the death of his brother Henry in 1612, and was declared Prince of Wales in 1616. Charles's proposed marriage to the Spanish Infanta was unpopular in England, and Charles himself eventually turned against Spain after his unsuccessful visit with Buckingham in Madrid in 1623. Jonson had prepared *Neptune's Triumph* for performance upon Charles's return to England, but the masque was never given because of an ambassadorial dispute. Except for his efforts in the negotiations for a Spanish bride, Charles took little part in politics before he succeeded his father in 1625. At first he was popular, but he almost immediately

offended his Protestant subjects by marrying the Catholic Henrietta Maria, sister of Louis XIII of France. Moreover, Charles's favorite, Buckingham, was unpopular, and his foreign ventures were misguided and unfortunate. Parliament would not willingly grant money to aid Charles's sister, Elizabeth of Bohemia, and the Protestants in the Thirty Years War. In a short period of time Charles's reign resolved itself into a bitter and vicious struggle for supremacy between the king and Parliament. This struggle resulted in the Puritan Revolution and Civil War. On January 30, 1649, Charles was executed for treason in levying war against Parliament.

Although the cult of Platonic love was fashionable at Charles's court, Jonson seems to have been on reasonably good terms with the monarch, but he probably was never so close to Charles as he had been to James. There is evidence that Jonson was summoned to court by Charles on several occasions and that Jonson could speak frankly with Charles both when he was Prince of Wales and when he was king. In the *Conversations* (ll. 467–69) Jonson said that he told Prince Charles that when he wanted words to express the worst villain in the world he would call him an Inigo. During Charles's reign Jonson was appointed chronologer of the city of London. Jonson wrote several poems to Charles: *Und.* LXIII, on the loss of his firstborn son; *Und.* LXIV, on his anniversary day in 1629; *Und.* LXXII, on Charles's birthday in 1632; *Und.* LXXXII, on the christening of his second son; and *Und.* LXXIX, a New Year's gift sung before the King. In response to *Und.* LXXVI, a petition, Charles increased Jonson's annual pension from the sum of 100 marks to one hundred pounds and also added a tierce of canary from the Whitehall cellars, which grant Jonson had to remind Charles in *Und.* LXVIII to supply. After the failure of *The New Inn* Charles gave Jonson an additional one hundred pounds, for which Jonson, now sick, thanked the King in *Und.* LXII. Another poem by Jonson ("Fresh as the day and new as are the Hours") is a song of welcome for Charles. The poem on Charles entitled "A Parallel of the Prince to the King" often ascribed to Jonson should probably be attributed to Thomas Freeman.

Charles was involved in a number of the masques and entertainments. As Prince of Wales he attended the performance of *The Entertainment at the Blackfriars* in 1620, and he had his fortune told in *The Gypsies Metamorphosed.* He danced in the following masques: *Pleasure Reconciled to Virtue* (his debut), *For the Honor of Wales, News from the New World, The Masque of Augurs, Time Vindicated, The Fortunate Isles,* and *Love's Triumph. Chloridia, The King's Entertainment at Welbeck,* and *Love's Welcome at Bolsover,* Jonson's last royal entertainment, were all performed before Charles.

Charles II (1630–1685). King of England 1660–1685. Second son of Charles I and Henrietta Maria. Jonson celebrated his birth in *Und.* LXV and LXVI. Three other poems on the prince's birth have been ascribed to Jonson at one time or another, but he probably did not write any of them: "Another Phoenix, though the first is dead"; "A Parallel of the Prince to the King" (probably by Thomas Freeman); and "A Petition of the Infant Prince Charles." Charles was Prince of Wales at the time of the Puritan Revolution. In 1645, for safety's sake, he was sent to the west of England with his council; a year later he was forced to escape to France, where he stayed with his mother and was tutored by Thomas Hobbes. In 1649 Charles made a desperate attempt to save his father by giving Parliament a blank petition to list any terms they desired. When his father was executed later in the year, Charles was proclaimed King in Scotland and in parts of Ireland and England. He was crowned in Scotland in 1651, after which he marched into England and was defeated by Cromwell at Worcester. He escaped to France where he lived in relative poverty, then went to Germany and later to the Spanish Netherlands. Aided by Charles's Declaration of Breda, General George Monck engineered the Restoration in 1660. Two years later Charles married Catherine of Braganza. Charles's reign was marked by a gradual increase in the power of Parliament, which he learned to circumvent, being a man of no mean political skill. Charles's wit, tolerance, and hedonism set the tone for the scintillating Restoration period in art and literature. Charles converted to Roman Catholicism on his deathbed. He had no legitimate children but many illegitimate ones by his various mistresses. He was succeeded by his brother James.

Charon. An old man who ferried the souls of the dead across the rivers of Hades, charging an *obolus,* a coin placed in the mouth of the dead before burial. In *Lovers Made Men,* he serves as the ferryman who delivers to Mercury the lovers who have been drowned and made ghosts by the charms of love.

Charybdis. A female monster that Zeus threw into the sea to punish her for stealing Hercules' cattle. She lay beneath the water on the Sicilian side of the Strait of Messina sucking in and then spewing forth great quantities of water three times a day to create a whirlpool. Opposite her, on the rocks on the Italian side of the strait, lived Scylla, a female sea monster who had once been a beautiful nymph. Scylla seized men from passing ships and ate them.

Chaucer, Geoffrey. One of the most important of all English poets. We know very little about his life. Born in London between 1340 and 1344, he was the son of a vintner, John Chaucer. Official records show that in 1357 he was serving as a page in the household of Prince Lionel, son of Edward III. By 1359–60 Chaucer was in the army of Edward III in France, where he was captured by the French. He was ransomed, and about 1366 he married a lady-in-waiting to the queen of Edward III. From 1370 to 1378 Chaucer was frequently sent on diplomatic missions on the Continent, and from 1374 on he held a number of official positions. The date traditionally given for his death is October 25, 1400. He is buried in Westminster Abbey.

Chaucer's literary career is usually divided into three periods: (1) His early work (to c. 1370), based largely on French models, included such works as the *Book of the Duchess* (1369) and a partial translation of the *Roman de la Rose.* (2) The work of his Italian period (to c. 1385) was strongly influenced by Dante and Boccaccio. Chief works of this period include *The House of Fame, The Parliament of Fowls,* and a prose translation of Boethius' *De Consolatione Philosophiae.* (3) In his last period, he achieved his greatest artistic triumphs. Major works include the unfinished *Legend of Good Women,* the prose fragment *The Treatise on the Astrolabe, Troilus and Criseyde,* and the *Canterbury Tales,* his masterpiece.

Jonson considered Chaucer one of the greatest poets of all ages. He owned a copy of Speght's 1602 edition of the *Works,* and he included Chaucer in the parade of poets in *The Golden Age Restored.* Echoes of his works are often heard in Jonson. *The Canon's Yeoman's Tale* was probably one of Jonson's sources for *The Alchemist,* and *The House of Fame* and *The Legend of Good Women* were certainly sources for *The Masque of Queens.* Chaucer is mentioned in *Timber* (ll. 1799, 1947). The Friar from the Prologue to the *Canterbury Tales* is alluded to in *The New Inn* (I. iii), and the Prioress in II. iii. Chaucer is referred to in *The Mag-*

netic Lady (III. v), and he is quoted twenty-seven times in *The English Grammar*. See also CUSTOM.

Cheerfulness. One of the servants of Humanity who appears on a triumphal arch in *Lovers Made Men*.

Chesil. A character in *Love's Welcome at Bolsover* who appears as a carver in Colonel Vitruvius' dance of the mechanics.

Chester, Robert. Author of *Love's Martyr* (1601), a rambling allegory on the Phoenix and the Turtle to which Jonson appended two poems ("The Phoenix Analyzed" and "Ode ἐνθουσιαστικὴ").

Chevalry. A symbolic character who appears in *The Speeches at Prince Henry's Barriers* and praises Meliadus for reviving knighthood.

Chev'rill. Literally, kid leather. *Epig.* XXXVII and LIV satirize under this name an unscrupulous lawyer.

chiaus. An imperfect adaptation of the Turkish word for messenger or herald which, because a clever Turk named Mustafa had fooled the Levant merchants and had been received at Windsor in 1607 as a representative of the Sultan, became synonymous in English with cheating. The term is used in *The Alchemist* (I. ii).

Child. An unnamed child appears as a character in *Neptune's Triumph for the Return of Albion*, serves as the Cook's assistant, and prepares a "metaphorical dish" for the first antimasque.

Child, First; Second Child; Third Child. In the induction to *Cynthia's Revels,* three children appear. The first child begins to speak the prologue, but the other two interrupt, arguing for the privilege of speaking it. The second child claims to have been the first to study the prologue. They draw straws. The first child wins, but before he can speak, the third child gives away the action of the play in a fit of spite, saying that he will play Anaides. The second child joins the third in mocking fashionable theater-goers and complaining of the "hard fortune" of being a player. The first child is amused by their mockery and at the third sounding speaks the prologue.

Chilmead, Edmund. See MUSICAL SETTINGS.

Chimaera. A triple-bodied, fire-breathing monster of divine origin slain by Bellerophon.

Chiswell, Richard. Bookseller who in 1692 was one of the publishers of the third folio of Jonson's *Works*.

Chloe. Albius' wife in *Poetaster;* one of Jonson's affected, position-conscious city women who is trying to break into court society, in the pattern of the Citizen's Wife in *Cynthia's Revels*. She despises her foolish husband's fussiness, saying that she only married him because she was assured she could dominate him. She openly flirts with Crispinus, eagerly accepting his courtly attentions and moving him to be a poet for her. She takes his foolish advice on court manners. The courtiers greet her warmly when they arrive at her house. Cytheris advises her on court customs. Chloe plays Venus at Ovid's masquerade and is happy to be invited but disappointed that her husband must accompany her. At the masquerade she eagerly flirts with Tucca, Ovid, and Crispinus. She is berated by Caesar along with the others when he breaks in.

Chloridia.
    Performed: February 22, 1631, at court.
    Published: 1631 in quarto by Thomas Walkley.
    Printer: unknown.
    Subtitled "Rites to Chloris and her Nymphs," this masque, Jonson's last at court, was intended to complement *Love's Triumph Through Callipolis*, which had been given by the king the previous month—the queen and her fourteen ladies providing an exact counterpart to the king and his fourteen nobles. Although Jonson and Inigo Jones collaborated on the work, the rupture between them came to a head in *Chloridia*, and the rather incongruous ending may well reflect the two men's disagreement about the appropriate design for the masque. Moreover, multiple entries in the antimasque, a practice Jonson opposed that had become popular, are noticeable in the work, and their inclusion suggests that Jonson, who was no longer predominant at court, had reluctantly yielded to popular taste.

    In an introductory statement, the authors explained that having been commanded by the king and queen to invent a new argument and a change of scene whereby the queen would have the same number of ladies as the king had lords in *Love's Triumph Through Callipolis*, they agreed that the work should provide a celebration of some rites done unto the goddess Chloris, who, in a general council of the gods, had been proclaimed goddess of the flowers and would be honored on earth by an absolute decree from Jupiter, who would have the earth, as well as the heavens, adorned with stars.

The ornament that encircled the scene was composed of foliage interwoven with all sorts of flowers. Naked children played and climbed among the branches, and in the midst of all there was a great garland of flowers in which was written "Chloridia."

The curtain was drawn to reveal a pleasant spring scene, with a serene sky with transparent clouds and verdant hills planted with young trees, whose lower slopes were covered with flowers. Streams came gliding down from the hills; they seemed to converge into a river in the distance. In one part of the sky, a bright cloud soon began to break forth; in it sat a plump boy in a richly embellished garment, representing the mild Zephyrus. Opposite him, in a purplish cloud, appeared the Spring, represented by a beautiful maiden, her upper garment green and under it a white robe wrought with flowers and on her head a garland. Announcing the gods' decree, Zephyrus called her forth, and she obeyed, and they both lauded in song the king as the cause of the new Spring. Afterwards, Zephyrus passed away through the sky. Spring descended to the earth and was received by the Naiads—nymphs who were the fountains and servants of the season.

The fountains and Spring then approached the king and explained, in unison, that Cupid, who had recently taken offense at being snubbed by the gods, had journeyed to Hell in a fury, there to stir up jealousy and to set heaven, earth, and hell at odds. The nymphs danced and returned to the scene, after which a part of the underground opened, and a dwarf postilion entered riding on a curtal (a horse with a docked tail) with cloven feet and accompanied by two lackeys. These danced and made the first of the eight entries of the antimasque, and then the postilion reported in a long speech how all had seen perpetual holiday and triumph in Hell since Cupid's arrival there, how Cupid had carried Jealousy and other goblins from hell to trouble the gods, and how the postilion himself had been commanded to raise Tempest and others to assist in an "exploit" against earth and the goddess Chloris—queen of the flowers and mistress of spring. His speech concluded, the postilion mounted his curtal and rode off, accompanied by his lackeys.

For the second entry of the anti-masque, Cupid, Jealousy, Disdain, Fear, and Dissimulation danced in together. In the third entry the queen's dwarf, richly attired as the Prince of Hell and attended by six spirits, danced in expression of the joy at Cupid's coming to Hell. The scene immediately changed to a horrible storm; the nymph Tempest, accompanied by four Winds, danced the fourth entry, followed by the fifth one consisting of three Lightnings. Imitating the sound, Thunder danced the sixth entry. The seventh entry was provided by Rain, represented by five persons whose hair was dressed to look wet and who sprinkled sweet water around the room as they danced. The eighth and last entry was danced by seven men with rugged white heads and beards, representing snow. When they had finished their dance, they returned to the stormy scene from whence they had come.

Instantly, the tempestuous storm was stopped by the providence of Juno, and the scene changed to the bower of Chloris, which was richly adorned with flowers and above which appeared a rainbow in the distance. In the most eminent place in the bower sat the goddess Chloris, accompanied by fourteen nymphs, lavishly attired. In joyful song, the nymphs, together with Rivers, Fountains, and Spring, celebrated the beauty of the new spring brought about by "Juno's soft command, and Iris' showers, / Sent to quench jealousie, and all those powers / 'Of *Love's* rebellious warres: / Whil'st *Chloris* sits a shining starre / To crowne, and grace our jolly song. . . ." Afterwards the goddess and her nymphs descended and danced their entrance, which was followed by another song in praise of spring. After these masquers performed a second dance, the scene changed into air, with a low landscape partly covered with clouds. Suddenly, the heavens opened, and Juno and Iris were discovered sitting in the clouds with many airy spirits above them.

In song Juno and Iris celebrated the triumph of Chloris and the defeat of Cupid, who had by now begged for pardon. Afterwards, out of the earth a hill arose, on which Fame was standing with a trumpet in her hand. On the hill also were seated four persons representing Poesy, History, Architecture, and Sculpture, all of whom together with the nymphs, Rivers, and Fountains composed the chorus. Fame mounted on her wings and in song praised Chloris, Juno, and Iris, who had all guarded the spring and defeated what Jealousy and her followers had sought to destroy. The chorus and Fame then proclaimed that great actions may be obscured by time but can be preserved by memory, and Poesy, History, Architecture, Sculpture, Juno, and Iris all pledged that they would help to immortalize the actions of the day. In a final speech the chorus then lauded the support of Fame, the beauties of the spring, and the glory of Chloris. The queen Fame now being hidden in the clouds, the hill sank, the heavens closed, and the masquers danced with the lords.

Chloris. Identified with Flora, the goddess of flowers. In *Chloridia,* a character played by the queen who appears with her fourteen nymphs as the goddess of flowers and the mistress of Spring.

Christian. One of the wenches in *The Gypsies Metamorphosed,* who discovers that the gypsies have picked her pockets.

Christmas. The first character to come onstage in *Christmas, His Masque,* he presents his children to perform before the king and his guests.

Christmas, His Masque.
Performed: At court, Christmas season 1616.
Published: 1640 in folio by Thomas Walkley at the beginning of the section on masques.
Printer: uncertain.
This work, probably performed at Whitehall, is actually a mumming. The performers came in procession, recited their lines, danced, and exited. It seems to be a burlesque of an entertainment at a city hall.

Dressed in round hose, long stockings, a close doublet, a high-crowned hat with a broach and wearing a long thin beard, Christmas entered with some guards, introduced himself, and announced that he had brought a masque from the city to be presented by his children, who were all excellent dancers. Led in by Cupid, who wore a flat cap and an apprentice coat and had wings on his shoulders, the children of Christmas danced forth, all appropriately attired: Mis-Rule, Carroll, Minc'd-Pie, Gamboll, Post and Paire, New-Yeares-Gift, Mumming, Wassall, Offering, and Babie-Cake. They all entered singing until Christmas noticed a disturbance and asked what it was all about, and Gamboll replied that someone from Friday Street wanted to be admitted to the show, but Christmas declared that anyone associated in any way with fasting was not a Christmas creature and would not be admitted, after which

the singing continued until it was again interrupted by a deaf old woman named Venus, who was the mother of the young boy playing Cupid and who wanted to watch her son perform before the king.

After considerable discussion and banter, Christmas reluctantly agreed to let Venus stay and called for the performance to proceed, but Carroll indicated that some of the properties were missing. Christmas commanded that the performance should go ahead without them, and the song continued, announcing that all of the characters would present a Christmas as of old. Then, to the sound of drum and fife, they all marched about, after which the song proceeded and introduced each character separately in an individual verse, ending with the introduction of Cupid, who invited all those present to view the sights he had brought. As Cupid attempted to deliver his lines, Venus, his mother, interrupted him with instructions and words of encouragement until Christmas, disgusted and frustrated, announced the end of the speeches and the start of dancing, all to the protestation of Venus, who promised to appeal to the king. All the characters then danced as Christmas lauded their performance. The masque ended with Christmas singing a song in which he explained that his children could do more than dance and that they would all be willing to return to entertain the court during every Christmas season.

Christian IV (1577–1648). King of Denmark and Norway 1596–1648. Son of Frederick II. He devoted his energy to building the navy, industry, and commerce. He visited England in 1606, and he and James I were entertained by Robert Cecil, 1st Earl of Salisbury, at Theobalds. Jonson wrote the entertainment for the occasion. Christian invaded Germany in 1625 as the champion of the Protestant cause during the Thirty Years War, and he maintained an anti-Swedish policy throughout most of his reign, which resulted in a war with Sweden (1643–45) in which he lost the Norwegian provinces of Jamtland and Harjedalen. Christian was succeeded by his son Frederick III.

Christophero. A steward to Count Ferneze in *The Case Is Altered.* He urges the servants below him to get to work and happily greets Valentine. When Onion asks him to advance Onion's suit to Rachel, Christophero decides that he loves her himself and will woo her for himself. He asks the Count to help him but is double-crossed when the count decides that he wants

Rachel for himself. Christophero asks Jaques for Rachel's hand, but Jaques treats him roughly, believing him to be a fortune hunter. Christophero and Angelo conspire to lure Jaques away from his daughter with a trail of gold and then steal her, but Christophero is double-crossed again by Angelo, who takes Rachel to an isolated place and tries to assault her. Christophero goes to the Count's complaining loudly but loses his hope of Rachel when Jaques reveals her true identity, and she is betrothed to Paulo.

Chromis. The name of one of the young satyrs in *Oberon, the Fairy Prince.*

Chronicler. An unnamed character who appears in *News from the New World Discovered in the Moon* and is interested in the news of the discovery as possible material for his book.

Chronomastix. A character symbolizing George Wither, who appears in *Time Vindicated to Himself and to his Honors* and scorns Time.

Chronos. Identified with Saturn as time itself.

Chuffe. Literally, chough or crow; churl; used as an aptronym for a usurer's kinsman who is satirized in *Epig.* XLIV.

Chute, Elizabeth (d. 1627), daughter of Sir George Chute, was buried in Sonning Church, Berkshire. *Und.* XXXV is an epitaph for her.

Chute, Marchette (1909–   ). Writer educated at the University of Minnesota. Author of several books on Renaissance writers and other subjects. In 1953 she published her very readable but uncritical biography of Jonson, *Ben Jonson of Westminster.*

Cicero, Marcus Tullius (106–43 B.C.). In Jonson's time often called Tully. The greatest Roman orator. He studied law and philosophy at Rome, Athens, and Rhodes and became a famous politician and philosopher. He served as curule aedile (69 B.C.), praetor (66 B.C.), and consul (63 B.C.); as leader of the senatorial party, he successfully prosecuted Catiline. Because he was unable to prove that he had legal sanction to execute five members of Catiline's group, he was exiled in 56 B.C. by his personal enemy Clodius, but he was recalled by Pompey the next year and hailed as a hero. Opposed to Julius Caesar, Cicero was leader of the party that forced him to convene the triumvirate at Lucca in 56 B.C. After the Civil War, Caesar forgave Cicero, and he lived in Rome in honor under the dictatorship. Marc Antony was Cicero's mortal enemy, and he attacked Cicero in the Senate. When Octavian (later Augustus) took Rome, he allowed Antony to place Cicero's name among the proscriptions, and Cicero was executed on December 7, 43 B.C.

Cicero's writings are voluminous, and among them are letters that reveal more of Roman life and politics than does any other source. His philosophical works, which are essentially Stoical, include: *De amicitia, De officiis, De senectute, De finibus, Tuscalanarum Quaestionum,* and *De natura deorum.* Among his rhetorical works are *De oratore, Brutus,* and *Orator.* His most widely read works are the orations, the most famous being the *Orations Against Catiline* and the *Philippics* against Antony.

Cicero's rhetorical and oratorical style is excellent, and his reputation as the great master of Latin prose has never waned. In the Renaissance every learned person spent time learning to imitate Cicero. Consequently, there are numerous echoes and paraphrases of Cicero throughout Jonson's works. *In Catilinam* is a major source for *Catiline.* Cicero is mentioned in *Timber* several times (ll. 899–900, 2282, 2389–96, 2496–99) and also quoted (ll. 2134–35). Cicero's definition of comedy is quoted in *Every Man out* (III. vi), and he is quoted in the *King's Coronation Entertainment.* These are only a few instances of how readily Cicero was at hand for Jonson.

In *Catiline,* Cicero is a "New Man" who wins a consulship and uses his governmental position and oratorical powers to save Rome from Catiline's conspiracy.

Cicero, Quintus. In *Catiline,* Cicero's brother, who helps prevent Vargunteius and Cornelius from assassinating his brother.

Cimber, Gabinius. In *Catiline,* one of the conspirators who supports Catiline's abortive attempt to seize power in Rome.

Cinxia. A symbolic character who appears in *Hymenaei* as one of the powers of Juno.

Cipus. One of the great citizens of the Roman state, upon whose head horns suddenly sprouted, portending that he was destined to become king, for which he voluntarily exiled himself, believing that his reign would not be for the good of the citizens.

Circe. Daughter of Helios, who lived on the island of Aeaea and was very powerful in magic, turning Odysseus' men into swine.

47

Citizen. Asotus' brother-in-law in *Cynthia's Revels*, who struggles to get into the courtship contest but is only knocked on the head for his pains and made to stay outside while his wife is admitted.

Clarendon, Edward Hyde, Earl of (1609–1674). English statesman and historian. In a manuscript of his life he lists Jonson as one of his early friends and states that Jonson was very kind to him until Hyde took up business. Hyde entered Parliament in 1640 and eventually offered his services to Charles I. In 1646 he followed Prince Charles into exile and became one of his chief advisers. In 1660 he was created Baron Hyde and in 1661 Earl of Clarendon. In 1660 his daughter Anne married James, Duke of York (afterwards James II). As Lord Chancellor, Hyde had difficulty in working with Parliament, and he was unpopular with the Restoration court. In 1667 Charles dismissed him, and he fled England and lived in exile until his death. Clarendon's *History of the Rebellion* is an indispensable account of the Civil War.

Claribel, Sir. In Spenser's *The Faerie Queen*, Sir Claribel, "the lewd," is one of six knights who compete for Florimel. In *The Alchemist* (I. ii), Face tells Subtle that Dapper is to be trusted and is "no cheating . . . Claribel."

Claridiana. A noble character, heroine of *The Mirror of Knighthood*, a work by D. Ortuñez de Calahorra, which was translated into English in 1580. In *The Alchemist* (I), Subtle compliments Dol after she settles a quarrel between himself and Face by saying that she is like Claridiana.

Clarion. The rich shepherd in *The Sad Shepherd*. He mourns for Earine and tells Robin Hood of the sour people who say that in merry making shepherds neglect their duties. He worries over Aeglamour's melancholy and tells Karolin to watch over Aeglamour. After he realizes that everyone has been deceived by Maudlin in the shape of Marion, he wonders that his eyes were fooled. He challenges Maudlin to speak out when she comes. He meets Karolin in the woods after Aeglamour has slipped away from him and goes to find Aeglamour himself.

Claros. Surname of Apollo derived from the name of a town where Apollo was worshipped.

Claudian. Claudius Claudianus (c. 370–c. 405), is usually regarded as the last of the classical Roman writers. He may have been a Christian. Born in Alexandria, he went to live in Rome, where he gained the patronage of the powerful general Stilicho. Claudian wrote eulogies of his patron and the emperor Honorius, poems attacking enemies of the emperor, epics on the wars against the Goths, an epithalamium for Honorius' marriage, an unfinished poem entitled *The Rape of Proserpine,* and numerous idylls and epigrams.

Jonson drew upon Claudian in many of his works, including the *King's Coronation Entertainment, A Panegyre, The Masque of Queens, The Entertainment at Highgate, The Haddington Masque, The Speeches at Prince Henry's Barriers, The Golden Age Restored, The Vision of Delight, Chloridia, Sejanus, Catiline,* and *Epig.* XIV, LXVII, and LXXVI.

Clay, John. In *A Tale of a Tub,* a tilemaker. He is the intended husband for Awdrey but is falsely accused of robbery, loses Awdrey, and is finally made a laughingstock.

Cleare, Dame Annesh. A rich London widow who married an unprincipled courtier during the reign of Edward I and drowned herself in a spring after he wasted her fortune and deserted her. A well in Hoxton, which supposedly comes from this spring, is named for her. In *Bartholomew Fair* (III. iii), Captain Whit makes a coarse reference to her.

clemency. In *Timber* (ll. 1158–96), Jonson, responding to Machiavelli's approval of the Prince's cruelty (*Il Principe,* chs. vii and viii), draws on Seneca (*De Clementia*) and argues that "no vertue is a *Princes* owne; or becomes him more, then his *Clemency:* And no glory is greater, then to be able to save with his power." Moreover, Jonson contends, Machiavelli's argument that restrained cruelty is ineffective is in reality also bad counsel, because cruelty in any degree is unwise, for cruel Princes will find that they cannot break the habit of cruelty and, in the end, will grow to hate themselves as much as their subjects hate them. On the other hand, the merciful Prince is loved, not feared, by his subjects, and consequently, the Prince "is guarded with his own benefits."

Clement, Dr. (Justice Clement). In *Every Man in His Humour,* a "merry old magistrate." (The version of the play in the folio of 1616 differs from that in the quarto of 1601—many of the characters have different names. Names used in the folio version are in parentheses here.) Lorenzo junior (Edward) and Prospero (Wellbred) speak admiringly of him, praising his good humour and "mad" wit. When Cob complains to him of being beaten for deriding the use of tobacco (of which Clement thinks highly), Clement is furious with Cob for his comments and plays at putting him in jail, which terrifies Cob and surprises Lorenzo senior (Knowell), who is with Clement. Clement urges Lorenzo senior to "be merry," to take life less seriously, and to stop worrying about Lorenzo junior's behavior. When the company comes before him with their various complaints, he unravels the complications Musco (Brainworm) has made with good humor and admiration for Musco's cleverness. He is merciful to Peto (Formal) for succumbing to Musco, comforts the discontented members of the company, and gives Lorenzo junior and Hesperida (Bridget) his blessing. He punishes Bobadilla and Matheo (Matthew), after mocking Bobadilla for pretending to be a soldier and discovering in a verse-making contest with Matheo that he is a plagiarist. He makes a short speech (in the folio version a long speech) in defense of true poetry and invites the company to dinner at his house.

Clement's servant. In the Q 1601 (F 1616) version of *Every Man in His Humor*, Clement's servant announces and escorts to Bobadilla, Matheo (Matthew), Musco (Brainworm), Giulliano (Downright), and Stephano (Stephen), when Clement is busy straightening out the complications of the plot.

Clench, Rasi'. In *A Tale of a Tub*, a farrier of Hamstead who is a petty constable and who assists Tobie Turfe in his efforts to find John Clay and a band of robbers.

Clerimont, Ned. In *Epicoene*, Clerimont is a close friend of Dauphine Eugenie. He joins Dauphine in plotting to make Dauphine Morose's heir and in making John Daw and Sir Amorous La-Foole appear ridiculous. He and Truewit, another friend, often discuss women.

Clerk. An unnamed member of the boys of Boeotia who perform an antimasque in *Pan's Anniversary*.

Cleyton, James, received his B.A. from Magdalen College, Oxford, in 1609, and his M.A. in 1611. He was rector of Fledborough in 1618 and of Harthills from 1625 to 1639. He prefixed verses to Sir John Beaumont's *Bosworth-Field* in 1629 and contributed an elegy ("Who first reform'd our stage with justest laws") to *Jonsonus Virbius*.

Clim-o'-the Clough. The name of an outlaw in an old ballad first printed in 1536. It was expanded to be a general term for out-

laws, and was even given to the Devil in Nashe's *Pierce Peniless* in 1592. In *The Alchemist* (I. ii), Face tells Subtle that Dapper is to be trusted by reassuring him that Dapper is "no cheating Clim-o'-the Clough."

Clock-keeper. An unnamed member of the boys of Boeotia who perform an antimasque in *Pan's Anniversary*.

Clod. One of the clowns who appears in *The Gypsies Metamorphosed* and discovers that the gypsies have picked his pockets.

Clothier. A member of the marketplace crowd in *Bartholomew Fair*.

Clotho, the eldest of the Fates, spins the thread of life.

Clove. In *Every Man out of His Humour*, a fop whose language may have been intended to satirize John Marston's turgid style.

Clun, Walter, an actor who played Falstaff and Iago, was murdered in 1664. According to Aubrey's Notes, Jonson, like Clun, had one eye lower than the other. Aubrey facetiously speculated that Jonson begot Clun.

Cob. A water bearer, who carries water from a reservoir to homes, using tankards broad at the bottom and narrow at the top, each holding about three gallons of water. His name is also the term for a herring's head. In *Every Man in His Humour*, Cob is husband to Tib and a source of low comedy. (The names in parentheses are those used in the 1616 folio version of the play, which differs from that of the 1601 quarto.) Cob makes extended puns to Matheo (Matthew) about his kinship to herring. He derides tobacco, proudly shows off the oaths he has learned from Bobadilla, and says that he thinks that poetry is worthless. In a long scene, he rails at fast days with Pizo (Cash). He and Bobadilla come close to fighting over the merits of tobacco; when he complains to Dr. Clement (Justice Clement), Clement threatens to throw him in jail for condemning tobacco. Cob is very jealous of Tib and tells her to lock herself up securely in their house. After Prospero (Wellbred) sends Thorello (Kitely) and Biancha (Dame Kitely) to Cob's house, each thinking that the other is being unfaithful there, Cob enters in the middle of the confusion and beats his wife for her apparent role of bawd in the situation. They are brought before Clement but have no speeches in the 1601 quarto version to show that they are happily reconciled. In the 1616 folio version, they speak of their reconciliation, Clement declares that night their bridal night since they are "married anew," and they eat with Stephen in the "butterie."

Cob, Pertinax. Pertinax means obstinate, sometimes stiff; Cob means a big man with sexual prowess. Jonson makes a witty play upon the sexual implications of this name in *Epig.* LXIX, and he further extends the joke in the character of Cob in *Every Man in His Humour,* with additional play upon the meaning of Cob as a red herring.

Cockrell. One of the clowns who appears in *The Gypsies Metamorphosed* and discovers that the gypsies have picked his pockets.

Cod. Literally, a perfume bag; also, the testicles. Jonson wittily plays upon these meanings in the Sir Cod satirized in *Epig.* XIX, XX, and L.

Cocytus. A murky river in Hades.

Cokeley. A jester who improvised at entertainments and who is mentioned in *Bartholomew Fair* (III. iv), *The Devil Is an Ass* (I. i), and *Epig.* CXXIX.

Coke, Sir Edward (1552–1634), eminent English judge and legal writer. Served as Solicitor-General (1592), Speaker of the House of Commons (1592–93), Attorney-General (1593–94), Chief Justice of the Common Pleas (1606), and Chief Justice of the King's Bench (1613). Coke championed the common law against the encroachments of the royal prerogative. Jonson praised him in *Und.* XLVI.

Cokes, Bartholomew. The foolish young Esquire of Harrow in *Bartholomew Fair.* Cokes comes to London to obtain a license to marry Grace, Justice Overdo's ward, and much to his guardian Waspe's dismay, shows his total foolishness in his conduct at the fair. He loses his purse twice, and his cloak and hat by his carelessness, and throws away great sums of money in childish, impetuous purchases of gingerbread, hobby horses, birds, and drums. Grace is disgusted by his boorishness and is easily persuaded by Quarlous and Winwife to leave him. Cokes is greatly impressed by Littlewit's vulgar, common puppet show, and annoys the other patrons by commenting loudly during it.

Colby. The unidentified friend to whom *Und.* XV is addressed.

Coleridge, S. T. (1772–1834). English poet, critic, and philosopher. At Christ's Hospital, where he was a charity pupil, Coleridge met his lifelong friend Charles Lamb. In 1793 he enlisted in the 15th Light Dragoons, but obtained an early discharge and returned to Cambridge. In 1794 he and Robert Southey made plans to establish a utopian community in America on the banks of the Susquehanna, but the project failed for lack of sufficient capital. Coleridge married Sara Fricker in 1795, and he collected his *Poems on Various Occasions* the following year. In 1797 Coleridge and his family went to live at Nether Stowey, where Coleridge and Wordsworth later planned their joint volume *Lyrical Ballads* (1798), the preface and poems of which established it as a germinal volume in the English Romantic movement. Included in the book was "The Rime of the Ancient Mariner," which has become Coleridge's most widely read work. After he had spent a year (1799–1800) in Germany translating Schiller's *Wallenstein,* Coleridge and his family settled in the Lake Country with the Southeys, where Coleridge wrote some of his best poetry. His drug habit was fixed by 1802 and by 1808 had led to estrangement from his family. After 1805 he gave several lectures on literature, and his criticism, particularly that on Shakespeare, is still valuable. In an effort to cure his addiction, Coleridge went in 1816 to live with Dr. James Gillman, where he remained until his death in 1834. In 1817 his *Sybilline Leaves* (poetry) and *Biographia Literaria* were published, and *Confessions of an Enquiring Spirit* appeared posthumously in 1840. Despite the devastating effects of opium upon his literary production in his last years, Coleridge remains one of the most influential writers in the English Romantic movement.

In his *Lectures on Shakespeare,* Coleridge criticized Sejanus' appealing for a sign to the divinity whose altar he proceeds to destroy (*Sejanus,* v) as "unspeakably irrational," but he placed *The Alchemist* along with *Oedipus* and *Tom Jones* among the "three best plots in literature." Coleridge also adapted *Und.* VII as "Mutual Passion, Altered and Modernized from an Old Poet."

Collier, Jeremy (1650–1726). English clergyman who was imprisoned as a nonjuror (he would not swear allegiance to William and Mary in 1689, as he considered himself still bound by the oath he had taken to the deposed king, James II) and later outlawed in 1696 for absolving two of those involved in an assassination conspiracy against William III. His principal claim to fame rests on his strong stand against the alleged immorality of the English stage.

In his *A Short View of the Immorality and Profaneness of the English Stage* (1698) Collier includes a section on immoral protagonists in which he complains that the practice on the English stage of making the protagonists debauched persons who find themselves happy at the conclusion of the play is against the law of comedy, which requires the rewarding of virtue and the punishment of vice. Collier specifically criticizes Dryden who had, in his preface to *The Mock Astrologer*, attempted to justify this practice in his own works, on the authority of Ben Jonson. Collier argues, contrary to Dryden, that neither *The Alchemist* nor *Epicoene* nor *Volpone* violates the comic law. Later in the same book Collier cites Jonson's dedicatory epistle to *Volpone* as the authority for the ideal that the poet cannot be a good poet without first being a good man. Earlier in the book Collier had criticized Vanbrugh's use of profanity in *The Relapse* and explained that the spirit of Vanbrugh's thought was derivative from Jonson's *Bartholomew Fair*. He also attacked Congreve for the use of profanity in *The Double Dealer*.

The attack on Congreve inspired a response from him. In his *Amendments of Mr. Collier's Faults and Imperfect Citations* (1698), Congreve defended himself on the authority of Ben Jonson, specifically *Bartholomew Fair*. In his reply to Congreve (*A Defense of the Short View* [1699]), Collier argued that Jonson's ill example was no excuse for Congreve to continue an atheistical practice. Collier concluded that since Congreve "endeavors to excuse himself upon the authority of Ben Jonson, I shall just mention what thoughts this poet had of his profane liberties, at a time when we have reason to believe him to be most in earnest. Now Mr. Wood reports from the testimony of a great prelate then present 'that when Ben Jonson was in his last sickness, he was often heard to repent of his profaning the scriptures in his plays, and that with horror.'"

Colonnia, Francisco. In *The Case Is Altered,* a nobleman in Milan, friend to count Ferneze and Angelo, master to Valentine. He has been traveling before the play opens and is warmly welcomed by the count on his return. He gently woos Phoenixella, urging her to forget her sadness at her mother's death. He is present at the resolution of the play and occasionally comments on the action, but plays no significant role in the denouement.

Colt. Used as an aptronym in *Epig.* XXXIX, the name implies lasciviousness.

Columbus, Christopher. The Italian adventurer credited with the discovery of America is mentioned in *Bartholomew Fair* (v. vi).

comedy. For their appreciation and criticism of Jonson's comedies, see John DRYDEN; Thomas SHADWELL.

comedy (theory of). In *Timber* (ll. 2625–77), Jonson, drawing upon Daniel Heinsius (*Ad Horatij de Plauto & Terentio judicium, Dissertatio,* 1618), includes a short discourse on comedy, noting first that the parts of a comedy and a tragedy are the same since they both strive to teach and to delight. Like Aristotle, Jonson argues that the moving of laughter is not always the end of comedy, but may be a fault in it. Since the ancient philosophers considered laughter inappropriate in a wise man, Plato thought Homer sacrilegious because he sometimes presented the gods laughing. According to Aristotle, to seem ridiculous is a part of dishonesty and is foolish. Hence, we find the moving of laughter in Old Comedy as in Aristophanes, who outdoes Plautus in this respect. Making the wise appear ridiculous in order to move to laughter is the reason Aristophanes, for example, presents Socrates in a basket in *The Clouds.*

commendatory poems. These are of two types: (1) those Jonson wrote for or about other people or their works and (2) those other people wrote for or about Jonson or his works. Most poems of the first type were not included in Jonson's *Works* until the Herford and Simpson edition, where they are in a section called Ungathered Verse. Many of the poems of the second type were used as prefatory pieces to particular works by Jonson.

Uncollected poems Jonson wrote to commemorate the works of others include:
1. "Certain Opening and Drawing Distiches." A series of thirteen distiches (A to N), most of them witty and some contemptuous, were prefixed to *Coryate's Crudities* (1611), an account by Thomas Coryate of his walking tour through Europe.
2. "*Comoedias trusatilis Plauti mola*" was prefixed to Thomas Farnaby's *L & M Annaei Senecae atque aliorum Tragoediae* (1613).
3. "*Cum Juvenale tuo, Farnabi, Persius exit*" was prefixed to Farnaby's *Auli Persii Flacci Satyrae sex* (1612),

as was the poem described at 8 below. The work had two title pages. They bore slightly different titles but the same imprint.

4. "In Authorem" was appended to Nicholas Breton's *Melancholicke Humours* (1600).

5. "Ode, ἀλληγοριϰὴ," originally appeared in Hugh Holland's *Pancharis* (1603).

6. "On the Author, Work, and Translator" was prefixed to James Mabbe's translation of *The Rogue* (1622).

7. "On the Honored Poems of his Honored Friend, Sir John Beaumont" was written for *Bosworth-Field* (1629) by Sir John Beaumont (1583–1627), brother of Francis Beaumont the dramatist.

8. *"Temporibus lux magna fuit Juvenalis auitis"* was prefixed to Thomas Farnaby's *Junii Juvenalis et Auli Persii Flacci Satyrae* (1612).

9. "The Ghyrlond of the Blessed Virgin Mary" was prefixed to Anthony Stafford's *The Female Glory* (1635). Some scholars dispute Jonson's authorship while others claim that if Jonson wrote the poem he must have done so when he was a Catholic, that is, between 1598 and 1612.

10. "The Vision . . . on the Muses of His Friend, M. Drayton" was written for Michael Drayton's *The Battaile of Agincourt . . .* (1627).

11. "To His Friend the Author Upon His *Richard*" was prefixed to Christopher Brooke's *The Ghost of Richard* (1614).

12. "To His Much and Worthily Esteemed Friend, the Author" was prefixed to *Cinthias Revenge: or Maenanders Extasie* (1613), a supposedly anonymous play that was probably written by John Stephens.

13. "To My Dear Son, and Right-Learned Friend, Master Joseph Rutter" was written for Rutter's *The Shepherd's Holy-Day* (1635).

14. "To My Old Faithful Servant" was written for Richard Brome's *The Northern Lass, A Comedy* (1632).

15. "To My Worthy and Honored Friend, Mr. George Chapman" was prefixed to Chapman's *The Georgicks of Hesiod* (1618).

16. "To the Author," prefixed to Thomas Wright's *Passions of the Mind in General* (2nd ed., 1604), lauds Wright for his study of the Renaissance theory of the passions.

17. "To the Memory of My Beloved, the Author, Mr. William Shakespeare" was prefixed to the Shakespearian First Folio (1623).

18. "To the Reader," prefixed to the Shakespearian First Folio (1623), is keyed to Martin Droeshout's portrait of Shakespeare which was also prefixed to the Folio.

19. "To the Right Noble Tom" was published in Thomas Coryate's *Coryate's Crudities* (1611).

20. "To the Worthy Author of The Husband" was prefixed to *The Husband*, an anonymous poem that is a development of Thomas Overbury's *A Wife* (1614).

21. "Truth is the trial of itself" was prefixed to James Warre's *The Touchstone of Truth. Wherin Veritie, by Scripture is plainely confirmed, and Errors confuted* (1624). Since Warre's work was directed against Catholics and Jonson was a Catholic for part of his life, some scholars do not believe Jonson wrote this poem although it is usually included in his canon.

22. "When late (grave Palmer) these thy grafts and flowers" was written for Thomas Palmer's, 'The Sprite of Trees and Herbes,' but the book was never published.

Uncollected poems Jonson wrote for or about other people include:

1. "An Expostulation with Inigo Jones" is one of the three caustic satires Jonson wrote about Jones; the poem was written shortly after the performance of *Chloridia* (1631) and the publication of *Love's Triumph* (1631). Jones resented his subordinate position on the title page of *Love's Triumph* and his claim to priority angered Jonson, who avenged himself by omitting Jones's name from the title page of the quarto of *Chloridia* and by writing three scathing satires on Jones (the other two satires are entitled "To a Friend: An Epigram on Him" and "To Inigo Marquess Would-Be: A Corollary.") The satires were apparently circulated in manuscript and were partly responsible for Jonson's losing favor with the king.

2. "A Grace by Ben Jonson" was delivered before James I, probably about 1617.
3. "Censure not sharply then but me advise" is an epistle to an unidentified friend of Jonson's.
4. "Charles Cavendish to His Posterity" is an epitaph for Cavendish (1553?–1619), Earl of Newcastle. The Earl left three children, one of whom (William) Jonson addressed in *Und.* LV and LXI.
5. "Epitaph [on Cecilia Bulstrode]" was sent with a covering note to George Garrard, an intimate friend of John Donne's and the one who informed Jonson of Cecilia's death. The poem is an enigma because it praises the virtue of the same woman severely satirized in the "Court Pucell" (*Und.* XLIX).
6. "Fresh as the day, and new as are the hours" was a welcome song addressed to Charles I.
7. "Shall the prosperity of a pardon still" criticizes Alexander Gill.
8. "Speech Presented unto King James at a Tilting in the Behalf of the Two Noble Brothers Sir Robert and Sir Henry Rich" was presented by the brothers on March 24, 1613.
9. "Tis a record in Heaven. You, that are" was an epitaph for Katherine, Lady Ogle, who died in 1629 and was buried at Bolsover.
10. "To My Detractor" is a response to John Eliot's verses that were critical of Jonson's verses to the first Earl of Portland.
11. "To the Memory of that Most Honored Lady Jane" was an epitaph for Lady Jane, eldest daughter of Cuthbert, Lord Ogle, and wife of Edward, 8th Earl of Shrewsbury. The Countess of Shrewsbury died on January 7, 1625 and was buried in Westminster Abbey. Jonson's verses were not used on her tomb.
12. "To the Most Noble, and Above His Titles, Robert, Earl of Somerset" celebrates the Earl's marriage to Frances Howard.

Poems written by others to commemorate Jonson's works include:

Alchemist (1612 quarto)
"To My Friend Mr. Ben Jonson Upon His *Alchemist*," by George Lucy.

Art of Poetry (1640)
1. "Proceed in thy brave rage," by an unidentified "I.C."
2. "Tis dangerous to praise; besides the task," by Barton Holyday.
3. "Twas not enough, Ben Jonson to be thought," by Lord Herbert of Cherbury.

Catiline (1611 quarto)
1. "To my Friend, Mr. Ben Jonson, Upon his *Catiline*," by Francis Beaumont.
2. "To His Worthy Beloved Friend Mr. Ben Jonson," by Nathan Field.
3. "To His Worthy Friend Mr. Ben Jonson," by John Fletcher.

Epicoene (1616 Folio)
"Upon the *Silent Woman*," by Francis Beaumont.

Magnetic Lady
"Upon Ben Jonson's *Magnetic Lady*," by Alexander Gill, was never published.

Sejanus (1605 quarto)
1. "How high a poorman shows in low estate," by William Strachey.
2. "In that, this book doth deign *Sejanus* name," by Hugh Holland.
3. "Sejanus, great, and eminent in Rome," by Sir Thomas Roe.
4. "So brings the wealth-contracting jeweler," by George Chapman.
5. "To Him that Hath so Excell'd on this Excellent Subject," by the unidentified ΦΙΛΟΣ.
6. "To the Most Understanding Poet," probably by Edmund Bolton.
7. "When I respect thy arguments, I see," by the unidentified "Cygnus."
8. "Ye ready friends, spare your unneedful bayes," by John Marston.

Volpone (1605 quarto)
1. "*Amicissimo & Meritissimo Ben: Ionson*," by John Donne.
2. "Magus would needs forsooth this other day," by Henry Parrot, was published in the *Mous-Trap* (1606).
3. "To My Friend Mr. Jonson," probably by Sir Thomas Roe.
4. "To My Good Friend, Mr.

Jonson," probably by Dudley Digges.

5. "To My Worthily-Esteemed Mr. Benjamin Jonson," probably by Edmund Scory.

6. "To the Ingenious Poet," by "I.C." (possibly John Cooke of Hartshill, Warwickshire).

7. "To the Reader, Upon the Work," probably by Sir Thomas Roe.

8. "To the True Master in his Art, Ben Jonson," by John Fletcher.

9. "To the Worthiest Master Jonson," by Nathan Field.

Works (1616)
"Raptam Thrëicii lyram Neanthus," by John Selden.

Works (1640)

1. "Each like an Indian ship or hull appears," possibly by William Hodgson, but some scholars believe it may be by Robert Anton since the verses seem to be borrowed from Anton's *The Philosophers Satyrs* (1616).

2. "Here is a poet! Whose muddled strains," by William Hodgson.

3. "Upon the Works of Ben Jonson," by John Oldham, was published in Oldham's *Poems and Translations* (1683).

Poems written about Jonson include:

1. "Ben is deceased, and yet I dare avow," by Nicholas Downey, was prefixed to Samuel Harding's *On Sicily and Naples, or, The Fatal Union* (1640).

2. "Had Rome but heard her worthies speak so high" was anonymously published in *Wits Recreations* (1640).

3. "Here Johnson lies who spent his days," by Thomas Willford, was included in an unpublished collection entitled 'Hyemall Pastimes' (poems from 1630 to 1640).

4. "Here lies Jonson with the rest," by Robert Herrick, was published in *Hesperides* (1648).

5. "Here lies the fox, then what need we," by Thomas Prujean, was published in *Aurorata* (1644).

6. "He who began from brick and lime," by Mildmay Fane, Earl of Westmorland, was published in *Otia Sacra* (privately printed in 1648).

7. "His prayer to Ben Jonson," by Robert Herrick, was published in *Hesperides* (1648).

8. "How comes the world so sad? For whom doth death," by George Stutvile, is an unpublished elegy.

9. "How! doest thou ask me why my ventrous pen," by Robert Heath, was appended to *Clarastella* (1650).

10. "I do not wonder that great Jonson's play," by the unidentified "C.G.," was prefixed to Thomas Nabbes's *The Unfortunate Mother* (1640).

11. "If great men wrong me, I will spare myself," possibly by Sir John Roe, was published in *Poems of John Donne* (1635).

12. "If that thy lore were equal to thy wit," by William Gamage, was published in *Linsi-Woolsi, or Two Centuries of Epigrammes* (1613).

13. "I love thy parts; so must I love thy whole," by John Davies of Hereford, was published in *The Scourge of Folly* (1611).

14. "In Benjaminum Jonsonum, Poetam Laureatum, & Dramaticorum Sui Seculi Facile Principem," by James Duport, was published in *Musae Subsecivae Seu Poetica Stromata* (1676).

15. "Inius te voco, Ionsoni, venito," by Charles Fitzgeoffrey, was published in *Affaniae* (1603).

16. "I would write of thee, Ben; not to approve," by William Cavendish, Earl (and afterwards Duke) of Newcastle, was first published in *Welbeck Miscellany, No. 2. A Collection of Poems* (1924).

17. "Jonson and his Peers," by George Daniel of Beswick, was published in *Poems Written Upon Several Occasions* (1646).

18. "Jonson's alive! the world admiring stands," by the unidentified "C.G.," was prefixed to Richard Brome's *The Antipodes* (1640).

19. "Jonson's Visits to the Peak," by Francis Andrewes, a London physician, was never published.

20. "Let Ignorance with Envy chat," by Thomas Bancroft, was published in *Two Books of Epigrammes and Epitaphs* (1639).

21. "Next these, learned Jonson in this list I bring," by Michael Drayton, was appended to *The Battaile of Agincourt* (1627).

22. "Next to Jonson sat—in ancient learning trained," by Charles Churchill, was published in *The Rosciad* (2nd ed., 1761).

23. "On Ben Johnson's Bust," probably by David Lewis, was published in Lewis' *Miscellaneous Poems* (1726).

24. "Our modern Poets to that pass are driven," by Thomas Heywood, was published in *The Hierarchy of the Blessed Angels* (1635).

25. "Poets are born not made, when I would prove," by Leonard Digges, was published in *Poems: Written by William Shakespeare. Gentleman* (1640).

26. "Poets, who others can immortal make," by Robert Wild, was published in *Dr. Wild's Poem in Nova Fert Animus* (1679, broadside).

27. "Put off thy Buskins (Sophocles the great)," by Henry Parrot, was published in *Laquei Ridiculosi* (1613).

28. "Regit/At quae maligna stella scenam?," by Edward Kemp, was published in *Senile Odium* (1633).

29. "Shall I alone spare paper? in an age," by Sir Thomas Salusbury, was probably intended for inclusion in *Jonsonus Virbius,* but was not printed until Sir Israel Gollancz published it in the *Times Literary Supplement,* October 8, 1935.

30. "Si cadus expletus merito Jonsonius audit," by J. Rogers, was published in *Senile Odium* (1633).

31. "Sir if my robe and garb were richly worth," by Richard James, was never published.

32. "Sons born of many a loyal muse to Ben," by Algernon Charles Swinburne, was appended to *Tristram of Lyonesse* (1882).

33. "The Country's Censure on Ben Jonson's *New Inn,*" anonymous and unpublished, was a response to Jonson's ode on leaving the stage.

34. "Thee, mighty Ben! we ever shall affect," by Robert Gould, was published in *Poems: Chiefly Con-*

sisting of Satyrs and Satyrical Epistles (1689).

35. "The fox, the lion's sight extremely feared," by Lucius Cary, Viscount Falkland, was never published.

36. "The Grave is now a favorite, we see," by Clement Paman of Sidney Sussex College, Cambridge, was never published.

37. "The Poet's Invitation to Ben Jonson's Ghost to Appear Again," by Samuel Sheppard, was published in *Epigrammes, Six Books* (1651).

38. "The State and men's affairs are the best plays," by Sir John Roe, was published in *Poems of John Donne* (1635).

39. "The sun which doth the greatest comfort bring," by Francis Beaumont, was published in "The Additions" to Shakespeare's *Poems* (1640).

40. "This is poetic fury! when the pen," by Lucius Cary, Viscount Falkland, was never published.

41. "Thou canst not die for though the stroke of death," by John Taylor, was published in *The Sculler, Rowing from Thames to Tiber* (1612).

42. "Thou had'st the wreath before, now take the tree," by Robert Herrick, was published in *Hesperides* (1648).

43. "To Ben Jonson Upon Occasion of his Ode to Himself," by Thomas Carew, was published in Carew's *Poems* (1640).

44. "To his False Friend Mr. Ben Jonson," by Inigo Jones, was never published.

45. "To His Noblest Friend Mr. Endimion Porter Upon Verses Writ by Benjamin Jonson," by John Eliot, was published in *Poems Consisting of Epistles and Epigrams, Satyrs, Epitaphs, and Elegies, Songs and Sonnets* (1658).

46. "To My Learnedly Witty Friend Mr. Benjamin Jonson," by John Davies of Hereford, was published in *Wits Bedlam* (1617).

47. "To this rare place where wit is taught," by Thomas D'Urfey, was published in *Collin's Walk Through London and Westminster, A Poem in Burlesque* (1690).

48. "Upon Ben Jonson's Picture" was anonymously published in *Ludus Scacchiae: A Satyr Against Unjust Wars* (1676).

49. "Vindiciae Jonsonianae," by R. Goodwin, is an unpublished response to Jonson's ode on the failure of *The New Inn*.

50. "You swore dear Ben you'ld turn the green cloth blue," by John Eliot, was published in *Poems Consisting of Epistles and Epigrams, Satyrs, Epitaphs, and Elegies, Songs and Sonnets* (1658).

51. "Your verses are commended and 'tis true," by John Eliot, was never published, but Jonson responded to it in "To My Detractor."

comoedia vetus. Comedy of the ancients, but Jonson does not always use the term to mean comedy of the classical writers. In the *Conversations* (ll. 409–15), Jonson's discussion of the use of the vice figure refers to the writers of Old English comedy. Cordatus' use of the term at the beginning of *Every Man out* refers to the ancient Greek and Roman writers of comedy.

Compass. In *The Magnetic Lady* the mathematics scholar who eventually marries Pleasance, the legitimate niece of Lady Loadstone.

Comus. A mirthful god of later antiquity, often associated with Bacchus. A character very suggestive of Silenus who appears in *Pleasure Reconciled to Virtue* as the god of cheer and the belly. He and his followers are derided by Hercules.

Concord. Personification of agreement between the Roman state and some other body within it. Concord's principal temple was near the forum.

Condell, Henry (d. 1627). An actor, who as one of the Chamberlain's Men and later as a King's Man, performed in *Every Man in His Humour, Every Man out of His Humour, Sejanus, Volpone, The Alchemist,* and *Catiline.* He also acted in the plays of Beaumont and Fletcher and Shakespeare's plays. He married in 1599 and had nine children. He and John Heminges (Heming) co-edited the First Folio of Shakespeare, published in 1623. Condell was one of the original sharers of the Blackfriars Theatre, and by 1612 he had acquired shares in the Globe, which he left to his wife.

Congreve, William (1670–1729). English dramatist. He studied law at the Middle Temple, but after publishing a novel (*Incognita*) and translations of Juvenal and Persius, he turned to writing plays and produced *The Old Bachelor* (1693), *The Double Dealer* (1693), *Love for Love* (1695), and *The Mourning Bride* (1697)—his only tragedy. He became entangled with Jeremy Collier in the controversy over the immorality of the English stage. Although coolly received, his last play, *The Way of the World* (1700), has come to be regarded as one of the comic masterpieces of the English language. After 1700 Congreve wrote little, held various minor political positions, and enjoyed the friendships of Swift, Steele, Pope, and Voltaire until his death.

In his *Amendments of Mr. Collier's Faults and Imperfect Citations* (1698), Congreve points out that Jeremy Collier has overlooked a passage in Jonson's *Timber* (ll. 1020–24, 2339–45) that justifies the presentation of vicious and foolish characters on the stage and in comedy. Congreve also wrote a letter to Dennis in which he explains that humor is from nature, habit from custom, and affectation from industry. (See Jeremy Collier and John Dennis in *Letters Upon Several Occasions . . . published by Mr. Dennis* [1696]). According to Congreve, Morose in *Epicoene* is a great character of humor while Sir John Daw is a character of affectation. Cob in *Every Man in His Humour* and most of the low characters in the *Bartholomew Fair* represent not humors but habits contracted from custom.

Constable, Henry (1562–1613). English poet. After graduating from Cambridge in 1580, he went to Paris, which was more comfortable than England for Catholics. There he wrote *Diana* (1592), a volume of sonnets alluded to in *Und.* XXVII. Constable also wrote four pastorals.

Contarini, Cardinal Gasparo, was the author of *De Magistratibus et Republica Venetorum* (1589; English translation by Lewis Lewkenor, 1599), a work referred to by Lady Politic in *Volpone* (IV. i).

Conti, Natale (Natalis Comes). Italian humanist whose *Mythologiae* (1551) summarized much of the mythological knowledge of European humanism in the sixteenth century and was used by Jonson as one of his authorities, especially for *The Masque of Blackness, Hymenaei,* and *The Haddington Masque.*

Conyers, George. Bookseller in London from 1686 to 1712 who specialized in practical manuals on various subjects, but who in 1692 was one of the publishers of the third folio of Jonson's *Works* and of the so-called Booksellers' Edition of 1716–17.

Cook. An unnamed cook appears as a character in *Neptune's Triumph for the Return of Albion,* argues that the art of poetry is analogous to the art of cookery, and presents two antimasques.

Cooke, Alexander. An actor, who as one of the King's Men played in *Sejanus, Volpone, The Alchemist,* and *Catiline.* He was also one of the principal actors in Shakespeare's plays. He appointed his fellow actors Henry Condell and John Heminges as trustees of his estate shortly before he died in 1614.

Cooke, Thomas. Groom of Prince Charles's Chamber who in 1620 was twice sent to Whitehall "to warn Mr. Ben Johnson the Poet, and the players at the Blackfriers to atend Hys Highnes the night following at Court."

Cophetua, King. A rich king of legend and ballad, usually of Africa, who disdained all women, married finally a beggar, and found her to be a good queen. Cob mentions him in *Every Man in His Humour* (1616 folio version, III. iv).

coranto (courante). A dance of Italian origin characterized by quick running steps. Later a similar but graver and more formal dance developed in the seventeenth century in France. This dance was often used in Jonson's masques, usually at the end.

Corbaccio. The old man in *Volpone* who, although in worse health than Volpone, foolishly hopes to outlive him and schemes to inherit his wealth. Mosca tricks him into disinheriting his son, Bonario, in favor of Volpone.

Corbet, Richard. Poet with whom Jonson stayed when he visited Oxford in 1619 to receive the honorary M.A. from the University. Although ten years his junior, Corbet was apparently a warm friend of Jonson's, and Jonson wrote an epitaph (*Und.* XII) for Vincent Corbet, Richard's father.

Corbet, Vincent, father of Richard Corbet, was a gardener who died in 1619 when he was nearly eighty. Jonson praised the elder Corbet in *Und.* XII.

Cordatus. In *Every Man out of His Humour,* a character who serves as a moderator and comments upon the action of the play.

Cordus, Cremutius. Writer of a controversial, honest, blunt history in *Sejanus.* He is praised by noble, high-minded Romans but feared and hated by Sejanus, Tiberius, and their followers for his criticism of the present age. He praises Germanicus and says bitterly that Sejanus' statue will ruin Pompey's theater. He is accused of treason after Silius is taken into custody, and his books are burnt, although he nobly defends himself by citing how critical works were tolerated by important men of the past, notably Julius and Augustus Caesar.

Corinna. Greek lyric poetess, who lived in the fifth century B.C. She lived for a long time in Thebes and used its local mythology as a subject for her poetry. In *Poetaster* (I. iii; IV. iii), Ovid addresses his mistress Julia as Corinna in his poems, so that no one will guess her identity.

Corn-cutter. 1. An unnamed member of the boys of Boeotia who perform an antimasque in *Pan's Anniversary.*
2. A member of the marketplace crowd in *Bartholomew Fair.*

Cornelius, Caius. In *Catiline,* one of the conspirators who supports Catiline's abortive attempt to seize power in Rome.

Cornucopiae. One of the horns of the she-goat that suckled Zeus, which reputedly produced whatever one wished.

Cornwallis, Sir William, the Elder (d. 1611), was the son of Sir Thomas Cornwallis of Brome Hall, Suffolk, the Controller of Queen Mary's household. Sir William, who was probably knighted in 1593, entertained the King and Queen at his house at Highgate in 1604; Jonson wrote the entertainment for the occasion.

Correggio, Antonio Allegri (1494–1534). Italian painter whose early work was influenced by Mantegna and Leonardo da Vinci. His most famous piece is the *Assumption of the Virgin* in the dome of the cathedral in Parma, and his ceiling decorations were widely imitated in the seventeenth century. He is mentioned in *Timber* (l. 1584) among painters of the last age who were excellent and imitated the ancients.

Corvino. In *Volpone,* Corvino is a merchant who viciously schemes to inherit Volpone's wealth. The extent of his corruption is shown when, although he professes to be insanely jealous of his beautiful wife's chastity, he eagerly attempts to prostitute her to Volpone and hypocritically calls her lewd and slanders her fiercely in court when she refuses.

Coryat, Thomas (c. 1577–1617). English traveller who spent some time at the court of James I, where he was the willing butt of many jokes. In 1608 he went on a journey that covered most of the continent and led to the publication of his *Crudities* (1611), for which Jonson wrote distiches, a prose character, and an anagrammatic poem. Jonson also wrote a verse panegyric, "Certain Verses upon *Coryate's Crudities*," that was prefixed to *Coryats Crambe* (1611). In 1612 Coryat set out on another journey, traveling to Asia Minor and Egypt, Palestine, Persia, and India, reaching Agra in 1616. Some of his letters from Agra were published in 1616 and the others appeared in 1618, one year after his death.

All of Jonson's references to Coryat in his own works are contemptuous: *Conversations* (ll. 640–41), *Bartholomew Fair* (III. iv, v), *Love Restored*, *Epig.* CXXXIX, and *Und.* XIII.

Corydon. Rustic name found in Theocritus and Virgil's *Eclogues*.

Cos. Foolish page to Amorphus in *Cynthia's Revels*. He goes to find the fountain of self-love, and possibly brings in its water. Mercury makes mocking asides about him. Cynthia includes him in the group of shallow courtiers to be punished at Crites' discretion. He marches, weeps, and sings the palinode with the other courtiers.

Costardmonger. A fruit salesman at the fair in *Bartholomew Fair*. He agrees to trip and spill a basket of pears so that Cokes will scramble for them and Nightingale and Edgworth can steal Cokes's cloak and hat.

Cotta. Roman senator in *Sejanus*, who foolishly supports Sejanus in hopes of gaining pesonal power. He speaks against Silius and Cordus when they are accused of treason and suggests that Cordus' books be burnt. He goes with Pomponius to bring Sejanus news that Macro has returned and that a Senate meeting is soon to take place. He is very flattered when Sejanus speaks kindly to him. At the Senate, he is quick to honor Sejanus, until Tiberius' letter is read; then he moves away. After Sejanus is disgraced, he is quick to deride him.

Cotton, Sir Robert (1571–1631). English antiquarian. He was one of Jonson's schoolmates at Westminster. Cotton's library, which was a literary center of London and contained collections of books, manuscripts, coins, and antiquities, became a part of the British Museum when it was

founded in 1753. Jonson frequented the Cotton Library and the country house in Connington. It was at Cotton's house that Jonson told the attorney general that he had seen the verses on the assassination of Buckingham, and according to the *Conversations* (ll. 261–72), Jonson's visions about the death of his son happened while he was staying at Cotton's house. Jonson mentioned Cotton in *Und.* XLIII. Apparently, some of the books Jonson had borrowed from Cotton were destroyed when Jonson's library burned in 1623.

counsel (how to give). In *Timber* (ll. 93–115), Jonson, paraphrasing Juan Luis Vives (*De Consultatione* [*Opera*, i. 169–71]), notes that to give effective counsel the counselor should have lived a good life, should offer advice modestly and respectfully only after careful meditation, should be circumspect and speak with humanity and sweetness, and should not allow himself to be subject to flattery. See also POET.

couplets. In the *Conversations* (ll. 5–11), Drummond records that Jonson said he had written a discourse on poetry against both Campion and Daniel wherein he proved couplets to be the bravest kind of verse, particularly when they are broken like hexameters. He also remarked that cross rimes and stanzas were all forced since they would lead one to conclude beyond eight lines.

courante. See CORANTO.

Covell, Lady. The unidentified subject to whom *Und.* LVI is addressed.

Coventry, Henry (1619–1686), was a fellow of All Souls College, Oxford, and the contributor of an elegy ("Might but this slender offering of mine") to *Jonsonus Virbius*. In 1661 he served as groom of the bedchamber to Charles II and from 1672 to 1680 was a principal secretary of state.

Cowse, Benjamin. Bookseller in London from 1714 to 1723 who was one of the publishers of the so-called Bookseller's Edition of Jonson's *Works* in 1716–17.

Cox, Captain, at Kenilworth. The ghost of Captain Cox, who was a Coventry mason known for his cunning and marvelous library, is the chief presenter in *The Masque of Owls*.

Crane, Francis, received a grant for life from the office of clerk of the Parliament in 1606. He served as secretary to Prince Charles, was knighted in 1617, and became famous as the director of the tapestry works established at Mortlake under the patronage of James I in 1619. Jonson inscribed a copy of the quarto of *Sejanus* for Crane in 1605, describing Crane as "my perfect friend."

Crassus, Marcus. In *Catiline*, a cautious Roman who, like Caesar, is sympathetic to Catiline and his conspiracy but is unwilling to risk any open commitment to his cause.

Crates. A Cynic philosopher and poet, beloved by many, who led a life of wandering poverty. In his fooling in *Volpone*, Androgyno claims that his soul once belonged to Crates.

Credulity. The name of one of the witches making up the antimasque in *The Masque of Queens*.

Crips (Crispe), Nicholas. City captain of London who gave a piece of ordnance and a carriage to the London company in 1635 and raised a regiment of horse for the King in the Civil War. He is mentioned in *Und.* XLIV¡

Crispinus, Ruf. Lab. A self-important, foolish gentlemen in *Poetaster*, who plagiarizes and writes affected poetry. He is meant as a caricature of Marston (see MARSTON for further information). He is very proud of his hereditary nobility but is in debt and wears worn clothes. He visits his cousin Cytheris at Albius' house, and flirts with Chloe, telling her how courtiers act. He vows to be a poet for Chloe, and sings proudly for the courtiers. On seeing Horace in the street, he tries to force an acquaintance with him; his pompous bragging and refusal to be put off annoy Horace. Horace tries to escape in several ways but is not successful until Minos brings the Lictors to arrest Crispinus for his debt. Tucca persuades the soliders to free Crispinus because he is impressed with Crispinus' position as a gentleman. At the masquerade, Crispinus sings to Chloe and plays the part of Mercury. He echoes Gallus' welcome to the masqueraders, takes part in the merriment, and sings with Hermogenes. As soon as Crispinus breaks into the masquerade, Caesar realizes that he is a foolish profaner of poetry. Crispinus accompanies Tucca and Lupus when they accuse Horace of treason to Caesar; he is tried by the true poets for Caesar's entertainment. At first Tucca advises him, but on learning that Caesar does not favor Crispinus, he turns against him and serves on his jury. A piece of his bad poetry is read in the trial, and he is sentenced to take a purgative administered by Horace. The purgative makes him vomit up many

affected words characteristic of his poetry (and Marston's poetry); Virgil then gives him a "diet" of good reading to help him develop taste for discretion in his writing. He and Demetrius are compelled to promise never to slander any noble Roman again.

His full name is Rufus Laberius Crispinus, composed of three men's names: Rufus is a satire on Marston's red hair, Laberius was a writer of "ignoble and sordid" mimes, and Crispinus was a bad poet who challenged Horace to see which of them could write faster.

Crites. A noble, wise, honorable courtier in *Cynthia's Revels*, beloved by Mercury and Arete. The shallow courtiers hate him and mock him for being a scholar and feeling superior to them. He makes mocking asides about their shallowness and foolishness. In soliloquies, he laments how men have fallen into being base creatures, only interested in material things. Hedon and Anaides are very offended when he does not notice their snub of him. Arete assures him that the court will soon be purified of corrupt men. Mercury joins with Crites in a scheme to make the courtiers appear foolish. Crites introduces the disguised Mercury as a Frenchman at the courtship contest and delights in his victory over Amorphus. Crites himself takes on Anaides and mocks him until he leaves the room in disgrace. He is discouraged when Arete tells him that he has been chosen to write a masque for Cynthia, but on learning that Cynthia has chosen this method, best to see the corruption of the courtiers, feels honored. Cynthia recognizes his worth and praises him for the masque. After she unmasks the courtiers, she allows Crites and Arete to decree their punishment. Arete gives her power to Crites, who mercifully and justly orders the courtiers to march around, weeping for forgiveness and singing a palinode, until they are purified.

critic. In *Timber* (ll. 2578–2624), Jonson observes that to judge of poets is only the faculty of poets. The duty of a true critic "is not to throw by a letter any where, or damne an innocent Syllable, but lay the words together, and amend them; judge sincerely of the Author, and his matter, which is the signe of solid, and perfect learning in a man." Such a critic was Horace. Jonson also cites Cato, the grammarian, who defended Lucilius, and Quintilian. Further, he notes Horace's judgment of Chaerilus against Joseph Scaliger, and Horace's defense of Laberius

59

against Julius. But, most important, he lauds Horace's defense of Plautus and Horace's esteem for Terence and Menander. Horace himself was so esteemed, Jonson records, that Augustus offered him the secretary of state office and invited him to the palace, but he politely refused.

Criticus. See JOHN DONNE.

Crooke, Andrew. Bookseller in London from 1630 to 1674 who published the third quarto of *Catiline* in 1669 and the fourth in 1674. Together with John Legatt Crooke, he acquired the copyright for *Bartholomew Fair* and *The Staple of News* in 1637. He probably also acquired the copyright to *The Devil Is an Ass* in 1640.

Crosse, William. See MUSICAL SETTINGS.

Cunningham, Francis (1820–1875). English scholar. Joined the Madras Army in 1838, won distinction as a field engineer, retired from service in 1861, and became a commentator and editor. He published editions of Marlowe (1870), Massinger (1871), and Jonson. In 1871 he published Jonson's *Works* in three volumes, and in 1875 he produced a revised reprint of Gifford's edition of Jonson. Although he greatly admired Gifford, Cunningham was aware of the shortcomings of Gifford's work, and he made many corrections in his edition. Cunningham intended to do his own elaborate edition of Jonson, but he did not live to complete the task.

Cupid. In Roman mythology, the god of love, son of Venus, identified with the Greek Eros.

1. Cupid is a character in *Cynthia's Revels*. He disguises himself as a page in order to invade chaste Cynthia's court and to disturb it by introducing love. He acts as a page to Philautia and mocks her and the other ladies for their foolishness and shallowness. He and Mercury make mocking asides during the courtiers' interaction. Mercury credits him with making Amorphus in love with Asotus. Cupid tries to make the other courtiers fall in love, but they cannot, since they have all drunk from the fountain of self-love. Cupid narrates the first masque disguised as the enemy of love but is unmasked by Cynthia, who gently banishes him from her court.

2. In *Time Vindicated to Himself and his Honors,* Cupid appears with Sport and promotes love among the audience by directing their dancing.

3. In *Lovers Made Men,* Cupid is shown to be responsible for the lovers' thinking that they are ghosts, and his will is finally reconciled with that of Mercury.

4. In *A Challenge at Tilt* two Cupids appear, both claiming to be the real Cupid. At the end of the work, they discover that they are both true Cupids, one being Eros, the first son of Venus and Mars, and the other Anteros, the second son of Venus and Mars.

5. In *Love Restored,* Cupid banishes the impostor Plutus and proclaims the power of genuine love in bringing harmony to the court.

6. A character represented as a boy who appears in *The Haddington Masque* as the son of Venus.

7. In *Chloridia,* Cupid is a rebel who, because he was snubbed by the gods, journeyed to hell in order to set earth, hell, and heaven at odds. He appears in the antimasque with Jealousy, Disdain, Fear, and Dissimulation, but he is later reported to have repented and begged pardon for his offense.

8. A character in *Christmas, His Masque,* Cupid appears as a young apprentice actor and leads the procession of the children of Christmas.

Curious. A symbolic character who appears in *Time Vindicated to Himself and to His Honors* and expresses interest in Chronomastix.

Curis. A symbolic character who appears in *Hymenaei* as one of the powers of Juno.

Curius, Quintus. In *Catiline,* a former senator ejected from the senate for infamous behavior who becomes a spy for Cicero and helps the consul put down Cataline's conspiracy to seize power in Rome. Caesar prevents him from receiving official reward after Rome is saved.

Curtius. According to Livy, Marcus Curtius was a Roman youth who, when the Forum fell in, mounted his horse and plunged himself in full armour into the chasm because he believed the strength of Rome to be in its arms and valor.

custom. In *Timber* (ll. 1926–79), Jonson, borrowing from Quintilian (*Instit. Orat.*), includes some observations on custom as the mistress of language, noting that by custom he does not mean vulgar custom but custom of speech which has the consent of the learned. Arguing that we should not be too quick to coin new speech or too dependent upon ancient speech, Jonson cites Virgil as one who loved antiquity and Lucretius as one whose style was scabrous and rough. Jonson also argues that many of his contemporaries are too fond of Chaucerisms and contends that words should not be played with too much, as in puns or paronomasia. The good author should adapt his style not only to custom but also to his matter, for "the congruent, and harmonious fitting of parts in a sentence, both almost the fastning, and force of knitting, and connexion: As in stones well squar'd, which will rise strong a great way without mortar."

Cutbeard. A barber in *Epicoene* who helps Dauphine make Morose marry Epicoene. He uses Latin phrases excessively. He masquerades as a learned Doctor, giving advice on divorce to Morose.

Cutting, Val. A roarer in *Bartholomew Fair*. He gets drunk with Knockem and his companions and quarrels with Quarlous.

Cybele. A fertility goddess, originally the great mother goddess of Asia, who was identified with Rhea by the Greeks and Romans.

Cyclope. A giant who appears in *Mercury Vindicated From the Alchemists at Court* as a tender of the fire of alchemy.

Cyclopes. Gigantic one-eyed beings who may have been born from the union of heaven and earth.

Cycnus. Kinsman of Phaëton who, after the latter's death, went lamenting throughout the world and was eventually changed into a swan.

Cygnus. Pseudonym of the unidentified author of a poem ("When I respect thy arguments, I see") on the play prefixed to the 1605 quarto of *Sejanus*.

Cyllarus. A centaur.

Cyllene. Birthplace of Mercury.

Cymbal. The master of the Staple of News in *The Staple of News* who presents himself as a suitor to Lady Pecunia.

Cynthia. Diana, or Artemis. *Cynthia's Revels* takes place at her court. The shallow courtiers have crept in and practiced their vices without her consent, but she knows of them. She is dignified and noble, pleased with Arete's attentions, Crites's honorable bearing, and the graceful masques presented to honor her. She casts out Cupid when she discovers him at her court but honors Mercury. She graciously gives Crites and Arete the right to punish the shallow courtiers.

Cynthia's Revels, or the Fountain of Self-Love.

Acted: 1600 by the Children of Queen Elizabeth's Chapel.

Published: 1601 in quarto by Walter Burre.

Printer: unknown.

Dedication. Jonson addresses the court, saying that, since it is revered as an example of the best way to live by the whole kingdom, it should be sure that its main interest is in honor and true beauty, rather than in material, shallow things. He signs himself its "servant, but not slave."

Induction. The first child, who seems ready to speak the prologue is disturbed by two others, who are jealous of him and want the honor for themselves. They draw straws to decide who will speak it; the first child wins. In anger, the third child spitefully gives away the action of the play, despite the protests of the other two. He then jokingly mocks fashionable theater-goers, and is joined by the second child, who also comments on the hard life of players and mocks men who set themselves up as critics. The first child speaks the prologue.

Prologue. Jonson says that he hopes his audience will thoughtfully and respectfully consider his unusual type of play and be able honestly to see the worth of his theme.

Act I. Cupid and Mercury meet; Cupid speaks of his power over the gods and his plan to disguise himself and invade Cynthia's court. Mercury is eager to take part in the plan but first goes to carry out Jove's orders to cause Echo to "take a corporal figure and ascend, / Enrich'd with vocal and articulate power." He allows Echo to speak about her sadness over Narcissus' death, something she has never been allowed to do before, because Jove pitied her. She makes a lengthy speech and ends by cursing the pool in which Narcissus died and making it a fountain whose waters cause extreme self-love. After her lament, she fades again to an echo, as Jove ordered. Amorphus sees her and pursues her, but she escapes. He drinks from the fountain and boasts about his travels and sophistication. Crites mocks Amorphus but agrees to introduce him to Asotus; Amorphus worries about how to make the best impression on Asotus. They exchange lengthy compliments on each other's clothes, Amorphus tells of his travels, and Asotus vows to copy his new friend's manners and to learn from him how to be a fashionable courtier. Cos is hired as a page by Amorphus, Prosaites by Asotus. Crites laments the base, shallow things men have become.

Act II. Mercury and Cupid meet. Mercury says that he has been hired as a page by Hedon and mocks him for his self-conscious concern with material, fashionable things. Hedon meets Anaides and tells him the clever oaths and ways of addressing Philautia that he has invented. Anaides tells him of a clever remark he has thought of for Moria. Mercury mocks Anaides to Cupid for being corrupt and self-interested. Amorphus teaches Asotus how to make a courtierlike face, mocking the expressions of all other types of people, especially scholars. Mercury mocks Amorphus for his shallow way of life and his boasting about his travels; he mocks Asotus for closely copying him. When Crites enters, Mercury praises him to Cupid for his honesty and wisdom. Argurion comes in, and Cupid tells of her fickle, flirtatious ways.

The other lady courtiers come in, and Cupid describes and mocks them to Mercury: Moria, for her ignorant conceit; Philautia, for her extreme pride; and Phantaste for her whimsical, shallow nature. He tells Mercury that Diana has other attendants who are pure and high-minded; these women have been slipped in without her notice. Prosaites sings a song praising a beggar's life; he and Cos go to fetch water from the fountain of self-love for the courtiers.

Act III. Amorphus comforts Asotus after he was apparently repulsed by the court during his first try at acting like a courtier. Amorphus tells him to steal lines from poets but debase their reputations in public. Crites passes Hedon and Anaides, who insult him and are very much angered when he takes no notice of their scorn. Crites, in a soliloquy, expresses his indifference to them because of their corruption. Arete greets him; he speaks bitterly to her of the shallow courtiers, listing their vices. Arete assures him that Cynthia will soon appear and purge her court, and leads him to speak with the other high-minded nymphs. Amorphus teaches Asotus the correct way of accosting a lady and flirting with her.

Act IV. Phantaste, Philautia, Argurion, and Moria gossip about the male courtiers, each telling which they prefer and mocking the others. Argurion tells how Moria mockingly encouraged her to flirt with Crites. Phantaste introduces a game in which they each tell what they would be if they could be anything they wanted. Moria says she would like to be able to see all the corruption at court and gossip about it,

Philautia that she would like the power of life and death over everyone, and Phantaste that she would either like to be able to change her shape at will or be the darling of the court for a year. Hedon and Anaides enter and flirt with them. Amorphus and Asotus enter; Asotus flirts with Argurion, and she falls in love with him, giving him many rich presents. Mercury accuses Cupid of causing this. They play two games of wit; in the second, Asotus makes himself appear very foolish. Anaides becomes jealous of Gelaia; Hedon sings to Philautia. Amorphus tells a fantastic story of how he was feasted by many nobles and how a king's daughter died of love-sickness for him. He sings. Asotus gives the presents Argurion gave him to the other courtiers to gain favor with them; Argurion sickens and faints. The water from the fountain of self-love arrives; all drink and call it good. Gelaia protests Anaides' treatment of her. Arete enters and tells them to make a solemn entertainment for Cynthia. After she departs, they mock her for being too serious and lament that their plans for merrymaking and so impressing Cynthia must be cancelled. The women say that they would not change places with Cynthia, and the men mock Crites. Amorphus proposes the courtship contest, to give his pupil Asotus a chance to show off his newly-learned skills. Mercury and Cupid mock them; Mercury says that Cupid's arrows are of no avail to people who are full of self-love.

Act V. Mercury reveals who he is to Crites and asks for his assistance in making the courtiers appear foolish. At first Crites is reluctant but agrees because of his respect for Mercury. Amorphus gives Asotus a final tutoring session; Asotus appears ridiculous even to his teacher. The crowd comes for the courtship contest; there is much confusion as Morphides tries to limit the number of people admitted. Asotus' sister is admitted, but her husband is turned away. The courtiers are all present. Amorphus reads a challenge; when no one comes forward, the courtiers act their accost to each other. Crites brings in Mercury, who is disguised as a Frenchman. The courtiers are impressed with him but become angry when he scorns them. Mercury disdains to compete with Asotus, challenging Amorphus instead. The first contest is the "bare Accost"; after much laughter and comment, the prize is awarded to Mercury. The next contest is the "better Reguard"; they split the prize. In the "solemn Addresse," the competitors primp and quarrel with various tradesmen, then speak to a lady. Amorphus wins. The last contest is the "perfect Close"; Mercury induces Amorphus to make a very foolish move, which disgraces him and makes Mercury the winner of the contest. Crites takes on Anaides at the "perfect Close" and mocks him cleverly, embarrassing him so that he leaves the room. Crites speaks to Mercury of his wish that the courtiers would reform. Arete comes to Crites and says that he has been chosen to write a masque in honor of Cynthia, including the shallow courtiers as players so that she can better see their corruption, of which she is already aware. Hesperus sings a song of praise to Cynthia, who appears with her nymphs. Arete praises her and speaks well of Crites; Cynthia says that she has already noticed him and thought him praiseworthy.

In the first masque, Cupid narrates, dressed as Anteros. The female courtiers, dressed as very virtuous figures, pay court to Cynthia, giving her a crystal ball. Cynthia expresses her delight and praises Crites. Mercury, dressed as a page, narrates the second masque, in which the male courtiers, dressed as very virtuous figures, pay court to Cynthia. In the dancing at the end of the masque, Amorphus appears clumsy. Cupid shoots his arrows and is angry when he finds that they have no power because of the courtiers' self-love. Cynthia speaks, praising the masques. She bids the courtiers to unmasque, and expresses her distaste that the corrupt courtiers played virtuous characters. She is surprised to see Cupid and banishes him from her court. She is happy to see Mercury and invites him to stay. She delegates to Arete and Crites the right to decide the courtiers' punishment; Arete delegates her share of the responsibility to Crites. Crites decrees that they should march, weep, and beg forgiveness in a palinode, and then when they are purified, return as worthy courtiers to Cynthia. Cynthia approves this. The courtiers beg for forgiveness, marching in pairs and singing a palinode, led by Amorphus and Phantaste; then Mercury sings with Crites and declares them purified and ready to grace Cynthia's court.

Epilogue. The speaker says that the author has told him to write an epilogue, but he cannot, since it would be dishonorable or distasteful to apologize for the children's acting, or the author's writing, or to promise a better play, and it would be unfitting, after a play about self-love, to praise it. He resolves his difficulty by saying gracefully: "By (——) 'tis good, and if you lik't, you may."

Cynthius. A title of Apollo, who was born at Mount Cynthius in Delos.

Cyparissus, son of Telephus, grieved so much at the death of his pet stag that he was turned into a mournful tree.

Cytheris. A noblewoman in *Poetaster,* who lives in Albius' house and is a cousin to Crispinus. She is apparently a favorite of the courtiers, who welcome her warmly when they meet her at Albius' house. She is Gallus' love. She advises Chloe on how to act in court, telling her of the fashions. She plays Pallas at Ovid's masquerade and is reprimanded along with the others when Caesar breaks in.

D

Daedalus. A legendary Athenian inventor and architect, famous for building the Labyrinth for Minos and for constructing wings for himself and his son. He appears as a character in *Pleasure Reconciled to Virtue* and instructs the masquers in subtle dancing. For Jonson's other uses of Daedalus, see C. F. Wheeler's *Classical Mythology* and A. H. Gilbert's *Symbolic Persons.*

Dagonet. King Arthur's fool. In *Bartholomew Fair* (v. v), a puppet calls Zeal-of-the-Land-Busy by this name.

D'Alva, Fernando Alvarez, Duke of (1508–1582). Fernando Alvarez was governor of the Netherlands from 1567 to 1573. In *The Alchemist* (IV. iii), Face, when speaking of the ancestry of the disguised Surly, guesses that he may have been conceived during the Duke's reign.

Dame. The chief of the witches who make up the antimasque in *The Masque of Queens.*

Damon and Phintias. Pythagoreans from Syracuse famous for their friendship. When Phintias (often erroneously referred to as Pythias) was condemned to death,

Damon sacrificed his own life as bond, but when Phintias returned to face death he was pardoned by the tyrant Dionysius.

Damplay. A gentleman who appears in the induction to *The Magnetic Lady* and comments on the action and characters as the play proceeds.

Danaë. Daughter of Acrisius. An oracle predicted she would bear a son who would kill her father. Acrisius attempted to prevent the fulfillment of the prophecy by imprisoning her, but Zeus impregnated her through a shower of gold, and she gave birth to Perseus who eventually accidentally killed his grandfather with a discus while participating in funeral games.

Danaüs. Son of Belus and Achinoe and twin brother of Aegyptus. Danaüs had fifty daughters—the Danaïds— and Aegyptus fifty sons. Danaüs ruled Lybia, and Aegyptus reigned in Arabia. When Belus died, the brothers quarreled, and Danaüs and his daughters fled to Argos in Greece, pursued by Aegyptus' sons who besieged Argos and demanded the Danaïds in marriage. Forced to consent, Danaüs instructed his daughters to kill their husbands on their wedding night, and all but Hypermnestra obeyed. She spared Lynceus, who in some versions of the legend killed Danaüs and became king himself. For their crime the Danaïds were condemned in Hades to eternally filling a sieve with water. Aeschylus' *Supplicants* is the only extant play of a trilogy dealing with the Danaïds.

Daniel, Samuel (1562–1619). English poet born near Taunton. The son of a music master, he was educated at Magdalen Hall, Oxford. He became tutor to William Herbert, son of the Countess of Pembroke. In 1592 he published his sonnet sequence *Delia* and his narrative *The Complaint of Rosamund*. His tragedy, *Cleopatra*, was published in 1594, the epic *The Civil Wars between the Two Houses of Lancaster and York* in 1595, with other books of the *Wars* following in 1599, 1601, and 1609. He is said to have become poet laureate after the death of Spenser, and about the same time he became tutor to Anne Clifford, daughter of the Earl of Cumberland. In 1604 he was appointed licenser of the plays of the Queen's Revels, for whom he wrote *Philotas* (1605). He was eventually made Groom, then Gentleman Extraordinary of Queen Anne's Privy Chamber. Daniel wrote two pastoral tragicomedies, and, as Jonson's rival, numerous masques, the most famous being *The Vision of the Twelve Goddesses* (1604). He was also the author of *A Defence of Rhyme* (1603) and a *History of England* (published posthumously in 1631). Although a mediocre poet, as Truewit suggests in *Epicoene* (II. ii), Daniel was often compared with and sometimes considered superior to Spenser and Jonson. The English Romantics admired Daniel for his purity of diction.

In the *Conversations* (ll. 23–24), Drummond records that Jonson remarked that Daniel was a good, honest man who had no children, but he was no poet. He also said Daniel was jealous of him (l. 152), a charge repeated in *Forest* XII. Later Jonson remarked that Daniel wrote of the civil wars but had not even one battle in the entire work (ll. 211–12). Actually, this statement is untrue. Battles were described in books III, IV, VI, and VIII. Jonson also claimed (ll. 5–11) that he had written a discourse on poetry against both Campion and Daniel, proving that couplets are the "bravest sort of verses." Littlewit in *Bartholomew Fair* was probably intended to represent Daniel, and Jonson made several allusions to Daniel or his works throughout the plays: *Every Man in* (1601 quarto version, v. iii; F 1616, v. v), *Every Man out* (III. iii), *Cynthia's Revels* (IV. i), *Volpone* (III. iv), *Bartholomew Fair* (IV. iii; v. iv), and *The Staple of News* (III. ii). See also COUPLETS.

Dante, Alighieri (1265–1321), the most outstanding figure of Italian letters, was born in Florence. After the death of his beloved Beatrice in 1290, Dante made a profound study of classical philosophy and Provençal poetry. He later married, had several children, and was active as councilman, elector, and prior of Florence. Dante opposed the temporal power of Pope Boniface VII and allied himself with the White Guelphs. When the Black Guelphs became victorious, Dante was dispossessed and banished in 1302, after which he served various princes but supported Emperor Henry VII as the potential ruler of a united Italy. During his exile, Dante wrote the *Divine Comedy*, a long vernacular poem in thirty-four cantos which established Tuscan as the literary language of Italy and gave rise to a vast literature. Dante's other works include *La vita nuova*, a collection of prose and lyrics celebrating Beatrice; *Convivio*, an allegory lauding both love and science; *De monarchia,* a treatise on the need for sovereign dominance in secular affairs; *De vulgare eloquentia,* rules for the Italian vernacular; and various lyrics, eclogues, and epistles. Dante died at the court of Guido da Polenta in Ravenna, where he is buried.

In *Volpone* (III. iv), Volpone and Lady Politic discuss the difficulty of understanding Dante.

Daphne. A nymph, the daughter of the river Peneus. Apollo fell in love with her and pursued her. She prayed to be rescued from him and was changed into a laurel, a tree sacred to Apollo.

Dapper. A foolish law clerk who comes to Subtle in *The Alchemist* and asks for a "familiar" to help him become lucky at gambling. Subtle draws him in by making him believe he is related to the Queen of Fairy and that he should prepare himself to meet her. Dol acts as the Queen of Fairy; Dol and Subtle take Dapper's money, make him go through ridiculous rituals, and give him a spider for a familiar, which they tell him he must allow to drink his blood.

Darrel, John. A Puritan preacher and exorcist, famous for his cures and their subsequent exposure. Darrel began his practice of exorcism in 1586 and was finally imprisoned for imposture in 1599; from then until about 1602 there appeared a number of pamphlets about him, some defending him, others attacking him.

Darrel and some of his notorious cases are mentioned in *The Devil Is an Ass* (v. iii).

D'Aubigny. See Esmé Stuart, Seigneur of AUBIGNY (afterwards Duke of Lennox).

Davenant (D'Avenant), Sir William (1606–1668). English poet, playwright, and theatrical producer, who succeeded Jonson as poet laureate in 1638. His life and works bridge the gap between the Elizabethan and Restoration periods. Among his best known works are *The Wits, The Platonic Lovers, Love and Honour,* and an unfinished epic poem, *Gondibert.* For his support of the royalist cause Charles I knighted Davenant in 1643; during the Puritan regime he was permitted to produce a series of plays often considered the first English operas, the most famous being *The Siege of Rhodes.* After the Restoration he and Thomas Killigrew received exclusive patents to produce plays, and Davenant divided his energy between managing the Duke of York's players and adapting old plays, especially Shakespeare's. Davenant imitated Jonson's *Staple of News* in his *News from Plymouth* (1635) and drew upon Jonson's *Love's Triumph* in his masque *Triumphs of the Prince d'Amour* (1635).

Davies, John, of Hereford (1565–1618). English poet who settled in London around 1600 after having served as a writing master at Oxford. He is best known for his religious and philosophical treatises, written in verse, two of the most famous being *Mirum in Modum* (1602) and *Microcosmos* (1603). He also published in 1611 *The Scourge of Folly,* a book of complimentary epigrams on contemporary poets including Jonson ("I love thy parts; so must I love thy whole").

His *Wit's Bedlam* (1617) also included a poem on Jonson, "To My Learnedly Witty Friend Mr. Benjamin Jonson."

Davies, Sir John (1569–1626). Poet and successful lawyer who served as solicitor general and attorney general in Ireland from 1603 to 1619. His works include popular epigrams and sonnets; *Nosce Teipsum* (1599), a long poem on the immortality of the soul; *Orchestra* (1596), an explication of the order of the universe; *Hymns of Astraea* (1599); acrostics on the name Elizabeth Regina; and tracts on the state of Ireland.

In the *Conversations* (ll. 190–93), Jonson said that Davies played on an epigram by Drayton, who had written that his mistress was the ninth [actually tenth] worthy. In ll. 629–30 Jonson discussed another of Davies's epigrams, and he quoted the opening couplet from *Orchestra* (ll. 388–89). Davies is mentioned in *Epig.* XVIII. See also James HOWELL.

Daw, Sir John. Epicoene's servant in *Epicoene,* who appears unaware that his "mistress" is a boy. He is a braggart and a fool who dismisses a long list of great authors as being of no consequence while bragging of his own poetry. He also claims to have had sexual relations with many women, including the "lady" Epicoene. He and his friend LaFoole are tricked into a mock quarrel by Truewit and are made to appear ridiculous.

Day, John (1574?–?1640). English dramatist who wrote for the stage from 1598 until his death. Working for Philip Henslowe, he collaborated with Thomas Dekker, Henry Chettle, and others. His allegorical masque *The Parliament of Bees* was published posthumously. In the *Conversations,* Jonson told Drummond that Day was a rogue (l. 51) and a base fellow (ll. 167–68).

Day, Thomas. An actor, one of the Children of the Chapel, who performed in *Cynthia's Revels* and *Poetaster.*

Decil. Publius Decius Mus, a Roman consul who supposedly dedicated himself to the gods so that the Romans might gain victory over the Latins. His son reputedly did likewise when he became consul.

death. In the *Conversations* (ll. 557-59), Drummond records that Jonson often recited the following verses about death:

So long as we may,
　let us enjoy this breath
For nought doth kill a man so soon,
　as death.

D'Eland, Robert. The Constable of Nottingham Castle in Jonson's fragment *Mortimer His Fall.*

Dee, John (1527-1608). English occultist who was known as both a magician and a mathematician. He was a favorite of Queen Elizabeth's, and he drew up valuable hydrographical and geographical materials on newly discovered lands for the queen. For a time Dee was associated with Edward Kelly, who claimed to have discovered the philosopher's stone. Dee published extensively on the occult, mathematics, natural sciences, and astrology. He is mentioned by Subtle in *The Alchemist* (II. vi). He died in seclusion and poverty.

De Dominis, Marco Antonio, Archbishop of Spalatro, came to England in 1616 to advocate a Universal Church without popes. He was appointed Master of the Savoy and Dean of Windsor by James II. Having failed to unite the English and Roman churches, he returned to Rome in 1622 and was received by Pope Gregory XV, after whose death De Dominis died as a prisoner of the Inquisition. He is mentioned in *The Staple of News* (III. ii).

Dekker, Thomas (1572?-?1632). English dramatist and pamphleteer. Little is known of his early life. He apparently began his literary career about 1598 working for Henslowe as a hack playwright. He was almost always in financial straits, but his years of working for Henslowe seem to have been lucrative. During this time he wrote one of his best known plays, *The Shoemaker's Holiday* (1600) and collaborated with Jonson and others on two plays now lost, *Page of Plymouth* and *Robert II King of Scots*. In 1604 he collaborated with Jonson on James's Coronation speeches, following the so-called War of the Theatres in which Jonson had attacked Dekker in *Poetaster* as Demetrius, "a dresser of plays about town." Many years later, Jonson told Drummond (*Conversations*, l. 51) that Dekker was a rogue. After collaborating with John Webster on several plays and with Thomas Middleton on the first part of *The Honest Whore* (1604; Part II, 1630), Dekker began writing pamphlets, the most important being *The Seven Deadly Sins of London* (1606) and *The Gull's Hornbook* (1609). In 1610 he returned to playwriting, but in 1613 he was imprisoned for debt in the King's Bench, where he remained for six years. He wrote plays in collaboration with Massinger, Ford, and others and is known to have had a hand in over forty plays, of which only about fifteen are extant.

In *Satiro-mastix* or *The Untrussing of the Humorous Poet* (1602) Dekker attempted to answer the attack on himself and John Marston that Jonson had leveled in *Poetaster*. In the dedication to *Satiro-mastix* Dekker gives his own account of the stage quarrel between himself and Jonson and later refers satirically to Jonson's early acting. In the play itself, Dekker presents a burlesque of Jonson in the character Horace, who is shown attempting to hammer out a lyric poem. Horace is later given a lecture on satire and how it should work. In the last scene Horace is dragged in dressed as a satyr crowned with a wreath of needles and is forced to take an oath in which he must swear many things—one of which is "not to bombast out a new play with the old linings of jests stolen from the temple's revels." See also Edward SHARPHAM.

De La Tour, Henri, Baron. See *LOVERS MADE MEN.*

Delia. Name used by Tibullus to celebrate Plania in his love poetry.

Delight. One of the central symbolic characters in *The Vision of Delight* who presides over the action of the masque and helps to turn the pleasures of the spring to the graces of the court.

Deliro. In *Every Man out of His Humour,* a doting citizen who eventually discovers that his wife is not worthy of his excessive admiration of her.

Delos. An island in the Aegean regarded as the birthplace of Apollo and Artemis.

Delphi. Place of the oracle of Apollo and Themis.

Delrio, Martin. Author of *Disquisitiones Magicae* (vol. 1, 1599; vol. 2, 1600), to which Jonson was heavily indebted for the material on witchcraft in *The Masque of Queens* and for the debate between Subtle and Surly in *The Alchemist* (II. iii).

Denbigh, Susanna, Countess of. Daughter of Sir George Villiers, sister of the 1st Duke of Buckingham, and wife of William Feilding, Earl of Denbigh. She was a patroness of Richard Crashaw, who dedicated his *Sacred Poems* (1651) to her. She is mentioned in the fortune of the Countess of Buckingham told in *The Gypsies Metamorphosed*.

Dennis, John (1657–1734). English critic and dramatist. His *Letters Upon Several Occasions* (1696) includes two to William Congreve. The first gives Dennis's opinion of Jonson's *Volpone*. Although Dennis liked the play, he points out four defects. First, the whole thing upon which the plot turns is unreasonable. Second, Corbaccio is exposed for a personal defect, which is contrary to the end of comic instruction. Third, the play has two characters who have nothing to do with its design. Fourth, the character of Volpone is inconsistent.

In the second letter, Dennis expresses his opinions on several of the plays. He calls the plots of *Volpone, The Alchemist,* and *Epicoene* very artful but says that those of *Volpone* and *The Alchemist* are more "dexteriously perplexed than to be happily disentangled" and that although the plot of *Epicoene* is more easily understood, the play may not be a very good comedy because it lacks a moral, probably because of Morose's character, which is too extravagant for instruction and really only appropriate for farce.

In general, Dennis finds Jonson's humor characters to be masterpieces and says his fools show a great deal more wit than his men of sense. According to Dennis, in all Jonson's works the thing most lacking is passion. See also William CON-GREVE.

Dennise. One of the Irish footmen who, speaking in an Anglo-Irish brogue, appears in *The Irish Masque at Court* and attempts to show his loyalty to the king.

Despenser, Hugh Le, sometimes incorrectly called the Earl of Gloucester, was an adherent of Edward II's and was executed by the barons in 1326. In *The Devil Is an Ass* (II. iv), Fitzdottrel alludes to him as one of those who was fatally connected with Gloucester.

de Prie, Jaques. A character in *The Case Is Altered.* He is living as a beggar under an assumed name; he is Melun, a former steward of Lord Chamont of France. He ran off with his master's gold and his master's infant daughter. Jaques is insanely suspicious of everyone, constantly fearing that some-

one is going to find and steal his gold. He warns his "daughter," Rachel, against thieves and suspects those who come courting her, including Christophero and Count Ferneze, of being fortune hunters. He hides his gold under a pile of dung to keep it safe, but Onion and Juniper find it and steal it. Angelo succeeds in luring Jaques away from home with a trail of gold and tricks Rachel into going with him to an inaccessible place while Jaques is gone. Jaques returns to find both Rachel and his gold gone and goes to the count, lamenting loudly. At the count's, he inadvertently lets out the secret of his true identity and Rachel's; the count recovers the gold from Onion and Juniper and gives it to Chamont's son, the rightful owner.

de Prie, Rachel. A character in *The Case Is Altered.* She is believed to be the daughter of Jaques de Prie, a beggar. Only Jaques knows that she is Isabel, the sister to Chamont, an important French soldier. She was stolen when a baby by Jaques, a former steward to Chamont's father, along with much gold. She is beautiful and noble; Paulo Ferneze is in love with her, and they pledge their faithful love before he goes off to war. Onion, Christophero, and Count Ferneze also seek her hand but are sent away by Jaques, who fears they are fortune hunters. Angelo betrays his friend Paulo's trust by luring Rachel away and trying to assault her, but she is saved by Paulo, who happens by just in time on his return from being imprisoned by the French. Jaques, when complaining of the theft of his gold to the count, inadvertently reveals who she is; the company wonders and rejoices. She is betrothed to Paulo at the end of the play.

DeQuester, Matthew. Newsmonger of Dutch descent who was confirmed in 1622 as Postmaster of England for Foreign Affairs. He is referred to in *The Staple of News* (I. ii) as Froy Hans Buz.

Dermock. One of the Irish footmen who, speaking in an Anglo-Irish brogue, appears in *The Irish Masque at Court* and attempts to show his loyalty to the king.

Desmond, James FitzGerald, Earl of, was the son and heir of the "rebel earl," Gerald FitzJames. Gerald, because he had embarrassed the English government in Ireland, was slain in 1583 and his head was displayed on London Bridge. In 1579 James, who was said to have been a godson of Queen Elizabeth's, was sent to Ireland and confined in Dublin Castle until 1584, when he was removed to London and kept in the

Tower until August 1600. In order to neutralize the pretensions of his cousin, James FitzThomas, he was created and restored in October 1600 as Earl of Desmond and became known as "The Queen's Earl" or "The Tower Earl." Later in October 1600 he was sent to Ireland in order to win over the Geraldine faction in Munster, but he was unsuccessful and returned in March 1601 to London, where he died unmarried in November. Jonson addressed *Und.* xxv to him.

Dessen, Alan C. (1935–   ). American scholar educated at Harvard and Johns Hopkins. Since 1973 professor of English at the University of North Carolina at Chapel Hill. Author of studies on Shakespeare and Elizabethan and Jacobean drama. His study of Jonson's moral comedy (1971) has been widely discussed.

Deucalion. Son of Prometheus. Zeus, angry at the irreverence of humans, flooded the earth. Prometheus had warned Deucalion, and he and his wife, Pyrrha, saved themselves in an ark. After the waters receded, an oracle instructed them to throw the bones of their mother (the earth) behind them. From the stones they threw sprang up men and women to re-people the earth. Deucalion and Pyrrha were the parents of Hellen, the eponymous ancestor of the Hellenes.

De Vere, Lady Susan. See Susan, Countess of Montgomery.

Devereux, Robert. See Essex.

Devereux, Walter, was a son of the 1st Earl of Essex and brother of Robert, the famous 2nd Earl, who was executed in 1601. Walter was killed at the siege of Rouen in 1591. According to the *Conversations* (ll. 580–81), Robert after the death of his brother carried a black shield void when tilting.

Devil Is an Ass, The.
Acted: 1626 at the Blackfriars by the King's Men.
Published: 1631 by Robert Allot.
Printer: John Beale.

Act I. Pug, a lesser devil, wants to visit earth, but Satan contends that Pug is too dull a devil to do well in London even if he were to be accompanied by Iniquity, who is out of touch with the times. When Pug insists upon going, Satan reluctantly agrees to let him go, tells him to assume the body of a thief who has just been hanged, and orders him to serve Fabian Fitzdottrel, a squire of Norfolk who desires to see a devil. Pug appears to Fitzdottrel, who doesn't believe that he is a real devil, and offers to be the squire's servant. Fitzdottrel accepts Pug's offer with the proviso that Pug will be beaten if he offends the squire. Shortly thereafter Engine, a broker, and Wittipol and Manly, two gallants, approach Fitzdottrel, offering him an expensive cloak if he will let Wittipol speak for fifteen minutes in the presence of Fitzdottrel to Fitzdottrel's lovely wife, whom the squire keeps locked up. Since he likes to be seen in public in expensive clothes, Fitzdottrel agrees even though his wife resists for fear of public scorn. In speaking to Mrs. Fitzdottrel, Wittipol attacks her husband and invites her to engage in an affair with him. When she does not respond to his offer, Wittipol answers in her stead, suggesting that since her husband is often out of the house attending plays there is ample opportunity for them to meet. Fitzdottrel assures Wittipol that he will henceforth take extra precautions, and feeling that he has gotten the best of the bargain, he sends his wife back to her room. Wittipol and Manly leave, Pug announces that Engine has arrived, and the broker tells Fitzdottrel that he has brought along a projector who the squire hopes will increase his wealth and status.

Act. II. The projector, Meercraft, assisted by Engine and a servant, Trains, interests Fitzdottrel in a project to reclaim flooded land throughout England; he promises to make the squire the Duke of Drown'd Land. As he observes the proceedings, Pug marvels at the subtle vices at work, and in order not to be outdone he decides to cuckold his master. Pretending to speak for Wittipol, Pug tries to seduce Mrs. Fitzdottrel, but she believes his advances to be part of a clever plot by her husband to test her, and when the squire discovers Pug's attempt, he beats the devil.

Meanwhile, at Manly's chambers in Lincoln's Inn opposite Fitzdottrel's residence, Wittipol continues his praise and admiration for Mrs. Fitzdottrel and decides to pursue her with song while Pug observes with envy. When Mrs. Fitzdottrel is discovered at her window listening to Wittipol, the squire strikes her, leads her away, and declares her to be unworthy of being a duchess. Later Meercraft assures Fitzdottrel that he knows a Spanish lady of great fashion who could teach his wife proper manners and behavior, and the projector makes arrangements for his goldsmith to prepare a token gift from Fitzdottrel to be presented to the renowned lady in order to solicit her services.

Act III. Thomas Gilthead, the goldsmith, desires his son Plutarchus to become a gentleman and has placed him with Justice Eitherside to read law although the son himself has no particular aspiration to be a gentleman. Everill, Meercraft's cousin, appears and demands money from the projector and threatens to expose him if he does not get it. Meercraft agrees to give him money if Everill will play his part in the current scheme. Together they are able to dupe Fitzdottrel into giving them more money, which they share, as Everill reminds Meercraft of Everill's importance in the various schemes, especially in another current one involving Lady Tailbush, a projectoress. Engine persuades Wittipol for love of wit to pose as the Spanish lady. Wittipol thinks that by doing so he will be assisting Meercraft, Lady Tailbush, and Amber, her gentleman usher, in a project involving the marketing of ladies' cosmetics. Charged with delivering a ring from Fitzdottrel, Pug goes to Lady Tailbush's, where the Spanish lady is reported to be dining. Determined to have a little venery while he is in human form, Pug attempts to ravish Pitfall, Lady Tailbush's servant, but he is thwarted as before.

Act IV. Complaining about the slowness with which Meercraft seems to be pushing her suit in court for a business venture, Lady Tailbush reports to Meercraft that Manly has been a suitor to her but that Everill has told her about discreditable things Manly has done. Lady Eitherside, wife of the lawyer and justice, arrives for a social visit; Wittipol, dressed as a Spanish lady, arrives soon after. Manly recognizes him but says nothing. Mr. and Mrs. Fitzdottrel and Pug enter. Fitzdottrel is greatly impressed with the Spanish lady, but Mrs. Fitzdottrel thinks her voice sounds familiar. After much discussion, Fitzdottrel puts his wife under the tutelage of the Spanish lady; he also gives the Spanish lady Pug, who now very much wants to return to hell, so she can train him to be Mrs. Fitzdottrel's messenger. With the encouragement and assistance of Manly, who has abandoned his suit for Lady Tailbush, Wittipol reveals his true identity to Mrs. Fitzdottrel and agrees to help her against her husband, and she recognizes Wittipol to be a virtuous friend. Because he is so enamored of the Spanish lady, Fitzdottrel offers to make her feoffee of his entire estate, but she persuades him that Manly would be a more appropriate choice. Fitzdottrel reluctantly agrees and signs the document, after which Wittipol reveals himself to Fitzdottrel, who is beside himself with anger. Wittipol assures Fitzdottrel that the estate will be used to his wife's advantage, after which Meercraft and the squire deliberate about how they can recover what has been lost.

Act V. Ambler, Lady Tailbush's gentleman usher, returns to the house of the projectoress and reports to Pitfall and Meercraft that while away he was engaged in an affair with a woman and was robbed of his clothes and money. Pug calls upon Satan to return him to hell, and when he and Ambler happen to meet, Ambler recognizes Pug as the thief who robbed him. Meanwhile, Meercraft, Everill, and Fitzdottrel plot to recover the estate; they plan to have Fitzdottrel claim that he was bewitched by his wife, but before they can put their scheme into action Gilthead and his son enter with Sledge the constable and other officers to arrest Fitzdottrel and Meercraft for failure to pay their debts. Meercraft is able to persuade Gilthead to drop the charges by offering him the opportunity to engage in a new project involving the marketing of forks. Before the constable leaves, Ambler drags in Pug and demands that he be arrested for thievery. Pug appeals to Fitzdottrel for help by telling him his true story, but the squire still refuses to believe that Pug is a real devil, and he is carried off to Newgate prison, where he is put in chains by Shackles, the keeper of the prison. While Pug bemoans his sad state, Iniquity appears to him and announces that Satan has decided to let him stay on earth for another month. Shortly thereafter Satan himself appears. He berates Pug for his inability to outdo the evil deeds of human beings on earth, indignantly declares him a disgrace to devils, and proclaims that Pug must return to hell immediately, whereupon Iniquity takes him on his shoulders. A loud explosion is heard, and Shackles and his men discover the dead prisoner and declare his quick demise the work of the devil, as they take the body off to be buried.

At Fitzdottrel's house the squire feigns a fit before Lady Eitherside, Lady Tailbush, Ambler, Trains, Pitfall, Meercraft, Everill, and Justice Eitherside, who seems to be persuaded that the squire has indeed been a victim of a conspiracy to bewitch him and defraud him of his land. Wittipol, Manly, and Mrs. Fitzdottrel arrive and observe the scheme in progress. Shortly thereafter Sledge, Ambler, and Gilthead come in and report what has happened at Newgate, whereupon Fitzdottrel realizes that he has been in the presence of a real devil after all, reveals his own sham, and finally tells the truth to shame the devil. Manly assures Fitzdottrel and all present that the maneuver to acquire the squire's estate was done to expose his folly, to protect Mrs. Fitzdottrel, and to insure that goodness would prevail in the end.

In the *Conversations* (ll. 409–13), Jonson said that he was attacked for this play because, according to *Comoedia Vetus*, in England the devil was brought in either with one vice or another, and when the play was over the devil carried away the vice, but Jonson presented the devil so overcome with the wickedness of the age that he thought himself an ass.

Devonshire, Sir William Cavendish, 2nd Earl of, employed Jonson to write an entertainment for the christening of his second son born on May 20, 1620. For this occasion Jonson created *An Entertainment at the Blackfriars.*

Diana. An Italian goddess, sometimes identified with the Greek goddess Artemis. She was goddess of the moon, of the country and forest, of the hunt, of springs and brooks, of chastity, and of childbirth, and she was worshipped mainly by women. In *Time Vindicated to Himself and to his Honors* she appears with Hippolytus and is discovered to be the one responsible for training the youthful beauties in the ancient arts, especially that of hunting, in order to honor Time.

Dido. Daughter of King Belus of Tyre. After the murder of her husband, she went to Africa and founded Carthage. According to the *Aeneid,* she had a tragic love affair with Aeneas. For Jonson's use of Dido, see C. F. Wheeler's *Classical Mythology.*

Digby children. The sons of Sir Kenelm and Venetia Digby. *Und.* LXXXIV is an elegy on their mother. In one section of the poem Jonson addresses his comments about their heritage and future to Venetia's sons Kenelm, John, and George. George died young.

Digby, Lady Venetia (d. 1633), was the daughter of Sir Edward Stanley of Tong Castle, Shropshire. In 1625 she secretly married Sir Kenelm Digby, whose mother was opposed to the match. Two years later, after the birth of two sons, the marriage was announced. Before she married Digby, Venetia was rumored to have been the mistress of the Earl of Dorset. To avoid scandal, Sir Kenelm had his wife painted by Van Dyck as a personification of Prudence. After her death he erected a monument to her memory at Christ Church. Elegies for her were written by William Habington, Joseph Rutter, Thomas Randolph, Owen Felltham, and Jonson, who commemorated her in *Und.* LXXXIV. Jonson often referred to Lady Digby as "my muse."

Digby, Sir Kenelm (1603–1665). Author, naval commander, and diplomat. Knighted in 1623, he won the battle of Scanderoon in 1628. He was interested in physical science, and after his wife's death in 1633 he retired to Gresham College for two years to study chemistry. He was a Catholic, and during the Commonwealth he was chancellor to Queen Henrietta Maria. He negotiated with Cromwell in the hopes of gaining toleration for Catholics. At the Restoration he was a member of the Royal Society. Jonson praised Digby in *Und.* LXXVIII and celebrated the virtues of his wife in *Und* LXXXIV. Jonson named Sir Kenelm his literary executor, and Digby supposedly edited the second volume of the 1641 folio. Digby gave Jonson a copy of Savonarola's *Triumphus Crucis* (1633).

Digges, Dudley (1613–1643), the third son of Sir Dudley Digges, diplomat and statesman, became a political writer and a fellow of All Souls College, Oxford. He probably wrote the poem ("To My Good Friend, Mr. Jonson") affixed to the 1607 quarto of *Volpone,* and he composed an elegy on Jonson ("I dare not, learned shade, bedew thy hearse") included in *Jonsonus Virbius.*

Dignitas. A figure in *The Masque of Beauty* who represents one of the elements of beauty.

Dillon (Deloune), Sir Lucas, is mentioned in *The Irish Masque.* The son of Sir Robert of Newton, who was Chief Justice of the Common Pleas in 1558 and Speaker of the Irish House of Commons, Sir Lucas himself was Chief Baron of the Exchequer in 1572.

Diodorus, Siculus. Ancient historian who flourished under Caesar and Augustus and wrote a world history in forty books covering from the earliest times to Caesar's Gallic War. Jonson used this history as one of the sources for his portrait of Penthesilea in *The Masque of Queens.*

Diogenes, Laertius (fl. 3rd century A.D.). Author of a compendium of ancient philosophy that contains valuable biographical information on ancient philosophers. At the beginning of Act I, scene ii, of *Volpone,* Jonson quotes from this work (in translation) biographical information about the transmigration of the soul of Pythagoras.

Diomedes. One of the bravest and greatest Greek warriors in the *Iliad.*

Dion, Cassius (also called Dio Cassius) (155?–235 A.D.). Roman historian and administrator, better known for his literary works than for his administrative abilities. His most famous work was a history of Rome (written in Greek) in eighty volumes, nineteen of which are extant. This history was one of Jonson's major sources for *Sejanus.* Jonson also used Dion for his portrait of Candace in *The Masque of Queens.*

Dionysus. Jonson's alternative name for Bacchus in *Oberon.*

Dioscuri. See CASTOR.

Dirce, wife of Lycus, captured and intended to kill Antiope, who was the mother, by Zeus, of Amphion and Zethus. Antiope's sons rescued her and murdered Dirce by tying her to the horns of a bull and then throwing her body in the spring which bore her name.

Discoveries. See *TIMBER, OR DISCOVERIES.*

Discovery, A. Jonson told Drummond (*Conversations,* 1. 406) that he intended to write a piece describing his journey to Scotland. Apparently the work was written, but it is listed in *Und.* XLIII as one of the pieces lost in the library fire of 1623.

Disdain. In *Chloridia,* a symbolic character who appears in the second entry of the antimasque.

Dissimulation. A symbolic character who appears in the second entry of the antimasque in *Chloridia.*

Ditchfield, Edward. City captain of London mentioned in *Und.* XLIV.

divinity, gleanings in. According to *Und.* XLIII, the fire which destroyed Jonson's library in 1623 consumed his gleanings in divinity over many years. These writings would have been most revealing about Jonson's conversion to Catholicism and his return to Protestantism.

Dixe, John. Rector of St. Andrew Undershaft from 1597 to 1613, who was one of the advisers assigned to Jonson when he was cited for recusancy in 1606.

Dobson, William. See PORTRAITS.

documents (legal and official). A number of legal and official documents that shed light on Jonson's life and activities are extant. They are: (1) A letter dated 1597 that

calls for the arrest and imprisonment of the actors, players, and authors of *The Isle of Dogs.* (2) The warrant to the keeper of the Marshalsea to release Jonson and his cohorts from prison. (3) The indictment (in Latin) against Jonson for the manslaughter of Gabriel Spencer on September 22, 1598, at Shordiche. (4) The 1606 citation of Jonson and his wife for recusancy. (5) A long deposition given by Jonson in the chancery suit of William Roe vs. Walter Garland in 1610, which sheds light on Jonson's relations with the Roe family. (6) A patent for Jonson's pension of 1616. (7) A patent of 1630 for an increased pension. (8) Some notices from the exchequer of receipt (miscellanea dated 1617) that make reference to Jonson. (9) Papers from the city archives of Edinburgh for 1618 that contain four specific references to Jonson. (10) A 1620 bill from Thomas Cooke, one of the grooms of the prince's chamber, that mentions several occasions on which Cooke had taken messages from court to Jonson. (11) A deed of assignment from Jonson to John Hull for thirty-six pounds of Jonson's pension to be assigned to Hull for a debt Jonson owed him. (12) A warrant for the reversion of the office of Master of Revels that would have benefited Jonson had he lived until the effective date. (13) Three documents relating to Jonson's appointment as chronologer to the city of London, one dated 1628 that announces the appointment of Jonson as chronologer to replace Thomas Middleton, who had died, and another dated 1631 that orders that Mr. Chamberlain "shall forebear to pay any more fees or wages to Ben Jonson, the city's chronologer, until he shall have presented unto this court some fruits of his labors in that his place," and one from 1634 that orders that Jonson's "yearly pension of 100 nobles out of the Chamber of London shall be continued and that Mr. Chamberlain shall satisfy and pay unto him all arrearages thereof." (14) A document from 1629 recording that Jonson was examined by the Attorney General about whether he had ever seen certain verses lauding the assassin of Buckingham and that Jonson told the examiner that the verses were written by Zouch Townley. (15) A document from 1629 showing that the dean and chapter of Westminster made a grant to Jonson in his sickness. (16) The warrant for the administration of Jonson's goods, which is dated 1637.

Dod, John (d. 1645). Puritan divine, Fellow of Jesus College, Cambridge. In the *Conversations* (ll. 513–16), Jonson told an

71

anecdote about a woman so attracted to Dod that she asked for and received her husband's permission to lie with Dod in order to produce an angel or saint, but when the child was born, it was only an ordinary one.

Dol Common. Subtle's bawdy colleague in *The Alchemist*. When Face and Subtle are duping various fools, Subtle pretending to be an alchemist, Dol contributes to the trickery by playing the parts of a beautiful woman, the Queen of Fairy, and a beautiful, mad noblewoman. She is forced to escape with Subtle and to leave the booty behind when Lovewit returns home unexpectedly.

Domiduca. A symbolic character who appears in *Hymenaei* as one of the powers of Juno.

Domitian (A.D. 51–96). Titus Flavius Domitianus, the son of Vespasian, became emperor in A.D. 81. Although he began his reign with an interest in order and public welfare, Domitian became despotic, causing many plots against him and drenching his last years in blood. Tacitus and Juvenal criticized Domitian's reign of terror caustically, but Martial celebrated the emperor. Domitian's wife finally had him stabbed to death. In *Epig.* XXXVI, Jonson compares his relationship to King James with that of Martial to Domitian.

Doni. Translator into Latin of the Fables of Pilpay, a collection of Oriental apologues. Doni's work was translated into English in 1601 by Sir Thomas North and was known as *The Moral Philosophy of Doni*. Sir Amorous alludes to this work in *Epicoene* (IV. iv).

Donne, George. Minor poet who prefixed verses to Ford's *The Lover's Melancholy* (1629) and *Chronicle History of Perkin Warbeck* (1634), and to Massinger's *The Great Duke of Florence* (1636). He also published an elegy on Jonson ("I do not blame their pains who did not doubt") in *Jonsonus Virbius*.

Donne, John (1571 or 1572–1631). English poet and divine. His father was a London ironmonger; his mother was the daughter of John Heywood, the interlude writer, and a niece of Sir Thomas More's. Donne was educated at Oxford and Cambridge and studied at Lincoln's Inn. From 1598 to 1602 he was secretary to Sir Thomas Egerton, lord keeper of the great seal, but lost his post when Egerton learned of his secret marriage to Anne More, niece of Egerton's wife. Although Donne was a Roman Catholic in his early life, upon the urging of James I he took Anglican orders in 1615 and became a great preacher. From 1621 until his death he was dean of St. Paul's and frequently preached before Charles I. His sermons reveal his deep concern with death, decay, and damnation. Donne wrote satires, epistles, elegies, and miscellaneous poems, all distinguished for their wit and profundity. He became the leader of the so-called metaphysical school of poetry, and his original, often obsure, style influenced many poets of his century.

Donne and Jonson were good friends, and there are many references to Donne in the *Conversations*. Jonson told Drummond that he esteemed Donne "the first poet in the world in some things" (ll. 117–18). Jonson respected Donne's judgment so much that he often submitted his poems to him for evaluation, and he knew several of Donne's poems by heart (ll. 118–20; 633–35). (Indeed, *Und.* XXXVIII–XLI are so similar in theme and style to some of Donne's poems that they cause perplexing problems of attribution.) Drummond also notes that Jonson said Donne's "Anniversary" was profane and blasphemous and told Donne that if he had written of the Virgin Mary the poem would have been something. Donne answered that he had described an idealized woman, not an actual one. Jonson also observed that Donne deserved hanging for not keeping accent (ll. 43–49). Jonson claimed that Donne had written his best pieces before he was twenty-five years old and said that Donne told him he had written his epitaph on Prince Henry to match Sir Edward Herbert in obscureness (ll. 120–22; 125–27). Still later in the *Conversations* (ll. 130–37), Drummond records that Jonson said that the general purpose of Donne's conceit of transformation (*metempsychosis*) was to have brought in all the bodies of the heretics from the son of Cain to Calvin, but he only wrote one sheet of the poem, and since he had been made a doctor repented and sought to destroy all of his poems. Jonson also told Drummond that Donne's poetry would not survive, because it would not be understood (l. 196).

Donne wrote a commendatory poem in Latin ("Amicissimo & Meritissimo Ben: Ionson") for the 1605 quarto of *Volpone* and an epitaph for Mrs. Bulstrode, whom Jonson had attacked as the court pucelle in *Epig.* XLIX. Jonson mentioned Donne's satires in *Epig.* XCIV, and he recommended in *Timber* (l. 1798) that students should read Sidney before they read Donne. In the *Conversations* (ll. 82–85, 417), Jonson said that his preface to the *Art of Poetry* (which was lost in the library fire of 1623) contained an apology for *Bartholomew Fair* in the form of a dialogue with Donne, who was represented as Criticus.

An extant letter from Jonson to Donne indicates how much Jonson valued Donne's friendship. The letter implores Donne not to believe something that Jonson had been accused of falsely, and declares, "But, there is a greater penaltie threatned, the losse of you my true friend; for others reckon not, who were never had, you have so subscribed your self." *Epig.* XXIII and XCVI praise Donne. See also Joseph HALL.

Donnell. One of the Irish footmen who, speaking in an Anglo-Irish brogue, appears in *The Irish Masque at Court* and attempts to show his loyalty to the king.

Doris. Daughter of Oceanus and Tethys and wife of Nereus.

D'Orlton, Adam. In Jonson's fragment *Mortimer, His Fall,* the politic Bishop of Worcester who counsels Mortimer against the envious Earl of Lancaster.

Dormer, Robert. See Robert Dormer, Earl of CARNARVON.

Dorset, Sir Edward Sackville, 4th Earl of (1591–1652). *Und.* XIII, a loose paraphrase of Seneca's *De Beneficiis,* is a long epistle to Sackville, whom Clarendon characterized as graceful, vigorous, witty, and learned. He was interested in Virginia and various projects for draining the Lincolnshire fens.

Doubt. A symbolic character in *The King's Entertainment at Welbeck* who welcomes the King.

Douce. "The Proud"; Maudlin's daughter in *The Sad Shepherd.* She is her mother's closest confidante and is proud and happy when she can dress in Earine's clothes and parade among the shepherds. She speaks with Karolin, and her appearance saddens Aeglamour, who believes her to be Earine's ghost.

Doulosis. A symbolic personage representing servitude who appears in a scene in Jonson's part of the *King's Coronation Entertainment.*

Dover, Robert (1575?–1652), founded around 1604 the Cotswold Games, which were annually celebrated at Whitsuntide. The games included wrestling, jumping, pitching the bar, handling the pipe, and dancing in the chase. The games died out during the Commonwealth but were revived under Charles II and finally ceased in 1852. Jonson wrote "An Epigram to my Jovial Good Friend Mr. Robert Dover" for *Annalia Dubrensia* (1636), a collection of poems published in honor of the games.

Dowland, John (1562–1626). English composer, the foremost lutenist and songwriter of his day. His *First Book of Songs or Airs* was published in 1597, and one of his songs is noted at the end of Act I, scene i, of *Eastward Ho.*

Downey, Nicholas. From Exeter College, Oxford, Downey published a poem on Jonson ("Ben is deceased and yet I dare avow") in Samuel Harding's *On Sicily and Naples, or the Fatal Union* (1640).

Downfall (Citizen's Wife.) Asotus' sister in *Cynthia's Revels.* She comes to court to see her brother play in the courtship contest, and leaves her husband outside without regret.

Downright, George. See GIULIANO.

Drake, Sir Francis (1540?–1596). English navigator and admiral, the first Englishman to circumnavigate the world (1577–80). He became famous and wealthy as a result of his marauding expeditions against the Spanish both in Spain and in Spanish settlements in the New World. In 1581 Queen Elizabeth knighted Drake aboard his ship, the *Golden Hind.* When the Spanish Armada invaded England in 1588, Drake served as a vice admiral of the English fleet. In 1589 Drake was joint commander of an unsuccessful invasion of Portugal. His last expedition was undertaken jointly in 1595 with his kinsman John Hawkins. They assaulted the West Indies, but this time the Spanish were prepared and the mission completely failed. Hawkins died in Puerto Rico, and Drake died of dysentery off Portobelo on the west coast of Panama and was buried at sea. Drake's voyage around the world in the *Golden Hind* is mentioned in *Every Man in* (I. iii) and *Eastward Ho* (III. ii; III. iii).

Drawer. In *Eastward Ho,* a nameless drawer at the Blue Anchor Tavern who warns Sir Petronel Flash and his party that because of an approaching storm, they should not sail for Virginia on the scheduled night. Later when they have all been shipwrecked, the drawer gives assistance to Winifred who had sailed with them and had found her way ashore.

73

Drayton, Michael. (1563–1631). The son of a prosperous tradesman, he received his educational training in the house of Sir Henry Goodyere, where he served as page and formed a lasting friendship with Anne Goodyere, the younger daughter of Sir Henry, who became the *Idea* in Drayton's series of sonnets (1593–1619). Reflecting the various poetical fashions of his day, Drayton wrote poems on English history and topography, including *England's Heroical Epistles* (1597–99). His most famous work is the *Poly-Olbion* (1612–1622). He also wrote satires (*The Owl*, 1604, and "The Moon Calf," 1627), a Spenserian though mock-heroic fairyland poem (*Nymphidia*, 1627), *The Battaile of Agincourt* (1627), and the idyllic *Muses' Elysium* (1630). In addition he wrote scriptural paraphrases, pastorals, popular ballads, myths, and for about ten years collaborated on some twenty plays for Henslowe and the Admiral's Men, one of them being *Sir John Oldcastle* (with Hathway, Munday, and Wilson) which was printed by Jaggard in 1619 as Shakespeare's. In the diary of the Stratford vicar, John Ward, an entry dated 1662–63 records the story that "Shakespear, Drayton, and Ben Jhonson, had a merry meeting, and itt seems drank too hard, for Shakespear died of a feavour there contracted."

In the *Conversations* (ll. 25–28), Drummond notes that Jonson said Drayton's *Poly-Olbion* would have been excellent if he had done what he promised—to write the deeds of all the worthies—but his long verses did not please Jonson. Jonson said that Drayton feared him and did not like him (l. 153). Jonson also said that Drayton was challenged for entitling one of his books *Mortimuriados* (ll. 188–89) and for calling his mistress the ninth worthy in an epigram (ll. 190–93). Jonson also told Drummond that Sir W. Alexander was unkind to Jonson because Alexander was Drayton's friend (ll. 161–62).

Although relations between Jonson and Drayton may have been strained at times, Jonson did write a commendatory poem ("The Vision of Ben Jonson on the Muses of His Friend Michael Drayton") for Drayton's *The Battaile of Agincourt* (1627), and Drayton appended to the same work an epistle to Henry Reynolds that includes Jonson in a roll-call of English poets ("Next these, learn'd *Jonson*, in this list I bring"). Jonson probably alluded to Drayton in *Forest* XII, but the "Epitaph on Michael Drayton," often attributed to Jonson, is probably by Francis Quarles.

Drebbel (Dribble), Cornelius (1572–1634). Dutch inventor, physicist, and mechanician. Drebbel was patronized by both James I of England and Rudolph II of Germany. Drebbel introduced microscopes, telescopes, and thermometers into England. He was also the inventor of the perpetual motion at Eltham mentioned in *Epicoene* (v. iii) and the first navigable submarine, which he tested on the Thames. Drebbel is discussed briefly in *News from the New World*.

Dresser. A character in *Love's Welcome at Bolsover* who appears as a plumber in Colonel Vitruvius' dance of the mechanics.

Drugger. In *The Alchemist*, the keeper of a tobacco shop who comes to Subtle for advice on building up his business. Subtle makes a punning family crest for him. Drugger then mentions Pliant, who lives near him, and expresses his despair that her brother will not allow her to marry anyone lower than a knight, and Subtle persuades Drugger to bring Pliant and Kastril to see Subtle. Drugger is induced by Subtle to speak boldly of Surly after Surly tries to win Pliant; then he is told to put on a Spanish costume and win Pliant himself. When Lovewit arrives unexpectedly and marries Pliant, Drugger's plans are ruined, and he is turned away when he comes back to protest.

Drummond, William, of Hawthornden (1586–1649). Scottish poet who was a friend of Drayton's and an acquaintance of Jonson's. He was a Royalist and an Episcopalian and wrote pamphlets and verses in support of the Royalist cause. He was the author of many sonnets, songs, elegies, satires, and hymns, his first published work being an elegy on the death of Prince Henry of Wales (1613) that Jonson thought was good. In 1623 he published what is generally considered his finest single work, *The Cypresse Grove*, a prose meditation on death. Drummond wrote a *History of Scotland* (covering the period 1423–1524), which was published posthumously in 1655. He also left manuscript notes, the originals of which have apparently since perished, that were published in an abridged form as *Conversations* in Drummond's *Works* (1711), on his conversations with Jonson during a visit Jonson paid him in 1619 while on his famous walking tour to Scotland. Although not always accurate in details, these notes give valuable insight into Jonson's personality and opinions. In addition to Drummond's *Conversations*, several letters (all dated 1619) have survived that reflect a friendly, if not an intimate, relationship between the two poets, and we know that Drummond presented Jonson a gift copy of George Buchanan's *Rerum Scoticarum Historia* (1586). According to the *Conversations* (ll. 110–16), Jonson thought Drummond's poems were generally good but that they "smelled too much of the schools and were not after the fancy of the time." The first collected edition of Drummond's poems was issued in 1636, and his complete works were printed in Edinburgh in 1711.

Drusus junior. In *Sejanus*, the second son of Agrippina and Germanicus, who is seen by Sejanus as an obstacle to his ascent to absolute power, since Drusus junior is in the line of succession to Tiberius' throne. He first appears bringing the news of Drusus senior's death to his mother, brothers, and followers. Although Tiberius expresses his love and concern for Drusus after Drusus senior's death, he is plotting against the boy; Sabinus reports that he praises him, attempting to play on the ambition of his "fierce nature" and make him jealous of Nero. Toward the end of the play, it is reported that Drusus is being held prisoner in Tiberius' palace.

Drusus senior. In *Sejanus*, son of Tiberius, heir to the throne, and chief opponent of Sejanus at the beginning of the play. Some noble Romans dislike him because he is "a riotous youth," but many respect him for opposing Sejanus and being kind to Germanicus' sons. When Sejanus orders him to move so that he can pass, Drusus becomes angry, strikes him, and speaks proudly against him. Sejanus then seduces Livia, Drusus' wife, and plots to poison him, an act that is quickly accomplished.

Dryden, John (1631–1700). English poet, dramatist, and critic born in Northamptonshire. Took his A.B. at Cambridge in 1654. He first came to public notice in 1659 with his *Heroic Stanzas*, commemorating the death of Oliver Cromwell, but in 1660 he celebrated the restoration of Charles II in *Astraea Redux*. He was elected to the Royal Society in 1662 and a year later married Lady Elizabeth Howard. *Annus Mirabilis* was published in 1667, and he was made poet laureate the following year. Dryden had a long and varied career as a dramatist, some of his best plays being *The Conquest of Granada* (in two parts, 1670–71), *Aureng-Zebe* (1675), *All for Love* (1677), and *Marriage à la Mode* (1672). His great political satire on Monmouth and Shaftesbury, *Absalom and Achitophel*, ap-

peared in two parts, the first in 1681, the second in 1682, the same year that *MacFlecknoe*, his attack on Thomas Shadwell, and *Religio Laici*, a poetical exposition of the Protestant layman's creed, were published. In *The Hind and the Panther* (1687) he announced his conversion to Catholicism. After the accession of the Protestant William III, Dryden lost his laureateship and court patronage; he spent the last years of his life translating Juvenal, Virgil, and other classical writers. Throughout his career Dryden wrote numerous illuminating critical prefaces, prologues, and discourses on literary excellence and principles, the most famous of which is his *Of Dramatic Poesy: An Essay* (1668).

Dryden's criticism on Jonson is substantial both in quality and quantity. His major criticism is to be found in *Of Dramatic Poesy, an Essay* (1668), in his prefaces to various works by others, and in several of his own works. Dryden's critical commentary on Jonson covers a wide range of topics and is generally laudatory, although at times Dryden is quite severe in his assessment of Jonson. In *Of Dramatic Poesy* the general topics discussed that are relevant to Jonson include: Jonson and the ancients, humor in tragedy, narrations in plays, the classical unities, French models, general appreciation of Jonson's dramatic art, and a detailed critical analysis of *Epicoene* and humor comedy.

In *Of Dramatic Poesy*, Dryden notes that Jonson held the ancients in high esteem: "He was not only a professed imitator of Horace, but a learned plagiary of all the others; you track him everywhere in their snow." Criticizing the English dramatists for mixing humor and tragedy, Dryden commented that "even Ben Jonson himself in *Sejanus* and *Catiline* has given us this Oleo of a play; this unnatural mixture of comedy and tragedy, which to me sounds just as ridiculous as the history of David with the merry humors of Golias." Citing Jonson's *Magnetic Lady* as an example, Dryden notes that Jonson has used narration in his play in imitation of Terence. Commenting on the unity of design in plays, Dryden observes that the more characters there are in a play the greater will be the variety of the plot. The idea is to construct the play in such a way that one will be led in "a labyrinth of design, where you see some of your way before you, yet discern not the end till you arrive at it." Dryden cites Jonson's *The Alchemist* and *The Silent Woman* as two plays that achieved this end but notes that *Volpone* falls short of this ideal. Speaking specifically of the unity of plays, Dryden contends that Jonson had not adhered to this unity in *Catiline*. Commenting on the indebtedness of English plays to French models, Dryden claims that "our plots are weaved in English looms." Jonson, in particular, has demonstrated the copiousness and the well-knitting of intrigue. Moreover, there is good precedent in English drama for the use of verse, especially in plays such as Jonson's *Catiline* and *Sejanus*.

In an extensive critical appreciation of Jonson, Dryden proclaims that Jonson was the most learned and judicious writer which any theater ever had, that Jonson's proper sphere was humor-comedy, and that he was deeply indebted to the ancients, both Greek and Roman, and borrowed boldly from them: "He invades authors like a monarch, and what would be theft in other poets is only victory in him." The only fault Dryden finds in Jonson's use of language is that he wove it too closely and laboriously in his serious plays and that he tended to romanize English too much. When we compare Shakespeare and Jonson, according to Dryden, we must acknowledge Jonson the more correct poet but Shakespeare the greater wit: "Shakespeare was the Homer or father of our dramatic poets; Jonson was the Virgil, the pattern of elaborate writing; I admire him, but I love Shakespeare."

In an extended critical analysis of *The Silent Woman*, the first example of a sustained criticism of an Elizabethan play, Dryden praises the play for its adherence to the classical unities and for its intrigue, claiming that "there is more wit in acuteness of fancy in it than in any of Ben Jonson's." Dryden explains in considerable detail the beauty of the plot and the artfulness of the dramatic techniques Jonson has employed in the play.

Dryden says that although the ancients made little use of humor in their old comedy and although the French have used it very sparingly in their comedies or farces, the English have made extensive use of humor in their comedy: "By humor is meant some extravagant habit, passion, or affection; particular . . . to some one person: by the oddness of which he is immediately distinguished from the rest of men; which being lively and naturally represented, most frequently begats that malicious pleasure in the audience which is testified by laughter. . . ." According to Dryden, the peculiar genius and talent of Jonson was to be able to represent humors in dramatic characters.

In his preface to *An Evening's Love, or The Mock-Astrologer* (1671), Dryden comments extensively on wit and judgment and proclaims that "Jonson is to be admired for many excellencies; and can be taxed with fewer failings than any English poet." According to Dryden, Jonson's great talent was to make men appear ridiculous on the stage, and "in that he needed not the acumen of wit but that of judgment." Thomas Shadwell in his preface to *The Humorist* (1671) refuted Dryden's claim that Jonson lacked wit. According to Shadwell, although one may argue that Jonson's works lack fire, he cannot claim that they lack either wit or judgment. "Nor can I think, to the writing of his humors (which were not only the follies, but vices and subtleties of men) that wit was not required, but judgment; where, by the way, they speak as if judgment were a less thing than wit. But certainly it was meant otherwise by nature, who subjected wit to the government of judgment, which is the noblest faculty of the mind." Later in the preface to *The Mock-Astrologer*, Dryden defends the charge against himself that his own comedies have violated the law of comedy that virtue must be rewarded and vice punished. He argues that no such law has been consistently observed in comedy and specifically cites Jonson's *The Alchemist* and *Epicoene* as examples in which the law has been violated.

In *A Defense of An Essay of Dramatic Poesy* prefixed to *The Indian Emperor* (Second edition, 1668), Dryden argues that in Jonson's *Bartholomew Fair*, which he considers to be the lowest kind of comedy, Jonson's technique of heightening his matter is clearly shown, in that he has not simply recorded the things that daily take place at the fair but has presented them in such a way that they become delightful.

In the Epilogue to the Second Part of his *The Conquest of Granada by the Spaniards* (1672), Dryden comments that

> They, who have best succeeded on the Stage,
> Have still conform'd their Genius to their Age.
> Thus *Jonson* did mechanique humor show,
> When men were dull, and conversations slow.

In his *Defense of the Epilogue to the Conquest of Granada* (1672) Dryden cites a number of what he considers to be serious faults in Jonson's language. He concludes that if Jonson with his vast learning and meticulousness made errors in language we cannot expect much correctness from Shakespeare or Fletcher. In the same work Dryden comments on Jonson's faults of style, the primary one of which Dryden considers to be "meanness of expression." According to Dryden, Jonson was "not free from the lowest and most groveling, kind of wit," and Dryden cites a number of examples from *Every Man in His Humour* to demonstrate his claim.

In several of his poems Dryden also comments critically on Jonson. In the Prologue to *The Tempest* adapted by Dryden and Davenant in 1670, it is claimed that Shakespeare imparted wit to Fletcher and to "laboring Jonson's art." In Dryden and Soames's translation of Boileau's *The Art of Poetry* (1683), the advice is given to "observe the town, and study well the court," and it is claimed that Jonson would have achieved greater fame had he himself adhered to this advice, but that since he was desirous of the people's praise he tended to mix buffoonery with wit and thus debased his work. In his commendatory poem to Congreve's *The Double Dealer* (1694), Dryden claims that Jonson was able to please because of his great strength of judgment but that in judgment Congreve is Jonson's equal. In "Prologue" to *Julius Caesar* from *Covent Garden Drollery* (1672), which some scholars deny was written by Dryden, we find a comparison between Shakespeare and Jonson in which it is said that Jonson's great talents lay in observing mankind and that "Jonson with skill, dissected humane kind, / And shew'd their faults, that they their faults might find: / But then, as all Anatomists must do, / He to the meanest of mankind did go, / And took from Gibbets, such as he would show."

du Bartas, Guillaume (1544–1590). French poet who served as a Huguenot soldier under Henri IV. Du Bartas is best known for his epic poems which were widely read in the English translation (1608) by Joshua Sylvester. In the *Conversations* (ll. 58–59) Drummond records that Jonson thought du Bartas not a poet but a versifier since he did not write fiction. See also Joshua SYLVESTER.

du Bellay, Joachim (1522–1560), became, together with Ronsard, the most important of a group of seven French poets known as the Pléiade. Du Bellay wrote their manifesto in which they asserted that French as a literary medium was the equal of Latin and Greek although the classics should serve as models. Spenser translated the

sonnets of du Bellay, Drayton imitated them in addressing his sonnets to Idea, and Shakespeare was indebted to them for various figures and phrases. In 1549 du Bellay called upon French poets to write odes in the classical form and in the same year published his own *Odes*. Although Ronsard was the first French poet to imitate the odes of Pindar, the attempt by du Bellay and Ronsard to imitate the classical ode eventually influenced the development of the English ode in general and Ben Jonson's odes in particular.

Dugges. A wet nurse who appears in *An Entertainment at the Blackfriars* and engages in a long quarrel with the dry nurse.

Duke, John. An actor who played in *Every Man in His Humour* in 1598 as one of the Chamberlain's Men. He later joined Worcester's company, which became Queen Anne's, and played with it from 1602–1609.

Dunn, Esther C. (1891–). American scholar educated at Cornell and the University of London. In 1960 was made Professor Emerita of English at Smith College. In 1925 she published her important book *Ben Jonson's Art: Elizabethan Life and Literature as Reflected Therein*.

Duperron, Jacques Davy, Cardinal (1556–1618), was appointed reader to the king of France, preached before the king at the convent of Vincennes, and gave the funeral oration on Ronsard. He became the faithful servant of Henri IV and instructed him in Catholicism. In 1604 he was sent to Rome and by his eloquence, for which he was greatly admired, he contributed to the election, after the death of Clement VIII, of Leo XI and later Paul V to the papal throne. While in Rome he was made a cardinal and in 1606 became Archbishop of Sens. After the death of Henri IV, he was active in the States-General in 1614. In the *Conversations* (ll. 69–71), Drummond notes that when Jonson was in France in 1613 he told Cardinal Duperron that Duperron's translations of Virgil were "naught."

Duppa, Bryan. Friend of Jonson's, Dean of Christ Church, and Bishop of Chichester, who in 1638 edited the volume of memorial poems on Jonson known as *Jonsonus Virbius*. See also James HOWELL.

D'Urfé, Honoré. Author of *Astrée*, a Platonic romance published in three parts from 1616 to 1620. D'Urfé is mentioned in *The New Inn* (III. ii).

D'Urfey, Thomas (1653–1723). English songwriter and dramatist. His comedies became forerunners of the ballad opera. In 1719 he published *Wit and Mirth*, a collection of his own witty, satirical songs and older tunes adapted to new words. This collection included musical settings for lines from *Bartholomew Fair, The Gypsies Metamorphosed*, and *The Masque of Augurs*. D'Urfey also published a poem on *Bartholomew Fair* in *Collin's Walk through London and Westminster: A Poem in Burlesque* (1690).

Dyer, Sir Edward (1543?–1607). Elizabethan poet educated at Oxford. Sidney and Spenser were friends of his, and in his day he was praised as an elegist. His most famous poem is "My Mind to me a Kingdom Is." In the *Conversations* (l. 229), Jonson said Dyer died unmarried.

Dyer (Diar), Sir James (1512–1582). Chief Justice of the Court of Common Pleas. A collection of his cases was edited, selected, and published by his nephews, R. Farewell and James Dyer, in 1585. There were several subsequent editions. In *Every Man out*, Fungoso refers to Dyer's work (II. iii).

Dyspragia. A symbolic personage representing unhappiness and appearing in a scene in Jonson's part of the *King's Coronation Entertainment*.

E

Eacus. See AEACUS.

Earine. "The Beautiful" shepherdess in *The Sad Shepherd*. Her name means "maiden of the spring" in Greek, and she is sister to Karolin. At the beginning of the play she is believed drowned, and all the characters, especially her lover Aeglamour, mourn deeply for her. It is revealed that she is Lorel's prisoner, shut up in a tree in the forest. He tries to woo her, but she is disdainful of his awkward, vulgar attentions.

Earle, John (1601–1665). English clergyman and author, best known for his *Microcosmographie* (1628), a collection of witty characterizations. Became Bishop of Salisbury in 1663. He translated into Latin Jonson's ode on himself affixed to the published version of *The New Inn*.

Ears. A symbolic character in *Time Vindicated to Himself and to his Honors* who is fascinated with Chronomastix.

Earth. The mother of all, from whom Spring was born. Earth appears as a character in *The Masque of Augurs* and requests that Jove allow the sovereign to have a long life.

Eastward Ho.

Acted: 1605 at the Blackfriars by the Children of the Queen's Revels.

Published: 1605 in quarto by William Aspley.

Printer: George Eld.

Written by Jonson, George Chapman, and John Marston. Although a number of scholars have tried to ascertain the precise contribution of each author to the play, there is little agreement about the matter. Despite, or perhaps because of, the multiple authorship, the play is one of the better made Elizabethan comedies. The play is often considered interesting because of its vivid portrayal of London society and of the life of apprentices and tradesmen. Because the play contains a passage deemed offensive to the Scots and because of its unlicensed publication, the authors were briefly imprisoned in 1605. Over the centuries, the play has remained fairly popular and has been performed both in the original and in several adaptations.

Act I. Touchstone, a wealthy London goldsmith, has two apprentices, Quicksilver and Golding, and two daughters, Gertrude and Mildred. To Touchstone's dismay, Quicksilver squanders his time and money reveling with the gallants and gentlemen of the town. Golding, on the other hand, is a conscientious and loyal apprentice. Touchstone's two daughters also have contrasting characters. Gertrude, the older, abhors being the child of a lowly tradesman, aspires to be a lady, and intends to marry an adventurous but actually penniless knight named Sir Petronel Flash. Mildred, the younger, is a modest and sober-minded daughter. Touchstone and his wife meet in their house with Sir Petronel and Gertrude to make arrangements for the marriage and for her dowry, which consists of some choice land. Displeased by the disdain of his daughter who is about to become a lady, and unimpressed with Sir Petronel, Touchstone reluctantly gives the couple his blessing, but Mrs. Touchstone enthusiastically supports this opportunity for her daughter to achieve a social status that she herself was never able to acquire. After the arrangements have been completed and everyone has left except Touchstone, Golding and Mildred, Touchstone offers Golding Mildred's hand in marriage. Although somewhat surprised by this sudden offer, Golding and Mildred, both being loyal to Touchstone, agree to consider the match.

Act II. Quicksilver appears drunk at Touchstone's shop, and Touchstone is so upset with him that he releases Quicksilver from his indenture and dismisses him. At the same time, Touchstone frees Golding and promises to make the wedding of Golding and Mildred surpass that of Gertrude and Sir Petronel. His future now uncertain, Quicksilver goes to see Security, an old usurer to whom Quicksilver is heavily indebted who is the panderer for Quicksilver's mistress, Sindefy. Security and Quicksilver plot to get Gertrude's land from Sir Petronel, who now desperately needs funds to finance a secret voyage to Virginia. In order to fulfill a promise to her and to keep track of developments, Quicksilver and Security tell Sindefy that they will get her a position as gentlewoman to Gertrude. When Winifred, Security's new young wife, overhears the plans, she expresses her disgust for the old usurer and his devious methods. When Sir Petronel arrives, Security offers to underwrite Petronel's expenses if he will sign over his wife's land to him. Later Gertrude arrives and agrees to make Sindefy her gentlewoman. The general arrangements now completed by the parties, Gertrude and Sir Petronel depart, the knight agreeing to breakfast with Security the following morning to work out the final details of their transaction.

Act III. Early the next morning, Sir Petronel, Quicksilver, Winifred, Security, and Bramble, Security's lawyer, meet at Security's and complete their deal, Sir Petronel agreeing to get Gertrude to sign a legal document transferring her land to Security for Sir Petronel's loan. Captain Seagull, Scapethrift, and Spendall—Sir Petronel's associates for the voyage—also arrive, and they all consent to meet at the Blue Anchor tavern that night before departing for Virginia. In the meantime, Gertrude herself prepares to board her coach and leave the city for Sir Petronel's supposed castle in the country while a group of curious townspeople gather excitedly to watch her departure. Shortly, Sir Petronel, Quicksilver, Touchstone, and Golding and Mildred (now married) arrive to see her off. Gertrude ridicules Mildred for marrying a common tradesman, Sir Petronel tricks Gertrude into signing her land away, and Gertrude leaves with great fanfare for a castle that does not exist.

Sir Petronel and Quicksilver make arrangements to have the money delivered to the Blue Anchor that night. Sir Petronel also requests that Security get his lawyer out of his house so that Sir Petronel may sneak out Bramble's wife with whom he has been having an affair and whom he now wants to take with him to Virginia. Amused, Security agrees and exits. Sir Petronel then instructs Quicksilver to go to Security's house and bring his young wife to the tavern because she is really the one he wants to take with him on the voyage. When Quicksilver leaves, Security reenters with one of his wife's gowns and suggests that it should be used to disguise Bramble's wife, and Sir Petronel readily agrees.

That night at the tavern Seagull and his associates carouse and exchange tall tales of the glory and riches of Virginia. Sir Petronel enters and announces to everyone's delight that a young gentlewoman will accompany them on their voyage. Security and Bramble show up to wish the voyagers a successful journey, and shortly thereafter Quicksilver enters accompanied by Winifred in disguise. Security makes several jokes with Bramble about cuckolding, and when Winifred begins to weep, Sir Petronel asks Security to comfort her. A drawer comes in and explains that because of a foreboding storm it will be very dangerous for the party to sail that evening, but all dismiss his fears as idle and continue their carousing. Bramble asks Security if the gentlewoman present is not really his wife, since she is dressed like her, but Security confidently assures him that she is not his wife. All now drunk, the voyagers leave the tavern and board a small boat to take them up the Thames to where their ship is anchored.

When Security returns home and discovers that his wife is missing, he immediately suspects that she has gone with Sir Petronel and hurriedly secures a small boat to pursue them.

Act IV. Because of the storm, Security's boat is wrecked on the Thames, and he washes ashore at the Cuckold's Haven— unhurt but frustrated. Close by, Winifred, also wrecked, finds her way to the shore and is given assistance by the friendly tavern drawer. Shortly thereafter and in the same general area, Quicksilver, Sir Petronel, and Seagull and his crew make their way to land. Believing they have been washed ashore in France, Sir Petronel tries to speak French to a local gentleman but discovers to his surprise that he and his group are actually on the Isle of Dogs. With all now lost except their lives, Quicksilver, who has stolen money from his former master, and the others consider ways to regain their losses, including a scheme for creating their own money. Meanwhile, Security and Winifred discover each other and are reunited, Security being persuaded by Winifred to believe that she has been out all night looking for him in the storm.

By this time Touchstone and his wife and Gertrude have figured out that Sir Petronel has no castle in the country, that he has stolen Gertrude's land, and that he has a ship bound for Virginia. To Touchstone's delight, Golding is appointed deputy alderman, and Sir Petronel and his cohorts are all captured and are brought before Golding for a hearing. Upon the testimony of Touchstone, Sir Petronel, Quicksilver, and Security are all imprisoned, and Touchstone feels that justice has finally prevailed although his sympathies are somewhat moved by the apparent sincerity of Sir Petronel's repentance when he openly weeps over his misdeeds.

Act V. Now destitute, Gertrude and Sindefy commiserate over their plight and consider various ways to secure funds to support themselves. Gertrude's mother arrives and pleads with Gertrude to swallow her pride and throw herself upon the mercy of her sister, who is now wealthy. Meantime, Touchstone receives numerous letters from the prisoners imploring his forgiveness, but he remains unmoved by their pleas. Wolf, the jail keeper, arrives and informs Touchstone that Sir Petronel, Quicksilver, and Security have all become exemplary repentant prisoners, but Touchstone is not impressed. Eventually, convinced that they have been mortified enough, Golding decides to intercede for the prisoners, and he directs Wolf to report to Touchstone that Golding himself has been imprisoned. When Touchstone receives the news, he rushes immediately to the prison to bail Golding out. Once he is at the prison, Quicksilver and Sir Petronel take the opportunity to show Touchstone that they are truly repentant. So moved is Touchstone that he realizes Golding's purpose in bringing him to the prison, forgives the prisoners, and is reconciled with them. Mrs. Touchstone, Gertrude, Mildred, Sindefy, and Winifred then arrive, and Gertrude and Sir Petronel are reconciled as are Gertrude and her father. Quicksilver agrees to marry Sindefy, Security providing her dowry. Although Security is concerned about having been cuckolded, through the intercession of Touchstone he is finally reconciled with Winifred. All parties now satisfied and happy, they leave the prison, Quicksilver remaining attired in his prison clothes as part of his self-enforced mortification and as an example to the townspeople.

Echo. A nymph vainly loved by Pan. She was torn to pieces by mad shepherds, but her fragments were hidden by Earth, and they now sing and imitate other sounds. Echo is a character in *Cynthia's Revels.* She is given a "corporall figure" and told to "ascend" by Mercury, at Jove's command, to speak her sorrow over Narcissus' death. She laments bitterly and at length; Mercury urges her to hurry, since Juno would be angry if she discovered Jove's pity toward Echo. Before returning to her doom of only echoing others' words, Echo curses the fountain in which Narcissus died, making it a fountain whose waters make men full of self-love. She is briefly pursued by Amorphus before she disappears.

Edgworth, Ezechiel. A cutpurse, or pickpocket, in *Bartholomew Fair.* He is good at his job, managing to steal Cokes's purse twice and, at Quarlous's urging, stealing the marriage license out of a box in Waspe's pocket. Justice Overdo shows his foolishness by believing that Edgworth is an honest but misguided young man. Toward the end of the play, Edgworth takes up with Win and Dame Overdo, who he believes are prostitutes.

editors of Jonson.

1616, *Works*, the first folio, possibly Jonson himself.

1631, *Plays*, possibly Jonson himself.

1640–41, *Works*, the second folio, possibly Richard Bishop and Thomas Walkley; Richard Meighen.

1692, *Works*, the third folio, editors unknown.

1716–17, Booksellers' edition, editors unknown.

1756, Whalley's edition in seven volumes. Editor, Peter Whalley.

1816, Gifford's edition in nine volumes. Editor, William Gifford.

1871, Cunningham's edition in three volumes. Editor, Francis Cunningham.

1875, revised reprint of Gifford's edition. Editor, Francis Cunningham.

1925–52, Oxford edition in eleven volumes. Editors, C. H. Herford, Percy and Evelyn Simpson.

The first folio, the *Plays* of 1631, the second folio, the third folio, and the Booksellers' edition were not true editions in the modern sense of the term. Traditionally, it has been thought that Jonson probably served as a kind of editor for the first folio, but exactly what role he played in its production is not clear. William Stansby, who was the printer and publisher for the first folio, may well have done some editing of the text he had available to work from. Likewise, Jonson may have edited some of the *Plays* of 1631, but Robert Allot, who was the publisher, may also have done some editorial work on the volume. How direct a hand Jonson had in the editing of either one of these volumes is unclear. Since the first volume of the second folio was printed by Richard Bishop, Bishop may well have edited some of the text. Part of the second volume of the second folio was issued by Richard Meighen and the other part by Thomas Walkley, and each of them may have done some editorial work on the project. Since the second folio is essentially the corrected reprint of the first, it seems very unlikely that much editorial work of any type was done. The third folio was a reprint of the second folio with some new and some revised material, which included *The New Inn, Leges Convivales*, the lines over the entrance of the Apollo Room at the Devil Tavern, and the recast version of the *English Grammar*. The Booksellers' edition was an uncorrected reprint of the third folio.

Whalley's was the first critical edition of Jonson's works. Since Whalley assumed that the first folio was printed under Jonson's own supervision, he did not consult quartos, although he did employ the duodecimo edition of the *Poems* of 1640 to correct the bad folio text of the *Gypsies Metamorphosed*. Whalley added critical notes, a preface explaining the critical principles upon which he had worked, and a life of Jonson with illustrative documents. His was the first edition of Jonson to include *The Case Is Altered*. Whalley did not make substantive changes in the text, but he did correct obvious errors and rearranged faulty verse. He printed from Theobald's copy of the Booksellers' edition.

Gifford was the first editor to collate the quartos and folios although he did not do so thoroughly, and he tended to adopt the critical method of his day, picking and choosing between quarto and folio readings, even though he believed the first folio to have been printed under Jonson's own supervision. Printing from a copy of Whalley's edition, Gifford modernized the text, marked scene divisions in the modern way, and put in scene locations instead of stage directions. His critical notes (he did not include any for the *Discoveries* and the *English Grammar*) were a great improvement over Whalley's. Since he was a classical scholar, Gifford was able to illuminate many of Jonson's borrowings from the classics. At times Gifford's attempt to vindicate Jonson from the charge of being an enemy of Shakespeare clouded his critical judgment, but despite his shortcomings as an editor, Gifford's edition served as the standard critical one for over a century.

Francis Cunningham's editions were essentially corrected reprints of Gifford's work.

The Oxford edition is the current standard critical one and is the most thorough, comprehensive, and exacting critical edition of Jonson to have been produced so far.

Edmondes, Clement (1564?–1622), was Remembrancer of the City of London in 1605 and Clerk of the Council in 1609. He was knighted in 1617 and served as a Member of Parliament for Oxford University in 1620. In 1600 Edmondes published an analysis of Caesar's *Gallic Wars*, which was supplemented by another volume in 1604; both volumes were reprinted in 1604 and in 1609. Jonson's *Epig.* cx and cxi were prefixed to the 1609 edition. Edmondes was appointed Secretary of State but died before assuming the position.

Edward II (1284–1327). King of England (1307–27). Son of Edward I and Eleanor of Castile. Married Isabella of France in 1308. He was a weak and self-indulgent monarch. Eventually he was deposed in 1327, forced to abdicate in favor of his son Edward III, and put to death by henchmen of the Queen and Mortimer, 1st Earl of March, who in alliance had led a movement to topple him and gain power for themselves. Edward II's son, Edward III, finally succeeded in gaining control of the reins of government in 1330 when he had Mortimer put to death and forced his mother into retirement. Jonson's fragment, *Mortimer*, would have dealt, in part, with these historical events.

Edward III. The king in Jonson's fragment *Mortimer His Fall* who at first refuses to believe the reports of his mother's extraordinary favors to Mortimer but finally investigates the charges, concludes that they are true, and has Mortimer executed.

Edward VI (1537–1553). Son of Henry VIII and Jane Seymour. Succeeded his father in 1547 under a council of regents, the majority of whom wanted to forward the Reformation. The government was actually controlled by Edward's uncle, Edward Seymour, Earl of Hertford (later Duke of Somerset) until he was overthrown by John Dudley, Earl of Warwick (later Duke of Northumberland), who gained complete ascendancy over Edward, who died of tuberculosis in 1553. After a struggle, Edward was succeeded by Mary —better known as Bloody Mary.

The allusion to the late Edward in *A Tale of a Tub* (I. v. 33) allows us to date the setting of the play in the reign of Queen Mary.

Edward the Black Prince (1330–1376). Son of Edward III, King of England 1327–1377. He achieved a popular reputation for his exploits, especially for his victory at Poitiers in 1356 when he captured the French king, John II. Edward did not live to succeed his father on the throne, but his son came to the throne after the death of Edward III as Richard II. Edward the Black Prince's exploits are lauded by Merlin in *The Speeches at Prince Henry's Barriers*.

Egerton, Thomas, Lord (1540?–1617). A friend of Essex's, he served as Solicitor-General in 1581, Attorney-General in 1592, Master of the Rolls in 1594, and Lord Keeper in 1596. In 1603 King James named him Lord Keeper and made him Baron Ellesmere and Lord Chancellor. Jonson praised Egerton's high reputation as a judge in *Epig.* LXXIV and addressed *Und.* XXXI and XXXII to him as a plea for a poor man.

Eglestone (Ecclestone), William. An actor who played in *The Alchemist* in 1610 and in *Catiline* in 1611 as one of the King's Men. From 1611–13 he was in the Lady Elizabeth's company but later rejoined the King's Men. He performed in the plays of Beaumont and Fletcher and was one of the principal actors in Shakespeare's plays.

Egmont, Lamoral, Count of. Flemish patriot killed by the Duke of Alva in 1568. In *The Alchemist* (IV. iii), Face insults the disguised Surly by saying that he might be "Egmont's bastard."

Eirene. One of the three Hours, daughters of Themis. Eirene personified peace.

Eitherside, Lady. The wife of Sir Paul Eitherside, the lawyer and justice, in *The Devil Is an Ass.*

Eitherside, Sir Paul. The lawyer and justice in *The Devil Is an Ass.*

Eld (Elde), George. Printer in London from 1604 to 1624 who printed *Sejanus* in quarto for Thomas Thorpe in 1605 and *Eastward Ho* for William Aspley in 1605.

Elder, William. See PORTRAITS.

Electra. Daughter of Agamemnon and Clytemnestra. Also sometimes considered to be a daughter of Atlas and one of the Pleiades and mother of the rainbow. In Jonson's part of the *King's Coronation Entertainment,* Electra is a symbolic personage representing one of the seven Pleiades, and she makes a speech.

Eleutheria. The Greek festival of liberty. A symbolic personage representing liberty in Jonson's part of the *King's Coronation Entertainment.*

Elich, Philippus Ludwigus. Author of *Daemonomagia* (1607), one of the authorities on witchcraft Jonson used in *The Masque of Queens.*

Eliot, John. Author of three poems critical of Jonson published in *Poems Consisting of Epistles and Epigrams, Satyrs, Epitaphs, and Elegies, Songs and Sonnets* (1658): "To His Nobelest Friend Mr. Endimion Porter Upon Verses Writ by Benjamin Jonson"; "You swore dear Ben you'd turn the green cloth blue"; and "Your verses are commended and tis true." Jonson's "To My Detractor" (uncollected) is his reply to the third poem, which was critical of Jonson's verses to the 1st Earl of Portland (*Und.* LXXVII).

Elizabeth, L. H. The unidentified subject of *Epig.* CXXIV.

Elizabeth, Princess (1596–1662). Daughter of James I of England. Her beauty attracted many of the royal suitors of Europe, and Jonson alluded to it at the end of *Prince Henry's Barriers.* In 1613 when Jonson was in France she married Frederick V, Elector of the Palatine. Jonson referred to her recent marriage in *The Irish Masque.* When her husband accepted the crown offered by the Bohemian Diet, she became Queen of Bohemia in 1619, but when Frederick was defeated the next year in the battle of White Mountain, she took up residence in Holland, where she endured privation and misfortune with courage. In 1661, against the wishes of Charles II, she returned to England, was given a pension, and died the following year. She had thirteen children, among them Princess Elizabeth, who was the patroness of Descartes, and Sophia, the mother of George I of England.

Elizabeth I (1533–1603). Queen of England 1558–1603. The daughter of Henry VIII and Anne Boleyn, Elizabeth was declared illegitimate in 1536 just before the execution of her mother, but in 1544 Parliament reestablished her in succession after Edward, her half-brother, and Mary, her half-sister. Since the possibility of her becoming a queen furnished a rallying point for discontented Protestants, Elizabeth was imprisoned but later regained some freedom by external conformity to Catholicism. When she became queen in 1558, one of her first acts was to reestablish Protestantism. As queen, she inherited religious strife, a huge government debt, and a war with France. Upon her death forty-five years later, England had witnessed a rebirth in literature, had become a united country, had developed into a sea power, had prospered in commerce and industry, and had begun colonization in the New World. Believing in the Tudor concept of strong rule and popular support, Elizabeth was able to select and work with competent counselors.

Although she had many suitors and often used the lure of marriage diplomatically, she never married. After England defeated the Spanish Armada in 1588, which was the result more of good fortune than of planning, her popularity began to wane, and the insurrection of her favorite, the Earl of Essex, darkened her last years. Although she has been accused of being vain, fickle, prejudiced, and miserly, Elizabeth was eminently successful as a queen, endowed with personal courage and a sense of her responsibility, and she kept the affection and allegiance of her subjects throughout her reign.

In the *Conversations* (ll. 338–47), Drummond records Jonson's saying of Elizabeth that she never saw herself in a true mirror after she became old, that she had dice that always threw fives or sixes to make her always win and consider herself fortunate, that her hymen was so tough that she was incapable of sexual intercourse although for delight she tried many men, that once a French surgeon was to attempt to cut it but she became afraid, and that King Philip, by special dispensation from the Pope, had intended to marry her. Also in the *Conversations* (ll. 202–3), Jonson said that Sir Walter Raleigh had written a life of Elizabeth; if that is so, the work has been lost.

Jonson introduced the queen into the original version of *Every Man out,* but subsequent versions left her out because many did not relish the idea. Elizabeth is addressed in *Cynthia's Revels,* and Cynthia was probably intended to represent Elizabeth.

Ellesmere, Thomas, Lord Egerton. See Thomas, Lord EGERTON.

eloquence. In *Timber* Jonson records several observations on this subject, drawn largely from M. Seneca (*Contraversiae,* iii, praefatio, 11–13), beginning with the statement that "*Eloquence* is a great, and diverse thing: nor did she yet ever favour any man so much, as to become wholly his" (ll. 419–37). In ll. 1682–84 Jonson observes in the course of a discussion on the education of children that "*Eloquence* would be but a poore thing, if wee should onely converse with singulars; speake, but man and man together." And in ll. 1865–68 he echoes Quintilian when he notes that talking and eloquence are not the same: "A foole may talke, but a wise man speakes, and out of the observation, knowledge, and use of things."

Elsmere, Thomas, Lord. See Thomas, Lord EGERTON.

Elyot, Sir Thomas (1490?–1546), was a diplomatist and author who popularized much of the knowledge of the Renaissance. His most famous work is *The Book Named The Governor* (1531), an important work in the evolution of English prose, which covers such topics as education, politics, and the principles that should guide the actions of those who are in authority. Elyot's medical treatise entitled *Castel of Helth* (1539) popularized the physiological theory of the humors from which Jonson later borrowed to develop his theory of humor comedy. In the *Discoveries* (l. 903), Jonson cites Elyot as an eloquent writer of his times.

Elysium. In Homer, an ideal land where heroes go at their death. In Latin literature, the part of the Underworld where the souls of the good and the noble go after death.

Empusa. A Greek bogy-woman who appears in fantastic forms and is an amorous fiend who eats her human lovers.

Enck, John J. (1921–1966). Educated at Haverford College and Harvard, Associate Professor of English at the University of Wisconsin in 1956. His important book, *Jonson and the Comic Truth,* was published in 1957.

Endymion. In mythology, a remarkably beautiful young man who was loved by the Moon.

Engine. A broker in *The Devil Is an Ass* who assists Meercraft, the projector.

Engineer. An unnamed member of the boys of Boeotia who perform an anti-masque in *Pan's Anniversary.*

England's Parnassus (1600), ed. Robert Allot, was a collection of "the choysest flowers of our moderne poets" which included verses by Jonson on murder, peace, and riches; passages from *Every Man in His Humour* and *Every Man out of His Humour;* and some of Jonson's lyrics—fourteen quotations in all from Jonson. The verses on murder, peace, and riches can be found in Herford and Simpson, vol. 8, p. 363 (in "Ungathered Verse").

English Gentleman. He appears in *The Irish Masque at Court,* reprimands the Irishmen for their crude dancing, and introduces the bard who praises the monarch.

English Grammar, The. A text by Jonson which contains two books, the first on etymology and the second on syntax. Since he had thought long about questions of style and language, it is not surprising that Jonson should have turned his attention to grammar. The work which has come down to us and which was first printed in the 1640 Folio with many errors was a second attempt at a grammar made late in life. Jonson's first attempt had perished when his library caught fire in 1623. There is little that is original in the work since Jonson relied very heavily (often without acknowledgment) on a number of authorities, particularly in the first part of the work, where he drew freely upon many of the following: Sir Thomas Smith's *De Recta & Emendata Linguae Anglicae Scriptione, Dialogus,* published by Robert Estienne at Paris in 1568; John Hart's *A Method or Comfortable Beginning for All Unlearned,* published in 1570; Richard Mulcaster's *The First Part of the Elementarie which entreateth chefelie of the right writing of our English tung,* printed by T. Vautroullier in 1582; William Bullokar's *Bref Grammar for English* (1586); P. Gr[eenwood]'s *The English Grammar called Grammatica Anglicana, a little epitome written according to the rules of art,* published at Cambridge in 1594; Alexander Gill's *Logonomia Anglica, Qua Gentis Sermo Facilius Addiscitur,* printed by John Beale in 1619 and reissued in 1621; Charles Butler's *The English Grammar, or the*

Institution of Letters, Syllables, and Words, in the English Tongue, published at Oxford in 1633; and Simon Daines's *Orthoepia Anglicana: or the First Principal Part of the English Grammar: Teaching the Art of Right Speaking and Pronouncing English, with Certain exact rules of Orthography and Rules of Spelling or Combining of Syllables and Directions for Keeping of Stops or Points Between Sentence and Sentence,* which was printed by Robert Young and Richard Badger for the Company of Stationers in 1640; and the works of Pierre de la Ramée, particularly his *P. Rami Grammatica. Parisiis, Apud Andream Wechelum, sub Pegaso, in Vico Bellovaco. Anno Salutis* (1572) and *P. Rami Scholae Liberales Artes* (Basel, 1578). Jonson also made some use of J. C. Scaliger's *De Causis Linguae Latinae Libri Tredecim* (Lyon, 1540).

Jonson was one of the first grammarians to pay consistent attention to phonetics, rude and elementary though his exposition of them may have been. Furthermore, since he believed that the exposition of English usage should not only be illustrated from Latin but should also be based upon it, one of his weaknesses was to try to press every possible analogy. Writing in an age which had no scientific study of comparative grammar, Jonson's scheme for the classification of English verbs is somewhat remarkable. Moreover, within certain limits he was a kind of spelling reformer.

In 1692 some unknown scholar carefully revised the *Grammar* and brought it up to date; this revised version, which carried no notice of the numerous changes that had been made in the text, was inserted in the one folio of Jonson's works published in that year. Whalley in 1756 and Gifford in 1816 reprinted the revised text in the belief that it reproduced the original text of 1640, and it was not until the Oxford edition of Herford and Simpson in the twentieth century that the original 1640 text was finally recensed.

In 1622 Jonson's "son," James Howell, published a text based upon Jonson's book. Howell's book was dedicated to Queen Catherine of Braganza and was entitled *A New English Grammar Prescribing as Certain Rules as the Language Will Bear for Forreners to Learn English: Ther is also another Grammar of the Spanish Castalian Toung, with some special remarks upon the Portugese dialect.* . . . See also James HOWELL; William WOTTON.

Ennius (239–?169 B.C.). Considered the father of Latin poetry. He introduced

84

hexameter as a literary form. His most important work is the first national Roman epic, *Annales*, which tells the history of Rome from the downfall of Troy until his time. He also wrote tragedies, comedies, and short miscellaneous poems. In *Poetaster* (I. i), Ovid says that Ennius, "though rude . . . a fresh applause in everie age shall gaine!" Later in the play (v. iii), after Crispinus has been purged of the affected words he favors, Virgil gives him a list of the best authors to read to develop his taste, but warns him to "shun . . . old Ennius" as "too harsh for a weake stomache."

Entertainment at Althorp, The.

Performed: June 25, 1603.

Published: 1604 by Edward Blount in quarto together with *The King's Coronation Entertainment* and *A Panegyre*.

Printer: Valentine Simmes.

This entertainment was written for Queen Anne and Prince Henry. On their journey from Edinburgh to London in 1603, they stayed four days at Althorp in the house of Sir Robert Spencer, who presented the entertainment for them.

In a wooded area through which the queen and prince would pass was hidden a satyr, who appeared suddenly before them at the sound of music announcing their arrival. The satyr expressed his sense of the presence of royalty in the woods, briefly played on his pipe, and then approached the queen and prince, examining their faces and exclaiming that they surely were of heavenly race. The satyr then ran into the woods as soft music played and a bevy of fairies and Mab, their queen, appeared dancing in a ring. Mab welcomed the queen to the woods while the satyr reappeared and proclaimed that Mab could not be trusted. The satyr then danced among the elves as they, in turn, made speeches in praise of Mab and concluded by pinching the satyr until he ran away. Mab asked the queen's pardon for this sylvan sport, and they all sang a song in praise of the queen, after which Mab made a complimentary speech and presented the queen with a jewel, asking the queen not to tell who gave her the gift. Mab and her train then danced away, and the satyr reappeared and introduced Sir Robert's son to the queen and presented the prince with some hunting gifts. Proclaiming that the satyrs would have the woods resound in celebration, the satyr and his train killed some choice deer, which had been released, as the woods re-

sounded with the sound of hunting music. Thus ended the first night's show.

On the following Monday was presented a morris dance of clowns with a single parting speech made by a clown called No-Body who was attired in breeches that came up to his neck with his arms coming out at his pockets and a cap covering his face.

Another parting speech was published but not delivered. The speech was to have been given by a youth, accompanied by the younger sons of many gentlemen. The speech praises the queen as a goddess and expresses the hope that the prince will develop fast in spirit as well as in years and become Europe's "richest gem without a paragon."

Entertainment at Highgate, The.

Performed: May Day, 1604.

Published: in 1616 folio by William Stansby.

Printer: William Stansby.

This private entertainment was written for King James and Queen Anne and was presented by Sir William Cornwallis the elder at his house at Highgate.

In the morning when the king and queen entered the gate, they were met by the Penates or household gods who received the royal couple with a speech of welcome and praise and led them through the house into the garden, where Mercury appeared and welcomed them to the Arcadian hill known as Cyllene, the place of Mercury's birth. He further explained that the garden was the tower of his mother Maia and noted how Aurora, Favonius, Flora, and Zephyre were awed by the presence of the king and queen, after which Aurora, Zephyre, and Flora sang a song in celebration of the arrival of James and Anne. Maia and then Mercury delivered speeches saluting the royal couple and urging them to come a-Maying again to Cyllene. This concluded the morning entertainment.

After dinner when the king and queen reentered the garden, Mercury saluted them and introduced his son Pan and the wood nymphs. Pan asked who the king and queen were, to which Mercury replied that they were gods on earth. After a brief speech, Pan offered the king and queen a drink and urged them and everyone to be joyful and to drink deeply. Mercury then concluded the entertainment with a speech proclaiming that the love of the king and queen should be flourishing as May and their house as fruitful, that their acts and fortunes should be ever good, and that they should ever live safe in the love rather than the fear of their subjects.

Entertainment at the Blackfriars, An.

Performed: 1620.

Published: February 1816 in *The Monthly Magazine, or British Register,* Part I, under the title *The Christening; A Masque by Ben Jonson, Not in his Works.* First included in a collected edition of Jonson's works in Gifford's edition of 1816.

This entertainment was apparently written for performance at the christening of Charles Cavendish, who was born on May 20, 1620. Cavendish was the second son of Sir William Cavendish, 2nd Earl of Devonshire.

At the entrance to the banquet, the guests were met by a Forester who welcomed them to the feast. In the passageway Dugges, a wet nurse, and Kecks, a dry nurse, inquired of Holdback, a midwife, whether the gossips or godparents were approaching. At the banquet itself everyone was welcomed by Holdback, and the new baby was praised. Shortly thereafter the two nurses began a quarrel about whether the wet nurse or the dry nurse should have the more prominent place. To calm things down, Holdback asked Kecks, the dry nurse, to sing, and she sang a song in praise of the new child, after which the two nurses resumed their dispute, each citing in detail her contributions to the rearing of the child. Holdback then delivered a long speech praising the importance of the midwife, after which the two nurses accused each other of various indiscretions.

Although the dispute was not settled, it ended when a mathematician or astrologer approached, reported the favorable signs attending the child's birth, and sang a light-hearted song about the battle between the two nurses and the need to cool their rage with water at the pump. Immediately following, watermen in the hall sang a song praising the gossips, lauding the festive banquet itself, and celebrating the new child.

Entertainment of the King and Queen at Theobalds, The.

Performed: May 22, 1607.

Published: in 1616 folio by William Stansby.

Printer: William Stansby.

This entertainment was written for King James and Queen Anne on the occasion of the transfer of the house at Theobalds to the king and queen from the Earl of Salisbury; Theobalds house, a seat of the Cecil family, was exchanged in 1607 for the manor of Hatfield. The house and its possessions were turned over to the queen during the ceremony.

The king, queen, princes (Prince Henry and Prince Joinville), and nobles entered the gallery after dinner and discovered a traverse of white, which, when drawn, revealed a gloomy, obscure place with only one light that was held by the Genius of the household. The Genius was sadly attired — his cornucopia about to fall out of his hand, his garland drooping on his head, and his eyes fixed on the ground. In this pensive posture he expressed his sorrow that he had to change lords and seek a new, unfamiliar habitation; he voiced his uncertainty about his obscure destiny. Out of the darkness was heard a voice telling Genius that he would know his fate. The darkness vanished, and a glorious Lararium or seat of the household gods was seen. Hovering in the air at one corner was a boy called Good Event. At the other corner Mercury and his Parcae were discovered. One of the Parcae was holding a Book of Adamant, which was open. Surprised by the scene Genius asked what was the significance of Mercury's meeting with Good Event. In reply Mercury requested the daughters of destiny to read Genius his fate from the Book of Adamant. Clotho explained that when, as now, underneath the roof are seen the greatest king and fairest queen then is the appropriate time for Genius to change lords, but Genius still wanted to know if his old lord was content to forsake the house of his fathers. Mercury assured Genius that he should obey and that the fate of both him and his lord was just. Lachesis then noted that the new lord whom Genius must serve and obey was he who governs with a smile this "lesser world, this greatest Isle" and that his lady great nature's second would gladly see. Atropos told Genius that his new lady was the grace of all that is and that he should believe and obey the fates. Whereupon Genius now realized that he should not mourn but rejoice, pledged his loyalty to his new lord and lady, and presented the house keys to the queen. There followed soft music and a song celebrating the blessed change and exclaiming that May never before looked so fresh and that duty thrives by the breath of kings.

Entertainment of the Two Kings at Theobalds, The.

Performed: July 24, 1606.

Published: in 1616 folio by William Stansby.

Printer: William Stansby.

This entertainment was written for King James and for Christian IV of Denmark when they both visited Theobalds, a seat of the Cecil family, on July 24, 1606.

When the kings entered the inner Court, above and over the porch sat the three Hours, representing Law, Justice, and Peace. The Hours delivered a short speech of welcome and praise, after which a brief speech of praise was delivered in Latin to Christian. On the walls were inscribed in Latin three epigrams of welcome and two for departure.

Envy. 1. Usually portrayed as an old woman dripping venom, surrounded by snakes and sometimes shown eating her own heart.

2. In *Poetaster,* Envy speaks a prologue, in which she speaks of the eager delight the poetasters will take in ruining Jonson's plays. She is angered when she realizes that the scene is Rome and despairs when no kindred spirits appear to help her wreak her vengeance on Jonson.

3. In *Timber* (ll. 258–321), Jonson includes a short essay on envy drawn largely from J. J. Scaliger's *Confutatio Stultissimae Burdonum Fabulae* (included in the Frankfort edition of *Opuscuta,* 1612, pp. 419–22).

Enyalius. A symbolic personage representing Mars or war in Jonson's part of the *King's Coronation Entertainment.*

Enyo. Greek goddess of the spirit of madness in warfare.

Eous. In mythology, the morning star identified with the eastern part of the world.

Epam. A tinker, one of the boys of Boeotia who performs an antimasque in *Pan's Anniversary.*

Epaminondas (418–362 B.C.). Theban general and statesman. An intellectual as well as a skillful tactician, he drove the Spartans out of Thebes and broke their total power over the Peloponnesus. He was instrumental in forming the Sacred Band, an elite corps of soldiers devoted to Thebes' freedom. He was first admiral of the Theban navy. He was noted for his nobility, patriotism, eloquence, and skill as a general. In *Poetaster* (v. iii), Tucca calls Mecoenas by this name. In *Timber* (ll. 362–64), Jonson, while discussing the wise tongue, mentions Epaminondas as a man who knew much but spoke little.

epic. See POEM.

Epicoene. A young boy in *Epicoene,* who is passed off by Dauphine Eugenie as a silent, soft-spoken woman. Dauphine, knowing that his irascible uncle, Morose, wishes to marry and disinherit him, tricks his uncle into marrying Epicoene. Immediately after the ceremony, Epicoene becomes loud, talkative, and aggressive. Dauphine gains favor with his uncle and is named his heir for helping Morose escape the marriage; he then reveals Epicoene's true identity and makes his uncle appear ridiculous.

Epicoene, or The Silent Woman.
Acted: 1609 at the Whitefriars by the Children of the Queen's Revels.

Published: May have been published in quarto in 1612 by Walter Burre, but no copy has ever been found. The play was published and printed by William Stansby in the 1616 folio.

Dedication: To Sir Francis Stuart, the second son of James Stuart, husband of Elizabeth, Countess of Moray, and Knight of the Bath. He was a member of the Mermaid Club. Jonson calls on him to judge the play not because it has pleased others but because it is offensive to no one and asks him to judge fairly because of the damage a careless criticism can do an author's reputation.

Prologue. Jonson says that early playwrights wrote to entertain the common people, but in his time a number of writers seem to be catering only to critics and highly educated people and disdaining the approval of the public. He, on the other hand, writes for everyone; there will be something in his plays to please all who come to see them.

"Another" Prologue. Jonson says that the goals of a playwright are "to profit and delight" his audience, not to slander public figures. He charges his audience not to look for portrayal of actual events, saying that the poet's job is to present "truths well fain'd" rather than truth and that anyone who finds slander in his play is misunderstanding him.

Act I. At his house Clerimont, a gentleman, asks his page to sing about Lady Haughty, and expresses his disgust that his page is freely admitted to her favor while he is kept away. His friend Truewit enters, and they speak of the folly of wasting life as gentlemen do, of the newly formed collegiate of women, and of the wisdom of a woman dressing herself with all the art she can muster. Truewit asks after their friend

Dauphine Eugenie, and they discuss the whims of Dauphine's uncle Morose, who has shut himself up in his house and has forbidden people to make noise in the street by his house because he cannot stand to hear any voice except his own. Dauphine himself enters and tells them that his uncle plans to marry and disinherit him. Clerimont says that he knew that Cutbeard, a barber, was searching for a wife on Morose's orders, and has found Epicoene, a "silent woman" in town. They speak of going to see her, but when Truewit hears that John Daw is her servant he leaves abruptly. Dauphine then tells Clerimont of Daw's ineffective attempts to court his mistress and mentions that he and Daw have been invited to the same dinner party by Sir Amorous La-Foole, a vain, foolish, social-climbing man. The page announces that La-Foole has come; he enters and invites Clerimont to dinner at Captain Otter's house. Clerimont and Dauphine bait La-Foole into name-dropping and bragging of his ancestry; then he rushes off to invite more guests.

Act II. Morose's servant comes to Morose and tells him, by physical signs, that Cutbeard is coming soon and will enter without making noise. Truewit bursts in with a horn on the pretense of being a messenger from court. Truewit tells Morose that his friends at court think him very unwise to marry, then goes into a long, loud railing speech against marriage that torments Morose. Truewit leaves, blowing his horn, and Cutbeard enters.

Clerimont and Dauphine go to Epicoene's house and try to dissuade her from going to La-Foole's feast, where she will be mocked by the collegiate women. They mockingly encourage Daw to recite his verses, of which he is very proud, and bait him until he dismisses a whole catalogue of great ancient writers as "not worthy to be nam'd for authors" and praises only a few lawyers. Truewit enters and tells them proudly that he has persuaded Morose not to marry; Dauphine and Clerimont despair and reveal that Epicoene is a gentlewoman in league with Dauphine to deceive Morose and win the inheritance for Dauphine. Cutbeard enters and tells them that Truewit's bungling has worked out well because Morose, thinking Truewit was sent by Dauphine, is all the more eager to marry and discredit his nephew.

Truewit and Clerimont speak with Daw of his friendship with La-Foole and then make him notice that Epicoene has gone with Dauphine and Cutbeard to see

Morose. They encourage Daw to take her departure as a slight and to act ridiculously melancholy at the feast.

Cutbeard takes Epicoene to Morose as Dauphine waits about to hear what happens. Epicoene speaks very softly and wins Morose's approval. Morose delights in images of his nephew's ruin. Cutbeard goes to tell Dauphine, Truewit, and Clerimont of his triumph, and Truewit plots to further torment Morose by converting La-Foole's dinner to a bridal feast at Morose's house. They speak of Tom Otter's nagging wife, his drinking habits, and the way he mocks his wife behind her back.

Act III. At Otter's house, Mrs. Otter nags her husband for lacking social graces and says that he shall not bring his drinking cups, which he has named his bull and bear, to the party. She says that he owes his social position entirely to her and nags him about his dress, which she provides. Dauphine, Clerimont, and Truewit enter; Mrs. Otter reveals that she is La-Foole's cousin, and they mock her pride in her position. Cutbeard enters and tells them that he has found a curate with a cold to marry Morose and Epicoene. Mrs. Otter tells her dreams in great detail. Daw enters, and Clerimont tells him that he has been deceived, for Dauphine has discovered that Epicoene recently married Morose. He reassures Daw, however, that Epicoene will still give him her favors, and Daw says that he forgives her. Clerimont begins a mock quarrel between Daw and La-Foole by telling Daw that La-Foole knew of the marriage and planned his dinner party as a bridal feast and an attempt to make Daw appear very foolish in his ignorance of his mistress's marriage. He suggests that Daw divert the collegiates, who are also invited to the feast, to Morose's and there have a happy dinner in honor of Epicoene, thus foiling La-Foole's plot. La-Foole enters, and Clerimont tells him that Daw has tried to disgrace him by stealing his guests and ruining his feast. Dauphine persuades La-Foole to dress like a servant and carry his food, which must outshine Daw's, to Morose's. Mrs. Otter is persuaded to go by Dauphine's insistence that at Morose's she will have all the honor of a guest and none of the work of a hostess. Captain Otter says that he wishes to bring his cups.

Meanwhile at Morose's house, Morose has just been married; he quarrels with the parson and, to his surprise, Epicoene begins to speak out and criticize him. Truewit comes in and, much to Morose's dismay, says that Cutbeard has told many people of his marriage and that there will soon be a feast at his house. Daw enters with the collegiates, who, on hearing of the plan to make Epicoene appear silent until marriage, declare that Epicoene has "wit" and set out to make her a collegiate. The entrance of musicians, Captain and Mrs. Otter, and La-Foole torments Morose even more.

Act IV. At Morose's Clerimont, Truewit, and Dauphine discuss Morose's disturbance, Dauphine's efforts to persuade him that Dauphine had nothing to do with the feast, and the appearance and courting of women. Dauphine says that he is in love with all the Collegiates, and Truewit promises to make them all in love with him that day. They then join Otter, Daw, and La-Foole in drinking and, after encouraging Otter to mock his wife behind her back, bring her in to hear his abuse. She flies into a rage, which terminates when Morose comes in, complaining loudly, with a sword. The collegiates instruct Epicoene in how she should treat her husband. Dauphine and Truewit meet with Morose and remind him that they warned him against marrying. Epicoene and the collegiates enter and torment Morose by loudly discussing various ways to cure him of his affliction. Morose asks Dauphine about divorce. La-Foole mocks Dauphine to the collegiates, but Truewit attempts to sway their opinion by having Epicoene praise Dauphine enthusiastically. Truewit sets up a mock quarrel between La-Foole and Daw by telling each of them, in private, that the other is looking for him in order to do him physical violence. He badly frightens each of them by elaborating on the malice and anger of the other; Clerimont and Dauphine look on in glee as Truewit hides La-Foole and Daw in separate rooms. He convinces the combatants that each must allow the other to beat him while blindfolded and later say nothing in order to end the quarrel; Dauphine actually does the beating. The ladies come in, discover the plot, and are taken with Dauphine's cleverness. They all praise him highly. Daw and La-Foole, according to their promise to Truewit, meet as friends and say nothing of their "quarrel." Morose again enters, is horrified at the noise and activity in his house and gives his trust to Dauphine. Dauphine plans to have Otter act as a parson and Cutbeard as a lawyer in order to "advise" Morose.

Act V. Clerimont entices La-Foole and Daw into bragging over their alleged conquests of many ladies, including Epicoene. In succession Lady Haughty, Centaure,

and Mavis come to Dauphine, each trying to gain his favor by criticizing her companions. Otter and Cutbeard come to Morose in disguise and in flowery, faulty, and enthusiastic Latin, describe at great length the conditions for divorce. The ladies discover what Morose is doing and berate him for acting so badly on his marriage day. Morose tries to escape from the marriage by saying that he is impotent, but Epicoene confounds him by saying that she will take him with all his faults. Truewit tells Morose that they have one last chance to free him; they bring in Daw and La-Foole, who freely boast of having been intimate with Epicoene. Cutbeard, however, says that since they have not been intimate with her since her marriage Morose has no cause for divorce. While Morose laments this scandal, Dauphine offers to deliver him from the marriage in return for being made his heir. Morose eagerly signs the papers. Dauphine then reveals that Epicoene is really a boy and tells Morose to go away. Truewit praises Dauphine's plot, which was hidden even from Clerimont and himself, and says that in addition to making a fool of Morose, Dauphine has also effectively disgraced La-Foole, Daw, and the collegiates. The play ends with an invitation to the audience to show their approval.

See also John Dryden.

Epidaurian serpent. See Lynceus.

epigram. In ancient Greece, an inscription, especially an epitaph, but the term came to mean a short poem expressing that which should be made permanently memorable. The epigram is characterized by compression, pointedness, clarity, balance, and polish. Although epigrams are found in the *Greek Anthology,* Jonson's model was Martial, who used the form for various themes and purposes: eulogy, celebration of friendship, compliment, epitaphs, philosophical reflection, jeux d'esprit, and satire. Numerous epigrams were written by sixteenth-century English writers, most notably John Heywood, but generally they did not conform closely to the classical type. Between 1596 and 1616 many collections of epigrams were published, the best known being a collection by Sir John Harington (1615).

Most epigrams during this period consisted of two parts, an introduction stating the occasion and establishing the tone and a conclusion sharply and tersely expressing the main point. In the *Conversations,* Jonson claimed that many epigrams in his day were poor because they expressed in the end what should have been understood by what was said (ll. 381–83), and he denounced Harington's epigrams as narrations (ll. 37–40) as well as those of John Owen (ll. 223–25). Jonson proclaimed his own epigrams to be the ripest of his studies, and he is generally considered the greatest writer of epigrams in English. See also POEM.

Epigrams. A collection of 133 of Jonson's poems, first published in the 1616 folio. Jonson apparently intended to publish a second volume of epigrams but never did so although he continued to write epigrams throughout his life. Many of them did appear in *The Underwood* and in his uncollected verse.

In the dedication of the *Epigrams* to the Earl of Pembroke, Jonson proclaimed the poems to be "the ripest of my studies." Primarily modelled on the epigrams of Martial, most of Jonson's epigrams are occasional (that is, connected with a particular event, person, or circumstance) and reflect a sincere moral purpose. Lacking only passionate love poetry, the collection in its variousness provides a view of Jonson's relations with some of the great and near-great men and women of his day, conveys the tenderness of love and friendship, and attacks social corruption. Although varied in subject matter, nearly all the poems are written in pentameter couplets. The last and longest poem in the collection—"On the Famous Voyage"—is not epigrammatic at all but rather is a kind of mock epic that many with Victorian taste still find offensive. All in all, the collection contains some of the best poetry of Jonson's age and in many ways anticipates the poetry of Robert Herrick and Alexander Pope.

epistle. A formal composition addressed to an individual or a group, sometimes written in verse. Jonson's verse epistles, unlike Ovid's and Drayton's, do not depict imaginary situations and persons but develop out of his own experience and relationships and are characterized by a minimum of poetic elaboration and a practical orientation and purpose, such as an appeal to the Lord High Treasurer for funds during illness (*Und.* LXXI).

epitaph. Originally an inscription to mark burial places, but epitaphs came to be commemorative verses or lines appearing on tombs or written as if intended for such use. Usually serious and dignified, some epitaphs are humorous, such as the one marking Shakespeare's burial place. Jonson's verse epitaphs are serious in tone and tend to be genuinely moving tributes to the dead. Those commemorating the death of children are particularly affecting, some of his most famous pieces of this type being the epitaphs on the boy actor Salathiel Pavy (*Epig.* CXX), Jonson's own daughter (*Epig.* XXII), and his first-born son (*Epig.* XLV). But he also wrote moving epitaphs on adults, such as those on Margaret Ratcliffe (*Epig.* XL), Vincent Corbet (*Und.* XII), and the anonymous Elizabeth, L. H. (*Epig.* CXXIV).

epithalamium. A bridal song or poem written to celebrate a wedding. The form was cultivated by ancient poets such as Pindar, Sappho, Theocritus, and Catullus, and by later writers such as Ronsard and Spenser. Unlike Spenser's famous *Epithalamion* written to celebrate his own marriage, Jonson's epithalamia are included in his masques performed in honor of marriages of the nobility—*Hymenaei* and *The Haddington Masque*. In the *Conversations* (ll. 404–5), Jonson notes that the untitled epithalamium in his printed works was composed for the marriage of the Earl of Essex.

Equites Romani. Minor characters in *Poetaster*; attendants and door guards to Caesar, who try to prevent Lupus, Tucca, Demetrius, and Crispinus from disturbing Caesar with their accusations about Horace.

Erasmus, Desiderius (1466?–1536). Dutch humanist. Born in Rotterdam. An ordained Catholic priest, he studied at the University of Paris and had many personal contacts in England, including Thomas More, Colet, and Henry VIII. A classical scholar, he edited the Greek and Latin classics and the Fathers of the Church (especially Jerome and Athanasius), and his Latin edition of the New Testament was based upon the original Greek texts. His original works are mostly satirical and critical. Combining vast learning with a fine style, a keen sense of humor, moderation, and tolerance, Erasmus deplored the religious warfare of his time because of the inhumanity and cultural decline that it induced, and his position on the Reformation was widely denounced, particularly by Luther, who initially considered Erasmus an ally because of his attacks on clerical abuse and lay ignorance. Eventually Erasmus was forced into open conflict with Luther, and he attacked the reformer's position on predestination in *On the Freedom of the Will*. Although eager for church reform, Erasmus, unlike Luther, remained a Catholic all his life.

Among Erasmus' most important works are *Adages* (1500), *Manual of the Christian Knight* (1503), *The Praise of Folly* (1509), *The Education of a Christian Prince* (1515), *Colloquia* (1516), his collected letters, and his editions of Greek and Latin classics and the writings of the Church Fathers.

Jonson seems to have been well versed in Erasmus; he borrowed from Erasmus' *Colloquia* in *Every Man out* (I. ii; III. iv, v), used *De Alcumista* as a source for *The Alchemist* and *Praise of Folly* and *Epistola Apologetica* as sources for *Volpone*, and in *Timber* (ll. 2304–34) adapted from Erasmus' *Epistola Apologetica* and also (ll. 1058–62) from his *Hyperaspistes Diatribae*.

Erebus. Primeval darkness, the son of Chaos.

Erechtheus. See ORITHYIA.

Eridanus. Mythical amber river, often identified with the Po by classical writers.

Erinyes, the Furies, or avenging goddesses, sprang from the blood of the castrated Uranus.

Eros. A character in *Love's Welcome at Bolsover*, who is the son of Venus and the brother of Anteros. See also CUPID.

Erycina. Surname of Venus used by Jonson in *Volpone* (III. vii).

Esculapius. See AESCULAPIUS.

essay. Since, like most of his contemporaries, Jonson considered the essay a tentative study or a rough sketch, the form did not have great appeal for him, and most of his references to the essay are derogatory (*Cynthia's Revels*, II. iii; *Epicoene*, II. iii; *Timber*, ll. 719–29), although, ironically, Jonson included several excellent essays in *Timber*.

Essex, Lady Frances Howard, Countess of. See Lady Frances Howard, Countess of SOMERSET.

Essex, Robert Devereux, 2nd Earl of (1567–1601), succeeded to the earldom upon the death of his father in 1576 and was placed under the guardianship of Lord Burghley. After taking his master's degree at Cambridge in 1581, he quickly won favor at court; he distinguished himself as a cavalry officer in the Netherlands and was knighted in 1587. When he returned to England, he became a favorite of the queen's, and this position involved him in a rivalry with Sir Walter Raleigh. Hun-

gering for adventure, he joined the expedition of Sir John Norris and Sir Francis Drake to Portugal, but he was ordered home by Elizabeth in 1589, and the next year he angered the queen by secretly marrying the widow of Sir Philip Sidney. After an unsuccessful expedition to Normandy in 1591 to help Henri IV, Essex returned home and, as advised by Francis Bacon, entered politics in an effort to seize power from Burghley, but Elizabeth was wary of his impetuosity and gradually conferred the power he wanted on Burghley's son, Robert Cecil. In 1596 Essex became a national hero when he shared command of the expedition that captured Cadiz, but the next year he failed completely in another Spanish expedition, much to the queen's displeasure. Shortly afterwards, however, she created him Earl Marshal, and he again attempted to gain power. In 1598 he affronted the queen in her private chambers, and she struck him. In 1599, upon his own demand, Essex was made Lord Lieutenant of Ireland and sent there with forces to quell the rebellion of Tyrone. He failed in his mission, made an unauthorized truce with Tyrone, returned to England against Elizabeth's orders, was confined by the Council, and became ill. He was tried for disobedience in 1600 by a special council and stripped of his offices. Although he was set free after several months, he was banned from court. Continuing to be popular, he planned a coup to unseat the enemy party and to establish his own about the queen. In order to accomplish his goal, he unsuccessfully sought the aid of the army in Ireland and opened negotiations with James VI of Scotland. Desperate, Essex made his attempt on February 8, 1601, but his support failed him, and he was easily defeated and arrested. At his trial Francis Bacon, whom Essex had patronized, contributed substantially to his conviction. After some hesitation, Elizabeth signed the death warrant, and Essex was executed.

Jonson may have symbolically represented Elizabeth's treatment of Essex in the Cynthia-Actaeon story in *Cynthia's Revels*. In *Timber* (l. 910), Essex is listed in the scriptorum catalogus as "noble and high." In the *Conversations* (ll. 368–70), Jonson said Essex wrote the prefatory epistle, signed A.B., to Sir Henry Savile's translation of Tacitus, and that the last book of Tacitus was not translated because of the evil it contains about the Jews. Later in the *Conversations* (ll. 580–84), Jonson reported that Essex, after the death in France of his brother, Walter Devereux, carried in tournaments a black shield with the motto *Par nulla figura dolori* and that once when the Queen was upset with him, Essex wore a diamond with the motto, *Dum formas minus*. According to Jonson, Essex patronized Spenser when he was in poverty (l. 175), and it is generally thought that Essex paid Spenser's funeral expenses.

Essex, Robert Devereux, 3rd Earl of (1591–1646). Son of the 2nd Earl of Essex. In 1604 James I restored the estates of his father to him and arranged for his marriage to Lady Frances Howard, daughter of Thomas Howard, Earl of Suffolk. The marriage, which was intended to heal one of several political ruptures caused by the execution of the 2nd Earl of Essex, took place in 1606 when the groom was fourteen and the bride thirteen. Jonson's *Hymenaei* was written to celebrate their wedding. The marriage ended in 1613 when the countess caused a great scandal by falling in love with Robert Carr, Earl of Somerset, and obtaining an annulment. Essex afterwards followed a military career and in 1626 joined the parliamentary opposition to Charles I. In 1639 he was second in command of the royal army in the first Bishops' Wars in Scotland and in 1641 was made privy councilor, but a year later he commanded the parliamentary forces at Edgehill and took Reading in 1643. In 1645 after failure, disgrace, and disagreement, he relinquished his command.

Estienne family. A famous Parisian and Genevan family of printers, whose surname was Latinized as Stephanus. The first of the line was Henri, who died in 1520. Henri's eldest son Robert (c.1500–1559) devoted himself to printing scholarly books; he published editions of classical authors, dictionaries, lexicons, and critical editions of the Bible. In *The Masque of Augurs*, Jonson used Robert's *Thesaurus Linguae Latinae*. Robert's brother Charles (1504?–1564) was educated in medicine but was a classical scholar as well. Charles wrote numerous books on medicine, agriculture, and other subjects. Jonson drew upon Charles' *Dictionarium . . . Poeticum* (1531 and 1573) for information for *The Masque of Augurs*. Henri (1531–1598), Robert's son and the last of the Estienne line, was a humanist scholar and a distinguished printer. He issued numerous editions of classical authors. Jonson used Henri's edition of Dion Cassius in *Sejanus* and his *Moschi . . . Idyllia* in *The Sad Shepherd* (II.vi).

Esychia. A symbolic personage representing quietness in a scene in Jonson's part of the *King's Coronation Entertainment*.

ethics. See POET.

Euclia. Corinthian festival in honor of Artemis. The personification of fair glory, as in the character representing fair glory who appears in *Love's Triumph Through Callipolis* and offers a song in praise of love and beauty.

Euclid. Greek mathematician of the third century B.C. famous for his *Elements*, a systematic exposition of the major propositions of elementary geometry, first translated into English by Sir Henry Billingsley in 1570. Euclid is mentioned in *The New Inn* (II. iv).

Eudaimonia. A symbolic personage representing felicity in a scene in Jonson's part of the *King's Coronation Entertainment*.

Eudemus. Corrupt physician in *Sejanus*. He is bribed with the promise of a title into agreeing to divulge Livia's secrets to Sejanus, and he arranges a meeting between them. Meeting with them, he suggests Lygdus as a good agent to administer poison to Drusus senior. He consults with Livia about her makeup, suggesting ways to make her more attractive to Sejanus. Late in the play, in grief over the murder of her children, Sejanus' wife, Apicata, vows to expose the involvement of Eudemus, Livia and Lydgus in Drusus' death.

Eugenie, Sir Dauphine. In *Epicoene*, a young knight. His high spirits are dampened by his uncle Morose, who cannot stand to hear any noise and who highly disapproves of his nephew. Morose threatens to disinherit Dauphine, but Dauphine tricks him into "marrying" Epicoene, a young boy who is supposed to be a silent, soft-spoken gentlewoman but who becomes loud and aggressive after marriage. When Dauphine agrees to deliver Morose from the marriage, Morose makes him his heir; Dauphine then makes his uncle ridiculous by revealing Epicone's true identity.

Eunomia. See HOURS.

Euphemus, heroic son of Poseidon and Europa, received a clod of earth that would have insured that his descendants would become rulers of Libya, but he lost it. He appears in *Love's Triumph Through Callipolis* as a messenger sent from heaven to inform the queen that certain depraved lovers have crept into Callipolis, the city where beauty dwells.

Euphorbus. Son of Panthoos who was killed by Menelaus. Pythagoras claimed to have been Euphorbus in a former incarnation.

Euphrosyne. 1. A symbolic personage representing gladness in Jonson's part of the *King's Coronation Entertainment.*

2. A character symbolic of gladness who appears in *The Haddington Masque* as one of the Graces and an attendant of Venus. See also GRACES.

Eupolis. Athenian comic poet of the fourth century B.C. whose satircal plays were greatly admired by the ancients. Eupolis probably collaborated with Aristophanes but later attacked him. Eupolis' contribution to the development of comedy is discussed briefly by Cordatus in *Every Man out* (After the second sounding. Grex).

Eupompus. Greek painter of the fourth century B.C. who founded the Sicyonic school and whose only work on record is *A Victor in The Olympic Games.* Jonson discusses his contribution to the development of painting in *Timber* (ll. 1555–56). See also PAINTING.

Euripides (c. 480–406 B.C.) Greek tragedian. He wrote between eighty and ninety plays, but only about eighteen are extant. Ranking with Aeschylus and Sophocles, Euripides is rationalistic and iconoclastic in his attitude toward the gods, tends to be interested in less heroic characters, and deals with problems and conflicts sometimes disturbing to his audience. Characteristic of his tragic form are a prologue, a *deus ex machina*, and choral passages of lyric power.

In *Timber* (ll. 2454–63), Jonson notes that Valerius Maximus recorded that Euripides, when told that Alcestis had said he could write a hundred poems in the time it took Euripides to produce only three, replied that the difference was that Alcestis' verses would last only three days while his own would last for all time. Later (ll. 2573–77), Jonson refers to Aristophanes' criticism of Euripides. Jonson borrowed from Euripides in *Timber* (ll. 33–35) and in *Volpone* (I. i), and he used him as one of his sources for *The Masque of Beauty, The Haddington Masque*, and *Oberon*.

Europa, daughter of Agenor, King of Tyre, was beloved by Zeus who disguised himself as a beautiful bull to seduce her, and she later bore him two or three sons.

Eustathius. Writer of the twelfth century whose romance *The Story of Hysmine and*

Hysminias was first printed at Paris in 1617 and is alluded to in *The Sad Shepherd* (I. v).

Evan. A Welsh attorney who appears in *For the Honor of Wales* and argues that a masque in which the Prince of Wales performs should have a Welsh setting.

Evans, Samuel, entered New College, Oxford, in 1625 and received his degree in 1632. In 1637 he was rector of Syresham, Northants, and was the contributor of a Latin poem ("Nec Sic excidimus: pars tantum vilior audit") to *Jonsonus Virbius.*

Evans, Willa McClung (1899–   ). American scholar, since 1964 Professor Emerita of English at Hunter College. An expert on the relationship between poetry and music, Professor Evans is the author of *Ben Jonson and Elizabethan Music* (1929).

Evans, William (d. 1636), porter to Charles I, was famous for his great height. He is alluded to in *The Magnetic Lady* (III. iii).

Everill. The champion of Meercraft in *The Devil Is an Ass.*

Every Man in His Humour.

Acted: 1598 at the Curtain Theatre in Shoreditch by the Chamberlain's Men. (This refers to the revised version. The original version was described on the title page as having been acted "sundry times.")

Published: Original version in 1601 in quarto by Walter Burre. Revised version in 1616 folio by William Stansby.

Printed: The printer for the quarto version is unknown. Stansby printed the 1616 folio version.

Prologue (found only in the 1616 folio version). Jonson says that his play will deal with ordinary, contemporary foibles, not with grand deeds long past or with serious crimes. It will be simple and true to life, not filled with sensational stage tricks. He hopes his audience, who have applauded unnatural plays about outrageous monsters, will like his natural play about men.

(Differing names and courses of action in the 1616 folio version are given in parentheses.)

Act I. The setting is a street before the house of Lorenzo senior (Knowell senior). He sends Musco (Brainworm), his servant, to wake Lorenzo junior (Edward) and laments his son's devotion to poetry, which he thinks is worthless, even though he enjoyed it in his youth. His nephew Stephano (Stephen) enters and asks to borrow a book on hunting and hawking, since these are the true marks of accomplishment in a contemporary young man (rather than Greek and Latin). Lorenzo senior mocks him and advises him to act less foolishly, to be more thoughtful and more independent of fashion. Prospero's servant brings in a merry letter from Prospero (Wellbred), which urges Lorenzo junior (Edward) to come at once to Florence (London). Stephano (Stephen) picks a meaningless quarrel with the servant but is quieted by Lorenzo senior (Knowell). The servant mistakenly gives Prospero's letter to Lorenzo senior, who is shocked at its familiar insolence. He secretly resolves to follow Lorenzo junior (Edward) to Florence (London) and patiently spy on his son and decide how to persuade him to a better way of life. Musco (Brainworm) delivers the letter to Lorenzo junior (Edward) and warns him that his father has read it, but Lorenzo junior (Edward) vows to go to Florence (London) anyway and to see the two foolish men Prospero (Wellbred) wants him to meet. He decides to take Stephano (Stephen) to provide more sport and mocks his foolish cousin to his face, but Stephano (Stephen) does not understand that he is doing so.

Matheo (Matthew) comes to Cob's house seeking Bobadilla, and listens to Cob's puns about his "herring" ancesters. He is surprised to learn that Bobadilla is staying there, and goes in to speak with him. Cob is angered at Matheo's (Matthew's) insult of his house, and he mocks Matheo (Matthew), revealing that Matheo is a fishmonger's son turned gallant poet, who fancies himself in love with Hesperida (Bridget). Cob rails at poetry in general, brags about the "dainty oaths" Bobadilla has taught him, and goes to work carrying water. Matheo (Matthew) goes in and greets Bobadilla, reading him some second-rate verses from a popular play, which Bobadilla praises highly. He complains that Giuliano (Downright) has threatened to beat him, and Bobadilla teaches him a fencing trick with bedposts. They leave to go to Prospero's (Wellbred's). [The F 1616 ends the act here, but the Q 1601 includes the next three scenes in the F 1616 in this same act.] In these three scenes, Thorello (Kitely), a foolish, rich merchant, praises his servant Pizo (Cash), complains to Giuliano of the dissolute conduct of Prospero and his friends in his house, and confesses that he is jealous of Biancha, his wife and Giuliano's sister. Bobadilla and Matheo come in and ask for Prospero, treating Thorello and Giuliano very insultingly; Thorello, who is a little

afraid of Prospero and his companion, dissuades Giuliano from acting violently. Thorello resolves to give Biancha no opportunity of being unfaithful to him with the gallants who meet in his house.

Act II. [In the F 1616 version, Kitely praises Cash, complains to Downright about Wellbred and his companions, and confesses his jealousy of Dame Kitely. Bodadilla and Matthew insult Downright and Wellbred; Kitely prevents Downright from acting violently. Kitely resolves to keep a close watch over Dame Kitely.]

Musco (Brainworm) enters, disguised as a begging soldier and planning to court favor with Lorenzo junior (Edward) by preventing his father from following him. He meets Lorenzo junior (Edward) and Stephano (Stephen), who do not recognize him, tells them of his military service, and easily convinces foolish, impetuous Stephano (Stephen) to buy his greatly overpriced sword. Lorenzo senior (Knowell) enters and speaks of the decline of reverence given to "Lord Reason" (of the disgraceful way that many modern children are brought up to be dissolute, licentious, and materialistic, and his fear that his son may, by contamination, become like them). Musco (Brainworm) meets him and begs from him; Lorenzo senior (Knowell) offers him a constructive job spying on Lorenzo junior (Edward), and Musco (Brainworm) takes it with glee. [The F 1616 ends the act here, but the Q 1601 continues for the next two scenes of the F 1616.] Prospero and Lorenzo junior have a warm meeting and join in baiting and mocking the three gulls—Bobadilla, Matheo, and Stephano. Bobadilla tells of the great battles in which he has taken part, and brags of his prowess as a soldier. Musco comes in and tells them that Lorenzo senior has followed Lorenzo junior to Florence; they are alarmed but vow to outwit him.

Act III. [In the 1616 version, Wellbred and Edward meet and mock the three gulls, and Bobadilla brags of his service and his military prowess. Brainworm brings the news that Knowell has followed his son to London; they are alarmed but vow to outwit him.]

Thorello (Kitely) makes a great show of having so much confidence in Pizo (Cash) that he will tell him an important secret but, at the last minute, loses his confidence for no good reason. He bids Pizo (Cash) watch over his wife while he is gone for a little while on business. Cob comes in, complaining and punning about the inhumanity of fasting days. Lorenzo junior (Edward) and Prospero (Wellbred) praise Musco (Brainworm) for his clever deception, learn that Thorello (Kitely) has gone to Clement's, and speak highly of Clement, a magistrate. Bobadilla speaks in lengthy praise of tobacco and gets into a fight with Cob, who hates the weed. Prospero (Wellbred) and Lorenzo junior (Edward) mock Stephano (Stephen) for picking up Bobadilla's habit of swearing absurdly and profusely. Cob brings Thorello (Kitely) the news that Prospero (Wellbred) and his friends have gone to Thorello's house and has a hard time convincing Thorello (Kitely) that they have not been trifling with Biancha (Dame Kitely) and Hesperida (Bridget). Thorello (Kitely) goes rushing home. Cob stays behind to complain of his beating by Bobadilla to Clement, but when Clement learns that Cob was beaten for deriding tobacco, which Clement values highly, he flies into a rage, plays at putting Cob in jail, and terrifies him before he lets him go. Clement tells Lorenzo senior (Knowell) to "be merry," not to take life so seriously, and not to worry so much about his son. [The F 1616 ends the act here, but the Q 1601 includes the next five scenes of the F 1616 in this same act.] Giuliano scolds Biancha for allowing Prospero and his companions in Thorello's house, even though she protests that she could not keep them away. Prospero and Lorenzo junior encourage Matheo to read his plagiarized verse to Hesperida, mocking him and encouraging the women to mock him also. Giuliano enters and, in anger, insults Prospero and his companions. They all draw, and Giuliano offers to fight his brother and Bobadilla, but they are parted. Thorello enters; Giuliano tells him that his brother and his companions started the fight. Biancha and Hesperida speak of how impressed they are with Lorenzo junior, and Thorello expresses his jealousy. Cob goes home, rails about Bobadilla to Tib, and warns her to stay locked up in their house and not be unfaithful to him. Prospero and Lorenzo junior send Musco to meet Lorenzo senior: Lorenzo junior confesses his love for Hesperida, and Prospero agrees to arrange a meeting and a marriage between them.

Act IV. [In the F 1616 version, Downright scolds Dame Kitely; Wellbred and Edward encourage Matthew to read his plagiarized verse to Bridget, who mocks him. Downright enters, insults them, and nearly begins a brawl with Wellbred and Bobadilla, which is prevented. He tells Kitely that the trouble was started by the young gallants. Bridget and Dame Kitely praise Edward, and Kitely becomes especially jealous of him. Cob rails about Bobadilla to Tib, and warns her to lock herself in and to try to stay faithful. Brainworm is sent to Knowell by Wellbred and Edward; Edward confesses his love for Bridget, and Wellbred agrees to arrange a match.]

Musco (Brainworm) returns to Lorenzo senior (Knowell), saying that Lorenzo junior (Edward) and his companions ambushed him and made him a prisoner, but that he heard that they were planning to meet at Cob's house, and then he escaped. Lorenzo senior (Knowell) leaves to catch his son there. Peto (Formal) asks Musco (Brainworm) to tell him of his military exploits while they drink; Musco (Brainworm), seeing an opportunity for further deception, gleefully agrees. Bobadilla brags about his prowess as a swordsman and about his plan with nineteen companions, for ridding Italy (England) of his "forty thousand" enemies by killing them all. Giuliano (Downright) enters and challenges Bobadilla to a fight; he disarms and defeats Bobadilla easily because Bobadilla is afraid to draw. He drops his cloak, which Stephano (Stephen) eagerly picks up. Musco (Brainworm) comes to Thorello (Kitely) dressed as Peto (Formal), and tells him that Clement wants him. Thorello (Kitely) leaves, asking Pizo (Cash) to watch over his wife. Prospero (Wellbred) tells Biancha (Dame Kitely) that her husband has gone to be unfaithful to her at Cob's house. Biancha (Dame Kitely) rushes there to catch Thorello (Kitely) in the act; she forces Pizo (Cash) to accompany her. Prospero (Wellbred) tells Hesperida (Bridget) of Lorenzo junior's (Edward's) love for her; she agrees to accompany Prospero (Wellbred) and meet him. Thorello (Kitely) comes back, angry at having been sent a false message; Prospero (Wellbred) tells him that his wife has gone to Cob's house. Thorello (Kitely) rushes there, thinking that she has betrayed him with Pizo (Cash). Bobadilla and Matheo (Matthew) have Musco (Brainworm), who is still disguised as Clement's man, draw up a warrant for Giuliano's (Downright's) arrest; they pay his fee by pawning a jewel from Matheo's (Matthew's) ear and Bobadilla's stockings. [The Q 1601 ends the act here, but the F 1616 goes on for the next two scenes of the Q 1601.] Knowell arrives at Cob's house and, thinking that his son is inside, demands that Tib open the door. Dame Kitely and Cash arrive; she demands that Tib send her husband out. Kitely arrives and accuses Dame Kitely of adultery, Cash of being her pimp, and Knowell of being her lover. In the confusion, Cob arrives and beats Tib for her apparent role in the situation. Kitely takes the whole group to Clement's. Brainworm, dressed up as a municipal officer, "arrests" Downright for Bobadilla and Matthew. He "arrests" Stephen in turn, at Downright's urging, for stealing his cloak, and is made to go before Clement.

Act V. In the Q 1601, Lorenzo senior arrives at Cob's and demands to be admitted. Biancha and Pizo come and demand that Thorello be sent out. Thorello comes and accuses his wife of adultery, Pizo of being a pimp, and Lorenzo senior of being her lover. Cob enters and beats Tib for her apparent role in the situation. Thorello takes them all before Clement. Musco, dressed as an officer, "arrests" Giuliano at Bobadilla and Matheo's urging, and arrests Stephano in turn at Giuliano's. They all go before Clement.

[The Q 1601 version continues the act, and the F 1616 version begins it, at Clement's, with Clement revealing that Prospero (Wellbred) caused the confusion between Thorello (Kitely) and Biancha (Dame Kitely).] Bobadilla, Matheo (Matthew), and Giuliano (Downright) enter; Clement mocks Bobadilla for being a "fresh water" soldier. When he learns that Musco (Brainworm) was only impersonating an officer, Clement threatens him with physical punishment and jail. Musco (Brainworm) reveals his deceptions, and says that Lorenzo junior (Edward) and Hesperida (Bridget) have gone to get married. Clement praises him for his clever powers of deception. Peto (Formal) enters sheepishly, having been tricked out of his clothes by Musco (Brainworm), but Clement gives Lorenzo junior's (Edward's) and Hesperida's (Bridget's) marriage his approval. On learning that Matheo (Matthew) is a poet, Clement engages him in a verse-making contest, but stops in disgust when he learns that all Matheo's (Matthew's) verse is plagiarized and second-rate. [In the Q 1601, Lorenzo junior makes a long speech in defense of true poetry and is seconded by Clement. In the F 1616, Clement makes a short speech in defense of true poetry and is seconded by Edward.] Clement sentences Bobadilla and Matheo (Matthew) to spend the night in jail, to be bound the whole next day in ridiculous costumes in the town square, and to write and sing a ballad of "repentence" (to stand and fast in the courtyard of his house while the others

feast inside) and sets Peto (Formal) to guard them. In the Q 1601, Giuliano speaks kindly to Prospero, and is reconciled with him. Clement realizes that Stephano (Stephen) is a fool but invites him to dinner with the company anyway (and tells him that he must eat in the "buttery" with Tib and Cob—Tib and Cob are reconciled.) Thorello (Kitely) and Biancha (Dame Kitely) are also reconciled, and Thorello (Kitely) makes a verse laughing at jealousy (recites a section of a jealous man's part in a play). Clement makes Musco (Brainworm) the honored guest at his dinner and invites the company, telling the discontented members to forget their cares (saying that he, Knowell, and Edward will discuss poetry at dinner and try to reach a reconciliation).

Every Man out of His Humour.

Acted: 1599 at the Globe and at court by the Chamberlain's Men.

Published: 1600 in quarto by William Holme.

Printer: Probably Adam Islip.

After the second sounding, Asper, the presenter, Cordatus, Asper's friend, and Mitis all enter. Asper immediately begins a caustic attack on this "impious world," claiming that he will "strip the ragged follies, / Naked, as at their birth." Cordatus tries to settle Asper down but only succeeds in inspiring him all the more in his disgust for the world. When Asper is reminded that an audience is present and that some may not be pleased with his ill humor, he launches into a long definition of humor as expressed in human behavior and announces that he will make the stage a mirror to reflect scornfully the "time's deformity." Requesting that Cordatus and Mitis serve as censors for his presentation, Asper leaves the stage to begin his play, and Cordatus, who has already seen the play but has reserved judgment of it, discusses with Mitis the general nature of the work and its relationship to classical comedy, and he further explains that the scene for the play is *Insula Fortunata*.

Following the third sounding, the Prologue enters and attempts to get Cordatus to introduce the play, but he politely refuses. While they are quibbling, Carlo Buffone, a jester, comes onstage with a boy and a bottle of wine. With a great flourish he offers a toast instead of a Prologue and briefly introduces the play, after which Cordatus explains to Mitis that Carlo is "an impudent common jester, a violent rayler, and an incomprehensible *Epicure*."

Act I. Macilente, a scholar who has traveled widely, enters and in a long philosophical speech rhetorically asks where in the vast world can be found a man who commands both his blood and his affection. He hears others approaching and decides to lie down until they pass. Carlo Buffone comes in with Sogliardo, a foolish man with land and money whose humor it is to become a gentleman at all costs. He seeks Carlo's advice and is told in detail the kind of clothes, manners, and debts he must acquire in order to be accepted into society. Overhearing their conversation, Macilente is appalled and attempts unsuccessfully to quarrel with Carlo's advice. When Sogliardo and Carlo leave to go meet Puntarvolo, a knight, Macilente expresses his hatred for creatures like Carlo.

Sordido, a farmer and Sogliardo's brother, comes in reading his almanac, hoping for many days of rain. His barns are already overflowing, yet he desires an even more bountiful harvest. Sordido's servant enters and serves him with a paper requesting him to bring his grains to market, but he decides that he will not only not market what he already has but harvest his crops, then bury them in the ground, and buy up the best crops available for his own household. In viewing the scene Mitis suggests to Cordatus that Macilente should have scorned the wretched Sordido, but Cordatus persuades him that had Macilente done so he would have expressed his actual hatred for Sordido instead of revealing his own humor of envy.

Act II. In the country before the house of the vainglorious knight Puntarvolo, appear Carlo, Sogliardo, and Fastidious Brisk, a dandified courtier who also has his page Cinedo with him. While they wait for the knight to receive them, they discuss his various idiosyncrasies, especially the way in which he courts his own wife. Presently they hear the cry of foxhounds, and, realizing that Puntarvolo is coming, they decide to hide so that they can observe his behavior.

Puntarvolo enters. He sees a gentlewoman at the window of his house and greets her in glowing terms although she insists that she is not the mistress of the house but merely the waiting gentlewoman. The two then engage in a long prearranged dialogue which is essentially a eulogy of Puntarvolo and which concludes with his requesting the gentlewoman to summon her mistress. At this point, Sordido, the elder brother of Sogliardo, and Fungoso, Sordido's son, approach Puntarvolo, who greets them while Puntarvolo's

wife appears at the window. When Puntarvolo notices her, he launches into a long laudatory dialogue with her until she descends to receive Puntarvolo, at which point she discovers Carlo and the others who have been observing. Puntarvolo then lavishly welcomes them all to his castle.

So impressed is Fungoso with Brisk's clothes that he persuades his uncle to give him money, ostensibly to buy law books but really to get new fashionable clothes like Brisk's. In the course of the conversation Puntarvolo describes the scheme he has concocted to insure his safe return from the journey he intends to make shortly.

Meanwhile, in the city at the house of Deliro, a rich man who dotes on his wife Fallace, Macilente calls upon Deliro and advises him not to be too obsequious to his wife, but Deliro insists that he is not worthy of his virtuous and incomparable wife. When Fallace enters, she complains of the excessive favors her husband bestows upon her. Fungoso, Fallace's brother, arrives attired like Fastidious Brisk, and Deliro implores him to help cheer up Fallace, but Fungoso only asks her for more money so that he can keep in fashion with Brisk. Shortly, Fastidious himself arrives in a new suit, much to the chagrin of Fungoso, who desperately plots to get more money. Macilente scorns all of them, but Fastidious requests money from Deliro in exchange for land. Deliro must leave to meet a man at St. Paul's, but Fastidious insists on accompanying him. When they leave, Fungoso, now with his new tailor, decides to go after them too. Left alone, Fallace reveals that she is attracted to Brisk although before leaving Deliro has urged her to open his own treasures and to take whatever she wants.

Act III. In the middle aisle of St. Paul's, Shift, a cheater, posts bills advertising his services as a gentleman usher and a practitioner of tobacco, and he is greeted there by two fops, Clove and Orange. Carlo and Puntarvolo enter, followed by two of the knight's serving men, one leading a dog and the other carrying a bag containing a cat. Presently Fastidious, Deliro, and Macilente arrive, and Fastidious promises Macilente that if Deliro will furnish him with proper clothes he will introduce Macilente to the most divine lady at court. Sogliardo comes in and announces that he has purchased a coat of arms and is now a true gentleman, and they discuss the virtues of Sogliardo's crest until Fungoso arrives with his tailor, whom the young man wants to fashion a suit for him modeled on the one Fastidious is wearing. When Shift is seen walking by flashing his rapier, Fastidious attempts to buy it from him because he fancies it, but Shift is reluctant to sell. Sogliardo requests that Shift go with him to dine and teach him how to take tobacco.

Meanwhile in the country, the depressed Sordido considers hanging himself and when a servant delivers a letter from Fungoso requesting more money to stay in fashion, he hangs himself from a tree but is rescued by some local rustics who curse him when they realize whom they have saved. Moved by their curses, Sordido repents of his wretched humor, promises to make amends for all his past errors, and realizes that "no life is blest that is not graced with love."

At an apartment at court, Macilente and Fastidious, both attired in new clothes, arrive, and Fastidious, while taking tobacco, tries to show off his mistress Saviolina, but Macilente finds her to be aloof, dull-witted, and unworthy of the admiration the gallants have given her. Fastidious asks Macilente not to reveal his disgrace and the shortcomings of his mistress to anyone else.

Act IV. In a room in Deliro's house Fungoso complains to his sister Fallace that their father is too cheap to keep his son in fashion like a true gentleman. Fallace bemoans having no friend in the world except her doting husband, and she again proclaims her admiration for Fastidious. Musicians hired by Deliro enter to serenade Fallace, and she is angered by her husband's incessant attempts to please her. Macilente is welcomed back from court by Deliro and tells him that Fastidious is scarcely known there and that the ladies consider him the simplest man they know. Deliro informs Macilente that Fastidious is greatly in debt to him and that he intends to sue Fastidious. Fallace angrily denounces Macilente as a traitor to Brisk. Deliro insists to Macilente that they should still try to appease her although Macilente does not think her worth the effort. In another room Fallace gives Fungoso money and asks him to warn Brisk of Deliro's malicious intent and the treachery of Macilente, but Fungoso privately decides to use the money for a new suit.

Meanwhile at his lodgings, Puntarvolo makes arrangements with his notary for his insurance scheme. Presently Macilente and Deliro arrive looking for Fastidious, and shortly after Sogliardo and Shift arrive. Shift has ingratiated himself with Sogliardo by telling tales of his great adventures and famous robberies. Brisk finally arrives, offers an elaborate excuse for being late, and launches into an embellished tale about a quarrel he has recently won. When they all leave to go to the notary, Macilente privately exclaims, "O, that there should be fortune / To clothe these men so naked in desert!" while back at Deliro's house Fungoso has his new suit fitted and makes credit arrangements with his new tailor. Later, with his insurance scheme settled, Puntarvolo declares himself ready at last to depart on his journey, but Brisk, who has now changed to a new suit and is accompanied by his dog, persuades him to go to court first, and they invite Carlo, Shift, Macilente, and Sogliardo to join them. Carlo insists that Sogliardo should become a courtier now that he is a new gentleman; behind Sogliardo's back, the others plot to present him at court as a true gentleman to Brisk's scornful mistress, thinking the courtiers will find the joke amusing. Carlo does not desire to go to court and agrees to make arrangements for supper for all at the Mitre Tavern. Fungoso, who now feels out of fashion in his new suit since Brisk has changed to yet another one, is reluctant to go with them but finally decides to do so since he remembers that he had a message for Brisk but can't recall exactly what it was. Observing all this action, Mitis comments to Cordatus that Macilente seems to have become more sociable, but Cordatus responds that "now does he, in this calm of his humour, plot, and store up a world of malicious thoughts in his brain, till he is so full with them, that you shall see the very torrent of his envy break forth like a land-flood: and, against the course of all their affections, oppose itself so violently, that you will almost have wonder to think how 'tis possible the current of their dispositions shall receive so quick and strong an alteration."

Act V. On the palace stairs Puntarvolo arranges for his dog to be kept by a groom, who would gladly sell the pet if he could. Shortly after Puntarvolo leaves, Sogliardo and Macilente enter. Macilente manages to get the dog from the groom and poisons it secretly as a mischievous jest. In her apartment Brisk and Fungoso tell Saviolina about the astonishing gentleman they have brought to see her, and she is eager to meet him. When she does so and hears his pretentious and artificial speech, she is very taken with the extraordinary gentleman until Macilente reveals that he is a counterfeit, at which point she throws Sogliardo out and leaves in anger, much to the amusement of all except Fungoso, who complains that his suit needs to be altered. Out on the palace stairs again, Puntarvolo looks for his dog. When he cannot find the dog, he blames Shift, who has come to court to see Sogliardo. When pressured, Shift finally admits that he has never been a thief as he had bragged to Sogliardo, and Fungoso finds the poisoned animal in the yard. When Sogliardo learns that Shift has never actually done any of the things he has claimed to do, he rejects him as a scoundrel. Macilente is delighted that they both have been dishumored, and all except the ostracized Shift prepare to go to dinner at the Mitre, where Carlo has been amusing himself with drink. When the others arrive, Carlo ridicules Puntarvolo about the death of his dog, and the knight finally strikes the clown and makes him lie down. Suddenly, the constable is heard outside. Puntarvolo tapes up Carlo's lips, and they all run out, except Fungoso, who hides under the table. Brisk is captured and escorted to jail. When the officers have departed, Macilente reenters, points out the hidden Fungoso to the tavern drawers, and leaves. The drawers demand payment from Fungoso for the meal since he is the only one left, and he protests that he is an invited guest and has no money. Macilente proceeds to Deliro's house, tells Deliro what has happened to Fungoso, and suggests that Fallace will be grateful and begin to look with favor upon her husband if he rescues her brother. Asking Macilente to tell his wife what he is up to, Deliro leaves, after which Fallace discovers Macilente and begins to berate him until he informs her that he has gotten her husband out of the house so that he could let her know that Brisk is in jail. Deciding that she has been mistaken about Macilente, she agrees to accompany him to the jail in order to bribe the jailor.

Later, back at the Mitre, Deliro rescues Fungoso, who abandons his humor of trying to stay in fashion. Meanwhile Fallace visits Fastidious in prison, kisses him, and tells him that she had tried earlier to get word to him through her brother about his potential arrest, but Brisk assures her that he never received her message. Fallace expresses her passion for Fastidious, and he kisses her in return just as Deliro and Macilente enter. Deliro's eyes are finally opened, and he pronounces his wife a lascivious strumpet. Declaring himself ruined by the law suits against him, Fastidious realizes the folly of his foppery, accepts his fate, and prepares to move to the cheaper ward in order to save charges. Macilente

finds that his own soul is finally at peace and that

I am as empty of all envy now,
As they of merit to be envied at.
My humour, like a flame, no longer
   lasts,
Than it hath stuff to feed it; and their
   folly
Being now raked up in their repentant
   ashes,
Affords no ampler subject to my sp-
   leen.
I am so far from malicing their states,
That I begin to pity them.

(In an epilogue for presentation before Queen Elizabeth, Macilente attributes his changed attitude to the presence and virtues of the sovereign.)

Execration. The name of one of the witches making up the antimasque in *The Masque of Queens.*

Exeter, Frances Cecil, Countess of (d. 1663). Daughter of William, 4th Lord Chandos, widow of Sir Thomas Smith, second wife of Thomas Cecil, 1st Earl of Exeter. Cecil died in 1623, and the Countess never married again. Her fortune was told by the Patrico in *The Gypsies Metamorphosed.*

Expectation. A gossip who appears in the induction and the intermeans to *The Staple of News.*

Eyes. A symbolic character in *Time Vindicated to Himself and to his Honors* who is fascinated with Chronomastix.

F

Fabian, Robert (d. 1513). English chronicler whose popular *New Chronicle of England and France,* covering events through the reign of Richard III, was posthumously published in 1516. He is mentioned by Puppy in *A Tale of a Tub* (i. ii).

fable. In *Timber* (ll. 2678–2815), Jonson, adapting from Daniel Heinsius (*De Tragaediae constitutione,* ch. 4), includes a long discourse on the magnitude of any epic or dramatic fable. According to Jonson, a fable is the "*Imitation* of one intire, and perfect Action; whose parts are so

99

joyned, and knitt together, as nothing in the structure can be chang'd, or taken away, without impairing, or troubling the whole; of which there is a proportionable magnitude in the members." In order to achieve this end, the epic fable asks a magnitude from other poems whereas the dramatic fable does not. That work is whole and perfect which has a beginning, a middle, and an end, but the action that may be whole for a tragedy or comedy may not be large enough in magnitude for an epic. On the other hand, the action of an epic must not be too vast, for that which happens to the eyes when we behold a body also happens to the memory when it contemplates action. Beholding a giant like Tityus, for example, the eye focuses on each part so that the whole is never perceived in one entire view. Likewise, if the action of a fable be too vast, the whole can never be comprehended in the imagination. An action becomes one and is entire when it is composed of many parts that grow or are wrought together and tend to one and the same end. As the best tragic poets and as Virgil and Homer realized, the action of one man—of a Hercules, a Theseus, an Achilles, or a Ulysses—does not necessarily make one entire action. Since the argument of an epic is far more diffuse than that of a tragedy, Virgil appropriately left out many things about Aeneas—how he fought Achilles, how he was snatched out of the battle by Venus— but executed how he came into Italy in twelve books. The rest of Aeneas' journey is not put as the argument of the work, but as episodes of the argument. Likewise, Homer left out many things about Ulysses and included only those things which tended toward one and the same end. An action, composed of diverse parts, may become one fable, as in the case of Sophocles' Ajax, whose battle with Hector, described at large by Homer, is left out of the action of Sophocles' play. "*For* the *whole,* as it consisteth of parts; so without all the parts it is not the whole; and to make it absolute, is requir'd, not only the parts, but such parts as are true. For a part of the whole was true; which if you take away, you either change the whole, or it is not the whole."

Face. Lovewit's housekeeper in *The Alchemist,* known to his master as Jeremy. He adopts the nickname Face when he takes Subtle and Dol into the house in his master's absence; he works as Subtle's assistant when Subtle pretends to be an alchemist. Together, they cheat many foolish people, including Dapper, Drugger, Mammon, Kastril, and Ananias, out of their wealth. When Lovewit returns home unexpectedly, Face's betrayal of Subtle and Dol and his success in winning Pliant for his master make Lovewit forgive him.

Factor. An unnamed character in *News From the New World Discovered in the Moon* who is interested in the news of the discovery because he writes a thousand or so weekly newsletters and plans to start a staple of news as soon as he can.

Fairfax, Edward (1580?–1635). In the *Conversations* (l. 32), Drummond records that Jonson said Fairfax's translation of *Godfrey of Bulloigne* was not well done. Fairfax published a book on witchcraft in which he interpreted the seizures of his two daughters as signs of witchcraft.

Falkland, Lucius Cary, Viscount. See Sir Lucius CARY.

Fallace. In *Every Man out of His Humor,* Deliro's wife whom Deliro idolizes. She dotes upon the dandified courtier Brisk.

Falsehood. The name of one of the witches in the antimasque in *The Masque of Queens.*

Fame. In classical literature, a god who lives in a house on a high hill and who spreads rumor throughout the world.

Fannius, Demetrius. A "dresser of plays" in *Poetaster,* who is foolish and spiteful, eager to slander anyone who offends him. He is a caricature of Thomas Dekker. His name combines the names of two men referred to by Horace: Demetrius, a musician whom Horace called a monkey and a backbiter, and Fannius, an inferior poet. He is shabbily dressed and a friend of Crispinus'. Histrio tells Tucca that Fannius has been hired to write a slanderous play about Horace and his friend to earn a lot of money. Fannius meets Tucca and accompanies the courtiers to Albius' house, where he says very little, except to slander Horace. He writes instead of taking part in Ovid's masquerade. He goes with Lupus, Tucca, and Crispinus to slander Horace to Caesar. He is made to swear that he will never again slander any noble Roman.

Farnaby, Thomas (1575?–1647), was the most distinguished classical scholar and schoolmaster of his day. His school had more than three hundred pupils, and his editions of the classics, with elaborate scholarly notes, remained very popular throughout the seventeenth century. He was a friend of Jonson's, and Jonson contributed commendatory verses in Latin to Farnaby's editions of Juvenal ("Temporibus lux magna fuit Iuvenalis auitis"), Persius ("Cum Iuvenale tuo, Farnabi, Persius exit"), and Seneca ("Comoedias trusatilis Plauti mola"). Jonson wrote a letter in Latin about Farnaby to Richard Brigges in a corner of Farnaby's edition of *Martial* (1615).

Fashioner. In *The Staple of News,* a tailor who serves Pennyboy Junior.

Fates. In Greek mythology, daughters either of Night or of Zeus, and Themis, often represented as three old women—Clotho, Lachesis, and Atropos. In Roman mythology the Fates are named Nona, Decuma, and Morta. The Fates appear in *Lovers Made Men* and inform Mercury that the lovers, who have become ghosts drowned by the charm of love, are not dead and can be transformed back into men.

fauns. Sometimes identified with satyrs and described as boisterous and rude, fauns should probably be associated with Faunus, Roman god of the woods, often depicted with horns and goat feet.

Faustus, Dr. A figure common in literature who sells his soul to the devil in return for knowledge or power. Marlowe's *Dr. Faustus* is an Elizabethan treatment of this subject. In *The Alchemist,* Surly calls Subtle a Faustus, and he is mentioned in *A Tale of a Tub* (IV. vi).

Favonius. Another name for Zephyr, the gentle wind of spring.

Fear. In *Chloridia,* a symbolic character who appears in the second entry of the antimasque.

Feather-maker. A craftsman called to take part in the courtship contest in *Cynthia's Revels,* who gives Mercury a feather during his staged primping.

Felltham, Owen (1602?–1668), was best known for his prose work *Resolves* (1623?). He contributed an elegy ("To write is easy; but to write of thee") to *Jonsonus Virbius* and answered Jonson's Ode on himself ("Come leave this saucy way") affixed to *The New Inn.*

Felton, John. Assassin of the Duke of Buckingham. In 1629, about three months after the assassination, Jonson was accused of having written a poem praising Felton, and the old poet was examined by the attorney-general, Sir Robert Heath, and exonerated.

Fen (Ven), Richard, City Colonel of London, is mentioned in *Und.* XLIV.

Fencer. An unnamed fencer in *Pan's Anniversary.* He and his followers challenge the Arcadians in their celebration of Pan's anniversary and the shepherd's holiday.

Fennor. See Richard VENNAR (Vennard).

Ferneze, Alessandro, became Pope Paul III in 1534. In the mountebank scene in *Volpone* (II), Volpone claims him as a customer.

Ferneze, Camillo. In *The Case Is Altered,* a young man who is actually the long-lost son of Count Ferneze of Milan but is believed by all, including himself, to be Gasper, a Frenchman. When he and his friend, young Lord Chamont, are taken prisoner by the Milanese, they vow to trade identities to deceive their captors into letting the more influential Chamont go free. Camillo stays in prison in Milan while Chamont is exchanged for Paulo; Phoenixella falls in love with him. When the exchange of identities is discovered, the Count, sure that Paulo is lost since the more important Frenchman has been freed, decides in anger to torture Camillo. Chamont arrives with Paulo just in time to save his friend; he then assembles evidence from his memory and from the Count's story of his lost son to realize that Camillo is the Count's older son. When Camillo's true identity is revealed, all rejoice.

Ferneze, Count. In *The Case Is Altered,* a rich count of Milan, who has recently lost his wife. He is father to Paulo, Aurelia, and Phoenixella. He believes that his older son, Camillo, died when very young during a great battle with the French many years ago. Milan is once again at war with the French, and the count mournfully tells his general, Maximilian, of the countess's death and the loss of his son and asks Maximilian to be very careful of Paulo when he takes him to war. The count realizes that Angelo is a rake and warns his daughters against him. When Christophero, his steward, tells the count that he loves Rachel, who is presumably a beggar's daughter, the count resolves to win her for himself because of her great beauty and "noblenesse." He goes to urge his suit to Jaques, but is put off by his raving. A messenger brings him the news that Paulo has been captured, and he laments that he thought of anything but his son. The count's army has captured two French soldiers, Lord Chamont and Gasper, and the count releases Chamont (whom he believes to be the less important Gasper) in exchange for Paulo. When the Count learns that he has been deceived about his prisoner's identity, he vows to torture Gasper, since he believes that the French, having their great leader back, will not bother to return his son. He pauses on the verge of killing Gasper; just at that moment, Maximilian returns with Paulo and Chamont. Chamont realizes that Gasper is actually Camillo, the Count's lost son; all rejoice at the news. Jaques inadvertently reveals who he is and who Rachel is; the company is surprised and happy. The Count catches Onion and Juniper, and makes them return Jaques's gold to Chamont. He is glad when Paulo is betrothed to Rachel, and happily offers Aurelia to Chamont.

Ferneze, Lord Paulo. Son to Count Ferneze of Milan in *The Case Is Altered.* He avoids his father long enough to confess his love for Rachel to his friend Angelo; he delays going to war against the French with Maximilian long enough to visit Rachel and to say goodbye to her, giving her into Angelo's care while he is gone. He is captured by the French, but after an exchange of prisoners complicated by deception, he arrives in Milan just in time to save Rachel from Angelo's dishonorable advances and Camillo from the Count's wrath. The Count is overjoyed to see him; he is betrothed to Rachel when he learns that she is really a noblewoman, not the beggar's daughter she seems.

Ferrabosco, Alphonso (d. 1628). Famous lutenist and composer who was also musical instructor to Prince Henry. Jonson praised Ferrabosco in *Epig.* CXXX, which was prefixed to Ferrabosco's *Ayres* (1609), and in *Epig.* CXXXI, and he acknowledged his collaboration in *The Haddington Masque* and *The Masque of Queens.* Ferrabosco wrote the music for *Love Freed, The Masque of Augurs,* and a cancelled passage of *Hymenaei,* and he played for *Oberon.* Ferrabosco's *Ayres* (1609) included the music for several songs from Jonson's works: "Come Away" (*Masque of Blackness,* 295–300); "Come, my Celia" (*Volpone,* III. vii. 166–83); "Why stays the Bridegroom" (*Haddington Masque,* 415–24); "So Beauty on the waters stood" (*Masque of Beauty,* 325–32); "If all these Cupids, now, were blind" (*Masque of Beauty,* 341–47); "It was no polity of court" (*Masque of Beauty,* 349–55); "Yes, were the Loves or false, or straying" (*Masque of Beauty,* 358–63); "Had those, that dwell in error foul" (*Masque of Beauty,* 369–73); and "When all the ages of the earth" (*Masque of Queens,* 743–48).

Ferret. In *The New Inn,* Lovel's servant, also called Stote and Vermin.

Festus, Sextus Pompeius. Roman lexicographer whose surviving work, *On the Meaning of Words,* is an abridgment of the lost glossary of M. Verrius Flaccus. This work served as one of Jonson's authorities on Roman antiquities, especially for *Hymenaei.*

Ficino, Marsiglio (1433–1499). Italian philosopher who, under the patronage of Cosimo de Medici, became the most influential exponent of Platonism in Italy during the fifteenth century. He translated many of the Greek classics into Latin, including Plato's dialogues and the writings of Plotinus. As the head of a new Platonic academy at Florence, he was important in the development of Renaissance humanism. In his major original work, *Theologica Platonica* (1482), he combined Christian theology and Neoplatonism.

Several of Jonson's masques reflect the influence of Ficino's Platonic concept of light, beauty, and love. These include *The Masque of Blackness, The Masque of Beauty, Love Freed, Oberon, Mercury Vindicated, News from the New World, Pan's Anniversary, The Vision of Delight, Love's Triumph,* and *Love's Welcome.*

Field, Nathan (1587–1620). Actor and playwright who was a pupil of Jonson's. At Jonson's invitation, Field prefixed verses to the 1607 quarto of *Volpone* ("To the Worthiest Master Jonson") and the 1611 quarto of *Catiline* ("To his Worthy Beloved Friend Mr. Ben Jonson"). He played in *Cynthia's Revels, Poetaster,* and *Epicoene* when he was a member of the Children of the Chapel. He joined the Queen's Revels in 1610 and the Lady Elizabeth's Company in 1613. As a member of the Revels–Lady Elizabeth combine, he performed in *Bartholomew Fair* in 1614, earning high praise from Jonson. Field also acted in some of the plays of Beaumont and Fletcher. He wrote two plays himself, *A Woman Is a Weathercock* (1612) and *Amends for Ladies* (1618) and was co-author with Massinger of *The Fatal Dowry.* In the *Conversations* (11. 164–65), Jonson stated that Field was his scholar and had read to him Horace's satires and some of Martial's epigrams. Field was notorious for his loose living.

Filcher. A doorkeeper at Littlewit's puppet play in *Bartholomew Fair.*

Filmer, Edward (d. 1669). Elder son of Sir Robert Filmer, author of *Patriarcha*—a defense of the divine right of kings. In 1629 Edward published *French Court-Aires,* translated from the French of Pierre Guedron and Antoine Boesset, for which Jonson wrote a commendatory poem ("To My Worthy Friend, Master Edward Filmer, On His Work Published").

Finio. A French page in *The Case Is Altered.* His master is the Frenchman Gasper, who is really the long-lost older son of Count Ferneze of Milan but does not know it.

Finnet, Sir John. Master of the ceremonies to James I and Charles I. His *Finetti Philoxenis* (1656) gives valuable insight into the fierce competition of foreign ambassadors to secure precedence at court for the performances of masques, including those written by Jonson.

fisher play. In the *Conversations* (ll. 402–3), Jonson said he intended to write a fisher or pastoral play set in Loch Lomond, but he never completed the project although Drummond sent him information on the lake after Jonson returned to London.

Fiske, Nicolas. Noted astrologer who became tutor to Lord Treasurer Weston's son in 1633. In Jonson's *The Devil Is an Ass* (I. ii), Fitzdottrel alludes to him as one who is unable to show man the devil.

Fitton. In *The Staple of News,* a court reporter who assists Cymbal in his efforts to win the hand of Lady Pecunia.

Fitz-Ale. 1. A character who appears as a ruffian in the antimasque of *The Fortunate Isles, and Their Union.*
2. A character in *The King's Entertainment at Welbeck,* whose daughter Pem is to be married to Stub.

Fitzdottrel, Fabian. A squire of Norfolk in *The Devil Is an Ass,* who is duped by Meercraft, the projector.

Fitzdottrel, Mrs. Frances. The wife of Fabian Fitzdottrel in *The Devil Is an Ass,* who with the assistance of Wittipol and Manly outwits her tyrannical and jealous husband.

Fitzherbert, Sir Anthony (1470–1538). Famous jurist. One of his most important works was his *Graunde Abridgement,* first published in 1514 in three volumes. Fitzherbert is mentioned by Fungoso in *Every Man out* (II. iii. Grex).

Flaccus. In *Catiline,* a praetor who helps prevent Cicero from being assassinated.

Flaccus, Quintus Fulvius. Roman politician of the second century B.C. He was consul four times and advocated that the allies of Rome be granted citizenship, but his proposals were rejected by the Senate. In *Poetaster* (III. v), Horace says that he must wait for the right time to approach Caesar, since at the wrong moment even "The humble words of Flaccus cannot clime / The' attentive care of Caesar."

Flaccus, Valerius. A Roman poet. Little is known of his life. His only known work is an epic on the Argonauts, the *Argonautica,* which was probably begun in A.D. 80 and closely imitates Apollonius' *Rhodius.* He was strongly influenced by Virgil and Ovid, and is less rhetorical than other authors of the period. He was unknown in the Middle Ages until 1416 when the Florentine humanist Poggio Bracciolini discovered at St. Gall a manuscript (now lost) of the first three books and part of the fourth book of the *Argonautica.* In *Epicoene* (II. iii), Daw dismisses him as worthless along with many other ancient writers. Flaccus' *Argonautica* was listed as one of Jonson's authorities for *The King's Entertainment* and *The Masque of Augurs.*

Flamen. A priest who appears in *Sejanus* to lead Sejanus' ceremony to Fortune.

Flaminio. See Flaminio SCALA.

Flash, Sir Petronel. In *Eastward Ho,* an adventurous but penniless knight who marries Gertrude, daughter of the wealthy goldsmith Touchstone, filches her dowry, and attempts to sail for Virginia. When he is shipwrecked, he is put in prison where he repents, is finally released, and is reconciled with his wife.

flattery. In *Timber* (ll. 1070–92), Jonson, drawing on Seneca (*Naturales Quaestiones,* iv, praefatio 7 and 9; *Epist.* lix. 11), notes that "Flattery is a fine Pick-lock of tender eares: especially of those whom fortune hath borne high upon their wings, that submit their dignity, and authority to it, by a soothing of themselves." He argues that one could not be taken in by flattery if he but "remember, how much more profitable the bitternesse of *Truth* were, then all the honey distilling from a whorish voice; which is not praise but poyson." The folly of some who like to be flattered, Jonson observes, has become so acute that when they are flattered modestly they think they are being maligned.

Later in *Timber* (ll. 1586–1635), Jonson includes a discourse on flatterers, attacking those who are parasites and obsequious sycophants. He argues that it is better to remain silent than to speak with flattery, "For it is not enough to speake good, but timely things." It is less dishonor to hear imperfectly than to speak imperfectly because the ears can be excused but the understanding cannot. Parasites and flatterers are called instruments of grace by great persons, but they are actually the organs of impotency and weakness. Flatterers and parasites "are commonly the off-scowring, and dregs of men, that doe these things, or caluminiate others: yet I know not truly which is worse; hee that malignes all, or that praises all. There is as great a vice in praising, and as frequent, as in detracting."

Flecknoe, Richard (d. 1678). English poet and dramatist. He wrote religious verse and prose, several plays, odes, and occasional verses. His works have long been forgotten, but his name was immortalized by Dryden's satire of Shadwell in the savage *MacFlecknoe*, which served as partial model for Pope's *Dunciad*.

In the section on the Elizabethan stage from *A Short Discourse of the English Stage* appended to *Love's Kingdom* (1664), Flecknoe claims that the Elizabethan period was the zenith of English poetry and acting. He argues that Jonson excelled in gravity and ponderousness of style and claims that his only fault was that he tended to be too elaborate. According to Flecknoe, if Jonson had mixed less erudition with his plays, they would have been more pleasant and delightful than they are, and when we compare Shakespeare and Jonson, we see the difference between nature and art.

Fletcher, Giles. Father of the poets Giles and Phineas, Dr. Fletcher was the uncle of the dramatist John Fletcher. He was one of the commissioners appointed to investigate and report on Jonson and his colleagues' part in the scandalous *The Isle of Dogs* in 1597.

Fletcher, John (1579–1625), was born in Sussex, the son of Richard Fletcher, vicar of Rye. The poets Phineas and Giles (the younger) Fletcher were John's cousins. John probably went to Benet College, Cambridge, but little is known of him before he began collaborating with Francis Beaumont about 1608 in the writing of plays for the King's Men. They wrote many plays together and developed the form of the romance tragicomedy. After Beaumont's marriage in 1613 and his death in 1616, Fletcher wrote several plays on his own and in collaboration with Massinger, Rowley, and others. *The Two Noble Kinsmen* and the lost *Cardenio* were written with Shakespeare, and Fletcher seems also to have had a hand in *Henry VIII*. It is difficult to separate the work of Fletcher from that of his collaborators, but he probably wrote the following on his own: *The Woman's Prize, The Faithful Shepherdess, Monsieur Thomas, Valentinian, Bonduca,* and *Wit Without Money*. Beaumont and Fletcher were very popular in their day, and the first folio of their plays was published in 1647. After the Restoration Fletcher was more popular than Shakespeare. Today the plays of Beaumont and Fletcher are thought to rely too heavily on contrivance and extravagance.

In the *Conversations* (ll. 55–56), Drummond records that Jonson said that next to himself only Fletcher and Chapman could make a masque. He said he loved Fletcher (l. 169) and that Fletcher and Beaumont had written *The Faithful Shepherdess* ten years before and that it was well done (ll. 227–28). (Actually, Fletcher was the sole author of the play.) Fletcher prefixed commendatory verses to the 1607 quarto of *Volpone* ("To the True Master in his Art, B. Jonson") and to the 1611 quarto of *Catiline* ("To his Worthy Friend Mr. Ben Jonson"), and Jonson wrote a poem (To the Worthy Author M. John Fletcher") for Fletcher's *The Faithful Shepherdess*.

Some think that Jonson may have collaborated with Fletcher and others on *The Bloody Brother*, a play of uncertain date and authorship, but there is little evidence to support this claim. There are also certain striking parallels between *The New Inn* (III. i) and Fletcher's *Love's Pilgrimage*, but these correspondences seem to have been incorporated into Fletcher's play by a reviser who adapted from Jonson's play for his own purposes.

Flora. Italian goddess of flowers, sometimes referred to as Chloris.

Florio, John (1553?–1625), who was born in London, became a university teacher of Italian and French. His Italian and English dictionary was published in 1598 and his famous translation of Montaigne's *Essays* in 1603. He was appointed tutor to Prince Henry, reader in Italian to Queen Anne, and a groom of the privy chamber. His patrons included Southampton and Pembroke. Both Jonson and Shakespeare knew Florio, and it is possible, but not likely, that Florio described or translated Bruno's

Candelaio for Jonson, and the work influenced his *Alchemist*. Jonson probably got a great deal of information about Italy from Florio, and it is highly probable that Jonson gathered his facts about Venetian mountebanks for *Volpone* from Florio. As a testimony of his love and friendship, Jonson gave Florio an inscribed quarto (1607) copy of *Volpone*. It seems clear that Jonson, like Shakespeare, was well acquainted with Florio's translation of Montaigne's *Essays*.

Fly. In *The New Inn*, a parasite and a former strolling gypsy who is eventually given the Inn by Lord Frampul.

folios. In 1616 Ben Jonson became the first Elizabethan or Jacobean dramatist to publish his plays in a folio as part of his literary works. Jonson was ridiculed by many of his contemporaries, who considered that his suggesting that his plays had literary merit and allowing them to be published in a collected edition of his works was a characteristic act of vanity. Despite the derision, the publication of his folio set a precedent. In 1623 Heminges and Condell produced the first folio of Shakespeare, and in 1647 the first folio of Beaumont and Fletcher's plays was published. The first folio of Jonson was published and printed by William Stansby (1597–1639), a man of considerable position in the London Book trade. It was one of the finest books Stansby ever produced. His task was not an easy one since he held copyright to only a few of Jonson's works and had to negotiate with various booksellers for the right to print the rest of the volume. Very little is known for certain about the printing history of the folio except that Stansby registered copy for the volume in January 1615 and completed the folio sometime in 1616. Traditionally, it has been assumed that Jonson carefully revised some of the plays included in the volume, corrected the copy, perhaps even supervised the printing, but this view has not been accepted by all Jonson scholars. If Jonson had a direct hand in the production of the volume, then we can reasonably assume that the texts included in it carried authority. On the other hand, if tradition is wrong in assuming that Jonson was directly involved in the production, then we might well question how much authority the text of the dramatic works of the folio might have as compared to those printed in quarto. Henry deVocht has consistently argued that the folio could not possibly have been corrected or supervised by Jonson since it contains inadequate reproductions of the text from earlier issues in

quarto. The Oxford editors, on the other hand, are convinced that the bulk of the evidence clearly indicates that the folio does have authority and that deVocht's position is based, to a great extent, upon logical inconsistencies and ignorance of work habits, practices, and procedures in the publishing and printing business in Jonson's day. Presumably the first folio contained all the works Jonson had completed up to 1615 which he wanted to be included in the volume. Two early works are not included—*Eastward Ho*, of which Jonson was only part author, and *The Case Is Altered*—and for some curious reason *Bartholomew Fair*, which was acted in 1614, was excluded.

The Plays of 1631. In 1631 Robert Allot published a folio containing three plays —*Bartholomew Fair*, *The Devil Is an Ass*, and *The Staple of News*. The printer was John Beale. This volume had a very limited circulation and was probably sent out as private gift copies to friends and patrons.

The Second Folio of 1640. Since twenty-four years elapsed between the publication of the first folio and that of the second, the 1640 folio was probably not a great financial success. The first volume of the second folio appeared in 1640 and was printed by Richard Bishop, who had bought Stansby's business from his widow in 1635. The first volume of the second folio was essentially a corrected reprint of the first folio. The first three plays of the second volume of the second folio—*Bartholomew Fair*, *The Devil is an Ass*, and *The Staple of News*— were issued by Richard Meighen, but the bulk of the volume—the masques and latest plays, *The Underwood*, the translation of *Ars Poetica*, and the prose works—was issued by Thomas Walkley, who claimed he had purchased the manuscripts, the works, and the right to publish them from Sir Kenelm Digby, whom Jonson had appointed as his literary executor. After a long legal battle with John Benson and Andrew Crooke over the right to publish the works, Walkley finally succeeded in getting the second volume out, probably in early 1641. Generally, the workmanship and the accuracy of the second folio compare quite unfavorably with those of Stansby's 1616 folio.

The Folio of 1692. The third folio was produced by a syndicate of leading booksellers—Henry Herringman, Edward Brewster, Thomas Bassett, Richard Chiswell, Matthew Wotton, and George Conyers. The chief partner, Herringman, had long contemplated such an edition and had acquired the copyright for Walkley's portion of the second folio in 1667. The third folio included *The New Inn, Leges Convivales*, and the lines over the entrance to the Apollo Room at the Devil Tavern, and it recast the *English Grammar*, eliminating archaisms and bringing the work thoroughly up to date. Except for this new or revised material, the folio of 1692 was essentially a reprint of the second folio. The printer was Thomas Hodgkin, who simplified the punctuation of the original, modernized the spelling, copied many blunders from the second folio, created new blunders of his own, and tried his hand at a few emendations.

A facsimile of the first folio of 1616, with an introduction by D. Heyward Brock, was published by the Scolar Press in 1976.

Follies. According to Jonson in *Love Freed*, children of the Sphinx, portrayed as twelve dancing she-fools.

Fond, Mistress. In *Eastward Ho*, one of the ladies who excitedly watches the departure of Gertrude in the coach which is to take her from the city to Sir Petronel Flash's castle in the country.

Ford, John (1586–?1640). English dramatist born in Devonshire who studied law but never practiced. Early in his career as a playwright, he collaborated with other dramatists like Dekker. Between 1627 and 1633 he produced his major tragedies— *'Tis Pity She's a Whore*, *The Broken Heart*, and *Love's Sacrifice*. His plays tend to focus on the conflict between passions and the laws of conscience and society. He published an elegy on Jonson ("So seems a star to shoot; when from our sight") in *Jonsonus Virbius*.

Foreman, Simon (1552–1611) was a noted astrologer and quack doctor. At the Overbury trial, a letter to Foreman from Lady Essex asking for love-philtres to alienate Essex's love into and to attract Somerset's was introduced into evidence. In Jonson's *The Devil Is an Ass* (I. ii), Fitzdottrel alluded to Foreman as one who is unable to show man the devil and later as "oracle Foreman" (II. viii). He is also mentioned in *Epicoene* (IV. i).

Forest, The. A book of fifteen poems by Jonson, who described the verses as a collection "of divers nature, and matter." *The Forest* was first published in the folio of 1616 together with the *Epigrams*, but the two books of verse are quite different. In general, the poems in *The Forest* are longer than Jonson's typical epigrams, and they

are more serious in tone and innovative in form. The collection contains some of Jonson's finest work. The title is a translation of "Silva," a title used for collections of occasional verse, especially by the Roman poet Statius.

I, "Why I Write not of Love," expresses in couplets the futility of attempting to capture love in verse.

II, "To Penshurst," in just over a hundred lines, celebrates the beauty, hospitality, and virtue of the Sidney family estate in Kent. At the time the poem was written, the head of the family was Sir Robert, brother of Sir Philip. The poem is the first example in English of its genre, the topographical poem, later imitated by Edmund Waller and achieving its greatest popularity in Denham's "Cooper's Hill."

III, "To Sir Robert Wroth," praises Wroth (1576–1614), who in 1604 married Lady Mary Sidney, daughter of Sir Robert Sidney, for his honest, hearty country life, away from the vices of the town and court.

IV, "To the World," is a dramatic monologue in which a gentlewoman, who has not been identified, declares her farewell to the false world.

V, "Song—To Celia," is a *carpe diem* song from *Volpone* (III. vii. 166–83), delivered when Volpone tries to seduce Corvino's virtuous wife Celia. The poem was inspired by Catullus.

VI, "To the Same," is another lyric addressed to Celia, asking for many kisses. Lines 19 to 22 appear in *Volpone* (III. vii. 236–39). Also inspired by Catullus.

VII, "Song—That Women Are But Men's Shadows," is an epigram that humorously compares women to men's shadows because when pursued, they flee, and when left, they follow. The song was adapted from a Latin poem by Barthemi Aneau. According to Drummond's *Conversations*, Jonson wrote the poem as a proof in verse of the idea of women being men's shadows, a notion which was in dispute between the Earl of Pembroke and his Lady and which Jonson was asked to settle.

VIII, "To Sickness," urges sickness and disease not to bother the best women, but to attack only men and corrupt women.

IX, "Song—To Celia," a love song addressed to Celia, is freely adapted from the *Epistles* of Philostratus. Commonly called "Drink to Me Only With Thine Eyes."

The tenth poem is untitled. In it the poet considers various mythological figures as possible Muses for his poem, dismisses them all, and decides that he will trust himself for inspiration. This poem and the next were first printed in an appendix (headed Praeludium) to Robert Chester's *Love's Martyr* (1601). The appendix also included poems by Marston, "Ignoto," Chapman, and Shakespeare, all on the theme of the Phoenix and the Turtledove, Platonic ideals for the perfect woman and the faithful man, respectively.

XI, "Epode," a long poem on morality, includes a passage based on the Renaissance psychology of morality, which held that ideally the senses would take perceptions to the heart, the home of the emotions, and from the heart perceptions would be referred to the tempering influence of the reason. The poem also praises genuine faithful love and argues that men may never sin without blame.

XII, "Epistle," is addressed to Elizabeth, Countess of Rutland (1584–1612), daughter of Sir Philip Sidney. Elizabeth married the Earl of Rutland in 1599. The poem laments the current power of gold and praises a love of poetry and the Muses as the countess's most ennobling attribute. The original conclusion of the poem was cancelled since it wished Elizabeth a son. Jonson learned, after writing the poem but before publishing it, that the Earl was impotent.

XIII, "Epistle," praises Katherine, Lady D'Aubigny (d. 1617), for her virtue as a woman and dedication as a wife. Katherine was the daughter of Sir Gervase Clifton. She married Lord Esmé, Seigneur D'Aubigny, in 1609.

XIV, "Ode," is addressed to Sir William Sidney (1590–1612), son of Sir Robert Sidney and grandson of Sir Philip. The poem was written on the occasion of William's twenty-first birthday and urges him to live virtuously and carry on the noble tradition of his heritage. Sir William was knighted in January 1611.

XV, "To Heaven," is one of Jonson's best religious poems. The persona admits to human sin and depravity but claims that his prayers are not inspired by discontent or weariness of life but rather by love of God.

For the Honor of Wales.

Performed: February 27, 1618.

Published: 1640 in folio by Thomas Walkley in the section of masques.

Printer: uncertain

This piece, written in part in a burlesque Welsh dialect, is actually a revised version of *Pleasure Reconciled to Virtue* with a new antimasque. The elaboration of the antimasque, which leads in Jonson's later masques to a lack of balance, begins with this work. On the whole, the audience ap-parently liked this piece better than *Pleasure Reconciled to Virtue*, but some thought the work was in poor taste, the Welsh setting suggesting a satire on Wales.

The scene was the same as that for *Pleasure Reconciled to Virtue* except that the mountain was Craig-Eriry instead of Atlas. Three Welsh gentlemen entered: Griffith, Jenkin, and Evan—an attorney. Although Griffith warned that one should always be polite in the presence of the king, Jenkin spoke very critically of the setting and characters in *Pleasure Reconciled to Virtue*, and he was unhappy about the role the Prince of Wales had been assigned in the work. Jenkin and Evan argued that it would have been more appropriate for the Prince of Wales to have had a Welsh setting and that the mountain should have been Craig-Eriry instead of Atlas. A quarrel developed between Howell and Rheese, who had been waiting outside. They came in, settled the disturbance, and asked if any of them had told the king about their suggested alterations in the masque, and in turn they each explained that the work should have been completely Welsh in every respect—for the honor of Wales—as they hoped to show.

To the sound of music two women entered and blessed the king, after which six stanzas of a song were offered, lauding various appropriate Welsh delights. After-wards there followed two Welsh dances. Jenkin then praised the dancers as being better than the pygmies of *Pleasure Reconciled* and promised an even more dazzling performance from the dancing Welsh goats, who are natural dancers and who would be superior to the dancing bottles of *Pleasure Reconciled*. After the dance of the goats, the women again sang in praise of the king and his family, after which the men and women all danced together. The work concluded with several speeches by Jenkin, Evan, and Griffith, all extolling the virtues of the king, insisting that pleasure could also come from Wales, and assuring the sovereign of the loyalty and prosperity of the Welsh under his just and gracious rule.

Fortesque, George, prefixed verses to Sir John Beaumont's *Bosworth-Field* (1629), Sir Thomas Hawkins's translation of *Odes of Horace* (1635), and J. A. Rivers's *Devout Rhapsodies* (1648). He contributed an elegy ("I parled once with death, and thought to yield") to *Jonsonus Virbius*.

Formal, Roger. See PETO.

Fortunate Islands. Traditionally, islands to which the souls of the blessed were transported, but Jonson uses the term to refer to England.

Fortunate Isles, and Their Union, The.

Performed: January 9, 1625.

Published: 1625 in quarto (no imprint). Reprinted in 1640 folio by Thomas Walkley in section of masques.

Printer: unknown.

A remodeled version of *Neptune's Triumph for the Return of Albion*, this masque was originally designed for presentation on Twelfth Night of 1625, as the title page of the quarto indicates, but, because of the king's ill health, it was postponed until January 9, 1625.

When the king was seated, Johphiel, an aery spirit and an Intelligence of Jupiter's sphere, ran in. On his bright yellow hair he wore a chaplet of flowers. His wings and clothes were light silks of various colors, and he wore blue silk stockings, pumps, and gloves and carried a silver fan. He announced that he had come from the sphere of Love "To wish good night / To your delight." A melancholy student named Mere-Fool, dressed in bare and worn clothes, entered and uttered a sigh. Surprised, Johphiel asked what kind of creature Mere-Fool was. He replied that he was a notary of the Rosicrucians and felt he had been abandoned by them because he had not seen any of the signs they had promised he would even though he had followed their detailed and rigorous requirements. Deciding to engage in a little sport with Mere-Fool, Johphiel promised that Mere-Fool would indeed see what he was seeking because Johphiel himself had been sent to Mere-Fool by Father Outis (nobody) and was to assure him that the brethren recognized his faithfulness and would duly reward him for it. Johphiel explained to Mere-Fool that so esteemed by the brethren was he that they expected him to become their new leader in the upper region since the former leader had died and left his legacy to Mere-Fool. When Mere-Fool asked how he was to assume power, Johphiel indicated that Mere-Fool would do so by inheriting the former leader's skill, which he had left Mere-Fool in a pot, and Johphiel presented Mere-Fool with the pot and rose as a sign of the transfer of power. Johphiel further noted that although Mere-Fool would have power he would remain poor but that Johphiel himself had the power to fulfill Mere-Fool's present wishes—

especially to see whatever ideas, spirits, or atoms he would like to see in the air. Mere-Fool then gave a list of people he would like to see, ranging from Zoroaster to Hermes Trismegistus, and Johphiel told him that he would see all of them in due course, but, in the meantime, he personally thought Mere-Fool should ask to see Scogan and Skelton. Somewhat astounded, Mere-Fool asked who they were, and Johphiel informed him that Scogan was a fine gentleman of the time of Henry IV who wrote in "ballad-royall" and that Skelton was the "worshipful *Poet* Laureat to King Harry."

Johphiel summoned Scogan and Skelton, and they appeared dressed in the habit of their day. Johphiel explained to them that Mere-Fool wished to see a famous person restored. In rhyme, Scogan and Skelton responded that Mere-Fool should by all means see the following: Howleglass, four knaves, Elinor Rumming, Fitz-Ale, Vapors, Marie Ambree, Long-Meg of Westminster, Tom Thumb, and Doctor Ratt. Johphiel agreed, and all of the above appeared and performed an antimasque and then vanished. Afterwards, Mere-Fool was disappointed that they had vanished so suddenly but expressed his gratitude for the grace the company of the Rosicrucians had extended him. Johphiel scorned Mere-Fool by explaining that what had been done in the antimasque was actually performed by the company of players, not the company of the Rosicrucians, and he declared that Mere-Fool would always be exactly what his name implied.

Johphiel then asked the king's pardon for the diversion and proclaimed the message of the Fates and Jove that the time had come when the Fortunate Isles should be united. To that end, Macaria (blessed), who heretofore had floated on the seas uncertain of her destination, had been instructed to attach herself that very night to Britannia and pay homage to Neptune. The scene then opened to disclose the masquers seated on Macaria's island. As the island moved toward the shore, Apollo and Harmony provided music while Proteus sat below. A song exhorting Macaria to dwell forever on Neptune's isles was offered. When the island had joined itself to the shore, Proteus, Portunus, and Saron approached the king while the masquers disembarked and prepared for their dance. Proteus, Portunus, and Saron offered a series of speeches lauding the glory of Neptune and his isles, after which the island withdrew and the masquers danced their entrance as the chorus called for a triumphant celebration.

To the accompaniment of loud music, the first perspective—the Palace of Oceanus—was discovered and the measures followed, after which the second perspective—the Sea—was shown, and Johphiel invited all to view the wonders of the deep. Proteus, Protunus, and Saron then approached the ladies of the audience and implored them to dance, and the revels ensued. When they were finished, Neptune's fleet appeared, ready to take the riches of the ocean home. In song Proteus, Portunus, and Saron each respectfully asked the king to excuse them so that they might return to their various charges. The chorus offered a final song in praise of the king, and the last dance was performed.

Fortune. In mythology, the Roman goddess Fortuna, identified in classical times with the Greek goddess Tyche, who was associated with chance and the acceptance of one's lot.

Fountains. Nymphs who appear in *Chloridia* and help to celebrate the glory of Chloris.

Foxe, John (1516–1587), was for a time tutor in the family of the Lucys. During the reign of Mary he lived in Germany, where he finished the Latin edition of his book of *Martyrs,* an account of the martyrs of the Christian church with particular reference to the Protestant martyrs of Foxe's own time. Upon his return to England, Foxe served as translator and editor for John Day, who in 1563 printed Foxe's *Acts and Monuments,* known as the *Book of the Martyrs.* Jonson alludes to the *Acts and Monuments* in several of his plays, specifically in *Every Man out of His Humor* (III. viii), *Epicoene* (I. ii), and *Eastward Ho* (V. ii).

Frampul, Lord. See GOODSTOCK.

Frampul, Lady Frances. In *The New Inn,* the supposed only daughter of Lord Frampul who eventually marries Lovel.

Francis. A character who appears in *The Gypsies Metamorphosed* and discovers that the gypsies have picked his pockets.

Francis (Fraunce), Abraham. Minor English poet of Jonson's day. In the *Conversations* (ll. 53–54), Drummond records that Jonson thought Francis a fool to write English hexameters.

Franciscina. The servant maid, a stock character of the *commedia dell'arte,* referred to by Corvino in *Volpone* (II) when he is accusing his wife, Celia, of being forward.

Francklin. An apothecary who supplied poisons for Overbury's murder and was executed in 1615. In Jonson's *The Devil Is an Ass* (I. ii), Fitzdottrel alludes to him as one who is unable to make the devil appear to man.

Frank. In *The New Inn,* the supposed son of Goodstock who turns out to be not a boy but a Lady and the daughter of Goodstock or Lord Frampul. Frank's real name is Laetitia, and in the play she eventually marries Lord Beaufort.

Fret. A character in *Love's Welcome at Bolsover* who appears as a plasterer in Colonel Vitruvius' dance of the mechanics.

Frisker. A "zany" actor in *Poetaster* (III. iv), whom Tucca invites Histrio to bring to dinner at his house. He has been alternately identified as a cariacature of William Sly or Armin, actors contemporary with Jonson.

Frost, John. An actor who played in *Cynthia's Revels* in 1601 as one of the Children of the Chapel.

Fuller, Thomas (1608–1661). English clergyman and author. He was an able preacher, a noted wit, and a royalist during the Civil War and Commonwealth. His most famous work was *The Histories of the Worthies of England* (1662), an invaluable collection of antiquarian information.

In a section on Westminster in *The Worthies,* Fuller records that Jonson was born in Westminister and when a child lived in Hart's-Horn-Lane near Charing-Cross; that Jonson's mother took a bricklayer for her second husband; that Jonson was first schooled in a private school in St. Martin's Church, then in Westminster School, and eventually was statutably admitted to St. John's College, Cambridge, where he continued for but a short period of time because of insufficient funding; that he returned to the trade of his father-in-law and helped in the building of the new structure of Lincoln's Inn, "when having a trowel in his hand he had a book in his pocket." Fuller also reported that Jonson had an elaborate wit and would remain silent in learned company and observe the several humors surrounding him; that his great skill was in the art of dramatic poetry; and that he taught the stage conformity to the laws of comedy. According to Fuller, Jonson's comedies were generally above the common people and were not at first well appreciated although upon the second reading they emerge as very meritorious. Fuller thought that the later plays were not as good as the earlier ones and speculated that the difference was probably due to old age. He mentions that none of Jonson's children survived him and that when Jonson died, he was buried near the base of the belfry in the Abbey church at Westminster. In the section on Warwickshire, Fuller records that there were many wit combats between Jonson and Shakespeare and that Jonson, although a man of greater learning, was usually outmaneuvered by Shakespeare's quickness of wit and invention.

Fulvia. In *Catiline,* an expensive and extravagant courtesan who assists Cicero in putting down Catiline's conspiracy to seize power in Rome.

Fulvius. In *Catiline,* one of the conspirators who supports Catiline's abortive attempt to seize power in Rome.

Fungoso. In *Every Man out of His Humour,* a student who is the son of Sordido and who attempts to keep up with the fashion of his day and wants to be considered a gentleman.

Furies. See ERINYES.

G

Gabor, Bethlehem (d. 1630). Prince of Transylvania who allied himself with the Protestant union in order to help in the recovery of the Palatinate. He is mentioned in *The Staple of News* (III. ii).

Gainsford (Gainford), Thomas. Captain and news purveyor famous in his day for his militant journalism, who probably died about 1624. He is alluded to in *The Staple of News* (I. iv) and *Und.* XLIII.

Galatea. A sea nymph who was beloved by the Cyclops, Polyphemus.

Galen. Second-century physician and writer born of Greek parents in Pergamum. After study in Greece, Asia Minor, and Alexandria, Galen returned to Pergamum to serve as physician to the gladiatorial school. After about 162 A.D. he resided chiefly in Rome, where he was noted for his lectures and writings and became court physician to Marcus Aurelius. Credited with over five hundred treatises, mostly on medicine and philosophy, Galen correlated earlier medical knowledge with his own discoveries, which were based in part on dissection of animals, and systematized medicine in accord with his own theories of purposive creation. His authority was unchallenged until the sixteenth century, and his work in anatomy and physiology was especially esteemed. He demonstrated that arteries carry blood instead of air, and he contributed to the knowledge of the brain, nerves, spinal cord, and pulse. Building on Hippocrates, he developed an influential theory of body humors and expounded his theory in *Of Temperaments.*

Jonson made sparse direct use of Galen although he was greatly influenced by him indirectly in his theory of humor comedy. Galen was one of the sources for *Oberon.* In the mountebank scene in *Volpone* (II. ii), Volpone claims that Galen would not have had to write so much if he had known of Volpone's oil. In *The Alchemist* (II. iii), Face proclaims that Subtle completely disregards Galen's traditional animal and vegetable drugs in favor of chemical ones.

Galileo Galilei (1564–1642), the great Italian astronomer, mathematician, and physicist, began his studies in medicine but soon turned to mathematics and physics at the University of Pisa, where he later (1589–92) served as professor and initiated experiments on the laws of bodies in motion which produced results so contrary to Aristotle that strong antagonism was aroused. In 1592 he began lecturing on mathematics at the University of Padua, where he remained until 1610. While there he constructed the first complete astronomical telescope in 1609; studied the moon, the Milky Way, Venus, and spots on the sun; and discovered three satellites of Jupiter. In 1610, he went to Florence as philosopher and mathematician to Cosimo II de'Medici and mathematician at the University of Pisa. In 1611 he visited the papal court to display the telescope, and in 1613 he published a work on sunspots in which he openly declared his acceptance of the Copernican system of the universe. Three years later the Copernician system was declared dangerous to faith and Galileo was called to Rome and warned not to teach it, but in 1632 he published another work supporting the Copernican view. Galileo was again summoned to Rome, tried by the Inquisition in 1633, and forced to abjure his beliefs and writings on this subject. After an indefinite period of imprisonment and enforced residence in Siena, he was allowed to live in seclusion at Arcetri near Florence, where he continued his scientific studies until his death in 1642. His last book, primarily devoted to physics, was published in 1638. Jonson makes one reference to Galileo, a jest about his burning glass in *The Staple of News* (III. ii).

Galla. In *Catiline,* a companion to the strumpet Fulvia.

galliard. A gay, lively dance with five steps to a phrase. The dance was popular in the sixteenth and early seventeenth centuries, and was often used during or at the end of Jonson's masques.

Gallus, Asinus. Noble Roman senator in *Sejanus,* feared and hated by Sejanus and Tiberius because of his ties to Agrippina. He joins Arruntius in mocking Tiberius' crafty speech to the Senate praising Sejanus, and seems to remain loyal to the noble Romans despite Arruntius' comment that he is working against Silius. He and Agrippina have a minor quarrel when he advises her to play along with Sejanus, but it is mended when news comes of how Sejanus saved Tiberius' life. Late in the play, Sejanus comments that he has "grub'd up" Gallus, along with many other followers of Agrippina.

Gallus, Cor. A gallant in *Poetaster,* who writes poetry and is a friend of Ovid's. Ovid senior criticizes him for his interest in poetry, but says that he is a gentleman. Cytheris is his love, and he meets her at Albius' house. He is good-natured, entreating both Crispinus and Hermogenes to sing. He plays Apollo at Ovid's masquerade. He addresses the guests at the banquet; Crispinus echoes him. Caesar upbraids him with the others when he enters the masquerade, but Gallus is pardoned because he is a gentleman. He praises Virgil to Caesar, and listens happily to the *Aeneid.* He is given permission by Caesar, with the other true poets, to try to punish the Poetasters. He helps Horace purge Crispinus. Unlike several of the other characters in *Poetaster,* he is not a caricature of one of Jonson's contemporaries.

Gamboll. A character dressed like a tumbler who appears as one of the children of Christmas in *Christmas, His Masque.*

Gamelia. A symbolic character who appears in *Hymenaei* as one of the powers of Juno.

Ganymede. Son of Tros, who was taken to Olympus by the gods or Zeus to be the gods' cupbearer because of his extraordinary beauty.

Gardiner, Stephen (1493?–1555). English prelate educated at Cambridge. He was appointed secretary to Thomas (later Cardinal) Wolsey, gained Henry VIII's favor by helping him divorce Katharine of Aragon, was made bishop of Winchester in 1531, and in 1535 published *De vera obedientia,* justifying royal supremacy in ecclesiastical affairs. After the accession of Edward VI, he was deprived of his bishopric and put in the Tower for five years, but when Mary came to the throne he was restored to power and made Lord High Chancellor. Gardiner was always controversial, being condemned by Catholics for his support of royal supremacy and by Protestants for his opposition to certain Reformation principles. Jonson lists him in *Timber* (l. 903) among those admirable in wit for their times.

Gargantua. The hero of a folktale well-known in the sixteenth century which is mentioned by Downright in *Every Man in* (1616 folio version, II. ii).

Gargaphie. The place where Actaeon was torn to pieces by his own hounds.

Garrard, George. Son of Sir William Garrard of Dorney. He was elected a fellow of Merton College, Oxford, in 1598 and master of Sutton's Hospital, the Charterhouse, in 1627. He was an intimate friend and correspondent of John Donne's. In 1609 Jonson apparently sent Garrard, whom he addresses as "my right worthy friend," an epitaph ("Stay, view this stone: and if thou beest not such," one of his uncollected poems) on Cecilia Bulstrode, the "court pucell" he so caustically satirized in *Und.* XLIX.

Garrick, David (1717–1779). English actor, manager, and dramatist. He was the greatest actor of the eighteenth-century English stage, and his friendship with other famous men like Dr. Johnson, Diderot, and Goldsmith resulted in detailed records of his life. In the coffeehouses of London, Garrick met the actors associated with Covent Garden, and after some work in the provinces he made his formal debut in 1742 as Richard III and was an immediate success. Noted for his versatility, he played contemporary dramatic roles as well as Shakespearean ones, and he was especially praised for his portrayal of King Lear. His straightforward style and diction swept the declamatory school from the stage. From 1747 until his retirement in 1776, he was the manager of Drury Lane, where he instituted many reforms. Some of these included concealing stage lighting from the audience and discontinuing the practice of having spectators sit on the stage. Besides training actors for his company, Garrick adapted many plays, composed prologues and epilogues, and wrote quite a few plays of his own. Reynolds, Hogarth, and Gainsborough painted portraits of him. He is buried in Westminster Abbey. In 1831 the Garrick Club for distinguished actors was established in London.

Garrick produced several of Jonson's plays. In 1751 he produced *Eastward Ho* and *Every Man in*, in which he played Kitely. His acting version of *Every Man in* was published the following year. He produced *Epicoene* in 1752 and 1776, and he had planned to do *Volpone* in 1757 but abandoned the project. Garrick was much celebrated for his production of *The Alchemist* and for his acting in the role of Drugger. He produced and acted in this play a couple of times a year from 1743 until his retirement in 1776.

Gasper. The name given Camillo Ferneze after he was found during a battle at Vicenza by Lord Chamont's father in *The Case Is Altered*. His real identity is not discovered by anyone, including him, until late in the play. See Camillo FERNEZE.

Gazer, Mistress. In *Eastward Ho*, one of the ladies who excitedly watches Gertrude depart in the coach which is to take her from the city to Sir Petronel Flash's castle in the country.

Geber. The most celebrated of the Arabian alchemists. He was a physician who lived during the eighth century. Many works on alchemy have been attributed to him, some of doubtful authenticity. These works influenced the development of medieval alchemy, indicated the use of laboratory experiments, and perpetuated the theory that metals are composed of sulfur and mercury and can be transmuted into gold. Jonson mentions Geber in *Mercury Vindicated*, and in *The Alchemist* (II. v) he quotes from one of Geber's most famous works, *Summa Perfectionis Magisterii in sua natura*.

Gelaia. A young woman dressed like a boy, who acts as page to Anaides in *Cynthia's Revels*. There is indication in the play that she is also his mistress. She complains when Anaides insults her, but does nothing really significant in the play. She is crit-icized by Cynthia and sentenced to march, weep, and sing the palinode with the other courtiers for punishment.

Gellius, Aulus. Roman writer of the second century who was a lawyer. He spent a year in Athens and wrote *Noctes Atticae*, a collection of commentary on law, antiquities, and various other subjects which is primarily valuable as a source of quotations from lost works. Jonson quotes from this work extensively in *Timber* (ll. 330–87), and he used it as one of his sources for the portrait of Artemisia in the *Masque of Queens*. According to Aubrey's notes, Jonson's studying chair looked like the one Gellius was usually portrayed working in.

Genius. In classical times, an attendant spirit.

George-a-Green. Huisher of the Bower, or master of Robin Hood's dogs and other animals in *The Sad Shepherd*. He carves the table for the feast from the "greene sword" and helps plan the feast. He mourns at Aeglamour's sad news of Earine's drowning. He is one of the witch hunters who goes to catch Maudlin.

Germanicus. Germanicus Julius Caesar lived from 15 B.C. until A.D. 19. He was in line to succeed Augustus and became popular early in his life as a soldier. He was made commander-in-chief of the Gallic and Germanic provinces. Although he never moved against Tiberius, he was disliked and feared by him for his popular affability and his republican sentiments. He offended Tiberius by traveling to Egypt (which Augustus had forbidden to senators), and quarreled bitterly with Piso. He married Agrippina, and was an eloquent scholar as well as a celebrated military man, writing comedies in Greek, Greek and Latin epigrams, and a Latin translation of a book by Aratus about natural phenomena. He fell mysteriously ill and died, reputedly of poison, at Antioch. His name appears often in *Sejanus*, for he is the very type of the wise, upright, and noble man to his wife, children, and friends and an inspiring presence feared by Sejanus and Tiberius.

Germinatio. A figure in *The Masque of Beauty* who represents one of the elements of beauty.

Gertrude. In *Eastward Ho*, Touchstone's immodest daughter, who aspires to be a lady. She marries Sir Petronel Flash, has her dowry filched by her husband, is estranged from her father, and becomes destitute, but is finally reconciled with both Touchstone and her husband.

Gesta Grayorum. The records of Gray's Inn. Since masques and revels were an ancient custom of the Inns of Court, particularly of Gray's and the Inner Temple, the *Gesta Grayorum*, first printed in 1688, contains contemporary accounts of masques and revels which give us an important insight into the development of these entertainments.

Giants. A mythological race of great strength and size who were valiant warriors although they were defeated in a war against the gods.

Gifford, William (1756–1826). Author, classical scholar, satirist, and editor. He edited the works of Philip Massinger (1805; 1813), John Ford (1827), and Jonson (1816). His edition of Jonson was published in nine volumes and marked a distinct advance over all previous ones. Gifford collated quartos and folios, modernized the text, glossed Jonson's classical borrowings, and attempted to vindicate Jonson from the charge of being an enemy of Shakespeare's. Although Gifford adopted the critical method of his day to pick and choose between quarto and folio readings, his edition served as the standard critical one for over a century and was reprinted in several revised versions by Francis Cunningham.

Gilbert, Allan H. (1888–   ). American scholar, since 1957 Professor Emeritus of English at Duke University. Author of numerous studies on literary criticism and Renaissance literature, including the useful *The Symbolic Persons in the Masques of Ben Jonson* (1948).

Giles, Thomas. In 1610 a dance master, servant to Prince Henry. Jonson acknowledges Giles as the inventor of dances for The *Masque of Beauty, Hymenaei, The Haddington Masque,* and *The Masque of Queens.* Giles also danced in *Oberon.*

Gill, Alexander (the elder) (1565–1635). High Master of St. Paul's School. He was Milton's schoolmaster, and his *Logonomia Anglica* (1619) was used by Jonson as one of his authorities for *The English Grammar*. In *Time Vindicated,* Jonson also alluded to Gill as the schoolmaster who "Is turning all his works too, into Latin, / To pure Satyric Latin. . . ."

Gill, Alexander (the younger). Son of the High Master of St. Paul's. In 1628 Gill was called before the Star Chamber for drinking the health of Felton, the assassin of the Duke of Buckingham, and speaking disrespectfully to the King. He was sentenced to degradation from the ministry, a fine, and loss of his ears. His father petitioned the King for mercy, and the sentence was not carried out, and he was pardoned in 1630. Gill satirized Jonson's *Magnetic Lady* in "Upon Ben Jonson's *Magnetic Lady*"; he was answered by Zouch Townly ("It cannot move thy friends firm Ben, that he") and by Jonson himself ("Shall the prosperity of a pardon still").

Gilthead, Thomas. A goldsmith in *The Devil Is an Ass,* who assists Meercraft, the projector.

Giraldi (Giraldus), Gregorio (1479–1552). An Italian scholar who summarized much of the mythological knowledge of European humanism. Jonson was greatly indebted to Giraldus' work in *The Entertainment at Highgate, The Masque of Blackness, The Masque of Beauty,* and *Hymenaei.*

Glaucus. A sea-god renowned for his prophecies.

Gloucester, Hugh le Despenser, married the eldest sister of Gilbert, Earl of Gloucester, who was killed at Bannockburn, and succeeded to a share of Gilbert's estate. He was sometimes incorrectly referred to as the Earl of Gloucester, who was actually Hugh's older brother Thomas. A supporter of Edward II, Hugh was executed by the barons in 1326, and Thomas was beheaded in 1400. In *The Devil Is an Ass* (II. iv), Hugh is called Spenser the younger.

Gloucester, Humphrey, Duke of (1391–1447), the youngest son of Henry IV, created Duke of Gloucester in 1414, protector during the minority of Henry VI, Duke Humphrey is mentioned in *The Devil Is an Ass* (II. iv) and *The Staple of News* (III. iii).

Gloucester, Thomas of Woodstock, Duke of, the youngest son of Edward III, was born in 1355, created Duke of Gloucester in 1385 by his nephew Richard II, and was murdered in 1397. He is mentioned in *The Devil Is an Ass* (II. iv).

Godelmannus, Johannes Georgius. Author of *De Magis, Veneficis, et Lamii* (1594), one of Jonson's authorities on witchcraft.

Godolphin, Sidney (1610–1643), was a devout royalist intimate with Falkland who contributed an elegy ("The Muses fairest light in no dark time") to *Jonsonus Virbius.* Godolphin was probably the author of

Und. LXXX. Godolphin fought for the king in the Civil War and was shot and killed in a skirmish at Chagford.

Golden Age. According to Hesiod and Ovid, that period of the world's history ruled by Cronus (Saturn) characterized by serenity, peace, and eternal spring. This age was followed by the Silver, ruled by Zeus and abounding in luxury; the Bronze, torn by strife; and the Iron, the present time, when justice and piety have fled.

Golden Age Restored, The.

Performed: January 6 and 8, 1615.

Published: 1616 in folio by William Stansby.

Printer: William Stansby.

After loud music, Pallas was discovered descending in her chariot to the accompaniment of softer music. She announced that since Jove could no longer endure the current condition of mankind he had decided to return Astraea (justice) and the Golden Age to earth. During her statement Pallas was interrupted by the sound of clashing arms, signaling the preparation of the Iron Age for battle to resist the return of the Golden Age, and she proclaimed that she would protect herself and frustrate the resistance with her shield. The Iron Age appeared and called forth his evils—Avarice, Fraud, Slander, Ambition, Pride, Scorn, Force, Rapine, Treachery, Folly, and Ignorance—and tried to rally them for combat, after which they danced to the confusion of martial music. Showing her shield, Pallas reappeared, scorned the weakness of the Iron Age and his evils, and banished them from the earth. They immediately disappeared.

Pallas then invoked Astraea and the Golden Age to return to power, and they descended and were welcomed. But Astraea and the Golden Age queried how they should reign on earth without a train, and Pallas assured them that Jove would provide for their support, and she summoned the Poets, who descended, proclaiming that Pallas was their best inspiration and that they would rekindle the light of the Golden Age. Throwing lightning from her shield, Pallas caused the darkness to yield, and a scene of light was discovered, and Astraea, the Golden Age, the Poets, and Pallas all celebrated the increase of peace, love, faith, and joy and the decrease of strife, hate, fear, and pain on earth, after which the first dance was performed. Afterwards, Astraea, Golden Age, Pallas, and the choir lauded the restoration

of nature in the new age, and the main dance followed; however, Pallas declared that even more had to be done to restore the true liberty of the previous Golden Age. In response, the Poets praised the harmony wrought by genuine love, and a dance with the ladies ensued. Ascending, Pallas reminded all that they should insure through their own lives that the flame of love and harmony would ever shine bright and make immortal the age of gold, and the choir lauded Jove with all the honor thankful hearts could give. Astraea expressed her delight in the change that had occurred in which Jove's presence had made a heaven on earth, and she proclaimed the earth to be her region where she would now gladly reside in the age of gold and "The law to mortals give." There followed galliards and corantos.

golden chain. In classical literature, a chain connecting heaven and earth.

Golden Fleece. In Greek mythology, the magic fleece of the winged ram that saved Phrixus and Helle from Ino. The fleece was sought by Jason and the Argonauts.

Golding. In *Eastward Ho*, the conscientious and loyal apprentice of the goldsmith Touchstone. He marries Mildred, Touchstone's modest daughter, becomes a deputy alderman, and eventually intercedes on behalf of Sir Petronel Flash, Quicksilver, and Security, who have been imprisoned for unscrupulous behavior.

Gondomar, Count. Diego Sarmiento de Acuña, Conde de Gondomar (1567?–1626), was the Spanish ambassador to England from 1613 to 1618 and 1620 to 1622. He had great influence over James I; he dissuaded the king from giving assistance to Frederick the Winter King at the outset of the Thirty Years War, and demanded the execution of Sir Walter Raleigh. Highly unpopular in England, Gondomar was attacked in Middleton's *A Game at Chess*, discussed in Jonson's *The Staple of News* (III. ii), and mentioned in *Und.* XLIV.

Goodfellow, Robin. The famous spirit from folklore who appears at court as a character in *Love Restored* and hopes to see the revels, but finds himself exposing Plutus, who has disguised himself as Cupid, and finally introduces the real Cupid to the audience.

Goodstock. In *The New Inn*, the host of the Inn who is actually Lord Frampul in disguise. He is the father of Frances and Laetitia.

Goodwin, William. Dean of Christ Church and Vice-Chancellor of Oxford in 1619 when Jonson received an honorary M.A. from the University.

Goodyere, Sir Henry (d. 1628), gentleman of the privy chamber to James I and an intimate friend of John Donne's, was knighted in 1599. He was a minor poet and prefixed verses to Coryat's *Crudities* (1611), Sylvester's *Lacrymae Lachrymarum* (1613), and wrote a number of other poems. Jonson recognized Goodyere's interest in hawking in *Epig.* LXXXV and praised his choice of books and friends in *Epig.* LXXXVI. Goodyere tilted in the *Barriers* of 1606.

Goose (Gosling). A showman named Gosling who is alluded to in *The New Inn* (I. v).

Gorgon. Phorcys, a sea god, the son of Pontus and Gaea, married his sister Ceto, and she bore a brood of monsters, including the Gorgons, the Graeae, Scylla, and the Sirens. The Gorgons were horrifying creatures with claws, frightening teeth, and serpents for hair.

Gower, John (1330?–1408). English poet. Chaucer, a contemporary of Gower's, called him "moral Gower." In the sixteenth and seventeenth centuries he and Chaucer were frequently cited together as masters of English poetry. Each of Gower's three major works, all characterized by metrical smoothness and moral criticism, was written in a different language. *Miroir de l'omme* (c. 1381, in French) is an allegorical manual of the vices and virtues; *Vox Clamantis* (c. 1381, in Latin) condemns the Peasants' Revolt and the baseness of all classes of society; *Confessio Amantis* (c. 1390, in English), Gower's masterpiece, is a collection of stories illustrating the Seven Deadly Sins. In *Timber* (ll. 1799–1802), Jonson warns not to let students taste Gower or Chaucer first lest they fall in love with antiquity. In *The Golden Age Restored*, Gower is portrayed as one of the old English poets who is a protagonist of the Golden Age restored, and in *The English Grammar* Jonson quotes from the *Confessio Amantis* twenty-nine times.

Grace. A symbolic character in *The Vision of Delight* who has no speaking part but accompanies Delight at the opening of the masque.

Graces. In Greek mythology, daughters of Zeus, usually three—Aglaia, Thalia, and Euphrosyne—who were exceptionally beautiful and were often associated with the Hours, the Muses, and Venus. The Graces appear in *Love Freed From Ignorance and Folly* as daughters of the morning and journey to the West to admire Phoebus, the sun god.

grammar. Jonson's interest in grammar is attested to not only by his publication of *The English Grammar* but also by at least two documents that have survived. In 1628 Joseph Webbe, M.D., wrote to Jonson asking his opinion of Webbe's latest book, which was entitled *Usus et Authoritas, Id est, Liber Loquens, Feliciter Incipit* (1626). Webbe's previous works included *An Appeal to Truth In The Controversy Between Art and Use* (1622) and *A Petition to the High Court of Parliament in Behalf of Ancient and Authentic Authors* (1623). Jonson's answer to Webbe's request has not survived. There is also extant a copy of a note to Mr. Caleb Morley, Master of Arts and sometime fellow of Balliol College, which indicates support for Morley's labors in "a Speedy and Certain Course for the attaining and retaining of languages and other parts of good literature proposed for the general ease and benefit of the studious in either kind" and which is signed by Jonson and several other individuals.

In the *Conversations* (ll. 617–21), Drummond records that Jonson raised some questions about the use of *they, them, those,* and *that,* and he also argued that *flouds* and *hills* should be masculine. See also James HOWELL; William WOTTON.

Gray, Philip. The unidentified subject of the sixteenth poem in Jonson's *Underwood.* Gray may have been the eldest son of Sir Edward Gray of Morpeth Castle. Philip entered Gray's Inn in 1598 and probably died in 1626.

Greene, Robert (1558?–1592). English writer whose short romances, written in the manner of Lyly's *Euphues,* replaced Sidney's *Arcadia* in popularity. His best plays, *Friar Bacon and Friar Bungay* (1594) and *The Scottish History of James IV* (1598), are a mixture of romance, fantasy, and history. His numerous tracts and pamphlets show both his acquaintance with the London underworld and his own unconventional way of life. *A Quip for an Upstart Courtier* (1592), a social allegory, is considered his best pamphlet, but his best known one is the *Groatsworth of Wit* (1592) because of its alleged attack on Shakespeare—one of the earliest printed references to the bard. Greene died in dire poverty. In *Every Man out* (II. iii), Carlo alludes to Greene's works, implying that they are little read, and *Groatsworth of Wit* is discussed in *Epicoene* (IV. iv).

Gresham, Edward. Noted almanac-maker and astrologer who was an agent of the Overbury murderers. He was also suspected of having had a hand in the Gunpowder Plot. In Jonson's *The Devil Is an Ass* (I. ii), Fitzdottrel alludes to Gresham as one who is unable to show man the devil.

Gresham, Sir Thomas (1519–1579). English merchant and financier. As royal financial agent in Antwerp after 1551 he was very effective, but some considered his methods to be frequently unethical. After the accession of Elizabeth, he lived in London but often went on diplomatic and financial missions. He accumulated a great private fortune, helped form the Royal Exchange, and endowed Gresham College in London. He is referred to as "grave Gresham" in *Eastward Ho* (IV. ii).

Griffith. A Welshman who appears in *For the Honor of Wales* and urges his companions to be circumspect before the king but also argues that a masque in which the Prince of Wales performs should have a Welsh setting.

Grisel. In *A Tale of a Tub*, one of the bridesmaids for Audrey's intended marriage to John Clay.

Groom of the Revels. A groom of the Revels appears in *The Masque of Augurs* and is very skeptical about the ability of a group of common laborers who want to present before the court a masque which they have devised and now want to perform.

Gryse, Sir Robert. Knighted on August 16, 1628, Sir Robert issued the same year a translation of *Argenis* (See John BARCLAY), which was published by the command of King Charles. In the *Conversations* (ll. 570–72), Jonson claimed that Sir Robert told the King an anecdote about a man, who, "being consumed," occupied his wife with a dildo and she never knew it until she discovered it one day when he had carelessly neglected to put it away.

Guarini, Giovanni Battista (1537–1612), wrote the famous pastoral *Pastor Fido* (1590), which was translated into English by Dymock in 1602. The work was considered a masterpiece of diction and had a great influence on pastoral style. In the *Conversations* (ll. 64–65; 611–13), Drummond records that Jonson thought Guarini did not keep decorum in his *Pastor Fido* because he made shepherds speak as well as he could. Lady Politic mentions Guarini to Volpone (III. iv) when she is trying to impress him.

Guenevere, Queen. Queen of the legendary King Arthur. Her illicit love for Sir Launcelot supposedly foreshadowed the downfall of Arthur's kingdom. She is mentioned in this connection in *Every Man out* (II. iii).

Giuliano (Downright). Older brother to Prospero (Wellbred), brother to Biancha (Dame Kitely) and Hesperida (Bridget) in the 1601 quarto version of *Every Man in His Humour* (names used in the 1616 folio version are in parentheses). (Downright is described as "a plaine Squier"; his name echoes the title of an old song, "A Downright Squire".) He is quarrelsome and straightlaced, hating poetry and being disgusted by the conduct of Prospero (Wellbred) and his friends, who he feels are dissolute. He scolds Biancha (Dame Kitely) for not preventing Prospero (Wellbred) and his friends from entering Thorello's (Kitely's) house, and mocks Matheo's (Matthew's) poetry before he even knows that it is bad. He insults his brother and his companions and threatens to fight his brother, but is prevented from doing so. When questioned by Thorello (Kitely), he asserts that his brother was responsible for the fight. When he meets Bobadilla later, he angrily challenges him to fight, and beats Bobadilla easily, since Bobadilla is afraid to draw. He goes off, forgetting his cloak, which Stephano (Stephen) picks up. Bobadilla and Matheo (Matthew) have Musca (Brainworm) arrest Giuliano (Downright) but he accuses Stephano (Stephen) of stealing his cloak and has him arrested, too. They go before Clement, who reveals that Musca (Brainworm) had no real warrant for Giuliano's (Downright's) arrest. At Clement's urging, he is reconciled to Prospero and goes to dinner with the others (he goes to dinner with the others, although he does not have a dramatized reconciliation with Wellbred).

Gyges. A shepherd who descended into a chasm in the earth and discovered a corpse wearing a golden ring that could make one invisible. Gyges later used this knowledge to murder the Gydian king and to succeed him on the throne.

Gypsies. Five gypsies appear in *The Gypsies Metamorphosed*, tell the fortunes of the nobility present, pick the pockets of some clowns and wenches, and finally are transformed into loyal admirers of the king and his virtues.

Gypsies Metamorphosed, The.
Performed: August 3; August 5; September, 1621.

116

Published: 1640 in a duodecimo entitled *Q. Horatius Flaccus: His Art of Poetry. Englished by Ben Jonson. With other Works of the Author, Never Printed Before.* Published by John Benson.

Printer: John Okes.

One of the longest and most popular of Jonson's masques, this work was performed three times in 1621 with several of the nobility (notably the Duke of Buckingham) playing some of the roles. It was given at Burley-on-the-Hill on August 3, at Belvoir on August 5, and finally at Windsor in a revised version sometime in early September.

At the entrance of the king at Burley, a speech of welcome was offered. At Windsor a prologue was given, noting that since the king had seen the work before, the performers would strive to make him merry and not weary.

A gypsy leading a horse loaded with five children entered, followed by another gypsy with a horse carrying stolen goods. The first gypsy, called the Jackman (actually the Jarkman), delivered a long speech proclaiming the children the five princes of Egypt and explaining that one of them was actually the offspring of the daughter of a justice and a relative of the gypsies' Captain. The second gypsy declared that the gypsy band hoped to fatten up their captured game when they found an appropriate spot. The Jarkman indicated that throughout their speeches the gypsies would be obscure about their intentions or purpose, but that anyone armed in canting might understand them. While the Jarkman played his guitar, the Captain of the gypsies and his followers danced their entrance. Afterwards the Jarkman sang a song describing the life of the gypsies and suggesting that the gypsies could perform a sleight of hand which would so please the audience that they could endure the gypsies' tawny faces and that the gypsies could accurately tell the fortunes of those present.

In a long speech the Patrico, or hedge-priest, urged the Captain and the other gypsies to forget their usual activities and to engage in good sport by attempting to turn the audience all into gypsies, and one of the other gypsies seconded this idea, which the Captain agreed to consider while the gypsies danced and sang. Following the singing, the Captain decided to tell the fortunes of some of those present. He began with the King, stressing the sovereign's love of peace and his ability to shape the fortunes of his subjects and even of the gypsies. Between dances the gypsies then told the fortunes of the Prince and the following ladies: Marquess of Buckingham, Countess of Rutland, Countess of Exeter, Countess of Buckingham, Lady Purbeck, and Lady Elizabeth Hatton. When the masque was performed at Windsor, in place of the ladies the fortunes of the following lords were given: the Lord Keeper, the Lord Treasurer, the Lord of the Privy Seal, the Earl Marshal, the Lord Steward, the Lord Marquis Hamilton, the Earl of Bruccleuch, and the Lord Chamberlain.

In song the Jackman and the Patrico summoned the clowns: Cockrell, Clod, Townshead, and Puppy. The clowns entered, became fascinated with the gypsies, and called forth a band of local musicians to play. With some local wenches, including Prudence, Meg, and Christian, they performed a country dance for the gypsies. Afterwards the gypsies offered to tell the fortunes of the clowns and wenches, and they eagerly accepted. When the fortunes were finished, the gypsies suddenly disappeared, and the clowns and wenches all discovered, much to their dismay, that their pockets had been picked. After the clowns had quibbled with each other for a while over their losses, the Patrico reappeared and assured them that everything would turn out for the best, and he proceeded to tell each one where his belongings might be found. The clowns were very impressed with the Patrico's restorative power, and they expressed a desire to know more about the gypsies, especially how came the Captain's "place firste to be called the *Devills arse.*" In response, the Patrico summoned his clerk, who delivered a long song entitled "Cock-Lorell" (the name of the first lord of the gypsies) which explained in detail the answer. After the song, the clowns were so inspired by the gypsies that they asked to join them. The Patrico then enumerated the criteria and the abilities they would have to acquire before they could become true gypsies, and afterwards the clowns expressed their great admiration for the Patrico and his abilities. The Patrico promised that he would demonstrate for them his greatest skill by causing a king and a prince to appear together with the gypsies who were formerly present but now were transformed into lords.

Immediately, the transformed gypsies danced their entrances, after which the Patrico explained that he now needed to deliver an appropriate blessing for his master and that before long his art would cause even the clowns to be transformed into knights. In a long monologue, the Patrico then blessed the sovereign and each of his five senses. Following the blessing, the Jackman, while ascending, announced in song that the sports were now ended and that the joys of all should be expressed in a hymn to the one responsible for their happiness. In a series of speeches the gypsies extolled the King's virtues and his fame, and the Captain concluded the masque on this note: "Love, Love his fortune then, and *vertues* knowne, / Who is the top of men, / But make the hapiness our owne: / Since, where the Prince for goodnes is renowned, / The subject with *felicitie* is Crownd."

An epilogue explained that the metamorphosis of the gypsies had been wrought by the power of poetry.

H

H., Elizabeth L(ady). The unidentified subject addressed in *Epig.* CXXIV.

Habington (Abington), William (1605–1654), was the author of *Castara,* a collection of poems in praise of his wife, Lucy Herbert (three editions: 1634; revised and expanded, 1635; again revised and expanded, 1640) and a play, *The Queen of Arragon* (1640). He contributed an elegy ("What doth officious fancy here prepare?") to *Jonsonus Virbius.* He prefixed verses to the 1647 folio of Beaumont and Fletcher.

Haddington, John Ramsey, Viscount (1580?–1626), came into prominence in 1600 when he killed the Earl of Gowrie and his brother Alexander Ruthven, extreme Protestants involved in an alleged conspiracy to kidnap James VI of Scotland. In 1606 James, who by then was also James I of England, created Ramsey Viscount Haddington and Lord Ramsey of Barns in the peerage of Scotland. In 1621 he was created Baron of Kingston-on-Thames and Earl of Holderness in the English peerage. Jonson wrote *The Haddington Masque* for the celebration of his marriage in 1608 to Elizabeth Radcliffe, daughter of Robert, 5th Earl of Sussex.

Haddington Masque, The.
Performed: February 9, 1608.
Published: 1608 by Thomas Thorpe

in quarto together with *The Masque of Blackness* and *The Masque of Beauty.*
Printer: unknown.

This masque was written in honor of the marriage of John Ramsey, Viscount Haddington, and Elizabeth Radcliffe, daughter of Robert, 5th Earl of Sussex, and was performed at court on February 9, 1608.

The scene discovered was a high, steep, red cliff extending up to the clouds. On each side was a pilaster covered with images of the spoils and trophies of Love and his mother. Beyond the cliff were seen only clouds. Suddenly, to solemn music, a bright sky broke forth and then were discovered two doves and two swans drawing forth a triumphant chariot, in which sat Venus, crowned with her star, and beneath her were the three graces—Aglaia, Thalia, and Euphrosyne. They all landed on the top of the cliff and gradually descended to the earth. Venus announced that Cupid, her son, had run away, and she feared that one of the beauties might have him. While describing the various attributes of Cupid, the graces conducted a search for him among the beauties present. Shortly, Cupid emerged from among the trophies with twelve boys representing the sports that accompany love. Reveling, they all danced forth in triumph, after which Cupid was captured by Venus and surrounded by the graces. Venus asked Cupid what triumph he was celebrating. Cupid replied that he could not tell, as Hymen entered, and Cupid made his escape. After asking Venus if she had done the proper thing in leaving her care and star on this night to come to earth, Hymen reminded Venus of the virtues of the king, who was present and had sanctioned the marriage. Venus then forgave Cupid for being present at the ceremony and asked Hymen to rehearse the virtues of the bride, and he did so. Hymen also informed Venus that Vulcan and his Cyclopes were forging some special piece with which to adorn the night. Vulcan appeared and claimed that he had done his best piece of work, after which the cliff opened and inside was discovered a cave filled with light in which a large artificial sphere turned and inside which the masquers under the twelve signs of the zodiac were placed. Vulcan explained that the sphere represented the heaven of marriage and the masquers the twelve sacred powers that preside at nuptials. Venus announced that she would return to heaven and that her light would ever shine within this sphere, and she and her graces returned to her chariot. As Vulcan called for Hymen's priests, who were the musicians, to sing, he was interrupted by Pyracmon, one of the Cyclopes, who asked the masquers representing the Zodiac to dance for the spectators. Vulcan agreed, and they all danced several dances while Hymen's priests sang the verses of an epithalamion alternately between the dances until the end.

Hadria, Cieco di. Luigi Groto (1541–85), famous as a blind actor, a writer of tragedies, comedies, and pastorals, and the translator of the first book of the *Iliad*. In *Volpone* (III. iv), Lady Politic Would-Be refers to him in an effort to impress Volpone with the scope of her reading.

Haggise. A watchman at the fair in *Bartholomew Fair*. He puts Waspe and Zeal-of-the-Land-Busy in the stocks, but Trouble-All attacks him and Bristle, and the prisoners escape.

Hall, Arthur. Translator of Homer's *Iliad* (1581) into alexandrine verse. In the *Conversations* (ll. 33–34), Jonson told Drummond that translations of Homer into long alexandrines "were but prose."

Hall, Joseph (1574–1656). English prelate and author. Educated at Cambridge. Made bishop of Exeter (1627–41) and of Norwich (1641–47). His vigorous defense of the episcopacy resulted in his imprisonment for high treason in 1641. He was eventually released, but his living was confiscated, and he lived in poverty until his death. His verse satires, modeled on Juvenal, appeared in two parts in 1597 and 1598. He also wrote prose satires, poems, meditations, autobiographical tracts, and prose characters in imitation of Theophrastus. In the *Conversations* (l. 609), Jonson said Hall wrote the prefatory poem to Donne's second *Anniversary*.

Hamersley, Sir Hugh (d. 1636). Lord Mayor of London in 1628 when Jonson was first appointed city chronologer. Sir Hugh was knighted in the same year. He is mentioned in *Und.* XLIV as a city captain.

Hamlet. In *Eastward Ho*, a footman who assists Gertrude when she leaves the city in her coach for Sir Petronel Flash's castle in the country.

Hannam, Captain. Jack Hannam, a captain in Drake's company in 1585 when they sailed for an expedition against Spain, was apparently the contemporary model for Tucca in *Poetaster*.

Hannibal. The famous Carthaginian general who invaded Rome after crossing the Alps. In *Catiline* (I), Sylla's Ghost predicts that Catiline will do things so horrible that Hannibal's evil deeds will pale in comparison.

Harington, Sir John (1561–1612), the godson of Queen Elizabeth, was educated at Eton and Cambridge. At court he was known for his indelicate humor. He retired to his home at Kelston to translate Ariosto's *Orlando Furioso,* published in 1591. In 1596 he published his Rabelaisian trilogy on Ajax. He served with Essex in Ireland and was knighted. Less popular at James's court than he had been at Elizabeth's, he wrote ironical accounts of the activities there, particularly about the hard drinking during the visit of Christian, King of Denmark. Harington was one of Prince Henry's tutors for a while. Shakespeare probably referred to his translation of Ariosto for the Claudio-Hero plot of *Much Ado*. His collection of epigrams was very popular during his day.

In the *Conversations* (ll. 35–40), Drummond records that Jonson said Harington's Ariosto was the worst of translations and that when Harington asked Jonson what he thought of his epigrams he told Harington that he really did not want to know the truth, for his epigrams were not real epigrams but narrations. Jonson may have represented Harington as Daw in *Epicoene,* and he punned on Harington's *The Metamorphosis of Ajax* at the end of *Epig.* CXXXIII.

Harmony (Harmonia). Daughter of either Ares and Aphrodite or Zeus and Electra, and wife of Cadmus, son of Agenor and founder of the city of Thebes.

Harper, Thomas. Printer in London from 1614 to 1656. In 1631 he printed *The New Inn* in octavo for Thomas Alchorne and in 1641 *The Devil Is an Ass* in folio.

Harpocrates. 1. The Roman god of secrecy and silence. In *Sejanus* (V), Lato persuades Sejanus' followers to tell him the news Macro has brought by saying, "I am Harpocrates."

2. Probably Harpocration, an Alexandrian lexicographer and author of the *Lexicon of the Ten Orators,* a work explaining sources and points of difficulty connected with words and phrases used by works of the imperial age. In *Epicoene* (II), Truewit wonders aloud, after rushing into Morose's silent house, if Harpocrates has been there regulating word usage.

Harpy. One of the supernatural birdlike creatures with clawed hands who were the wind-spirit daughters of Thaumas and Electra (daughter of Oceanus). The Harpies, whose names were Aello, Ocypete, and Celaeno, supposedly snatched people away like a wind.

Harrington, Lucy. See Lucy Harrington, the Countess of BEDFORD.

Harvey, Gabriel (1545?–1630), was educated at Cambridge and in 1570 elected a fellow of Pembroke Hall, where he formed his friendship with Edmund Spenser, who later celebrated him as Hobbinal in *The Shepherd's Calendar*. For a while he practiced as a lawyer in London. Harvey was a fanatical supporter of the movement to apply classical rules of prosody to English poetry. He was ridiculed by a number of his contemporaries, including Thomas Nashe and Robert Greene. Jonson may have been mocking the alleged superficial erudition of Harvey through the language and character of Juniper in *The Case Is Altered*.

Haterius, Quintus (d. A.D. 26). Roman senator and rhetorician. A minor character in *Sejanus*. In *Timber* (ll. 669–70), Jonson cites him as an example of a man whose eloquence needed to be clogged, since it was so overflowing.

Haughty, Lady. A lady collegiate in *Epicoene*, full of pride and independence. Truewit wins her affections for Dauphine Eugenie. Clerimont accuses her of being overly concerned with her appearance.

Hawkins, Sir Thomas (d. 1640), succeeded to the family estates in 1617 and was knighted in 1618. In 1629 he prefixed verses to Sir John Beaumont's *Bosworth-Field*. He contributed an elegy ("To press into the throng where wits thus strive") to *Jonsonus Virbius*. Sir Thomas translated a number of works including Horace's *Odes and Epodes* (1625, 1631); Nicolas Caussin's *The Holy Court* (1626, 1634, 1638); Pierre Matthieu's *The Histories of Aelius Sejanus and Phillippa The Catanian* (1632); Nicolas Caussin's *The Christian Diurnal* (1632); Etienne Binet's *The Lives of St. Elzear, Count of Sabran and of his Wife* (1638).

Heath, John. The title page of his *Two Centuries of Epigrammes* describes him as "Bachelour of Arts, and fellow of New Colledge in Oxford." See POETS (RUNNING JUDGMENTS ON).

Heath, Sir Robert. Attorney-General who examined Jonson on October 26, 1629,

about his knowledge of verses on John Felton, which seemed to approve Felton's assassination of the Duke of Buckingham.

Hebe, the daughter of Zeus and Hera, cupbearer to the gods and wife of Hercules, was often associated with youth and was called Juventas by the Romans.

Hecate, Greek goddess of the underworld, was associated with the moon and identified with Selene as well as Artemis and Persephone. As an Underworld goddess, she was thought to send demons to earth to accompany the souls of the dead, and she was considered to be a protector of sorcerers. She was worshipped at crossroads.

Hector. Son of Priam and Hecuba and one of the greatest Trojan warriors in the *Iliad*.

Hedon. A vain, foolish gallant in *Cynthia's Revels*, probably intended to be a caricature of John Marston. Mercury acts as his page, and mocks him for his concern with fashionable, material things. Hedon takes pride in the oaths and graceful sayings he can compose and is angry when Crites does not notice his snub. He is called "Ambition" by Philautia. He plays the games of wit with the other courtiers and sings a song he wrote to Philautia. He drinks from the fountain of self-love with the others and mocks Crites. He watches and comments on the courtship contest. After playing in the second masque, he is discovered and criticized by Cynthia, who allows Crites to decide his punishment. He marches, weeps, and sings the palinode with the others.

Heinsius, Daniel (1580–1655). Dutch classicist who became one of the most famous Renaissance scholars, editing numerous Latin works, composing Latin poetry himself, and writing in Dutch as well. His son Nikolaas (1620–81) rivaled his father as a Latin editor and author.

Jonson used Daniel's classical reconstruction of Horace's text of the *Art of Poetry* (published in 1610) in preparing his translation of the piece, and he also used him as a source for *The Haddington Masque*. Substantial sections of *Timber* are borrowed from Daniel Heinsius' works: *De Satira* (ll. 2596–98); *De Tragoediae Constitutione* (ll. 2555–77; 2706–2820); *Ad Horatii de Plauto & Terentio judicium, Dissertatio* (ll. 2586–90; 2602–24; 2625–77).

Helen. Daughter of Zeus and Leda and wife of Menelaus, king of Sparta. Paris, prince of Troy, abducted her, causing the Trojan War. She was regarded in antiquity as the most beautiful woman in the world, and she was worshipped in Sparta as a goddess of marriage.

Helicon. Largest mountain of Boeotia whose summit contained the sanctuary of the Muses. On its slopes lay Ascra, home of Hesiod. Slightly below the summit was located the spring Hippocrene (the inspiration of poets), struck by Pegasus' foot from the rock. See also PARNASSUS. In *Timber* (l. 2424), Jonson notes that poets mean poetic inspiration when they refer to Helicon.

Heliodorus of Emesa. Third century Syrian Greek writer of whom little is known. He wrote *Aethiopica*, one of the oldest and best of the extant Greek romances. The work was first printed at Basel in 1534, and was translated by Thomas Underdowne in 1569. Heliodorus is mentioned in *The New Inn* (III. ii) and *The Sad Shepherd* (I. v). The poem "An Oracle of Heliodorus," a loose paraphrase from the second book of *Aethiopica*, is sometimes ascribed to Jonson but probably was not written by him.

Hell. Either Hades, the home of disembodied spirits, or Tartarus, home of those who expiate the crimes of their earthly existence.

Hell, Prince of. A character, played by the queen's dwarf, who appeared with six infernal spirits in the third entry of the antimasque in *Chloridia*.

Heminges (Heming), John (d. 1630). As a member of the Chamberlain's and later the King's men, Heminges played in *Every Man in His humour*, *Every Man out of His Humour*, *Sejanus*, *Volpone*, *The Alchemist*, and *Catiline*. After 1611 he appears to have become a theater business manager, and Jonson's allusion to him in *Christmas His Masque* (ll. 135–37) would seem to bear this out. He acquired considerable financial interest in the Globe and Blackfriars theaters and apparently became quite wealthy and powerful. In 1623 he and his friend Henry Condell co-edited the first folio of Shakespeare.

Henri III (1551–1589). Son of Henri II and Catherine de' Medici, born in 1551. He succeeded his brother Charles IX in 1574. A weak, debauched, and unscrupulous ruler, he left France torn by civil strife and mired in financial anarchy when he died.

Volpone alludes to Henri when he is trying to seduce Celia (*Volpone*, III. vii).

Henri IV (1553–1610). King of France 1589–1610. Son of Antoine de Bourbon

and Jeanne d'Albret and the first of the Bourbon kings of France, Henri succeeded to the throne in 1589 after the death of Henri III. In 1600 he married Marie de' Medici, who became regent during the minority of their son Louis XIII after Henri IV's assassination in 1610. Henri's reign saw the transition of French arts and letters from the Renaissance to the French classical period. Tolerant and moderate like his contemporary Montaigne, Henri was gallant, witty, and concerned for the common people. Among Frenchmen he is often considered the most popular French king.

In the *Conversations* (ll. 425–32), Jonson told a jesting anecdote about Henri IV, and he alluded to the king in *Und.* LXVII.

Henrietta Maria (1609–1669), the daughter of Henri IV of France, became the queen of Charles I of England in 1625. She was a woman of good character who was devoted to her husband, but she lacked political judgment, and her Catholicism made her suspect and often unpopular in England. Her attempted negotiations with the Pope, foreign powers, and army officers greatly contributed to the suspicions against Charles and helped precipitate the civil war. After 1644 she lived in France and continued to seek foreign aid for Charles I until his execution in 1649. After the Restoration she returned to England but resumed living in France in 1665. Her religious views may have influenced her two sons, Charles II and James II, although she herself was unsuccessful in converting them to Catholicism.

Jonson was never close to the Queen, but she was associated with some of his masques, namely *The Fortunate Isles*, *Love's Triumph*, *Love's Welcome at Bolsover*, and *Chloridia*, in which she was the leading masquer. Henrietta Maria made Platonic love fashionable at court, and Jonson probably intended the court of love in *The New Inn* to allude to this fashion. Jonson addressed several poems to the Queen. *Und.* LXIII offers condolences to the King and Queen on the loss of their first-born child. *Und.* LXVI was addressed to the Queen when she was lying in with her second pregnancy, and *Und.* LXVII celebrates her birthday. *Und.* LXXIX was a New Year's gift in 1635 to the royal couple in which the Queen is represented as Mira.

Henry, Earl of Lancaster. Envious cousin of Edward III in Jonson's fragment *Mortimer His Fall*, who opposes Mortimer and finally triumphs over him.

Henry Frederick, Prince of Wales (son of James I) (1594–1612). The eldest son of James I and Queen Anne was an athletic young man who was popular and promising. In 1610 he was made Prince of Wales, and Jonson provided the speeches for the barriers held to celebrate the occasion. In the barriers Henry took the name of Meliadus. Jonson, whose own first-born son would have been about the same age had he lived, liked the Prince and admired him. When the Prince asked Jonson to annotate *The Masque of Queens*, Jonson obliged and dedicated the work to him. Jonson also had written *The Entertainment at Althorp* for the entertainment of the Prince and his mother, and *Oberon* was commissioned by Henry himself, who was the chief masquer in it. Henry's sudden death from typhoid fever in 1612 shocked the country, so popular was the Prince and so often was he compared to his namesake Henry V. Many elegies and epitaphs were written, but the epitaph on Prince Henry sometimes ascribed to Jonson was not by him.

In the *Conversations* (l. 111), Jonson praised Drummond's epitaph on the Prince and reported (l. 125) that Donne told him that he had written his epitaph on the Prince to match Sir Edward Herbert in obscurity. Jonson also said (l. 585) that his motto for the Prince was *fax floria mentis honestae*. Also in the *Conversations* (ll. 493–94), Jonson remarked that a little man drinking a toast to Prince Henry between two tall men claimed that he made up the H.

Henry V (1387–1422). King of England 1413–1422. Son of Henry IV. Henry was determined to regain lands in France held by his ancestors, and he launched a series of invasions of France, winning victories at Harfleur and at Agincourt—one of the most famous battles in English history. In England Henry received enthusiastic acclaim for his military victories, and this tended to overshadow English political and economic unrest. In 1420 Henry married Catherine of Valois and agreed to rule France in the name of her father, who accepted Henry as his successor, but Henry continued conquests in France to consolidate his holdings and eventually fell ill while engaged in these campaigns and died. Henry lifted England from the near anarchy of his father's reign to civil order and a high spirit of nationalism. His charismatic personality, military successes, and care for his less fortunate subjects made him a popular hero, but the wars he waged placed the crown heavily in debt and left England with economic and military problems which could not be dealt with later by Henry V's son during his reign.

According to *Und.* XLIII, Jonson had written a history of Henry V which was destroyed in the library fire of 1623. Henry V is also lauded in Merlin's long speech in *The Speeches at Prince Henry's Barriers*.

Henry VIII (1491–1547). King of England 1509–1547. Second son of Henry VII, created Prince of Wales in 1503, Henry was educated in the new learning of the Renaissance and developed skill in music and sports. He ascended to the throne in 1509 and soon after married his brother Arthur's widow, Katharine of Aragon, on a dispensation granted by the Pope. Henry inherited from his father a full exchequer and a precedent for autocratic rule. In 1521 he earned from the Pope the title of Defender of the Faith for a treatise against Luther, but by 1527 he had decided to divorce Katharine on the grounds that the dispensation under which they were married was illegal. In 1533 Henry married Anne Boleyn. Thomas Cranmer, who had been made Archbishop of Canterbury, declared the marriage to Katharine invalid. The Pope excommunicated Henry, and by the end of 1534 the break with Rome was complete, and Henry had become the head of the English church. In 1536 Anne Boleyn, who had given birth to Elizabeth but no male heir, was convicted of adultery and incest and beheaded. In 1537 Henry married Jane Seymour, who bore a son (later Edward VI) and died. In 1540 Henry married Anne of Cleves, but he disliked her, and soon divorced her. He then married Catherine Howard, but in 1542 she met the fate of Anne Boleyn. In 1543 Catherine Parr became Henry's sixth queen. As a young man he was accomplished, but as he grew older his moral fiber deteriorated, and he became despotic, egotistical, and vicious, although his despotism was tempered by a growing political maturity. Although he dominated Parliament, that institution increased significantly in importance during his reign. Under Henry's strong hand, England enjoyed a relatively peaceful and prosperous transition at a time when reformation, revolution, and severe wars were ravaging the rest of Europe.

Jonson told Drummond in the *Conversations* (l. 235) that his maternal grandfather had served Henry VIII, who is alluded to in *A Tale of a Tub* (I. ii) and in *The Masque of Owls.*

Henslowe, Philip (d. 1616). Theatre manager, financier, and owner. In the 1580s he was known as a dyer, in the 1590s he was described as a pawnbroker, and throughout his career he was always a buyer of property. In 1592 he was appointed a Groom of the Chamber, and in 1603 he became Gentleman Sewer of the Chamber. In 1604 he became joint Master of the bear baiting game at Paris Garden with Edward Alleyn, who was married to Henslowe's stepdaughter. Henslowe was quick to realize the future of the theatre business, and during his career he was either owner of, or held interest in, Paris Garden, the Rose, the Theatre at Newington Butts, the Fortune, and the Hope. When he died, Henslowe's property was inherited by Alleyn, upon whose death Henslowe's *Diary*, among other papers, passed to the Library of Dulwich College, where they were forgotten until they were rediscovered in 1790 by Edmund Malone. These documents shed a great deal of light on Henslowe's relations with the theatre, on theatre management and finance, and on the Elizabethan stage generally. Henslowe's *Diary*, which is a kind of account book, covers the years 1592–1603. From the *Diary* we learn that in July 1597 Jonson was employed by Henslowe as a playwright. Between 1597 and 1602 there are at least a dozen entries in the diary which indicate that Henslowe paid Jonson for work which he had done for him or lent him money for work he was supposed to do for him in the future. Either Jonson did not complete these projects, or the works themselves have not survived.

Heralds. Two unnamed heralds appear in *News from the New World* and announce the discovery of the New World by a poet.

Herbert of Cherbury, Edward, Lord (1583–1648), brother of the poet George Herbert, was a philosopher, traveller, and soldier. He was knighted in 1603 and created Lord Herbert of Cherbury in 1629. He prefixed a brief tribute ("Twas not enough Ben Jonson to be thought") to Jonson's translation of the *Ars Poetica*, as is noted in the *Conversations* (ll. 85–86) by Drummond, and Jonson addressed *Epig.* CVI to him. Herbert also wrote an epitaph on Cecily Bulstrode, whom Jonson had attacked in *Und.* XLIX, and the Lord presented Jonson with a gift copy of Martin de Roa's *Singularum Locorum ac Rerum Libri*

V (1600). In the *Conversations* (ll. 125–27), Jonson said that Donne had told him that he had written his epitaph on Prince Henry to match Herbert's in obscurity.

Herbert, Philip. See Philip Herbert, Earl of MONTGOMERY.

Herbert, Sir Henry. Master of the Revels whose lost office book recorded information on several of Jonson's works. Herbert licensed *The New Inn* on January 19, 1629, and *The Magnetic Lady* on October 12, 1632. He entered on his office book a performance on January 9, 1625, of *The Fortunate Isles* and the failure of the performance at court in 1634 of *A Tale of a Tub.* According to Herbert's account, *The Alchemist* was played for his benefit on December 1, 1631, and *Epicoene* was performed at the Court of St. James on February 18, 1636.

Hercules. The son of Zeus and Alcmena, Hercules (or Heracles) was a Greek hero noted for his courage, his amazing physical strength, and his ability to endure great toil, danger, and agonizing personal sorrow. He was particularly famous for his accomplishment of the so-called twelve labors. In *Timber* (ll. 973–75), Jonson, while castigating the vulgar for "grudging" against their sovereign, notes that "a Prince has more business, and trouble with them, then ever *Hercules* had with the Bull. . . ."

Herford, C. H. (1853–1931), was educated at Trinity College, Cambridge. From 1887 to 1901 he was Professor of Language and Literature at University College, Aberystwyth. In 1901 he was appointed to the independent Chair of English Literature at Manchester University, remaining there until his retirement in 1921. He was literary critic for the *Manchester Guardian* until his death.

One of the most accomplished English scholars of his day, Herford was elected a Fellow of the British Academy in 1926 and was awarded a number of honorary degrees. He edited the works of a number of authors including Spenser and Shakespeare. He was the senior editor of the Oxford edition of Jonson's *Works* and was responsible for the first two volumes published in 1925. Percy Simpson was his co-editor, and Simpson and his wife completed the edition in 1952. The Herford and Simpson edition is the standard critical one for Jonson.

Hermaphrodite. A bisexual divinity who, according to Ovid, was the union in one body of the son of Hermes and Aphrodite, and the nymph Salmacis.

Hermes. A Greek god who was the son of Zeus and Maia. He supposedly invented the lyre and was the messenger of the gods. He was the god of secrets, cunning, tricks, the arts, markets, roads, merchants, and thieves, and he dealt in dreams and led souls to Hades. The Romans often identified him with Mercury.

Hermione, the daughter of Helen and Menelaus, was as beautiful as Aphrodite. She probably became the wife of Orestes and the mother of Tisamenus.

Herne, Hierome. In 1610 one of Prince Henry's musicians, Herne was one of the choreographers for the dances in *The Masque of Queens* and *The Haddington Masque*, and he played in *Oberon*.

Hero. A priestess of Aphrodite at Sestos who was beloved by Leander, who lived at Abydus. Hero would hold a lighted torch at night to guide Leander as he swam across the Hellespont to visit her. When he was drowned in a storm, she threw herself into the sea.

Herodotus (484?–425 B.C.). Called the father of history. Little is known about his early life. By 447 B.C. he was in Athens and may have helped to found the Athenian colony of Thurii in southern Italy in 443, where he probably spent the rest of his life completing his history, the first comprehensive attempt at secular narrative history and the starting point of Western historical writing. Concerned primarily with the Persian Wars, the earlier books of the history contain numerous pieces of information about the ancient world as Herodotus understood it, with digressions and stories illustrating the diverse cultures of his and earlier times. Although not always accurate, the work is important for its scope, rich diversity, and anecdotal style.

Herodotus served as one of Jonson's sources for the portrait of Thomyris in *The Masque of Queens* and for the Silenus in *Oberon*.

Heroic Virtue. A symbolic character in *The Masque of Queens*.

Heroologia. In the *Conversations* (ll. 1–5), Drummond notes that Jonson said he had intended to complete an epic poem entitled *Heroologia* about the worthies of England roused by fame; the poem was to be dedicated to the country and was to be written in couplets because Jonson disliked all other rhymes. He apparently never completed the project.

Herrick, Robert (1591–1674). Generally considered the greatest of the Cavalier poets and the most important of the Sons of Ben. Herrick was born in London and spent most of his childhood in Hampton. Apprenticed in 1607 to his uncle who was jeweler to the King, Herrick remained in London until 1613. He took his A.B. at Cambridge in 1617 and his M.A. in 1620. Sometime before 1627 he took holy orders, and the same year he was chaplain on the Duke of Buckingham's unsuccessful expedition to the Isle of Ré. In 1629 he was given the country living of Dean Prior in Devonshire, where he remained until 1647 when he was ejected because of his royalist sympathies. He was restored, however, in 1662 and remained there until his death. Most of his work is contained in *Hesperides* (1648) which, when it was first published, also included his sacred songs called *Noble Numbers*. Influenced by Jonson and the classics, Herrick's greatness lies in his simplicity, careful design and detail, and management of words and rhythms. His reputation declined considerably soon after his death, but in the nineteenth century he was again recognized as a great lyricist.

Herrick wrote several poems on Jonson, including "His Prayer to Ben Jonson"; "A Bacchanalian Verse"; "An Ode for him"; "Thou had'st the wreath before now take the tree"; "After the rare archpoet Jonson dy'd"; and "Here lies Jonson with the rest." Herrick imitated Jonson's "To Penshurst" (*For.* II) in his "A Panegyrick to Sir Lewis Pemberton," and he borrowed from his master in "Epithalamie to Sir Thomas Southwell."

Herringman, Henry. Bookseller in London from 1653 to 1693 who in 1692 was one of the publishers of the third folio of Jonson's *Works*.

Hesiod. Greek didactic poet who lived in the eighth century B.C. Little is known about his life except that he was probably born in the village of Ascra. His major poem is *Works and Days*, which includes moral lessons, practical advice on how to live, the story of Pandora, and descriptions of the five ages of man. With Homer, he is credited with first composing descriptions and genealogies of the gods.

In *Poetaster* (I. i), Ovid composes a verse that proclaims that Hesiod's fame will last "while vines doe beare, / Or crooked sickles crop the ripened ear." Later in the play (v. iii), Virgil includes Hesiod in the list of the best Greeks Crispinus should read after he is purged.

Hesiod serves as one of Jonson's sources for *The Masque of Queens, The Masque of Augurs,* and *A Panegyre,* and he is quoted in *Timber* (ll. 357–60). Jonson prefixed a commendatory poem ("Whose work could this be, Chapman, to refine") to Chapman's translation (1618) of Hesiod's *Geor-*

Hesperida (Bridget). Sister to Biancha (Dame Kitely), Giuliano (Downright), and Prospero (Wellbred), in the Q 1601 (F 1616) version of *Every Man in His Humour.* She listens to Matheo's (Matthew's) poetry, mocking him for his foolishness. She is attracted to Lorenzo junior (Edward), and is glad when Prospero (Wellbred) offers to be a matchmaker for them. She marries Lorenzo junior (Edward), and their marriage is celebrated at Dr. Clement's (Justice Clement's) feast.

Hesperides. Daughters of Atlas who guarded (with the aid of the dragon Ladon) a tree that bore golden apples. As one of his twelve labors, Hercules killed Ladon and obtained the apples.

Hesperus. The evening star.

Heylyn, Peter (1599–1662). The author of *Cosmographie* (1652) in which, in Book I, he proclaims that Jonson is "equal to any of the ancients for the exactness of his pen and the decorum which he kept in dramatic poems, never before observed on English theatre." Heylyn studied at Oxford. He was deprived of his living under the Commonwealth but was made Dean of Westminster after the Restoration.

Heyward, Edward (d. 1658), entered Corpus Christi College, Cambridge in 1600 and the Inner Temple in 1604. He wrote lines for Drayton's *Barons' Wars* (1610), Browne's *Britannia's Pastorals* (1613), and for the Jonson folio of 1616 ("May I subscribe a name? Dares my bold quill"). According to the *Conversations* (ll. 605–6), John Selden dedicated his *Titles of Honor* to Heyward as "my most beloved friend and chamber-fellow," and Jonson celebrated Heyward in *Und.* xiv, addressed to Selden and prefixed to Selden's work.

Heywood, John (1497?–1580). English dramatist important in the development of English comedy. He was the most famous writer of the interlude, a short comic dialogue; some of his best-known ones are *The Play of the Weather* (1533) and *The Four P's* (c. 1543). He also wrote epigrams, proverbs, and ballads. In the *Conversations* (ll. 573–77), Jonson told an anecdote

about Heywood's being so attired in velvet by Queen Mary that he hardly knew himself. Heywood is mentioned in *A Tale of a Tub* (v. ii).

Heywood, Thomas (1574?–1641). Prolific English dramatist who was also an actor. His best play was *A Woman Killed With Kindness* (1603), one of the finest examples of domestic tragedy in English. He replied to the Puritan attacks on the stage in his *Apology for Actors* (1612). In the addresses to the readers for two of his other notable works, *The Fair Maid of the West* (1631) and *The London Traveler* (1633), he ridiculed Jonson for publishing his plays as literary works, and in his *The Hierarchy of the Blessed Angels* (1633), in describing the modern poets, he wrote: "And famous Johnson, though his learned Pen / Be dipt in Castaly, is still but Ben."

Hill, Nicholas (1570?–1610), was the author of *Philosophia, Epicurea, Democritiana, Theophrastica, proposita simpliciter, non edocta* (1601). Jonson alludes to this work in the *Conversations* (ll. 452–58) and in *Epig.* cxxxiii.

Hilts, Basket. In *A Tale of a Tub,* Squire Tub's governor, who assists the Squire in his unsuccessful efforts to marry Audrey.

Himerus. According to Hesiod, a companion of the Muses and Graces.

hinges of the world. According to the ancients, the heavens turn on the North Pole and the lower universe turns upon another hinge. The four winds also operate on hinges.

Hippocrates (460?–?370 B.C.). Famous Greek physician who is generally recognized as the father of medicine. Born on the island of Cos, he studied under his physician father, traveled for some time, and returned to Cos to practice, teach, and write. The Hippocratic or Coan school that formed around him was of major importance in separating medicine from superstition and philosophical speculation and placing it strictly on a scientific basis. Although Hippocrates followed the current belief in his day that illness resulted from an imbalance of four bodily humors, he thought the disturbance was influenced by outside forces and the humors were glandular secretions. In contrast to the rival Cnidian school, Hippocrates believed that medicine should build the patient's strength through appropriate diet and hygienic measures, resorting to more drastic measures only when necessary. Of the large body of writings associated with the Coan school, only a few are actually ascribed to Hippocrates himself although his influence is pervasive throughout these works, the most important of which include *The Aphorisms* and *Airs, Waters, and Places*. Although the so-called Hippocratic oath cannot be credited to him directly, it obviously represents his ideals, and it is still administered to medical students at most modern medical schools.

In the *Conversations* (l. 141), Jonson said Hippocrates should be read for health, and in *Volpone* (II. ii) Volpone claims in the mountebank scene that had Hippocrates possessed his great oil he need not have spent so much time in study and writing. Hippocrates is also mentioned in *The Magnetic Lady* (III. iii) and was one of the sources for *Oberon*.

Hippocrene. One of the springs sacred to the Muses, supposedly created when Pegasus struck the ground with his hoof causing water to flow.

Hippolytus. Son of Theseus and the Amazon Hippolyte. After the death of his mother, Hippolytus was passionately beloved by his stepmother Phaedra. When Hippolytus rejected her advances, she hanged herself after leaving a letter accusing her stepson of incest. Theseus banished Hippolytus despite his son's protestations of innocence and, with the aid of Poseidon, caused Hippolytus to be killed. Theseus later learned the truth from Artemis, who, according to some versions of the myth, restored Hippolytus to life.

History. A symbolic character who appears in *Chloridia* and supports the efforts of Fame to immortalize great actions.

Histrio. An actor in *Poetaster*. Tucca calls him over and berates him for not saluting him, stating that he hates players because they mock worthy people like himself. Histrio makes Tucca approve of him, however, by inviting him to dinner and assuring him that he produces comedy, not satire. He is impressed by the performance of Tucca's pages and asks for them on loan. He shows what a foolish slanderer he is when he reveals that he has hired Demetrius to write a play abusing Horace because "it will get us a huge deal of money." He foolishly "informs" on Ovid and his friends to Lupus after they borrow properties for the masquerade, and he rushes into the masquerade with indignant Caesar and Lupus. He stands by Lupus when Horace is angry at Lupus for misleading Caesar, and Horace calls him a "base unworthy groome." He goes with Lupus,

Demetrius, and Crispinus to arrest Horace; Caesar realizes that he is foolish and sends him away to be whipped.

Hodges, John. City captain of London mentioned in *Und.* XLIV.

Hodgkin, Thomas. Printer and bookseller in London from 1677 to 1713, who in 1692 printed the third folio of Jonson's *Works* for a syndicate of booksellers and publishers.

Holdback. A midwife who appears in *An Entertainment at the Blackfriars* and tries to settle a dispute between a wet nurse and a dry nurse.

Holdfast. In *Eastward Ho*, a jail keeper who watches Security, Quicksilver, and Sir Petronel Flash when they are imprisoned.

Holland, Abraham. Poetaster who composed the Latin verses accompanying Robert Vaughan's portrait of Jonson, which was used as a frontispiece to the first volume of the 1640 folio.

Holland, Hugh. A Westminster man who was the author of *Pancharis* (1603), a long poem on Owen Tudor, which was dedicated to King James. Jonson's "Ode α᾽λληγορικὴ" was affixed to the work. Holland himself had prefixed verses ("In that, this book doth deign Sejanus name") to *Sejanus* and to the Shakespeare folio. Holland, who was Jonson's good friend and, like him at the time, a Catholic, died in 1633. Jonson alluded to *Pancharis* and to his own ode in *Und.* XXVII.

Holland, John and John Isaac. John and John Isaac Holland were supposedly the first Dutch alchemists. They lived in the first half of the fifteenth century. Their works were used as a reference by Paracelsus. In *The Alchemist* (I. ii), Subtle says that with their help, Dapper will have such good luck at cards that he will think that Isaac's spirit is in him.

Holme, William. Bookseller in London and Chester from 1589 to 1615 who in 1600 published two quartos of *Every Man out of His Humour*.

Holofernes. An Assyrian general and tyrant slain by Judith in the Apocrypha book of Judith. In *Every Man in His Humour* (1601 quarto version, III. iv), Bobadilla calls Giuliano by this name in a derisive way. In the 1616 folio version (IV. ii), Bobadilla calls Downright by this name.

Holyday, Barton. Translator of Juvenal and Persius, whose commendatory poem ("'Tis dangerous to praise; besides the task") was prefixed to Jonson's translation (1640) of Horace's *Art of Poetry*.

Homer. According to Aubrey's notes, a bencher overheard Jonson quoting Homer while he was laying bricks with his stepfather. To be sure, Jonson knew his Homer well, and he often referred to him in his own works. The burlesque banquet of the gods scene in *Poetaster* is probably modeled on the council of the gods scene in the *Iliad*. Homer served as one of the sources for *The King's Coronation Entertainment, The Masque of Beauty, Hymenaei, The Haddington Masque, The Masque of Queens,* and *Oberon*. Jonson mentioned Homer in *The New Inn* (I. vi), *Poetaster* (I. ii; v. iii), and *Timber* (ll. 354–57; 536–38; 1197–98; 2638–40; 2770; 2814). In the *Conversations* (ll. 33–34), Drummond notes that Jonson said the translation of Homer (referring apparently to Chapman's and Hall's *Iliad*) in long Alexandrines was merely prose, but later (ll. 124–25), Drummond indicates that Jonson knew part of Chapman's translation by heart.

honesty. In the *Conversations* (ll. 631–32), Drummond records that Jonson loved to be called honest above all and had a hundred letters so calling him. In *Timber* (ll. 84–92), Jonson, borrowing from Juan Luis Vives (*De Consultatione* [*Opera*, i. 169–71]), notes that honesty is one of "the chiefe things that give[s] a man reputation in counsell" and that honesty can be gotten only by "living well."

Honor. According to Cicero, a diety. She was often portrayed as a female figure clad in a loose robe covering only one shoulder, and she was placed in the Temple of Fame alongside Virtue.

Honthorst, Gerrit van (1590–1656). Dutch painter. When he was in Italy (c. 1610–20), he gained a sound understanding of the works of Caravaggio, carried on the Caravaggesque tradition when he returned to Holland, and introduced the Italian manner of illusionistic decoration dependent on the Carracii into Dutch interiors. In 1628 Charles I invited him to England, and he decorated Whitehall and painted portraits of the King and nobility. Also during his six months' visit in England, he probably painted what has come to be known as the most famous portrait of Ben Jonson.

Hooker, Richard (1554?–1600). Famous English theologian and clergyman. He studied and lectured at Oxford and preached at a number of churches. His *Of the Laws of Ecclesiastical Polity* (in eight books, three of which were published posthumously) was a major influential analysis of church government, the intellectual concepts of Anglicanism, and its influence on the theory of government (civil and ecclesiastical) as based on reason. In the *Conversations* (ll. 142–43), Jonson recommended the reading of Hooker to Drummond, and in *Timber* (l. 907) he listed Hooker among those who were masters of wit and language.

Hopkins, Hester. J. P. Collier, a nineteenth-century editor of *Eastward Ho*, cited an entry in the register of St. Giles, Cripplegate, of the marriage on July 27, 1623 of "Beniamyne Johnson and Hester Hopkins," but that entry is the only evidence that Jonson may have married a second time, and it is known that Jonson had no wife living with him at his last house in Westminster.

Horace. Quintus Horatius Flaccus (65–8 B.C.), one of the greatest of the Latin poets. Born at Venusia in southern Italy, he studied at Rome and Athens and fought with Brutus and the republicans at Philippi in 42 B.C. When he returned to Rome, he was introduced by Virgil to Maecenas, who became his close friend and patron, giving Horace his famous Sabine farm where he lived thereafter except for lengthy visits to Rome.

Horace's first book of *Satires* appeared in 35 B.C. Other works followed steadily; the *Epodes* about 30 B.C., the second book of *Satires* in 29 B.C., three books of *Odes* about 24 B.C., and the first book of *Epistles* around 20 B.C. About 13 B.C. Horace published a fourth book of *Odes,* a second book of *Epistles,* a hymn (the *Carmen saeculare*), and his famous *Ars Poetica* or *Epistle to the Pisos.*

A master of poetic form, Horace's early poems show the influence of the Greek Archilochus, but his later works reveal a complete and individualized adaptation of Greek meters to Latin. As he matured, Horace turned his themes from personal vilification to more generalized satire and eventually to literary criticism. His works give a vivid view of contemporary Roman society and represent particularly well the spirit of the Augustan age of Rome—a time of peace during which the arts were earnestly cultivated. Horace's influence on English poetry in general has been immense, and his influence on Jonson in particular was profound. Jonson seems to have identified himself in spirit and, to an extent, in character with the ancient Roman master.

In *Poetaster,* Horace is portrayed as a noble poet, who is supposed to represent Jonson. Crispinus traps him on the street and bores him by trying to court his favor and reading him verses; he cannot escape until Minos comes to arrest Crispinus. Trebatius cautions him to stop writing satiric verse, but he says that it is his nature to write such verses and that the corrupt age in which he lives incites him to write them. He does not believe Lupus' story of the "treasonous" masquerade and is upset when Caesar breaks into the masquerade and upbraids the people there. He praises Virgil highly, reassuring Caesar that there is no jealousy among true poets, and listens eagerly to the *Aeneid.* When Lupus bursts in and accuses Horace of treason, Caesar refuses to listen. Horace is permitted to arrest, try, and punish the poetasters, who slander him. He gives Crispinus pills that purge him of the affected words he writes, and he is highly praised by Caesar.

In *Timber* (ll. 2475–82), Jonson notes that the poet should follow the advice of Horace to imitate the best writers by drawing forth the best and choicest flowers and, like the bee, turning all into sweet honey. The poet should also observe how the best writers themselves have imitated—how, for example, Virgil and Statius imitated Homer and how Horace imitated Archilochus and Alcaeus.

In the *Conversations* (ll. 74–76), Drummond reports that Jonson read to him Jonson's translation of Horace's ode "*Beatus ille qui procul negotiis . . .*" and his translation of Petronius Arbiter's epigram "*foeda et brevis est veneris voluptas. . . .*" Jonson recommended that Drummond read Horace (ll. 140–41), and Jonson read to Drummond Jonson's preface to his translation of Horace's *Ars Poetica* which he wrote while staying at Lord D'Aubigny's house (ll. 182–86). The preface contained an apology for *Bartholomew Fair* and was in the form of a dialogue with Criticus, who represented Donne. Although Jonson had announced his intention to publish the preface and his translation as early as his address to the readers in the 1605 quarto of *Sejanus* and obviously had the preface and translation with him when he visited Drummond, the preface was lost in his library fire of 1623. The translation itself somehow miraculously survived and was published later. Jonson referred to Horace's *Ars Poetica* in *Und.* XLIII, in *Timber* (ll. 1569–71; 1889–91), and in *The Staple of News* (IV. iv), and he used it as one of his sources for *Oberon.*

Considering Horace an author of much civility (*Timber* ll. 2590–91) and mentioning him specifically in the "Ode to Himself") and in *Und.* XLII, Jonson composed his *Und.* XLIV in the spirit of Horace's attacks upon national degeneracy. Moreover, Jonson made frequent use of Horace's *Satires.* The dialogue between Horace and Trebatius in Act III of *Poetaster* is a free rendering of the first satire in Horace's second book of *Satires.* Jonson cited the *Satires* in *The Masque of Queens,* and he borrowed from them, for instance, in *Every Man out* (I. iii), *Poetaster* (III. i-iii; IV. iii; V. iii), *Volpone* (I. i, ii, iv; II. vi), *The Devil Is an Ass* (II. iv), *The Staple of News* (I. i), *Epig.* II, *Epig.* XCVIII, *For.* IV, *Und.* XV, and *Und.* XLVIII.

Jonson also imitated Horace's *Epistles;* he mentioned them in *Every Man out* (II. i), *Bartholomew Fair* (II. i; IV. vi), and *The King's Coronation Entertainment;* and borrowed from them in *Every Man in* (II. v), *Cynthia's Revels* (I. iv), *Sejanus* ("To the Readers"), *For.* X, *Leges Convivales,* and in an uncollected poem ("I had you for a servant, once, Dick Brome").

Horace's *Odes* serve as one of the sources for *The King's Coronation Entertainment;* are cited in *The Haddington Masque, Love's Triumph,* and *Timber* (l. 2367); and are borrowed from in *For.* XII, *Und.* XXVI, *Und.* LXXVII, and *Leges Convivales. Und.* LXXXVI and LXXXVII are translations of *Epode* II and *Ode* IX (Bk. III), respectively.

The *Epodes* are used as one of the sources for *The Masque of Queens,* and *Und.* LXXXV is a translation of Horace's second *Epode.* See also ARISTOTLE; ART OF POETRY; CRITIC; POEM; READING.

Hoskyns, John. Distinguished lawyer who lived from 1566 to 1638 and was author of *Directions for Speech and Style.* According to a late tradition recorded by Aubrey, Hoskyns was Jonson's intellectual father. Hoskyns may also have been the friend who sent Jonson to school. The section on letter writing in *Timber* (ll. 2128–60) is taken from Hoskyns's *Directions.*

Hostia. The mistress of Propertius, called Cynthia in his poems. She shared his interest in literature and encouraged him to develop his talent as an elegiac poet. Their affair began in 28 B.C. and lasted until 23 B.C. He wrote about her even after her death. In *Poetaster* (I. iii), he mourns for her.

Hours. According to Hesiod, the daughters of Themis and Zeus, whose names were Dike (Justice), Eunomia (Order), and Irene (Peace). Sometimes they

128

were associated with the Graces and were considered to guard the gates of heaven.

Howard, Edward. In Howard's *The Women's Conquest* (1671), the second prologue "personated like Ben Johnson rising from below" presents a character who denounces "the stage's crimes" and in typical Jonsonian fashion proclaims

Did I instruct you (well ne're half an age)
To understand the grandeur of the stage,
With the exactest rules of comedy,
Yet now y'are pleased with wits low frippery,
Admitting farce, the trifling mode of France,
T'infect you with fantastick ignorance,
Forgetting 'twas your glory to behold
Plays wisely form'd, such as I made of old.

In an essay on *Criticism and Censure* Howard praised Jonson excessively, claiming "I dare affirm that he is yet unparalleled by the world, and may be some succeeding ages: he gave our English tongue firmness, greatness, enlarged and improved it, without patching of French words to our speech, according to some of our modern pens. . . ."

Howard, Lady Frances. See Frances Howard, Countess of SOMERSET.

Howard, Henry, Earl of Northampton. See Ben JONSON.

Howell. A Welshman who appears in *For the Honor of Wales* and offers a song for the pleasure of the king.

Howell, James (1593–1666). A literary son and friend of Jonson's, educated at Hertford and Jesus Colleges, Oxford. Appointed steward to a patent-glass manufactory, he went abroad in 1616 to find materials and workmen and for four years traveled in Holland, Flanders, France, Spain, and Italy, observing men and manners and acquiring extensive knowledge of modern languages. He later served as a clerk to the Privy Council, but was imprisoned for eight years for debt, during which time he supported himself by translating and composing a variety of works. In 1661 he became historiographer-royal, the first who ever enjoyed that title. He was one of the earliest Englishmen to make his living by the pen. His forty or so publications include translations from Italian, French, and Spanish; controversies; pamphlets; and books on history, politics, and philology. Howell is probably best remembered for his literary, informative, and entertaining *Epistolae Ho-Elianae, or Familiar Letters* (1645, 1647, 1650, and 1655).

In his *Epistolae Ho-Elianae* (1645), Howell declares that Jonson was indeed inspired with divine enthusiasm when he wrote *Volpone, The Alchemist, Catiline, Sejanus,* and *The Epigrams,* but not so inspired in *The Magnetic Lady.* In another letter Howell says he is sending Jonson a copy of John Davies's *Welsh Grammar* (1592) and tells Jonson a complicated French story about romantic intrigue that he thinks may be of some use to him. Howell included with the *Grammar* a poem (" 'Twas a tough task, believe it, thus to tame") for Jonson. In his own *New English Grammar* (1662), modeled on Jonson's, Howell declares that the more Jonson researched grammar, the more perplexed he became.

Apparently Howell helped save Jonson's library from a second disastrous fire about ten years after the first one in 1623. Howell published an elegy on Jonson ("And is thy glass run out? Is that oil spent") in *Jonsonus Virbius.*

Hudson, Jeffery. Queen Henrietta Maria's dwarf, alluded to in *Chloridia.*

Huffle, Hodge. In *The New Inn,* a notorious cheater and companion of Bat Burst who drinks and carouses with Colonel Tipto.

Hugh, Chanon (Canon). In *A Tale of a Tub,* the vicar of Pancras, who poses as Captain Thums, assists at various times both Squire Tub and Justice Preamble in their efforts to wed Audrey, and eventually performs the marriage ceremony for Audrey and Pol Martin.

Hull, John. A London founder to whom Jonson assigned part of his pension payment in 1621.

Humanity. She appears as the central figure on a triumphal arch in *Lovers Made Men.* Her lap is full of flowers, which she scatters with her right hand while holding a golden chain in her left.

humor. See John DRYDEN; Thomas SHADWELL; John WEEVER.

humor and tragedy. See John DRYDEN.

Humors. Four symbolic characters who appear in *Hymenaei* and attempt to disrupt the ceremony.

humors, theory of. In the fifth century B.C., Hippocrates promulgated the physiological theory that four humors enter into the composition of man's body and that the right proportion of these humors leads to health while an imbalance of them brings about illness. In *Of the Nature of Man*, Polybus, Hippocrates' son-in-law, explained that "the body of man has in itself blood, phlegm, yellow and black bile. . . . His health is most perfect when these elements are evenly proportioned to one another in combination, quality, and quantity, and are perfectly mingled. He has pain when one of these elements is defective or excessive or is isolated in the body, uncompounded with the others." In the second century A.D. Galen developed the theory further in his *Of Temperaments*, combining it with the notion of spirit mingling with the humors in different proportions and producing four basic temperaments: the sanguine, buoyant type; the phlegmatic, sluggish type; the choleric, quick-tempered type; and the melancholic, dejected type. Thomas Linacre published a Latin translation of Galen's work in 1521 and thus circulated the theory in England, but it was Linacre's pupil, Sir Thomas Elyot, who popularized the idea in his *Castel of Helth* (1539). Elyot connected the humors with the ages of man and the seasons of the year and, as Hippocrates had done, prescribed a diet for each humor, The only contemporary of Jonson's to analyze the humors was Robert Burton, who did so in an introductory subsection of his *The Anatomy of Melancholy*. After the sixteenth century, Galen's theory began to be displaced by the chemical doctrines which resulted from the study of alchemy, but the humor theory persisted until early in the eighteenth century, any personality aberration or eccentricity being referred to as a humor.

Although Chapman's *An Humourous Day's Mirth* (1597) was the first humor play, Jonson was the first playwright to develop a theory of comedy derived from the theory of humors and to use humor characters to portray various types of irrational and immoral behavior. He was also the first to make the exhibition of humors the sole function of comic plot. The display of humors gave him ample opportunity to focus his satirical eye upon individual and local social traits, habits, and conduct and to ridicule them. Three of his plays are primarily humor comedies (*Every Man in, Every Man out, Magnetic Lady*), but others also contain humor characters. Jonson explained his own humour theory of comedy most succinctly in the induction to *Every Man out*, but he also discussed humor theory in *Every Man in* (1601 quarto, III. i;

1616 folio, III. iv) and in the induction to *The Magnetic Lady*. In addition, four symbolic humors dance in *Hymenaei*.

Of Jonson's followers, perhaps Thomas Shadwell was the one to make the most use of humor theory for dramatic purposes.

Huygens, Sir Constantyn (1596–1687), a friend of the Dutch ambassador in London, was knighted in 1622. Both Jonson and Donne were friends of his. In 1658 he translated into Dutch nineteen of Donne's poems as well as Jonson's *Epig.* XXXIII on Sir John Roe, and he paraphrased *Epig.* XLII on Giles and Joan. Huygens owned a copy of the 1616 folio of Jonson and a quarto manuscript of *The Gypsies Metamorphosed*. He was present at three of Jonson's masques—*News from The New World, The Masque of Augurs*, and *Time Vindicated*. In 1622 Huygens prefixed an autographed note in Latin for Jonson to his Broadsheet poem *Constantinus Hugenius Academiae Oxoniensi Perpetuum Florere* (1622).

Hydra. A multi-headed water serpent who was the offspring of Typhon and Echidna and who grew two new heads each time one was cut off. As his second labor, Hercules killed the monster by burning the neck after he cut off each head.

Hymen. In Greek mythology, the personification of marriage represented as a beautiful youth carrying a bridal torch and wearing a veil.

Hymenaei.
Performed: January 5 and 6, 1606, in the old Banqueting House at Whitehall.
Published: 1606 by Thomas Thorpe in quarto.
Printer: Valentine Simmes.
This masque was written in honor of the marriage of Lady Frances Howard and the Earl of Essex, whose marriage had been arranged to heal a political feud. After the annulment of the marriage in 1613, Jonson attempted to suppress references to the occasion of the original performance.
The masque was performed on two consecutive nights. On the first night, when the scene opened, an altar was discovered. Five pages and one youth representing the bridegroom approached the altar, after which Hymen (god of marriage) entered with three youths and another one impersonating the bride. They were followed by two singers, auspices, and the musicians. When all were in place, a song

was sung bidding all the profane to leave the sacred rites of union about to begin, after which Hymen praised the king and queen as the force of union in the commonwealth. To the sound of contentious music, there then appeared a microcosm or globe representing man, out of which emerged eight men—four representing the four Humors and four representing the four Affections. After a short dance, they drew their swords and attempted to disrupt the ceremony. Hymen urged them to save the virgins and summoned Reason forth from the globe to control the Humors and Affections. Reason appeared and reprimanded them for disturbing the sacred rites of union, and, amazed, the rioters sheathed their swords while Reason ranked the persons, ordered the ceremony, and then explained the symbolic significance of the ritual.

The upper part of the scene composed of clouds opened and Juno, sitting in a throne, was discovered. Above her in the regions of fire was Jupiter brandishing his thunder. Beneath Juno was the rainbow Iris, and on the two sides were eight women representing the powers of Juno. Reason hailed the presence of Juno and explained that Order was awaiting Juno's powers on the earth. Juno and her train descended while a song was offered noting that they were the powers the Humors and Affections had to obey. When the song ended, they all danced forth, led by Order, the servant of Reason. Order was commanded to rank the powers in their proper place while Reason explained their function. By this action the men were paired with the women, and they danced forth while a song celebrating union was sung, and they all concluded holding hands in the figure of a chain. Then Reason lauded the harmony wrought by the presence of Hymen and Juno as the dancers danced with others in galliards and corantos while Hymen and Reason hailed the coming night for love. The dancers ended in the figure of a circle with Reason standing in the middle, celebrating the approaching union of the bride and groom and the union of the commonwealth brought about by the king. Then to the sound of soft music, they all departed led by Hymen, the bride, and the auspices while the musicians recited a long epithalamion.

The following night, all the previous scenery having been removed, the Barriers were performed. At one end of the hall, to the sounds of battle, appeared a mist out of which emerged two women identically dressed, one named Opinion and the other Truth. Each one claimed to be genuine truth, and they decided to settle the issue by debating whether the married or the virgin state were preferable, Truth taking the former position and Opinion the latter. The verbal debate raged inconclusively until both decided to settle the matter by having champions for each side engage in combat. Marching music sounded at the lower end of the hall and thirty-two knights equipped for battle entered— sixteen on each side. Truth called for them to fight and declared that if her champions failed she would retire and reappear in greater power to make her position prevail, to which Opinion replied with an insult about Truth's quitting her side. The knights then participated in mock combat until a striking light filled the hall, and an angel appeared and announced that Truth would shortly appear in a second number to reconcile the issue and the battle. Truth reappeared and explained that Opinion had merely posed as Truth and had falsely argued for the virgin state. She urged all the champions to yield to Hymen, stressing that it is a conquest to yield to right, and proclaimed that the king before whom she bowed would support her position and had the wisdom to see and understand genuine truth. Then all were led forth, hand in hand, reconciled and triumphant.

hyperbole. See STYLE.

Hypsicratea. According to Jonson, the wife of Mithridates, known for her loyalty to and love of her husband. She was Queen of Pontus and appears as one of the virtuous queens in *The Masque of Queens.*

Hypsipyle. The daughter of Thoas, king of Lemnos, who helped her father to escape when the women on the island agreed to murder all the men. She may also have had a love affair with Jason.

I

Icarius. The father of Penelope.

Ida. Mountain in Phrygia where the judgment of Paris occurred.

Idmon. Heroic son of Apollo who could foretell the future and who was killed by a wild boar when he was on the expedition with the Argonauts.

Idomen. Idomeneus, legendary valiant king who led the Cretan forces against Troy. On the way home he vowed to sacrifice to Poseidon the first thing to meet him if the god would save him from a terrible storm which had arisen. When Idomen was met by his son, the old warrior felt obliged to fulfill his vow, and Crete was punished for the son's sacrifice with a dreadful plague. As a result, Idomen was banished, and he fled to Italy.

Ignorance. One of the witches who make up the antimasque in *The Masque of Queens.*

impresa. A miniature symbolic picture or emblem that is interpreted by an epigrammatic motto. These emblems were popular at court, especially for tournaments and jousts, and poets were often called upon to devise appropriate ones for the nobility. Camden, Daniel, and Drummond all wrote learnedly on the subject, and Francis Quarles published a famous seventeenth-century emblem book. In the *Conversations* (ll. 578–85), Jonson told Drummond about three impresas — his own, that of Essex, and one Jonson furnished for Prince Henry.

Jonson's own impresa was a compass with one foot in the center, the other foot broken, and the motto, *Deest quod duceret orbem.*

In July 1619, Drummond sent Jonson information for his proposed Scottish poem about impresas worked by Queen Mary in the embroidery of a bed of state. Many of Jonson's masque characters seem to be conceived of in the impresa tradition, and we know that Jonson was greatly indebted to the *Iconologia* of the Renaissance mythologizer Caesare Ripa.

Impudence. The name of one of the witches making up the antimasque in *The Masque of Queens.*

Indagine, John de (Johan van Hagen). Author of *Introductiones Apotelesmatiae Elegantes . . .* (1522), who is mentioned in *The Gypsies Metamorphosed.*

induction. An old word for *introduction*, which, when used in drama, indicates a presenter engaged in preliminary dialogue before the beginning of the play proper. Jonson and other dramatists made use of inductions in some of their plays. In *Every Man out*, Jonson used the induction to lecture the audience on the true principles of comedy and to explain his theory of humor comedy. Although he never used the induction again as a manifesto for literary theory, Jonson did employ an induction in several other plays: *Cynthia's Revels, Bartholomew Fair, The Staple of News,* and *The Magnetic Lady.*

Ingeland, Thomas. Author of *The Disobedient Child*, a prodigal son story which may have influenced the plot of *Eastward Ho* and *The Staple of News.*

Iniquity. The vice in Jonson's *The Devil Is an Ass.*

Innys, William. One of the leading booksellers in London in the early eighteenth century (1711–32) who was one of the publishers of the so-called Booksellers' Edition of Jonson's *Works* in 1716–17.

inscriptions. At least a dozen inscriptions (seven in Latin) written by Jonson have survived. The inscriptions are addressed to Robert Jermyn; Lucy, Countess of Bedford; William Camden; Sir John Roe; Queen Anne; Joachim Morsius; Captain Francis Segar; Francis Crane; Sir Robert Townshend; John Florio; Alexander Glover; and Henry Theobald.

Insulae Fortunae. See FORTUNATE ISLANDS.

Interest, Sir Moth. In *The Magnetic Lady*, the brother of Lady Loadstone and a usurer who holds the inheritance for Lady Loadstone's niece.

Io Paean. Io refers to the wanderer, and a paean is a song in praise of Apollo or a victory song.

Irene. A symbolic personage representing peace and appearing in a scene in Jonson's part of the *King's Coronation Entertainment.* See also HOURS.

Iris, daughter of Thaumas and Electra (daughter of Oceanus), was the goddess of the rainbow, the messenger of the gods, and a special servant of Hera.

Irish Gentlemen. They appear in their mantles instead of their best garments and dance before the king in *The Irish Masque at Court.* Later, by the transforming power of the king, they appear appropriately attired for masquing.

Irish Masque at Court, The.
Performed: December 29, 1613, and January 3, 1614.
Published: 1616 in folio by William Stansby.
Printer: William Stansby.
Performed twice, this masque was part of the series of festivities honoring the marriage of the Earl of Somerset and Lady Frances Howard. The masquers were apparently disguised as Irishmen in accord

with the convention often followed in the masque of the wandering foreigner visiting the prince. The masquers speak in a burlesque Anglo-Irish jargon, but there is no evidence that Jonson was proficient in Irish.

After the king was seated, a man dressed like a citizen ran out before the audience, followed by four Irish footmen named Denmise, Donnell, Dernock, and Patrick. Speaking in an Anglo-Irish brogue, they identified themselves and asked which one of the spectators was the king—King Yamish, as they called him. When the king was pointed out, they approached, blessed him, and assured him of his many loyal subjects in Ireland, and then they began to quarrel among themselves over who was to be their spokesman. Finally, they all spoke in turn and told the king that they had heard news in Ireland of a great marriage that was to take place, and they had brought over a dozen of their most distinguished masters to dance at the wedding; unfortunately, the wild Irish sea had caused them to lose their fine garments; and so the masters would now have to dance in their mantles. The footmen appealed to the audience for their indulgence under the circumstances, and promised them that the dancers would still perform brilliantly and demonstrate their loyalty in spite of the hardship. The footmen themselves then danced to the bagpipes and offered a song, after which they introduced their masters, who danced in their Irish mantles to the music of harps.

After the dance, the footmen spoke again until they were interrupted by a civil gentleman who was accompanied by a bard. The gentleman informed all of the Irishmen that the king had seen enough of their coarse dancing and called upon the bard to celebrate appropriately the glory and majesty of the king. The bard approached and to the accompaniment of the harp sang a song about the power of the king's presence in transforming his subjects into new creatures. As he sang, the masters' mantles fell from their shoulders and their masqueing apparel was discovered beneath, and the now gloriously attired masquers danced forth, after which the bard offered a final song in praise of the transforming power of the monarch.

Iron Age. A symbolic character who appears in *The Golden Age Restored* and resists the return to the golden age on earth. See also GOLDEN AGE.

Ironside, Captain. In *The Magnetic Lady*, the brother of Compass and a soldier who eventually marries Lady Loadstone.

Isabel. In Jonson's fragment *Mortimer His Fall*, the queen mother who raises Mortimer to power through her extraordinary favors to him.

Isabel. See Rachel DE PRIE.

Islip, Adam. Printer in London from 1591 to 1640 who in 1600 may have printed in quarto *Every Man out of His Humour* for William Holme.

Islip, Simon. Abbot of Westminster under Henry VII, known for his ingenious devices playing on his name. He is mentioned in *The New Inn* (I. i).

Item, Timothy. In *The Magnetic Lady*, the apothecary to Dr. Rut.

Iterduca. A symbolic character who appears in *Hymenaei* as one of the powers of Juno.

Ixion, husband of Dia, murdered his father-in-law Deioneus when he came to collect the promised bridal gifts. Zeus purged Ixion of his guilt, but when Ixion tried to seduce Hera, Zeus punished him by creating an image of Hera from the cloud Nephele which bore Ixion the Centaurs. Ixion was also punished by being bound to a continuously turning wheel in the Underworld which could only be temporarily stopped by the beautiful music of Orpheus.

J

Jack, Black. In *A Tale of a Tub*, Lady Tub's butler.

Jackman. The first gypsy in *The Gypsies Metamorphosed*, who plays the guitar and sings several songs.

Jackson, Gabriele Bernhard (1934–). American scholar, educated at Yale University, since 1970 Professor of English at Temple University. Author of an influential study of vision and judgment in Jonson's plays (1968) and editor of *Every Man in* in the Yale Ben Jonson.

James I (1566–1625). King of England 1603–1625. The son of Lord Darnley and

Mary, Queen of Scots, James became James VI of Scotland after the forced abdication of his mother in 1567. He was placed in the care of the Earl of Mar. Taught primarily by George Buchanan, the young king matured in his studies and developed an interest in learning and theological debate. During his minority, Scotland was ruled by a series of regents, and the young monarch found himself entangled in a complicated struggle between the remnants of his mother's Catholic party, who favored an alliance with France, and the Protestant faction, which wanted an alliance with England. Influenced by his favorite, James Stuart, Earl of Arran, James began his personal rule in 1583, and in 1586, considering his prospects for the English throne, he allied himself with Queen Elizabeth I, causing a break with the party of his mother, whose execution in 1587 he calmly accepted. By shrewd politics and force, James succeeded in subduing the feudal Scottish baronage, in establishing royal authority, and in asserting the authority of the state over the church. Against the wishes of Elizabeth, he married Anne of Denmark in 1589, and in 1603 he succeeded to the English throne as James I by virtue of his descent from Margaret Tudor, daughter of Henry VII.

Although he was initially received enthusiastically as the new monarch, James had little understanding of Parliament or the changing conditions in the kingdom. His anti-Puritan attitude, his inconsistent policy toward English Catholics, and his attempt to arrange a marriage between a Spanish princess and Prince Charles all caused distrust, and his reliance upon favorites with few qualifications produced more discontent. Parliament complained of the abuses of monopolies, James' neglect of the navy, and his insistence upon the concept of the divine right of monarchy. In 1611 James dissolved Parliament and, except for the Addled Parliament of 1614, ruled without one until 1624. By 1619 George Villiers, 1st Duke of Buckingham, was the king's confidant and adviser on all matters. When James died in 1625, his son Charles inherited colonies in North America, a war against Spain, and a kingdom in which the Puritan revolution was well begun.

A well-educated man, James was active as a writer during his life. Some of his best known works include: *His Majesty's Poetical Exercises* (1591), a collection of his own poems and translations; *Demonology* (1597), a treatise on witchcraft; *True Law of Free Monarchy* (1598), an assertion of the divine right of kings; and *Basilikon Doron* (1599), a treatise on the art of government.

James' own love of learning and writing encouraged considerable literary activity during his reign, although the king had little concept of intellectual freedom. From 1617, the establishment of an Academy of Letters, of which Jonson would have been a member, was discussed, but the project died with the king.

Jonson took seriously his part of the *King's Coronation Entertainment*, and he wrote several other entertainments for the King's private amusement (including *The Entertainment at Highgate, The Entertainment of Two Kings at Theobalds, The Entertainment of King and Queen at Theobalds, The King's Entertainment at Welbeck*, and *Love's Welcome at Bolsover*), and he created numerous masques for the king's court over the years of his reign.

Although Jonson was imprisoned in 1604 for his part in some incidental satire on the Scots and a caricature of James in *Eastward Ho*, over the years he developed a good relationship with James. In *Timber* (ll. 999–1002), Jonson, after discussing the necessity for princes to be merciful, records that James deserved great praise because he allowed men to visit and pity those who were incarcerated in his prisons. He apparently could be very candid with the King. In *Conversations* (ll. 330–32), Jonson told Drummond that he would not flatter the King, although he saw death, and later (ll. 561–63), he said that he had told James that his teacher Buchanan had corrupted his ear. According to Aubrey's notes, Jonson told James that the king had disappointed him in choosing a certain W. Wiseman for sheriff and got the monarch to change his mind. Aubrey also records that Jonson gave an extemporaneous grace before the King which included a blessing for Raph, a drawer at a local tavern. A 1619 letter from Drummond indicates that the king regretted Jonson's absence from the court.

Jonson addressed *Epig.* iv, xxxv, and li to James, compared the monarch to Aeneas in *The Haddington Masque*, and told his fortune in *The Gypsies Metamorphosed*, the Prologue of which for the Burley performance was addressed to the King, who was so pleased with the masque that he himself composed a poem in honor of Marquess Buckingham, host for the performance. Although it seems unlikely that Aubrey's note that James made Jonson write against the Puritans is accurate, the poet did address the Prologue of *Bartholomew Fair* to the King. Jonson had a copy of *His Majesty's Poetical Exercises* (1591) in his personal library, and he prudently quoted from the *Demonology* (1597) in *The Masque of Queens*.

In 1616 James gave Jonson an annual pension which was increased by Charles in 1630. In 1621 James issued to Jonson a warrant for reversion of the Office of Master of the Revels, but Jonson never gained the position because the holder of the office outlived him.

James II (1633–1701). King of England 1685–1688. The son of Charles I and younger brother of Charles II, James, as the young Duke of Albany and of York, was surrendered in 1646 to the parliamentary forces during the civil war, but escaped to the Continent in 1648 and served in the French and Spanish forces. After the Restoration he returned to England, married Anne Hyde, and was converted to Catholicism about 1668. James's first wife died in 1671, and he married the Catholic Mary of Modena, an act which alienated many Englishmen. In 1677 James consented to the marriage of his daughter Mary (later Mary II) to the Protestant Prince William of Orange (later William III), and the couple became the heirs presumptive to the throne after James. When Charles II died in 1685, James ascended peacefully to the throne, but was deposed three years later in the Glorious Revolution, which put William and Mary on the throne. James fled, was captured, and was allowed to escape to France, where he died in inglorious exile in 1701 although several unsuccessful efforts were waged to restore him to power.

Jonson's *Und*. LXXXII celebrates the christening of James.

Janiculo, Stephano. A sham prince, known as Bodgan, Prince of Moldavia, who is alluded to in *Epicoene* (v. i). He visited England in 1601 and enlisted the support of Elizabeth, was imprisoned by the Turks in Constantinople but escaped disguised as a woman in 1606, and returned to England in 1607. King James gave him a grant, and the next year issued a warrant for the Levant Company to secure his restitution. In 1608 Janiculo announced in Venice that he was going to marry Lady Arabella Stuart, a cousin of James, but he was already married to a Venetian woman. Except for causing some excitement, nothing ever came of this announcement, although Lady Arabella was eventually confined to the Tower for marrying Sir William Seymour without James's permission.

Januarius. A character in *The Masque of Beauty,* who appears as the prince of months.

Janus. An ancient Italian god with two or more faces looking in different directions. He was the god of beginnings, and the month of January was sacred to him. Janus also guarded gates and doors, and in ancient Rome the doors of his temple were open during war and closed during peace. He was considered an important god, being named at the beginning of any list of gods in a prayer.

Japetus. Father of Prometheus.

Jason. Son of Aeson, the rightful king of Iolcos in Thessaly. When Aeson's half brother Pelias usurped the throne and either killed or imprisoned Aeson, Jason was smuggled away to be reared by the centaur Chiron. When Jason later tried to gain the throne, Pelias gave Jason what the unlawful king thought would be an impossible task: to obtain from Aeëtes, king of Colchis, the Golden Fleece, which had magic powers and was guarded by a giant serpent. For this purpose, Jason built the ship *Argo,* and with the aid of Aeëtes' daughter Medea, whom he promised to marry, Jason was successful in his mission. He later abandoned Medea and was killed when part of the *Argo* fell on him as he slept under the stern.

Jealousy. In *Chloridia,* a symbolic character who appears in the second entry of the antimasque.

Jenkin. A Welshman who appears in *For the Honor of Wales,* criticizes *Pleasure Reconciled to Virtue,* and insists that a masque in which the Prince of Wales performs should have a Welsh setting.

Jephson, Sir William. A friend of Jonson's who was knighted in 1603 and to whom Jonson addressed *Epig.* CXVI.

Jermyn, Robert, of Rushbrook, the eldest son of Sir Thomas Jermyn, was baptized in 1601 and died of the fever in 1623. Jonson wrote an epitaph in Latin for him (*Quid diurnare magnos invides Parca?*).

Jerome, Saint (347?–?420), was a Father and Doctor of the Church who was acclaimed for his exposition of Scripture and whose scholarly texts became the basis for the Vulgate. During his life Jerome was involved in many theological and scholarly controversies, and his correspondence with Augustine is of particular interest. In *Timber* (ll. 2306–7), Jonson, in the course of a discussion on aspersions, alludes to St.

Jerome's comment (*Epist.* cxxv) that where the discussion of faults is general no one is injured.

Jeronimo (Hieronymo). An Italian fencer alluded to in *The New Inn* (II. v).

Jeweller. A craftsman called to take part in the courtship contest in *Cynthia's Revels*. He offers Mercury a jewel for hire during Mercury's staged primping and is criticized for his high prices.

Joan. In *A Tale of a Tub,* one of the bridesmaids for Audrey's intended marriage to John Clay.

John, Earl of Cornwall. Brother of Edward III in Jonson's fragment *Mortimer His Fall,* who joins with the king to investigate the charges against Mortimer.

John of Gaunt, Prince (1340–1399), was the fourth son of Edward III. As the Duke of Lancaster, he enjoyed rich holdings that made him the wealthiest and most influential noble of his day in England. In 1396 John married Catherine Swynford, who had long been his mistress and who had borne him several children. In 1397 Richard II declared their children, under the name of Beaufort, to be legitimate. John died in 1399, soon after the King had exiled his eldest son, the Duke of Hereford (later Henry IV). The Tudor royal line was descended from John and Catherine. Gaunt was Geoffrey Chaucer's patron.

Gaunt's relationship with Catherine and the Beauforts is alluded to in *The New Inn* (V. v).

Johnson, Richard. See George WITHER.

Johnson, Robert. Composer of a musical setting for Jonson's song "From the famous Peak of Darby" (*Gypsies Metamorphosed*), first published in John Playford's *The Musical Companion, In Two Books* (1673).

Johnston, George Burke (1907–   ). American scholar. Since 1974 Professor Emeritus of English at Virginia Polytechnic and State University. Author of the first major study of Jonson as a poet, *Ben Jonson: Poet* (1945), and other publications on English literature of the Renaissance.

Johphiel. Described by Jonson as an aery spirit and an Intelligence of Jupiter's sphere, Johphiel appears as a character in *The Fortunate Isles, and Their Union* who engages in sport with Mere-Fool and delivers to Neptune (the king) the message from the Fates and Jove that the isles of Neptune will be united and blessed.

Joinville, Prince (1571–1640), was the son of the Duke of Guise. His name was Charles de Lorraine. He had been imprisoned for his part in the internal troubles of France and had made his peace with Henri IV in 1594. In 1607 Joinville came to England and was present at Jonson's *Entertainment of the King and Queen at Theobalds.* Richelieu eventually forced Joinville to leave France, and he died abroad.

Jones, Inigo (1573–1652), the son of a clothmaker, was able to travel in Europe at the expense of the Earl of Rutland. In Italy he studied the remains of Roman architecture and the Renaissance buildings of Palladio. When Jones returned to England, he established himself as the earliest of England's great architects, designing settings for masques at the court of James and later Charles and performing other architectural services for the crown. He was also sponsored by the Earl of Arundel. After repeated visits to Italy, Jones became the king's surveyor general of works in 1615. In 1616 he began work on the Queen's House (Greenwich), the first English one to embody Palladian principles. From 1619 to 1622 he built the royal banqueting hall at Whitehall, again using classic principles he had learned in Italy. He also made designs for St. Paul's Cathedral and Covent Garden and constructed other houses in London and the country. By the time he died in 1652, Jones's work had marked the beginning of classical architecture of the late Renaissance and Georgian periods in England.

Jones and Jonson had a long relationship which began amicably but ended in bitterness while they were employed to make masques for the court. It seems likely that Jones may have been a member of the group who met regularly at the Mermaid, and Jonson told Drummond (*Conversations,* ll. 317–21) a story about dining with Jones at Lord Salisbury's. The two artists first worked together on *The Masque of Blackness,* and Jonson readily acknowledged Jones's contribution to the work, as he also did in *Hymenaei, The Haddington Masque,* and *The Masque of Queens.* But by 1611 or so the relationship between the two had become strained, and Jonson suppressed any mention of Jones's part in *Oberon, Love Freed, Pleasure Reconciled, Pan's Anniversary, The Masque of Augurs, Time Vindicated, Neptune's Triumph,* and *The Fortunate Isles.* When Jones objected to his name's being listed second on the title page of *Love's Triumph,* Jonson retaliated by leaving his name completely off the title page of *Chloridia,* and the break between the two was final. By 1631 Jones's reputation as a masque maker had reached its peak while Jonson's had declined, and Jones then stood with Charles where Jonson had with James a decade before.

Jonson had not accepted defeat quietly. He satirized Inigo with a vengeance in *Tale of a Tub* (In-and-In Medlay), *Bartholomew Fair* (Lanthorn Leatherhead), "An Expostulation with Inigo Jones," "To a Friend, An Epigram of Him," "To Inigo Marquis Would-be," *Epig.* CXV and CXXIX, and *Love's Welcome* (Iniquo Vitruvius). In the *Conversations* (ll. 467–72), Jonson said he told Prince Charles that when he wanted words to express the greatest villain in the world he would call him an Inigo. Later Jonson said that Jones accused him of calling him a fool behind his back, but Jonson said he only called him an errant knave (ll. 470–72).

Jones's only known response was "To His False Friend, Mr. Ben Jonson," left in manuscript. A contemporary account does record that Jones attended the first performance of *The Magnetic Lady* and was elated to see how bad it was. According to Archdeacon Plume's notes on Ben Jonson, Inigo dared not call Jonson a jackanapes, but it seems doubtful that Jones would have had any great fear of Jonson, although he probably did respect the power of the old poet's pen. George Chapman left in manuscript a savage attack upon Jonson that was probably provoked by Jonson's treatment of Jones. Apparently Jonson had no knowledge of the poem, or he would, even from his sickbed, have responded in kind.

Jonson, Ben. Jonson's life and career are outlined chronologically below:

1572–73. Born near London sometime between May 5, 1572 and January 19, 1573, possibly on June 11, 1572. His father, a minister, died sometime in 1572, and Jonson was born a month after his father's death. Within two or three years his mother married a master-bricklayer, of whom little is known, and the family moved to Charing Cross, where Jonson spent his childhood and attended private school in St. Martin's Church until a friend put him to school at Westminster, where William Camden was probably his master.

1588. Removed from school and put into the business of his stepfather.

1591–92?. Volunteered and fought in Flanders.

Sometime between 1592 and 1595,
probably on November 14, 1594, married Anne Lewis. First son (Benjamin) born in 1596. (A daughter who died at six months was also born sometime during these years, presumably after the marriage.)

July, 1597. Employed as playwright for Henslowe.

August–October, 1597. Imprisoned for acting in and for part authorship of *The Isle of Dogs,* a play the authorities felt was seditious.

September, 1598. Every Man in His Humour acted by Lord Chamberlain's Men at The Curtain with Shakespeare playing a leading role.

September 22, 1598. Kills Gabriel Spencer, a fellow actor in Henslowe's Company, in a duel in Hoxton Fields and is imprisoned in Newgate.

October, 1598. Tried at Old Bailey and escapes gallows by pleading benefit of clergy. Goods confiscated and Tyburn brand placed on his thumb. While in prison converted to Catholicism. *The Case Is Altered* acted by the Children of the Chapel Royal.

1599. Collaborated with Dekker and others for Admiral's Company in writing two lost tragedies—*Page of Plymouth* and *Robert II King of Scots.*

1599–1600. Every Man out of His Humour acted by Lord Chamberlain's Men at new Globe Theatre.

1599–1602. "War of the Theatres":

1599. Jonson offended by Marston's portrait of him as the poet and philosopher Chrisoganus in *Histrio-mastix;* Jonson apparently satirizes Marston's turgid style in *Every Man out* (Chamberlain's play).

1600. Marston satirizes Jonson as Brabant Senior in *Jack Drum's Entertainment* (a Paul's play).

1601. Jonson apparently satirizes Marston as Hedon and Dekker as Anaides in *Cynthia's Revels* (a Chapel play). Marston satirizes Jonson as Lampatho Doria in *What You Will* (probably a Paul's play). Jonson (portrayed as Horace) ridicules Dekker as Demetrius and Marston as Crispinus in *Poetaster* (a Chapel play). Dekker, probably assisted by Marston, ridicules Horace in *Satiromastix* (a Chamberlain's and Paul's play).

September 25, 1601. Jonson paid two pounds by Henslowe for additions to Kyd's *Spanish Tragedy.*

June 22, 1602. Jonson paid ten pounds by Henslowe for further additions and advance on book called "Richard Crookback" (Richard III).

1602. Jonson living in seclusion with Sir Robert Townshend.

1603–1607. Jonson probably living with Esmé Stewart, Lord D'Aubigny.

1603. Son Benjamin, age 6, dies. *Sejanus* acted by Lord Chamberlain's Men (now known as King's Men). Accused by the Earl of Northampton, Jonson was called before the Privy Council on the charge of popery and treason.

June, 1603. Performance of *King's Entertainment at Althorp,* Jonson's first royal entertainment.

March, 1604. Performance of *King's Coronation Entertainment* and *A Panegyre.*

May, 1604. Performance of *Entertainment at Highgate.*

January, 1605. Performance of *Masque of Blackness.*

1604 or 1605. Eastward Ho written in collaboration with Chapman and Marston and acted by the Children of the Queen's Revels (formerly called the Children of the Chapel). Chapman and Jonson imprisoned because of a supposed slight in the play against the Scots and especially King James.

May 4–September 4, 1605. Jonson wrote letters to powerful persons including Suffolk and Salisbury, urging them to work for his and others' speedy release from prison. All later released.

October 9(?), 1605. Jonson attends a Catholic supper party given by Robert Catesby, later discovered to be a principal conspirator in Gunpowder Plot.

November 7, 1605. Jonson commissioned by Lord Salisbury two days after the abortive Gunpowder Plot to convey a promise of safe conduct to an unnamed foreign priest who had offered to help the state. Working through the chaplain of the Venetian ambassador, Jonson was unable to find the priest, and he so informed Salisbury the following day.

January, 1606. Performance of *Hymenaei* and *Barriers.*

April, 1606. Jonson and his wife cited for recusancy.

July, 1606. Performance of *Entertainment of the Two Kings at Theobalds*

1606. Volpone acted at Oxford and Cambridge and by King's Men at the Globe Theatre.

January, 1608. Performance of *The Masque of Beauty.*

February, 1608. Performance of *The Haddington Masque.*

February, 1609. Performance of *The Masque of Queens.*

1609. Epicoene acted by Children of the Queen's Revels.

January, 1610. Performance of *Prince Henry's Barriers.*

1610. The Alchemist acted by the King's Men.

1610(?). Jonson returns to Anglican religion.

1610. Jonson gives deposition in Chancery suit of William Roe *versus* Walter Garland.

January, 1611. Performance of *Oberon, the Fairy Prince.*

February, 1611. Performance of *Love Freed From Ignorance and Folly.*

1611. Catiline acted by the King's Men.

1612–13. Jonson travels in France as tutor to son of Sir Walter Raleigh.

January, 1612. Performance of *Love Restored.*

1612. Jonson probably begins to prepare material for the first folio of his works.

September 4, 1612. Jonson witnesses a theological debate between Protestant and Catholic champions in Paris.

June 29, 1613. Jonson witnesses the burning of the Globe Theatre in London.

December, 1613, and January, 1614. Performance of *A Challenge at Tilt* and *The Irish Masque.*

October, 1614. Bartholomew Fair acted by Lady Elizabeth's Men.

January, 1615. Performance of *Mercury Vindicated.*

January, 1616. Performance of *The Golden Age Restored.*

February, 1616. King James grants Jonson an annual pension of 100 marks.

1616. Publication by William Stansby of the first folio of *Works.*

1616. The Devil Is an Ass acted by the King's Men.

December, 1616. Performance of *Christmas His Masque.*

February, 1617. Performance of *Lovers Made Men.*

December, 1617. Performance of *Vision of Delight.*

1618–19. Jonson travels on foot to Scotland.

January, 1618. Performance of *Pleasure Reconciled to Virtue.*

February, 1618. Performance of *For the Honor of Wales.*

September, 1618. Jonson stays at Leith with John Stuart.

September and October, 1618. Jonson's presence in Edinburgh recorded in City Archives.

December, 1618–January 17,

1619. Jonson stays with William Drummond at Hawthornden.

July 17, 1619. Jonson awarded honorary M.A. by Oxford University.

May(?), 1620. Performance of *Entertainment at Blackfriars.*

January, 1621. Performance of *News from the New World.*

October 5, 1621. Jonson nominated by warrant of reversion to Office of Master of the Revels.

August and September, 1621. Performance of *The Gypsies Metamorphosed.*

May, 1622. Performance of *Masque of Augurs.*

January, 1623. Performance of *Time Vindicated.*

October 20, 1623. In a deposition given in Chancery Court Jonson is associated with Gresham College in London (probably as a lecturer in rhetoric).

October or November, 1623. There was a fire in Jonson's lodgings, and many books and manuscripts were destroyed.

1623(?)–1624(?). Performance of *Pan's Anniversary.*

January, 1624. Performance of *Neptune's Triumph.*

August, 1624. Performance of *Masque of Owls.*

January, 1625. Performance of *The Fortunate Isles.*

1626. The Staple of News acted by the King's Men.

1628. Jonson paralyzed by a stroke.

September, 1628. Jonson appointed chronologer of the city of London (a sinecure).

January 19, 1629. The New Inn acted by the King's Men. Jonson given a grant by Dean and Chapter of Westminster.

October 26, 1629. Jonson examined by the attorney general, Sir Robert Heath, about his knowledge of verses which approved the stabbing of the Duke of Buckingham by John Felton.

March 26, 1630. Jonson's royal pension increased by Charles to 100 pounds per year plus an annual tierce of canary from the cellars of Whitehall.

January, 1631. Performance of *Love's Triumph through Callipolis.*

February, 1631. Performance of *Chloridia.*

1631. Plays (*Bartholomew Fair, The Devil Is an Ass,* and *The Staple of News*) published in folio by Robert Allot.

1632. The Magnetic Lady acted by King's Men.

1633. A Tale of a Tub acted by Queen Henrietta's Men.

May, 1633. Performance of the *King's Entertainment at Welbeck.*

January, 1634. Repeat performance of *A Tale of a Tub* at Whitehall.

July, 1634. Performance of *Love's Welcome at Bolsover.*

November, 1635. Only remaining son died.

August 6, 1637. Jonson died in Westminster, apparently intestate.

August 9, 1637. Burial in Westminster Abbey.

March, 1638. Publication of *Jonsonus Virbius.*

1640–41. Publication of second folio of *Works* (in two volumes).

Drummond's notes (the *Conversations*) have been an immensely valuable although not entirely reliable source of information. The following items are from ll. 233–335.

Jonson's grandfather came from Carlisle, served King Henry VIII, and was a gentleman. Jonson's father lost his estate under Queen Mary and was thrown into prison. When he was released, he became a minister. Jonson himself was born one month after his father's death. He was brought up in poverty. He was put in school by a friend [probably William Camden], but was afterwards withdrawn and put to work as a wright or bricklayer, which he detested. He served in the Low Countries, where he killed an opponent in single combat before the two armies. After his return to England and his studies, he killed another man in a duel, for which he was imprisoned and nearly went to the gallows. While in prison he was converted to Catholicism by a priest who visited him, and thereafter he was a Papist for twelve years. He was given honorary M.A.'s by both universities. Jonson's wife was "a shrew yet honest," and for a period of five years he did not live with her but stayed instead in the home of Lord Aubigny. When he was imprisoned during the reign of Queen Elizabeth, his judges could not get him to talk, so they put two spies in with him, but he had been warned by the jailkeeper. He later wrote an epigram on the spies.

At the time James came to the throne, the plague was in London and Jonson was staying in the country at the home of Sir Robert Cotton with Camden. There he had one night a vision of his eldest son with the mark of a bloody cross on his forehead. Amazed, he prayed, and in the morning related the vision to Camden, who persuaded him it was only a fancy not worth worrying about, but he soon received a letter from his wife telling him his son had died of the plague. In the vision his son looked manly and of the size that Jonson expected him to be at the resurrection.

Sir James Murray reported him to the King for writing something against the Scots in *Eastward Ho,* and he voluntarily imprisoned himself with Chapman, one of the co-authors of the play. (Marston, the other co-author, escaped imprisonment.) Although the rumor was that they would have their ears and noses cut, they were exonerated and afterwards had a banquet to which Camden, Selden, and other friends were invited. During the banquet, Jonson's mother drank to him and showed him an envelope containing strong poison which she said she had intended to mix in his drink in prison if the decision had gone against him. She also had intended to take the poison herself.

His quarrel with Marston, on whom he wrote *Poetaster,* began when Marston represented him on the stage.

Jonson considered that wanton wives made much better mistresses than did maidens. Two strange incidents happened to him in this regard. A man made his own wife court Jonson, and Jonson enjoyed her favors for over two years before he realized that the husband knew about the relationship. Another woman Jonson enjoyed many times, but she would never consent to the last act.

As tutor, he accompanied the son of Sir Walter Raleigh to France. The youth got Jonson dead drunk, put him on a cart, pushed him through the streets, and said that Jonson was a more lively image of the Crucifix than any the French had. The boy's mother was amused, claiming that his father was so inclined in his youth, but Sir Walter himself was not pleased.

Jonson claimed that he could set horoscopes but did not trust them. Once he tricked a lady who had made an appointment to see an astrologer. Jonson disguised himself in a long robe and a white beard, and the lady kept the appointment.

Every New Year's Day the Earl of Pembroke sent him twenty pounds to buy books.

After he was reconciled to the Church, at his first communion in the spirit of true reconciliation he drank the whole cup of wine.

Being at the end of Lord Salisbury's table with Inigo Jones, Jonson was asked why he was not happy, and he replied that he did not think he dined with the Lord unless he ate from his serving dish.

Jonson said that he had spent a whole night looking at his big toe about which in his imagination he had seen Tartars, Turks, Romans, and Carthaginians fighting.

Northampton was his mortal enemy, had him called before the Council for *Sejanus,* and accused him of both popery and treason.

On several occasions, Jonson claimed, he had sold all of his books out of necessity.

Jonson said he had a mind to be a clergyman, and wished he had the opportunity to preach one sermon before the King because he would not flatter even if he were to die.

Drummond concluded the *Conversations* (ll. 680–99) with what are apparently his own impressions of Jonson. He said that Jonson was a lover and praiser of himself and a scorner of others, that he was a man both passionately kind and passionately angry who often interpreted the best words or deeds for the the worst, that he was well versed in both Catholicism and Protestantism, and that he was oppressed with fantasy which had mastered his reason. He added that Jonson's inventions are smooth and easy but that he excels in a translation. As a last barb, Drummond says that after Jonson's *The Silent Woman* was first acted there were found verses on the stage indicating that the play was well named since there was never any man to give plaudits to it.

Jonson scholarship. Jonson scholarship may be broadly divided into the following areas: 1) life, background, contexts, and influences; 2) dramatic achievement and the Elizabethan and Jacobean theater; 3) poetic achievement; and 4) specialized studies.

The first two centuries after Jonson's death added little to our understanding of his life and works. During the seventeenth century a number of commendatory verses and contemporary poems on Jonson's individual works were published, and a few notes on his life were recorded. Following his death in 1637, a number of elegies were published, many of which were collected in *Jonsonus Virbius.* Although a few of these elegies contain literary criticism, most of them are merely laudatory poems. After the Restoration, Fuller and Aubrey recorded notes on Jonson's life and works, some of which were inaccurate, but the most important criticism of the period was that of Dryden, who understood and extolled the virtues of Jonson's comedy. In 1756 Chetwood published his memoirs on

Jonson, but the book contributed little to Jonson scholarship.

Modern Jonson scholarship actually began in the nineteenth century. In 1819 Hazlitt explained Jonson's virtues as a comic writer, and in 1836 Coleridge included notes on Jonson in his *Literary Remains*. J. A. Symond's study (1896) found fault with Jonson's lack of romantic temperament. A. C. Swinburne (1889) criticized Jonson's inability to sing and to create sympathy for his characters although he admired his sententiousness. Because it became so influential, Swinburne's sympathetic study of Jonson is often considered to mark the beginning of modern Jonson criticism. At the end of the century Woodbridge (1898) analyzed Jonson's comedies with particular attention to his classicism, and Penniman and Small published studies on Jonson's role in the War of the Theatres.

Twentieth-century scholarship has run the gamut in subjects and significance. Castelain's mammoth general study of Jonson was published in Paris in 1907, the same year that Nason's study on Jonson's heraldry was published in New York. In 1911 Bakerville analyzed English elements in Jonson's early comedy, and in 1912 Kerr assessed Jonson's influence on English comedy in general. In 1919 G. G. Smith published a sympathetic general study of Jonson, but probably the most influential study of Jonson in the early twentieth century was T. S. Eliot's 1919 essay which called for a total reassessment of Jonson's achievements. *The Jonson Allusion Book* appeared in 1922, and in 1925 the first volume of the Herford and Simpson edition of the works was published by Oxford University Press. This edition, completed in 1952, became the standard critical one for Jonson. Dunn's study (1925) on life and art as reflected in Jonson's works did not prove to be so influential as the later study on drama and society by L. C. Knights (1937). Evans's study (1929) on Jonson and Elizabethan music is still the standard work on the subject, but her book should be supplemented with Chan's more recent one (1981) on music in the theater of Jonson. Hillberry's analysis of Jonson's ethics (1933) is still a useful reference, and Palmer's general study (1934) continues to be worth consulting. Noyes's carefully researched book (1935) on Jonson's plays as performed on the Restoration and eighteenth-century stages added much to our understanding of Jonsonian theater, especially when considered with Frickers's more recent but less reliable study of Jonson's plays in performance (1972). Leg-

gatt's perceptive analysis of Jonson's vision and art was published in 1981.

Jonson's classicism has proved to be a subject of intense interest. Schelling's seminal study of Jonson and the classical school appeared in 1898, and Wheeler's study on classical mythology in Jonson's works appeared in 1938. In 1939 McEuen assessed the classical influence on the Tribe of Ben, and in 1941 Proebstef analyzed Jonson's progress from classicism to realism in the comedies. In 1901 Lumley assessed the influence of Plautus on the comedies, and more recently Duncan has considered Jonson and the Lucianic tradition (1979).

The relationship between Jonson and Shakespeare has also interested many critics. In 1939 Rendall published his study of Jonson and the First Folio of Shakespeare. Bentley's two-volume study (1949) compared the reputations of Shakespeare and Jonson in the seventeenth century. Musgrove's study of the two dramatists appeared in 1957. Grene's interesting comparative study of the comic patterns and attitudes of Shakespeare, Jonson, and Molière was published in 1980.

Jonson's dramatic theory and practice has attracted the attention of many scholars. In 1947 Baum studied the satiric and the didactic in Jonson's comedies, and Townsend explained the art of the comedies with special reference to *Bartholomew Fair*. In 1957 Enck attempted to determine Jonson's comic truth, and in 1959 Bamborough wrote a general introduction to Jonson with particular attention to the comedies. Partridge's highly influential study of the major comedies appeared in 1958, and later Thayer (1963) and Knoll (1964) published important general studies of the plays. In 1967 Champion attempted to reassess Jonson's so-called dotages, and Davis studied the achievement of the Sons of Ben in Caroline England. Gibbons included Jonson in his general study of the satiric comedy (1968), as did Donaldson in 1970.

There have also been a number of studies on particular aspects of Jonson's plays. Jackson (1968) has analyzed vision and judgment in the plays, and Dessen (1971) has considered Jonson's moral comedy. Johansson has analyzed religion and superstition as seen in the plays (1950) and has described the law and lawyers of Elizabethan England as reflected in Jonson's dramatic works (1967). Bryant has viewed Jonson as a compassionate satirist (1972), and Arnold has analyzed Jonson's Cavalier heroes (1972). Two studies have assessed the Aristophanic aspects of Jonson's plays: Dunn (1969) and Dick (1974). DeLuna's study of the historical implications of *Catiline* was published in 1967.

Until fairly recently critics have tended to stress Jonson's dramatic achievement and to ignore his poetic accomplishments. The first major study of Jonson as a poet was published by Johnston in 1945. Nichols's general study appeared in 1969, and Gardiner's analysis of the development of Jonson's poetry was published in 1975. Parfitt published his study of Jonson as public poet and private man in 1977, and in 1981 Peterson explained Jonson's artistic use of imitation and praise.

Like the poetry, the artistry of the masque has been generally neglected by scholars until recently. In 1948 Gilbert explained the symbolic persons in the masque, but Orgel's seminal study of the art of the Jonsonian masque did not appear until 1965, followed the next year by Meagher's analysis of method and meaning in the works. In 1975 appeared Randall's extensive analysis of the background and historical implications of *The Gypsies Metamorphosed.*

Jonson's language has been the focus for a great deal of scholarship. King (1941) has studied the language in *Poetaster,* Sackton (1948) has focused on rhetoric as dramatic language in Jonson's works, and Penniman (1951) has also analyzed the language of the dramatic works. A. C. Partridge has produced two linguistic studies of Jonson's language, one on the syntax of the plays (1953) and one on the accidence of the plays, masques, and entertainments (1953). Trimpi (1962) has explained Jonson's plain style, and Barish (1960) has contributed an influential study of Jonson's language of prose comedy. Stagg (1967) has done an index to the figurative language of the tragedies, and Beauline (1978) has studied Jonson and Elizabethan comedy with particular attention to Jonson's dramatic rhetoric.

Other twentieth-century scholarship on Jonson has ranged widely in subject. In the 1950s de Vocht published a series of studies on the text of Jonson's plays in which he generally argued for the authority of the quartos over the first folio, but his views were rejected by the Oxford editors and have been pretty much ignored by subsequent editors. Although no major critical biography on Jonson has yet appeared, Chute published a popular biography in 1953. Boughner (1968) has assessed Machiavelli's influence on Jonson, and in 1970 Redwine collected Jonson's

literary criticism into a single volume.

During the quadricentennial, two international conferences were held in Canada to celebrate the occasion, one at the University of Waterloo and one at the University of Toronto. These celebrations were attended by scholars from throughout the world, and the papers from the conference were subsequently published in individual volumes.

Jonson has proved to be a figure of international scholarly appeal. German scholarship on Jonson has been particularly prolific, and some of the most important studies have been contributed by von Baudissin (1836), Schmidt (1847), Saegelken (1880), Soergel (1882), Hoffschulte (1894), Koeppel (1895 and 1906), Reinsch (1898), Grossmann (1898), Holstein (1901), Hofmiller (1901), Brotanek (1902), de Vogt (1905), Aronstein (1906), Birck (1908), Pfeffer (1934), and Tiedje (1963). The French have also contributed, in addition to Castelain, with the studies by Reyher (1909) and Messiaen (1948). Italian studies have come from Praz (1937) and Capone (1969). Wada's study of Jonson was published in Tokyo in 1963, and Gottwald's analysis of Jonson's comedy appeared in Wroclaw in 1969.

For further details on Jonson scholarship, see the Selected Bibliography.

Jonson's correspondence. About twenty or so letters written by Jonson and to him have survived. Seven of the letters were written by Jonson in 1605 during his imprisonment along with Chapman for the unauthorized publication of *Eastward Ho.* Each of the letters solicits aid from an important person to help in freeing him and his cohort from prison. The letters suggest that Jonson and Chapman were imprisoned "unexamined and unheard," protest their innocence, state that their arrest is apparently a result of the King's anger, and imply that some others are guilty. In one letter Jonson proclaims that since his first error, which was presumably his imprisonment for his part in the lost play *The Isle of Dogs*, he has tried to keep his work from being offensive in any way, and he challenges his accusers to examine all his past works to determine "whether I have ever (in anything I have ever written private, or public) given offensive to a nation, to any public, order or state, to any person of honor, or authority." Not all of the letters are dated nor are they addressed to a specific person, but presumably they were all written in 1605 and were probably addressed to the following: the Earl of Suffolk, the Earl of Salisbury, the Countess of Bedford, Lord D'Aubigny, the Earl of Montgomery, the Earl of Pembroke, and another unnamed lord.

Other letters by Jonson which have survived include: a letter to a Mr. Leech, who was probably John Leech, secretary to the Earl of Pembroke. This letter requests Mr. Leech's assistance in "a business of so great charity." Another letter is addressed to Mr. Thomas Bond, secretary to the Lord Chancellor of England. This letter requests Mr. Bond's help in "furthering this gentleman's suit." The gentleman is unnamed.

In yet another letter to the Earl of Salisbury, Jonson apologizes for being unable to complete a task which the earl had apparently asked him to do, but concludes, "I shall yet make further trial and that you cannot in the meantime be provided: I do not only with all readiness offer my service, but will perform it with as much integrity as your particular favor, or his majesty's right in any subject he hath, can exact."

A letter addressed to Dr. Donne attempts to clear Jonson of an accusation which has been made against him and states, "but there is a greater penalty threatened, the loss of you my true friend; for others I reckon not, who were never had, you have so subscribed yourself. Alas, how easy is a man accused that is forsaken of defense!"

Several letters from William Drummond to Jonson, all dated 1619, are extant. One explains that Drummond is sending an epigram to Jonson that he had requested and suggests that if there is any other thing Drummond can do for him, he will be glad to do it. Another letter from Drummond, of which there is also a rough draft, thanks Jonson for writing to a Mr. Fenton and remembering Drummond in that letter quite fondly. A letter from Jonson to Drummond, also dated 1619, requests a number of things from Drummond, including "that you inquire for me whether the students' method at St. Andrew's be the same with that at Edinburgh and so to assure me or wherein they differ." Another 1619 letter from Drummond to Jonson goes into an elaborate explanation of the "impressaes and emblems on a bed of state wrought and embroidered all with gold and silk by the late queen Mary, mother to our sacred sovereign, which will embellish greatly some pages of your book and is worthy your remembrance."

Five letters, all undated but presumably written about 1631, are addressed to

the Earl of Newcastle, and they all are letters requesting money from the earl, who is frequently described as "my best patron."

A letter from Jonson to Sir Robert Cotton requests that Sir Robert lend Jonson a book for one day.

A letter written in Latin by Jonson in a corner of Thomas Farnaby's edition of Martial (1615) is addressed to Richard Briggs, who was from 1602 to 1630 headmaster of Norfolk School.

Jonson's family. Although the details are sketchy, we have some information on Jonson's family. In the *Conversations* (ll. 233–35), Jonson told Drummond that he thought his grandfather originally came from Annandale but moved to Carlisle and that he served Henry VIII. Jonson's father (ll. 236–39) lost all of his estate, which was apparently considerable, under Queen Mary, was imprisoned and became a minister. Jonson himself was born about a month after his father's death in 1572 or 1573. According to Aubrey's notes, Jonson's mother married a bricklayer after the death of her first husband. In the *Conversations* (ll. 278–83), Jonson relates that his old mother had intended to give him poison, after she had taken it herself, if the sentence had been execution when Jonson was imprisoned for his part in the allegedly offensive *Eastward Ho*. Sometime between 1592 and 1595 Jonson probably married Anne Lewis. In the *Conversations* (ll. 254–55)," he describes her as "a shrew yet honest" and says he did not live with her for five years when he resided with Aubigny. When both he and his wife were cited for recusancy in 1606, Jonson denied the charge against her, so she apparently did not share his faith during his Catholic period. We do not know when she died. He may have married a second time, but it seems unlikely. See Hester HOPKINS. The woman who cared for Jonson after his stroke and received his pension, as reported by Izaak Walton to Aubrey, was not his wife. Jonson's first child was probably Mary, the child of her parents' youth commemorated in *Epig.* XXII. His first son Benjamin died of the plague at seven years of age in 1603. In the *Conversations* (ll. 260–72), Jonson tells of his visionary premonition of his son's death when Jonson was staying in the country at the house of Sir Robert Cotton. Benjamin is movingly commemorated in *Epig.* XLV. Other probable children include: Joseph, baptized in 1599; a second son Benjamin, baptized in 1608 and died in 1611; and Elizabeth, baptized in 1610. There probably were other children, both legitimate and illegitimate, but they have not been documented. Apparently, no legitimate children survived Jonson.

Jonson's library. Jonson was known by his contemporaries as a poet with a well-furnished library. Every New Year's Day Lord Pembroke gave Jonson twenty pounds to buy books with, and there is ample evidence that the money was well spent. Approximately 200 items included in Jonson's collection have been identified. Both John Selden and Barten Holyday mention borrowing from Jonson's collection. Jonson's own marginal notes to *Sejanus* and *The Masque of Queens* suggest the breadth and depth of his collection. We know that his library included manuscripts, scriptures, English works (including translations and chronicles), Greek and Roman writers, Renaissance and later writers, antiquities and scholarship, and languages and grammar. Jonson prefixed verses to at least twenty-three works published by his friends (see COMMENDATORY POEMS) and so must have had copies of those books, but not many of them have been traced.

It was Jonson's habit to inscribe his books with his motto — "Tanquàm Explorator" — and his name, and he frequently annotated them, sometimes writing names in the margins, sometimes making underlinings that suggest literary ideas, and sometimes writing notes that suggest his studies in a new field.

In the autumn of 1623 a fire destroyed most of Jonson's library, an event which he commemorated with a certain amount of humor in *Und.* XLIII. Ten years later he narrowly escaped another fire. There was also another threat to Jonson's collection. As he told Drummond of Hawthornden, he had sometimes had to sell his books to raise money.

For a list of the books known to have been in Jonson's library, see W. C. Hazlitt's *Contributions toward a Dictionary of Book Collectors*, Part 8, pp. 3 and 4; Robert W. Ramsey's "Books from the Library of Ben Jonson," in *Transactions of the Royal Society of Literature* 27 (1897): 139–53, 155–57; and Herford and Simpson, I, pp. 250–71; XI, pp. 593–603. *See* BIBLE for lists of the scriptures in Jonson's library and the obvious Biblical allusions in his works.

Jonsonus Virbius: or, The Memory of Ben Jonson Revived by the Friends of the Muses, a collection of thirty-three elegies on the death of Jonson, was edited by Bryan Duppa, Bishop of Chichester, printed by Elisabeth Purslowe for Henry Seile, and first published in 1638. According to Aubrey, Lord Falkland was responsible for the name of the volume. Hippolytus, the favorite of Diana, was given the name Virbius when Aesculapius restored him to life after his murder. Many writers had apparently sent poems to Duppa to be included in the volume, but some arrived too late for insertion, Sir William Davenants' among them. In general David Masson was right when he said: "The gist of all the panegyrics, various as they were in style, was that English poetry had died with Ben. The panegyrics themselves went near to prove it" (*Life of Milton* [1881], I, 467). The contributors to the volume, following the order of the poems, were: Lord FALKLAND, Richard SACKVILLE, John BEAUMONT, Thomas HAWKINS, Henry KING, Henry COVENTRY, Thomas MAY, Dudley DIGGES, George FORTESCUE, William HABINGTON, Edmund WALLER, James HOWELL, John VERNON, Sidney GODOLPHIN, James CLEYTON, Jasper MAYNE, William CARTWRIGHT, Joseph RUTTER, Owen FELLTHAM, George DONNE, Shackerley MARMION, John FORD, Ralph BRIDEOAKE, Richard WEST, Robert MEADE, Henry RAMSAY, Francis WORTLEY, Thomas TERŒ RENT, Robert WARING, William BEAW (Bew), and Samuel EVANS. There was also an anonymous contribution.

Jordan. In *The New Inn*, a chamberlain who is considered an officer of the house of militia by Colonel Tipto.

Josephus, Flavius. (A.D. 37–?95). Jewish soldier and historian. He was a Pharisee who was made governor of Galilee at the beginning of the war between the Romans and Jews. He eventually won the favor of the Roman general Vespasian and took his name Flavius, causing criticism of his conduct. Josephus' fame rests upon his historical writings, which include *The Jewish War*, *Antiquities of the Jews*, and *Against Apion*. Josephus is quoted in *The Masque of Queens*.

Jove. Another name for the Roman god Jupiter identified with the Greek god Zeus. The chief god of the Romans, he is discovered in *The Masque of Augurs* in heaven with the Senate of the gods, and he verifies the interpretation of the augury offered by Apollo. Jove does not appear in *The Golden Age Restored* but is proclaimed to be the instigator of the new golden age on earth. In the masque the audience was to identify the king with Jove.

Joyce. In *A Tale of a Tub*, one of the bridesmaids for Audrey's intended marriage to John Clay.

Jug. In *The New Inn*, a tapster who is a good source of news.

Juga. A symbolic character who appears in *Hymenaei* as one of the powers of Juno.

Juggler. An unnamed member of the boys of Boeotia who perform an antimasque in *Pan's Anniversary*.

Jugglers. Performers in the second antimasque in *Time Vindicated to Himself and his Honors*.

Julia. Daughter to the emperor Augustus Caesar in *Poetaster*, love of Ovid, who celebrates her in his poetry as Corinna. Ovid says that he will risk his father's disapproval and desert law in favor of her and poetry. She goes to Albius' house to meet Ovid and shows her good sense and good humor by her comments to Cytheris and Chloe, Albius and Hermogenes. She shows her high spirits when she plays Juno at Ovid's masquerade. On invading the masquerade, her father flies into a rage at her profanity and association with what he considers to be low characters, and, after threatening to kill her, shuts her up in a balcony and later speaks to banished Ovid, telling of her distress and her love for him.

Julian de Campis. Pseudonym of Julius Sperber, a councillor of Dessau in the duchy of Anhalt, and author of *Sendbrieff oder Bericht An Alle welche von der Newen Brüderschaft des Ordens vom Rosen Creutz . . .* (1615) and other works on mystical theology. Sperber died in 1616. Julian is mentioned in *The Fortunate Isles*.

Juno. The chief goddess of the Romans and the wife of Jupiter who was identified with the Greek goddess Hera. Originally Juno was considered the goddess and protector of women, especially their sexual life, but she later became the great goddess of the state and was worshipped together with Jupiter and Minerva at the temple on the Capitol. Juno was a moon goddess. As the goddess of childbirth, she was called Lucina, and as the goddess of good counsel she was referred to as Moneta.

Juniper. A cobbler, friend to Onion, in *The Case Is Altered*. He tries to speak a prologue to the play but is prevented by Onion, who urges him to hurry and serve the count. He asks Antonio Balladino to write a song for Onion's wooing of Rachel. He is glad to see Valentine, and jokes with him about his travels. When Onion talks back to the count, who is acting unreasonably and is sacked, Juniper has his friend reinstated in service. He helps persuade Christophero to speak to Rachel on Onion's behalf, with a joking, bawdy speech. He is present during Onion's fencing bout with Martino, joking with the other servants, and offers a remedy for Onion's wounded head. He goes with Onion to see Rachel, and flees in terror when Jaques catches them outside his house and threatens to turn loose his dog. He is overjoyed when Onion discovers Jaques's gold, and, dressing himself like a "gentleman," Juniper gets very drunk. He is forced to return the money, however, when Jaques reveals to the count that it was stolen from Chamont.

Jupiter. Chief god of the Romans identified with the Greek god Zeus. He was the husband of Juno and was originally a sky god associated with rain, thunder, and lightning. He had many epithets and names suggesting his association with victory and conquest in war. Like Zeus, Jupiter could foretell the future and gave man indications of its course through signs and prophecies. He was the prime protector of the state and represented law and morality. The oak tree was sacred to Jupiter, and the eagle was his bird.

Justine. Marcus Junianus Justinus, a third-century Roman historian who compiled an epitome in Latin of Pompeius Trogus' *Historiae Philippicae*. In *The Masque of Queens*, Jonson is indebted to Justinus' *Epitome Trogi Pompeii* for Penthesilea and Thomyris.

Justinian (483–565). A strong Byzantine emperor best known for reforming and codifying the laws and administration of the empire. Volpone, in disguise, taunts Voltore by wondering at the fact that lowly Mosca, who never studied Justinian, should be the heir instead of the learned Advocate (v).

Juvenal. Decimus Junius Juvenalis was the greatest of the Roman satiric poets. He was probably born about 50 A.D., but since he was not well known during his lifetime few details of his life are available. He was apparently desperately poor and may have been exiled by Domitian, of whom he writes bitterly. His verses established the model for the satire of indignation in contrast to the less harsh ridicule of Horace. All of Juvenal's extant works were published under Trajan and Hadrian. He is known primarily for his sixteen hexameter satires in five books, probably written between 100 A.D. and 128 A.D., and giving a vivid portrait of life in Rome under the empire. The biting tone of his verse has seldom been equaled, and he powerfully denounced the lax society, the brutal tyranny, the immorality of women, and the criminal excesses of Romans as he perceived them. The finished rhetorical form and the epigrammatic character of his verse have made many of his sayings famous, and he had a profound influence on the Middle Ages and has served as the model for many verse satirists through the ages.

Jonson had copies of Juvenal in his personal library, and his works often reflect the profound influence the Roman had upon him, as the following catalogue of various allusions to Juvenal indicates: *Every Man in* (II. v); *Every Man out* (Ind.; III. vi); *Poetaster* (II. i; III. i; Apol. Dia.); *Volpone* (I. v; II. iv, vii; III. iv, v, vi; IV. v, vi; V. xii); *Epicoene* (II. ii); *The Alchemist* (II. ii); *Bartholomew Fair* (I. iii; v. vi); *Cynthia's Revels* (mottoes; Ind.; II. ii; III. iii; IV. i; V. i); *The Magnetic Lady* (II. vi); *Sejanus* (Arg.; I-V); *Catiline* (III): *Mortimer* (I. i); *Masque of Blackness; Hymenaei; Masque of Queens; Haddington Masque; Epig.* CI; *Timber* (ll. 387 and 1311). See READING.

K

Karolin. "The Kind" shepherd in *The Sad Shepherd*, brother to Earine. He laments Earine's drowning and Aeglamour's sadness, sings to try to cheer Aeglamour, and is dispatched to follow and to watch over him. Aeglamour forces Amie to kiss Karolin after his song; Amie falls ill with lovesickness for Karolin. He meets Douce and, while speaking with her, loses Aeglamour. Lionel tells him to go and comfort Amie.

Karre, Robert. See Sir Robert CARR.

Kastril. Dame Pliant's brother in *The Alchemist*. He is very foolish and hotheaded and comes to Subtle for lessons in quarreling. Subtle persuades him to give up his close guard of his sister, hoping to marry her to the disguised Surly. When Surly reveals himself, Face sets Kastril to insulting him and to picking a quarrel with him. After Lovewit returns, Kastril comes back to the house, abusing his innocent sister's name, and demanding entry. He is pacified when he finds that his sister has married Lovewit.

Kate. In *A Tale of a Tub*, one of the bridesmaids for Awdrey's intended marriage to John Clay.

Kean, Edmund. (1787?–1833). English actor who embodied the Romantic temper. His energy and violent emotions brought about a radical change in the prevailing classical style of acting of the period. His 1814 appearance at Drury Lane as Shylock is a landmark in theatrical history. He went on to become a famous Shakespearean in both England and the United States. In 1816 Kean revived *Every Man in* at Drury Lane and was applauded for his portrayal of Kitely.

Kecks. A dry nurse who appears in *An Entertainment at the Blackfriars* and engages in a long quarrel with the wet nurse.

Keep. In *The Magnetic Lady*, the nurse of Lady Loadstone's niece.

Kelly, Edward (1555–1595), alias Talbot, rose in the favor of the Emperor Rudolph II by claiming that he possessed the philosopher's stone. He was imprisoned in 1593 and 1595 when Rudolph tried to force him to show results from the stone. He was killed while attempting to escape from prison. In *The Alchemist* (IV. i), Mammon claims that the Emperor has been courting Subtle more ardently than Kelly.

Kemp, William. A famous comedian who acted in *Every Man in His Humour* in 1598 as a member of the Chamberlain's men. An allusion in *Every Man out of His Humour* (IV. viii. 145–46) suggests that he had probably left that company by 1599. Kemp also acted in Shakespeare's plays and was an original shareholder in the Globe. It seems likely that he played Peter in *Romeo and Juliet* and Dogberry in *Much Ado*. He later sold his share in the Globe. From February 11 to March 11, 1600, he danced from London to Norwich, a journey that he wrote about in *Kemp's Morris to Norwich* (1600) and that is alluded to in *Epig.* CXXXIII.

Kernan, Alvin B. (1923–), since 1977 has been Mellon Professor of Humanities at Princeton University. He has published numerous studies on Renaissance drama, and his books on satire have shed much light on the art of Jonson's comedies. Professor Kernan has also edited *Volpone* and *The Alchemist*.

Kerwyn, Andrew. Paymaster of the works whose accounts include charges for work done and arrangements made for *The Masque of Beauty*, *The Masque of Queens*, and *The Golden Age Restored*.

Kerwyn, Margaret. Widow of Andrew Kerwyn, paymaster of the works, who took over her husband's business after his death and made the arrangements for *Mercury Vindicated*.

Killigrew, Thomas (1612–1683). English dramatist and theater manager born in London. He followed Prince Charles into exile in 1647, and after the Restoration was made groom of the bedchamber and chamberlain to the Queen. In 1660, Charles II granted to Killigrew and Sir William D'Avenant exclusive patents to build new theaters and to establish new companies. Killigrew formed the King's Servants at the Theatre Royal in Drury Lane in 1663, where they acted as "old stock plays" *Every Man in*, *Every Man out*, *Catiline*, *Bartholomew Fair*, *The Devil Is an Ass*, *Sejanus*, garbled versions of Shakespeare, and Killigrew's own plays. In Killigrew's *Thomaso* (Part I, iv. ii), he borrowed heavily from Volpone's speech to the crowd during the mountebank scene.

Kimhi, David (1160?–?1235). The most famous member of a family of grammarians and Biblical scholars who worked at Narbonne. His most famous work is the *Mikhlol*, a Hebrew grammar. He also wrote Biblical commentary. In *The Alchemist* (IV), Dol, while trying to convince Mammon that she is mentally disturbed, wildly mentions Kimhi along with many other religious figures.

Kindheart. An itinerant toothdrawer mentioned in the Induction to *Bartholomew Fair*.

King, Henry (1592–1669), the eldest son of John King, Bishop of London, was appointed Bishop of Chichester in 1642. He contributed an elegy ("I see that wreath which doth the wearer arm") to *Jonsonus Virbius*. An intimate friend of Donne's, King preached in 1662 the funeral sermon of Bishop Duppa, editor of *Jonsonus Virbius*. King's *Poems* were collected in 1657.

King's Coronation Entertainment, The.
Performed: March 15, 1604.
Published: 1604 by Edward Blount in quarto together with *Panegyre* and *The Entertainment at Althorp*.
Printer: Valentine Simmes.
This entertainment was written for King James as he progressed to his coronation. Jonson and Dekker collaborated on the speeches. Jonson wrote the speeches for the first and seventh triumphal arches in London as well as the later speeches in Westminster. At Fenchurch the scene represented was the city of London, and the symbolic personages were Monarchia Britannica, Theosophia, Genius Urbis, Bouleutes, Polemius, Tamesis, Euphrosyne, Sebasis, Prothymia, Agrypnia, Agape, and Omothymia. The congratulatory speeches were delivered by Genius Urbis and Tamesis.
At Temple Bar the scene was the temple of Janus and the symbolic figures were Irene, Plutus, Enyalius, Esychia, Tarache, Eleutheria, Doulosis, Soteria, Peira, Eudaimonia, Dyspragia, Genius Urbis, and Martialis. Only Genius and Martialis spoke and engaged in a dialogue in praise of the King and Queen.
In the Strand at Westminster the scene was the Pleiades, and the only speaker was Electra, representing one of the seven Pleiades. She lauded the significance of the day and the virtues of the King and proclaimed herself a comet of good omen for his reign.

King's Entertainment at Welbeck, The.
Performed: May 31, 1633.
Published: the second volume of the folio of 1640 issued by Thomas Walkley.
Printers: probably Bernard Alsop and Thomas Fawcett.
This entertainment was written for King Charles when he was invited to Wel-

147

beck by the Earl of Newcastle in 1633. The performance was given on May 31.

At dinner a song of welcome was sung in the form of a dialogue between the passions of Love and Doubt. After dinner when the king and lords were ready to ride, two persons were discovered in the crowd. One was dressed in a cassock of black buckram, the other in a herald's coat. One was called Accidence, and the other Fitz-Ale. They introduced themselves and explained that Fitz-Ale had a daughter named Pem, who was to be married to a bold champion named Stub, and they invited all to join in the celebration. In honor of his bridal day, Stub had challenged six brave bachelors, supposedly descended from Robin Hood, to a tilting contest. Stub and the six tilted in turn, as Accidence and Fitz-Ale applauded each champion, after which Accidence introduced the bride, dressed as a May lady, and her six attendants, one of whom was Alphabet, the daughter of Accidence. As a song in celebration of the union of Pem and Stub was sung, all shared the bridal cake, drank, and danced. After a period of frivolity, a gentleman interrupted the festivities. In a long speech he reprimanded all those engaged in the activities for their rudeness in trying the king's patience with their sport, called for reverence for the monarch, praised and blessed the king, his queen, and his son, and wished good fortune for the king and his realm.

Kitely. See THORELLO.

Kitely, Dame. See BIANCHA.

Knaves. Four knaves appear in the antimasque of *The Fortunate Isles, and Their Union.*

Knevet, Master. A Catholic who engaged in a disputation at Paris in 1612 on the doctrine of the real presence. His opponent was a Protestant minister by the name of Daniel Featley. Jonson witnessed the debate and later certified the published account of it as accurate.

Knight, Mr. Bookkeeper of the Blackfriars playhouse who made payment to Sir Henry Herbert, Master of the Revels, for the license to allow *The Magnetic Lady* to be acted in 1632.

Knights, L. C. (1906–   ). British scholar educated at Cambridge, where since 1973 he has been King Edward VII Professor of English Literature Emeritus. He has written widely on a variety of subjects. His *Drama and Society in the Age of Jonson* (1937) is a seminal work that remains provocative for students and scholars.

Knipperdollinck, Bernt, a draper by trade, was one of the leaders of an Anabaptist uprising in Munster in 1534–36. The "Kingdom of God" established there was marked by "despotism and debauchery"; it was crushed by the Bishop of Munster. In *The Alchemist* (II. v), Subtle asks Ananias if he is connected with this faction.

Knockem, Dan Jordan. A "horse-courser, and ranger o'Turnbull" in *Bartholomew Fair*. He is a rogue who enjoys eating and drinking with Ursula and encourages her and joins her in her quarrel with Winwife and Quarlous. He gets drunk with his companions and persuades Mrs. Overdo and Win to act like prostitutes, then attends the puppet show with them.

Knoll, Robert E. (1922–   ). Scholar of English literature. Since 1962 Professor of English at the University of Nebraska. Author of *Ben Jonson: An Introduction* (1964), which focuses on the influence of indigenous rather than classical sources on Jonson's plays.

Knollys, Sir William (d. 1632). Controller of the Household and member of the Privy Council in 1597 when Jonson was imprisoned for his role in the offensive *Isle of Dogs*. Knollys was present when Jonson and his cohorts were charged. Sir William was eventually made Earl of Banbury.

Knowell, Edward, junior. See LORENZO JUNIOR.

Knowell, Edward, senior. See LORENZO SENIOR.

Knox, John (1505?–1572), was a Scottish religious reformer who became the founder of Scottish Presbyterianism. His single-minded zeal made him a strong influence on the Protestant movements in England and on the Continent. His *History of the Reformation in Scotland* (1584) was posthumously published. It is a striking record of that conflict but reflects his strong bias. Knox is mentioned in *Bartholomew Fair* (I. iii).

Kyd, Thomas (1558–1594). English dramatist born in London whose literary fame rests on the incredibly successful *Spanish Tragedy* (1587). Kyd may also have been the author of an earlier lost version of *Hamlet* used by Shakespeare. In 1593 Kyd was accused of unorthodox religious and moral views. He died in poverty.

Although he mentioned Kyd disparagingly in his eulogy on Shakespeare prefaced to the First Folio, Jonson probably played the hero's part in *The Spanish Tragedy* early in his acting career, and Henslowe records that he paid Jonson (1601–1602) to write additions for him to this popular play. In the Induction to *Every Man out*, Jonson alludes to Kyd's translation of Garnier's *Cornelia* (1594). Like many other dramatists of his day, Jonson made frequent allusions to *The Spanish Tragedy*, usually in an unfavorable light: *Every Man in* (I. i; v); *Eastward Ho* (Ind.; II. i); *Bartholomew Fair* (Ind.); *Cynthia's Revels* (Ind.); *Poetaster* (III. iii); *The Alchemist* (IV. vii); and *The Staple of News* (I. iv).

L

Laberius. A Roman knight required by Julius Caesar to act in his own mimes in 45 B.C. during a dramatic contest with Publilius Syrus. Horace considered Laberius' work inferior. Mentioned in *Timber* (l. 2601).

La Boderie, Antoine Lefevre de. Author of *Ambassades en Angleterre* (1750), which contains information on the competition of foreign ambassadors to secure precedence at court masques and makes specific references to *The Masque of Beauty, The Masque of Queens,* and *Speeches at Prince Henry's Barriers.*

Lachesis. See FATES.

Laco, Gracinus. Captain of the watch in *Sejanus*. He first appears overseeing the captive Nero, and tells the fates of Drusus junior and Agrippina. Although Arruntius accuses him of being Sejanus' spy, which seems to be borne out when he speaks with Sejanus' friends, Lepidus' opinion that Laco "has the voyce to be an honest Romane" proves true when he is regarded as "a friend most welcome" by the men who plot to overthrow Sejanus. He brings them intelligence, aids them, and stands guard outside the Senate. He enters with a guard and prevents Sejanus and his followers from escaping.

Lactantius (c. 260–340). Lucius Caelius Firmianus was a Christian author and apologist. He was Latin tutor to Constantine's son Crispus. Some of his best known works include *The Divine Institutions*, the

Epitome, On God's Wrath, and *On the Death of the Persecutors*, a chief source for the history of the persecutions. He is alluded to in *The King's Entertainment in Passing to his Coronation.*

Lacy, John. A dancing master who became an actor after the Restoration and developed into Charles II's favorite comedian. He also wrote four plays, one of them a coarse version of *The Taming of the Shrew*, called *Sauny the Scot*. Aubrey reports that Lacy said Jonson would often wear a coat with slits under the armpits and that Ben got a catalogue of the Yorkshire dialect from him which Jonson later used in *A Tale of a Tub* (actually *The Sad Shepherd*). Lacy died in 1681, but *Sir Hercules Buffoon* (1684) contains a passage by Lacy that proclaims Jonson would have given a hundred pounds to have been author of some lines by Taylor, the water poet, which declare that poets are to be esteemed above princes.

Laelius. Roman general and consul who lived around 200 B.C. He led an expedition to Africa and won renown as a commander. In *Poetaster*, Horace praises him as "great with fame" and not jealous, and speaks of his friendship with Scipio (III. v).

Laetitia. A figure in *The Masque of Beauty* who represents one of the elements of beauty.

La-Foole, Sir Amorous. A foolish knight in *Epicoene*, who is a social climber and a braggart. He invites many people to parties, brags of his pedigree, and claims to have had sexual relations with many women, including the "lady" Epicoene. He and his friend John Daw are tricked into a mock quarrel by Truewit and are made to appear ridiculous.

Laing, David. Born in 1793, the son of an Edinburgh bookseller, Laing was an antiquary who followed his father's trade for thirty years and from 1837 until his death was librarian of the Signet Library. He made many contributions to the *Transactions* of the Society of Antiquaries of Scotland. In 1833 he published in *Archaeologia Scotia* Sir Robert Sibbald's (1641–1722) transcript of Drummond's conversations with Jonson. Sibbald was an Edinburgh physician and antiquary who had made a copy of Drummond's manuscript which was apparently lost. Laing's publication of Sibbald's copy eventually led to making Drummond's record available to the general public. Laing died in 1878.

Lais. Probably an obscure courtesan mentioned by Athenaeus and Claudian. For Jonson's use, see C. F. Wheeler's *Classical Mythology*.

Lake, Lady of the. The name of a character who appears in *The Speeches at Prince Henry's Barriers* and calls forth King Arthur and Merlin.

Lamb, Charles (1775–1834). English essayist born in London and educated at Christ's Hospital, where his friendship with Coleridge began. In 1796 Lamb's sister wounded their father and killed their mother, and Lamb had himself declared her guardian to save her from permanent commitment to an asylum. After 1799, they lived together and collaborated on several books for children, the most famous being *Tales from Shakespeare* (1807). Lamb wrote four unsuccessful plays, but his dramatic essays, *Specimens of English Dramatic Poets* (1808), established his reputation as a judicious critic and did much to revive the popularity of Elizabethan drama. *Specimens* included selections from and commentary on *Poetaster*, *The Alchemist*, *The Case is Altered*, and *The New Inn*.

Lamb was also interested in the influence of *Leges Convivales* on poets like Drayton. From 1800 until his death Lamb wrote intermittently for periodicals, his best known contributions being *Essays of Elia* (1820–25). Lamb was pensioned in 1825. His style was distinctive and masterful, and he was a talented conversationalist who was friendly with most of the major literary figures of his day.

Lambe. An astrologer who was twice indicted for magical practice in 1608 and put into prison, where he was allowed to receive clients. He was pardoned and released through the influence of the Duke of Buckingham, who patronized him. A powerful storm that broke over London in 1626 was thought to be his work. In 1628 he was attacked by a mob outside the Fortune Theatre, and although rescued from them, he died the next day. Lambe is mentioned in *The Staple of News* (I. iv; III. iv).

Lamia. A grief-stricken woman whose name was used to frighten children. Lamia's own children were killed by Hera, who was jealous of her husband's love for Lamia. Thereafter, Lamia stole and killed the children of happy mothers. Later her name was also used for a woman who lured a youth to his death.

Lancelot, Sir. Also Launcelot. In Arthurian legend, the bravest and most celebrated knight at the court of King Arthur, who became the lover of Guinevere and was also loved by Elaine (daughter of King Pelles), by whom he fathered Sir Galahad, and by Elaine, the Lily Maid of Astolat, who died for love of the great knight. Lancelot is mentioned in *Every Man in* (II. iii) and *Und.* XLIII.

Landus, Constantius, Count of Campiano. His text and commentary on Catullus' Epithalamium were published in Pavia in 1550. He is alluded to in *Hymenaei.*

Langley, Francis (1550–1601), became the owner of the manor of Paris Garden, builder of the Swan Theatre, and a member of the Goldsmith Company. Like Henslowe, Langley became a theatre financier. In his "An Expostulation with Inigo Jones" Jonson alludes (ll. 21–22) to Langley's apparent ridicule of Jones.

language. In *Timber* (ll. 1863–65), Jonson observes that letters which are the bank of words restore themselves to an author as the pawns of language. Later in the same passage (ll. 1870–73), borrowing in part from Quintilian, he notes that he loves pure and neat language which is plain and customary. Again in *Timber* (ll. 2031–89), he includes a long metaphorical passage, drawn from Vives (*De Ratione Dicendi*, II), on the theme that language most shows a man, stressing that language is the image of the parent of man, which is his mind, and discussing in this respect structure, periods, the levels of language, periphrasis, phrasing, and redundancy.

Lanier, Nicholas (1588–1666), was born into a French family of musicians at court. He became attached to the household of Prince Henry. When Charles I ascended the throne, Lanier was appointed master of the king's music and given an annual pension. He was a painter as well as musician, and his purchases of paintings in Italy formed the basis of Charles's great collection.

Lanier worked with Jonson on several masques. He composed the music for *Lovers Made Men*, the first English opera; for *The Masque of Augurs*; and for *The Gypsies Metamorphosed*. He also set to music a song from *The Sad Shepherd* (I. v. 65–80) and some lines from *Und.* LXXIX for a pastoral song for the king on New Year's Day in 1633.

Lanney, Cornelius de. An alchemist who in 1565 undertook to produce fifty thousand marks a year for Queen Elizabeth but failed and was consigned to the Tower in 1567, where he probably died.

Latiaris. Cousin to Sabinus in *Sejanus*. He appears early in the play as one of Sejanus' lackeys and is mocked by the noble characters in the play. At the Senate, he speaks against Silius and Cordus. He plots to betray his cousin, tricking him into criticizing Tiberius where he can be overheard, then arresting him for treason, in hopes of gaining favor for himself with Sejanus. He tells Sejanus that he and the others have been summoned to the Senate, arousing Sejanus' suspicions, and he is very flattered when Sejanus salutes him. He attends the Senate eagerly to support Sejanus and so advance his own position, speaking disdainfully of Arruntius and Lepidus. Tiberius' letter names him as a dangerous accomplice of Sejanus, and he is led out under arrest.

Latimer, Lord. In *The New Inn*, a lord and companion to Lord Beaufort, who eventually marries Prudence.

Lapithes. According to several ancient writers, the name of the groom's tribe at the wedding feast of Pirithous and Hippodamia, who did battle with the intoxicated centaurs after the ferocious creatures attempted to do violence to the bride.

Lares. In Roman religion, guardian spirits who may have been ghosts of the dead and, since they were considered destructive, had to be propitiated. Sometimes they were thought to be farm deities, but more often they were identified as household gods who were worshipped in close connection with the Penates.

Latona. The Roman name for Leto, the daughter of the Titans Coeus and Phoebe and the mother of Apollo and Artemis by Zeus. Because they feared the wrath of Hera, no town would welcome Leto when she was about to give birth to the twin gods. She was finally received by Delos, where she bore her two sons.

La Tour, Henri, Baron de (1555–1623). Afterwards Duc de Bouillon, Henri came to England as ambassador extraordinary for the Court of France in 1617. Lord Hay, who had been ambassador in France, entertained him lavishly. *Lovers Made Men* was performed in his honor.

Laud, William (1573–1645), studied at St. John's College, Oxford, and was ordained in 1601. He became President of St. John's

in 1611, Dean of Gloucester in 1616, Bishop of London in 1628, Chancellor of Oxford in 1629, and Archbishop of Canterbury in 1633. Hostile to Puritans and Calvinism, Laud made Oxford a royalist stronghold and later attempted to enforce High Church worship. A supporter of both Charles and the Earl of Strafford to the end, Laud was impeached by the Long Parliament in 1640, found not guilty of treason by the House of Lords in 1644, and condemned to death by the Commons by a bill of attainder.

Laud apparently objected to the oaths in the performance of *The Magnetic Lady*, and Jonson alluded to him in *Und.* LXXV in his capacity as Bishop of London.

Laughter. A symbolic character in *The Vision of Delight*, who has no speaking part but accompanies Delight at the opening of the masque.

la Warr, Henry West, Baron De (1603–1628), was the 13th Baron De la Warr. He succeeded to the title in 1618. His father was a member of the Council of the Virginia Colony, and the names of Delaware state, bay, and river commemorate him. Lord Henry served as a member of Parliament in 1621 and as captain of the Earl of Oxford's regiment of foot soldiers in 1624. Jonson's *Und.* LX is an epitaph on him.

Lawes, Henry. Composer of musical settings to several of Jonson's songs: *Poetaster* (II. ii. 163–72, 179–88), *Cynthia's Revels* (IV. iii. 242–53), and *Haddington Masque* (88–156).

Lawes, William. Composer of a musical setting for one of Jonson's songs: *Epicoene* (I. i. 92–102).

laws. In *Timber* (ll. 2555–77), Jonson, drawing upon Daniel Heinsius (*De Tragaediae Constitutione*, I), records that one should not confine a poet's liberty to laws because before there were laws many excellent poets fulfilled them. Of these, he cites Sophocles, Demosthenes, Pericles, and Alcibiades. He explains that whatever nature dictated as laws, the wisdom of Aristotle formed into an art. Aristophanes rightly ridiculed many things in Euripides, not because of art but because of truth, for judgment is never absolute if reason does not accompany it.

Leander, a young man who lived in Abydos, fell in love with a girl, Hero, who was a priestess of Aphrodite at Sestos, and swam the Hellespont every night to see her. One night the light she set up to guide him went out and he was drowned. In *Bartholomew Fair*, in Littlewit's puppet show adaptation of the story to fit the vulgar tastes of his audience, he is "a Diers sonne, about Puddle-wharfe" who woos Hero with a pint of sherry (v. iii).

learning. In *Timber* (ll. 924–47), Jonson notes, "I have ever observ'd it, to have beene the office of a wise Patriot, among the greatest affaires of the *State*, to take care of the *Common-wealth* of Learning . . . and nothing is worthier the study of a States-man, then that part of the *Republicke*, which wee call the *advancement* of Letters." He cites Julius Caesar, who, "in the heat of the civill warre, writ his bookes of *Analogie* . . ." and ends with a highly laudatory tribute to Francis Bacon and his *Advancement of Learning* (1605). According to Arthur Shillinglaw (*Times Literary Supplement*, April 18, 1936), Jonson's tribute to Bacon was borrowed almost verbatim from a 1621 letter of Fr. Fulgenzio Micanza, a Venetian patriot, to the first Earl of Devonshire.

Leatherhead, Lanthorn. A hobby-horse seller in *Bartholomew Fair*. He cries his wares until Cokes buys his shop from him, then absconds with Cokes's money. His wares are wrecked by Zeal-of-the-Land Busy, whom he has placed in the stocks. He then takes his place as Master of Littlewit's puppet show, moving and conversing with the puppets, and has those around him call him Lanthorn when Cokes is around, to prevent Cokes from recognizing him as the man who cheated him.

Leatherleg. In *The Staple of News*, a shoemaker who serves Pennyboy Junior.

Lecca, Portius. In *Catiline*, one of the conspirators, who supports Catiline's abortive attempt to seize power in Rome.

Leda. Daughter of Thestios, king of Aetolia, and wife of Tyndareus, king of Sparta. She was beloved by Zeus who came to her in the form of a swan. From her union with Zeus came Helen and Polydeuces. She was also the mother of Clytemnestra.

Leech, Edward. Gentleman who was paid to make preparations for the performances of *Vision of Delight* and *News from the New World*.

Leech, John. One of the extant letters by Jonson was addressed to John Leech, asking him to grant an unspecified favor to an unnamed third person. The John Leech

addressed was probably the John Leech who was secretary to the Earl of Pembroke, Jonson's patron.

Legatt, John. Printer at Cambridge and London from 1620 to 1658. Mary Allot, widow of Robert, transferred the copyright for *Bartholomew Fair* and *The Staple of News* to Legatt and Andrew Crooke in 1637.

Legenda Aurea. A collection of saints' lives written by Jacobus de Voragine, Archbishop of Genoa, in the thirteenth century and mentioned in *Und.* XLIII.

Leges Convivales. A poem by Jonson that lists twenty-four tavern laws for the Tribe of Ben, which met frequently in the Apollo room of the Devil Tavern. The poem is in Latin and was first published in Daniel Tossanus' tribute to John James Frey, *Oratio Panegyrica* (Basel, 1636). The *Leges* was published by Alexander Brome in his *Songs and Other Poems* (London, 1661). Brome provided a verse translation opposite the original Latin version. The folio of 1692 printed the *Leges* for the first time in an edition of Jonson. The *Leges* was apparently composed about 1624 when the Apollo room was built. The *Leges* outlines the code of conduct and behavior for the meetings of the Tribe of Ben and contains echoes of Horace and Martial. Another one of Jonson's poems ("Over the Door at the Entrance into the *Apollo*") served as the verses of welcome for the guests in the Apollo room. These verses were also first printed in the Jonson folio of 1692 and were reprinted in Dryden's *Miscellany Poems* (1716).

Leicester, Robert Dudley, Earl of (1532–1588). The son of the Duke of Northumberland, Dudley was knighted at an early age and brought into the society of Queen Elizabeth I. He helped his father in the plot to place Lady Jane Grey on the throne, for which he was sent to the Tower and condemned to death, but he was pardoned and, for service in France, restored to his rights. When Elizabeth took the throne in 1558, Dudley was made master of the horse and later a privy councilor. He was soon acknowledged as the queen's favorite and the most probable choice for her husband, but by 1563 Elizabeth realized the impracticality of marriage to Dudley, although her personal affection for him continued, and he remained in a powerful position at court. In 1564 Elizabeth created him Earl of Leicester. Upon the approach of the Spanish Armada, Leicester was appointed captain general of the armies. He died suddenly and mysteriously. Throughout his life Leicester was a patron of literature and drama.

Jonson mentioned Leicester in *Every Man out* (III. iv) and *The Masque of Owls*. In the *Conversations* (ll. 350–52), he told Drummond that Leicester had given his wife some medicine for faintness, not knowing that it was poison, that it was given to him when he returned from court, and he died. The accuracy of this story has never been verified.

Leicester, Robert Sidney, Viscount Lisle, Earl of (1563–1626), a younger brother of Sir Philip Sidney, became a soldier and man of affairs. He served as a member of Parliament for a long time, and he carried thanks to James VI of Scotland for his aid in defeating the Spanish Armada. He was created Earl of Leicester in 1618. He spent his later years as a sponsor of colonial exploration in North America and as a patron of music and literature. Jonson told Drummond that Leicester's eldest son resembled Sir Philip Sidney in appearance (*Conversations*, ll. 230–32).

Lemnos. The place where Vulcan fell when he was expelled from heaven by Jove. The island was considered sacred to Vulcan.

Lennox, Charlotte (1720–1804), an unsuccessful actress, married and became a writer. She wrote poems, plays, and novels, the best known of which are *Harriot Stuart* (1751); *Henrietta*, which she dramatized as *The Sister*; and *The Female Quixote* (1752). In 1751 she adapted *Eastward Ho*, which was successfully performed at Drury Lane under the title *Old City-Manners*. Her work was praised by both Dr. Johnson and Fielding.

Lennox, Esmé Stuart, Duke of. See Esmé Stuart, Seigneur of AUBIGNY.

Lentulus, Publius. In *Catiline*, a senator formerly ejected from the senate for infamous behavior but later restored. Lentulus actively supports Catiline's conspiracy to seize power in Rome and is ultimately arrested and executed.

Leo Africanus. Moorish traveler in Africa and the Near East who lived c. 1465 to 1550. Captured by pirates, he was sent as a slave to Pope Leo X, became a Christian, and taught Arabic in Rome, where he wrote in Arabic a description of his journeys in Africa that was published in Italian in 1526 and translated into English in 1600 (*The History and Description of Africa*). His

work was for a long time the only known source on the Sudan. Jonson refers to it in *The Masque of Queens*.

Lepidus, Marcus. A wise, noble, high-minded Roman senator in *Sejanus*. He does not exclaim in surprise or horror during Silius' accusation and death like most of the other noble senators, speaking only to urge Tiberius to be merciful to Silius' children in the confiscation of his goods. He exclaims in disgust to Arruntius when Cordus' books are burnt, and when he hears of Sabinus' death, but cautions Arruntius to be more discreet in order to survive the accusations of the age. He expresses his "wonder" while Arruntius rails bitterly at the Senators who rush to honor Sejanus, and sits apart with Arruntius while the other Senators clamor for favor. He speaks of the fickleness of fortune after Sejanus' downfall, and makes his only strong public comment on hearing of the murder of Sejanus' children.

Lerna. The place where the monstrous hydra destroyed by Hercules lived.

L'Estrange, Sir Nicholas (d. 1655), became a baronet in 1629 when his father bought the title for him. He is best known for his *Merry Passages and Feasts* (1650–55), a manuscript collection of some 600 anecdotes, one of which records that Shakespeare was the godfather to one of Ben Jonson's children.

Lethe. The plain or river of oblivion in Hades from which the dead souls drank before their reincarnation so they would forget their past.

Leucothoe. A sea goddess who was originally Ino, a daughter of Cadmus and Harmonia, but was transformed by Neptune. Ino aided the shipwrecked Odysseus.

Lewis, Anne. Jonson's wife. He probably married her on November 14, 1594. How many children they had is not clear. When Anne died and how long Jonson lived with her is also uncertain. Probable children Jonson fathered with Anne include: Joseph, baptized December 9, 1599; Benjamin, baptized February 20, 1608 and buried November 18, 1611; Elizabeth, baptized March 25, 1610 (who may have been Jonson's child by another woman). It seems clear that Anne was not alive when Jonson died in 1637.

Lewis of Madrid. Don Luis Pacheco de Narvaez, a pupil of Carranza's. He and Carranza were recognized as the great authorities on Spanish fencing. Lewis published at Madrid *Libro de las granderas de la Espada* (1600). An appendix to it was issued in 1612 and a handbook of fencing in 1625. Lewis is mentioned several times in *The New Inn* (II. v; IV. iii, iv).

Libanius. Fourth-century Greek sophist and rhetorician whose *De Muliere Loquaci* was edited by the French scholar Morellus and published at Paris in 1597. Jonson was indebted to Libanius in *Volpone* (III. iv–v) and for part of the plot of *Epicoene*.

Liberty. See Eleutheria.

Lickfinger. In *The Staple of News*, a master cook and erstwhile poet who serves the Pennyboys and their friends.

Lictors. 1. Characters in *Poetaster;* they were ancient Roman officers who attended the chief magistrate and carried fasces to symbolize their power. In *Poetaster,* they serve Lupus. They go with Minos to arrest Crispinus but are put off when Tucca convinces Minos to drop his charges. They are present when Histrio brings his charges of the masqueraders' treason to Lupus, and they go with him and Caesar to break up the masquerade. They go to Caesar when Lupus and his associates charge Horace with treason, and Caesar orders them to turn against their master and fit him with a pair of ass's ears. They stand by during the trial of the Poetasters, punishing Tucca.

2. In *Sejanus*, lictors are present at the first Senate meeting, where, after the prosecution of Silius and Cordus, a Praetor tells them to "resume the fasces." They lead in the accused Nero, and are present at the second Senate meeting, where they stand guard.

Lightnings. In *Chloridia*, three symbolic characters who appear in the fifth entry of the antimasque.

Lily, William (1468?–1522). Scholar and teacher of grammar who became the first high master of St. Paul's School sometime after 1512 and co-author of the old Eton *Latin Grammar*. He is referred to in *Tale of a Tub* (III. vii) and *The New Inn* (II. iv).

Linacre, Thomas (1460–1524). English humanist and physician. He took his M.D. at Padua, returned to England about 1492, and became tutor to Prince Arthur and later physician to Henry VIII. Interested in the humanist revival, he wrote a Latin grammar for Princess Mary. Among his other pupils were Erasmus and Sir Thomas More. Linacre founded readerships in medicine at Oxford and Cam-

bridge, and he translated into Latin many of Aristotle's and Galen's works. His translation of Galen's *Of Temperaments* helped circulate the theory of humors in England. Linacre was the founder and first president of the Royal College of Physicians.

Ling, Nicholas. Bookseller in London from 1580 to 1607. The title page of the third quarto (1600) of *Every Man out of His Humour* indicates that it was printed for him, but the printer is unknown and the date is doubtful since Ling transferred the copyright to John Smethwicke in 1607.

Linus. In Greek mythology, the son of Apollo and Psamathe of Argos who was devoured by dogs when abandoned by his mother who was in turn murdered by her father. Out of this legend developed the Linus song, a dirge sung at harvest time for the dying vegetation. In another tale Linus taught music to Hercules, who killed his teacher when Linus tried to punish him. According to another legend, Linus was killed by Apollo, who tolerated no rivals in music.

Lionel. "The Courteous" shepherd in *The Sad Shepherd*, brother to Amie. He is a guest at Robin Hood's feast who mourns for Earine and is saddened by Aeglamour's melancholy. He is present when Maudlin takes Marian's shape, and when Maudlin comes to the bower, and when Amie falls ill of lovesickness. He tells Karolin to go visit Amie to comfort her.

Lipsius, Justus (1547–1606). Joest Lips was a Flemish scholar celebrated as an authority on Roman literature, history, and antiquities. He edited many Latin works, but his edition of Tacitus was particularly well known. Jonson used the Tacitus edition for *Sejanus*, and he was indebted to Lipsius in *The English Grammar* (Bk. II, Chapt. IX) and *Timber* (ll. 525–36; 1235–39). In ll. 2428–29 Jonson alluded to Lipsius' comment that no poet was ever great without a rich share of divine inspiration.

Little John. Robin Hood's bow-bearer in *The Sad Shepherd*. He enthusiastically leads Marian on her stag hunt and comments as she describes it to Robin. He is one of the witch-hunters who goes to catch Maudlin.

Littleton, Sir Thomas (1422?–1481). English jurist who became a sergeant-at-law in 1453 and a judge in 1466. He is best known for his *Tenures*, a work in French on the types of estates in land in England. This book was one of the earliest printed books in England, and it was greatly admired for its concise, simple quality. In Sir Edward Coke's expanded edition, *Tenures* served as the standard text on property law until the nineteenth century. He is mentioned in *The Staple of News* (IV. iv).

Littlewit, John. A proctor in *Bartholomew Fair* who imagines himself clever and witty but who is really foolish. He plots to take his wife, Win, into Bartholomew Fair to see his puppet show against the wishes of his Puritan mother-in-law, Dame Purecraft. His carelessness of his wife and lack of ability to judge others is most apparent when he leaves Win in the company of two disreputable, drunken men (whom he says are "very good men"), and they persuade her to act like a prostitute. Littlewit is free and familiar with Quarlous and Winwife, who realize that he is a fool.

Littlewit, Win. John Littlewit's wife in *Bartholomew Fair*. Although she is often called beautiful, Win is as foolish as her husband. She is eager to go see his puppet show at the Fair and, while there, she is easily persuaded by Knockem and Captain Whit to act like a prostitute.

Livia. Corrupt wife of Drusus senior in *Sejanus*. She is persuaded and possibly seduced by Sejanus into betraying her husband, whom she plots to poison. In her eagerness to make Sejanus fall in love with her, she worries with Eudemus over her make-up. Tiberius refuses to let Sejanus marry her, however, after Drusus is dead. At the end of the play, when Sejanus' wife finds her children strangled, she vows to expose Livia's part in the poisoning.

Livia Drusilla (56 B.C.–A.D. 29). Given the title Augusta by her husband, Augustus Caesar. She was first married to T. Claudius Nero, and bore him future emperor Tiberius, but was divorced so that she could marry Augustus. She was well loved by him for her dignity, beauty, propriety, and intelligence; she even gave him counsel. After his death, she tried to continue her influence and came into conflict with Tiberius. Although some malicious rumors were circulated about her, she remained popular until her death. In *Sejanus*, she is held up as a model of womanhood; her granddaughter Livia and Agrippina, the wife of her grandson Germanicus Caesar, are compared to her. She is also an unwitting influence on Sejanus' plots to discredit Agrippina and her friends when he sends word to her that Tiberius is threatened and spreads a rumor that she is threatened by Agrippina (II. i, iii, iv, vii). Later in the play, Tiberius

tells the Senate that he is concerned over his son's death, since Augusta is old and he is aging (III. ii).

Livy (59 B.C.–A.D. 17). Titus Livius was born at Patavium (Padua). He became a Roman historian and, with the support of Augustus, wrote a history of Rome in 142 books, much of which is now lost. Although his work is weak in critical method and use of sources, it is noted for its vividness, fervor, and devotion to republican ideals. His *History* was admired by Tacitus, Seneca, Quintilian, and Plutarch; Philemon Holland's English translation (1600) increased Livy's reputation and influence during the Renaissance. Jonson alluded to Livy in *The Masque of Augurs* and *Epig.* CI, and he is mentioned by Daw in *Epicoene* (II) as one of the worthless ancient writers. See also READING.

Loadstone, Lady. In *The Magnetic Lady*, the Magnetic Lady herself who eventually marries Captain Ironside.

Locusta. An infamous female poisoner who helped Agrippina kill Claudius and Nero destroy Britannicus.

Lollia Paulina. A woman of great ancestry and wealth who was forced to marry the Emperor Gaius (Caligula) in A.D. 38 but was divorced by him the following year. In A.D. 48 she was an unsuccessful candidate for the hand of Claudius after the death of Messalina. Through the influence of Agrippina, she was banished the following year; eventually she committed suicide.

Lomond, Loch. Lake between Dumbartonshire and Stirlingshire in West Scotland; the largest and one of the most beautiful of Scottish lakes. Jonson was very much interested in Loch Lomond and told Drummond in the *Conversations* (ll. 402–3) that he intended to write a fisher or pastoral play set in Lomond, but he never realized the project although Drummond made a note to himself (ll. 644–45) to send Jonson descriptions of Lomond. In a May 10, 1619, letter to Drummond, Jonson asked him to keep his promise to send information on the loch, and Drummond replied in a July 1, 1619, letter that he had done so. Even before his journey to Scotland Jonson had in *The Masque of Beauty* set his scene on a floating island and indicated in a note that such an island had been reported to exist in Lomond.

London. In his plays, poems, and masques Jonson made extensive use of specific London settings and places. According to Chalfant, the references to London and its

155

environs contribute to the unity of place in the plays, enhance Jonson's satiric purposes, and enrich the nonsatiric aspects of a characterization or a work. The most frequently mentioned London references in Jonson's works include the Exchanges (Royal and New), Cheapside, St. Paul's, Moorfields, the Tower of London, the Strand, the Inns of Court, Blackfriars, Smithfield, Bankside, the Thames, the Counters, Newgate Prison, and Tyburn. Jonson's London dramas may be said to include: *Every Man out, Eastward Ho, Epicoene, The Alchemist, Every Man in* (folio version), *Bartholomew Fair, The Devil Is an Ass, The Staple of News, The New Inn, The Magnetic Lady,* and *A Tale of a Tub.* Although set in Venice, *Volpone* also contains several London references. *A Tale of a Tub* has the greatest number of London references, over twenty-five. The London dramas average about twenty London references apiece. For specific information on Jonson's use of London references, see the index to the Oxford edition of the *Works* and Fran C. Chalfant's *Ben Jonson's London: A Jacobean Placename Dictionary* (Athens: University of Georgia, 1978).

London Prodigal, The. A play published anonymously in 1605 which probably influenced the plot of Jonson's *The Staple of News.*

Longinus, Lucius Cassius. In *Catiline,* one of the conspirators who supports Catiline's abortive attempt to seize power in Rome.

Long Meg of Westminster. A virago whose exploits were celebrated in *The Life of Long Meg of Westminster . . .* (1620) and in a lost play of the Admiral's Men recorded in Henslowe's *Diary* in 1594–97. She appears as a character in the antimasque of *The Fortunate Isles, and Their Union.*

Longus. Third century A.D. Greek writer of the novel *Daphnis and Chloe.* Nothing is known about his life. *Daphnis and Chloe* was first published in French in 1559 and in Greek in 1598. This pastoral story influenced the *Aminta* of Tasso and was very popular in France and England in the seventeenth and early eighteenth century. Jonson mentioned Longus in *The Sad Shepherd* (I. iii).

Lord Keeper. See John WILLIAMS.

Lorel. "The Rude," a swineherd, son to Maudlin, in *The Sad Shepherd.* His name means a "worthless person," and he is vulgar and crude. He shuts Earine up in a tree and tries to woo her by offering her hedgehogs and badgers. His mother berates him for his awkward attentions to Earine, but even when he speaks more smoothly, Earine disdains his affections.

Lorenzo junior (Edward Knowell junior). A young gallant, son of Lorenzo senior (Knowell) in the 1601 quarto version of *Every Man in His Humour.* (Differing names and courses of action in the 1616 folio version are given in parentheses.) He is a little alarmed when he learns that his father has read Prospero's (Wellbred's) letter, but vows to go to Florence (London) anyway, and join his friend in mocking Bobadilla, Matheo (Matthew), and Stephano (Stephen) for being fools. He despises his cousin Stephano (Stephen), openly calling him a fool when he buys the disguised Musco's (Brainworm's) overpriced sword. He is merry when he meets Prospero (Wellbred), and joins him in baiting the three gulls. He is surprised to see Musco (Brainworm) and worried at the news that his father has followed him, but he greatly admires Musco's (Brainworm's) powers of deception. He encourages Matheo (Matthew) to make a fool out of himself by reading his plagiarized verses to Hesperida (Bridget). He falls in love with Hesperida (Bridget), and, with Prospero's (Wellbred's) help, meets and marries her. Clement sends for them while he is busy straightening out Musco's (Brainworm's) deceptions, and gives the marriage his blessing. He makes a long plea for true poetry (seconds Clement's defense of true poetry), as opposed to the vulgar poetry popular at the time, and attends Clement's dinner with his new wife (to discuss poetry with his father).

Lorenzo senior (Knowell). Father to Lorenzo junior (Edward) in the 1601 quarto version of *Every Man in His Humour.* (Differing names and courses of action in the 1616 folio version are given in parentheses.) He laments his son's devotion to poetry, which he feels is worthless, even though he, too, valued it in his youth. He makes a speech of trust in reason (of criticism of the way modern parents rear their children to be licentious) and is angered by the dissolute foolishness of many modern fashionable people. He is shocked when he intercepts a letter from Prospero (Wellbred) to Lorenzo junior (Edward), and vows secretly to follow his son to Florence (London) and spy on him and his friends. With a common sense that makes him a well-meaning, only disillusioned, father, not one of Jonson's old fools, he mocks foolish Stephano (Stephen) and understands that he should try gently to persuade Lorenzo junior (Edward) to a better way of life, rather than railing at him. His plan of watching his son's movements in Florence (London) is foiled, however, when he fails to recognize Musco (Brainworm), who is disguised as a soldier and who is in sympathy with Lorenzo junior (Edward). Lorenzo senior offers him a job spying on Lorenzo junior (Edward). Musco (Brainworm) sends him on a wild goose chase to Cob's house, where he is mistaken by Thorello (Kitely) for Biancha's (Dame Kitely's) lover. When Dr. Clement (Justice Clement) reveals Musco's (Brainworm's) deceptions, Lorenzo senior is consoled by Prospero and joins the dinner at Dr. Clement's with his son and the others (he laughs at the deception and admires Brainworm's skill, then goes to Justice Clement's dinner with his son and the others to discuss poetry).

Louis XI (1423–1483). King of France 1461–1483. Louis was the son and successor of Charles VII. As dauphin he was almost constantly in revolt against his father, and when he began his reign in 1461 he dismissed many of his father's best advisers. Louis began the arduous task of centralizing all authority in the crown, and by force and shrewd diplomacy he established an efficient central administration that encouraged industry, expanded domestic and foreign trade, and laid the basis for the absolute monarchy of Louis XIV. During the Wars of the Roses, he supported the York party, and he succeeded in buying off Edward IV when he invaded France in 1475. During his last years, Louis was in near self-imprisonment at Tours, squandering extravagant sums on the cults of his favorite saints.

In *Timber* (ll. 1317–22), Jonson records an anecdote, attributed to Louis, about the wheel of fortune.

Louis XIII (1601–1643) King of France 1610–1643. Louis succeeded his father, Henri IV, in 1610 under the regency of his mother, Marie de' Medici. In 1615 he married Anne of Austria. From 1630 onward he entrusted the government to others, first to Cardinal Richelieu and later to Mazarin. Louis's reign was remarkable for the establishment of the French Academy and for the work of St. Francis of Sales, Descartes, and Corneille. Jonson referred to Louis XIII in *Und.* LXVII.

Love. 1. A symbolic character in *The Vision of Delight* who has no speaking part but accompanies Delight at the opening of the masque.

2. A symbolic character in *The King's Entertainment at Welbeck* who welcomes the king.

3. A symbolic and mythic character who appears in *Love Freed from Ignorance and Folly* as the captive of the Sphinx, who represents ignorance.
See also CUPID.

Lovel. In *The New Inn,* a gentleman, soldier, and scholar who is the melancholy guest at the inn and who eventually marries Lady Frances Frampul.

Love Freed From Ignorance and Folly.
Performed: February 3, 1610.
Published: 1616 in folio by William Stansby.
Printer: William Stansby.

Although originally planned for Christmas 1610, for various technical and political reasons the work was not performed at court until Febuary 3, 1610. Jonson was assisted by Inigo Jones and Alphonso Ferrabosco in the preparation of the masque, but he does not mention them in the text.

After the king was seated, loud, strange music was heard, and a Sphinx, representing ignorance, danced forth, leading Love bound. As the Sphinx approached, she led the enslaved Love, proclaiming that the tyrannical Love was now only a powerless prisoner. Cupid protested such treatment and replied that he had only striven to keep the world alive and that without him all would be in chaos, and he appealed to the audience for compassion and promised to narrate how the Sphinx had captured him out of malice.

Love explained that in the East there once lived eleven glorious and beautiful daughters of the morning, the eldest of whom was their queen who desired to wed Phoebus. With Love as their guide, the daughters all decided to journey to the West to see Phoebus in his glorious sun palace. No sooner had the party arrived on the island in the West than the Sphinx surprised them all, captured the daughters and threw them into prison, and bound Love, explaining that the daughters would be freed only if they could solve a riddle, or if they would let Love be sacrificed for them. Heroically, the women refused to allow Love to be sacrificed, and Love himself promised either to solve the riddle or give his life to save them.

After scorning Love, the Sphinx gave him the riddle, the resolution of which involved finding a world that was without a world wherein what was done was done by an eye that moved and yet was fixed and in whose powers were mixed two contraries that until now fate had not known where or how to join. Cupid attempted to solve the riddle quickly, giving the answer "Woman," but trying to make all the attributes fit confounded him, and the Sphinx in triumph called for Love's destruction, after which twelve females and fools representing folly danced for joy. As he was being escorted off to his death, Love made a last desperate appeal to the audience for help, and twelve priests of the Muses appeared to aid him. They suggested that Love should look upon the brightest, shining face in the audience, and Cupid immediately realized that the answer to the riddle as well as the object of the search was the king of Albion. The riddle resolved, the priests banished the Sphinx and the follies, proclaiming "Sphinx must flie, when Phoebus shines, / And to ayde Love enclines." Love then called forth the Graces, who were the daughters, to receive the lustrous king, the now discovered object of their journey. They approached, singing in praise of love, and crowned Cupid as their savior, after which a masque dance was performed, and a priest praised the glorious beauties who were saved. There followed revels, a final masque dance, and a song celebrating love and beauty and the glorious sun enthroned in the West.

Love Restored.

Performed: Twelfth Night, 1612.
Published: 1616 in folio by William Stansby.
Printer: William Stansby.
This masque was first performed at court on Twelfth Night 1612 by the King's Servants. Jonson does not describe the performance in the text.

Masquerado appeared and apologetically explained that although everyone expected a masque to be presented it was unlikely that one would be given because of various complications among the presenters. Plutus, the god of money, entered disguised as Cupid and rebuked Masquerado for apologizing and argued that there should be no more masqueing at court because the custom was merely an idle and costly one of no significance. Excited, Robin Goodfellow appeared, and tried to ascertain whether there was to be a masque or not, and Plutus emphatically insisted that there was to be no masque, nor should there be one. Upset at the news, Robin expressed his disappointment in not being able to witness the celebrated revels and went on in great detail to explain the difficulties he had encountered in gaining entrance to the scheduled presentation, after which Plutus commanded both Robin and Masquerado to leave and declared that he would have no more talk of these superfluous excesses. Masquerado then exclaimed that Plutus looked like Cupid, but Robin perceptively pointed out that Plutus was actually an impostor who had stolen Cupid's attire and was now attempting to usurp "all those offices in this age of gold, which Love, himself perform'd in the golden age." Robin further indicated that he could guide all to the real Love, whose majesty and glory would allow the entertainment to proceed, but Plutus proclaimed that nothing was likely to succeed without his sanction and aid. The real Cupid entered in his Chariot, guarded by the masquers, while a song was sung noting that tyrannical money always attempts to quelch desire and that if in all courts love is cold, so are its sports. Cupid then retrieved his bow and quiver from Plutus, banished him from the rites, and declared that majesty always triumphs through the genuine love reflected in the courtly graces and the harmony of honor, courtesy, valor, urbanity, confidence, alacrity, promptness, industry, hability, and reality. There followed dances and three songs celebrating the power of love.

Lovers Made Men.

Performed: February 22, 1617.
Published: 1617 in quarto with no imprint; quarto reprinted in the section of the masques in 1640 folio by Thomas Walkley.
Printer: uncertain.
Produced by Nicholas Lanier, who designed the scenery and wrote the music, this masque was actually the first English opera. It was presented in honor of Henri, Baron de la Tour (1555–1623), who came to England on January 26, 1617, as an ambassador extraordinary for the Court of France. The work was commissioned by Lord Hay, who had served as ambassador in France, and it was performed at Lord Hay's house as part of his extravagant entertainment of Baron de la Tour (afterwards Duc de Bouillon).

Before the scene there was a triumphal arch on which sat the figure of Humanity, her lap full of flowers, which she scattered with her right hand while holding a golden chain in her left. Her two servants, Cheerfulness and Readiness, attended her, one on either side. The scene discovered was a boat in which was seen Charon, putting off from shore after having landed some ghosts whom Mercury had received and encouraged to come toward the River Lethe, who appeared lying down like an old man with the Fates sitting beside him on his bank and a grove of myrtles behind them. Noticing that the ghosts were growing faint, Mercury urged them on and showed them his golden rod. When Lethe asked Mercury who the ghosts were, he explained that they were lovers who, tossed upon the frantic seas from which Venus had sprung, had been drowned by love—all but one were dead. The Fates told Mercury, however, that none of them were actually dead, and Mercury realized that Love had apparently charmed them into thinking they were ghosts. The Fates declared that the ghosts should all drink from Lethe's stream, which would make them forget Love's name and allow them to recover. They stooped to the water, came forth and danced an antimasque enacting their behavior in love, returned to the grove, and reappeared changed into men again, to the joyful exclamation of Mercury and the Fates. After the chorus celebrated their transformation and their second birth, the transformed lovers danced their first masque. Afterwards Cupid appeared, lauded their dancing, and attempted to charm them again, but they were warned by Mercury to beware, and they danced their main dance. Cupid approached after the dance and explained that they should not allow themselves to be subject to Mercury's will alone, but to Love's as well, and he encouraged them to express their own appreciation of love by dancing with the ladies. They did so, and the revels followed. After some discussion, Cupid agreed never to force himself upon lovers without the approbation of Mercury, and the chorus celebrated the joyful reconciliation of all parties.

Love's Triumph through Callipolis.

Performed: January 9, 1631.

Published: 1630 in quarto by Thomas Walkley.

Printer: John Norton, Jr.

Co-authored by Jonson and Inigo Jones, this masque was presented at court in honor of Queen Mary by King Charles, who was assisted by fourteen of his lords and gentlemen.

In an introductory statement entitled "To make the Spectators Understanders,"

Jonson and Jones explained that, since masques should be mirrors of man's life and should both delight and instruct, when they were commanded by the king to produce a work worthy of his majesty's and his lords' participation that would also reflect honor on the court and befit the dignity of the sovereign's heroic love for his queen, the authors decided on the following argument as one appropriate for the masque.

There appeared a person of good character named Euphemus, who was sent down from heaven to Callipolis, the city where Beauty or Goodness dwells. Discovering the queen enthroned, Euphemus announced to her that Love had received word that in the suburbs of Callipolis certain depraved lovers who knew neither the name nor the nature of love correctly had sneaked in and proclaimed themselves Love's followers, but actually the whole life of these lovers was one of continuous vertigo of a torture on the wheel of Love rather than one showing any motion either of order or measure. Suddenly, the depraved lovers leaped forth, led by a mistress, and in antic gesticulation and action redolent of the old Roman pantomime they danced an antimasque of a distracted comedy of love, expressing their confused affections in the scenic persons and habits of the four prime European nations. The depraved lovers represented were: a boasting lover, a whining lover, an adventurous lover, a phantastic lover, a bribing lover, a jealous lover, a sordid lover, a proud lover, an angry lover, a melancholic lover, an envious lover, and a sensual lover.

When the depraved lovers had finished their dance and exited, Euphemus descended, singing of the harmony that genuine love produces. He approached the queen and praised her as the "top of beauty" and requested her to grace Love's triumph through the streets of Callipolis on this night. He further stated that although Love was eager to appear he did not want to do so until the air had been purified of all infected love, after which he would flow forth like a rich perfume in the air. The chorus then walked about with their censers while they explained that the diseased race of those tortured on the wheel of love had now been frightened away from the labyrinth of true love. As they spoke, the prospect of a sea appeared, and when the chorus finished, the triumph was discovered in the distance. Led by Amphitrite—the wife of Oceanus—with the sea gods Nereus, Proteus, Glaucus, and Palaemon attending her, the triumph consisted of fifteen lovers and as many Cupids with lighted torches, all of whom ranked themselves seven on a side with the king between the two groups. The king represented heroical love, and the other lovers and their counterparts were the provident and the judicious; the secret and the valiant, the witty and the jovial, the secure and the substantial, the modest and the candid, the courteous and the elegant, and the rational and the magnificent.

Amphitrite implored these perfect lovers to remain for a while in the temple of beauty and to make vows to the ladies present since true love must have an object and must be reciprocal. In a series of short speeches, Amphitrite and Euphemus then lauded the queen as the epitome of love and beauty, after which the Cupids danced and the masquers made their entrance. When they were finished, Euclia, or fair glory, appeared in the heavens, singing a paean about love bringing order out of chaos. Upon seeing a work of Neptune in which the Muses sat in a hollow rock that filled part of the sea prospect, Euclia proclaimed that Neptune's waves were calling forth the Muses to sing the birth of Venus' day.

Afterwards, the scene changed to a garden, the heavens opened, and four persons—Jupiter, Juno, Genius, and Hymen—appeared sitting in the form of a constellation and calling in song upon Venus, whom they expected shortly. Venus then appeared in a cloud, and, pushing through the constellation, descended to earth, after which the clouds vanished, and she was discovered sitting in a throne and singing. When Venus was finished, she arose and approached the queen, and Venus' throne disappeared. In its place there sprang up a palm tree with an imperial crown on the top, and from its roots were seen lilies and roses intertwined and covering the stem and the crown. Together Venus and the chorus sang:

> Beauty and Love, whose story is mysteriall,
> In yonder Palme-tree, and the Crown imperiall,
> Doe from the Rose, and Lilly so delicious,
> Promise a shade, shall ever be propitious
> To both the Kingdomes . . .
>   . . . . . .
> And who this King, and Queene would well historify,
> Need onely speake their names: Those them will glorify.

MARY, and CHARLES, CHARLES, with his MARY, named are,
And all the rest of Loves, or Princes famed are.

The last dance followed, and the masquers exited.

Love's Welcome at Bolsover.

Performed: July 30, 1634.
Published: in the second volume of the 1640 folio issued by Thomas Walkley.
Printers: probably Bernard Alsop and Thomas Fawcett.

This entertainment was written for King Charles and his queen when they visited the Earl of Newcastle in 1634. It was Jonson's last royal entertainment.

At the banquet a welcoming song was sung celebrating love as a lifting of the senses to the knowledge of pure intelligence where the soul resides and explaining that love feasts on itself and thus is a circle. After the banquet the king and queen were entertained by Colonel Vitruvius (a satirical portrait of Inigo Jones) and his oration on the dance of the mechanics. In his speech Vitruvius introduced each mechanic: Captain Smith, the blacksmith; Chesil, the carver; Maul, the Freemason; Squire Summer, the carpenter; Twybil, the carpenter's apprentice; Dresser, the plumber; Quarrel, the glazier; Fret, the plasterer; and Beater, the mortar man. The mechanics all danced while Vitruvius applauded them.

When the dancing ended, a second banquet was set before the king and queen by two loves names Eros and Anteros, who descended from clouds. One love served the king, and one the queen. The two loves engaged in a long verse dialogue explaining that since they were both sons of Venus they were actually brothers and that their function was to report the graces from the king's side to the queen's. The two loves quarreled briefly over a palm which they finally decided to divide between them, showing that the two were really one. They concluded their dialogue on a note of mutual love and attributed their attitude to their being in the presence of the circular court of the king and queen—the school of pure love.

Philalethes interrupted the two loves and pointed out that they were in the divine school of love where the true lessons of love are taught and made demonstrable to the senses. Philalethes advised Eros and Anteros to stop their verse dialogue, return to themselves, and admire the miracle they serve—the king and queen who are the whole divine school of love. All should study and contemplate the royal couple as the ideal of true love. Then followed lavish praise of the king and queen and the wish that their own palms should ever be the types of true victory. The entertainment ended on a final note of joyous welcome to the royal couple.

Lovewit. The master of the house in *The Alchemist*, Face's employer. He departs from the city in fear of the plague, leaving Face behind to take care of his house. When he returns unexpectedly, he is at first confused, then angered by the use to which Subtle, Face, and Dol have put his house. Face pacifies him, however, by giving him the chance to marry Dame Pliant.

Lowin, John (1576–?1669). Actor who joined the King's Men in 1603 and acted in *Sejanus*. He performed in *Volpone, The Alchemist, Epicoene,* and *Catiline* as well. He also acted in Shakespeare's plays, especially doing Falstaff, and in the plays of Beaumont and Fletcher. When Heminges died in 1630, Lowin bought shares in the Globe and Blackfriars Theatres. ∆ Bosola

Lownes, Matthew. Bookseller in London from 1591 to 1625. The 1602 quarto of *Poetaster* was published by Lownes and probably printed by Rich and Bradock. The title page of *Poetaster* in the 1616 folio reads "Printed by W. Stansby for M. Lownes."

Lucan (A.D. 39–65). Marcus Annaeus Lucanus was born at Córdoba. Seneca was his uncle. Lucan's wealthy family took him to Rome, where he received an excellent education in rhetoric and philosophy. The Emperor Nero liked Lucan and appointed him quaestor, but eventually the two had a falling out. Nero forbade Lucan to recite or publish his poems, which he had begun to write as a young man. In retaliation, Lucan joined the conspiracy of Piso to depose and murder Nero. Lucan was arrested and forced to commit suicide in 65. Lucan's only extant work is *On the Civil War*, an epic poem in ten books dealing with Julius Caesar's struggle against the Senatorial party of Rome. This work is often erroneously referred to as *Pharsalia*.

Jonson told Drummond (*Conversations*, ll. 66–67; 611–14) that Lucan read in parts was good, but taken all together he was no poet. In *Epicoene* (II), Daw dismisses him as one of the worthless ancient writers. Jonson did a verse translation from Lucan ("Just and fit actions . . ."), included among his uncollected poems, and he frequently

alluded to him: *Bartholomew Fair* (IV. vi), *King's Entertainment in Passing to his Coronation, Masque of Queens, Hymenaei, Sejanus* (passim), *Catiline* (I; III; IV; v), and *Und.* XXXIII.

Lucian (A.D. 120–?200). Lucianus, a Greek born at Samosata in Syria, was apprenticed early in life to a sculptor but soon left the profession and until he was forty traveled in Greece and Italy earning his living as a rhetorician. He gave up rhetoric, settled in Athens, and began studying philosophy with the Stoci Demonax and composing satirical dialogues. When he was old, the Emperor Commodus appointed him to a position in Egypt.

Over eighty works have been attributed to Lucian, some of which are probably not by him. He wrote in an easy, masterly Attic prose, and his wit, satire, and characterizations give his works a vigor that has been highly admired and imitated. His works may be classified in the following groups: (1) rhetorical writings such as *Phalaris* and *Apology for an Incorrect Greeting*; (2) literary works such as *Lexiphanes, How to Write History,* and *True History;* (3) mock philosophical writings like *Dialogues of the Dead* and *Hermotimus*; (4) satires on various subjects, the best known of which is *Dialogues of the Gods*; and (5) miscellaneous writings including a parody of Oedipus called Swiftfoot.

Jonson had a copy of Lucian in his library and made considerable use of him both directly and indirectly in his works. Jonson apparently knew most of Lucian's writings well, judging from the range of Lucian's works upon which Jonson drew as indicated in the following selective list. *Adversus Indoctum* was used in *Poetaster* (v. iii); *De Saltatione* in *The Masque of Beauty; Dialogues of the Gods* in *The Haddington Masque, Oberon, Neptune's Triumph,* and *Cynthia's Revels* (I. i). *Encomium Demonsthenis* is discussed in *Cynthia's Revels* (I. iv) and was used in *For.* XI. *Gallus* was employed in *Volpone* (I. ii); *Hermotimus* in *The Sad Shepherd* (III. iv); *Icaromenippus* in *News from the New World; Lexiphanes* in *Poetaster* (v. ii); *Timon* in *Love Restored; True History* in *News from the New World*; and *Sale of Lives* in *Volpone* (I. ii).

Lucifer. Another name for the evening star Hesperus.

Lucilius (148–103 B.C.). The first great Roman satirist. It was he who dictated the form of satire. In *Poetaster*, Trebatius calls him "wise," and Horace "both our better" (III. v).

161

Lucina. The Roman goddess of childbirth associated with the Greek Eileithyia. Also often identified with Juno, Trivia, and Luna.

Lucrece, wife of Tarquinius Collantinus, stabbed herself to death after she had been violated by Sextus, son of Tarquinius Superbus. This incident led to a popular uprising which resulted in the expulsion of the Tarquins from Rome.

Lucretius (94–55 B.C.). Roman philosophical poet. Little is known of his life. He wrote *De rerum natura*, a didactic and philosophical poem in six books that explains the atomistic philosophy of Democritus and Epicurus. In the poem, Lucretius tries to prove that all things happen by natural causes and that belief in the supernatural is unnecessary and superstitious. He also writes of physics, ethics, cosmology, and psychology. In *Poetaster*, Ovid says that Lucretius' fame will last until "earth, and seas in fire and flames shall frie" (I. i).

As indicated by the annotations in his personal copy, Jonson had read Lucretius with care, but he included few borrowings from the Roman poet in his works. In *Timber* (ll. 1946–47), Jonson refers to Lucretius as "scabrous and rough" in custom, and later (ll. 2368–69), he quotes him on poetry. In *Hymenaei*, Lucretius is cited as one of the authorities for the attributes of Venus displayed in the masque. See POEM.

Lucullus. The wealthy conqueror of Mithridates, king of Pontus, a Roman province on the Black Sea in northeast Asia Minor. In *Poetaster* (I. ii), Tucca calls Ovid senior "my noble Lucullus."

Lully, Raymond (1235–?1315). A philosopher born in Majorca who was rumored to have found the philosopher's stone and to have developed an elixir from it. In 1266 Lully had a vision that turned him to religion. He became a Franciscan tertiary and fanatically devoted himself to the conversion of Islam. On his third unsuccessful proselytizing trip to Moslem countries, Lully was stoned to death in North Africa. An authority on Arabic languages and Moslem culture, Lully was a prolific writer, and later generations attributed to him many works on alchemy and magic that were not his. His chief work was *Ars magna*, a defense of Christianity against the teachings of Averroës in which Lully set forth a curious method of expressing all knowledge symbolically and maintained that philosophy (including science) was not divorced from theology and that every

article of faith could be demonstrated logically.

In the mountebank scene (II. ii), Volpone proclaims that Lully's elixir would never have become famous had his own elixir been known in medieval times. Although a martyr, Lully was most frequently associated with alchemy and is alluded to in *Mercury Vindicated* and *The Alchemist* (II. v).

Lupus, Asinius. A foolish, vengeful magistrate in *Poetaster*. He derides players and playwrights to Ovid senior, and encourages Ovid junior to continue studying law. When Histrio tells him of Ovid's order of costumes for the players, he thinks that they are planning treason, and rushes to tell Caesar. After Caesar punishes the masqueraders, Horace upbraids Lupus for his action in bringing Caesar to the innocent, if frivolous, masquerade. Lupus, angry at Horace, plans vengeance on him for his reproof. He breaks into Caesar's palace and accuses Horace of treason on trumped-up charges; Caesar realizes that he is foolish, and has him carried out to be whipped and fitted with a large pair of ass's ears.

Luscus. A servant to Ovid senior in *Poetaster*, who appears only to warn Ovid junior to give up "villainous poetry" and study law as his father wishes. He realizes that Tucca is interested in borrowing money from Ovid senior and jokes about it.

Lyaeus. An epithet for Bacchus indicating the wine god's freeing men's minds from cares.

Lycaeum. One of the Arcadian mountains associated with Pan.

Lycophron. Greek poet and grammarian, who lived in the third century B.C. He arranged the works of the Greek comic poets for the Alexandrian library and wrote a long poem about the Trojan War, the *Alexandra* or *Cassandra*. In *Poetaster* (v. iii), Virgil includes Lycophron in the list of poets Crispinus should read with a tutor in order to develop literary taste and discretion, but in *Epicoene* (II) Daw dismisses him as worthless along with many other ancient writers.

Lycurgus. The traditional founder of the Spartan constitution and military, whose legislation was believed to have been approved by the oracle at Delphi. Whether Lycurgus was a god or a historical person and, if the latter, when he lived are uncertain. In *Timber* (ll. 1006–7), Jonson states that the Prince must command himself as well as others and notes that "the wise *Licurgus* gave no Law, but what himselfe kept."

Lydgate, John (1370?–?1450), a Benedictine monk, was one of the most prolific English poets of his day. Little is known about his life or the chronology of his works, which may be divided into three categories: (1) poems written in imitation of Chaucer, whose disciple Lydgate professed himself to be; (2) lengthy translations, of which *The Fall of Princes* is one of the best known; (3) short pieces including fables, saints' lives, and devotional, philosophical, and occasional poems. Lydgate was one of the most influential poets of his day, but his fame diminished rapidly after his death.

Along with Chaucer, Lydgate appears in *The Golden Age Restored* as one of the poets summoned forth by Pallas. His *Fall of Princes* is quoted extensively in Book II of *The English Grammar* on syntax: chapt. II, ll. 65–68; chapt. III, ll. 53–55, 80–82, 135–37; chapt. V, ll. 51–53; chapt. VI, ll. 29–31; chapt. VII, ll. 16–18, 74–76, 88–89, 94–96, 109–112; chapt. VIII, ll. 12–15, 62–64; chapt. IX, ll. 61–63.

Lyly, John (1554?–1606). English courtier, prose writer, and dramatist. Served as a member of Parliament (1589–1601). His best known and most influential work was *Euphues*, published in two parts (*The Anatomy of Wit* [1578] and *Euphues and his England* [1580]). An early example of the novel of manners, *Euphues* tried to establish an ideal of perfected prose style which became known in the 1580s as Euphuism and was characterized by wide use of simile and illustration, balanced construction, alliteration, and antithesis. Lyly's early plays, the most popular of which were *Campaspe* (1584) and *Endimion* (1591), followed the euphuistic style, but his later works such as *Mother Bombie* (1594) employed the robust, realistic style of Roman comedy. Many Elizabethan playwrights, including Shakespeare and Jonson, are indebted to Lyly for his innovation of prose as the vehicle for comic dialogue and for his development of romantic comedy.

Although there is only one reference to Lyly in Jonson' work (*Every Man out*, v. x), it seems that Jonson was influenced by Lyly in several ways. Jonson probably borrowed from Lyly's method of relating Greek myth to contemporary and courtly issues, particularly in the masques. Subtle in *The Alchemist* seems to be modeled in part on the alchemist in Lyly's *Gallathea*, Hannibal Puppy in *A Tale of a Tub* appears

to be akin to Licio and Petullus in Lyly's *Midas*, and Jonson's Awdrey in the same play was probably influenced by Silena in Lyly's *Mother Bombie*.

Lynceus. An Argonaut famous for his keen sight.

lyric. See POEM.

Lysander. Fourth century B.C. Spartan naval commander and statesman who established oligarchies in each of Athens' allied states and, in Athens, the Thirty Tyrants. In *Timber* (ll. 1007–8), Jonson, while discussing the necessity for the prince to keep his own laws, notes that Lysander did not do so.

Lysippus. A worker in bronze. Alexander the Great was said to have forbidden any other worker than Lysippus to represent him. See ORATORS.

M

Mab. Queen of the fairies in *The Entertainment at Althorp*.

Mabbe, James (1572–?1642), was a scholar who did valuable work making English translations of Spanish works. In 1622 he published *The Rogue* for which Jonson wrote a commendatory poem ("Who tracks this Authors, or Translators Pen"). Jonson's library contained a copy of Mabbe's *Celestina* (London, 1631).

Macaria. One of the daughters of Hercules. Also the poetical name for several of the Grecian Isles.

Machaon. One of the skilled physician sons of Aesculapius, who was the god of healing.

Machiavelli, Niccolò (1469–1527). Italian author and statesman, one of the outstanding figures of the Renaissance. A native of Florence, he entered political office as a clerk and became increasingly important throughout the time of the Florentine republic (1429–1512). In 1506, for instance, as defense secretary, he instituted a major reform by replacing the prevailing mercenary system with a citizens' militia. Machiavelli undertook several important diplomatic missions. He met Cesare Borgia twice and was sent by Florence to Louis XIII of France in 1504 and 1510, to Pope Julius II in 1506, and to Emperor Maximilian I in 1507. When the Medicis returned to Florence in 1512, he was dismissed, and the next year he was imprisoned and tortured for his alleged complicity in a plot against them. After he was released, he retired to his estate, where he wrote his major works, but he did humiliate himself in vain before the Medicis to be restored to office. When the Florentine republic was briefly reestablished, he was distrusted by the republicans, and he died disappointed and embittered.

His best known work is *The Prince* (1532), which describes in practical, amoral terms how a prince may gain and maintain power. The book has always caused problems in interpretation. It has been variously seen: as sincere advice, as a plea for political office, as a detached analysis of Italian politics, as an example of early Italian nationalism, and as political satire on Medici rule. Although Machiavelli was a lover of liberty and republican values, his name, because of this book, has become synonymous with amoral cunning and absolute power. More indicative of Machiavelli's politics are his *Discourses on Livy* (1531), the first work of general political theory to depart from Platonic and scholastic concepts, and *History of Florence* (1532), a masterpiece both as literature and as history. He also wrote poems and plays, including the ribald comedy *Mandragola* (1524), and his important correspondence has been preserved.

Jonson knew *The Prince* well and discussed it in *Timber* (ll. 1127–96), and he has Sir Politic misquote from Machiavelli in *Volpone* (IV. i).

Macilente. In *Every Man out of His Humour*, a scholar who is eventually cured of his humor of envy.

Macro, Sertorius. Prefect chosen by Tiberius to curb Sejanus' power in *Sejanus*. Tiberius asks him to watch Sejanus while he is away from Rome; in a soliloquy, Macro reveals his own unscrupulous corruption and lust for power. When he hears that Sejanus is back in favor for saving Tiberius' life, he swears to redouble his efforts to make Sejanus fall. Macro advises Caligula to hurry to Tiberius and beg for mercy bringing stories of Sejanus' treasonous behavior, then meets with Regulus and Laco and plots to call a Senate meeting to overthrow Sejanus. He craftily makes Sejanus let down his guard when they meet by hinting to him that he is to be honored at the meeting. He arrives in the Senate after a letter from Tiberius has been read, denounces Sejanus, and reassures the Senators that Sejanus' former power has been transferred to him. Although many thoughtless Senators praise him, Arruntius says that Macro may soon be as tyrannical as Sejanus; this seems to be beginning by the end of the play when news is brought that Macro has cruelly murdered Sejanus' children.

Macrobius. Latin writer of about the fourth century whose *Saturnalia* incorporates important quotations from other authors and whose commentary on Cicero's *Dream of Scipio* was well known in the Middle Ages and influenced Chaucer. Jonson was fond of Macrobius and used him as a source for information and ideas in *The Masque of Beauty* and *Hymenaei*.

Madge. In *A Tale of a Tub*, one of the bridesmaids for Awdrey's intended marriage to John Clay.

Madrigal. In *The Staple of News*, a poetaster who is one of the suitors to Lady Pecunia.

Maecenas. Caius Maecenas, Roman statesman and wealthy patron of the arts, born between 74 B.C. and 64 B.C., became a trusted adviser of Octavian Augustus. In later life he retired and devoted his time to the famous literary circle that included Horace, Virgil, and Propertius. To the great poets of his day, he proved himself to be a good friend and a generous patron. His name has become synonymous with the wealthy and munificent patron of the arts. Jonson mentions him in this connection in *Poetaster* (III. i). He also refers to Maecenas' frequent quarrels with his wife, at the end of *The New Inn* (V. v).

Maenalus. One of the two Arcadian mountains associated with Pan.

Magellan, Ferdinand (1480?–1521). Portuguese navigator. After being rejected by Manuel I, Magellan went to Spain in 1517 with a plan to reach the Moluccas by a western route. His plan was approved by Charles I (later Emperor Charles V), and he set sail in 1519 with five ships and 255 men. In 1521 Magellan reached the Marianas and shortly thereafter the Philippines, where he was killed while supporting one group of natives against another. A year later one of the original ships completed the first voyage around the world. Although he did not live to complete the voyage, Magellan provided the knowledge and determination to guide the ships over a vast unknown portion of the earth—a great navigational achievement. This voyage also proved the roundness of the earth, revolutionized ideas about the relative proportions of land and water, and revealed the Americas as a new continent separate from Asia. Jonson mentions Magellan in *Bartholomew Fair* (v. vi).

Magnetic Lady, The.
Acted: 1632.
Published: 1640 in the third volume of the second folio by Thomas Walkley.
Printer: unknown.

In the induction Master Probee and Master Damplay, two gentlemen who declare themselves delegates of the people, interrupt the boy of the house and ask to see the poet of the day. After telling them a little about the playwright, the boy invites the two gentlemen to sit beside him to watch the play which is about to begin, and he suggests that they should feel free to criticize the playwright's work, keeping in mind that "a good play is like a skein of silk which if you take by the right end you may wind off at pleasure . . . but if you light on the wrong end you will pull all into a knot or elf-lock. . . ." The gentlemen accept the boy's offer and comment on the play after each act, expressing their views of the characters and situations and expounding a theory of comedy.

Act I. Compass, scholar of mathematics, tells Captain Ironside, a renowned soldier, about the house of Lady Loadstone, where many interesting gentlewomen and men of various dispositions and professions gather to socialize, and he invites the soldier to join them. There are many guests at the house since Lady Loadstone has a fourteen-year-old niece named Placentia whose parents are deceased. Placentia is ripe for a husband and has several suitors, the most prominent among them being Practice, a lawyer, and Sir Diaphanous Silkworm, a courtier. Placentia's father left her a considerable fortune to be paid upon her marriage with approval of Lady Loadstone, but Lady Loadstone's brother, Sir Moth Interest, a usurer who holds the fortune, tries to discourage Placentia's suitors although Compass has been instrumental in bringing eligible suitors to the house. Placentia, who is presently not feeling well, was reared by Lady Loadstone's garrulous parasite Polish, whose daughter Pleasance is Lady Loadstone's waiting woman. Lady Loadstone, who is concerned about her niece's health and her future, is counselled by Parson Palate, prelate of the parish, and

Dr. Rut, her physician. When Sir Interest presents his own candidate for Placentia's hand (a suitor named Bias who is a subsecretary with good political prospects), Compass finds the man not very acceptable and a mild quarrel erupts in which Sir Moth reminds Compass that although the scholar himself has a reversion for surveyor of the projects general, he is not yet in that potentially lucrative office.

Act II. Keep, Placentia's nurse, and Pleasance try to make the despondent Placentia feel better by assuring her that she shall soon have a husband, either the lawyer favored by Lady Loadstone or the courtier preferred by Polish, but Needle, Lady Loadstone's steward and tailor, insists that Placentia's current disposition has a physical cause, and Polish agrees, proclaiming that Placentia is "leavened." Dr. Rut's diagnosis is that she is suffering from "tympanites" and, in order to be cured, needs to spend about a month in the fresh air in the country and then return to town with a husband. Lady Loadstone agrees to send her niece to the country, and when Polish urges her mistress also to choose a husband for Placentia right away she announces that Practice is her choice. Polish responds by arguing for Sir Diaphanous Silkworm, claiming that he will be able to make Lady Loadstone a countess.

Meanwhile, Palate has surreptitiously accepted money to work for the cause of Sir Diaphanous, and he tells the courtier not to worry because he knows that Practice secretly loves Pleasance. When speaking on behalf of Lady Loadstone, Compass offers Placentia's hand to Practice; the lawyer politely refuses and hints that he is committed to another. Later, when pressured, Palate admits to the astonished Lady Loadstone that the lawyer prefers Pleasance, but the parson insists that Pleasance's mother must not know. With Practice out of the running, Sir Moth instructs the lawyer to draw up a contract for Bias and Placentia with a dowry at a reduced amount in consideration of the usurer's services for the last fourteen years. When Practice objects to Sir Moth's dishonesty, the old usurer delivers a stirring speech in defense of the love of money and infinite wealth, after which a disgruntled and hungry Captain Ironside enters and threatens all present, and they disperse in fear. Pleasance announces that dinner is served, and as Compass proceeds to the dining room, he asks her privately if she has any suits pending in court since he understands that she has retained Practice for counsel and "are to be joined a patentee with him." She is very perplexed by Compass's question and decides to study it, thinking that "this riddle shows / a little like a love trick. . . ."

Act III. Shortly after Timothy Item, Dr. Rut's apothecary, arrives at one room in Lady Loadstone's house, a quarrel breaks out in the dining room, swords are drawn, Captain Ironside humiliates Sir Diaphanous in front of the dinner guests, and the gentlewomen swoon. Placentia faints and is carried from the room by Keep. Sir Moth falls into a fit of the "happyplex," and Lady Loadstone fears for the good reputation of her house. Sir Diaphanous consults with Practice about how he may repair his own damaged reputation through legal means, and as advised by Compass, the courtier decides to send Captain Ironside a written challenge. Sir Moth is treated by Dr. Rut with the assistance of Item and advised to cleanse his body, but the doctor and apothecary are called away by nurse Keep, who reports that Placentia has fallen into a worse fit than before. Sir Diaphanous asks Bias to deliver his written challenge to Ironside, but the politically shrewd subsecretary politely refuses while confiding to Compass that he would gladly deliver the challenge if he could be assured that the captain would kill the courtier, who is actually a nuisance at court. When the captain himself enters, Sir Diaphanous challenges the experienced soldier to a duel in which they will fight without their doublets on. The captain is merely amused, but Practice suggests that it would be better to have a cup of wine than to fight shirtless. Sir Diaphanous proclaims that his valor is of a different nature, and he launches into a long discourse on the nature of true valor, which is finally interrupted by Keep, who calls out Needle and instructs him to proceed with dispatch to bring the midwife, Mistress Chair. Sir Moth reenters and announces that according to Dr. Rut, Placentia is in labor. Sir Diaphanous is reconciled with Ironside when he realizes that he and all the other suitors have been saved by this strange discovery brought about by the Captain's aggressive behavior at dinner. They speculate that Compass, who has left the room hurriedly and has consistently tried to get Placentia an appropriate suitor, is responsible for the "slip."

Act IV. Although he is not responsible, the noble and honorable Compass makes arrangements with Practice for a license to marry Placentia discreetly in order to save Lady Loadstone the embarrassment of her niece's giving birth to an illegitimate child, while Sir Moth still tries to swindle Bias into a deal for her. The scholar also learns from Practice that the reversion has fallen upon him. Later Compass overhears a quarrel between Polish and Keep in which he finds out that Placentia is really Polish's daughter and Pleasance is actually Placentia since Polish, unknown to Lady Loadstone, switched the cradles of the two children in infancy and changed their identities. Afterwards Pleasance tells Compass that Placentia has given birth to a boy, and by an ingenious stratagem Compass has Palate marry him and Pleasance.

Meanwhile Chair, the midwife, makes arrangements for the new child to be sent out of the house with Needle to a nurse and devises a plan in which she will claim that her own daughter actually gave birth to the child. Later Sir Moth celebrates the birth of an heir who will be ineligible for inheritance held by the old usurer, and he praises Compass for being responsible for the deed, but Compass himself chastises the old man and in the presence of Ironside, Sir Diaphanous, Palate, Pleasance, and Lady Loadstone reveals the true identities of Pleasance and Placentia, announces his marriage to Pleasance, and asks for Lady Loadstone's approval, which is granted, much to the displeasure of Sir Moth, who demands proof of Compass's claims.

Act V. Needle complains to Item that the whole house is divided because of the apparent mistake Dr. Rut made in diagnosing Placentia as being in labor, and Item makes a plan to restore the Doctor's reputation in the household, in which Needle will feign sleepwalking and will be cured by the physician. Polish chastises Pleasance for marrying against Polish's wishes. Compass makes peace with Practice by giving the lawyer his reversion, and in return Practice urges Compass to sue Sir Moth for his wife's dowry. Lady Loadstone tries to persuade Sir Moth that he was mistaken in thinking Placentia had given birth to an heir by Compass, and Compass himself accuses Polish of hiding Compass's wife, out of malice, somewhere in the house. Later Doctor Rut and Sir Moth encounter Needle talking in his sleep about some treasure buried in the garden, and afterwards the old usurer renegotiates a deal with Bias, who is now again interested in Placentia since she apparently did not have a baby. Palate reports that Pleasance has been found where her supposed mother had hidden her. Compass confronts Polish with the truth about the identity of Pleasance and Placentia and demands that Polish reveal the father of her daughter's illegitimate child. Before Polish can be forced to respond, Rut rushes in and informs all that Sir Moth has fallen into a well while looking for a treasure in the garden. The old usurer is saved by Needle, and after drying himself off wants to know if Bias and Placentia are yet married. He is assured that they are, and Moth pronounces that Bias shall receive his portion of the inheritance the next day and after that none will then be left to satisfy Compass. At Compass's direction a sergeant then enters and arrests Sir Moth, who is being sued for five hundred thousand pounds by Compass and Pleasance, and the usurer has to post bail or be imprisoned. Captain Ironside agrees to post Moth's bail if the usurer will assure Pleasance's dowry, but Moth protests that he has no other portion to bestow since he has already given it to Bias and Placentia. Enraged, Compass insists that the new child be produced as its mother, Polish, and Chair will be charged with murder. With this threat Polish finally confesses all and announces that Needle is actually the father, whereupon Bias demands to be released from his contract and Sir Moth finally agrees to pay Pleasance her rightful portion. Out of gratitude to Ironside for his initially and ultimately bringing about the truth and saving her daughter, Lady Loadstone offers herself and her entire estate to Ironside, who accepts her, denounces any further warfare except in her defense, and promises to consider what would be an appropriate portion for Needle and Placentia when they are married with the captain and his Magnetic Lady.

Maia. In Greek mythology the daughter of Atlas and the mother by Zeus of Hermes. The month of May is named after her.

Maids. Minor characters in *Poetaster*, servants to Chloe and Albius, who appear only when they are preparing to welcome the courtiers.

Malice. The name of one of the witches making up the antimasque in *The Masque of Queens*.

Mammon, Sir Epicure. A foolish knight in *The Alchemist*, who comes to Subtle in hope of getting the philosopher's stone for himself. He tells Surly and Face of all the rich and corrupt pleasures he will buy with the stone, then hypocritically assures Subtle that he has only the loftiest and most noble of motives. Face tells him that Dol is a beautiful, but mad, noblewoman; Mammon sneaks in to see her and is dismayed when she begins raving about ancient and religious figures. Subtle rushes in and pretends to be shocked by the display; he tells Mammon that all hope of winning the stone is gone. Mammon returns in anger when Lovewit comes back home but is turned away.

Manly, Eustace. The friend of Wittipol in *The Devil Is an Ass*, who helps him to rescue Mrs. Frances Fitzdottrel from her tyrannical husband.

manners. In *Timber* (ll. 948–58), Jonson, paraphrasing Seneca (*Epist.* cxiv. 3. 11), includes a short discussion on corrupt manners and concludes that "Wheresoever, manners, and fashions are corrupted, Language is. It imitates the publicke riot. The excesse of Feasts, and apparell, are the notes of a sick State; and the wantonnesse of Language, of a sick mind."

Manners, Francis. See Francis Manners, Earl of RUTLAND.

Mannington, George. Author of *A Woeful Ballad* (1576) discussed in *Eastward Ho* (v. v).

Mansfield, Ernest, Count of. Commander of the army of Frederick, Elector Palatine and King of Bohemia. Mansfield visited England in 1624 and is mentioned in *Und.* XLVII.

Maria, Infanta of Spain, daughter of Philip III of Spain and sister of Philip IV, was proposed as a bride for Prince Charles of England, but the proposed marriage never happened. Jonson alludes to the Infanta and the proposed marriage in the Prince's fortune in *Gypsies Metamorphosed.*

Marian. Robin Hood's lady in Sherwood Forest in *The Sad Shepherd*. She is an enthusiastic huntress, passing the time until Robin's return by catching a stag for the feast, but she is disturbed by the ominous crow that croaked at its death. She enjoys seeing Robin and telling him of her hunt. After Maudlin disguises herself as Marian and insults Robin and his men, Marian is baffled and hurt at his coolness until they realize that they have been deceived. She pities Amie's malady and scolds Maudlin, being grateful when the stag is returned.

Markham, Gervase (1568–1637). A hack poet who wrote a great deal but is better known for his literary thefts. His chief works are on horses and country life— *Cavelarice; or the English Horseman* (1607) and *Country Contentments* (1615). Markham was said to have imported the first Arabian horse into England. In the *Conversations* (ll. 166–68), Jonson said Markham, Day, and Middleton were all base fellows and not faithful poets.

Marlowe, Christopher (1564–1593), dramatist and poet, was born in the same year as Shakespeare, and educated at Cambridge. His first play, *Tamburlaine the Great,* was produced in 1587, the same year he earned his M.A. Other important plays include: *Dr. Faustus* (c. 1588), *The Jew of Malta* (c. 1589), and *Edward II* (c. 1592). His best known nondramatic pieces include *Hero and Leander* (1598) and the lyric "Come Live with Me." Marlowe's titanic dramatic heroes epitomize the aspiring temper of the Renaissance, and his strong blank verse prepared the way for Shakespeare's plays, in which works some scholars see traces of Marlowe's hand.

Marlowe led a colorful life. In 1593 Thomas Kyd, with whom Marlowe had lived at one time, supported charges that Marlowe held and propagated lewd and immoral religious views. Before Marlowe could appear for questioning, he was stabbed to death in a brawl in a tavern. Although a coroner's jury decided the assailant had acted in self-defense, some believe the murder may have been a result of Marlowe's activities as a government agent.

Jonson's elegy on Shakespeare prefaced to the First Folio contains the famous description of Marlowe's "mighty line," recognizing the strength of his blank verse and its importance for Shakespeare. Jonson mentioned *Dr. Faustus* in *Tale of a Tub* (IV. vi) and *Tamburlaine* in *Every Man in* (1601 quarto version, III. ii), *Timber* (l. 777), and *Eastward Ho* (II. i). He also referred to *Hero and Leander* in *Every Man in* (1601 quarto version, III. iv; 1616 folio version, IV. ii) and in *Bartholomew Fair* (V. iii), and he borrowed, with few changes, from Marlowe's translation of Ovid's *Amores* in *Poetaster* (I. i).

Marmion, Shackerley (1603–1639), was educated at Thame and at Wadham College, Oxford. He became a dramatist and published several works: *Holland's Leaguer* (1632), *The Legend of Cupid and Psyche* (1637), and *The Antiquary* (1641). He considered himself a member of the Tribe of Ben, and he contributed an elegy ("I cannot grave nor carve else would I give") to *Jonsonus Virbius* and included a poem on the Apollo in his *A Fine Companion* (1633).

Mars. Thought to be the son of Juno, Mars was frequently mentioned as the lover of Venus and the father of Cupid, Penthesilea, and Romulus and Remus. The name Mars, originally that of a Roman vegetation deity, came to be that of the god of war, the Roman name of the Greek god Ares. His weapon was a spear, and his sacred animal was the wolf.

Marshall, William. See PORTRAITS OF JONSON.

Marston, John (1575–1634). English dramatist born at Coventry, the son of a lawyer. His mother was Italian. After Oxford, he followed his father's wishes and entered the Middle Temple, but he soon abandoned law for literature, publishing his verse satires in 1598 under the pseudonym W. Kinsayder. The next year he began writing plays for the Admiral's Company. From 1600 to 1603 he wrote for the Paul's boys, during which time he became involved in the War of the Theatres, and after 1604 he worked for the Queen's Revels at the Blackfriars, of which syndicate he became a member. By 1608 he had taken holy orders and retired from the stage. In 1616 he was given a living at Hampshire, where he remained until shortly before his death.

Although Marston initially admired Jonson, they seem to have had a hot and cold relationship. Marston apparently intended to compliment Jonson in the character of Chrisogamus in *Histriomastix* (1599) and in the portrait of Brabant senior in *Jack Drum's Entertainment* (1600), but Jonson found the portraits offensive, as he told Drummond in the *Conversations* (ll. 284–86). Jonson seems to have ridiculed Marston's vocabulary in *Every Man out* (III. iv) and may have satirized him in the character of Hedon in *Cynthia's Revels,* while Marston may have represented Jonson as Lampatho in *What You Will* (1601), and most certainly he criticized Jonson's penchant for theorizing in the play. Moreover, if we can believe the *Conversations* (l. 160), Jonson, at some time, had beaten Marston and taken a pistol from him. But Marston was also attacked by someone other than Jonson, notably in the anonymous *Whipping of the Satire* (1601), in which Marston and Jonson are both ridiculed. In retaliation for Marston's portraying him on the stage, Jonson satirized Marston as Crispinus in *Poetaster,* and the War of the Theatres was in full force. Although the men apparently had many quarrels, both private and public, by 1604 they seem to have been reconciled, for in that year Marston warmly dedicated his *Malcontent* to Jonson, and the next year

Marston prefixed a commendatory poem (in English, with a Latin title, "Amicis, Amici Nostri Dignissimi, B.J. Dignissimis, Epigramma. D. Johannes Marstonius") to the quarto of *Sejanus*. Marston, Jonson, and Chapman collaborated on *Eastward Ho*, but on publication the play was adjudged offensive, and Jonson and Chapman were imprisoned. Marston, who was mainly responsible for the offensive passages, escaped. This fact, as is implicit in Jonson's comments in the *Conversations* (ll. 275–76), seems not to have endeared Marston to Jonson, who did not forgive others with alacrity. Another of Jonson's sarcastic comments to Drummond leads one to believe that Jonson never fully accepted Marston as a true friend. Marston was married to the daughter of the Rev. William Wilkes, one of James's chaplains. In the *Conversations* (ll. 206–7), Jonson remarked that Marston wrote his father-in-law's sermons and his father-in-law wrote his comedies. As perhaps a final statement, Marston alluded to Jonson's past cruelty toward him in the address to the readers of his *Parasitaster* (1606). Jonson did have a copy of Marston's collected plays in his personal library. See also WAR OF THE THEATRES; John WEEVER.

Martial (c. A.D. 40–c.104). Roman poet born at Bilbilis in Spain. He was well educated and went to Rome in 63, where he became a friend of Quintilian and the younger Seneca. For many years in Rome Martial was dependent upon the bounty of wealthy patrons, a subject which he writes about in his epigrams. After living and writing in Rome for a long time, he was awarded the rank of tribune and the *ius trium liberorum,* which entitled him to tax exemptions and other privileges. Martial's *Liber Spectaculorum* appeared in honor of Titus' opening of the Colosseum in 80, and *Xenia* and *Apophoreta* were published in 84. The first of Martial's twelve books of epigrams, for which he is best known, appeared in 86. His epigrams reveal his great skill in adapting the form to a variety of uses, and the range of his subjects is wide, including the hardship of being dependent on patronage, vice, affectation, folly, the immortality of poetry, the pretentiousness of females, and the inadequacy of the physician. These epigrams suggest an urbane and witty poet who was an astute and detached critic of his society. The only subject on which he seems to be hypocritical is the Emperor Domitian, whom he flatters out of necessity. In 100 Martial returned to his native Spain, where he lived until his death about four years later.

Jonson was very fond of Martial and was much indebted to him. He left a heavily annotated copy of Scriverius' *Martial* (1619) in his personal library, and he gave a copy of Thomas Farnaby's 1615 edition to Richard Briggs. Jonson recommended Martial to Drummond in the *Conversations* (l. 15) and made frequent references to him in other discussions with Drummond (ll. 108–9; 140–41; 164–65; 610). He used mottos from Martial for a number of his works: *Poetaster, King's Coronation Entertainment, Panegyre, Lovers Made Men, Neptune's Triumph, Cynthia's Revels,* and *Time Vindicated.* Martial served as a source for *The Masque of Queens* and *King's Coronation Entertainment*; Jonson borrowed from him in *Poetaster* (v. iii), *Cynthia's Revels* (IV. i), and *Bartholomew Fair* (I. iii); and rules seventeen and twenty-four of *Leges Convivales* were taken from Martial, who is also mentioned in *The Magnetic Lady* (II. vii, Chorus). *Epig.* XXVI is on the ghost of Martial, and *Und.* LXXXIX is a translation of Martial's *Epig* LXXVII (Bk. VIII). Many of Jonson's poems either echo Martial or are derived from him, some of the most notable being *Epig.* XLII, LXXI, CI, CXII; *For.* II; *Und.* LXXVI, LXXVIII.

Martialis. A flamen who engages in a dialogue with Genius in a scene in Jonson's part of the *King's Coronation Entertainment.*

Martin, Pol. In *A Tale of a Tub,* the usher for Lady Tub, whom she makes a gentleman and who eventually woos and marries Awdrey.

Martin, Sir Richard (1570–1618), studied at the Middle Temple and was called to the bar in 1602. He served as recorder of London just before his death. Together with Jonson, Donne, Sir Robert Cotton, Christopher Brooke, Inigo Jones, and others, Martin was a member of the Fraternity of Sirenical Gentlemen. As a distinguished lawyer, Martin vouched for the innocence of *Poetaster* and won the king's favor when a lawsuit against Jonson was threatened. Out of gratitude, Jonson dedicated the play to Martin.

Martino. A servant to Count Ferneze in *The Case Is Altered.* He greets Valentine at the beginning of the play and is one of the servants whose inability to find Paulo exasperates Count Ferneze. He plays a minor role in the play, only appearing to beat Onion and to break his head in a fencing match, possibly (although he is not named) as one of the servants who bring in Camillo at the end of the play, and to laugh at the drunken Juniper and Onion in their new finery with the other servants.

Marton, Thomas. An actor who played in *Poetaster* as one of the Children of the Chapel.

Mary I (1516–1558). Queen of England 1553–1558. Daughter of Henry VIII and Katharine of Aragon. Although she was a pawn in her father's political intrigues, she was given a separate household as Princess of Wales in 1525, but two years later her father began negotiations for divorce, and Mary, remaining loyal to her mother and to Catholicism, spent the next nine years in misery. In 1536 she was finally forced to acknowledge herself as illegitimate and to repudiate Catholicism, for which she was later absolved by the Pope. During the spread of Protestantism under the reign of her half brother, Edward VI, she stubbornly remained faithful to Catholicism in defiance of the Act of Uniformity. Following the short-lived reign of Lady Jane Grey after Edward's death, she ascended the throne in 1553, supported by an overwhelming number of loyal subjects. Although in the early part of her reign she showed considerable tolerance toward her political opponents, she and her advisers insisted on two policies—her marriage to Philip (later Philip II of Spain) and the restoration of papal supremacy in England, both of which were realized by 1554 despite violent opposition. The next year there began the religious persecutions which lasted throughout the rest of her reign and earned her the title of "Bloody Mary." In 1555 Philip, frustrated by his unsuccessful attempt to win coronation in England, left his wife and went to his dominions in the Netherlands. In 1557 England was reluctantly drawn into the war between Spain and France, causing increased hostility of the English people toward their queen, who died the following year.

In the *Conversations* (l. 236), Jonson said his father lost his estate under Mary, and he told an anecdote about the queen and John Heywood (ll. 573–77). *Tale of a Tub* is set during the reign of Mary, who is referred to several times in the play: I. iv; II. i, ii, v, vi; IV. i; V. ii.

Mary, Queen of Scots. Daughter of James V of Scotland and Mary of Lorraine, born in 1542 and crowned Queen of Scotland when six days old. A staunch Catholic, she lived in France and in 1558 was married to the dauphin, later Francis II, who died in 1561, after which Mary returned to Scotland and began her turbulent reign which ended in her being forced to abdicate in 1567. She was imprisoned but escaped. After her army was defeated, she fled to England where she was held prisoner by Elizabeth until her execution in 1587 after she was convicted of conspiring to assassinate Elizabeth. Mary's son, James VI of Scotland, became James I of England upon the death of Elizabeth in 1603.

In the *Conversations* (ll. 178–79), Jonson told Drummond that Duessa in Spenser's *Faerie Queen* was supposed to represent Mary.

masque. The form of entertainment characterized by a procession of masked figures. Because of the gradual evolution of the form and a lack of adequate records, it is impossible to determine exactly when the masque came into existence, but we do know that in 1377 a band of 130 Londoners rode disguised as esquires, knights, cardinals, emperor, pope, and devil to Prince Richard at Kennington, entered the hall, and after playing at dice with him, danced with the company. This disguising or mumming eventually evolved into the elaborate entertainments known as masques.

Originally the participants were disguised, probably carrying torches, and brought with them musicians, and usually brought presents, but by the fifteenth century the spectacular and mimetic elements in the masques were emphasized, leading to a divorce between performers and spectators. In the early sixteenth century the original practice of spectators' joining in the dance, which had survived in Italy, returned to England as something new, as can be seen in the famous Epiphany spectacle of 1512, participated in and given by the young Henry VIII. For a time masques and mummings were distinct, but by the middle of the sixteenth century the various elements of the two had been fused together, and the masque of Elizabeth's reign combined the original dancing and the participation of both performers and spectators with the allegorical pageantry of the mummings.

When James I ascended to the throne, the court masque developed rapidly, mainly because of Queen Anne's interest in the Revels and the consequent employment of poets and dramatists such as Chapman, Beaumont, and Jonson, and of Inigo Jones, the famous architect and scene designer. During this period masques became incredibly expensive types of entertainment and, at the same time, became more dramatic in form, particularly with Jonson's development of the antimasque. The glorious era of the masque ended with the Puritan revolution.

From its inception to its fullest development certain characteristics of the masque were consistently retained: (1) the dance executed by the disguised persons or masquers was the culminating and indispensable event toward which the whole preceding action led; (2) the abrupt entrance of the disguised persons (ostensibly strangers) into the festive hall was the highlight; (3) the masquers took part with the courtly spectators in the dance.

Between 1603 and 1634, Jonson wrote more than thirty-five masques and entertainments, most of which he created to entertain the king, the queen, or important noblemen. Jonson's idea of the masque was quite different from that of many of his fellow masque writers and theorists, notably Daniel, Bacon, and Jones. Essentially, Jonson believed that the masque should be not merely spectacular but literary, and in order to justify this view he made a distinction between the body and the soul of the masque. With the exception of Chapman, Jonson was nearly alone in his day in making such a distinction and in viewing masques as literary. As he explained in his preface to *Hymenaei* (1606), Jonson believed that the masque has two parts, the body and the soul. One appeals to the understanding and the other to the sense. The first part constitutes the soul, the second the body. The body of the masque depends upon the architect's ingenuity; the soul depends on the author's ability as a poet. In the masque the body is the scenery, the costumes, and all the mechanical devices necessary to manipulate the stage. The soul of the masque is the story or the ideal that is developed through the action that takes place on the stage. Jonson's insistence that the soul of the masque should always take precedence over the body precipitated his famous quarrel with Inigo Jones. Although the Elizabethen masque was, for the most part, mimed, with any necessary explanation given by a presenter, Jonson's masque dialogue and songs became important elements, and he added variety with the introduction of the antimasque, a comic or grotesque interlude providing contrast to the main masque itself. Moreover, unlike his fellow masque writers, Jonson employed the masque as a means whereby he might tactfully counsel the nobility. Jonson was staunchly convinced that the poet was more important to the masque than the architect since the poet was the one who was able to integrate harmoniously the music, dancing, and dialogue through poetry into a work of literary significance, and under his guidance the genuine masque reached its highest

form of development, and probably exerted considerable influence upon the later development of professional English opera.

Following is a complete chronological list of Jonson's masques and entertainments. The entertainments are not genuine masques but do sometimes exhibit some of the characteristics of the form. See also ANTIMASQUE and individual title entries; POET LAUREATE.

Chronological list of masques and entertainments:

1603	*The Entertainment at Althorp*
	A Panegyre
1604	*The King's Coronation Entertainment*
	The Entertainment at Highgate
1605	*The Masque of Blackness*
1606	*Hymenaei*
	The Entertainment of the Two Kings at Theobalds
1607	*An Entertainment of the King and Queen at Theobalds*
1608	*The Masque of Beauty*
	The Haddington Masque
1609	*The Masque of Queens*
1610	*The Speeches at Prince Henry's Barriers*
1611	*Oberon, The Fairy Prince*
	Love Freed From Ignorance and Folly
1612	*Love Restored*
1613–14	*A Challenge at Tilt*
	The Irish Masque
1615	*Mercury Vindicated From the Alchemists at Court*
1616	*The Golden Age Restored*
	Christmas, His Masque
1617	*Lovers Made Men*
	The Vision of Delight
1618	*Pleasure Reconciled to Virtue*
	For the Honor of Wales
1620(?)	*Entertainment at the Blackfriars*
1621	*News from the New World Discovered in the Moon*
	The Gypsies Metamorphosed
1622	*The Masque of Augurs*
1623	*Time Vindicated to Himself and to his Honors*
1620–24	*Pan's Anniversary*
(1624)	*Neptune's Triumph for the Return of Albion* [never performed]
1624	*The Masque of Owls*
1625	*The Fortunate Isles and Their Union*
1631	*Love's Triumph Through Callipolis*
	Chloridia
1633	*The King's Entertainment at Welbeck*
1634	*Love's Welcome at Bolsover*

Masque of Augurs, The.

Performed: January 6, 1622, and May 5 or 6, 1622 (enlarged version).

Published: in quarto in 1622 (no imprint). Revised and enlarged text published in 1640 folio by Thomas Walkley in section of masques.

Printers: unknown.

The first masque to be given in the existing Banqueting Hall at Whitehall, this work was first performed on January 6, 1622. It was revised and enlarged, especially in the comic scenes, and performed again probably on May 5, 1622. The producer and scene designer was Inigo Jones, and the music was composed by Alphonso Ferrabosco and Nicholas Lanier.

The scene was the court buttery, and most of the characters discovered there were from St. Katharine's (a London neighborhood). Notch, a brewer's clerk who claimed that he had seen the lions before, now wanted to see the king, but Slug, a lighterman, warned that there was as much danger in going too near a king as too near the lions. The Groom of the Revels entered and informed Notch and his cohorts that they would have to leave. Following a short quarrel, Notch asked the groom if the king and the court expected to see a masque that night, and the groom replied that they did but not while Notch and his company were present. Notch's response made it clear that the only reason he and the others had come was to express their love for the sovereign by performing for him a masque they had made. Although the groom initially objected to the idea, Vangoose, who spoke in a burlesque German-English and who was the inventor of the proposed masque, so interested the groom that he agreed to consider their offer. Notch, Slug, and Lady Alewife explained that since they were all from the alehouse in St. Katharine's, whose sign was three dancing bears, they had thought it appropriate to bring John Urson, a bearward, and his dancing bears to perform for the court. They argued, too, that if they were not good enough for a masque, they should at least be allowed to provide an antimasque. After being assured that the bears would pose no danger for the ladies in the audience, the groom agreed to let them perform.

With his bears, John Urson entered and sang a long ballad about the pleasures of the alehouse at St. Katharine's. The groom was very impressed, but Vangoose promised that he could produce an even more interesting show by the use of his special mirrors. Notch, however, insisted that Vangoose should not be too spectacular but rather should offer something simple like Welsh pilgrims, and Vangoose seized upon the idea of presenting pilgrims. The groom protested that he did not understand what pilgrims had to do with a masque, but Vangoose assured him that the more absurd an antimasque was the better it was considered to be, and he conjured up the second antimasque, a perplexed dance of deformed pilgrims who strayed and danced aimlessly until a light suddenly broke forth above and frightened the pilgrims away. Then the main masque began.

Descending, Apollo announced his arrival in song. When he was near the earth, he summoned his sons (Linus, Orpheus, Branchus, and Idmon), and they, together with Phoemonoe, responded to his call. After he had descended, Apollo showed his sons where the king was sitting, addressed him in laudatory terms, advanced to the king and announced that at the command of Jove, he had established a College of Augurs on earth in honor of the king and that he had made the sovereign's son the president. Apollo further explained that Mars had also contributed to the Salian rites and that the augurs were even now enclosed in a distant temple in contemplation, each being guided by a star. The masquers were discovered with their torch bearers while Apollo and the chorus offered a song. Following a dance by the torch bearers, the augurs laid down their staves and danced their entrance. When they had finished, Apollo and his sons interpreted the augury, signs of which were all favorable and emphasized the sovereign's love of peace, his just rule, and his deserved fame. Then ensued the main dance and the revels, after which Apollo approached the king and informed him that Apollo himself could not tell everything about the king's good fortune since the Fates kept some things even from the gods.

Suddenly, the heavens opened, and Jove, with the Senate of the Gods, was discovered as Apollo began his ascent. Jove announced that no augury was valid unless he personally ratified it, and Apollo requested that Jove do so. In response Jove asked what the mortals wanted, and all, together with Earth, replied: "That Jove will lend us this our Sovereigne long; / Let our grand-children, and not wee, / His want or absence ever see." Jove assured them that their wish would be blessed, and the chorus broke forth in praise. The whole scene closed, and the masquers danced their exit.

Masque of Beauty, The.

Performed: January 10, 1608.

Published: Thomas Thorpe in quarto 1608 together with *The Masque of Blackness*.

Printer: unknown.

This masque is a companion piece to *The Masque of Blackness*, which had been performed in January of 1605. *The Masque of Beauty*, according to Jonson, was written at the request of Queen Anne, who wanted Jonson to create another work about the daughters of Niger newly beautified, add four more to their train, and provide an explanation for their absence from court for almost three years. The masque was performed on January 10, 1608, in the new Banqueting House at Whitehall.

Boreas, one of the cold winds and a messenger, approached and asked which one of those present was the son of Neptune. Januarius, prince of months, reprimanded Boreas for not recognizing those present, to which Boreas responded that he was bringing a message from the twelve Aethiopian dames who had previously come to Britania to cleanse their blackness and gain true beauty and who had been commanded to return within a year. Januarius remembered the nymphs but noted that although they had been beautified they had not returned as they were supposed to do; in fact, almost three years had elapsed and they still had not come back. Boreas then reported that the twelve had been on their way when Proteus had told them of four others who also wanted to come and be beautified, but Night, who was envious and considered the change from blackness to beauty to have been done to spite her, had caused the nymphs to be shipwrecked. However, by chance the nymphs had landed on a floating island, but Night had caused the island to be set adrift, where Boreas had met one of the nymphs who had asked him to report what had happened to them.

Vulturnus, a warm, calm wind, then entered and explained that the isle had been found and that Aethiopia, the silver-moon, had made it into the center of beauty for the earth. On the island the queen and the nymphs sat on a throne which turned with the motion of the world, while moving contrary to them was a world of little loves and chaste desires who lighted their beauty. To this isle the spirits of the antique Greek poets and singers had now come to sing hymns in celebration of the beauties. To the sound of the hymns two fountains flowed—one called lasting youth and the other, chaste delight. Vulturnus reported that the island was now floating close by Albion and that Aethiopia had desired that the other four nymphs should also be beautified by Neptune's son.

At this point a curtain was drawn and the island was discovered floating on calm waters. On the island were placed the sixteen masquers by couples. Over the roof of the throne were figures representing the elements of Beauty—Splendor, Serenitas, Germinatio, Laetitia, Temperies, Venustas, Dignitas, Perfectio, and Harmonia. Upon the six steps to the throne were Cupids who served as torch bearers. In the Arbors were placed the musicians who represented the spirits of the old poets. The loud music closed and the musicians sang a song celebrating the bringing of light into the world, when love moved from out of chaos, and claiming that night should yield to light as blackness had to beauty, for the world was made for love, and where she reigns she allows no shade. When the song ended, Vulturnus spoke to the figure of the River Thamesis, represented by Thomas Giles (the choreographer for the masque), and asked him to receive the nymphs. The wind then departed, and Thamesis received the nymphs, after which they danced forth and stopped in the figure of a diamond while a song was sung celebrating the creation of beauty by love. There was another dance and two more songs extolling beauty and love. Then were danced galliards and corantos while a song was offered praising women as the soul of the world—true harmony. Januarius lauded their beauty and proclaimed that beauty's perfect throne had been made peculiar to the land by their presence and the light of Albion. The nymphs danced back to their throne, and the scene closed with a song calling for youth and pleasure to flow while the state remained as fixed as the island was now, so that beauty's sphere would know that the Elysian fields are located in this land.

Masque of Blackness, The.

Performed: January 6, 1605.

Published: Thomas Thorpe in quarto in 1608 together with *The Masque of Beauty*.

Printer: unknown.

This masque was written for Queen Anne and was performed at Whitehall in the Old Banqueting House in 1605.

The scene was a small woods with hunting fields onto which flowed an artificial sea. In front of the sea were six Tritons, and behind them a pair of sea maids between which were two great sea horses, and upon their backs rode Oceanus and Niger. Oceanus was in human form with blue flesh while Niger was in form and color an Aethiope. These two induced the masquers which were twelve Negro nymphs who were the daughters of Niger. The nymphs were attended by many Oceanae who served as light bearers. The masquers were placed in a concave shell which was made to move on the waters. On the sides of the shell swam six huge sea monsters who carried on their backs twelve torch bearers.

One of the Tritons together with two sea maids sang a song welcoming to the West Niger, son of Oceanus, and his beauteous black race, after which Oceanus enquired why Niger and his train had traveled so far West. Niger answered that since other women were considered more beautiful than his daughters they had been told by a luminary face reflected in a lake to find a land whose name ended in *tania* where Sol leaves in the climate a greater light that forms beauty with his sight. When Niger asked what land they were in, Oceanus replied that they were in Albion, named after and ruled by Neptune's son. Suddenly the moon, called Aethiopia, was discovered triumphant in a silver throne crowned with a sphere of light. Niger greeted the moon with joy and praise and asked her to shine on his daughters and beautify them. Aethiopia replied that she was the face his daughters had seen in the lake and that Britania was the land ruled by a Sun that has the power to blanch an Aethiope. The daughters were then called forth, for this sun was temperate and refined all things on which it shone. The Tritons sounded and the Aethiopians and the Oceanae danced on shore.

After the dance Aethiopia explained to the nymphs that the night was growing old and that the light could no longer be held. She noted that only Niger should return to the lake while the daughters should remain for a feast with Oceanus. She further advised that the daughters should repeat the ritual by bathing in the Ocean every full moon and should journey again to Albion after a year to dry their perfected faces in the sun. The nymphs danced, then returned to the sea, entered their shell, and departed while a song was sung celebrating the winning of Neptune's son in sight of Albion.

Masque of Owls, The
Performed: August 19, 1624.
Published: in the second volume of the 1640 folio issued by Thomas Walkley.

Printed: probably by Bernard Alsop and Thomas Fawcett.

This entertainment was performed before Prince Charles at Kenilworth on August 19, 1624. The presenter was the ghost of Captain Cox, a Coventry mason who possessed a good library.

The ghost of Captain Cox, mounted on his hobby-horse, appeared and explained that since he was reputed to be learned and had previously entertained Queen Elizabeth, he was pleased to reappear and entertain the Prince. He then proceeded to present six owls who had all endured some kind of misfortune. The first owl was a tobacconist, and the second a cheese monger. The third was a "native bird" undone by the Puritanism of Coventry. (An alternate version, probably used at the performance, substituted a dishonest scrivener for the third owl.) The fourth was a "Bankrupt of worth" who had acquired a "Serjeant's place" and ended up worse off than in his previous condition. The fifth was a "Don, a Spanish reader," who now had no "Scholler to teach." The last owl had sworne himself out of his estate by repeatedly breaking the law against swearing.

Masque of Queens, The.
Performed: February 2, 1609, at Whitehall.
Published: 1609 in quarto by Richard Bonion and Henry Walley.
Printer: Nicholas Okes.
This masque was originally planned for the Christmas season of 1608 but was not performed until Febraury 2, 1609. It was commissioned by Queen Anne at the request of King James. Jonson dedicated the masque to Prince Henry, who had asked Jonson to annotate the work for him. In his preliminary remarks to the masque Jonson formally introduced the antimasque for the first time, although, as he explained, he had included an antimasque in *The Haddington Masque* performed in 1608.

The scene discovered was an ugly, smoking Hell from which emerged twelve witches or hags to the accompaniment of infernal music. They began to dance until one of the witches noted that their chief, or dame, was not present and urged the others to call upon the dame with charms to appear with them. The hags recited three charms, after which the dame made her entrance and introduced the witches one by one as follows, proclaiming them all to be the faithful opposites of true fame and glory: Ignorance, Suspicion, Credulity, Falsehood, Murmur, Malice, Impudence, Slander, Execration, Bitterness, Rage, and Mischief. The dame exhorted the witches to disturb the solemnity and peace of the night and to report what mischief they each had been doing, and each hag in turn reported her devious activities. After their recitation, the dame delivered a long invocation, boasting about all the power attributed to witches by the ancients. Following her invocation, the hags chanted various other charms and then engaged in a magical dance. Suddenly, a blast of loud music was heard; the witches and their Hell vanished and in their place appeared a magnificent building representing the House of Fame, in which were discovered twelve masquers sitting on a triumphant throne erected in the form of a pyramid encircled with light. From this scene emerged a person representing Heroic Virtue who spoke in praise of virtue and true fame, denouncing the efforts of the witches to disrupt the glories of the night, declaring that true fame derives from virtue and is immortal, and announcing the imminent appearance of Bel-Anna, the epitome of all virtue, and eleven other virtuous queens immortalized in the House of Fame.

The scene changed and Fame herself, daughter of Heroic Virtue, appeared and declared that the queens would ride in triumph in Fame's own chariots while the hags would be led as captives before them. In state about the stage rode the triumphant procession of queens: Penthesilea, Camilla, Thomyrsis, Artemisia, Beronice, Hypsicratea, Candace, Voadicea, Zenobia, Amalasunta, Valasca, and Bel-Anna. To the accompaniment of a song urging all to celebrate the triumph of virtue and fame, the procession continued around the stage until the queens alighted from their chariots and engaged in several dances, after which they returned to the chariots which took them in triumph back to the House of Fame, as a concluding song in praise of virtue and fame was sung.

Masquerado. A character who appears disguised at the beginning of *Love Restored* and announces that because of various complications among the presenters no masque will be given as scheduled.

masquers and tilters.

Arundel, Alathea Talbot, Countess of (d. 1654), third daughter of Gilbert, 7th Earl of Shrewsbury, married Thomas, Earl of Arundel, in 1606. She danced in *The Masque of Beauty* and *The Masque of Queens.*

Arundel, Thomas Howard, Earl of (1585–1646), also Earl of Surrey and Earl of Norfolk, was a patron of the arts and collected paintings as well as guns, coins, classical marbles, and rare books and manuscripts. His father had died in the Tower in 1595 under attainder, his estates forfeit to the Crown. But upon the accession of James, the title was restored, and Thomas came to court in 1605. He danced in *Hymenaei* and *The Haddington Masque,* tilted in *Prince Henry's Barriers,* and had his fortune (as Earl Marshal) told in *The Gypsies Metamorphosed.*

Auchmouty (or Achmouty), John. a Scot who came to England in the reign of James, who made him a groom of the bedchamber and gave him a pension in 1620. He danced in *The Irish Masque, Pleasure Reconciled,* and *For the Honor of Wales.*

Badger, Sir Thomas (d. 1638), was granted the office of master of the harriers for life in 1605 and given a pension in 1625. He tilted in *Prince Henry's Barriers.*

Berkeley, Lady Elizabeth, daughter of Sir George Cary, the 2nd Lord Hunsdon, married Thomas Berkeley, son and heir of Henry, the 7th Lord Berkeley, in 1596. She danced in *Hymenaei.*

Bevill, Lady Frances, danced in *The Masque of Blackness.* The widow of Sir William Bevill of Kilkhampton, Cornwall, in 1602 she married Francis Manners, who became the 6th Earl of Rutland. She died of smallpox in 1605.

Bowey, Thomas. One of the masquers who danced in *Neptune's Triumph.*

Bowy (Bovey or Buy), James, Sergeant of the Cellar, danced in *News from the New World, Pan's Anniversary, The Masque of Augurs,* and *Time Vindicated.*

Boyd, Andrew, danced in *The Irish Masque.* He was granted the office of Surveyor of Coals in the North of England in 1616 and was knighted in 1620.

Brooke, Sir William, danced in *Love's Triumph.* He was made a knight of the Bath at the coronation of Charles I in 1626.

Buccleuch, Walter Scott, Earl of (d. 1633), became the 2nd Lord Scott of Buccleuch in 1611 and Earl of Buccleuch in 1619. He was one of those whose fortunes were told by the gypsies when *The Gypsies Metamorphosed* was performed at Windsor in 1621.

Buckingham, Katharine, Marchioness of (d. 1649). Daughter of Francis Manners, 6th Earl of Rutland, and his first wife Frances, daughter of Sir. H. Knevet, Katharine married George Villiers, 1st Duke of Buckingham on May 16, 1620. The duke was murdered in 1628, and she married the 1st Marquis of Antrim in 1635. Katharine had her fortune told in *The Gypsies Metamorphosed.*

Buckingham, Mary Villiers, Countess of. Daughter of Antony Beaumont, Mary married Sir George Villiers and afterwards Sir Thomas Compton. She was the mother of the 1st Duke of Buckingham, the king's favorite. In 1618 when her son was made Marquess of Buckingham, she was created Countess of Buckingham. She had her fortune told in 1621 in *The Gypsies Metamorphosed.*

Carey, Sir Robert (1560?–1639), jousted in the *Barriers* of 1606. He was created Earl of Monmouth in 1626.

Carey, Thomas (d. 1635), son of Sir Henry Carey and groom of the bedchamber, danced in *The Fortunate Isles.* He was granted a pension for life in 1625.

Carlisle, Lucy Hay, Countess of (1599–1660), the second daughter of Henry Percy, Earl of Northumberland, and the second wife of James, Lord Hay, Earl of Carlisle, danced in *Chloridia.*

Carnarvon, Anna Sophia, Countess of. The daughter of Philip Herbert, Earl of Montgomery, in 1625 she married Robert Dormer, Earl of Carnarvon. She danced in *Chloridia.* She died of the smallpox in 1643.

Carnarvon, Robert Dormer, Earl of, was created 1st Earl of Carnarvon in 1628, fought for the king in the civil war and was killed in 1643 at the first battle of Newbury. He danced in *Love's Triumph.*

Carr (Ker), Sir Robert (1578–1654). Carr was made Gentleman of the Prince's Bedchamber in 1625 and created Earl of Ancrum in 1633. He probably took part in *The Golden Age Restored* and *For the Honor of Wales.*

Cary, Mistress Sophia, danced in *Chloridia.*

Cavendish, Lady Anne, daughter of William, 2nd Earl of Devonshire, married Robert, Baron Rich. A well-known patroness of literature, she danced in *Chloridia.*

Chandos, Grey Bridges, Lord (d. 1621). The 5th Baron Chandos, commonly called the King of Cotswold, jousted at the wedding of the Earl of Somerset in 1614.

Chichester, Lady Frances (d. 1615). Second daughter of John, 1st Lord Harington of Exton, and sister of Lucy, the Countess of Bedford, Lady Frances married Sir Robert Chichester of Rawleigh, Devon. She danced in *The Masque of Beauty.*

Clifford, Lady Anne (d. 1676), daughter of George, 3rd Earl of Cumberland, was tutored by the poet Sam Daniel. In 1609 she married Richard Sackville, Lord Buckhurst. After his death, she married Philip Herbert, 4th Earl of Pembroke and Montgomery, in 1630. She danced in *The Masque of Beauty* and *The Masque of Queens.*

Compton, Lord William (d. 1630), who tilted at the wedding of the Earl of Somerset in 1614, was created Earl of Northampton in 1618 and made a Knight of the Garter in 1629.

Constable, Sir William (d. 1655), who tilted in the *Barriers* of 1606, was knighted in 1599 and created a baronet in 1611. He fought on the side of Parliament in the Civil War.

Cromwell, Sir Oliver, the uncle of the Protector, was knighted in 1598. He lavishly entertained James I on his coming to England, and he tilted in the *Barriers* of 1606.

Dalison, Sir Roger, jousted in the *Barriers* of 1606. He was made High Sheriff of Lincoln in 1601, knighted in 1603, and created a baronet in 1611.

Darcy, Thomas, jousted in *Prince Henry's Barriers.* The only son of Thomas, Baron Darcy of Chiche, he died without issue before his father's death.

Denbigh, Susanna, Countess of. Daughter of Sir George Villiers, sister of the 1st Duke of Buckingham, and wife of William Feilding, Earl of Denbigh. She was a patroness of Richard Crashaw, who dedicated his *Sacred Poems* (1651) to her. She is mentioned in the fortune of the Countess of Buckingham told in *The Gypsies Metamorphosed.*

Denbigh, William Feilding, Earl of (d. 1643), was created Baron in 1620 and Earl of Denbigh in 1622. The Earl played the second gypsy in *The Gypsies Metamorphosed.*

Derby, Elizabeth, Countess of, the eldest daughter of Edward de Vere, Earl of Oxford, married William Stanley, 6th Earl of Derby, in 1594. She danced in *The Masques of Blackness and Beauty* and *The Masque of Queens.*

Digby, Sir John (1580–1653), jousted in the *Barriers* of 1606. Knighted in 1607, created Baron Digby of Sherborne in 1618, and Earl of Bristol in 1622, Sir John was for many years ambassador at Madrid.

Dingwell (Dingwall), Lord. Richard Preston, Knight of the Bath, Gentleman of the King's Privy Chamber and instructor in arms to Prince Henry, was created Lord of Dingwell in the peerage of Scotland in 1609, and Earl of Desmond in the peerage of Ireland in 1619. He jousted in *Prince Henry's Barriers* in 1610 and at the wedding of the Earl of Somerset in 1614. In 1628 he drowned in the Irish Channel.

Doncaster, James Hay, Viscount (d. 1660). The son of the 1st Earl of Carlisle. Succeeded to his father's title in 1636 and in 1639 established his hereditary right to the island of Barbados where he resided during the Civil War. He danced in *Love's Triumph.*

Dorset, Richard Sackville, 3rd Earl of (1589–1624), the first husband of Lady Anne Clifford, jousted at the wedding of the Earl of Somerset in 1614.

Drury (Drewry), Sir Robert (d. 1615). Knighted by Essex at the siege of Rouen (1591–92), Sir Robert also served in the Low Countries. He was one of John Donne's chief patrons–Donne's famous *Anniversaries* were written as elegies upon the death of Drury's youngest daughter, Elizabeth. Sir Robert jousted in the *Barriers* of 1606.

Dutton, Sir Thomas (d. 1614), was knighted in 1603 and made Sheriff of Cheshire in 1611. He tilted in the *Barriers* of 1606.

Dymock (Dimock), Master. Probably a son of Sir Charles Dymock, champion of England at the coronation of Charles I. Master Dymock danced in *Love's Triumph.*

Effingham, Anne Howard, Lady (d. 1638), wife of William, eldest son of the admiral Lord Howard of Effingham, danced in *The Masque of Blackness.* She is buried in Westminster Abbey.

Effingham, William Howard, Lord (1577–1615), the eldest son of the Earl of Nottingham, was summoned to Parliament as Baron Effingham during his father's lifetime. He tilted in the *Barriers* of 1606.

Egerton, Lady Penelope, 6th daughter of John, 1st Earl of Bridgwater, and wife of Sir Robert Napier of Luton, Bedfordshire, danced in *Chloridia.*

Erskine, James. Probably the son of John Erskine, Earl of Mar, and the half-brother of the earl's son John, who succeeded his father in 1634. Afterwards James, whose mother was the daughter of the Earl of Lennox, became the Earl of Buchan. James is probably the Mr. Erskine listed by Jonson as one of the masquers in *The Haddington Masque.* John may also have performed in the masque.

Erwin (Irwin), Sir William, gentleman usher of the Prince's Privy-chamber and a dancing tutor to Prince Henry, danced in *Pleasure Reconciled* and *For the Honor of Wales.*

Exeter, Frances Cecil, Countess of. Daughter of William, 4th Lord Chandos, widow of Sir Thomas Smith, second wife of Thomas Cecil, 1st Earl of Exeter. After Cecil's death in 1623, the countess remained a widow until her own death in 1663. Her fortune was told by the Patrico in *The Gypsies Metamorphosed.*

Gauteret (Gunteret), Henry. A German who tilted in the *Barriers* of 1606 and was knighted in 1608.

Gerard (Garrard), Lady Elizabeth (d. 1613). Daughter of Robert Woodford of Brightwell and second wife of Thomas, Baron Gerard of Gerard's Bromley, Lady Elizabeth danced in *The Masque of Beauty.*

Gerard, Lord Thomas (d. 1618). Son of Sir Gilbert Gerard, Lord Thomas was created Baron Gerard of Gerard's Bromley, Staffordshire, in 1603. He tilted in the *Barriers* of 1606.

Gerrard, Sir Thomas, of Bryan (d. 1652). Knighted in 1603 and created a baronet in 1611, Sir Thomas served as a member of Parliament in 1628. He tilted in the *Barriers* of 1606.

Gordon, Sir Robert. A favored Scot who tilted in *Prince Henry's Barriers.*

Goring, George (1608–1657), was a brilliant figure at court. Created Earl of Norwich in 1644, he was a royalist general in the Civil War. He danced in *Love's Triumph.*

Gray, Sir John (d. 1611). Knighted by the Earl of Essex in 1596, Sir John tilted in the *Barriers* of 1606.

Guildford, Elizabeth, Lady. Elizabeth Somerset, the eldest daughter of Edward, 4th Earl of Worcester, and wife of Sir Henry Guildford of Hemsted Place in Kent, was married at Essex (now Somerset) House in 1596 at the same time as her sister Catherine, and the marriage was celebrated in Spenser's *Prothalamion.* She danced in *The Masque of Beauty* and *The Masque of Queens.*

Hamilton, James, 2nd Marquis of (1589–1625), succeeded to the title in 1604. He was a gentleman of the King's Bedchamber, Lord Steward of the Household, and a privy councillor. In 1619 he was created Earl of Cambridge and Baron of Emerald in Cumberland. He had his fortune told in *The Gypsies Metamorphosed,* and he danced in *Pleasure Reconciled* and *For the Honor of Wales.*

Hamilton, James, 3rd Marquis of (1606–1649), succeeded to the title in 1625. He danced in *Love's Triumph.*

Hastings, Lady Dorothy. Lady Dorothy was the second daughter of George, 4th Earl of Huntingdon. Her first husband was Sir James Stuart, who was killed in a duel in 1609. Her second was Robert Dillon, Earl of Roscommon. She danced in *Hymenaei.*

Hatton, Lady Elizabeth (Lady Coke).

The fourth daughter of Thomas Cecil, 1st Earl of Exeter, Lady Elizabeth married Sir William Hatton, who died in 1597. In 1598 she married Sir Edward Coke. She danced in *The Masque of Beauty* and had her fortune told in *The Gypsies Metamorphosed*.

Hay, Lord James (d. 1636). Knighted by James I, James was created Lord Hay in the Scottish peerage in 1606, a knight of the Bath in 1610, Baron Hay of Sawley in 1615, Viscount Doncaster in 1618, and Earl of Carlisle in 1622. He danced in *Hymenaei* and *The Haddington Masque* and tilted in the *Barriers* of 1606 and at the Earl of Somerset's wedding in 1614. For part of his entertainment of Baron de la Tour in 1617, Lord Hay commissioned Jonson to write *Lovers Made Men*.

Herbert, Lady Anne. Daughter of Henry, second Earl of Pembroke, Lady Anne danced in *The Masque of Blackness*.

Herbert, Sir William (d. 1655). Made a night of the Bath in 1603 and created Baron Powys in 1639, Sir William tilted in the *Barriers* of 1606.

Holland, Henry Rich, Earl of (1590–1649), was knighted in 1610. A favorite of both James I and Charles I, he was created Baron Kensington in 1623 and Earl of Holland in 1624. He fought for the king in the Civil War and was captured and executed in 1649. He danced in *Love's Triumph*, and Jonson wrote a speech for him and his brother presented at a tilting on March 24, 1613.

Houghton (Hawton), Sir Gilbert (d. 1647), the eldest son of Sir Richard Houghton, was knighted in 1604 and succeeded to the baronetcy of his father in 1630. He served as M.P. for Lancashire from 1614–23 and as high sheriff in 1643. He fought for King Charles in the Civil War. Noted for his skill in dancing, he danced in *Pleasure Reconciled* and *For the Honor of Wales*.

Houghton, Sir Richard (d. 1630). Sheriff of Lancashire in 1598, knighted in 1599 and created a baronet in 1611, Sir Richard was a personal favorite of James I. He tilted in the *Barriers* of 1606.

Howard, Sir Charles (d. 1622), fourth son of Thomas, Earl of Suffolk, danced in *Pleasure Reconciled* and *For the Honor of Wales*.

Howard, Sir Charles (1579–1642), second son of the Earl of Nottingham, was knighted in 1603 and succeeded his father in 1624. He served as M.P. in 1597, 1601–11 and 1614, and was Lord Lieutenant of Surrey in 1627. He tilted in the *Barriers* of 1606.

Howard, Sir Edward (d. 1675), the seventh son of Thomas, 1st Earl of Suffolk, was made a Knight of the Bath in 1616 and created 1st Baron Howard of Escrick in Yorkshire in 1628. He tilted in the *Barriers* of 1606.

Howard, Lady Elizabeth (afterwards Lady Knollys) (d. 1658), daughter of Thomas, 1st Earl of Suffolk, was born in 1586, married William, Baron Knollys (afterwards Earl of Banbury) in 1605, and after his death Edward, 4th Lord Vaux, in 1632. She danced in *The Masque of Blackness* and *Hymenaei*.

Howard, Sir Francis (d. 1651), was knighted in 1604. He tilted in the *Barriers* of 1606.

Howard, Henry. Third son of Thomas, 1st Earl of Suffolk, Henry participated in the *Challenge at Tilt* in 1614.

Howard, Sir Thomas (d. 1669), second son of Thomas, Earl of Suffolk, was made a knight of the Bath, created Baron Howard of Charlton in 1605 and Viscount Andover in 1622, and became a knight of the Garter in 1625 and Earl of Berkshire in 1626. He danced in *Hymenaei*, *Pleasure Reconciled*, and *For the Honor of Wales*, and he tilted at the Earl of Somerset's wedding in 1614.

Howard, Sir William. There were three Sir William Howards in 1630, and it is not clear which one danced in *Love's Triumph*: (1) a son of the Earl of Suffolk, knighted in 1616; (2) a son of the Earl of Arundel, knighted in 1626; or (3) a son of Lord William Howard, knighted in 1628.

Howard, Lady, wife of the Sir William Howard who danced in *Love's Triumph*, danced in *Chloridia*.

Huntingdon, Elizabeth Hastings, Countess of (d. 1633). Elizabeth Stanley in 1603 married Henry Hastings, who succeeded his grandfather as 5th Earl of Huntingdon in 1604. She danced in *The Masque of Queens*.

Kennedy (Kennethie), Sir John (d. 1668), in 1615 succeeded his uncle as the 6th Earl of Cassilis. Danced in *The Haddington Masque*.

Killigrew, Sir Robert (1579–1633), father of the dramatist Thomas Killigrew, was knighted in 1603. Jousted in the *Barriers* of 1606.

Leigh, Sir John. Probably the Leigh who was knighted in 1603. He tilted in the *Barriers* of 1606 and was one of the masquers at the marriage of Sir Philip Herbert and Lady Susan de Vere in 1604.

Lennox, Ludovic Stuart, 2nd Duke of (1574–1624), succeeded to the title in 1583. Highly favored by James I, Stuart was made Baron Settrington in the county of York and Earl of Richmond in 1613 and Earl of Newcastle-on-Tyne and Duke of

Richmond in 1623. He tilted in the *Barriers* of 1606, *Prince Henry's Barriers,* and at the wedding of the Earl of Somerset in 1614. He danced in the *Haddington Masque,* and his fortune was told in *The Gypsies Metamorphosed.* He was Lord Steward of the Household in 1621.

Maunsell, Sir Lewis (d. 1638), son of Sir Thomas, who was created a baronet in 1611, was knighted in 1603 and succeeded to his father's title in 1626. He tilted in the *Barriers* of 1606.

Maunsell, Sir Robert (1573–1656). Knighted in 1596 and served as M.P. from 1601 to 1628. He tilted in the *Barriers* of 1606.

Monson, Sir Thomas (1564–1641), who was knighted in 1588, was a favorite with James I, who appointed him his master falconer and in 1611 master of the armory at the Tower. He was implicated in the Overbury murder and imprisoned for three years until he was able to clear himself. Thomas Campion dedicated to Monson *A Book of Airs* (1601) and *The Third and Fourth Book of Airs* (1617). He tilted in the *Barriers* of 1606.

Montagu, Henry, Baron (d. 1642), recorder of London in 1603, was knighted in the same year, was made Lord Chief Justice in 1616, Lord High Treasurer and Baron Montagu and Viscount Mandeville in 1620, Lord President of the Council in 1621, and Earl of Manchester in 1626. He was one of Charles I's trusted followers. His *Manchester al Mondo,* reissued frequently in the seventeenth century, was published anonymously in 1631. His fortune was told as Lord Treasurer in *The Gypsies Metamorphosed.*

Nevill, Lady Mary (d. 1649), daughter of Thomas Sackville, 1st Earl of Dorset and co-author of *Gorboduc,* married Sir Henry Nevill, afterwards 9th Lord Abergavenny. She danced in *The Masque of Beauty.*

Newport, Anne Blount, Countess of (d. 1699), daughter of John, Baron Boteler of Brantfield, in 1627 married Mountjoy Blount, later the Earl of Newport. In 1637 the countess became a Catholic. Suspected of being a royalist intriguer, she was allowed to leave the country in 1653. She danced in *Chloridia.*

Newport, Mountjoy Blount, Earl of (1597?–1665), the illegitimate son of the Earl of Devonshire and Lady Penelope Rich, became the Earl of Newport in 1628. He fought for the king in the Civil War. He danced in *Love's Triumph.*

Norris, Francis, Lord (1579–1622), succeeded his grandfather as 2nd Lord

Norris in 1601 and became Viscount Thame and Earl of Berkshire in 1620. He participated in the *Challenge at Tilt.* In 1622, while imprisoned in the tower for quarrelling with Lord Scroope before the Prince of Wales, he mortally wounded himself with a crossbow.

North, Dudley, Lord (1581–1666), eldest son of Sir John North, succeeded his grandfather as 2nd Baron North in 1600. He was an accomplished musician and poet. He participated in the *Challenge at Tilt.*

Nottingham, Charles Howard, Earl of (1536–1624), as Baron Howard of Effingham, commanded the English fleet that routed the Spanish Armada and was created Earl of Nottingham in 1596. He rendered distinguished service to Elizabeth in both military and civil affairs. He served as Lord High Constable at the *Barriers* of 1606, in which his victory over the Armada was lauded.

Ogilby, John. A dancing master who was one of the minor characters in *The Gypsies Metamorphosed.*

Oxford, Diana Cecil, Countess of. In 1624 Lady Diana Cecil married Henry de Vere, 8th Earl of Oxford. She danced in *Chloridia.*

Palmer, Humphrey. One of the dancers in *News from the New World, Pan's Anniversary,* and *The Masque of Augurs.*

Palmer, Roger. Second son of Sir Thomas Palmer, cupbearer to Prince Henry and Prince Charles. He became the master of Charles's household and was made a knight of the Bath in 1626. A skilled dancer, he performed in *Pleasure Reconciled* and *For the Honor of Wales.*

Peter, Katherine, Lady. Second daughter of Lord Worcester, Katherine Somerset in 1596 married William, Baron Peter of Writtle, at the same time that her sister Elizabeth, Lady Guildford, married Sir Henry Guildford of Hemsted Place in Kent, and the marriage was celebrated in Spenser's *Prothalamion.* Lady Peter danced in *The Masque of Beauty* and died in 1624.

Porter, Endymion (1587–1649), a dependent of the Buckingham family, was a poet. He became the groom of the bedchamber to Prince Charles. He played the third gypsy in *The Gypsies Metamorphosed.*

Porter, Olivia (d. 1663), daughter of the Duke of Buckingham's favorite sister, married the poet Endymion Porter about 1620. She danced in *Chloridia.*

Purbeck, Frances, Lady (d. 1645). Youngest daughter of Sir Edward Coke and Lady Elizabeth Hatton, Frances married Sir John Villiers in 1616 over her mother's strong objection. In 1619 her husband was created Baron Villiers of Stoke, Buckinghamshire, and Viscount Purbeck of Dorset. In 1621 he lost his mind, and Frances deserted him and cohabited with Sir Robert Howard, to whom she bore one son. Her fortune was told in *The Gypsies Metamorphosed*.

Raleigh, Carew (1605–1655). The second son of Sir Walter, restored in blood in 1628, and made a gentleman of the privy chamber in 1635. He probably danced in *Love's Triumph*.

Radcliffe (Ratcliffe), Elizabeth, Viscountess Haddington. The daughter of Robert, 5th Earl of Sussex, who tilted in the *Barriers* of 1606, Elizabeth was considered one of the prime beauties of the kingdom. She died of smallpox in 1618, only ten years after her marriage to John Ramsey, Viscount Haddington. Jonson's *Haddington Masque* was written to celebrate their marriage. All three of Elizabeth's children—Charles, James, and Bridget—died young.

Reynolds (Reynell), Sir Carey (d. 1624). Knighted in 1599, gentleman pensioner to Queen Elizabeth and James I, Sir Carey tilted in the *Barriers* of 1606.

Rich, Penelope Devereux, Lady (d. 1607). Penelope Devereux, the "Stella" of Sidney's sonnets, married Robert, Lord Rich, about 1581. At the time she performed in *The Masque of Blackness* (1605) she was openly cohabiting with Charles Blount, Lord Mountjoy. In 1605 she was divorced and married Blount later the same year.

Rutland, Cecily Mannners, Countess of. Daughter of Sir John Tufton of Hothfield and sister of Nicholas, 1st Earl of Thanet. Her first husband was Sir Edward Hungerford. In 1608 she married her second husband, Francis Manners, who became the 6th Earl of Rutland in 1612. Two sons from this marriage died in infancy, supposedly from the effects of sorcery. The countess died in 1653 and was buried in her brother's vault in Westminster Abbey. The Countess had her fortune told in the Belvoir performance of *The Gypsies Metamorphosed*.

Rutland, Francis Manners, Earl of (1578–1632). Francis Manners became the 6th Earl of Rutland in 1612, when he was also keeper of Sherwood Forest. In 1619 he was warden and chief justice of the royal forests north of the Trent, and in 1623 he was admiral of the fleet to bring Prince Charles home from Spain. He participated in the *Challenge at Tilt*. He is referred to in the Burley and Belvoir per-

formances of *The Gypsies Metamorphosed*. He was host for the Belvoir performance.

Sackville, Mistress Cecily. Daughter of Robert, 2nd Earl of Dorset, Mistress Cecily married Sir Henry Crompton. She danced in *Hymenaei*.

Sanquhar (Sankier), Robert, Lord Crichton of, danced in *The Haddington Masque*. He was hanged in the Great Palace Yard in 1612 for having arranged the murder of John Turner, to whom he had lost an eye in a fencing match in 1605.

Savage, Dorothy. Daughter of Sir Thomas, afterwards Viscount, Savage of Rock Savage, Cheshire, and sister of Lady Jane Pawlet, Mistress Dorothy married Lord Andover, heir to Thomas Howard, Earl of Berkshire. She danced in *Chloridia*.

Savage, Mistress Elizabeth. Daughter of Sir Thomas, afterwards Viscount, Savage of Rock Savage, Cheshire, and sister of Lady Jane Pawlet, Mistress Elizabeth married Sir John Thimbelly, of Irnham, Lincolnshire. She danced in *Chloridia*.

Scroope, Lord Emanuel. Emanuel, the last Lord Scroope, was Lord President of the King's Council in the North in 1618–19 and was created Earl of Sunderland in 1627. He tilted at *The Challenge at Tilt*.

Somerset, Lady Blanche (d. 1649), sixth daughter of Edward, 4th Earl of Worcester, married Thomas, 2nd Baron Arundell of Wardour, in 1607. She danced in *Hymenaei*.

Somerset, Sir Thomas (d. 1632), third son of Edward, 4th Earl of Worcester, Sir Thomas was sent to Scotland along with Sir C. Percy to announce the death of Elizabeth to James. In 1626 he was created Viscount Somerset of Cashel, Tipperary. He danced in *Hymenaei* and tilted in the *Barriers* of 1606, *Prince Henry's Barriers*, and at the Earl of Somerset's wedding in 1614.

Southampton, Henry Wriothesley, 3rd Earl of (1573–1624), was Shakespeare's patron. Imprisoned for two years until the accession of James I for his part in the Essex rising, the Earl also played a prominent role in the development of colonial enterprise. He tilted in *Prince Henry's Barriers* and danced in *Oberon*.

Stanley, Sir Robert (d. 1632), son of William, 6th Earl of Derby, was made a knight of the Bath in 1626. He and his elder brother, Lord Strange, danced in *Love's Triumph*.

Strange, Charlotte Stanley, Lady (d. 1663). Daughter of Claude de la Trémoille, Duc de Thouan, Lady Charlotte in 1626 married James, Lord Strange, afterwards 7th Earl of Derby. At the outbreak of the civil war when her husband joined the king's forces, Lady Strange remained at the family estate (Latham House), which by May 1643 was the only place held by the king's adherents. On February 28, 1643 Latham was besieged by Sir William Fairfax, but Lady Strange, dressed in men's clothes, successfully conducted the defense of Latham, thereby winning the admiration of the parliamentarians who proclaimed her a better soldier than her husband. She danced in *Chloridia*.

Strange, James Stanley, Lord (1607–1651), was the eldest son of William, 6th Earl of Derby. In the Civil War he fought on the royalist side and succeeded to his father's title in 1642. After the battle of Worcester, Lord Strange was captured, tried, and beheaded in 1651. He and his younger brother, Sir Robert Stanley, danced in *Love's Triumph*.

Stuart, Lady Arabella (1575–1615), was the only child of Charles Stuart, 5th Earl of Lennox. Because she was a cousin of King James's, restrictions were put on her marriage. In 1610 she married William Seymour, for which she was imprisoned, but in 1611 she escaped from the Bishop of York who had charge of her by playing an epicene part in boy's clothes, an episode which may have been alluded to in Jonson's *Epicoene* (v. i). She was recaptured and put in the Tower, where she died in 1615. She danced in *The Masque of Beauty*.

Suffolk, Catherine Howard, Countess of, was the eldest daughter of Sir Henry Knyvet of Charlton, Wiltshire. In 1583 she married her second husband, Thomas Howard, 1st Earl of Suffolk and Lord High Treasurer. In 1619 the two were tried on the charge of embezzling the Treasury funds, with Francis Bacon as the prosecutor. The same year her beauty was ruined by the smallpox. She danced in *The Masque of Blackness*.

Sussex, Robert Radcliffe, Earl of (d. 1629), succeeded to the title in 1593. George Chapman included a sonnet in his honor in the *Iliad* of 1598. Radcliffe tilted in the *Barriers* of 1606.

Villiers, Sir John (1591?–1657). Viscount Purbeck, the eldest son of Sir George Villiers of Brooksby, Leicestershire, was probably the fourth gypsy in *The Gypsies Metamorphosed*. He was the brother of the King's favorite, the Duke of Buckingham. In 1616 he married Frances, the youngest daughter of Sir Edward Coke and Lady Elizabeth Hatton, but she deserted him in 1621 when he lost his mind.

Walden, Theophilus Howard, Lord (1584–1640), was the eldest son of Thomas, 1st Earl of Suffolk, whom Theophilus succeeded in 1626. He danced in *Hymenaei* and *The Haddington Masque*, and tilted in the *Barriers* of 1606 and at the Earl of Somerset's wedding in 1614.

Walsingham, Audrey, Lady. Ethelreda or Audrey, daughter of Sir Ralph Shelton, was the wife of Sir Thomas Walsingham. The two were appointed Chief Keepers of the Queen's Wardrobe, and she was given a pension in 1604. She danced in *The Masque of Blackness* and *The Masque of Beauty*.

Weston, Mistress Anne. Daughter of Richard, Earl of Portland, and wife of Basil Feilding, heir of the first Earl of Denbigh, Mistress Anne danced in *Chloridia*.

Willoughby de Eresby, Robert Bertie, Lord (1572–1642), succeeded to his title in 1601. He was knighted for valor in 1597. He was created Earl of Lindsey in 1626, Lord High Admiral in 1636, and General of the King's forces in 1642. He danced in *Hymenaei* and tilted in the *Barriers* of 1606. In 1642 he was mortally wounded at Edgehill.

Windsor, Catherine Somerset, Lady. (1590–1641), the seventh daughter of the 4th Earl of Worcester, was the wife of Henry, 6th Lord Windsor. She danced in *The Masque of Beauty* and *The Masque of Queens*.

Winter, Anne, Lady. Third daughter of Lord Worcester, Anne Somerset married in 1597 Sir Edward Winter of Lydney, Gloucestershire. She danced in *The Masque of Beauty* and *The Masque of Queens*.

Woodhouse, Sir William. Knighted by the Earl of Essex in 1591, Sir William tilted in the *Barriers* of 1606.

Worcester, Edward Somerset, 4th Earl of (1553–1628), succeeded to the title in 1589. A favorite with both Elizabeth and James he was made Master of the Horse and Lord Privy Seal. At the *Barriers* of 1606 he was Earl Marshal, his fortune was told in *The Gypsies Metamorphosed*, and he is mentioned in *For the Honor of Wales*.

Wray, Edward. The younger son of Sir William Wray, Edward was made a groom of the bedchamber through the influence of the Duke of Buckingham, but he lost his post in 1622 when he ran away and married the daughter of Lord Berkshire. He danced in the *Masque of Augurs*.

Zinzen (alias Alexander), Henry and Sir Sigismund, tilted at the Earl of Somerset's wedding in 1614. They were brothers, members of an Italian family (the Zinzanos) that settled in England during the reign of Mary. Some members of the family took as their surname the Christian name of the family patriarch, Alexander Zinzan. In 1607 Henry received the office of the brigandry. In 1617 Sir Sigismund was a lieutenant in the Low Countries.

Masuccio. Author of *Il Novellino* (Naples, 1476), from which the intrigue in *Eastward Ho* is borrowed.

Mathematician. An unnamed mathematician or astrologer appears in *An Entertainment at the Blackfriars* and reports a favorable omen for the new child being christened.

Matheo (Matthew). A gallant in the 1601 quarto version of *Every Man in His Humour*. (Differing names of characters and courses of action in the 1616 folio version are given in parentheses.) He is very conscious of being a fashionable poet, but since he recites only plagiarized verses, claiming them for his own, he is the personification of the very sort of foolish and vulgar poet that all the people of taste in the play despise. He meets Bobadilla at Cob's house and tells him that Giuliano (Downright) has threatened to beat him. He reads verses from a popular second-rate play, claiming that they are "simply the best that ever [I] heard." Prospero (Wellbred) and Lorenzo junior (Edward) mock and bait him along with Bobadilla and Stephano (Stephen), especially when they encourage him to read plagiarized verse (which he claims to have written that morning) to Hesperida (Bridget), whom he wishes to impress. He runs away when he and Bobadilla are accosted by Giuliano (Downright) but plans with Bobadilla to make out a warrant for Giuliano's arrest. He pawns a jewel which he wears in his ear in order to raise the fee Musco (Brainworm) demands. After Musco (Brainworm) "arrests" Giuliano (Downright), he goes with the others to Clement. On discovering that he is a poet, Clement challenges him to a verse-making match, but is disgusted to learn that he is only a plagiarist of second-rate, famous verse. He is sentenced to a night in jail and a day bound in the town square, after which he and Bobadilla will write and sing a ballad of "repentance" (sentenced to stand and fast in Clement's courtyard with Bobadilla while Clement entertains the others inside at dinner).

Matthew, Master. See MATHEO.

Maudlin. In *The Sad Shepherd*, the "Envious" witch of Papplewick, a village on the road between Nottingham and Mansfield, near Newsted Priory. She tells Aeglamour

that Earine has drowned when, in reality, her son Lorel has shut Earine up in a tree. She appears disguised as Marian, steals Robin Hood's stag, and causes great discontent in the company. When her deception is discovered, the company speak of her evil nature and their fear and hatred of her. She berates Lorel for wooing Earine in a vulgar and awkward way. She again tries to upset Robin's company by disguising herself as Marian but is discovered. Robin steals her magic belt, and she is made to be very angry.

Maul. A character in *Love's Welcome at Bolsover* who appears as a Freemason in Colonel Vitruvius' dance of the mechanics.

Maurice of Nassau, Prince of Orange. See Maurice Nassau, Prince of ORANGE.

Mavis, Mistress. A lady collegiate and friend of Lady Haughty in *Epicoene*. She is proud and independent and professes loyalty to her friends until, in competition for Dauphine Eugenie, she criticizes them behind their backs.

Maximilian. A Milanese general in *The Case Is Altered*. He woos Aurelia, who is taken with him, and, in his colorful, bombastic way of speaking, vows to take good care of Count Ferneze's son Paulo when he takes him to war with the French. The count is very angry when he returns after Paulo's capture, but Maximilian brings Chamont and Camillo with him to arrange a trade. After their exchange of identities is discovered, the count is more angry than ever at Maximilian, and refuses even to speak with him. Maximilian steadfastly holds that Chamont will honor his promise and return; he tries to dissuade the count from killing Camillo. He is happy, with the rest, when Paulo returns with Chamont, Camillo's identity is revealed, and Chamont's gold and sister are restored. He good-naturedly drops his courtship of Aurelia when she is betrothed to Chamont, hinting that he will begin wooing Phoenixella, even though she is a "profest virgin." He ends the play with a happy speech, asking for a "faire March."

Maximilian, Duke of Bavaria (1573–1651), elector (1623–51) and Duke (1597–1651) of Bavaria, was one of the outstanding figures of the Thirty Years War and an ardent supporter of the Catholic Reformation. In response to the Protestant Union, he formed the Catholic League and brought the League's army to the support of Emperor Ferdinand II against Frederick the Winter King. By the

Peace of Westphalia in 1648, Maximilian gained Frederick's electorate and the Upper Palatinate. He is mentioned in *The Staple of News* (III. ii).

Maximus, Valerius. See EURIPIDES.

May Lord, The. In the *Conversations* (ll. 393–403), Jonson told Drummond that half his comedies were not in print and that he had written a pastoral play entitled *The May Lord* in which he himself was represented as Alken, the Countess of Bedford as Ethra, Overbury as Mogibell, and the old Countess of Suffolk as an enchantress. Other names were given to Somerset's lady, Pembroke, the Countess of Rutland, and Lady Wroth. In the first story Alken comes in mending a broken pipe, and, contrary to other pastorals, Jonson introduces clowns making mirth and foolish sport. Jonson also said he intended to write a fisher or pastoral play set in Loch Lomond. *The May Lord* has not survived, and there is no convincing evidence that *The May Lord* should be identified with *The Sad Shepherd*.

May, Thomas (1595–1650). Translator, playwright, and historian who published translations of Lucan's *Pharsalia* (1627), renderings of the *Georgics* (1628), *Selected Epigrams of Martial* (1629), and Barclay's *Argenis* (1629). Jonson wrote a commendatory poem for the *Pharsalia* ("When, Rome, I reade thee in thy mighty paire"). May eventually turned Parliamentarian probably because he was upset that Davenant was appointed Poet Laureate at Jonson's death. In Andrew Marvell's satire *Tom May's Death*, Jonson is portrayed as upbraiding May for his apostasy. May contributed an elegy ("Though once high Statius o're dead Lucan's hearse") to *Jonsonus Virbius*.

Mayne, Jasper (1604–1672), was a student of Christ's Church, Oxford, in 1627. In 1629 he published the *City Match*, and in 1658 he published the *Ammorous War*. Brian Duppa was his patron, and he contributed a long elegy ("As when the vestal hearth went out, no fire") to *Jonsonus Virbius*. Eventually, Mayne became Archdeacon of Chichester. Mayne considered himself one of the members of the Tribe of Ben.

Meade, Robert (1616–1653), was educated at Westminster and Christ Church, Oxford, receiving his B.A. in 1638 and his M.A. in 1641. In 1633 he prefixed verses to Abraham Cowley's *Poetical Blossoms*. He contributed an elegy ["Our bays (me thinkes) are withered, and they look"] to *Jonsonus Virbius*. Meade's comedy, *The Combat of Love and Friendship*, was printed in 1654. In 1640 Meade became a captain in the army, and in 1646 he took his M.D.

Meagher, John Carney (1935–   ). American scholar educated at Notre Dame, Princeton, University of London, and McMaster University. Since 1970 he has been Professor of English, St. Michael's College, University of Toronto and since 1973 Professor of Theology. He has published widely on theology and Renaissance literature. His important study, *Method and Meaning in Jonson's Masques*, was published in 1966.

Mecaenas. In *Poetaster*, Mecaenas is a true poet and noble friend of Horace, Virgil, and Caesar. Crispinus tells Horace that he will force himself on Mecaenas, since he very much wants to meet him. Horace assures him that there is no jealousy among noble poets. Lupus tells Macaenas of the "treason" of Ovid's masquerade and brings him with Caesar and the others to surprise the masqueraders. He has pity on them, and asks Caesar to forgive them. Mecaenas realizes that Lupus is jealous and foolish, and tells him that Caesar will punish him for his empty accusations. Mecaenas is pleased when Caesar states his respect for true poetry and when Virgil comes to read the *Aeneid* to them. He helps Horace purge Crispinus and is praised by Caesar. Mecaenas, unlike most of the characters in *Poetaster*, is not a characterization of one of Jonson's contemporaries.

Medea. Daughter of King Aeëtes of Colchis and the niece of Circe. Like Circe, Medea was a sorceress. She fell in love with Jason and helped him obtain the Golden Fleece. When Jason left Colchis, she went with him and lived as his wife for many years, bearing him several children. When Jason later wished to marry the daughter of King Creon of Corinth, Medea sent her an enchanted wedding gown which burned her to death. The many experiences of her violent and tragic life are treated extensively in Greek and Roman poetry and drama.

Medlay, In-And-In. In *A Tale of a Tub*, a cooper of Islington who produces a masque for Squire Tub. The character was intended to be a caricature of Inigo Jones.

Medusa. The most famous of the three Gorgons, who were sisters. Medusa was once a beautiful woman, but she offended Athena, who changed her hair into snakes and made her face so hideous that all who looked at her were instantly turned to stone. When Medusa was pregnant by Poseidon, Perseus killed her, and Chrysaor and Pegasus sprang from her blood when she died.

Meercraft. The projector in Jonson's *The Devil Is an Ass*, who purports to have a number of schemes to make his clients rich.

Meg. One of the wenches who appears in *The Gypsies Metamorphosed* and discovers that the gypsies have picked her pockets.

Megaera. One of the Furies and the first wife of Hercules.

Meighen, Richard. Bookseller in London, 1615–41, who published the first three plays—*Bartholomew Fair, The Devil Is an Ass*, and *The Staple of News*—of the second volume of the second folio (1641).

Meliadus. A young knight representing Prince Henry who appears in *The Speeches at Prince Henry's Barriers* and revives chivalry and knighthood.

Mellifleur. "The Sweet" shepherdess in *The Sad Shepherd*. She mourns for Earine's drowning and Aeglamour's melancholy with the rest of the company. She goes with Marian to comfort Amie when she falls ill of lovesickness and vouches to the company that Marian was not the disguised Maudlin who offended Robin Hood and his men.

Melpomene. A symbolic character used to denote attractiveness.

Melun. The real name of Jaques de Prie, who is posing as a beggar in *The Case Is Altered*. He was formerly a steward to Lord Chamont's father, and is living under an assumed name in Milan because he ran off with Chamont's gold and his infant daughter. His real identity is not known until late in the play. See JAQUES DE PRIE.

Memnon. A mythical king of Ethiopia who went to the aid of his uncle Priam during the Trojan War, killed Antilochus, and was himself slain by Achilles, after which Zeus made him immortal. A famous statue of Memnon at Thebes was said to sing each dawn.

memory. In *Timber* (ll. 479–507), Jonson, borrowing from the Elder Seneca (*Controversiae*, praefatio, i. 2–5), observes that "*Memory*, of all the powers of the mind, is the most *delicate*, and *fraile*: it is the first of our *faculties*, that Age invades." Noting that Seneca, the Elder, had a miraculous mem-

ory, Jonson indicates that he himself until he was past forty could recite everything he had ever written and that he could still repeat whole books and poems of selected friends.

Menander. Athenian comic poet. Born in Athens about 342 B.C., he drowned about 291 B.C. He wrote more than one hundred plays, largely of everyday, domestic complications and love stories, and was highly esteemed for his wit, skill in characterizations, inventiveness, and clever maxims. He was the most famous writer of New Comedy. *The Curmudgeon* is his only complete play now extant; we have only fragments of others. Both Plautus and Terence made adaptations of plays by Menander; the adaptations survived and strongly influenced seventeenth-century comedy. In *Poetaster* (I. i), Ovid says that Menander's fame will last "whil'st slaves be false, fathers hard, and bawdes be whorish, / Whil'st harlots flatter." According to the ode written by the unidentified I.C. on Jonson's "Ode to Himself," which is prefixed to Jonson's translation of *The Art of Poetry* (1640), Jonson physically resembled the image of Menander on an ancient medal. See also CRITIC.

Menelaus. A king of Sparta, the son of Atreus and the brother of Agamemnon. Menelaus was married to Helen, whose abduction by Paris was said to have begun the Trojan War.

Mercatori. The three merchants in *Volpone* who plot with Peregrine to make Politic-Would-Be leave Venice.

Mercury. 1. In Roman religion Mercury was the god of commerce, and he was honored at the Mercuralia, a festival held in mid-May and attended primarily by traders and merchants. He soon became associated with the Greek god Hermes, son of Zeus and Maia, and like Hermes, Mercury was a herald of the gods, especially Jupiter.

2. Mercury is a character in *Cynthia's Revels*. He disguises himself as a page and serves Hedon in order to view the disguised Cupid's sport at Cynthia's court, after carrying out Jove's orders to help Echo rise from earth. He mocks Hedon's shallowness and vices, and mocks the other courtiers, including Anaides, Asotus, and Amorphus. He praises Crites for his honorable conduct and his wisdom. He and Cupid make mocking asides during the courtiers' interaction. Mercury discovers himself to Crites, and they work together to make the courtiers appear foolish. Dis-

guising himself as a Frenchman, Mercury beats Amorphus at the courtship contest. He narrates the second masque, and is honored by Cynthia. The courtiers ask for his defense against their follies.

3. Appears as a character in *Pleasure Reconciled to Virtue* and honors Hercules by crowning him with a garland of poplar.

4. A messenger-god who appears in *Mercury Vindicated From the Alchemists at Court* and triumphs over the forces of alchemy.

5. In *Lovers Made Men* he receives the lovers who have been drowned by love, causes them to drink from the River Lethe and forget their past, and finally reconciles his own will with that of Cupid.

6. He appears on a floating island with the other gods in *Neptune's Triumph for the Return of Albion*. He has no speaking part.

Mercury Vindicated From the Alchemists At Court.

Performed: January 1 and 6, 1616.

Published: 1616 in folio by William Stansby.

Printer: William Stansby.

This masque was probably performed at Whitehall on January 1 and 6, 1616. Its dramatic form is that of a triumph in which the splendor of the denouement suggests the victory of the hero. Nature and natural forces, represented by Mercury and the king, triumph while art, represented by Vulcan and the alchemists, is humbled.

After loud music, the workshop of an alchemist was discovered, and a Cyclope, tending the fire, sang in praise of the fire of alchemy as the soul of art and the superior of nature. After the song, Mercury appeared at the tunnel of the middle furnace and attempted to escape, but was noticed by Vulcan, who called for Mercury to stay. Running about the room, Mercury stopped and delivered a long speech, imploring someone to save him and denouncing the spurious and devious art of the alchemists. Vulcan entered with a group of alchemists who encircled Mercury while he defended himself with his caduceus and proclaimed the futility of Vulcan and the alchemists in trying to capture him, scorning their claim to be able to create superior creatures through their artistry. In response, Vulcan berated Mercury and called forth the creatures made by the alchemists to convince Mercury of their power, and several imperfect creatures appeared and danced about Mercury. In contempt, Mercury reviled Vulcan for offering such inferior creatures in defense of the fire of alchemy as opposed to the excellence of the natural sun, and he proclaimed that Vulcan and his party of impostures should be banished and melted before the majestic light of the sun, so that all sensible people might be able to see and judge the difference between the ridiculous monsters created by the alchemists and the glorious creatures made by nature.

The whole scene changed to the glorious bower wherein sat Nature with Prometheus at her feet and the twelve masquers, who were her sons, standing before him. Slowly, Prometheus descended and Nature followed, singing in praise of the glory of the sun and the creatures bathed in its light, after which the twelve masquers danced forth, and Prometheus and Nature engaged in a dialogue lauding their beauty. There followed the main dance and a dance with the ladies of the audience in which the masquers demonstrated the love and harmony created by Nature. Prometheus announced the time to depart from the presence of such beauty, after which Nature voiced the reluctance of all to leave the glorious warmth and life-giving presence of the sun.

Mere-Fool. A melancholy student and a notary of the Rosicrucians who appears as a character in *The Fortunate Isles, and Their Union* and is made sport of by Johphiel.

Meres, Francis (1565–1647), was born at Kirton in Lincolnshire and educated at Pembroke, Cambridge, where he took his B.A. in 1587 and his M.A. in 1591. He became rector and schoolmaster at Wing, Rutland. In 1598 he published a collection of apothegms on philosophy and the arts entitled *Palladis Tamia: Wit's Treasury*, which contained an invaluable discourse comparing English poets with the Greek, Latin, and Italian poets, in which he superficially assesses the work of English writers from Chaucer to his own day. In *Palladis Tamia*, Jonson is referred to as one of the dramatists who is "best for tragedy." Meres's assessment seems to show that several of Jonson's tragedies have not survived and that Jonson's reputation as a comic playwright had not yet been established.

Merlin. In Arthurian legend, a magician, seer, and teacher at the court of King Vortigern and later at the court of King Arthur. When Merlin revealed the secrets of his knowledge to the enchantress Vivien, she imprisoned him forever in an oak tree. Merlin appears as a character in *Prince*

Henry's Barriers and is mentioned in *Und.* XLIII.

Merope. One of the Pleiades who was the wife of Sisyphus. Merope was thought to be an invisible star because she hid her face with shame for having married a mortal while all of her sisters mated with gods.

Merry Devil of Edmonton, The. An anonymous play first published in 1608 and mentioned in the Prologue to *The Devil Is an Ass* and in *The Staple of News* (I. vi, first intermean).

metaphor. In *Timber* (ll. 1898–1925), Jonson, drawing upon Vives (*De Ratione Dicendi*, I), includes a discussion of translation of metaphor in his comments on the dignity of speech. Jonson argues that in the use of metaphor we must serve only necessity or commodity. Metaphors should not be far-fetched, affected, or deformed. Later in the same passage (ll. 2015–19), Jonson reiterates Quintilian's warning that we should not mix metaphors inappropriately.

Metaphor, Miles. In *A Tale of a Tub*, the clerk of Justice Preamble, who assists the Justice in his unsuccessful efforts to marry Awdrey.

Metoposcopy. The art of judging one's character by telling one's fortune from his forehead or face. Subtle practices this art in *The Alchemist* (I. iii).

Mezentius. A king of Caere in Etruria whose aid was sought by Turnus against the invading Aeneas. In the *Aeneid,* Mezentius is portrayed as an atheist tyrant who was eventually killed by Aeneas.

Michaelangelo. Born Michelangelo Buonarroti in Tuscany in 1475, Michaelangelo became a sculptor, painter, architect, and poet. He died in 1564, the year of Shakespeare's birth. Although he thought of himself primarily as a sculptor, he is perhaps best known for his paintings on the ceiling of the Sistine Chapel. His most famous sculpture is the *David*. He is considered by many to be one of the most brilliant and creative men ever to have lived.

Jonson alludes to Michaelangelo in *Und.* LXXVII and mentions him in *Timber* (l. 1583) as an excellent painter who emulated the ancients.

Midas, king of Phrygia, befriended Silenus. As a result Dionysus gave Midas the power to turn everthing he touched into gold. When he discovered that his food also turned to gold, he asked to be relieved of this gift, and Dionysus allowed him to wash away his power in the Pactolus River, which has had gold sands since that time. In another instance, Midas received ass's ears because he preferred the music of Pan in a contest with Apollo. He was able to disguise his shame with a headdress but had to tell his barber, who whispered Midas' secret into a hole in the ground, and the weeds which grew out of the hole betrayed Midas's secret whenever the wind blew through them.

Middleton, Thomas. (1580–1627). English dramatist. Graduated from Oxford in 1598. Little is known of his early life although it is highly probable that he entered Gray's Inn at some point. By 1602 he was writing for Henslowe, collaborating with Dekker in the Admiral's *The Honest Whore* (1604) and also working for the Children of St. Paul's. Between 1604 and 1611 he wrote realistic, satirical comedies about London life, aimed at exposing contemporary vice: *Michaelmas Term, A Trick to Catch the Old One, A Mad World, My Masters, The Roaring Girl* (with Dekker), and *A Chaste Maid in Cheapside*. From 1613 to 1618 he wrote primarily tragicomedies, and from 1621 to the end of his career he wrote his most notable plays, including the tragedies, *The Changeling* (with William Rowley) and *Women Beware Women*. In 1620 he was appointed City Chronologer of London, a post he held until his death, after which Jonson was appointed to it, in 1628. Middleton's *A Game of Chess* (produced 1624) was considered offensive political satire, and Jonson even sneered at it in *The Staple of News* (III. ii). Throughout his career Middleton also wrote civic pageants and masques, one of which, *The Inner Temple Masque,* Jonson probably alluded to unfavorably in *Timber* (ll. 710–18) and *News from the New World.* Middleton's *More Dissemblers Beside Women* was performed in place of Jonson's *Neptune's Triumph* in 1624 when Prince Charles returned to England without a Spanish bride.

Jonson called Middleton a "base fellow" in the *Conversations* (ll. 167–68). He did allude to Middleton's *Blurt Master Constable* in *Tale of a Tub* (II. ii). Although similar to *The New Inn* in its concluding scenes, *The Widow* was most likely written by Middleton himself without Jonson's collaboration. See also Gervase MARKHAM.

Midwinter, Daniel. Bookseller in London from 1698 to 1725 who was one of the publishers of the so-called Booksellers' Edition of Jonson's *Works* in 1716–17.

Mildred. In *Eastward Ho,* the faithful and modest daughter of Touchstone, who marries Golding, Touchstone's loyal apprentice.

Millar, [Edward?]. City captain of London mentioned in *Und.* XLIV.

Milliner. A craftsman who is called to take part in the courtship contest in *Cynthia's Revels.* He sells Amorphus some ribbons during the staged primping.

Milton, John (1608–1674). English poet born in London, educated at St. Paul's School and at Christ's College, Cambridge, where he wrote poetry in Latin and English while he was a student, including "On the Morning of Christ's Nativity" and probably "L'Allegro" and "Il Penseroso." His increasing dislike for the ritualism developed in the English church led him away from the ministry to poetry, and he resolved to become a poet and retired to his father's estate at Horton, where he wrote the masque *Comus,* modeled on Jonson's *Pleasure Reconciled to Virtue,* and "Lycidas," an elegy on the death of his friend Edward King. After the death of his mother in 1638, Milton went to Italy, where he traveled widely, studied, and met Galileo. When he returned to England the following year, he wrote several pamphlets in support of the efforts of the Presbyterians to reform the English church. In 1643 he married Mary Powell, who left him shortly thereafter but returned two years later. During her absence Milton wrote two pamphlets defending the morality of divorce for incompatibility.

In 1644 he published his most famous prose piece, *Areopagitica,* an eloquent argument for the freedom of the press which grew out of his dissatisfaction with Parliament's strict censure of the press. Milton gradually separated himself from the Presbyterians, and in 1649 he published *The Tenure of Kings and Magistrates,* which supported the imprisonment of King Charles and declared the right of subjects to depose and put to death an unworthy king. When Cromwell came to power, Milton was appointed secretary of foreign tongues, and he continued to defend the Commonwealth. In the midst of his official business and pamphleteering, Milton went blind and had to depend upon several secretaries, one of whom was Andrew Marvell.

After the death of his first wife, Milton married Catherine Woodcock in 1656, but she died two years later, and in 1663 he married Elizabeth Minshull, who survived him.

At the Restoration, Milton was forced into hiding, and some of his writings were burned, but he was included in the general amnesty and lived quietly until his death. In 1667 Milton published his blank verse epic in twelve books, *Paradise Lost,* which he had probably begun to work on before the Restoration. *Paradise Regained* and *Samson Agonistes* were published before his death, but Milton's unorthodox theological Latin pamphlet *De doctrina Christiana* was not discovered and published until 1825. Although he has always been considered one of the greatest English poets, Milton's personal life, politics, and theology have always been controversial.

Milton seems to have looked to Jonson primarily as a model of the poet as teacher of virtue, and as a masque writer. Both Milton and Jonson wrote elegies on the death of Lady Jane Pawlett, Marchioness of Winchester, but the works differ substantially in style and tone.

Minc'd-Pie. A character who appears as one of the children of Christmas in *Christmas, His Masque.*

Minerva, originally a Roman goddess of arts and trades, became identified with the Greek goddess Athena and was considered a goddess of war and wisdom as well as crafts. She was sometimes thought to be the inventor of musical instruments. Minerva was a popular goddess and was worshipped with Jupiter and Juno.

Minos. 1. In Greek mythology, king of Crete, son of Zeus and Europa, and the husband of Pasiphaë, who bore him Ariadne and Phaedra. When Minos failed to sacrifice a white bull to Poseidon, the god caused Pasiphaë to conceive a passion for the bull, by whom she bore the Minotaur, a monster with the head of a bull and the body of a man. Daedalus constructed the labyrinth in which the monster was confined. Every year Minos sacrificed seven young men and seven maidens to the Minotaur. Theseus joined a group of the victims and eventually killed the Minotaur. Minos became the most prosperous king of the Mediterranean, known for his justice as well as his power. He became one of the three judges of Hades.

2. A foolish apothecary in *Poetaster,* to whom Crispinus is in debt. He is possibly a caricature of a man to whom Marston was in debt. He brings in the lictors to arrest Crispinus, but frees him after Tucca flatters him and offers to stand as bail for his prisoner. Minos is even convinced by Tucca to lend more money to Crispinus. He is present when Lupus declares that he suspects the masqueraders of treason, and he breaks into the masquerade with Caesar but plays no major part in the action.

Minotaur, the, offspring of Pasiphaë and a bull, had the face of a bull and the body of a man. The Minotaur was confined in the labyrinth constructed by Daedalus and was eventually killed by Theseus.

Minutius. One of Sejanus' lackeys in *Sejanus,* who hopes to rise in power with him. He gossips with Laco, Pomponius, and Terentius about Sejanus' power and signs that it is failing while Arruntius mocks them. He brings the news to Sejanus of the rope that appeared around the new statue and is very flattered when Sejanus salutes him. He is not mentioned again in the play.

Mirth. A gossip who appears in the induction and the intermeans in *The Staple of News.*

Mischief. The name of one of the witches making up the antimasque in *The Masque of Queens.*

Mis-Rule. A character dressed in a short cloak with yellow ruffles and a velvet cap who appears as one of the children of Christmas in *Christmas, His Masque.*

Mithra. An ancient god of Persia whose cult became a popular religion, especially among the Roman legions, for whom Mithra was the ideal divine comrade. The fundamental aspect of the Mithraic system was the dualistic struggle between the forces of good and evil. The central myth associated with Mithra was the story of his capture and sacrifice of the sacred bull from which sprang all the beneficient things of the earth. Mithracism, which had many similarities to Christianity, declined rapidly in the late third century A.D.

Mitis. In *Every Man out of His Humour,* an acquaintance of Cordatus, the narrator of the play.

Mnasyl. The name of one of the young Satyrs in *Oberon, the Fairy Prince.*

Momus. A son of night, Momus eventually became the personification of censure and criticism.

Monarchia Britannica. A symbolic personage represented as a woman richly attired appearing in a scene in Jonson's part of the *King's Coronation Entertainment.*

Monmouth, Robert Carey, Earl of. See Sir Robert CAREY (CARY).

Montaigne, Michel de (1533–1592), was the son of a rich French Catholic landowner. His mother was of Spanish Jewish descent. His famous essays greatly influenced English literature. He studied law, held a magistracy until 1570, and served as mayor of Bordeaux from 1581 to 1585. Between 1571 and 1580, he wrote the first two books of his *Essais,* the third book of which was written between 1586 and his death in 1592. The essays, which were trials or tests of his thinking on a variety of subjects, focus on an examination of himself, reflect Montaigne's conviction that man must discover his own nature if he is to live in peace and dignity, and are characterized by his lucid style and skeptical attitude. In *Timber* (ll. 724–25), Jonson calls Montaigne the master of the essayists, and Lady Politic mentions him to impress Volpone in *Volpone* (III. iv).

Monteagle (Mounteagle), William Parker, 4th Baron (1575–1622), is most famous for the letter he received in 1605 giving a clue to the Gunpowder Plot. He was awarded a pension which was in arrears when he died in 1622. *Epig.* LX lauds Monteagle as the saver of his country. He tilted in the *Barriers* of 1606.

Montgomery, Philip Herbert, Earl of (1584–1650), was the younger brother of William, Earl of Pembroke, Jonson's patron. Shakespeare's First Folio was dedicated to "this incomparable pair of brethren." Philip married Lady Susan de Vere in 1604, became Earl of Montgomery in 1605, Knight of the Garter in 1608, and fourth Earl of Pembroke upon his brother's death in 1630. He danced in *Hymenaei, The Haddington Masque, The Vision of Delight, Pleasure Reconciled, For the Honor of Wales,* and *Love's Triumph,* and he tilted in Prince Henry's *Barriers* and in the *Challenge at Tilt.* There is extant an undated letter from Jonson to Montgomery asking for the Earl's aid.

Montgomery, Susan, Countess of (1587–1629), was the daughter of Edward de Vere, 17th Earl of Oxford. In 1604 she married Sir Philip Herbert, who became Earl of Montgomery in 1605. She was held in high esteem by John Donne and George Chapman, and Jonson lauded her in *Epig.* CIV. She danced in *The Masque of Blackness, The Masque of Beauty, Hymenaei,* and *The Masque of Queens.*

Moon. A symbolic character in *The Vision of Delight* who has no speaking part but accompanies night. See also ENDYMION.

Mooncalf. Ursula's assistant, or tapster, at her pig-roasting in *Bartholomew Fair*.

Moore. The character Muly Mahamet in the play *The Battle of Alcazar*, written by George Peele (1558–97). In *Poetaster* (III. iv), one of Tucca's pages plays the part of "the Moore" for Histrio.

More, Sir Thomas (1478–1535). English statesman celebrated in the Roman Catholic Church as a saint. He received a Latin education in the household of Cardinal Morton and at Oxford. He was greatly influenced by the new learning. He numbered Colet, Lyly, and Erasmus among his friends and was himself an ardent humanist. A successful London lawyer, he also served on diplomatic missions. He entered the service of Henry VIII in 1518 and was knighted in 1521. He held several important government offices and was made Lord Chancellor in 1529, despite his disapproval of Henry's divorce from Katharine of Aragon. He resigned in 1532, ostensibly because of ill health. When he refused to subscribe to the Act of Supremacy, he was imprisoned in the Tower in 1534 and finally beheaded on a charge of treason in 1535.

More's *Utopia* (published in Latin in 1516 and in English in 1551) portrays an ideal society founded on reason. Among his numerous other works are a *History of Richard III,* used by Shakespeare; several polemical tracts against the Lutherans; devotional works; poems; meditations; and prayers. More's biography by his son-in-law, William Roper, has been the principal source for all subsequent biographies. More was beatified in 1886 by Pope Leo XIII and canonized in 1935 by Pius XI.

Jonson mentions More in *Timber* (l. 902) as one of those considered admirable in their times because they were eloquent, and he used numerous illustrations from More's *History of Richard III* in *The English Grammar*. Part of *Eastward Ho* (III. iii), probably by Chapman, was adapted from *Utopia*. More was apparently the first to use the phrase "a tale of a tub" in literature in the sense of a stupid or absurd story.

Morforius. See PASQUIL.

Moria. A foolish female courtier in *Cynthia's Revels.* She is older than the other women and loves to reminisce about when she was the belle of the court. Cupid mocks her for her folly. She gossips with the ladies about the men, saying that she prefers Hedon. She is accused of mockingly trying to induce Argurion to flirt with Crites. When asked by Phastaste what she would be if she could be anything, she says that she would like to be aware of all the immoral activities at court and free to gossip about them. She plays the games of wit with the other courtiers and drinks from the fountain of self-love. She takes part in the first masque but is discovered by Cynthia and sentenced to be punished at Crites' will. She marches, weeps, and sings the palinode with the other courtiers.

Morison, Sir Henry, the eldest son of Sir Richard Morison, Lieutenant-Governor of the Ordnance and nephew of the traveller Fynes Morison, was probably the Henry Morison admitted to Brasenose College in 1622. He was knighted in 1627 and died in 1629. Sir Lucius Cary and Morison, whose sister was married to Cary, are the subject of Jonson's *Und.* LXX, the first Pindaric ode in English, which celebrates the virtue and friendship of these noble men and condoles with Cary on Morison's death.

Morley, George (d. 1684), was appointed Bishop of Winchester in 1662. According to a note Izaak Walton wrote to John Aubrey, Morley saw Jonson often when the poet was ill and Jonson supposedly told Morley that he lamented having profaned the scriptures in his plays.

Morning. See AURORA.

Morose. An irascible man in *Epicoene* who cannot stand to hear anyone speak except himself and who orders his servants to communicate only with signals and signs. He disapproves highly of his nephew, Dauphine Eugenie, and marries Epicoene, a supposedly "silent woman," in order to disinherit him. His plan fails when Dauphine tricks him into making him heir, then reveals that Morose's new "wife" is really a boy.

Morphides. Cousin to Amorphus in *Cynthia's Revels,* who only appears to try to keep order among the crowd attempting to get into court to see the courtship contest.

Morsius (Moers), Joachim (1593–1643). Famous Dutch scholar. Professor of history and of Greek at Leyden and afterwards Professor of History at the Danish University of Soroë. He visited England in 1619 and 1620. Jonson wrote an inscription in Latin for Morsius' album on January 1, 1619–20.

Mortgage. In *The Staple of News,* the nurse to Lady Pecunia.

Mortimer. The tragic hero of Jonson's fragment *Mortimer His Fall.* He was created Earl of March by the extraordinary favor of Isabel, mother of Edward III, but because of his excessive pride, scorn of the nobility, and familiarity with the queen was finally executed.

Mortimer His Fall.
The fragment of a tragedy. Only the Argument and about seventy lines of dialogue have survived.

Published: 1640 in folio by Thomas Walkley.

Printer: unknown.

Although when this fragment was first published in 1640, an editorial note at the end of it indicated that Jonson died before he finished the play, the general opinion now seems to be that the play was a project which Jonson started early in his career but abandoned for some reason. According to Jonson's rather sketchy argument, the action would have been developed along the following lines of plot.

The first act reveals Mortimer's pride and security in having been raised to the title of Earl of March by the favor of Isabel, the queen mother, and includes the counsels of Adam D'Orlton, politic Bishop of Worcester, against the Earl of Lancaster, the envious cousin of the king, Edward III. The chorus of ladies celebrates the worthiness of Isabel in rewarding the services of Mortimer and the Bishop. The second act focuses on the king's love and respect for his mother and his refusal to believe the reports of her extraordinary favors to Mortimer. Edward attributes all such charges to Lancaster's envy. The chorus, now of courtiers, lauds the king's worthiness of nature and affection for his mother, extols his piety, and celebrates their own good fortune under such a monarch. Through a vision experienced by the blind Earl of Lancaster, the third act reveals to the king's brother, the Earl of Cornwall, the horror of their father's death and the cunning way in which Mortimer had arranged for the death of their uncle. The chorus of country justices and their wives report how they were deceived into thinking that the old king was alive by being led to believe, through the use of lighting and disguises at court, that they had seen the old king dining at Corfe Castle. In the fourth act the king's attitude toward Mortimer begins to change, and he meets in conferences with his brother.

They decide to explore the charges against Mortimer and to employ W. Mountacute to get the keys of the Castle of Nottingham into the king's power and to persuade the constable of the castle, Sir Robert D'Eland, to join their party. The chorus describes Mortimer's vain sense of security, his scorn of the nobility, his familiarity with the queen (including the king's surprising Mortimer in the queen's bedchamber), and the general joy at Mortimer's finally being sent to execution. The fifth act relates the triumph of the Earl of Lancaster and the celebration of the king's justice.

The fragment of the text itself contains only Mortimer's opening speech in which he proudly proclaims his rise to power and a short dialogue of mutual admiration between Mortimer and Isabel.

Morus. A page to Asotus in *Cynthia's Revels.* Argurion acts affectionately toward him after she is thrown over by Asotus. Asotus promises to treat him very well. He is criticized by Cynthia and sentenced to march, weep, and sing the palinode with the other courtiers.

Mosca. In *Volpone,* Mosca is Volpone's Parasite, his crafty servant who schemes to add to his master's riches by capitalizing on the greed of corrupt Venetians. Mosca's craftiness and double-dealing are fully revealed toward the end of the play, when he attempts to betray Volpone and to claim his master's wealth for himself.

Moschus. Greek bucolic poet of the Theocritus school whose idyl on Europa is among his few extant works. From this work Jonson borrowed the idea of the runaway Cupid in *The Haddington Masque.*

Moseley, Humphrey. Bookseller in London from 1630 to 1661, who became the chief publisher of the finer literature of his age, publishing the collected works of Milton, Cartwright, Crashaw, D'Avenant, Denham, Donne, Fanshaw, Howell, Vaughan, and Waller. In 1658 Moseley acquired from Thomas Walkley copyrights for *The Devil Is an Ass, The Magnetic Lady,* and the third volume of Jonson's *Works.* In his preface to the *Last Remains of Sir John Suckling* (1659), Moseley cited Digby's publication of Jonson's fragments *The Sad Shepherd* and *Mortimer* as precedents justifying his own publication of Suckling's fragmentary tragedy *The Sad One.*

Moseley was also the author of the Preface to the Reader for William Cartwright's *Comedies, Tragicomedies with other Poems* (1651), in which Jonson is proclaimed to be the faithful judge and professor of poetry who has given his approval to his literary son William Cartwright.

Motives. In his *Athenae Oxonienses* (1818), Antony à Wood included in his list of Jonson's works "His *Motives*—Printed 1622, Oct." No trace of such a work has ever been found. If such a work ever existed, it may have been connected with the gleanings in divinity that according to *Und.* XLII were lost when Jonson's library burned in 1623.

Mountacute, W. A character in Jonson's fragment *Mortimer His Fall* employed by the king to secure the keys to Nottingham Castle.

Mounteagle, William, Lord. See MONT-EAGLE.

Mountforde, Thomas (d. 1632), was appointed prebendary of Harleston in St. Paul's Cathedral in 1597. He was one of those appointed to serve as spiritual adviser to Jonson when he was cited for recusancy in 1606.

Mountjoy, Charles, Lord, succeeded Essex in 1601 in the Irish command and proceeded to crush Tyrone's rebellion in short order. In "Ode ἀλληγορικὴ," one of his uncollected poems, Jonson alludes to the harmony and strength of Mountjoy's command.

Mousetrap-man. A member of the marketplace crowd in *Bartholomew Fair*.

Much. Bailiff, or steward in charge of providing food to Robin Hood in *The Sad Shepherd*. He gathers all kinds of food for the feast, and is horrified when he hears of Earine's drowning. He stays to take the Cook's place, along with Friar Tuck, while the witch hunters go to catch Maudlin, who cursed the Cook.

Mulcaster, Richard (1530?–1611), educated at Eton, King's College (Cambridge), and Christ Church (Oxford). In 1561 he became headmaster of the Merchant Taylors' School, where Spenser was his pupil. In 1586 he resigned, and in 1596 he was appointed High Master of St. Paul's. Holding advanced views on education, Mulcaster was a firm believer in the value of the classics, but he argued that not all boys could benefit from a purely classical education, and he advocated elementary teaching in English. His *Elementary* (1582) is in part an elementary course in English and in part a defense of English instead of Latin as a medium for the writing of serious books. Jonson relied very heavily, without acknowledgment, on Mulcaster's *Elementary* in *The English Grammar*.

Mulciber. A name associated with Vulcan.

mumming. See MASQUE.

Mumming. A character dressed in a pied suit with a visor who appears as one of the children of Christmas in *Christmas, His Masque*.

Munday, Anthony (1560?–1633), the son of a London draper, was first an actor and then was apprenticed to the printer John Allde, whom he left in 1578 to journey to Rome, where he collected material for an attack on English Catholics in France and Italy. When he returned to England, he wrote a number of anti-Catholic tracts, and in 1584 he apparently gave up acting when he was given the court post of Messenger of the Chamber as a reward for his anti-Catholic efforts. He began writing plays, publishing his first extant one in 1585 and writing for Henslowe and the Admiral's from 1594 to 1602. In 1598 Meres, rather perplexingly, noted him as one of "the best for comedy" and as "our best plotter." Munday also wrote ballads and lyrics, translated romances, edited the 1618 edition of Stow's *Survey of London*, and created pageants for the City and City Companies. His plays are undistinguished, and most of them were written in collaboration for the Admiral's. In 1598 he wrote *The Downfall of Robert Earl of Huntingdon* and, with Chettle, *The Death of Robert Earl of Huntingdon*, both Admiral's plays about Robin Hood which may have inspired Shakespeare's *As You Like It*.

Munday was often ridiculed by his contemporaries. He was satirized as Posthaste in *Histriomastix* and as Balladino in *The Case Is Altered*.

Muralt, Béat-Louis de. In *Lettres sur les Anglois et les Francois* (1725), de Muralt offers a comparison between Jonson and Molière as comic dramatists: " . . . je dirois que Ben Johnson, quoi que véritablement grand Poëte, à certains égards, est inférieur à Molière en beaucoup de choses. . . . Après tout, il faut avoüer que Ben Johnson est un Poëte judicieux, admirable à distinguer & à soutenir les caractères qu'il entreprend, & dont les bonnes Pièces sont excellentes dans leur espèce. Mais laissons là leurs bons Poëtes; ce ne sont guère ceux-là qu'on oppose à Molière."

Murmur. The name of one of the witches making up the antimasque in *The Masque of Queens*.

Murray, Sir James, who was knighted on August 5, 1603, was one of the gentlemen of the Privy Chamber in ordinary to Prince Henry in 1610. According to the *Conversations* (ll. 273–76), Murray was the one who "delated" Jonson to James for allegedly writing something against the Scots in *Eastward Ho*, causing Jonson voluntarily to imprison himself with one of the co-authors—Chapman.

Musaeus. A Greek poet of the fourth century A.D. who wrote a famous poem on Hero and Leander.

Musco (Brainworm). Servant to Lorenzo senior (Knowell) in the 1601 quarto version of *Every Man in His Humour*. (Differing names and courses of action in the 1616 folio version are given in parentheses.) He is extremely clever and crafty, ingratiating himself with Lorenzo junior (Edward) by telling him that Lorenzo senior (Knowell) has read Prospero's (Wellbred's) letter. He disguises himself as a begging soldier to try to foil Lorenzo senior's (Knowell's) pursuit of Lorenzo junior (Edward) to Florence (London) and, for fun, sells a greatly overpriced sword to foolish Stephano (Stephen). He meets Lorenzo senior (Knowell) and is hired to spy on his son. Going to Lorenzo junior (Edward), he tells him that his father has followed him; Lorenzo junior (Edward) and Prospero (Wellbred) praise him for his powers of deception. Returning to Lorenzo senior (Knowell), Musco (Brainworm) tells him that he has been trapped and made a prisoner by Lorenzo junior (Edward) and his companions, but has overheard that they will be meeting at Cob's house and has escaped. He goes with Peto (Formal) to a tavern, where he gets Peto (Formal) drunk and dresses up in his clothes as Dr. Clement's (Justice Clement's) assistant. Going to Thorello (Kitely), he tells him that Clement wants him, and gives Prospero (Wellbred) time to make Biancha (Dame Kitely) think that Thorello (Kitely) is cheating on her. He meets Bobadilla and Matheo (Matthew), who asks him to serve a warrant to Giuliano (Downright). He dresses up as a varlet, his last disguise, and "arrests" Giuliano (Downright), hoping for money from him to avoid the arrest. When Giuliano (Downright) "arrests" Stephano (Stephen) in turn, he is forced to go before Clement who, upon learning of his clever deceptions, praises him and makes him the honored guest at his dinner.

Muses. The daughters of Zeus and Mnemosyne, the Muses, sang and danced at the festivities of Olympians and heroes, often led by Apollo. They were considered goddesses of the arts and in postclassical times were assigned to particular arts: Calliope, epic poetry; Clio, history; Euterpe, the flute; Melpomene, tragedy; Terpsichore, dance; Erato, the lyre; Polyhymnia, sacred song; Urania, astronomy; Thalia, comedy. Functions and names of the Muses vary widely and the names of other muses are also known.

musical settings. About twenty-five of Jonson's songs are known to have been set to music by about a dozen different musicians during the seventeenth and early eighteenth centuries, although Jonson himself was only close to two contemporary musicians—Alphonso Ferrabosco and Nicholas Lanier. Jonson described Ferrabosco and Lanier as "that excellent pair of kinsmen." Jonson gave Ferrabosco high praise for his setting of the songs of *Hymenaei*, and his music was also noted in *The Haddington Masque* (ll. 351–52). Jonson gave Nicholas Lanier credit for both the scene and the music in *Lovers Made Men*. Lanier was also paid for the original music in *The Gypsies Metamorphosed*. There is also extant a pastoral song sung at court on New Year's Day, 1669, which was modeled on Jonson's *Und*. LXXIX and which is attributed to Nicholas Lanier.

The standard work on the subject of musical settings for Jonson's works is Willa McClung Evans's *Ben Jonson and Elizabethan Music* (1929), which includes settings and musical criticism. Evans should be supplemented with Mary Chan's *Music in the Theatre of Ben Jonson* (1980).

Following is a list of the musicians and songs that were set to music between 1608 and 1750:

1. Edmund Chilmead. "Why, this is a sport" (*The Gypsies Metamorphosed*, ll. 706–31). Extant in a manuscript signed by Mr. Chilmead (1611–54). This work was probably prepared as a revival for the masque.

2. William Crosse. "Hear me, Oh God." (*Underwood*, I. 2). Extant in manuscript and used as an anthem in the Chapel Royal in 1635.

3. Alphonso Ferrabosco. Ferrabosco's *Ayres* (1609) include eight songs taken from Jonson's works: "Come away, come away" (*Masque of Blackness*, ll. 295–300). "Come, my Celia, let us prove" (*Volpone*, III. vi. 166–83). "Why stays the bridegroom to invade" (*Haddington Masque* ll. 415–24). "If all these cupids, now, were blind"; "It was

no policy of court" (*The Masque of Beauty*, ll. 341–55). "Yes, were the loves or false, or straying" (*The Masque of Beauty*, ll. 358–63). "So beauty on the waters stood" (*The Masque of Beauty*, ll. 325–32). "Had those that dwell in error foul" (*The Masque of Beauty*, ll. 369–74). "When all the ages of the earth" (*The Masque of Queens*, ll. 743–48).

4. Robert Johnson. "From the famous Peak of Darby" (*The Gypsies Metamorphosed*, ll. 121–44). Published in John Playford's *The Musical Companion, In Two Books* (1673). Since Nicholas Lanier was paid for the music at the performance of this masque in 1621, Johnson's setting was most likely for a revival.

"See the Chariot at hand here of love"; "Do but look on her eyes, they do delight"; "Have you seen but a bright lily grow" (*Underwood*, II. 4). All the above are ascribed to Jonson and reproduced in V. Jackson's *English Melodies*.

5. Nicholas Lanier. In addition to the music in *Lovers Made Men* and *The Gypsies Metamorphosed*, Lanier is also credited with the following: "Though I am young, and cannot tell" (*The Sad Shepherd*, I. v. 65–80), reproduced in *Select Musical Ayres and Dialogues* by J. Wilson et al. (1652).

6. Henry Lawes. "If I freely may discover / She should be allowed her passions" (*Poetaster*, II. ii. 163–72, 179–88). "O, that joy so soon should waste!" (*Cynthia's Revels*, IV. iii. 242–53). "Beauties, have yee seen this toy" (*Haddington Masque*, ll. 86–156). The songs are in Lawes's autographed manuscript.

7. William Lawes. "Still to be neat, still to be drest" (*Epicoene* I. i. 92–102). Written for revival of the play in 1665 and published anonymously in John Playford's *Select Ayres & Dialogues* (1669).

8. Edmund Nelham. "Buzz, quoth the blue fly" (*Oberon*, ll. 210–17). Published in *Catch That Catch Can: Or The Musical Companion* (1667).

9. James Oswald. "Drink to me only with thine eyes" (*Forest*, IX). This, the most popular of Jonson's songs, has been given many settings. The earliest setting which has survived has been attributed to James Oswald. The setting was entitled "The Thirsty Lover" and was published by S. Babb in 1774–75.

10. Martin Peerson. "See, see, o see who here is come a Maying" (*Entertainment at Highgate*, ll. 93–112). Published in *Private Music, or the First Book of Ayres and Dialogues* (1620).

11. Henry Youll. "Slow, slow, fresh fount, keep time with my salt tears" (*Cynthia's Revels* I. ii. 65–75). Published in *Canzonets to Three Voices* (1608).

12. William Webb. "Come noble nymphs and do not hide" (*Neptune's Triumph*, ll. 472–503, and *Fortunate Isles*, ll. 586–617). Published in *Select Ayres and Dialogues* by J. Wilson et al. (1659).

13. Musical settings of uncertain authorship. There is extant an eighteenth-century setting in manuscript of the witches' chant from *The Masque of Queens*, ll. 155–204.

Included in T. D'Urfey's *Wit and Mirth: or Pills To Purge Melancholy* (1700) and *Songs Complete, Pleasant and Divertive* by J. Bow, H. Purcell, et al. (1719) are: "My master's and friends, and good people, draw near, / And look to your purses" (*Bartholomew Fair*, III. v. 69–156). "Cock Lorell would needs have the devil his guest" (*Gypsies Metamorphosed*, ll. 1061–1125). "Though it may seem rude / For me to intrude" (*Masque of Augurs*, ll. 165–225).

Musicians. In *Sejanus*, a chorus of musicians ends each act.

Mute. Morose's servant in *Epicoene*, who communicates according to his master's wishes only by body signals and signs.

Mutes. Characters who appear as the supporters of Chronomastix in the first antimasque in *Time Vindicated to Himself and his Honors*.

mythology. It is commonly believed that Jonson was a man of great classical erudition, but, in fact, he was no more learned than many men of his age such as Chapman or Heywood. Jonson was not primarily a scholar but a poet, and he took from classical mythology and antiquities whatever he could use to embellish his own works. In the spirit of his age, Jonson was very interested in symbolism and allegory, and he drew heavily upon mythology to give authenticity and authority to his own creations. He was particularly adept at finding and elaborating upon parallels between classical mythology and antiquities and contemporary people and events. Although much of his knowledge was firsthand, Jonson relied greatly upon compendia of classical civilization and mythology such as Johannes Rosinus' *Romanarum antiquitatum libri decem*, Barnabas Brissonius' *De veteri ritu nuptiarum*, Casare Ripa's *Iconologia*, and Lilius Gregorius Gyraldus' *De deis gentium*.

From his experience with *Cynthia's Revels*, Jonson must have realized that myth lacks the vitality to invigorate even a shallow dramatic plot, and consequently, after this play he resumed his practice of including only learned allusions to mythology in his plays. Frequently, according to

Wheeler, the allusions are used to embellish the play, to soften Jonson's satire or tragedy, or to dazzle his audience. Often mythology contributes to both direct and indirect characterization in the plays. Generally, myth content in the comedies of contemporary London and Venice is proportionately small while it increases significantly in the comedies and tragedies of Rome. In addition to employing myth for ornamentation and characterization, Jonson also uses it to develop his criticism of contemporary life, particularly in applying mythological parallels to his satirical attacks upon his literary rivals.

Symbolical characters and mythological gods and goddesses are the warp and woof of Jonson's masques, and classical mythology often animates the poems.

For detailed information on Jonson's use of mythology, see Charles Francis Wheeler's *Classical Mythology in the Plays, Masques, and Poems of Ben Jonson* (Princeton: Princeton University Press, 1938) and Allan H. Gilbert's *The Symbolic Persons in the Masques of Ben Jonson* (New York: AMS Press, 1948).

N

Nabbes, Thomas (d. 1645). Minor playwright and poet. He wrote tragedies, comedies, and masques, the best known of which are *Microcosmus* and *Spring's Glory*. He was one of the young men attracted to Jonson in his later years. Nabbes's *Tottenham Court* (1634) may have been influenced by Jonson's *Tale of a Tub*.

Naevius, Gnaeus. Latin poet born about 270 B.C. who began writing plays in 235 B.C. He died in north Africa about 201 B.C. Naevius was an outspoken Roman citizen; he attacked Roman statesmen and was imprisoned for his actions. He is best known for his *Bellum Poenicum*, the first Roman epic and national drama. This work greatly influenced Ennius and Virgil. In *Timber* (ll. 2345–48), Jonson quotes Naevius' epitaph, citing its elegance of language.

Naiads. In Greek mythology, nymphs of streams, rivers, and lakes.

Nano. In *Volpone*, Volpone's dwarf, who entertains him and accompanies him when he pretends to be a mountebank.

Napier, John (1550–1617). Scottish mathematician who invented the logarithm, introduced the decimal point in writing numbers, and published *Mirifici Logarithmorum Canonis Descriptio* (1614). This work was translated into English by E. Wright in 1616, one year before Napier's death. In *The Magnetic Lady* (I. vi), we are told that Sir Interest uses logarithms to calculate the utmost profit of stock. This may be the first literary allusion to logarithms.

Narcissus. A beautiful boy who, although he was loved by the nymph Echo, cared only for himself and paid no attention to her. Ovid relates how Narcissus fell in love with his own image reflected in the water of a well and eventually died of anguish because he could not reach the one he loved.

Nashe, Thomas (1567–1601) English satirist. Little is known of his life although his first publications appeared in 1589. One of his first successes was *Pierce Penniless His Supplication to the Devil* (1592), a caustic satire on contemporary society. His staunch anti-Puritanism involved him in the Martin Marprelate controversy and a scurrilous pamphlet battle with Richard and Gabriel Harvey. His best known work, *The Unfortunate Traveler* (1594), was a forerunner of the picaresque novel of adventure. His brief career in playwriting produced *Summer's Last Will and Testament* (1592), a satirical masque, and the lost fragment *The Isle of Dogs*, which was completed in 1597 by Jonson and led to the imprisonment of Jonson and several others. The play was considered seditious, but Nashe, who left town, was never imprisoned, and in his *Lenten Stuff* (1599), he blamed the problems with the play on Jonson's additions. Jonson makes no references to Nashe in his works, but Nashe alludes to *The Case Is Altered* in *Lenten Stuff*.

Nasutus. In *Poetaster*, one of the characters in the "Apologetical Dialogue," who wonders if Jonson has been offended by the talk about his play and all the slander against him and questions the author, giving him the opportunity to reveal his feelings.

Nathaniel. In *The Staple of News*, the first clerk of the Staple office.

Natta, Pinnarius. One of Sejanus' lackeys in *Sejanus*, who appears in the first scene of the play and is mocked by the noble Romans for his corrupt loyalty to his patron. He acts as a spy for Sejanus and accuses Cordus of treason. He tells Sejanus of the monster which came from the head of the statue of Sejanus and attends the second senate meeting, where he is arrested with Latiaris for being a follower of Sejanus.

Nature. 1. Although usually not personified by ancient writers, nature was often conceived of as the generative power of the universe, and she was sometimes portrayed as a naked woman with her breasts full of milk and with a vulture in her hand.

2. She appears with her twelve sons in *Mercury Vindicated From the Alchemists at Court* and triumphs over the art of alchemy.

3. In *Timber* (ll. 124–28), Jonson, borrowing largely from Juan Luis Vives (*In Libros de Disciplinis Praefatio* [*Opera*, i. 324]), records that nature is not "so spent, and decay'd, that she can bring forth nothing worth her former yeares." The passage indicates that Jonson was aware of the controversy, current in his day, over the decay of nature. The central works published on the subject were Godfrey Goodman's *The Fall of Man, or the Corruption of Nature, proved by the light of our Natural Reason* (1616) and George Hakewill's *An Apology of the Power and Providence of God in the Government of the World* (1627). See also PAINTING; POETRY.

Necessity. Often closely associated with the Fates.

nectar. The drink of the gods, usually thought of as some kind of honey drink, which made those who took it immortal.

Needle. In *The Magnetic Lady*, the steward and tailor to Lady Loadstone, who fathers an illegitimate child by Pleasance.

Neighbors. In *The Alchemist*, the neighbors crowd around Lovewit when he returns home and tell him, in a shocked way, of all the strange happenings at his house in his absence. After Face protests that he is innocent and they must be mistaken, however, the neighbors quickly change their mind and express uncertainty about their former claims.

Nelham, Edmund. See MUSICAL SETTINGS.

Nemesis. An offspring of Night. In Greek literature Nemesis is the personification of the wrath of the gods at man's pride and presumption. The Roman poet Tibullus celebrated his love for a woman he called "Nemesis."

Neoptolemus. Also called Pyrrhus. The son of Achilles and Deidamia, Neoptolemus came to Troy after the death of Achilles to take part in the Trojan War. He appears in the works of many classical writers, and he is usually portrayed as a gentle and wise young man who was renowned for his bravery and physical strength.

Neptune. Originally an Italian god identified by the Romans with the Greek god Poseidon, Neptune was the ruler of the seas and of islands.

Neptune's Triumph for the Return of Albion.
Performed: Scheduled for January 6, 1624, but never actually performed.

Published: 1623–24 in quarto with no imprint. Reprinted in 1640 folio by Thomas Walkley in section of masques.

Printer: unknown.

Planned for Twelfth Night 1623–24, this masque was postponed because of problems over precedence between the French and Spanish ambassadors to be invited, and it was actually never performed in its original form. Jonson had written the masque in honor of Charles's return to England on October 5, 1623, without a Spanish bride—a return welcomed with great relief and enthusiasm because the proposed marriage with Spain was thoroughly unpopular. Although it was never performed, quarto copies of the masque (with no imprint) were printed for the actors and court patrons. Since the masque was not given as scheduled on Twelfth Night 1623–24, the original version had lost its relevance and importance, but Jonson remodeled the masque in the following year when the engagement of Charles and Henrietta Maria was announced, and he entitled the new version *The Fortunate Isles and Their Union*.

When the king was seated, and the music had ceased, the scene, which consisted of two erect pillars dedicated to Neptune, was discovered. The Poet entered to give the argument; he was approached by the Master Cook, who inquired what his business was. The Poet informed the Cook that he was there to present a masque, to which the Cook replied that since they were in his region—the banqueting house—any activity there had to meet with his approval. Surprised, the Poet asked who addressed him. The Cook told him, then asked who the Poet was. The Poet explained that he was merely his majesty's "unprofitable servant," who was called upon once or so a year to deliver a "trifling instrument of wit." In response, the Cook questioned whether the Poet had ever been a cook, and the Poet said that he surely had not. The Cook stated that if he had never been a cook then he could not be a good poet since the art of either was the "wisdom of the mind." Elaborating, the Cook noted that a cook must please the palates of the guests just as a poet must know the palate of the times, and both must satisfy expectation and curiosity even if the guests expect more than they are likely to appreciate or understand, for there is a palate of the understanding as well as the senses. Taste likes relishes, sight fair objects, hearing delicate sounds, smell pure scents, and feeling soft and plump bodies, but the understanding encompasses all of these, and all have their origin in the kitchen, where the art of poetry is learned just the same as the art of cookery. After a long eulogy of the cook's abilities given by the Cook himself, the Poet was convinced and recognized the Cook as a brother, but the understanding the Cook requested that as a favor to him the Poet explain his device for the masque, and he proceeded to do so.

The Poet explained that the mighty Neptune had recently sent his son Albion forth on a mission and, wishing to find out about him, had dispatched a floating island to him which had now brought Albion safely back to Neptune's court. The Cook was impressed with the device, but made some suggestions about how he would have staged it within a kitchen scene and asked if the bare island was the complete device. The Poet replied that the island had a tree—the tree of Harmony—which was shaped like an arbour, in which sat Albion and his companions, who were the masquers. The Cook asked if there were an antimasque, and the Poet said that one was not necessary, but the Cook argued that the device could not be truly poetic without one, and he informed the Poet that he could show him how much of a genuine poet he himself was by providing a metaphorical dish. The Cook called forth a child from the boiling house and instructed him to prepare a special dish in a big pot with persons representing the various ingredients, the desired characteristics of which were discussed in detail. When the dish was ready, the various persons emerged from the pot and danced an antimasque.

Afterwards, the Poet called for the opening of the scene, and the island was discovered with the masquers sitting in their several locations. The heavens opened, and Apollo with Mercury, some Muses and the goddess Harmony, made music as the island advanced, with Proteus sitting below and Apollo and the chorus singing a song imploring Proteus to report to Neptune the safe and joyous return of Albion. When the island had joined itself with the shore, Proteus, Portunus, and Saron came forward and approached the king with song while the masquers disembarked. There followed a series of speeches praising the sovereign and lauding the triumphant return of his son. When these were completed, the island withdrew, and the masquers danced their entrance while the chorus called for a full celebration of the triumph.

After the masquers' dance, the scene was changed to the Palace of Oceanus where Albion had been a guest, and the main dance followed. A second prospect of the sea then appeared, and the wonders of the deep were revealed as Proteus, Portunus, and Saron approached the ladies of the audience and, singing, implored them to dance. The revels ensued, after which Neptune's fleet was discovered, ready to take the riches of the deep home again. The Cook reentered and offered another dish—one of pickled sailors—and an antimasque of sailors was performed. To the accompaniment of lutes and coronets, songs were then provided by Proteus, Portunus, and Saron, excusing themselves from the celebration and indicating their desire to return to the sea. The chorus called for unity and peace in the kingdom under Neptune's glorious reign, and the last dance was performed.

Nereus, a sea god, was the son of Pontus, the husband of the Oceanid Doris, and the father of the Nereids. Nereus was said to be the father of fifty daughters. Like Proteus he could constantly change his shape, and he had the gift of prophecy.

Nero. Oldest son of Germanicus and Agrippina in *Sejanus,* seen by Sejanus as an obstacle to his ascent to absolute power, since he stands in line to Tiberius' throne. Nero first appears with his mother, brothers, and followers, expressing his disdain of Tiberius' spies and his horror at Drusus senior's death. Although Tiberius expresses his love and care for Nero after Drusus senior dies, Nero is soon accused of treason and banished to Pontia by the Senate.

Nestor, son of Neleus and father of Antilochus, became the wise king of Pylos. In the *Iliad,* Nestor was portrayed as a vigorous warrior and a respected advisor who traveled with the Greeks to the Trojan War. In the *Odyssey,* the gods allowed him to return unharmed to Pylos after the war because of his piety and prudence. Nestor lived to a ripe old age and the details of his death are uncertain.

Nevil, Sir Henry (1564?–1615), was knighted in 1599 and served as a member of Parliament from 1584 to 1614. He was implicated in the Essex plot, imprisoned, fined, and released in 1603. Because of his sympathy with the popular party, he was not in favor with the king. In 1612 when Nevil applied for the secretaryship of State, he was denied the position. Jonson praised Nevil in *Epig.* CIX for his fame, titles and honor.

New Inn, The.

Acted: 1629 by the King's Men.

Published: 1631 in octavo by Thomas Alchorne.

Printer: Thomas Harper.

Act I. Assisted by his supposed son Frank, Goodstock, a gentleman and a scholar neglected by the times, operates a new inn in Barnet called *The Light Heart*. In keeping with the name of his establishment, the host wants all of his guests to be happy, but one of the current guests is a melancholy gentleman soldier and scholar named Lovel, who was once a page to old Lord Beaufort and is now the guardian of the old lord's son. The host and Ferret, Lovel's quick-witted servant, are unsuccessful in trying to improve Lovel's disposition. Presently, Prudence, a chambermaid, arrives at the inn and announces that her mistress, Lady Frampul, and her party composed of young Lords Beaufort and Latimer, Colonel Tipto, and Trundle, the coachman, are coming to the inn for a day of festive merrymaking. Prudence has been elected sovereign of the sports for the day, and she invites Lovel to participate, and he reluctantly agrees to do so at the host's insistence. Lady Frances Frampul is reputed to be the sole remaining daughter of Lord Frampul who left his lady and their two daughters Frances and Laetitia many years ago, after which his wife became melancholy and also left home; Laetitia was then lost and the estate descended to Frances. To the host, Lovel confesses that he secretly has loved Lady Frances for a long time but has not expressed his love to her because his ward, the young Lord Beaufort, loves her too. Although Lovel resolves to continue to love but not to confess it, the host finally does succeed in getting Lovel to cheer up since he will at least be able to enjoy Lady Frances's company for a while.

Act II. Lady Frampul is angered by her tailor, who has promised to make Prudence a new suit for the occasion at the new inn but has apparently not done so, and the lady has to have Prudence fitted with some of her own apparel. While they criticize the tailor, Prudence points out to

Lady Frances that it is not appropriate that a woman of her rank and quality should go to a public inn accompanied only by her chambermaid and be surrounded by so many men. Lady Frampul concurs, and together they agree to persuade the host to let them dress up his son as a girl and to present her to the company as a kinswoman named Laetitia Sylly. The host goes along with the plan provided that his son may be accompanied by an old Irish charwoman who is his nurse and who dotes on the boy.

Meanwhile, Lords Beaufort and Latimer and Colonel Tipto have discovered Fly, the inn parasite, a witty fellow, formerly a strolling gypsy, whom the lords decide should now become Prudence's pet. They also designate Pierce, the drawer; Jordan, the chamberlain; Jug, the tapster; and Peck, the hostler, as the militia of the house which will be commanded by Sir Glorious Tipto. Later, richly dressed, Sovereign Prudence makes her grand entrance followed by Lady Frances and Frank disguised as Laetitia and accompanied by the nurse. Lord Beaufort is greatly attracted to Laetitia, and Lord Latimer is much taken with Prudence, but Lady Frances discovers Lovel in a sad mood and, upon command of Queen Prudence, bestows a kiss upon the melancholy Lovel, who finds the kiss to be both nectar and at the same time to provide a sting. Queen Prudence commands that a court of love shall be established and that for the next two hours the only case tried shall be that of love and gentle courtship, and all prepare to carry out her injunction.

Act III. At a lower room in the inn, Colonel Tipto is delighted to hear of the arrival of some new guests at the inn—Bat Burst, a broken citizen, and his companion Hodge Huffle, a notorious cheater. In yet another room set up for a tribunal, Prudence sits as justice over the love case of Lovel versus Lady Frances. As appellant, Lovel is called upon to define and prove the existence of love, and his argument is so cogent and vivid that the defendant, Lady Frampul, becomes enamoured of both the man and his matter, repents, and is reconciled to the church of love and willingly bestows another kiss upon Lovel. Although some of the spectators doubt the sincerity of her changed attitude, Lady Frances actually does not completely commit herself because she wants to enjoy a second remaining hour of love decreed by Sovereign Prudence. Upon news of the arrival of a new lady and a new coachman named Barnaby, the court temporarily dissolves.

Act IV. When the new lady, richly dressed and accompanied by her footman, arrives, she falls into the hands of Colonel Tipto and the house militia who have all been drinking and carousing, and when they begin to treat her uncivilly a quarrel breaks out. She is in jeopardy until she is rescued by the valorous Lovel and is invited to join Lady Frampul and the other ladies and lords in another room. When she does so, Lady Frampul recognizes her rich attire as the dress intended for Prudence, and the newcomer is discovered to be Pinnacia Stuff, wife of the tailor, and her footman to be Nick Stuff, the tailor himself, who likes to have his wife dress up in the fancy clothes he makes for noble ladies so that he can pretend to be her footman and then ravish her. Pinnacia is stripped of her dress, and she and her husband are sent home in disgrace. Afterwards Lady Frampul petitions the court to change the suit from love to valor, and it is agreed to do so, whereupon Lovel delivers a stirring defense of valor and receives as just reward a second kiss from Lady Frampul. Sovereign Prudence then declares the court permanently dissolved and the game ended, and Lovel immediately falls into a more profound melancholy than before and retires for bed. Lady Frampul chastises Prudence for not allowing the game to be extended. The two quarrel briefly but are reconciled when Lady Frampul promises to work everything out and that Prudence shall still get her new dress.

Act V. Fly announces to the host that Lord Beaufort has been secretly married to Laetitia, and Goodstock anticipates the mirth that will abound when Beaufort discovers that he has married a boy. Prudence enters attired in her new dress and upon the insistence of her lady is employed to arouse the melancholy Lovel. The host tells everyone the news of Beaufort's marriage, and it is confirmed by Lord Latimer. Lord Beaufort himself then comes in and demands that his bridal bed be prepared, but the host forbids it and shows him that he has married a boy. The old nurse frantically charges in and complains to the host that her daughter has been ruined in marriage and to the astonishment of all she reveals that the host's supposed son is really a girl—the old nurse's own daughter who is the daughter and co-heir of Lord Frampul and Lady Frances Frampul's long-lost sister. The old nurse explains that she herself is actually Lord Frampul's wife, whereupon Goodstock removes his own disguise and reveals himself to be none

other than Lord Frampul, and the whole Frampul family is joyfully reunited. Lord Frampul then gives Frances to Lovel, who is ecstatic, and the Lord affirms the marriage of Laetitia and Beaufort. The old Lord gives the New Inn to Fly and offers money to Prudence, but Lord Latimer asks for her hand without dowry because her virtue is sufficient, and all retire to celebrate their newfound joy in the New Inn.

Newcastle, Margaret Cavendish, Countess (afterwards Duchess) of (1624?–1674), youngest daughter of Sir Charles Lucas and second wife of William Cavendish, Duke of Newcastle, was the foremost English woman writer of her day. She achieved recognition for her poems, plays, essays, scientific treatises, letters, orations, and fantasies. She was also praised for her biography of her husband, the duke, which was published in 1667. In her *Sociable Letters* (1674), the duchess comments that her husband considered Ben Jonson to be an excellent reader. In commentary contained in her *Plays* (1662), the duchess explains that her own plays may be condemned because they do not conform to the unity of time, but she argues that a comedy which attempts to adhere to the unity of time would be flat and dull and that although she understands that Jonson believed that in order for a comedy to be good it had to adhere to the unity of time he violated this principle in his own comedies, specifically in *Volpone* and *The Alchemist*. In a poem which serves as a general prologue to all of her plays, the duchess informs her audience that they should not expect to see plays such as Jonson's *The Alchemist*, *Volpone*, or *Epicoene* because they are masterpieces and probably took a long time to write. She goes on to comment on Jonson's strengths, citing his brain, which was very strong, his language, which was significant and free, and his great learning, and comparing him to Shakespeare. suggesting that Shakespeare had a fluent wit and wrote from nature.

Newcastle, William Cavendish, Earl (afterwards Duke) of (1592–1676). English soldier, politician, and nobleman of great wealth. He was created Viscount Mansfield in 1620 and Earl of Newcastle in 1628. In 1638 he became privy councilor and governor of the Prince of Wales and supplied financial and military support to the royalist cause during the Puritan Revolution, even leading troops in the northern counties. After some early successes, he was defeated with Prince Rupert in 1644 and retired to the continent, but he returned with Charles II at the Restoration and was created Duke in 1665. Newcastle was noted for his horsemanship and skill at arms, and he taught Charles II to ride. In 1658 he published at Antwerp *La Méthode et Invention Nouvelle de dresser les Chevaux.* Newcastle's second wife, Margaret Lucas, was the first Englishwoman to attain recognition as a writer, and before the duke's death in 1676 she wrote a famous biography of her husband.

Newcastle wrote several plays and books himself and was a lifelong patron of the arts. Jonson was particularly close to the duke, as can be seen from the five extant letters Jonson wrote to him. Jonson wrote *The Entertainment at the Blackfriars* for the christening of the duke's son, and he prepared *The Entertainment at Welbeck* and *Love's Welcome at Bolsover* upon commission of Newcastle. *Und.* LIII and LIX praise the duke, who left in manuscript a poem to Jonson's ghost "I would write of thee, Ben; not to approve," which was first published in *Welbeck Miscellany, No. 2. A Collection of Poems* (1924).

News from the New World Discovered in the Moon.

Performed: January 17 and February 29, 1620.

Published: 1640 in folio by Thomas Walkley in the section of masques.

Printer: uncertain.

Two heralds, a printer, a chronicler, and a factor were discovered, the heralds announcing that excellent free news was available to those who would care to listen. The printer expressed interest in the news, whether it were true or not, because he needed some copy. The chronicler needed some accurate material for his book. The factor, who was in the business of disseminating news throughout England by writing some thousand newsletters or so a week and who planned to start a staple of news soon, was also interested, but only in news that was reliable. During a discussion of the matter, the printer claimed that since news was for the common people it did not make any difference whether it were true or not, but the factor argued that news which was printed was not really news while the printer maintained that most people would not believe anything that was not printed. The chronicler stated that he had been cheated so often with unreliable news that he had to spend more time correcting his book than composing it. The heralds assured them that they would all be satisfied and informed them that the news was from the moon and had

been learned by a poet who had visited there and had discovered a new, inhabited world. The heralds then responded to several questions about the nature of the new world and its inhabitants. When asked how the poet had journeyed to the moon, one of the heralds explained that there were only three ways to go—the way of Endymion, the way of Menippus, and the way of Aetna. The poet had gone the way of Menippus—on the wings of his muse.

The heralds continued to elaborate on certain aspects of the life and various traits of the moon's inhabitants. Of particular interest, the heralds noted, was the fact that the inhabitants carried on all their activity in the clouds and that they had only one main island, called the Island of the Epicoenes, because both sexes were created there while their parents enjoyed all pleasures and delights. When the epicoenes had tasted the springs of pleasure, the females laid eggs from which were hatched a race of creatures called Volatees, which resembled man but were really a kind of fowl partly covered with feathers. The Volatees entered and performed their antimasque.

The heralds then explained to the audience that so far they had only attempted through their muse to offer delight, but now they hoped to create belief because a group of human beings who had been animated and enlightened by the glorious light of the sovereign had been rapt in wonder far above the moon all this time and had now returned, hoping that their dancing might be formed to the music of the king's peace and that they might gain his favor, which only could thaw the cold they had contracted in traveling through the colder region. They descended, shook off their icicles, and offered a song extolling the warming light of the sovereign. The first dance was performed and another song of praise followed, after which the main dance and the revels ensued. Two more laudatory songs and a dance were given, and the heralds concluded with short speeches extolling "Fame, that doth nourish the renowne of Kings, / And keeps that fayre, which envie / would blot out."

New-Yeares-Gift. A character dressed in a blue coat who appears as one of the children of Christmas in *Christmas, His Masque.*

Nicholas, Harry. Anabaptist mystic Henrick Niclaes, leader of the sect of "the Family of Love," which was banned by Elizabeth in 1580. He wrote several pamphlets. In *The Alchemist* (v. v), Lovewit mistakes Drugger for one of the Brethren and calls him by this name.

Nicholson, John. Bookseller in London from 1686 to 1715 who was listed as one of the publishers of the so-called Booksellers' Edition (1716–17) of Jonson's *Works*.

Niger. A character in *The Masque of Blackness* who is the son of Oceanus and who brings his daughters to Albion to be beautified.

Night. 1. Nyx, a great cosmogonical figure who was feared and respected by Zeus. In Hesiod she was born of Chaos and was the mother of Aether, Hemera, and lesser powers.

2. A symbolic character in *The Vision of Delight* who appears, sanctions the activities of Delight, and summons Phant'sie from the cave of clouds.

Nightingale. A ballad singer in *Bartholomew Fair*. He is an accomplice to Edgworth and sings a song about cutpurses while Edgworth picks Cokes's pocket. He trips the costardmonger and, with Edgworth, steals Cokes's cloak and hat while Cokes scrambles for the spilled fruit.

Niniveh. A famous puppet play. Others included Jerusalem, Rome, the City of Norwich, Sodom and Gomorrah, and the Gunpowder Plot. Jonson frequently refers to Niniveh: *Every Man out* (Second Sounding; II. iii), *Bartholomew Fair* (v. i), "The Character" prefixed to *Coryat's Crudities*. Usually called "motions," these puppet shows were apparently quite popular. Most likely the puppets were hand puppets. They were presented by the master of the motions who spoke the dialogue, as is the case in *Bartholomew Fair* (v) where Jonson gives us the libretto for a show on Hero and Leander. Sometimes the motions were burlesques of a play. For example, Niniveh, which is often alluded to in old plays, was probably built on Lodge and Greene's *A Looking Glass, for London and England* (1598), and Rome was apparently the puppet play of Julius Caesar. Allusions to all these motions are frequent in the seventeenth century, and there are some records of performances. *Wit and Drollery*, for instance, records in 1656 a performance of Sodom and Gomorrah, in which the tempest of fire would most likely have been a great attraction. The most durable of the shows seems to have been The Gunpowder Plot, for in 1762 G.A. Stevens, reflecting on the vanished glories of Bartholomew Fair, wrote of "Punch's whole play of the Gunpowder Plot."

Niobe, the daughter of Tantalus and the wife of Amphion, had seven daughters and seven sons. In her vanity she claimed that she was at least equal to Leto who had only two children, Apollo and Artemis. For her pride, Niobe was punished by Leto's children, who killed all of Niobe's children, and Niobe wept until she was transformed into a stone from which her tears continued to fall.

Nisbet, James. Town councillor and afterwards baillie of Edinburgh who was one of those directly responsible for the vote of the Edinburgh Magistrates and Town Council to make Jonson an honorary burgess. Jonson mentions Nisbet in a 1619 letter to Drummond of Hawthornden.

Nisbet, Sir William. A wealthy merchant who was Lord Provost of Edinburgh in 1618 and was one of those directly responsible for the vote of the Edinburgh Magistrates and Town Council to make Jonson an honorary burgess. Jonson mentions Nisbet in a 1619 letter to Drummond of Hawthornden.

nobility. In *Timber* (ll. 1127–38), Jonson, drawing upon Machiavelli (*Il Principe*, ch. ix. 4), notes that nobles who genuinely serve the Prince and the commonwealth not for spoil should be honored and loved. Those nobles who serve to avoid business and care the Prince may use with safety. Those nobles who serve with the premeditated thought of their own profit the Prince should take heed of and consider his enemies. See also SOVEREIGNTY.

Noctifer. Another name for the evening star Hesperus.

Nomentack. A Virginia Indian chief, servant of Powhatan, who was brought to England as a hostage in 1605, with an Englishman left in his place. He was murdered in the Bermudas in 1610 on his way home. In *Epicoene* (v. i), La-Foole claims that John Daw made a "map" of him when he visited England.

Northampton, Henry Howard, Earl of (1540–1614), son of the poet Henry Howard, Earl of Surrey, was a well-known English courtier. As a member of the powerful Catholic Howard family, he was suspected of heresy and treason with Mary, Queen of Scots. He was attached to Robert Devereux, 2nd Earl of Essex, and to Essex's enemy, Robert Cecil (later Earl of Salisbury). Howard was distinguished for his great learning and notorious for his unprincipled public life. James I made him a privy councillor in 1603, Earl of Northampton in 1604, Lord Privy Seal in 1608, and the king's principal minister in 1612 after Salisbury's death. Howard supported the divorce of his grandniece, Frances Howard, from the 3rd Earl of Essex and was responsible for the imprisonment of Sir Thomas Overbury. According to the *Conversations* (ll. 325–27), Northampton accused Jonson of popery and treason after the performance of *Sejanus* in 1603.

Northern. A clothier from the North who drinks and quarrels with Knockem and his companions at Ursula's booth in *Bartholomew Fair*.

Norton, John, Jr. Printer in London from 1621 to 1645 who in 1630 printed in quarto *Love's Triumph Through Callipolis* for Thomas Walkley.

Norwich, The City of. See NINIVEH.

Nose. A symbolic character who appears in *Time Vindicated to Himself and to his Honors* and is fascinated with Chronomastix.

Notch. A brewer's clerk who appears in *The Masque of Augurs* and, together with his cohorts, offers to present a masque before the court.

notes and records (contemporary). Several contemporary notes and records about, and presumably by, Jonson have survived, the most extensive of which is the *Conversations* with William Drummond of Hawthornden, which probably took place in 1619 when Jonson made his famous walking tour of Scotland. Apparently, Drummond jotted down his notes about their conversations just as they occurred and then summed up his impressions in a final note of characterization. The accuracy and reliability of the *Conversations* is uncertain. The *Conversations* were first printed in an abridged form in *The Works of William Drummond of Hawthornden* (ed. Bishop John Sage and Thomas Ruddiman. Edinburgh, 1711). Whether or not the *Conversations* are completely reliable, they do provide some interesting insight into Jonson's opinions, character, and biographical facts.

John Aubrey's notes about Jonson (Aubrey ms. 6 in the Bodleian, folio 108) also provide some insight into the poet's life and character. Aubrey (1626–1697) was an antiquary who liked to collect gossip and trivial information about noteworthy people. His notes on Jonson tend to be more gossip than fact and contain a number of inaccuracies. One interesting aspect of his notes is that he does include a note from Izaak Walton (1593–1683), who wrote the life of John Donne. Walton's note to Aubrey was presumably written during Walton's eighty-seventh year, and his note, like most of Aubrey's, tends also to be more in the realm of gossip than fact.

Yet another record of Jonson's life is contained in the notes of Archdeacon Plume (1630–1704), a native of Maldon, to which he left his library, including his notebooks. His notes are highly abbreviated and also tend to be more gossip than fact. They add nothing to our knowledge of Jonson's life.

In many ways the most interesting record of Jonson's life is a series of memoranda supposedly written by himself. These memoranda were first published by David Hughson (the pseudonym of Edward Pugh) from "An ancient manuscript preserved at Delwich College" in his *London*, volume 4, page 40 (issued in 1807). The memoranda contain brief comments about the composition of *Volpone*, *Catiline*, *The Alchemist*, *Epicoene*, *Tale of a Tub*, and *The Devil Is an Ass*. That Jonson wrote these memoranda is questionable. Professor Mark Eccles (*Mod. Lang. Notes*, 51 [1936], 520–23) has shown that they were written by Lewis Theobald, who, assuming the name of a Ben Jonson claiming to be descended from the poet, printed them in *The Censor*, May 11, 1715.

Noye, Sir William. Appointed attorney general in 1631, Noye was well known for his support of Charles I's extending the royal prerogative and encroaching upon popular rights. According to Plume's notes, when Noye was at his commencement dinner for his law degree and Jonson was waiting outside, the poet sent in some clever verses, punning on Noye's name: "An Impromptu to Sir William Noye." These verses are not usually included in Jonson's canon.

Noyes, Robert Gale (1898–1961). American scholar educated at Brown and Harvard, later was Professor of English at Brown. His carefully researched and very useful book on Jonson, *Ben Jonson on the English Stage: 1660–1776*, was published in 1935.

Numa Pompilius succeeded Romulus to become the second king of Rome. He was considered a wise and judicious ruler.

Nuncio. In *The Case Is Altered*, a messenger, who makes only one appearance, bringing Count Ferneze the news that Paulo has been captured by the French.

Nuntius. A messenger in *Sejanus*. He brings Arruntius, Lepidus, and Terentius the news of how Sejanus' children were murdered after his death, how Drusus Senior's wife vowed revenge on those who poisoned her husband, and how the mob began to repent its action.

Nurse. In *The New Inn*, a poor charwoman who is nurse to the host's supposed son Frank but eventually turns out to be Lady Frampul in disguise.

nymphs. 1. Female divinities associated with various natural objects and portrayed as the daughters of Zeus. There were an infinite variety of nymphs, some of whom represented and were associated with various localities while others were identified with the part of nature in which they dwelt and yet others were associated with functions of nature. Some were portrayed as young, beautiful, and gentle although they were sometimes associated with the wilder aspects of nature. Some were even shown as vengeful and malicious. The nymphs were considered to be mortal, although they usually were thought to live very long lives. Some of the most important classes of nymphs were the Naiads (nymphs of streams, rivers, and lakes), the Nereids (daughters of Nereus who lived in the depths of the sea), the Dryads (nymphs of forests and groves), and the Oceanides (daughters of Oceanus).

2. In *Chloridia* two types of nymphs appear. The Naiads receive Spring when she descends to earth. Fourteen nymphs, played by the Queen's ladies, serve as attendants to Chloris, played by the Queen herself.

3. Three unnamed nymphs appear at the beginning of *Pan's Anniversary* and strew flowers about while offering songs in praise of Pan.

O

Oberon. The prince of the fairies in *Oberon, the Fairy Prince* who appears with his knights and helps to praise the glory of the English court.

Oberon, The Fairy Prince.

Performed: January 1, 1611.
Published: 1616 in folio by William Stansby.
Printer: William Stansby.
This masque was performed at court on January 1, 1611, with Prince Henry as

Oberon. Although Jonson did not give them credit in the published text, Alfonso Ferrabosco wrote the music, and Inigo Jones provided the staging for the work.

The scene discovered was a large rock surrounded by wilderness. At one corner of the cliff the moon began to rise slowly above the horizon, and a satyr was seen. He approached and called for his cronies and, hearing no reply, sounded his horn. After three soundings, he was answered; Silenus came leaping forth, accompanied by several satyrs asking what they were to do. Silenus informed the satyrs that the night was to be one solemn to the Fairy Prince and his knights, and the satyrs queried whether they would get to see Oberon and whether he was as magnificent as they had heard. Silenus described the glories and virtues of Oberon, after which the satyrs speculated on the blessings Oberon might bestow upon them when he appeared.

The rock opened and inside was seen a glorious palace with transparent walls and gates. By the gates lay two armed sylvans asleep. Astonished, the satyrs approached the palace and discussed various mischievous ways to awaken the sylvans but finally decided to strike a charm in their ears. They did so, and the sylvans awoke in amazement. Silenus and the satyrs playfully reprimanded the sylvans for their careless watch, but the sylvans responded that the gates would not open before the second crowing of the cock, so that their guard was sufficient even though they slept. The satyrs decided to sport until the opening of the gates, and they sang and danced until the crowing of the cock when the gates opened and inside the palace was discovered the nation of the fairies. In the distance sat the knights who were the masquers and behind all sat Oberon in a chariot which, to the accompaniment of loud music, began to move forward, drawn by two white bears and guarded on each side by three sylvans. The chariot slowly approached the front of the scene as a song in praise of James was offered, and the satyrs began to jump about for joy. A sylvan reprimanded the satyrs for their sport and lack of decorum on such a solemn occasion when all should pay homage to the court, after which Silenus praised the virtues of the king, and the sylvans invited all to observe the rites to be performed by Oberon and his knights in honor of the crown. Two fairies then offered a song of praise, followed by a fairy dance and another song, after which Oberon and his knights performed two dances and two songs. Measured corantos and galliards were performed, followed by a sylvan's song urging Oberon and his men to return home. Phosphorus, the day star, appeared and announced the dawning of a new day, after which all danced back into the palace to the accompaniment of a song. The star vanished, and the whole scene closed.

Oceanides. Nymphs who were the daughters of Oceanus, the god of the water surrounding the earth.

Oceanus. The Titan son of Uranus and Gaea, the husband of Tethys, and the father of the river gods and the sea nymphs, or Oceanides. In the *Iliad,* Oceanus is considered the father of the gods. He was portrayed as a powerful but tiny old man. Early in Greek mythology Oceanus was regarded as the god of the water surrounding the earth.

ode. An elaborate poem of praise, dignified in language, solemn and intellectual in tone, that has an exalted theme. Originally a Greek poetic form used in drama, the ode was choral and was accompanied by music. The classical masters of the ode were Pindar and Horace. Influenced by French poets such as Du Bellay and Ronsard, English poets attempted to imitate and modify the forms of the classical masters, and Jonson and several of his contemporaries made such efforts. Although Jonson wrote several odes, most of them are not particularly distinguished. His main contribution to the development of the English ode was *Und.* LXX, which was the first attempt in English to imitate the tripartite structure (strophe, antistrophe, epode) of Pindar as opposed to the homostrophic form of Horace.

Oedipus. In Greek legend the son of Laius, king of Thebes, and his wife Jocasta. Warned by an oracle that he was fated to be killed by his son, Laius abandoned Oedipus on a hillside. He was rescued by a shepherd and brought to the king of Corinth, who adopted him and reared him as his son. When Oedipus was a man, he learned from the oracle at Delphi that he would kill his father and marry his mother. Oedipus fled Corinth to escape his fate. At a crossroads he quarreled with and killed an imperious stranger, who was Laius. Oedipus went on to Thebes, which was besieged by the Sphinx. Oedipus solved the riddle of the Sphinx and gained the hand of the widowed Queen Jocasta, thus unwittingly fulfilling the prophecy. The marriage produced two sons, Polynices and Eteocles, and two daughters, Antigone and Esmene. A plague descended on Thebes, and an oracle explained that the only way to get rid of it was to banish the murderer of Laius. Through various revelations, Oedipus learned the truth. In horror he blinded himself, and Jocasta committed suicide. In Homer, Oedipus continued to reign over Thebes until he was finally killed in battle, but the more common version of his story has it that he was exiled by Creon, after which his sons battled for the throne. Details of Oedipus' death are not clear, but Sophocles portrays him as wandering blindly around the countryside guided by his faithful daughter Antigone.

Oenone. A nymph skilled in the art of healing who was loved by Paris but was abandoned by him for Helen. In revenge Oenone sent their son Corythus to guide the Greeks to Troy. When Paris was mortally wounded, he asked Oenone to heal him, but she refused. After he died, she committed suicide.

Offering. A character dressed in a short gown with a staff in his hand who appears as one of the children of Christmas in *Christmas, His Masque.*

Okes, John. Son of Nicholas Okes and printer in London from 1636 to 1644, who in 1640 printed Jonson's poems in both quarto and duodecimo for John Benson.

Okes, Nicholas. Printer in London from 1606 to 1639. In 1609 he printed *The Masque of Queens* in quarto for Richard Bonion and Henry Walley. In 1635 he printed the second quarto of *Catiline* for John Spenser.

Oldham, John (1653–1683), the son of a nonconformist minister, was educated at Oxford where he became a private tutor. Oldham made paraphrases from the classical satirists adapted to contemporary London, and he translated Greek, Latin, and French poets. He included in his *Poems and Translations* (1683) a long ode on Jonson ("Upon the Works of Ben Jonson"). Oldham's early death in 1683 elicited eloquent tributes from Waller, Dryden, and others.

Oldisworth, Nicholas. Author of a verse epistle to Jonson dated 1629, "Die Jonson: Cross not our religion so"; the poem is in manuscript. Oldisworth may have visited Jonson in his home after he was confined to his bed.

Oldys, William (1696–1761), was an antiquary who wrote a number of lives, his best known being that of Raleigh (1740). He collected a number of anecdotes on famous people that survive in ms. (British Museum), but much of his information is of doubtful authority. Oldys recorded several notes and anecdotes about Jonson including the anecdote about Sir Walter Raleigh's son getting Jonson drunk, some information about the origin of the phrase over Jonson's tomb, and some verses supposedly by Shakespeare and Jonson occasioned by the motto to the Globe Theatre.

Olivares, Conde. Gasparo de Guzman (1587–1645), was a favorite of King Philip IV of Spain and became his chief minister in 1622. Olivares is mentioned by Lovel in *The New Inn* (IV. iv).

Oliver, Peter. See PORTRAITS OF JONSON.

Olympus. In Greek religion the summit of Mount Olympus which was the site of the house of the gods.

Omothymia. A symbolic personage representing unanimity and appearing in a scene in Jonson's part of the *King's Coronation Entertainment*.

Onion, Peter. A "groom of the hall to Count Ferneze" in *The Case Is Altered*. With his constant punning, especially on his name, Onion provides low comedy for the play. He urges Juniper, his constant companion, to hurry and serve Ferneze; after confessing his love for Rachel, he commissions Antonio Balladino to write him a love song to woo her. He is happy to see Valentine, and sadly tells him of the death of the Countess Ferneze. When the Count berates him for his inability to find Paulo immediately, and for his speech, he talks back to the Count and is fired. Juniper gets him reinstated. He asks Christophero to speak to Rachel for him. He fences with Martino and has his head broken but quickly recovers and goes with Juniper to speak with Rachel. Jaques catches them outside his house and suspects them of trying to steal his gold; when he lets loose his dog, Onion climbs a tree. From there he discovers Jaques's hidden gold. He and Juniper steal it and, dressing like "gentlemen," get drunk, but they are forced to return it when Jaques reveals to the Count that he stole it from Chamont.

Opinion. 1. A symbolic character who appears in the Barriers for *Hymenaei* and argues for the virgin state's being preferable to the married state.

2. In *Timber* (ll. 43–49), Jonson records that "*Opinion* is a light, vaine, crude,

and imperfect thing, settled in the Imagination. . . ." His observations on this subject are partly indebted to Seneca (*Epistles*, 13, 4).

Ops. Roman goddess of harvest, the wife of Saturn by whom she bore Jupiter and Juno. She was later identified with the Greek goddess Rhea.

Opsius. One of Sejanus' followers in *Sejanus*, who hopes to gain power by his loyalty. His only action in the play is hiding while Latiaris tricks Sabinus into criticizing Tiberius, then jumping out and arresting Sabinus.

Orange. In *Every Man out of His Humour*, a fop.

Orange, Maurice of Nassau, Prince of. Son of William the Silent, who inherited the principality of Orange in southern France and became stadholder of the Netherlands. As Princes of Orange, Maurice and his brother Frederick Henry succeeded their father as stadholders. Maurice is mentioned in *Und.* XLIV.

orators. In *Timber* (ll. 862–923), Jonson drawing upon M. Seneca (*Controversiae*, iii, praefatio), includes a discussion on oratory, noting that "I *have* knowne many excellent men, that would speake suddenly, to the admiration of their hearers; who upon study, and premeditation have beene forsaken by their owne wits; and no way answered their fame: Their eloquence was greater, then their reading: and the things they uttered, better then they knew." He cites the following in particular for their mastery of wit, invention, language, judgment, and eloquence: Francis Bacon, Cicero, Sir Thomas More, Sir Thomas Wyatt, Henry Howard, Sir Thomas Chaloner, Sir Thomas Smith, Sir Thomas Elyot, Bishop Stephen Gardiner, Sir Nicholas Bacon, Sir Philip Sidney, Richard Hooker, Robert Devereux, Sir Walter Raleigh, Sir Henry Savile, Sir Edwin Sandys, and Lord Egerton.

Later in *Timber* (ll. 2528–43), Jonson observes that the poet is the nearest borderer upon the orator, especially the comic poet, because he excells in the moving of men's minds and in the stirring of their affections: "What figure of a Body was *Lysippus* ever able to forme with his Graver, or *Apelles* to paint with his Pencill, as the Comedy to life expresseth so many, and various affections of the minde?"

Order. A symbolic character who appears in *Hymenaei* as the servant of Reason.

Orestes. The only son of Clytemnestra and Agamemnon and the brother of Electra and Iphigenia. After Clytemnestra and her lover Aegisthus killed Agamemnon, Orestes, who was still a boy, was sent to live in exile, but since he was the senior male in the house it was his duty to punish the murderer, and he was commanded by Apollo to avenge the crime. With the assistance of Electra and his friend Pylades he killed his mother and her lover. After this murder he was haunted by the Furies until he reached Athens, where he was tried and acquitted by the Areopagus, the tribunal of Athenian judges. But not all of the Furies accepted the verdict, and Orestes was commanded to steal the sacred image of Artemis from Tauris. With the assistance of Iphigenia he stole the image and safely returned to Greece. According to some accounts, he later married Hermione, the daughter of Menelaus and Helen.

Orestilla, Aurelia. In *Catiline*, Catiline's wife, for whom he murdered his former wife and son, who aids Catiline in his conspiracy by holding a meeting of the feminine auxiliary of conspirators.

Orgel, Stephen Kitay (1933–). American scholar educated at Columbia University and Harvard. He has taught at Harvard and the University of California at Berkeley, and since 1976 he has been Professor of English at Johns Hopkins University. He wrote *The Jonsonian Masque* (1965), one of the two major studies on the art of Jonson's masques, edited the Yale edition of the complete masques (1969), and has written and edited numerous other publications on Jonson and the Renaissance.

Orion. Boeotian hunter who violated Merope. Her father Oenopion blinded Orion, but his vision was restored by the rays of the sun. Several versions of Orion's death suggest that he was killed by Artemis.

Orithyia. The daughter of Erechtheus, a king of Athens.

Orpheus. The celebrated Thracian musician who was considered the son of Apollo. So beautifully did he play the lyre that his music was said to move rocks and trees and to calm wild animals. Orpheus married the nymph Eurydice. When she died Orpheus made an unsuccessful attempt to recover her body from Hades. In grief he became a recluse who wandered for many years. There are several versions of his death, some suggesting that he met a violent end. See also PRINCE.

Osbalston, Lambert, master of Westminster School, and later prebendary of the Chapter of Westminster, was one of those who made a grant from the Dean and Chapter of Westminster to Jonson in 1629 during his illness.

Ostler, William. An actor who played in *Poetaster* as a member of the Children of the Chapel. After he had joined the King's Men, he performed in *The Alchemist* and *Catiline*. He also acted in the plays of Webster, Fletcher, and Shakespeare. In 1611 he became the son-in-law of John Heminges and later became a housekeeper in the Globe and Blackfriars theaters. He died in 1614.

Otrera. Mother of Penthesilea, queen of the Amazons.

Otter, Mistress. Captain Otter's wife in *Epicoene*. She continually nags her husband about his manners and is very conscious of her own social position. She flies into a fit of anger when she overhears her drunken husband mocking her.

Otter, Thomas. A retired sea-captain in *Epicoene*, who names his drinking glasses the bear, the bull, the horse, the deer, and the ape. He is totally bullied by his socially conscious, foolish wife; he mocks her behind her back at Morose's house when he is drinking with Clerimont, Dauphine, Truewit, La-Foole, and Daw and comes to grief when she overhears his taunts. He masquerades as a parson, giving advice on divorce to Morose.

Overall, John. Dean of St. Paul's from 1602 to 1614, who was appointed as an adviser and counselor to Jonson when he was cited for recusancy in 1606.

Overbury, Sir Thomas (1581–1613), was knighted in 1608 and was made server to the King through the influence of Robert Carr, Earl of Somerset, but Carr and Overbury became enemies when Overbury advised Carr not to marry Lady Essex. In 1613 Overbury was lodged in the Tower, where he was poisoned at the instigation of Lady Essex in one of the sensational crimes of the day. Jonson addressed *Epig.* CXIII to Overbury, but according to the *Conversations* (l. 170), the two who were once friends later became enemies. Jonson also said (ll. 213–19) that he served as intermediary in Overbury's pursuit of Elizabeth Sidney, Countess of Rutland, daughter of Sir Philip Sidney, and that Overbury was represented as the character Mogibell in Jonson's lost pastoral *The May Lord* (l. 395). Overbury was the author of *The Wife*, published posthumously in 1614, which Jonson read in manuscript to the Countess of Rutland on Overbury's behalf (ll. 215–16). Overbury also wrote notable character sketches in the Theophrastian tradition.

Overdo, Adam. A justice of the peace in *Bartholomew Fair,* who thinks that he is wise and just and disguises himself so that he can go into the fair and search for corruption. He shows that he is foolish when he thinks that cutpurse Edgworth is a misguided young man and mistakenly signs his ward, Grace, away to Winwife. He throws off his disguise at the end of the play and roars about the corruption he has found, but he is silenced when Quarlous reveals how foolishly he has acted.

Overdo, Dame. Adam Overdo's wife in *Bartholomew Fair.* She pretends to wisdom and gravity at the beginning of the play, often quoting her husband but, once in the fair, shows her foolishness by getting very drunk and allowing Knockem and Captain Whit to persuade her to act like a prostitute.

Ovid (43 B.C.–A.D. 18). Publius Ovidius Naso studied law and held several minor offices, but his real interest was always in poetry, and he enjoyed early widespread fame as a poet. Ovid was known to Augustus, and his literary friends included Tibullus, Propertius, Gallus, and Aemelius Macer. Ovid married three times and had a daughter, Perilla, by his wife. In 8 A.D., for some unknown reason, Ovid was exiled from Rome to Tomis, where he died ten years later.

His works may be classified in three groups: erotic poems, mythological poems, and poems of exile. Most of his poems, which were written for pleasure, are in elegiacs. The love poems include *Amores,* forty-nine short poems, mostly lauding the charms of Corinna, the poet's mistress; *Epistulae heroidum,* imaginary letters by ancient heroines to their absent lovers; *Ars amatoria,* three books with complete instructions on how to get and keep a lover. The most important mythological poem, Ovid's masterpiece, is the *Metamorphoses,* a collection of myths cleverly woven together. The poems of exile include *Tristia* and *Epistulae ex Ponto.* Ovid has always been praised for his natural verse style, his wit, and his ability as a storyteller. He believed that his poetry would bring him immortality, and his belief has been justified. In the Middle Ages, he was a popular poet, often noted and alluded to by Chaucer and Gower; in the Renaissance no

Latin poet had a greater influence, and he is still influential today on contemporary poets.

Like Spenser, Marlowe, and Shakespeare, Jonson was very attracted to Ovid. The young Ovid is a central character in *Poetaster,* and he is frequently referred to or built upon in other plays such as *Every Man in* (II. v), *Volpone* (III. vii), *Epicoene* (III. iii), *Cynthia's Revels, The Alchemist* (I. ii), *Bartholomew Fair* (II. iv), *Tale of a Tub* (III. vii), and *The New Inn* (III. ii). Ovid's works served as an important source for a number of entertainments and masques: *King's Coronation Entertainment, Masques of Blackness* and *Beauty, Hymenaei, Haddington Masque, Masque of Queens,* and *Masque of Augurs.* In *Timber* (ll. 2425–27), Jonson alluded to Ovid's comment that there is a god within and we glow when he stirs us, and this inspiration comes from heaven.

Ovid, Marc (Ovid senior). Father to Ovid in *Poetaster.* He appears only in the first few scenes of the play, when he upbraids and mocks Ovid junior for preferring writing poetry to studying law. He rails at poetry and poets in general, saying that none ever succeeded in life, as evidenced by their lack of material goods. He threatens to disinherit Ovid junior if he does not dismiss poetry. He is flattered by Tucca, who wants to borrow money from him, and lends him six drachmas, even though he realizes that Tucca is a fool. Unlike some of the characters in *Poetaster,* he is not a caricature of one of Jonson's contemporaries.

Ovid, Publius. Young poet in *Poetaster.* Ovid loosely resembles the historical Ovid. He is more interested in writing poetry than in studying law; his father is angry at him and threatens to disinherit him if he neglects his studies. Ovid tries to become interested in law by putting it into verse but is distracted when Tibullus brings him a note from Julia, his mistress, whom he addresses in his poetry as Corinna. He goes to Albius' house with the others, and tries to comfort melancholy Propertius. He good-humoredly jokes with the others. He plays Jupiter at the masquerade, ordering and overseeing it. When Caesar breaks into the masquerade, he upbraids Ovid with the others, and banishes him from court. Ovid laments his banishment bitterly, then delights in a meeting with Julia, swearing to stay under her chamber window adoring her even though her father might disapprove.

Owen, John. Author of eleven books of epigrams issued in 1606, 1607, 1612, and

1613(?). As a collection, Owen's epigrams became very famous on the Continent. In the *Conversations* (ll. 223–25), Jonson said Owen was a pedantic schoolmaster who made his living off the posteriors of children and whose epigrams were merely narrations.

Owleglas. Also Howleglass. A strange-looking character who appears in the antimasque for *The Fortunate Isles, and Their Union.*

P

Pacheco de Narvaez, Luis. Referred to as Don Lewis in *The New Inn* (II. v), he was one of the great authorities on Spanish fencing. See LEWIS OF MADRID.

Pacue. A page to Gasper (really Camillo Ferneze) in *The Case Is Altered.* He swears to Camillo and Chamont that he will not reveal the secret of their exchanged identities, but they realize that he is foolish and not to be trusted. Onion mocks him when they joke together. Count Ferneze's decision to torture Camillo comes after Pacue slips and reveals the exchange of identities to one of the Count's daughters. Finio hires him to the drunken Juniper as a servant.

Page of Plymouth. A lost tragedy upon which Jonson collaborated with Thomas Dekker and others in 1599.

Page (to Paulo). A boy in *The Case Is Altered,* who fetches Angelo for Paulo, brings him the news that his father is looking for him, and delivers the message to his father that he is coming presently.

painting. In *Timber* (ll. 1522–40), Jonson, borrowing from Quintilian (*Instit. Orat.* XII. x), argues that whoever does not like painting is injurious to truth and all the wisdom of poetry because painting is the invention of heaven and most akin to nature. Painting so enters and penetrates the innermost affection that it often overcomes the power of speech and oratory. Noting that although there are diverse graces in painting, Jonson claims that some men so aspire to truth than they are rather lovers of likeness than beauty.

Later in *Timber* (ll. 1549–85), Jonson includes a short discourse on the progress of painting taken for the most part from Antonio Posseirno's *Bibliotheca Selecta Qua agitur De Ratione Studiorum* (Rome, 1593). He notes that painting took feigning from poetry, and from geometry she took rule, compass, lines, proportion, and symmetry. He cites Parrhasius in particular for his use of symmetry, and he observes that Eupompus gave painting "splendor by numbers." From optics painting took perspective, and from moral philosophy it took "soule, the expression of Senses, Perturbations, Manners." From the ancient plastic arts of moulding in clay came sculpture, and "Socrates taught *Parrhasius,* and *Clito* (two noble Statuaries) first to expresse manners by their looks in Imagery." Jonson mentions also the ancients Polygnotus, Aglaophon, and Zeuxis, who after Parrhasius was the law-giver to all painters. In conclusion Jonson notes that in this latter age there were several famous painters in Italy, who were excellent and emulated the ancients: Raphael de Urbino, Michael Angelo Buonarotti, Titian, Antony of Correggio, Sebastian of Venice, Julio Romano, and Andrea Sartorio (del Sarto). See also STYLE.

Palaemon. Greek equivalent to Portunus, a sea god whose function was to guard the ports. Palaemon appears as a sea god attendant upon Amphitrite in the triumph in *Love's Triumph through Callipolis.*

Palate, Parson. In *The Magnetic Lady,* the prelate of the parish who performs the various marriages in the play.

Pales. An Italian deity of shepherds.

Palladis Tamia. See Francis MERES.

Pallas. An epithet associated with Athena and Minerva. Pallas appears as a character in *The Golden Age Restored* and announces the return to earth of the golden age.

Palmer, Thomas, took his B.A. from Brasenose College in 1554 and his M.A. in 1557. He became Principal of Gloucester Hall in 1563 but was forced to resign the post the following year because of his Catholicism. In 1566 he was deprived of his fellowship at St. John's College, where he lectured on rhetoric. He withdrew to his estate in Essex but continued to be persecuted. A noted orator, he was applauded by William Camden. In 1598–99 Palmer wrote *The Sprite of Trees and Herbes,* a book containing 223 emblems on the subject of plant life. Jonson, who was a Catholic at the time, composed a prefatory poem for the volume, but the book was never published, and the poem is now included in Jonson's uncollected verse ("When late [grave Palmer] these thy graffs and flowers").

Palmerin of England. Anthony Munday's 1602 translation of the Portuguese Francisco de Moraes' *Palmerin de Inglaterra* (1544), alluded to in *Eastward Ho* (v. i) and mentioned with contempt in *Und.* LXIII.

palmistry. Form of divination in which significance about human destiny is discerned by studying the characteristics of the hand and palm. Palmistry is discussed in *The Alchemist* (I. iii; IV. ii) and is used by the gypsies in *The Gypsies Metamorphosed* to tell the fortunes of the nobility.

Paman, Clement. Paman was from Sidney Sussex College, Cambridge; was prebendary of St. Patrick's, Dublin, from 1661 to 1663; and Dean of Elphin from 1662 to 1664. He contributed a long elegy ("The grave is now a favorite, we see") to *Jonsonus Virbius.*

Pan. A pastoral god of fertility who was worshipped principally in Arcadia. He was thought to be the son of Hermes, Zeus, or some other god. Pan was portrayed as a merry, ugly man with the horns, ears, and legs of a goat. He was sometimes ill-tempered, and he liked to frighten unwary travellers. His myths deal with amorous affairs. In one of these myths he pursued the nymph Syrinx, but before he could capture her her sister nymphs changed her into a reed. Thus Pan plays the reed in memory of her and is credited with the invention of the shepherd's flute. Pan was supposed to make flocks fertile, and when he did not his image was flogged to stimulate them. Later when Pan was worshipped in other parts of Greece and Rome, he became associated with the Greek Dionysus and the Roman Faunus, both gods of fertility.

Panchia. An island east of Arabia which was often associated by ancient writers with China. Supposedly there was located on the island a temple which contained a large golden column on which were written the deeds of Uranus, Kronos, and Zeus.

Pancridge, Earldom of. One of the mock-titles of the Finsbury Archers, constituted by Henry VIII in 1539 into a fraternity of St. George. The Earl of Pancridge is mentioned in *A Tale of a Tub* (III. vi), *The Devil Is an Ass* (II. i), and one of Jonson's uncollected poems ("To Inigo Marquess Would-Be: A Corollary").

Pandora. A woman created by Hephaestus upon the command of Zeus who wanted to avenge himself upon Prometheus. The gods gave Pandora charm, curiosity, and deceit. She was given a box containing many evils and was warned never to open it. Though he had been warned never to accept a gift from Zeus, Epimetheus, the brother of Prometheus, received Pandora as a wife and was so charmed by her beauty that he permitted her to satisfy her curiosity about the contents of the box. Pandora opened it and out flew all the evils and sorrows that human beings have endured since. But last out of the box was hope, which has provided some solace for man.

Panegyre, A.
Performed: March 19, 1603.
Published: 1604 by Edward Blount in quarto together with *The King's Coronation Entertainment* and *The Entertainment at Althorp.*
Printer: Valentine Simmes.
This panegyric of 163 lines was written for King James on the occasion of his entrance to his first session of Parliament in 1603. Jonson drew only slightly upon the ancient panegyrics in honor of a Roman emperor, alluding specifically to the speech of the younger Pliny on the accession of Trajan in A.D. 98 and Claudian's verse tribute to Honorius in A.D. 406. In essence, Jonson's panegyric expresses the joy and good fortune of the kingdom in receiving their new king and counsels the new sovereign that kings rule more effectively by example rather than coercion and that subjects more easily obey when they are led rather than compelled.

Panisci. Pan's attendants who generally associate with satyrs and sylvans.

Panvinius, Onuphrius. Author of *Reipublicae Romanae Commentarii* (1588), one of Jonson's authorities on archaeology.

Pan's Anniversary.
Performed: June 19, 1620 (according to the folio).
Published: 1640 in folio by Thomas Walkley in the section of masques.
Printer: uncertain.
The subtitle of this masque, *The Shepherd's Holy-day,* the nymphs' strewing flowers at the opening of the work, and the performance date given in the folio suggest that this masque was probably performed on King James's birthday, June 19, but on that day in 1620 James was at Greenwich, and there is no independent record of a performance there or anywhere else.

The scene was Arcadia. Three nymphs entered strewing various flowers about and singing of the rites of Pan to be celebrated on this the shepherd's holiday with sports, dances, and delights. The nymphs were followed by an old shepherd with a censer and perfumes. He thanked the nymphs and asked them to continue their shower of flowers. To loud music, the scene opened, and in it the masquers (who were Arcadians) were discovered sitting around the Fountain of Light with the musicians dressed like the priests of Pan standing below them. Flourishing his sword, a fencer came forth and announced to the old shepherd that he had brought along certain bold boys of Boeotia who had come to challenge the Arcadians at their own sports and dancing on the shepherds' own holiday. The old shepherd pointed out to the fencer that the bravest spirits of Arcadia were currently gathered in consultation about the Fountain of Light to consider what honors they might bestow upon Pan's anniversary that would befit the music of his peace. Scorning their efforts, the fencer, in a series of long, bombastic speeches, lauded the various merits and talents of his boys: a tooth-drawer, who was the foreman of the group; Epam, the tinker; a juggler; a corn-cutter; a tender-box-man; a clock-keeper; an engineer; a tailor; and a clerk, who was a philosopher. Following their introduction, this group danced an antimasque. Afterwards the old shepherd reprimanded them for being presumptuous although delightful, and he banished them from the scene, summoned the Arcadians, and commanded them to dance in accord with the enlightened spirit of the fountain.

To a hymn in praise of Pan, the masquers descended and performed their first dance, followed by another laudatory hymn and the revels. Afterwards the fencer, now impressed, reentered with a company of gamesters who performed a second antimasque. When they had finished, the old shepherd condemned their stupidity manifested in a country which had an air too pure for gross brains and ordered them to return to Boeotia, where they truly belonged. A final hymn was offered to Pan, imploring his blessings of fruitfulness and prosperity. The old shepherd then proclaimed that all Arcadians should return to their charges and explained that they should not trust their flocks to hirelings for too long or too often, lest they and their flocks be deceived by them.

Pantalones. Old men, stock characters in the *commedia dell'arte*. In *The Vision of Delight,* they dance in the first antimasque with six Burratines. In *Volpone* (II. iii), Corvino accuses Celia of making him worthy of this name.

Parabosco, Girolamo. Italian poet, author of some verses which Jonson had apparently translated and was fond of reciting, according to the *Conversations* (l. 92).

Paracelsus (1493?–1541). Philippus Aureolus Paracelsus, whose real name was Theophrastus Bombastus von Hohenheim, was a Swiss physician and alchemist. He traveled widely and acquired considerable knowledge of alchemy, chemistry, and metallurgy. Although his egotism and contempt for accepted theories made him many enemies, he gained wide popularity, lectured and wrote extensively in German (not Latin), and greatly influenced his own and succeeding generations. He has always been a controversial figure. He was one of the first to combine medicine and chemistry. He opposed the humoral theory of disease as taught by Galen, advocated the use of specific remedies for specific diseases, introduced many chemicals into use as medicines, and made a number of astute medical observations, such as noting the hereditary pattern in syphilis. Paracelsus was a prolific writer, producing numerous medical and occult works. Although it tends to overlook his controversial side, Robert Browning's poem "Paracelsus" gives just recognition to his accomplishments.

Jonson frequently refers to Paracelsus. He is mentioned in *Volpone* (II. ii); Subtle is called an "excellent Paracelsian" in *The Alchemist* (II. iii); Epicoene laments that Paracelsus gives her no cure for Morose (IV. iv); Paracelsus serves as one of the sources for *The Masque of Queens,* and he is mentioned by his real name in *Mercury Vindicated.* He is also mentioned in connection with Mercury in *Epig.* CXXXIII.

Parasitaster, or The Fawn. See John MARSTON.

Parker, William. See William Parker, Baron MONTEAGLE.

Parnassus. 1. A mountain range in Phocis that was sacred to Apollo and the Muses.

2. In *Timber* (l. 2425), Jonson notes that when poets refer to Parnassus they refer to their poetic inspiration. Later in *Timber* (ll. 2488–91), he indicates that one cannot suddenly become a poet by dreaming he has been in Parnassus or has washed his lips in Helicon.

Parnel. In *A Tale of a Tub,* one of the bridesmaids for Awdrey's intended marriage to John Clay.

paronomasia. See CUSTOM.

Parrhasius. See PAINTING.

Parrot. A notorious informer alluded to in *Epig.* CI.

Parrot, Henry. Epigrammatist who published five collections of epigrams, some of which he had plagiarized: *The Mous-Trap* (1606), *Epigrams* (1608), *Laquei Ridiculosi* (1613), *The Mastive* (1615), and *Cures for the Itch* (1626). Jonson's *Epig.* LXXI is probably a criticism of Parrot, who had attacked Jonson in an epigram ("Put off thy Buskins [Sophocles the great]) in *Laqueri Ridiculosi* and in another one ("Magus would needs forsooth this other day") included in *The Mous-Trap.*

Partridge, Edward B. (1916–   ). American scholar educated at Columbia University. He has taught at several American colleges and universities, but since 1965 he has been Professor of English at Tulane University. He has written several studies on Jonson and has edited *Bartholomew Fair* and *Epicoene.* In 1958 he published his highly influential study *The Broken Compass: A Study of the Major Comedies of Ben Jonson.*

Pasfield, Zacharias. Prebendary of Newington in St. Paul's in 1604 who died in 1616. He was one of those designated as spiritual advisers to Jonson when he was cited for recusancy in 1606.

Pasiphaë. The wife of Minos who became enamoured of a bull and gave birth to the Minotaur.

pastoral. See *THE MAY LORD.*

Paterculus, Velleius. Retired Roman officer who became an amateur historian and wrote *Historiae Romanae* for his friend M. Vinicius when he assumed the consulship in A.D. 30. This work is a valuable source for the reigns of Augustus and Tiberius although Paterculus' admiration for his old chief Tiberius and even his ministers like Sejanus is sometimes unbounded. Jonson used this work as one of his sources for *Sejanus.*

Patrick. One of the Irish footmen who, speaking in an Anglo-Irish brogue, appears in *The Irish Masque at Court* and attempts to show his loyalty to the king.

Patrico. The hedge-priest of the gypsies who appears in *The Gypsies Metamorphosed.*

Paulina, Lollia. See LOLLIA Paulina.

Pausanias. Traveler and geographer of the second century who was probably born at Lydia and whose *Description of Greece* is an invaluable source for the topography, monuments, and legends of ancient Greece. Jonson used Pausanias as one of his sources for *The King's Entertainment in Passing to his Coronation, The Masque of Beauty, The Haddington Masque,* and *Neptune's Triumph.*

Pavy, Salomon. Boy actor in the Children of Queen Elizabeth's Chapel whose name appears in the actor-lists of *Cynthia's Revels* and *Poetaster.* In 1602, Pavy died in his thirteenth year, and Jonson commemorated his death in *Epig.* CXX.

Pawlet, Lady Jane. See Lady Jane Pawlet, Marchioness of WINCHESTER.

Payne, Robert. Divine and friend of Hobbes who may also have been chaplain to the Earl of Newcastle. In a letter (1634?) to the Earl, Jonson described Payne, who was in the Earl's employ, as "my right learned friend."

Peace. A symbolic character in *The Vision of Delight* who appears in the company of the Hours and offers a song about the amazing change to the pleasures of spring which has taken place in the masque. See also IRENE.

Peck. In *The New Inn,* the hostler.

Pecunia. In *The Staple of News,* the grand lady who is the ward of Richer Pennyboy and has many suitors but finally marries Pennyboy junior.

Peerson, Martin. See MUSICAL SETTINGS.

Pegasus. 1. A winged horse created from the blood of Medusa after she was beheaded by Perseus. With a slash of his hoof, he created Hippocrene, a spring sacred to the Muses. Pegasus assisted Bellerophon in killing the Chimaera.
    2. In *Timber* (l. 2425), Jonson notes that when poets refer to Pegasus they refer to their poetic inspiration.

Peira. A symbolic personage representing danger and appearing in a scene in Jonson's part of the *King's Coronation Entertainment.*

Pem. A character in *The King's Entertainment at Welbeck,* who is the daughter of Fitz-ale and is to be married to Stub.

Pembroke, Mary Sidney, Countess of. According to the *Conversations* (ll. 204–5), Sir Philip Sidney had translated some of the psalms which circulated under the name of the Countess, who died in 1621. An epitaph for her ("Underneath this sable Hearse") originally attributed to Jonson was probably written by William Browne of Tavistock.

Pembroke, William Herbert, Earl of (1580–1630). English courtier and patron of letters, son of Mary, Countess of Pembroke, and nephew of Sir Philip Sidney. Tutored by Samuel Daniel, William succeeded his father to become the 3rd Earl of Pembroke in 1601. He was a prominent figure at the courts of Elizabeth and James I. He was appointed privy councilor in 1611, furthered the exploration and colonization of America, and served as lord chamberlain of the royal household from 1615 to 1625 and lord steward from 1626 to 1630. While he was chancellor of Oxford, Pembroke College was named in his honor in 1624.

Pembroke was Jonson's patron, and he gave Jonson twenty pounds at the beginning of every new year to buy books. An extant letter also indicates that Jonson called upon the earl for help on other occasions. The earl was instrumental in getting the honorary degree from Oxford for Jonson in 1619. Jonson dedicated the *Epigrams* and *Catiline* to him and lauded him in *Epig.* CII and in *The Gypsies Metamorphosed.* Pembroke danced in *The Haddington Masque* and tilted at the Earl of Somerset's wedding in 1614. Shakespeare's First Folio was dedicated to William and his younger brother, the Earl of Montgomery.

In the *Conversations* (ll. 364–67), Jonson said that the Earl, when speaking with his wife, claimed that women were but men's shadows, but she denied it and asked Jonson to decide the issue. He agreed with the Earl, and she, as penance, told Jonson to prove it in verse—hence his epigram on the subject (*Forest* VII).

Pen (Penn), William. An actor who played in *Epicoene* as one of the Children of the Revels but later joined the Prince's Men.

Penates. Roman household gods, primarily guardians of the storeroom, that were worshipped in connection with the Lares and with Vesta. Household offerings were made to images of the Penates before each meal. The Penates were also public gods who protected the community and state.

Penelope. The daughter of Icarius, the wife of Odysseus, and the mother of Telemachus. In the *Odyssey,* she is portrayed as a chaste and faithful wife, who, while Odysseus was away, rejected the offers of many suitors who tried to persuade her

that Odysseus would never return. As a result of pressure from the suitors, she at last promised to marry the man who could bend the great bow of Odysseus, but none could do so except Odysseus, who had returned disguised as a beggar. With the aid of the bow, Odysseus slaughtered the suitors and revealed himself to Penelope. In another version of the legend, Penelope was unfaithful to Odysseus and was banished upon his return.

Pennyboy, Frank. In *The Staple of News,* the father of Pennyboy junior. When he first appears, he is disguised as an old canter but finally reveals himself to his prodigal son.

Pennyboy, Junior. The son and heir of Frank Pennyboy and the nephew of Richer Pennyboy and suitor to Pecunia in *The Staple of News,* who becomes a penitent prodigal and finally wins the hand of Lady Pecunia.

Pennyboy, Richer. The uncle of Pennyboy junior in *The Staple of News,* who is a usurer and the guardian of Lady Pecunia.

Pennyless Pilgrimage, The. See John TAYLOR.

Penthesilea. 1. Queen of the Amazons who led a troop of Amazons against the Greeks during the Trojan War. She was eventually killed by Achilles, who fell in love with her dead body.

2. Penthesilea is one of the queens in *The Masque of Queens.*

Pepys, Samuel. English diarist and public official born in 1633, who became secretary to his relative Sir Edward Montagu (later Earl of Sandwich) in 1660, the same year he became a clerk in the navy office. By 1668 he was one of the most important navy officials and owned a large estate. He was made secretary to the admiralty in 1672. In 1679 he sat in Parliament, but was charged with betraying naval secrets to the French, was imprisoned in the Tower, vindicated in 1680, and reappointed secretary to the admiralty and elected president of the Royal Society in 1684. At the accession of William III Pepys was forced into retirement, where he wrote his *Memoirs* (1690) of the royal navy. When he died in 1703 Pepys left his valuable library, including his diary in cipher, to his nephew and in turn to Magdalene College, Cambridge, from which he had graduated in 1653. Covering January 1, 1660 to May 31, 1669, when failing eyesight forced him to stop writing, Pepys's diary provides an intimate record of the daily life and reflections of an ambitious and observant man in London and gives a graphic picture of social life and conditions of the early Restoration.

Pepys records having seen several of Jonson's plays performed. In 1661 he saw *Bartholomew Fair* and thought it "admirable" but "prophane and abusive," and *Epicoene*, which he considered an "excellent play." In 1663 he saw *The Alchemist* with Walter Clun (who was murdered the next year) as Subtle and again in 1669, when he records missing Clun in the lead. Pepys also saw *Catiline* in 1669.

Peregrine. In *Volpone*, Peregrine is an English gentleman traveling in Venice. He quickly sees that Politic Would-Be is a very foolish man and baits him throughout the play. He joins with three merchants in embarassing Sir Politic and making him leave Venice.

Perfectio. A figure in *The Masque of Beauty*, one of the elements of beauty.

Perfumer. A tradesman called to take part in the courtship contest in *Cynthias's Revels*. He recommends scents, and lists their ingredients, to Amorphus and Mercury during their staged primping.

Perseus. The heroic son of Zeus and Danaë. With the aid of the gods Perseus was able to kill Medusa, one of the Gorgons, and gain possession of her head, which had the power to petrify anyone who looked directly at it. Using Medusa's head as a weapon, Perseus turned Atlas into a mountain and saved the maiden Andromeda, whom he later married. Perseus then rescued his mother from the tyrant Polydectes of Seriphos and killed him. While participating in a discus contest, Perseus accidentally killed his grandfather Acrisius, thus fulfilling an oracle's prophecy that Danaë would bear a son who would kill her father. Several versions of what eventually happened to Perseus exist. Perseus was the father of Electryon, who was the grandfather of Hercules.

Persius. (A.D. 34–62). Aulus Persius Flaccus was a Stoic satirist. He was also a wealthy Etruscan knight. He opposed Nero and satirized current literary tastes, vices, and follies. He was greatly admired in medieval times, but because of his obscurity, digressions, and forced imagery, he has been little admired since then. His works show, however, skillful use of sound and rhythm, powerful use of the vernacular, and a sympathetic view of the human condition. Donne admired him. In *Epicoene* (II. iii), Daw dismisses him as worthless

along with many other ancient writers. However, in the *Conversations* (ll. 140–41), Jonson mentions Persius as one of those ancient poets to be read for delight. Jonson gave his friend Sir John Roe a copy of Casaubon's *Persius*, and he cited Persius' satires as one of his sources for the *King's Coronation Entertainment*. Jonson also used a motto from Persius on the title page of *Timber* and quoted from him in the work (ll. 2312–13) and in *Bartholomew Fair* (IV. vi).

Peto (Roger Formal). Clerk to Dr. Clement (Justice Clement) in the 1601 quarto version of *Every Man in His Humour*. (Differing names and courses of action in the 1616 folio version are given here in parentheses). He offers to buy Musco (Brainworm) a drink in exchange for the story of his exploits as a soldier; Musco (Brainworm) makes him so drunk that he falls asleep, steals his clothes, and goes to work deceptions, leaving Peto (Formal) only a suit of armor in which to dress himself when he awakens. When he sheepishly comes to Clement at the end of the play, dressed in armor, after Musco's (Brainworm's) deceptions have been revealed, Clement jokes about his armor, then good-naturedly accepts him back, not embarrassing him any more.

Petrarch (1304–1374). Francesco Petrarca was born in Tuscany. He spent his youth there and in Avignon and Bologna. In 1326 he took lesser ecclesiastic orders and entered the service of Cardinal Colonna although he also traveled widely and wrote numerous lyrics, sonnets, and *canzoni*. The following year he met Laura, who inspired his great vernacular love lyrics. His verses became famous, and in 1341 he was made laureate at Rome. After the deaths of Colonna and Laura in 1348, he devoted himself to the struggle for Italian unification, argued for return of the papacy to Rome, and served the viscount of Milan. In his declining years Petrarch enjoyed great fame. After his death in 1374 his influence continued to spread, and he was recognized as one of the greatest of the humanists. He realized that Platonic thought and Greek studies could provide a new cultural framework, and he spread this Renaissance view through his writings and personal influence. He also contributed to the new learning by the discovery of Latin manuscripts and by his important epic *Africa*, which stressed the virtues of the Roman republic. Often considered the first modern poet, he perfected the sonnet form and developed a poetic style which became a model for Italian literature for three centuries. Although he also wrote in the vernacular, Petrarch took great pride in his Latin, which he had mastered as a living language, and in his Latin works. Early English translators of his sonnets and songs include Chaucer, Spenser, Surrey, and Wyatt. In the *Conversations* (ll. 60–63), Drummond notes that Jonson cursed Petrarch for redacting verses to sonnets. Lady Politic in *Volpone* (III. iv) describes Petrarch as passionate, and Laura is alluded to in *Und.* XXVII.

Petreius. In *Catiline,* the leader of the Roman forces against Catiline's army who vividly and poetically reports the defeat and death of Catiline.

Petronius Arbiter. Roman satirist who was probably the C. Petronius referred to by Tacitus as *arbiter elegantiae* in the court of Nero. Although a profligate lover of luxury, so accomplished was Petronius in elegance that he became director of Nero's entertainments. About A.D. 66, a rival for Nero's favor caused Petronius to be arrested. He ended his life by opening his veins, but made dying leisurely by engaging in festivity with his associates. His most important work known to us is his *Satyricon,* a romance interspersed with verse. Composed of several satires, this work gives a vivid picture of the life and manners of the period and provides important examples of the colloquial language. Petronius' Latin style is considered one of the best of its time, and in the *Conversations* (l. 138) Jonson praised his Latin and read his own translation (ll. 78–81) of a spurious Petronius epigram, which Jonson later published as *Und.* LXXXVIII. Petronius also served as one of the sources for *The Masque of Queens,* and Jonson was indebted to him for phrases and ideas in a number of his works. See also HORACE.

Phaëton, son of Helios the sun god and the nymph Clymene, tried to drive his father's golden chariot but could not control its horses. The horses broke from their course, and the earth began to blaze with fire, which created the Libyan Desert. The whole world would have been destroyed if Zeus had not killed Phaëton with a thunderbolt.

Phantasms. Symbolic characters who dance the second antimasque in *The Vision of Delight.*

Phantasos. Loosely associated with Phant'sie.

Phantaste. A foolish courtier in *Cynthia's Revels.* Cupid describes her as being vain and shallow, acting on her whims. She gossips with the other women about the male courtiers, saying that Amorphus is the finest. She devises the game in which each of the female courtiers tells what they would be if they could be anything, and says that she would choose either to be able to change her shape at will, or to be the darling of the court for a year. She directs the playing of the games of wit. She mocks Arete, and proudly says that she would not change places with Cynthia after drinking water from the fountain of self-love. She is present during the courtship contest and often comments during it. She is disguised and plays a noble character in the first masque but is unmasked and criticized by Cynthia, who sentences her to be punished by Crites. She weeps and marches with the other courtiers, leading them in the palinode (with Amorphus) by reciting the fopperies they forsake.

Phant'sie. One of the central symbolic characters in *The Vision of Delight,* who at the command of Night, creates a waking, fantastic dream and helps to change the pleasures of Spring to the graces of the court.

Phaon. A legendary ferryman in Lesbos who was made so handsome and charming by Aphrodite that Sappho fell desperately in love with him. When he rejected her, she threw herself from the Leucadian rock.

Philalethes. 1. A character in *Love's Welcome at Bolsover,* who delivers a long speech on love in praise of the King and Queen.

2. One of the pseudonyms of Ortensio Landi of Milan whose *Forcianae Quaestiones* (Naples, 1536) served as one of the sources for Jonson's portrait of Valasca in *The Masque of Queens.*

Philautia. A foolish courtier in *Cynthia's Revels,* called "Honor" by Hedon. Cupid acts as her page, and mocks her to Mercury for being very conceited. She gossips with the other female courtiers about the men, saying that, if she could be anything, she would choose to have the power of life and death over the other courtiers. She flirts with Hedon and plays the games of wit with the other courtiers. She greatly enjoys water from the fountain of self-love and mocks Arete, saying that she would not change places with even Cynthia. She is present at and comments on the courtship contest. She takes part in the first masque but is discovered and criticized by

Cynthia, who allows Crites to decide her punishment. She marches, weeps, and sings the palinode with the others.

Philip II. King of Spain. The son of Charles I of Spain, he became Philip II when his father abdicated in his favor in 1556, shortly before Elizabeth became Queen of England. Philip II was on the Spanish throne when the English defeated the Armada in 1588. According to the *Conversations* (ll. 346–47), Jonson told Drummond that Philip had special dispensation from the Pope to marry Queen Elizabeth.

Phillips, Augustine (d. 1605). An actor who, as a member of the Chamberlain's Company, played in *Every Man in His Humour, Every Man out of His Humour,* and *Sejanus.* In 1599 he became one of the original shareholders in the Globe Theatre, and he later performed in a number of Shakespeare's plays.

Philostratus. Flavius Philostratus, second century Greek Sophist, was born into a famous literary family in Lemnos. In later life he settled in Athens. Some of his works include *Life of Apollonius of Tyana* and *Lives of the Sophists.* Jonson was fond of him and used him as one of his sources for *The Masque of Beauty, Oberon, Pleasure Reconciled,* and *Gypsies Metamorphosed.* He also quoted from him in *Catiline* (II) and in *Timber* (ll. 1522–28). *For.* IX is based upon Jonson's gleanings from Philostratus.

Phlegethon. One of the infernal rivers in Hades.

Phlegra. The location in Macedonia where the battle between the gods and the giants was reputed to have taken place.

Phoebe. See DIANA.

Phoebus. A character in *Love Freed From Ignorance and Folly,* who is a sun god and who symbolizes King James.

Phoemonoë. 1. Sometimes considered to be the first prophetess of Apollo, the first one who sang in hexameter verse, and the first Phythian priestess.

2. A character who appears when summoned by Apollo in *The Masque of Augurs.*

Phoenixella. Daughter to Count Ferneze in *The Case Is Altered.* She is apparently gentle and mild, a "profest virgin," mourning for her mother long after her mother's death. Francisco woos her, but she gently protests her grief and lack of desire to engage in the "ceremonies" of courtship.

She is much taken with the prisoner Gasper and laments her father's decision to torture him when a fraud is discovered in the exchange of Chamont for Paulo. Phoenixella is surprised when Gasper is revealed to be her brother Camillo. At the end of the play, Maximilian hints that he will try to win her even though she does not seem to favor him.

Phosphorus. 1. The morning star sometimes represented as a youth bearing a torch.

2. A character who appears as the day star in *Oberon, The Fairy Prince* and announces the waning of the night and the dawning of the new day.

Phronesis. In *Cynthia's Revels,* a mute nymph, said to be very lovely and high-minded, who attends Cynthia.

Picklock. A lawyer and reporter of Westminster who appears in *The Staple of News* and attempts to defraud Frank Pennyboy and Pennyboy Junior of their estate.

Pie (Pye), Sir Robert (d. 1662). Treasurer's Remembrancer of the Exchequer and Clerk of the Warrants who owed his appointment to the Duke of Buckingham. He was honest, outspoken, and straightforward. He was knighted in 1621. He is mentioned in *Und.* LVII.

Piedmantle. In *The Staple of News,* a heraldet who is one of the unsuccessful suitors to the Lady Pecunia.

Pierce. In *The New Inn,* a drawer who is knighted by Colonel Tipto and styled Sir Pierce.

Pierio Valeriano. Author of *Hieroglyphica sive de Sacris Aegyptiorum Literis Commentarii* (Lyon, 1595), one of Jonson's sources and authorities for Greek and Roman symbols in *The Masques of Blackness* and *Beauty* and *The Masque of Queens.*

Piety. Pietas, Roman deity of loyalty.

Pigmies (Pygmies). 1. Dwarfs ridiculous in appearance who live in Africa, India, or Scythia, the Pigmies are discussed in Greek mythology in connection with their legendary battle against the cranes. Pigmies disguise themselves as rams or ride on rams and goats and battle the cranes to protect their fields or even attempt to destroy the eggs of the cranes.

2. Pygmies appear in the second antimasque in *Pleasure Reconciled to Virtue* and threaten to attack Hercules while he is asleep but flee when he awakens.

Pilgrims. A group of confused, deformed Pilgrims perform a perplexing dance which constitutes the second antimasque in *The Masque of Augurs.*

Pindarus (Pindar) (518?–438 B.C.) Celebrated Greek lyric poet. He was admired from early in his life for his music and poetry and honored for his devotion to traditional religion. He wrote in the Ionic dialect, and many of his works were set to music. Fragments of his *Hymns, Paeans, Processional Songs,* and *Dirges* and forty-four complete *Epinicia (Victory Odes)* are extant. In the seventeenth and eighteenth centuries, many poets attempted to imitate his famous odes. In *Poetaster* (v. iii), Virgil includes Pindarus in the list of poets Crispinus should read with a tutor in order to develop literary taste and discretion. In the *Conversations* (1. 141), Jonson told Drummond that Pindar should be read for delight, and he mentioned him in the "Ode to Himself" appended to *The New Inn,* in *News from the New World,* and in *Timber* (11. 362–64). Pindar was one of the sources for *Hymenaei,* and *Und.* LXX was the first attempt in English to imitate the tripartite structure of the Pindaric ode.

Pitfall. The servant of Lady Tailbush in *The Devil Is an Ass.*

Pizo (Thomas Cash). Servant to Thorello (Kitely) in the 1601 quarto version of *Every Man in His Humour.* (Differing names and courses of action in the 1616 folio version are given here in parentheses.) Thorello (Kitely) brags that Pizo is a completely trustworthy servant (Kitely says that he was a foundling he sponsored after he showed promise). He carries out business communications for his master and orders his affairs. Thorello (Kitely) begins to tell him an important secret but stops when he suddenly decides he does not trust Pizo (Cash), for no good reason. Pizo questions Cob when Cob rails against fast days, and pulls Cob away from a fight with Bobadilla. Thorello (Kitely) leaves Pizo in charge of Biancha (Dame Kitely) when he goes off on business; Pizo (Cash) is compelled to follow Biancha (Dame Kitely) when she rushes off to Cob's house at Prospero's (Wellbred's) suggestion to catch her husband in adultery. Thorello (Kitely) calls him a pimp when he finds Pizo (Cash) there and takes him, along with the others, before Dr. Clement (Justice Clement). He is sent to guard Bobadilla and Matheo (Matthew) in jail (in Clement's courtyard).

Placentia. In *The Magnetic Lady,* the woman who is thought to be the niece of Lady Loadstone but actually turns out to be the daughter of Polish.

Plancina. Munatia Plancina, wife of Cn. Calpurnius Piso, lived during Tiberius' reign. She was in Syria with her husband when Germanicus and Agrippina came there, and was a friend of Livia's. She quarreled with Agrippina, being domineering, and was accused by Agrippina of murder when Germanicus died in A.D. 19. She was pardoned, because of Livia's influence, when her husband was condemned in A.D. 20, but committed suicide when she was accused again in A.D. 33. In *Sejanus* (I. iii), she is mentioned as one of Eudemus' patients.

Plato (427?–?347 B.C.), was born of noble Greek parents. In 407 B.C. he became a pupil and friend of Socrates', but in 388 he left Athens and lived at the court of Dionysius the Elder, tyrant of Syracuse. When he returned to Athens, he founded the Academy, where he taught mathematics and philosophy until his death. Plato's work has been handed down to us in the form of dialogues and epistles. The early dialogues, which present Socrates in conversations that illustrate his main ideas, include *Apology,* the defense of Socrates; the *Meno,* concerned with the teaching of virtue; and the *Gorgias,* which discusses the absolute nature of right and wrong. That there is a rational relationship between the soul, the state, and the cosmos is the general theme of the great dialogues of Plato's middle years—the *Republic, Phaedo, Symposium, Thaetetus, Phaedrus, Timens,* and *Philebus.* Plato's theory of Ideas or Forms is discussed in the *Republic,* where it is illustrated by the famous cave analogy, and in the *Phaedo.* The path to the highest good—the supreme Idea in a world of flux—is shown in the *Symposium* as the ascent by true lovers to eternal beauty and in the *Phaedo* as the pilgrimage of the philosopher through death to the world of eternal truth. Many of the late dialogues are devoted to technical philosophical problems. The most important dialogues include *Parmenides* and the *Sophist.* Plato's last and most extensive work, the *Laws,* analyzes the nature of the state in practical terms. Since he touched upon almost every problem which has concerned subsequent philosophers, Plato's teachings have been among the most influential in Western thought and civilization.

The idealized world of the masques shows Jonson's general indebtedness to Plato, and *The New Inn* (III. ii) is also particularly dependent upon Platonic ideas. In

Timber (11. 1832–37), Jonson wrote that since Plato had to labor to learn, so must we. Some of Plato's works served as sources for *Masque of Queens, Love's Triumph,* and *Oberon.* Specific dialogues are often referred to, alluded to, or quoted from: *Apology* in *Timber* (11. 849–51); *Cratylus* in *Haddington Masque; Gorgias* in *For.* x; *Phaedrus* in *Timber* (11. 2416–17); *Republic* in *Timber* (11. 2638–40); and *Symposium* in *The New Inn* (III. ii) and *Oberon.*

Platt, Sir Hugh. Author of a standard work on cosmetics entitled *Delights for Ladies to Adorn Their Persons* (1602). Platt is referred to in this connection in *Und.* XXXIV.

Plautia. A noblewoman, Tibullus' love, in *Poetaster.* She attends the "slight banquet" at Albius' house, and has little to say. She plays Ceres at Ovid's masquerade, where she has a minor role. She is upbraided along with the others when Caesar breaks in.

Plautus (254?–184 B.C.). Titus Maccius Plautus, Roman comic poet. Adapted from Greek New Comedy, Plautus' comedies provide vigorous representations of middle- and lower-class life. Written in masterful idiomatic Latin and governed by ingenuity of situation and by coarse humor, his plays were very popular in his day, and his works have greatly influenced later literature with imitations and adaptations by many writers of a number of his twenty-one extant works. Characteristic of his plays are the stock comic figures which have often been imitated—the knavish, resourceful slave; the young lover and his mistress; the courtesan; the grouchy, avaricious father; the parasite; and the braggart soldier.

Jonson was heavily indebted to Plautus for comic characters and situations. In the *Conversations* (11. 420–23), he told Drummond that he had intended to imitate Plautus' *Amphitryo,* but had given up the idea, and he mentioned the same play at the end of *Every Man out.* Several of Plautus' works served as sources for parts of Jonson's plays: *Aulularice* for *The Case Is Altered* and *The Staple of News* (II. iii); *Captivi* for *The Case Is Altered; Casina* for *Epicoene;* and *Mostellaria* for *The Alchemist. Aulularia* is alluded to in *The Magnetic Lady* (II. vi, Chorus II) and *Miles Gloriosus* in the same play (II. vii, Chorus). *Cistellaria* is mentioned in *Every Man out* (III. viii) and *Trinummus* is quoted from in *Timber* (11. 397–404). Also in *Timber* Jonson gives judgments on Plautus by Lucius Aelius

Stilo (11. 2550–51), Varro (11. 2552–54), and Horace (11. 2602–18).

play. In *Timber* (11. 1093–1109), Jonson records: "I *have* considered, our whole life is like a *Play:* wherein every man, forgetfull of himselfe, is in travaile with expression of another." He further notes that we so insist on imitating others that we cannot return to ourselves when it is necessary. Continuing the analogy, Jonson argues that "Good *men* are the Stars, the Planets of the ages wherein they live, and illustrate the times," and he notes that God has always allowed good men to exemplify the ideal, as, for example, Abel, who illustrated innocence; Enoch, purity; Noah, trust in God's mercy; and Abraham, faith. These men, "plac'd high on the top of all vertue, look'd downe on the Stage of the world, and contemned the Play of *Fortune.* For though the most be Players, some must be *Spectators.*"

Pleasance. In *The Magnetic Lady,* the waiting woman to the magnetic lady who actually turns out to be her legitimate niece.

Pleasant Notes Upon Don Quixot. See Edmund GAYTON.

Pleasure. A symbolic character who does not speak but appears sitting with Virtue at the foot of Atlas in *Pleasure Reconciled to Virtue.*

Pleasure Reconciled to Virtue.
Performed: January 6, 1618.
Published: 1640 in folio by Thomas Walkley in the section of masques.
Printer: uncertain.

Although Prince Charles made his first appearance as a masquer in this work, the masque as a whole was generally considered a disappointment, if not a complete failure. A few weeks after the initial presentation the masque was performed again with a new elaborated antimasque entitled *For the Honor of Wales,* but the audience response was about the same. Milton read the original version, and his own *Comus* reflects the influence of Jonson's masque.

The scene was a mountain which was discovered to be Atlas. The top of the mountain was in the figure of an old man, and a grove of ivy was at his feet. To wild music, out of the grove was brought forth in triumph Comus, the god of cheer and the belly. His head was crowned with roses, and those who waited upon him were crowned with ivy. One of those in the company of Comus was carrying the bowl of Hercules. As Comus approached, a song was offered, lauding the god of the bowl bearer, who delivered a long speech extolling the pleasure of the belly, after which the first antimasque of dancing wine bottles was performed.

Hercules entered, condemned the participants as monsters of vice, and commanded that the grove disappear, which it did. In its place appeared the musicians, sitting at the foot of the mountain with Pleasure and Virtue seated above them. In song the choir invited Hercules to rest at the foot of the mountain from his labors in support of virtue, and they called for a crown to be prepared for his head. After Hercules had lain down, the second antimasque of pygmies appeared, and they intended to attack Hercules while he slept, but because of the noise caused by their dancing he awoke, and the pygmies all ran into holes to hide. Mercury then descended from the hills with a garland of poplar with which to crown Hercules and delivered a long speech, praising Hercules as the active friend of virtue who had most recently defaced the voluptuous Comus and his followers and whom Atlas now wished to show that the time had arrived when there should be a cessation of conflict between Pleasure and Virtue to be effected on this very night by the presence of Hesperus, the glory of the West. Pleasure being reconciled to Virtue, Virtue herself would bring forth on this night twelve princes who had been reared on the rough mountain near the head of Atlas, one of whom was of the bright rose of Hesperus. Virtue had now entrusted these princes with pleasure, and she had no fear that "they should grow soft, or wax effeminat here, / Since in hir sight, and by hir charge all's don, / *Pleasure* ye servant, *Vertue* looking on."

To the accompaniment of music and song, the twelve princes came forth as the masquers from the lap of the mountain, all preceded by Daedalus. Hercules enquired of Mercury who the leader of the procession was, and Mercury informed him that the leader was Daedalus the wise who would show the masquers how they might prove any labyrinth even though it was of love. While the masquers assembled, Daedalus offered a song, exhorting the masquers to dance with such subtlety that no one would be able to tell which lives were pleasures and which were not, "for Dauncing is an exercise / not only shews ye movers wit, / but maketh ye beholder wise, / as he hath powre to rise to it." There followed several other songs by Daedalus

and dances by the masquers, as they all moved through the labyrinths of beauty and love and concluded with a dance with the ladies of the audience, followed by the revels. The final song celebrating the brief sporting with pleasure which had taken place was provided by Mercury, who ended his song in praise of the rewards and glories of rigorous virtue. The masquers performed their final dance and returned to the scene from which they had entered. The scene closed and was again seen to be the same mountain discovered at the beginning of the masque.

Pleiades. The seven daughters of Atlas and the nymph Pleione, who were the attendants of Artemis and were transformed into stars by the gods when they were pursued by Orion. The names of the Pleiades were: Maia, Merope, Electra, Celaeno, Taygeta, Sterope (or Asterope), and Alcyone.

Pliant, Dame. A beautiful, rich, extremely foolish young widow who is jealously guarded by her brother Kastril, in *The Alchemist*. When he goes to Subtle for quarreling lessons, he brings her along; Subtle and Face each plot to win her. They mock the disguised Surly by allowing him to court her. When Surly reveals his identity, she is confused and says that she will consider marrying him. She is guarded by Dol until Lovewit's return, and she is quickly persuaded to marry the master of the house.

Pliny the Elder (A.D. 23?–79). Caius Plinius Secondus was a Roman naturalist who was a friend and fellow soldier of Vespasian's. He died of asphyxiation on Vesuvius, having gone to investigate the eruption. His only extant work is an encyclopedia of natural science, *Historia naturalis,* dedicated to Titus. The work deals with the nature of the physical universe, geography, anthropology, zoology, botany, medical uses of plants, animal curatives, and mineralogy, including an account of the uses of pigments and a history of fine arts.

In *Epicoene* (IV. iv), Epicoene asks Daw if Pliny mentions any cure for Morose's malady, and in the *Conversations* (ll. 433–34), Jonson said that when anyone drank on him he cited Pliny that he had been called *ad prandium non ad poenam et notam.* Pliny is also cited on painting in *Timber* (ll. 1543–48; 1567–71), and he served as one of Jonson's sources for the *King's Coronation Entertainment, The Masque of Blackness, The Masque of Beauty, Hymenaei,* and *The Masque of Queens.*

Pliny the Younger (A.D. 62?–?113). Caius Plinius Caecilius Secondus, nephew and ward of Pliny the Elder, orator and statesman, was quaestor in 89, tribune in 91, praetor in 93, and consul in 100. His fame rests on his letters, which were probably written for publication. These provide a good picture of Roman life and are written in good Latin. According to the *Conversations*, Jonson said Pliny's Latin was excellent (l. 138) and that Drummond should read his epistles (ll. 12–14), and he expressed considerable interest in one of his epistles in particular (ll. 624–26). The *Epistles* are mentioned in *Every Man in* (1601 quarto, II. iii; 1616 folio, III. i) and in *Timber* (ll. 1542–48) and served as sources for *King's Coronation Entertainment* and *Masque of Blackness.* Several of Jonson's epigrams are indebted to the *Epistles,* and Pliny's *Panegyricus* was one of the models for *A Panegyre.*

Plowden, Edmund (1518–1585). Eminent English jurist. His chief work, *Les Commentaries,* was first published in 1571. He is mentioned by Fungoso in *Every Man out* (II. iii, Grex).

Plume, Thomas (1630–1704). Archdeacon of Rochester at the time of his death. He founded the Plumean professorship of astronomy at Cambridge. At his death he left several notebooks of contemporary gossip, including notes on Jonson's life that are generally considered unreliable.

Plutarch (A.D. 46?–?120). Greek essayist and biographer. He traveled in Egypt and in Italy, where he lectured on philosophy in Rome and in Athens. He eventually returned to his native Boeotia, where he served as a priest at the temple of Delphi for the last thirty years of his life. His greatest work is *The Parallel Lives,* biographies arranged in pairs comparing one Greek life with one Roman one. The English translation of this work by Sir Thomas North had a significant effect upon English literature, providing, for example, the material for Shakespeare's *Coriolanus, Julius Caesar, Antony and Cleopatra,* and *Timon of Athens.* Although his facts were not always accurate, Plutarch was a peerless biographer and a reasonable critic of culture and character. Since his primary purpose was to portray character and to analyze its moral implications, his biographical technique included the use of considerable anecdotal material. Also of in-terest are his *Morals,* essays and dialogues on ethical, literary, and historical subjects. Plutarch's frequent quotations from the old dramatists are often the only records we have of those works.

Plutarch is mentioned several times in *Epicoene* (I. i; II. iii; IV. iv). *The Lives* is referred to in *The Devil Is an Ass* (III. ii) and was a source for *The Masque of Blackness* and *Catiline* (V). The *Morals* is alluded to in *Timber* (ll. 113–15; 364–69; 1510–12), *Catiline* (III), and *Und.* XIII. *Quaestiones Romanae* was one of the sources for *Hymenaei.*

Plutarchus. The son of Thomas Gilthead, the goldsmith, in *The Devil is an Ass.*

Pluto. Son of Cronus and Rhea, who was the god of the underworld. After the fall of the Titans, Pluto and his brothers divided the universe, and Pluto received everything underground. With Persephone as his queen, Pluto ruled over Hades. He was also identified as a god of the earth's fertility.

Plutus. 1. Son of Demeter and Iasion. Originally associated with the abundance of crops, Plutus came to be the god of wealth.

2. A symbolic personage representing wealth and appearing in a scene in Jonson's part of the *King's Coronation Entertainment.*

3. The god of wealth appears disguised as Cupid in *Love Restored* and declares that there will be no more masqueing at court because it is an idle and expensive custom of no significance.

Po. Another name for Eridanus, a mythical amber river.

Pocahontas, Princess, of Virginia (1595?–1617). The daughter of the American Indian chief Powhatan, Pocahontas used to visit the English settlers at Jamestown, where she may have saved the life of Captain John Smith, who later wrote about her in his *The General History of Virginia* (1624). In 1613 she was captured by Captain Samuel Argall, taken to Jamestown, and held as a hostage for English prisoners in the hands of Powhatan. While at Jamestown, she converted to Christianity and was baptized as Rebecca. A settler named John Rolfe fell in love with her; and with the permission of her father and the governor they were married in 1614. Their union brought peace with the Indians for eight years. With several other Indians and her husband, Pocahontas visited England in 1616. She was received as a princess and presented to the king and queen. She attended Jonson's *Vision of Delight*. When preparing to return to Virginia in 1617, she became ill and died at Gravesend, where she was buried. Her only son Thomas Rolfe was educated in England, went to Virginia in 1640, and became wealthy. She is discussed in *The Staple of News* (II. v).

Pocher. A beadle in *Bartholomew Fair*, who speaks with the watch when they have Busy in the stocks.

Pod, Captain. A well-known puppet master mentioned in *Every Man out* (IV. v), *Bartholomew Fair* (v. i), and *Epig.* XCVII.

Podalirius. One of the skilled physician sons of Aesculapius.

poem. In *Timber* (ll. 2356–73), Jonson notes that a poem is not necessarily a whole work in many verses, but sometimes a single verse makes a perfect poem or, another word for poem, carmen. He cites examples from Virgil (*Aeneid*, III), Martial (*Epig.* VII), Horace (*Odes*), and Lucretius, and further indicates that the ancient oracles were called *Carmina* and that whatever sentence, howsoever long, was called an epic, lyric, elegiac, or epigrammatic poem. At the end of *Timber* (ll. 2816–20), Jonson includes a random note echoing one of Martial's epigrams about admiring a poem that does not flow smoothly but hobbles along. See also POESY; POEMS ASCRIBED TO JONSON.

poems ascribed to Jonson. None in the following list is likely to be the authentic work of Jonson, and the poems are not usually included in his canon, but all of them have been attributed to him at one time or another.

1. "A Highway Robbery" was first published in Captain Charles Johnson's "The Life of William Tracey" in *A General History of the Lives and Adventures of the Most Famous Highwaymen, Murderers, Street Robbers, etc.* (1734).

2. "Another [Epigram] on the Birth of the Prince," which celebrates the birth of Charles I, does not appear in the 1616 folio of Jonson's *Works*.

3. "An Impromptu to Sir William Noye," according to Plume, was composed by Jonson for Noye when Noye was at his commencement dinner for the degree of sergeant at law.

4. "An Oracle of Heliodorus" was first published in Willis's *Current Notes September*, vol. 1 (1851), by an unidentified "A.F.W." who claimed that he had a copy

of Underdowne's translation of Heliodorus on the title page of which was Jonson's autograph and this poem.

5. "A Parallel of the Prince to the King" was probably written by Thomas Freeman, since this poem is the fourth of a set of eight odes on the birth of Prince Charles entitled *Carmina illustrissimi Principis Caroli nativitatem celebrantia*, ascribed to Freeman.

6. "A Petition of the Infant Prince Charles" was probably not written by Jonson since it sharply contrasts with the official poems in which Jonson celebrated Charles' birth.

7. "Epitaph on an Honest Lawyer" was first published in *The Life and Errors of John Dutton* (1705).

8. "Epitaph on Michael Drayton" appears on Drayton's monument in Westminster Abbey and was probably written by Francis Quarles, Drayton's close friend.

9. "Epitaph on Prince Henry," first published in William Camden's *Remaines, Concerning Britain* (1614), was probably not written by Jonson since there are a number of manuscript copies of the poem, all of them anonymous.

10. "Epigram on Richard Burbage" was first printed in H.J.C. Grierson's *The Poems of John Donne* (1633).

11. "Horace, Odes II.iii," first published in John Ashmore's *Certain Selected Odes of Horace, Englished* (1621), probably not by Jonson since it is completely at variance with Jonson's theory and practice of translation.

12. "Master Jonson's Answer to Master Withers," first published in *A Description of Love* (1625), was probably written by Richard Johnson.

13. "On My Friend and Adopted Son, Mr. Thomas Jordan," first published in Jordan's *Poeticall Varieties* (1637), is probably not by Jonson since Jordan has never been considered one of the sons of Ben.

14. "On the Birthday of Prince Charles" was probably written by Thomas Freeman since this poem was the first of a set of eight odes on Charles entitled *Carmina illustrissimi Principis Caroli nativitatem celebrantia*, ascribed to Freeman.

15. "On the Countess Dowager of Pembroke" was written by William Browne of Tavistock and was first printed anonymously in the third edition of Camden's *Remaines, Concerning Britain* (1623).

16. "On the Family Vault of Lord Zouch at Harringworth" was first published in John Bridges's *The History of Northamptonshire* (1791).

17. "On the Good Wives Ale" was first printed anonymously in *Wits Recreations* (1641) and was probably written by Thomas Randolf.

18. "On the Steeple of St. Mary's Church, Newcastle" was first published in W. Gray's *Chorographia* (1649).

19. "Scorn, or some humbler fate" is an ode in manuscript, first ascribed to Johnson by W.D. Briggs.

20. "The Crown Inn at Basingstoke" was first published in *The Merry-Thought* (c. 1730).

21. "The Half-Moon Tavern in Aldersgate Street" was first printed in William Winstanley's *The Lives of the Most Famous English Poets* (1687).

22. "To Lord Bacon" is a poem in manuscript which offers pious advice to Bacon on the day (May 3, 1621) he was sentenced for his crimes and is probably not by Jonson since it is inconsistent with the attitude Jonson expressed toward Bacon in *Timber* (ll. 943–45).

poesy. 1. A symbolic character who appears in *Chloridia* and supports the efforts of Fame to immortalize great actions.

2. In *Timber* (ll. 2375–2400), Jonson, drawing in part upon Johannes Buchler of Gladbach (*Reformata Poeseos Institutio, ex R. P. Iacobi Pontani potissimum libris concinnata*, 1633), distinguishes between a poem and poesy. The poem is the work of the poet. Poesy is the skill of the poet or the craft of making. The poem is the thing done, the doing is poesy, and the doer is the poet. Jonson contends that poesy is the queen of arts because, according to Aristotle, the study of poesy offers mankind a certain rule and pattern of living well and happily and disposes men to all civil offices of society. Moreover, according to Cicero, poesy nourishes and instructs our youth, delights our age, adorns our prosperity, comforts our adversity, entertains us at home, keeps us company abroad, watches, divides the times of our work and sport, shares in our country recesses and recreations, and is the absolute mistress of manners and nearest of kin to virtue. Whereas philosophy is said to be a rigid and austere poesy, so poesy is a sweet and gentle philosophy which leads and guides us by the hand to action with ravishing delight and incredible sweetness.

poet. 1. An unnamed poet appears as a character in *Neptune's Triumph for the Return of Albion*, engages in a long discussion with a Cook about the art of poetry, and presents the masque which he has devised for the evening.

2. In *Timber* (ll. 1020–45), while discussing the malignity of the learned, Jonson, drawing in part on Quintilian (i, prooem. 9–14), notes that "I could never thinke the study of *Wisdome* confin'd only to the Philosopher: or of *Piety* to the *Divine:* or of *State* to the *Politicke.* But that he which can faine a *Common-wealth* (which is the *Poet*) can governe it with *Counsels,* strengthen it with *Lawes,* correct it with *Iudgements,* informe it with *Religion,* and *Morals;* is all these. Wee doe not require in him meere *Elocution;* or an excellent faculty in verse; but the exact knowledge of all vertues, and their contraries: with ability to render the one lov'd, the other hated, by his proper embattaling them."

Later (ll. 1873–76), echoing Quintilian, Jonson observes that the reason a poet should have all knowledges is that he should not be ignorant of many, especially those he will handle.

And in ll. 2347–55, Jonson includes a definition of the poet, explaining that the poet is a maker or feigner, and that his art is that of imitation in which he expresses the life of man in fit measure, numbers, and harmony. A true poet is not merely a versifier, but one who feigns and forms a fable and writes things like the truth.

In a long discourse (ll. 2400–2618), Jonson expounds on the qualifications of the genuine poet, noting at the outset that the poet should proceed through the disciplines of grammar, logic, rhetoric, and ethics. The first requirement of the poet is that he possess natural wit, or that he be able to "powre out the treasure of his minde." Second, he must exercise or be willing to write and rewrite until his wit and ability arrive at the dignity of the ancients. The third requirement is imitation or the ability to convert the substance or riches of another poet to his own use. The fourth is "an exactnesse of Studie, and multiplicity of reading, which maketh a full man, not alone enabling him to know the *History,* or Argument of a *Poeme,* and to report it: but so to master the matter, and Stile, as to shew, hee knowes, how to handle, place, or dispose of either, with *elegancie,* when need shall be." And finally, to nature, exercise, imitation, and study must be added art, which can lead the poet to perfection. See also ORATORS.

Poetaster, or the Arraignment.

Acted: 1601 at the Blackfriars by the Children of the Chapel.

Published: 1602 in quarto by Matthew Lownes.

Printer: unknown.

Dedication. To Richard Martin. Jonson praises him for being virtuous, and expresses scorn for the men who have tried to ruin his good name. He expresses his gratitude to Martin for standing by him.

Prologue. After the second sounding, Envy enters and speaks of her malice toward Jonson's play. She says that she wants to ruin the audience's enjoyment of it but is foiled when she learns that the scene is Rome. When no kindred spirits rise to share her bitterness, she sinks, and after the third sounding an armed character (Prologue) enters and explains his armament by saying that this is a dangerous age when playwrights slander each other publicly. He charges the audience to judge the play fairly and objectively, saying that Jonson's mind is "above [the] injuries" of his detractors.

Act. I. Ovid is composing poetry when Luscus, the servant of Ovid senior, enters and begs him to forsake poetry and return to studying law, as his father wishes. Although warned that his father is coming, Ovid continues reading his poetry aloud. Ovid senior enters, mocks him, and derides poets, playwrights and actors. Tucca, a military captain, and Lupus, a magistrate, enter and second Ovid senior's opinions. They contend that no poet has become rich; therefore no poet has been successful. Ovid goes off to study law; Tucca, who reveals that he habitually borrows money, borrows six drachmas from Ovid senior. Pyrgus, one of Tucca's pages, mocks Tucca's foolishness. Ovid senior threatens to disinherit Ovid if he continues working on poetry to the exclusion of law. Tibullus, a young gallant who is a friend of Ovid's, comes to bring Ovid news from Julia, Caesar's daughter, and finds that Ovid has been putting law into verse. On hearing from Julia, Ovid vows to desert law for love and poetry.

Act II. Albius, a jeweller, eagerly welcomes Crispinus, a self-important gentleman who writes poetry, to his house. Crispinus has come to visit his cousin Cytheris. Albius is very excited that courtiers are coming to his house, and his fussiness irritates his wife, Chloe, who reveals that she only married Albius because she thought she could rule him. He seems henpecked, and she openly flirts with Crispinus, who expresses pride in his aristocratic background. Crispinus teaches Chloe the foolish fashion of deriding visitors before they arrive; he thinks Albius a fool for not understanding it. The courtiers Cornelius Gallus, Ovid, Tibullus, Propertius, Julia,

Plautia (the lover of Tibullus), and Hermogenes arrive. Julia and Plautia compliment Chloe and greet Cytheris warmly. Ovid expresses concern for Propertius, who is still mourning for his dead love, Cynthia, and has no taste for mirth. Chloe is impressed with the poets; Crispinus vows to become one to please her. Hermogenes is entreated to sing but does not until Crispinus proudly sings and is praised. Crispinus goes off to find a poet's outfit as the courtiers go in to eat.

Act III. Crispinus meets Horace and, since he is eager to be a poet, forces himself on him. He brags and speaks affectatiously; Horace soon realizes that he is a fool and makes up several excuses to try to escape, but Crispinus sticks persistently with him. Crispinus says that he will soon force himself on Mecaenas, too. Aristius, Horace's friend, comes in, and seeing that Horace is trapped, teasingly goes off, leaving him with Crispinus. Minos, an apothecary to whom Crispinus owes money, brings in the Lictors to arrest Crispinus; Horace finally sneaks away, thanking Apollo. The Lictors are about to drag Crispinus away when Tucca enters with his pages, and takes a fancy to Crispinus because he is a nobleman. The changeable, whimsical Tucca alternately berates and flatters Minos and the Lictors until Minos agrees to free Crispinus, and Tucca reconciles them. Histrio, an actor, passes without saluting; Tucca calls him over to berate him. Pyrgus mocks Tucca. Histrio invites Tucca to dinner, and Tucca introduces him to Crispinus. Tucca even persuades Minos to give Crispinus more money. Tucca discusses plays with Histrio, expressing his anger at the profane satires and his longing for a purely entertaining bawdy comedy. The two pages, the Pyrgi, enact passages from several plays; all are impressed, and Histrio asks to borrow them for his theater, but is denied. Demetrius is introduced as a vengeful "dresser of plays," who has been hired to write a play abusing Horace. Horace complains to Trebatius, a jurist and friend of Caesar's, that he has made many enemies since he began to write satire; Trebatius urges him to give it up and write safer verse, such as praise to Caesar. Horace insists, however, that his driving inspiration and the corruption of the times will make him continue to write satires.

Act IV. At Albius' house Cytheris reassures Chloe that she is well dressed for court and will be well received there; she tells Chloe about fashionable manners at court. Gallus, who loves Cytheris, and

Tibullus come to invite them to Ovid's masquerade at court, in which all the courtiers will play the part of gods. Tibullus tells them the part each courtier will play and assigns Chloe to be Venus. Against Chloe's wishes Albius is invited and assigned to play Vulcan. Horace enters and tells them that Propertius, in his grief, has locked himself in Cynthia's tomb. Crispinus and Albius enter; Horace flees. Tucca warmly greets Albius and flirts with Chloe. Crispinus plays and sings a song he claims to have written; several people, including Tucca, praise him; Tibullus reveals disgustedly that he plagiarized the whole song from Horace. Tucca, Demetrius, and Crispinus bitterly mock Horace; they plan to discredit him. Tibullus and Gallus mock them and lead the ladies to the masquerade. Histrio comes to Lupus and the Lictors and tells them that the masqueraders borrowed properties which seemed to predict treason. They rush off to deal with the "treason."

At court Ovid, the courtiers and poets, and Tucca masquerade as gods; Gallus gives a courtly speech welcoming them, and Crispinus echoes him. Chloe flirts with Tucca and Ovid, and all enjoy playing their parts. Ovid and Julia have a mock quarrel, and Crispinus and Hermogenes sing. Caesar breaks in and is shocked and horrified at the "impious sight"; he threatens to kill his daughter for associating with such low characters. He angrily questions the masqueraders, banishes Ovid, and locks his daughter away. Horace and Mecaenas try to persuade him to be merciful but cannot. Tucca sneaks away but comes back and marvels at what has happened. Horace expresses his anger at Lupus' sensational charges. Ovid enters and soliloquizes on his sorrow over his lost love; Julia comes to a window above him, and they speak of their love and sorrow.

Act. V. Caesar reinstates Tibullus and Gallus in his favor because they are "gentlemen." He says that he values and reverences true poetry; Horace, Tibullus, Gallus, and Mecaenas praise him. A servant brings the news that Virgil is at hand; they all speak well of him. Virgil enters; he and Caesar speak gracefully to each other. Virgil sits in Caesar's chair at Caesar's insistence and reads a section of the *Aeneid* which he has just completed, which all have been eagerly awaiting. Tucca, Lupus, Crispinus, and Demetrius force themselves into the room, noisily interrupting Virgil's reading and accusing Horace of plotting treason. Horace reveals that Lupus grossly misread the meaning of the emblem he

thought was treasonous. Caesar has them bring in Histrio as a witness; Caesar sends him out to be whipped without even questioning him. Lupus is fitted with a pair of ass's ears, and Virgil praises Caesar for his tact and wisdom. Tucca sees how opinion is going and quickly begins to court favor with Mecaenas. Caesar appoints the true poets as judges of Crispinus and Demetrius in a trial. Tibullus reads the accusation, and Tucca tells them how to plead. Tucca manages to maneuver himself onto the jury; Virgil administers the oath. Samples of each of their poetry is read; Tucca praises them, but quickly changes his mind when Horace speaks out against them. Caesar sends for a "case of vizards" to put on Tucca. Crispinus and Demetrius are declared guilty, Tucca is fitted with the masks, and Horace forgives Demetrius for his envy. Horace administers a purgative to Crispinus, who vomits up, quite graphically, the affected words he uses in his poetry. Virgil gives him a list of writers whom he should read as a diet to refine his literary taste, and sends him away to be locked up for a week or two. Demetrius is sentenced to act honestly and plainly instead of puffing himself up.

Both are required to swear that they will no longer slander any noble Romans. The true poets praise Caesar; he praises true poetry and condemns slanderers; the play proper ends with a song about apes and foolish men, who cannot bide their folly.

Jonson has a short apology to the reader for the Apologetical Dialogue he includes as "all the answers I ever gave, to sundry importent libells then cast out . . . against me, & this Play."

Apologetical Dialogue. Nasutus and Polyposus wonder if the author has been hurt by the libels against him. Jonson says that he is not offended by the ugly things his enemies said against him, but Polyposus reminds him that "the Multitude are delighting, believing him hurt." The author speaks of his disdain for the mass of people and for those who slandered him; he tells Polyposus that, although many people think he has maliciously slandered them in *Poetaster*, he only meant to express disapproval of their vices, and purposely set the play in Rome to show that all ages are full of corruption and malice. He maintains that he honors honest lawyers, noble soldiers, and honorable players. He rails against inferior poets and playwrights who slander him, saying that he writes in a great satiric vein, whose roots go back to the Greeks. He says that he will next try a tragedy (*Sejanus*), and asks the others to leave him while he begins work on something "high, and aloof, / Safe from the wolf's black jaw, and the dull ass's hoof."

Some of the characters in this play are supposed to be satirical portraits of Jonson's contemporaries. Scholars generally agree that Crispinus is meant to represent John Marston; Minos, an unidentified man to whom Marston owed money; Demetrius, Thomas Dekker; Horace, Ben Jonson. For more information on the controversy of which this play was a part, see WAR OF THE THEATERS.

poetomachia. See WAR OF THE THEATERS.

poetry. In *Timber* (ll. 1509–21), Jonson observes that there are interesting similarities between poetry and painting since both involve imitation, and he notes that Plutarch's contention that poetry is a speaking picture and painting a mute poetry is a sound one. Citing the parallels between poetry and painting, Jonson argues that they both invent, feign, and devise many things and accommodate all they invent to nature; they both have pleasure and profit as their common end; and they are both artificers. Of the two arts, however, poetry is more noble because it can speak to the understanding whereas painting speaks only to the sense.

Later in *Timber* (ll. 2290–2303), Jonson records some other observations about poetry, noting, in particular, that "*Poetry*, in the Primogeniture, had many peccant humours, and is made to have more now, through the Levity, and inconstancie of mens Judgements. Whereas, indeed, it is the most prevailing Eloquence, and of the most exalted *Charact.*" See also PAINTING.

Poets. The poets appear in *The Golden Age Restored* as the train of Astraea and the Golden Age and praise the return to earth of love and harmony.

poets (running judgments on). In *Timber* (ll. 587–668), Jonson includes a short critical essay on the quality of poetry in his day and laments that we "heare those things commended, and cry'd up for the best writings, which a man would scarce vouchsafe, to wrap any wholsome drug in. . . ." Claiming that the bad poets are actually lauded for their vices by the ignorant, Jonson notes that Cestius was preferred to Cicero in his time, that John Heath's *Epigrams* and John Taylor's *Skullers Poems* are acclaimed in Jonson's own day, and that Taylor's works are more appreciated than Spenser's. Commenting that Shakespeare should have blotted a thousand lines, Jonson indicates that he had an "excellent *Phantsie*, brave notions, and gentle expressions: wherein hee flow'd with that facility, that sometime it was necessary, he should be stop'd . . ." and that he sometimes "fell into those things, could not escape laughter," as when he had Caesar claim that Caesar never did wrong but with just cause. All in all, however, Jonson concludes that Shakespeare "redeemed his vices, with his vertues. There was ever more in him to be praysed, then to be pardoned."

Poldavy. In *Eastward Ho*, a tailor who fits Gertrude when she is about to become a lady.

Polemius. A symbolic personage appearing in a scene in Jonson's part of the *King's Coronation Entertainment* and representing the military force of the city.

polemos. Greek for "war."

Polish. In *The Magnetic Lady*, the parasite to the Magnetic Lady, who eventually turns out to be the mother of Pleasance.

Politian (1454–1494) Angelo Poliziano, humanist, poet, and critic, was patronized by Lorenzo de' Medici. In *Epicoene* (II), John Daw includes him in the catalogue of authors he despises.

Politianus, Angelus. Author of *Miscellanea* (1489), one of Jonson's authorities for archaeology.

Pollio, Trebellius. See TREBELLIUS POLLIO.

Pollux. A Latin name for Polydeuces. See DIOSCURI.

Pollux, Julius. Egyptian Greek lexicographer of the second century, who compiled a Greek lexicon for Emperor Commodus. Jonson used Pollux as one of his sources for *Hymenaei* and *Oberon*.

Poluphagus. A name meaning "eating to excess." In *Poetaster* (III. iv), Tucca invites Histrio to supper but tells him not to invite his gluttonous friend Poluphagus. Poluphagus has been identified as a satire on either Armin or Sincklo, actors contemporary with Jonson.

Polygnotus. See PAINTING.

Polyphemus. A Cyclops who was a shepherd and the son of Poseidon. In the *Odyssey*, he imprisoned Odysseus and his men in his cave, but the giant became drunk with wine given him by Odysseus and was blinded. Odysseus and his men escaped by hiding under the giant's sheep as they left the cave. In a later legend the giant had a futile love for the nymph Galatea.

Polyposus. In *Poetaster,* one of the characters in the "Apologetical Dialogue," who wonders if Jonson has been offended by the talk about his play and all the slander against him and questions the author, giving him an opportunity to reveal his feelings.

Pompey (106–48 B.C.). Gnaeus Pompeius, Roman general and administrator. As a young man, he distinguished himself by many victories. He was made a senator and continued fighting in the east and against pirates. He was made consul, but his popularity decreased, and he became involved in intrigues. He fought against Caesar, was defeated, and was murdered while trying to flee. He was a skillful administrator and had a constitutional position resembling that of Augustus. In *Sejanus* (I. i), Cordus is reputedly writing annals which begin in Pompey's time and Sabinus says that Germanicus had "Pompey's dignitie." Later in the play (I. iv), a statue of Sejanus is built in Pompey's theater, and Cordus attempts to defend himself by saying that Titus Livius praised Brutus and Cassius as well as Pompey, yet remained in favor with Augustus. Pompey is also alluded to several times in *Catiline* (I; III).

Pomponatius (1462–?1524). Pietro Pomponazzi, Italian philosopher, was an authority on Aristotle, and the author of a heretical tract on the immortality of the soul. After dismissing a long list of authors, including Homer and Virgil, as "not worthy to be nam'd for authors," John Daw in *Epicoene* (II) claims to respect Pomponatius.

Pomponius. One of Sejanus' followers in *Sejanus.* He expresses his happiness at Sejanus' increasing power to Laco, Minutius, and Terentius, in a conversation mocked by Arruntius. He brings Sejanus word that Macro has come to Rome, and he is sent to warn Trio, a consul, of the changed circumstances. He foolishly helps spread the rumor that Sejanus will gain great power at the Senate meeting. He at first acclaims Sejanus, saying that he hopes to rise with him, but is quick to deride him after Sejanus falls into disgrace.

Pomtinius. In *Catiline,* a praetor who helps prevent Cicero from being assassinated.

Pooly (Poley), Robert. An informer who was a government messenger at various dates from 1588 to 1601. He is alluded to in *Epig.* CI.

Pope, Alexander (1688–1744) English poet. Born in London to Roman Catholic parents, he was afflicted during his childhood by an illness that ruined his health and deformed his body. Since he was a Catholic, he was debarred from a Protestant education, and he was essentially self-taught. In his early years, he attracted the attention of William Wycherly, William Walsh and others, and before he was seventeen he was admitted to London society and encouraged as a prodigy. He had a short-lived friendship with Addison and his group, but his Tory leanings led him to a warm friendship with Swift and involvement with the Scriblerus Club. His early poetry was essentially descriptive and included, among others, *Pastorals* (1709), *Windsor Forest* (1713), *Essay on Criticism* (1711), *The Rape of the Lock* (1714), and "Eloisa to Abelard." In his middle period Pope did translations and editions of Homer and Shakespeare, amassing a considerable fortune for his merely competent efforts. In the last period of his career, he wrote moral poems and satires, including *The Dunciad, Imitations of Horace, An Essay on Man,* and *Moral Essays.* Throughout his career he was well known for his quarrels and for making enemies.

Joseph Spence's *Anecdotes, Observations, and the Characters of Books and Men,* ed. Singer (1820), records Pope's opinion that Jonson and Shakespeare were not enemies because Betterton had assured Pope that such was not the case. Pope also did not believe, as Dryden did, that Jonson's verses on Shakespeare's death were in any way intended to be satirical.

Pope, Thomas (d. 1604). A comedian and acrobat who, as one of the Chamberlain's Men, played in *Every Man in His Humour* and *Every Man out of His Humour.* He was one of the original housekeepers of the Globe and acted in Shakespeare's plays.

Popham, Sir John, the Lord Chief Justice from 1592 until his death in 1607, was noted for his severity on the bench. He is alluded to as the "greatest justice" in the dedication of *Poetaster* to Richard Martin.

Poppaea Sabina. Roman empress, the wife of Nero. While married to Otho she became Nero's mistress and finally married the emperor in A.D. 62. She exerted great influence over Nero, inducing him to have his mother, his former wife, and the philosopher Seneca killed.

Porphyrius of Tyre (A.D. 233–304). A Neoplatonist who was the pupil of Plotinus and the master of Iamblichus. Jonson used him as one of his sources in *The Masque of Queens* and mentioned him in *The Fortunate Isles*.

Porta, Baptista. Giovanni Battista della Porta, author of *De Furtivis Literarum Notis* (Naples, 1563), which was frequently reprinted, and *Magia Naturalis* (1562). Jonson mentioned Porta in *Epig.* XCII and used his *Magia* as one of the sources for *The Masque of Queens*.

Porter, Alan (1899–1942). Poet, editor, teacher of psychology, and associate professor of English at Vassar College. Porter, at the request of the Philalethean Society of Vassar, completed Jonson's fragment *The Sad Shepherd,* and the entire work was performed by the students on May 18, 1935 at the College outdoor theater. In 1944 Jonson's fragment with Porter's continuation of the play was published by the John Day Co. of New York in the Living Drama Series, edited by William Kozlenko.

Porter, Henry (d. 1599). Dramatist. His only extant play, which was first published in 1599, is the rural comedy, *The Two Angry Women of Abingdon,* which some have compared to Shakespeare's *The Merry Wives of Windsor.* In 1598 Meres mentioned him as one of the best for comedy. Porter's *Two Angry Women* may have had a slight influence upon Jonson's *Tale of a Tub, Every Man in His Humour,* and *Eastward Ho.* He was stabbed to death by the playwright John Day.

Portland, Hierome, Lord Weston, 2nd Earl of (1605–1663). In 1630 and 1632 Lord Hierome was sent to Paris and Turin for diplomatic negotiations. He became the 2nd Earl of Portland on his father's death in 1635. Jonson addressed *Und.* LXXIV to him and celebrated his marriage in *Und.* LXXV.

Portland, Richard, Lord Weston, 1st Earl of (1577–1635), was apparently an important patron in Jonson's later years. Jonson addressed *Und.* LXXI, LXXIII, LXXVII to him and also mentioned him in LXXV and LXXVIII. In 1621 Weston was made Chancellor and Under-Treasurer of the Exchequer, and in 1628 he was created Baron Weston. Later in 1628 he was made Lord High Treasurer and became one of the major enemies of Parliament. In 1630 and 1631 he helped bring about peace with Spain, and in 1632 he was created Earl of Portland. Lord Falkland alludes to Portland in his elegy published in *Jonsonus Virbius.*

portraits of Jonson. Three different engravings appeared in the early editions of Jonson's works. Issued separately sometime before 1627, Robert Vaughan's portrait was prefixed to the 1640 quarto edition of the *Poems* and the 1640 folio edition of the *Works.* If Jonson sat for this portrait, he probably did so before his stroke in 1628. The Vaughan portrait is the best in quality of those which appeared in the early editions of Jonson. John Benson prefixed to the duodecimo edition of the *Poems* in 1640 a portrait by William Marshall, who engraved from 1591 to 1646. The Marshall portrait is of poor quality and the features were copied from Vaughan. The 1692 folio of Jonson's *Works* contained a frontispiece by William Elder, who worked from 1680 to 1700 and was very popular with booksellers. Elder's portrait is an idealized version of Vaughan's engraving. Although superior to Marshall's, Elder's engraving reveals little artistic skill but does show some degree of technical accomplishment.

The oil portraits of Jonson that have survived are of a uniform type, and there are over twenty known copies of them. The best of these was acquired in 1935 by the National Portrait Gallery (London). The portrait has a certain resemblance to the Vaughan engraving, shows the influence of Rubens and Van Dyck, and is perhaps the best version we possess of a portrait done from life. Portraits of this type are often ascribed to Gerard Honthorst, but in this case it seems unlikely that Honthorst painted it. In an inventory of the Duke of Buckingham's pictures at York House in 1635, there is listed a picture of Ben Jonson by Abraham Blyenberch. No such portrait has ever been identified, and there is some speculation that the portrait in the National Gallery may actually be by Blyenberch.

In 1943 a portrait of Jonson attributed to Rubens was sold at auction. In the portrait Jonson holds a scroll of verses, namely, *Und.* LVII, in which Jonson thanks Mr. Berges for a gift of ink. The portrait commemorates the poem, but little is known about the painter or the occasion for the work. Nothing at all is known about the portrait of Jonson by Sir William Borlase commemorated in *Und.* LII. In 1888 a portrait of Jonson attributed to Gheerart Jansen (1593–c. 1662) was sold, although it is now attributed to William Dobson (1610–1646). In the portrait Jonson is seated at a table with books, holds a pen in his right hand, and has a landscape behind him. The atmosphere, setting, and theatrical pose suggest the eighteenth century.

A miniature by Peter Oliver (c. 1594–?1648) engraved by J. Houbraken (1698–1780), labeled "Ben Jonson," and published in *Heads of the Illustrious Persons of Great Britain* (1743) is probably not a representation of Jonson but may well portray a younger brother of Peter Oliver.

Portunus. Often identified with Neptune himself, Portunus was sometimes considered the god of ports. In *Neptune's Triumph for the Return of Albion*, he appears as one of the characters who lauds Neptune and celebrates Albion's joyous return. He also appears in a similar role in *The Fortunate Isles, and Their Union*, where he praises Neptune's glory. See also PALAEMON.

Pory, John. Newsmonger who together with Jonson and others on September 4, 1612, witnessed a theological debate in a private residence in Paris between a Catholic champion named Knevet and a Protestant minister named Daniel Featley. On January 7, 1606, Pory had written a detailed report to Sir Robert Cotton of the performance of *Hymenaei*. Pory's letter of September 20, 1632, to Sir Thomas Puckering, in which he expressed surprise at the announcement that Jonson, who Pory thought was dead, had written a new play (*The Magnetic Lady*), helps to establish the probable date of composition for that work.

Possevino, Antonio (1534–1611), a noted diplomatist and Jesuit who traveled extensively on political missions for the Papacy. He was also the author of *Bibliotheca Selecta Qua Agitur De Ratione Studiorum* (Rome, 1593), a kind of catalogue of the major authorities to study in the arts and sciences. Jonson borrowed heavily from this work for his commentary on painting in *Timber* (ll. 1549–67; 1581–85).

Post and Paire. A character who appears as one of the children of Christmas in *Christmas, His Masque.*

Posthumus, Julius. A follower of Sejanus' in *Sejanus*, one of the men who hopes to gain power by endorsing him. Jonson hints at his historical role as Mutilia Prisca's lover when Sejanus asks him to get an audience with Augusta through his "kindest friend," and tell her things to make her fear for her son Tiberius' life, and so further alarm him. He does not appear again in the play.

Postilion. A dwarf from hell who appears riding on a curtal in *Chloridia* and reports the perpetual holiday and triumph in hell following Cupid's arrival there.

Potkin. In *Eastward Ho*, a tankard bearer who assists Gertrude when she leaves the city in her coach for Sir Petronel Flash's castle in the country.

Practice. In *The Magnetic Lady*, a lawyer who is one of the suitors to Lady Loadstone's niece.

Praecones. Heralds in *Sejanus*. They appear during the Senate meetings, and during Sejanus's ceremony to fortune.

Preamble, Justice. In *A Tale of a Tub*, a justice of Maribone who tries unsuccessfully to marry Awdrey. Also known as Bramble.

Preston, Sir Richard. See Richard Preston, Lord DINGWELL (Dingwall).

Priapus. Son of Aphrodite and Dionysus. Priapus was a fertility god of gardens and herds. He was usually represented as a grotesque little man with a very large phallus.

Priests (of the Muses). Twelve priests of the Muses appear in *Love Freed From Ignorance and Folly* and aid Love's escape from the Sphynx, who represents ignorance.

Primalion. Short title for *The Second Book of Primaleon of Greece. And Prince Edward of England. Continuing the Course of Their Rare Fortunes, Knightly Adventures, Success in Love, and Admirable Escape from Very Perilous Enchantments,* translated by Anthony Munday, 1596. *Primalion* is alluded to in *The New Inn* (I. vi).

prince. In *Timber* (ll. 986–98), Jonson records that "*After God, nothing is to be lov'd of man like the Prince: He violates nature, that doth it not with his whole heart.*" He goes on to stress that the prince, since he is the arbiter of life and death, should be merciful, so that his punishments should be corrective rather than destructive: "Why are prayers with *Orpheus* said to be the daughters of *Iupiter*; but that Princes are thereby admonished, that the petitions of the wretched, ought to have more weight with them, then the Lawes themselves?"

Later in *Timber* (ll. 1250–91, Jonson, borrowing in part from Iustus Lipsius (*Politica*), notes that if only men realized the responsibilities of the prince, fewer men would want to be one. The prince is the pastor of his people, is the soul of the commonwealth, and should strive to be just rather than powerful. He should defend his subjects and appoint his ministers on the basis of worth. He should realize how easily he can be deceived since so many court arts are studied. Above all, the prince must remember that eventually he must account not only for himself but also for those whom he has entrusted with responsibilities: "And if *Piety* be wanting in the *Priests, Equity* in the Iudges, or the *Magistrate* be found rated at a price; what Iustice or Religion is to be expected? Which are the only two Attributes make *Kings* a kinne to Gods. . . ."

Prince of Moldavia. Stephano Janiculo, would-be suitor of Lady Arabella Stuart. In *Epicoene* (v), La-Foole claims that John Daw made a "map" of him.

Printer. An unnamed character in *News From the New World Discovered in the Moon* who is interested in the news of the discovery because he needs some copy.

printers and printing. A list of the sizes and known printers and publishers of Jonson's works through the seventeenth century is given below.

Work(s)	Size(s) & Printer(s)	Publisher(s)
Every Man out of His Humour	Q1(1600) Richard Bradock(?) Q2(1600) Peter Short (?) Q3(1600)	William Holme William Holme Nicholas Ling
Every Man in His Humour	Q(1601)	
Cynthia's Revels	Q(1601)	Walter Burre
Poetaster	Q(1602)	Matthew Lownes
King's Entertainment, A Panegyre, Entertainment at Althorp	Q(1604) Valentine Simmes	Edward Blount
Sejanus	Q(1605) George Eld	Thomas Thorpe
Eastward Ho	Q1,Q2,Q3(1605) George Eld	William Aspley
Hymenaei	Q(1606) Valentine Simmes	Thomas Thorpe
Volpone	Q(1607)	Thomas Thorpe
The Masque of Blackness, The Masque of Beauty, The Haddington Masque	Q(1608)	Thomas Thorpe
The Case Is Altered	Q(1609) Nicholas Okes	Bartholomew Sutton William Barrenger
The Masque of Queens	Q(1609) Nicholas Okes	Richard Bonion Henry Walley
Catiline	Q1(1611) Q2(1635) Nicholas Okes Q3(1669) Q4(1674)	Walter Burre John Spenser Andrew Crooke William Crooke and Andrew Crooke
Epicoene	Q1(1612) [may never have existed; no copy has ever been found] Q2(1620) William Stansby	William Stansby
The Alchemist	Q1(1612) Thomas Snodham	Walter Burre
Works	F1(1616) William Stansby	William Stansby
Lovers Made Men	Q(1617)	
The Masque of Augurs	Q(1622)	
Time Vindicated	Q(1623)	
Neptune's Triumph	Q(1624)	
The Fortunate Isles	Q(1625)	
Love's Triumph	Q(1630) John Norton, Jr.	Thomas Walkley
Chloridia	Q(1631)	Thomas Walkley
The New Inn	Octavo(1631) Thomas Harper	Thomas Alchorne
Plays [Bartholomew Fair, the Devil Is an Ass, The Staple of News]	F(1631) John Beale	Robert Allot

Probee. In *The Magnetic Lady,* a gentleman who appears in the induction to the play and comments on the actions and characters in the play as it proceeds.

Proclus (410?–485). Neoplatonic philosopher born in Constantinople. A synthesizer of Neoplatonic ideas, Proclus kept the elements of Plotinus but introduced a principle of triadic development in the series of emanations. He wrote several commentaries on Platonic dialogues and two treatises on Platonic theology. Jonson used Proclus as one of his sources for *The King's Coronation Entertainment* and mentioned him in *The Fortunate Isles.*

Prodromus (Theodorus). Greek romance writer who some time before the twelfth century wrote *The Loves of Rhodanthe and Dosicles,* first printed at Paris in 1625. Jonson alludes to Prodromus, whose proper name was Theodorus, in *The Sad Shepherd* (I. v).

Prologue. An "armed Prologue" in *Poetaster,* who enters after Envie has sunken, and explains his armor by the fact that in Jonson's "dangerous age," men seek to injure each other publicly on the stage. He asks the audience to view the play fairly and objectively, saying that Jonson is "above their injuries."

Prometheus. 1. The Titan son of Iapetus and of Clymene or Themis, who became the great benefactor of mankind. Since he foresaw the defeat of the Titans by the Olympians, he sided with Zeus and thus was spared the punishment of the other Titans. According to one account, Prometheus created mankind out of clay and water, and when Zeus mistreated man, Prometheus stole fire from the gods for man and taught man many useful arts and sciences. Prometheus' sympathy for mankind angered Zeus, who plagued man with Pandora and her box of many evils and chained Prometheus to a mountain peak in the Caucasus. In some versions of the myth, Prometheus was released by Hercules, but in other versions Zeus freed Prometheus when he revealed to the mighty god that it would be dangerous for Zeus to marry Thetis, who was fated to bear a son who would be more powerful than his father.

2. In *Mercury Vindicated From The Alchemists at Court,* this fire-god appears in the company of Nature and lauds the supremacy of natural fire and beauty over the fire of alchemy.

Propertius. 1. Propertius Sextus, born between 54 and 47 B.C. He was a Roman lyric poet and an elegist, best known for his love poems in praise of his mistress, Cynthia. He became a member of Maecenas' circle of poets and probably knew Virgil and Horace. In *Epicoene* (II. iii), Daw dismisses him, along with many other ancient authors, as a writer of no merit. Propertius was one of the sources for the portrait of Penthesilea in *The Masque of Queens,* and his elegies served as one of the sources for *Hymenaei.*

2. A gallant in *Poetaster* who writes poetry and is a friend of Ovid's. He is melancholy because his mistress, Cynthia, has recently died; Ovid and Tibullus express their concern for him. He goes to Albius with the others but apologizes for not being "sociable," and takes no major part in the scene. He shuts himself up in Cynthia's tomb; no mention is made of him for the rest of the play. Unlike several of the characters in *Poetaster,* he is not a caricature of one of Jonson's contemporaries.

Prosaites. A foolish page to Asotus, called "the beggar" in *Cynthia's Revels.* He sings a song about the joy of being a beggar, and goes with Cos to get water from the fountain of self-love for the courtiers. He is criticized by Cynthia, who sentences him to be punished at Crites' discretion. He marches, weeps, and sings the palinode with the others.

Proserpine. Persephone, the goddess of fertility and the queen of the underworld, was the daughter of Zeus and Demeter. She was seized by Pluto as a beautiful young maiden and held captive by him in the underworld. Demeter eventually persuaded the gods to let her daughter return to earth. Persephone had to remain in the underworld for four months of every year, however, because she had eaten a pomegranate—the food of the dead. When Persephone left the earth, the flowers withered and the grain died, but when she returned life was renewed; hence she came to symbolize the annual vegetation cycle.

Prospero (Wellbred). A young gallant, friend to Lorenzo junior (Edward) and brother to Giuliano (Downright), Hesperida (Bridget), and Biancha (Dame Kitely) in the 1601 quarto version of *Every Man in His Humour.* (Differing names and courses of action in the 1616 folio version are given here in parentheses.) Prospero sends Lorenzo junior a merry letter, asking him to come to Florence (London) and meet his two foolish acquaintances, Bobadilla and Matheo (Matthew). He is overjoyed at meeting Lorenzo junior, but worried to learn that Lorenzo senior (Knowell) has read his letter. He and Lorenzo junior enjoy baiting and mocking the three gulls, and he comforts Lorenzo junior when he learns that his father has followed him. He encourages Matheo to make a fool out of himself by reading his plagiarized verses to Hesperida, and loses his temper when Giuliano (Downright) threatens his companion and insults him. He offers to arrange for Hesperida to meet Lorenzo junior and to marry him, and persuades her to do that. He sends Thorello (Kitely) and Biancha (Dame Kitely) to Cob's house, making each suspect the other of being unfaithful, and each appear foolish. His merry good humor holds when he is brought before Dr. Clement (Justice Clement); he mocks Matheo and is reconciled to Giuliano and Lorenzo senior there, joining them at Clement's dinner (and attends the dinner, even though he is not openly reconciled to Downright and Knowell).

Prospero's (Wellbred's) servant. In the 1601 quarto version of *Every Man in His Humour,* he is the carrier of a merry, artificially styled letter from Prospero (Wellbred) to Lorenzo junior (Edward). (Differing names and courses of action in the 1616 folio version are given here in parentheses.) He begins the complications of the plot by mistakenly giving the letter to Lorenzo senior (Knowell). Stephano (Stephen) tries to pick a quarrel with him, but he leaves before Stephano succeeds.

Proteus. 1. Sea deity who tended the seals of Poseidon and could transform himself into any shape he wanted. However, if he were seized and held, he would foretell the future.

2. The old man of the sea who, according to Greek legend, was a seer constantly changing his shape to avoid answering questions. In *Neptune's Triumph for the Return of Albion,* he appears as one of the characters on the floating island who praises Neptune and celebrates Albion's return. He also appears in a similar role in *The Fortunate Isles, and Their Union,* where he extols Neptune's glory. In *Love's Triumph,* he is one of Amphitrite's attendants in the triumph.

Prothymia. A symbolic personage representing promptitude who appears in Jonson's part of the *King's Coronation Entertainment.*

Prudence. 1. A wench who appears in *The Gypsies Metamorphosed* and discovers that the gypsies have picked her pockets.

2. In *The New Inn,* the chambermaid to Lady Frances Frampul, who serves as sovereign of sports in the New Inn and who eventually marries Lord Latimer.

Prynne, William. English political figure and Puritan pamphleteer born in 1600 and graduated from Oxford in 1621. Admitted to the bar in 1628, Prynne's attacks on Arminian doctrine made him an enemy of Archbishop Laud, and his criticism of the stage in *Histriomastix* (1632), which was interpreted as an aspersion on the King and Queen, earned him imprisonment in 1633 and the loss of his ears in 1634. He continued his Puritan propagandizing in jail and in 1637 was fined, sentenced to life imprisonment, and branded with the letters S.L. (seditious libeler). Prynne was released by the Long Parliament in 1640, and he supported the Parliamentary cause and vindicatively prosecuted his old enemy Laud. In 1648 he entered Parliament himself, but was expelled for opposing the demands of the army and the execution of Charles I. Thereafter he attacked the Commonwealth in violent pamphlets and worked for the Stuart cause. He was again imprisoned from 1650 to 1653. After the Restoration he was keeper of the Tower records until his death in 1669. Jonson refers to him as "Scribe Prin-Gent" in *The Magnetic Lady* (I. v).

Psellus, Michael (1018–?1079). Professor of philosophy, under Constantine IX (1042–1055), at the Academy in Constantinople. He was appointed State Secretary and except for a brief retirement in a monastery (1054–55), was a member of all the governments at Constantinople until the reign of Michael VII (1071–78), under whom he became Prime Minister. A man of encyclopedic learning and great literary ability, Psellus had a keen love of classical and patristic literature and was passionately devoted to Plato and the Neoplatonists. He was a prolific writer, publishing scientific and philosophical treatises on mathematics, music, astronomy, physics, metaphysics, ethics, theology, alchemy, demonology, medicine, jurisprudence, and topography. His literary masterpiece, *De Daemonibus* (1577), was one of Jonson's sources for *The Masque of Queens*.

Psyche. Personification of the human soul. Psyche was so lovely that Eros (Cupid) fell in love with her and visited her by night. He forbade her to look on him since he was a god. When she disobeyed, he abandoned her, and she ceaselessly searched for him, performing difficult and dangerous tasks. At last she was reunited with Eros and made immortal.

Puck-Hairy. A "merry Andrew," or woods being, with a "hairy," or leafy dress in *The Sad Shepherd*. He is, at first, attached to Maudlin, and must do her bidding and protect her although she "growes high in evil." As her familiar spirit, or goblin, he warns her to be canny in her hatred of Robin Hood.

Pug. The lesser devil in Jonson's *The Devil Is an Ass* who desires to visit earth.

Puntarvolo. In *Every Man out of His Humour,* a vainglorious knight.

Puppets. In *Bartholomew Fair,* characters in Littlewit's puppet show, which radically changes the story of Hero and Leander. They interact with Lanthern and Busy.

Puppy. 1. One of the clowns who appears in *The Gypsies Metamorphosed* and discovers that the gypsies have picked his pockets.
 2. In *Bartholomew Fair,* a Western man who comes to Bartholomew Fair to wrestle before the Lord Mayor. He gets drunk with Knockem and his friends and quarrels.

Puppy, Hannibal. In *A Tale of a Tub,* Tobie Turfe's man who eventually marries Lady Tub's woman, Dido Wispe.

Purbeck, John Villiers, Viscount. See Sir John VILLIERS.

Purecraft, Dame. Win's mother and John Littlewit's mother-in-law in *Bartholomew Fair.* She is a rich Puritan widow who is besieged by suitors, including Winwife and Zeal-of-the-Land Busy. She has been told by a fortune-teller that she will only be happy with a gentleman madman so, after Littlewit tricks her into going to the fair, she eagerly accepts the attentions of pretended madman Quarlous and marries him before she learns that he is not truly mad.

Purslowe, Elizabeth. Printer in London from 1633 to 1646 who printed *Jonsonus Virbius* for Henry Seile in 1638.

Puttenham, George (d. 1590). English author. He is best known for a work which was anonymously published in 1589 but attributed to him—*The Art of English Poesie.* This book was generally considered the best treatise on English versification of its time and reveals discriminating taste and wide classical knowledge. Jonson had a copy in his library, and he told Drummond in the *Conversations* (ll. 418–19) that the book had been written twenty years before (scholars believe it was actually thirty years before) and had been kept in secret.

Pylades. A friend of Orestes who helped him to murder his mother Clytemnestra and her lover Aegisthus.

Pyracmon. 1. One of the Cyclopes.
 2. He appears as a symbolic character in *The Haddington Masque.*

Pyrgus (Pyrgi). Two pages to Tucca in *Poetaster.* One of them goes with Tucca when he tries to borrow money from Ovid senior and mocks Tucca. Both pages mock Tucca later, when he persuades Minos to free Crispinus. The Pyrgi perform passages from various plays for Histrio and Demetrius. They attend Ovid's masquerade, where one of them plays Ganymede, and sneak away with Tucca when Caesar breaks in.

Pyrrhus. Achilles' son, who killed Priam on the night the Greeks took Troy. In his fooling in *Volpone* (I), Androgyno claims that his soul once belonged to Pyrrhus.

Pythagoras (582?–507 B.C.). Greek pre-Socratic philosopher. He migrated from Samos to Crotona and established a secret religious society. We know little of his life and writings. Since his followers came to worship him as a demigod and to attribute all their doctrines to him, it is nearly impossible to distinguish his teachings from theirs. The Pythagoreans are best known for two teachings: the transmigration of souls and the theory that numbers constitute the real nature of things. The Pythagoreans performed purification rites and followed moral, ascetic, and dietary rules in order to achieve a higher rank in their subsequent lives. They also considered the sexes equal, treated slaves humanely, and respected animals. The Pythagoreans were influential mathematicians and geometricians. They made important contributions to medicine and astronomy and were among the first to teach that the earth was round and revolved about a fixed point. At the end of the fifth century B.C. the Pythagoreans were forced to flee Magna Graecia because people became enraged at their interference with traditional religious customs. At the beginning of the Christian era a short-lived Neo-Pythagoreanism developed which borrowed elements from Jewish and Hellenistic thought and emphasized the mystical aspects of Pythagorean ideas.

Pythagoras is mentioned in *The Masque of Blackness*, *The Gypsies Metamorphosed*, and *The Fortunate Isles* and is alluded to in *Hymenaei*. In *Volpone* (I. ii), Androgyno claims that his soul once belonged to Pythagoras, and Dol mentions him in her frenzy in *The Alchemist* (IV. v).

Python. A huge serpent sent by Hera to persecute Leto when she was pregnant by Zeus with Artems and Apollo. Python was eventually killed by Apollo. The Pythian games celebrated the triumph of Apollo over Python.

Q

Quarlous, Tom. A clever gamester in *Bartholomew Fair* who, with his companion Winwife, exposes the folly and corruption of many people with whom he comes into contact, including Littlewit, Waspe, Busy, and the rogues of the fair. He engineers the plan to have Edgworth steal Cokes's marriage license from Waspe, and, by disguising himself as a madman, manages to get Justice Overdo's signature on it. He wins Purecraft for his wife by pretending to be the "gentleman mad-man" a fortune-teller said she should marry, and he saves the whole company, at the end of the play, from Justice Overdo's wrath by exposing all the folly Overdo committed while in disguise.

Quarrel. A character in *Love's Welcome at Bolsover* who appears as a glazier in Colonel Vitruvius' dance of the mechanics.

quartos. A number of Jonson's works, which are listed below, were published in quarto, some before they were published in folio, and some after. See also PRINTERS AND PRINTING.

Every Man out of His Humour	Q1(1600), Q2(1600), Q3(1600)
Every Man in His Humour	Q(1601)
Cynthia's Revels	Q(1601)
Poetaster	Q(1602)
King's Entertainment, A Panegyre, Entertainment at Althorp	Q(1604)
Sejanus	Q(1605)
Eastward Ho (collaboration)	Q1, Q2, Q3(1605)
Hymenaei	Q(1606)
Volpone	Q(1607)
The Masque of Blackness, The Masque of Beauty, The Haddington Masque	Q(1608)
The Case Is Altered	Q(1609)
The Masque of Queens	Q(1609)
Catiline	Q1(1611), Q2(1635), Q3(1669), Q4(1674)
Epicoene	Q1(1612) [may never have existed; no copy has ever been found], Q2(1620)
The Alchemist	Q(1612)
Lovers Made Men	Q(1617)
The Masque of Augurs	Q(1622)
Time Vindicated	Q(1623)
Neptune's Triumph	Q(1624)
The Fortunate Isles	Q(1625)
Love's Triumph	Q(1630)
Chloridia	Q(1631)
Poems	Q(1640)

Quicksilver. In *Eastward Ho*, the disloyal apprentice of the goldsmith Touchstone, who is dismissed by his master, helps Security get Gertrude's land for a loan to her husband, attempts to sail to Virginia, is shipwrecked, imprisoned, repents, and finally is released through the efforts of Golding.

Quintilian (c. A.D. 35–c. 95). Roman rhetorician. He taught rhetoric in Rome, where Pliny the Younger and possibly Tacitus were his students. Vespasian endowed him with a salary and eventually made him consul. His most famous work was *Institutio oratoria*, a complete survey of rhetoric in twelve books. Quintilian's style was among the most elegant of his time, combining good taste and moderation. He was very influential in antiquity and the Renaissance. Jonson was greatly indebted to Quintilian, especially to his ideas on rhetoric.

In the *Conversations* (ll. 12–14), Jonson recommended Quintilian to Drummond and told him that books 6, 7, 8 should be thoroughly digested. Quintilian is mentioned in *The Devil Is an Ass* (I. iv) and paraphrased in *Every Man in* (II. v). Throughout *Timber* Jonson borrows extensively from Quintilian on a variety of topics: on wit (ll. 575–86; 669–80); on ignorance of writers (ll. 745–59); on characteristics of the genuine poet (ll. 1038–45); on painting (ll. 1529–40); on education (ll. 1644–96); on style (ll. 1697–1754); 1770–1820); on learning (ll. 1821–57); on words (ll. 1885 ff.); on metaphor (ll. 1915–25); on custom (ll. 1926–45); on translation and allegory (ll. 2014–23); and on brevity (ll. 2228–29). Book I, chapters I and VII, of Jonson's *English Grammar* is also indebted to Quintilian.

Quire. A choir appears in *The Golden Age Restored* and helps to celebrate the return to earth of the golden age.

R

Rabelais, François (1490?–1553). French writer and physician. The son of a wealthy lawyer, he early became a novice in a Franciscan monastery. He studied Greek and Latin and made inquiries into science, law, philology, and letters. He became known and respected by the humanists of his day, including Budé. Under suspicion because of his humanism, Rabelais petitioned Pope Clement VII for permission to transfer to the Benedictine monastery of Maillezais, whose scholarly bishop became his friend and patron. In 1530 Rabelais received his degree in medicine at the University of Montpellier, and in 1532 he went to Lyons, then an important intel-

lectual center, where he practiced medicine, edited various Latin works, composed burlesque almanacs, and published *Gargantua* (1532) and *Pantagruel* (1532). So popular were these two works that Rabelais developed them into an elaborate romance and published two other volumes in 1546 and 1552 about these famous giants. (A fifth book appeared after his death; whether Rabelais wrote it is questionable.) One of the world's great masterpieces of wit and humor, Rabelais's romance also contains serious discussions of education, politics, and philosophy, all reflecting the breadth of Rabelais's learning and his zest for living. Rabelais made several trips to Rome with his friend Cardinal Jean du Bellay, lived with the Cardinal's brother, Guillaume, for a time, was patronized by Francis I briefly, and probably spent some time in hiding when his book was condemned by the Sorbonne. He taught medicine in 1537 and 1538 at Montpellier, and after 1547 was given sinecures, from which he resigned before his death in Paris in 1553.

Jonson mentions *Gargantua* in *Every Man in* (1601 quarto, I. iv), and he alludes to *Pantagruel* in *The Staple of News* (IV. ii) and in *Neptune's Triumph*.

Radcliffe, Sir John, who was knighted in 1599, was the surviving brother of Margaret Radcliffe, whom Jonson commemorated in *Epig.* XL. Jonson praised Sir John for his "great marks of virtue" in *Epig.* XCIII. Radcliffe gave Jonson a manuscript of Juvenal's *Satires* and Horace's *Ars Poetica*. Radcliffe died in the Isle of Rhé in 1627 while fighting against the French.

Radcliffe, Margaret. See Margaret RATCLIFFE.

Radcliffe, Robert. See Robert Radcliffe, Earl of SUSSEX.

Rage. The name of one of the witches making up the antimasque in *The Masque of Queens*.

Rain. In *Chloridia*, five symbolic characters who appear in the seventh entry of the antimasque, dance, and sprinkle sweet water about the room.

Rainolds (Reynolds), John (1549–1607). English clergyman and Oxford scholar. He was a leading Puritan of his day. He recommended to King James that a new translation of the Bible be undertaken, and he assisted in the translation of the Prophets for the new version. He published *The Overthrow of Stage Plays* (1599 and 1600), in which he attacked plays in general and humor plays in particular. One of the plays he probably had in mind was Jonson's *Every Man in His Humor*.

Raith, James. See James WRITH.

Raleigh, Sir Walter (1552?–1618). English statesman and man of letters. Although listed as an undergraduate at Oxford in 1572, he had served in the Huguenot army in France in 1569. Little is known of his activities after he returned to England, but by 1580 he was serving in Ireland, where he first met Edmund Spenser, whose patron he later became. When Raleigh returned to London in 1581, he went to court and became a favorite of Queen Elizabeth's. As an important courtier he was granted wine monopolies in 1583, knighted in 1584 and given valuable estates, made warden of the stanneries in 1585, and appointed captain of the queen's guard in 1587. He conceived and organized the expeditions to America which ended in the lost colony on Roanoke Island, Virginia. Probably because of his conflict with Robert Devereux, 2nd Earl of Essex, Elizabeth's new favorite, Raleigh left court in 1589, but after the Queen's quarrel with Essex over his marriage Raleigh returned to court and was granted an estate at Sherborne in 1592. Later in the year he was imprisoned in the Tower by Elizabeth when she learned of his affair with a maid of honor at court, Elizabeth Throckmorton, who later became his wife. Raleigh was later sent to Dartmouth to quell a riot and for this service he won his freedom.

Barred from court, he entered Parliament, but he became notorious for his association with the poetic group known as "the school of night," which was led by Thomas Harriot, included Marlowe and Chapman, and was considered atheistic because of their skepticism and critical interpretation of Scripture.

Determined to find the fabled El Dorado, Raleigh and Laurence Kemys embarked for Guiana in 1595. Raleigh published his *Discovery of Guiana* in 1596, and in the same year he also helped save an English expedition against Cádiz from disaster. In 1597 his capture of Fayal without waiting for Essex precipitated a violent quarrel between the two. In 1600 Raleigh was appointed governor of Jersey, but his fortunes began to fall when he differed with Robert Cecil in the political tempest over Essex's treason and death. When James ascended the throne in 1603, Raleigh's enemies convinced the new monarch that Raleigh was opposed to his succession, and most of Raleigh's offices and monopolies were taken away. On rather insubstantial evidence, he was convicted of treason, but was saved from the block by reprieve, and settled down in the Tower with his wife and son, where he devoted himself to literature, science, and the writing of his *History of the World* (1614). In 1616 Raleigh was released from the Tower to lead another expedition to Guiana in search of gold. He was charged not to entrench on Spanish possessions. The expedition was a disaster—storms dispersed his fleet, many of his men died of disease, many deserted, Raleigh himself fell very ill with fever, his son Walter died. He at last returned to England by way of Newfoundland, and in 1618, at the demand of the Spanish ambassador, who was angered at the expedition's capture of the new Spanish town San Tómas (not to mention the many Spanish ships Raleigh had plundered in the 1590s), Raleigh was executed under the original sentence for treason handed down in 1603.

Raleigh left a number of political essays, philosophical treatises, and a body of verse that was highly praised by his contemporaries. Much of the verse is now lost, and several of his prose works seem to be missing, such as the life of Queen Elizabeth that Jonson told Drummond in the *Conversations* (ll. 202–3) Raleigh had written.

Jonson apparently knew Raleigh well. In the *Conversations* (ll. 295–305), he told an anecdote about Raleigh's notoriously knavish young son, to whom Jonson served as governor in France in 1613. The boy got Jonson drunk, put him on a wagon, and drew him through the streets of Paris, proclaiming him to be the most lively image of the crucifix they had yet seen. The boy's mother was delighted by the sport, claiming his father was so inclined in his youth, but Sir Walter was not amused. In *Timber* (ll. 910–12), Jonson cited Raleigh for his good judgment and style.

In the *Conversations* (ll. 197–99), however, Jonson said that Raleigh esteemed fame more than conscience because the best wits of England had been employed in his *History*, that Jonson himself had sent Raleigh a piece on the Punic Wars, which Raleigh had altered and used in the *History* without acknowledgment (ll. 200–201). In spite of this, Jonson did write a prefatory poem (*Und.* XXIV) explaining the symbolic frontispiece for the volume.

According to Jonson in the *Conversations* (ll. 20–22), Spenser had given Raleigh a written explanation of his allegory in the *Faerie Queen*, and the explanation indicated that the blating beast was supposed to symbolize the Puritans, and Duessa the Queen of Scots (ll. 177–79).

In 1623 Jonson gave testimony in Chancery Court in support of a suit by Raleigh's widow. Because of his knowledge of the man, Jonson was able to verify Sir Walter's handwriting on an important document.

Raleigh, Walter, the younger. Son of Sir Walter, he matriculated at Corpus Christi College, Oxford, in 1607 and took his degree in 1610. He was killed on his father's Guiana expedition in 1618, the same year his father was executed for treason. See also Sir Walter RALEIGH.

Ralph. Drawer at the Swan Tavern by Charing Cross who served Jonson good Canary. According to Aubrey, Jonson commemorated Ralph in an impromptu grace before the King ("Our King and Queen the Lord God bless").

Ramsay, Henry. Contributor of an elegy ("Let thine own Sylla [Ben] arise and try") to *Jonsonus Virbius*. He received his B.A. in 1639 from Christ Church, Oxford.

Ramsey, Mary, Lady (d. 1596). Second wife of Sir Thomas Ramsey, Lord Mayor of London in 1577. She was a benefactress of Christ's Hospital and other institutions. She is mentioned in *Eastward Ho* (IV. ii).

Ramus (de la Ramée), Petrus (Pierre) (1515–1572). French humanist and philosopher who attempted to break away from Aristotelian and scholastic traditions. He wrote a number of influential works, among them *Dialecticae Institutiones* (1543) and *Aristotelicae Animadversiones* (1543). As a result of his attack on Aristotle, his teaching position was threatened, but Ramus was established in a chair of rhetoric and philosophy in 1551 at the Collège de France through the efforts of Cardinal de Lorraine. Ramus sympathized with the religious reforms of his day. In 1568 he fled to Germany. He returned to Paris in 1570 and was killed in the St. Bartholomew's Day Massacre in 1572. So-called Ramist logic, emphasizing clarity, precision, testing, and definite boundaries between subjects, was very influential in the early sixteenth and seventeenth centuries, particularly in Protestant lands — Switzerland, Scotland, and much of Germany. From its English stronghold at Cambridge, Ramist logic affected Francis Bacon, Milton, and many others, and it

may have encouraged the scientific spirit in general throughout Europe.

In his *English Grammar*, Jonson was heavily dependent upon Ramus' *Grammatica* (1572), and he made considerable use of his *Scholae in Liberales Artes* (1578).

Randall, Dale B. J. (1929–). American scholar educated at Western Reserve University, Rutgers University, and the University of Pennsylvania. Since 1970 he has been Professor of English at Duke University. Specializing in seventeenth-century English literature, he has published studies on a variety of subjects. His *Jonson's Gypsies Unmasked: Background and Theme of The Gypsies Metamorphosed*, an important and provocative study, was published in 1974.

Randolph, Thomas (1605–1635). English poet and dramatist who became one of Jonson's literary sons. From Westminster, Randolph went to Trinity College, Cambridge, in 1623 and was elected a fellow in 1629. He showed early promise of distinction, and Jonson took him under his wing, but Randolph's fine promise of genius was cut short by his early death, probably the result of intemperate habits. Randolph left a number of poems and several plays. *Aristippus* and *The Conceited Pedlar* are academic interludes; *The Jealous Lover* is a clever comedy; *The Muse's Looking-glass* is a satire in pseudo-dramatic form; and *Amyntas* is a pastoral play.

In *Poems with the Muse's Looking-glass and Amyntas* (1638), Randolph included two poems on Jonson: "A Gratulatory to Mr. Benjamin Jonson for his Adopting of him to be his Son" and "Ben, do not leave the stage." "An Eclogue to Mr. Jonson" is included in *Poems* (1638), and a Latin reply to Jonson's "Ode to Himself" was published in *A Crew of Kind London Gossips* (1633). In a manuscript of *Aristippus*, Randolph wrote that Jonson knew that the spring of the Muses is the fountain of sack.

"On the Good Wives' Ale," a poem sometimes ascribed to Jonson, was probably written by Randolph.

Raphael (Raffaello Sanzio) (1483–1520). Major Italian painter. Born in Urbino. He was very prolific and achieved recognition for his altarpieces, portraits, tapestries, and scenes at the Vatican. He was patronized by both Julius II and Leo X, and in 1514 he succeeded Bramante as chief architect of the Vatican. Raphael was very indebted to ancient sculpture for his mythological and biblical figures. Jonson mentions

Raphael in *Und.* LXXVII and in *Timber* (l. 1583). See also PAINTING.

Raphael Volaterranus (1450–1521). Raphael Maffei of Volterra was the author of *Commentarii Urbani Libri XLV*. He translated a number of classical authors including Xenophon. Jonson used Raphael as one of the scources for his portrait of Valasca in the *Masque of Queens*.

Rasis. Famous Persian physician born about A.D. 850 who was known as Rhazes or Rasis. He was the first to distinguish smallpox from measles. His works on medicine were widely circulated in Arabic, Greek, and Latin versions, and his writings often provided the basis for medical training until well into the seventeenth century. Jonson mentions him in *Tale of a Tub* (IV. i) and *The Magnetic Lady* (III. iii).

Ratcliffe, Lady Elizabeth. See RADCLIFFE (Ratcliffe), Elizabeth, Viscountess Haddington.

Ratcliffe (Radcliffe), Margaret. Daughter of Sir John Radcliffe, celebrated in *Epig.* XCIII. She died in 1599, grief-stricken over the death of her brother. Jonson wrote an epitaph for her which was not placed on her tomb but does appear as *Epig.* XL.

Ratsey, Gamaliel. An English highwayman noted for wearing a very ugly mask; two pamphlets were written about him. In a quarrel in *The Alchemist* (I. i), Face tells Subtle that he will expose his corruption and make him look as bad as Ratsey.

Ratt, Doctor. A curate in *Gammer Gurton's Needle* (1575), he appears as a character in the antimasque for *The Fortunate Isles, and Their Union*.

Reade, Simon. A doctor from Southwark who was accused in 1607 of having successfully invoked three spirits to find a thief who had stolen money from Toby Matthew. Reade was pardoned in 1608. In *The Alchemist* (I. ii), Subtle feigns caution in dealing with Dapper in order to dismiss Dapper's suspicions and kindle his enthusiasm, and he gives Reade's accusation as a reason for his caution.

Readiness. One of the servants of Humanity who appears on a triumphal arch in *Lovers Made Men*.

reading. In the *Conversations* (ll. 12–16), Drummond notes that Jonson recommended his reading the following: Quintilian, who would tell Drummond the faults of his verses as if he had lived with him; Horace; Plinius Secundus's *Epistles;* Tacitus; Juvenal; and Martial, whose epigram *Vitam quae faciunt beatiorem* Jonson had translated. Later in the *Conversations* (ll. 138–50), Jonson recommended Petronius, Plinius Secundus, and Tacitus as those who spoke the best Latin, and he said that the sixth, seventh, and eighth books of Quintilian should be thoroughly digested while Juvenal, Perse, Horace, Martial, and Pindar should be read for delight. For church matters, Hooker should be read; for antiquities, Selden. Tacitus should be read for the secrets of the Council and Senate and Suetonius for those of the Cabinet and Court. The best subject for a heroic poem was King Arthur's fiction, and Sidney had intended to transform all of his *Arcadia* to stories of King Arthur.

Reason. A symbolic character who appears in *Hymenaei* and calms the disruptive Humors and Affections.

Redwine, James D., Jr. Born in 1932, Redwine is an American scholar who was educated at Duke, Columbia, and Princeton. Since 1976 he has been Edward Little Professor of English and Literature at Bowdoin College in Brunswick, Maine. In 1970 he published a useful compilation of Jonson's literary criticism.

Register. In *The Staple of News*, the register for the Staple office.

Regulus. One of the two Roman consuls in power during *Sejanus*. Macro returns to his house to plot against Sejanus, and Regulus helps him make his plans, running in and out so quickly as to anger Macro. His name heads the invocation to the Senate with Trio's; he calls them to order and reminds them of their purpose, then listens to Tiberius' letter denouncing Sejanus. He calls for guards to keep order in the Senate and to keep the accused from escaping and shows his true feeling against Sejanus when he exclaims, "thanks, to the gods" when Macro speaks of Sejanus' fall.

religion. In *Timber* (ll. 1197–1212), Jonson notes, quoting H. Farnese (*Diphthera Iouis*, 1607, p. 105), that the strength of empire is in religion because nothing more commends the sovereign to his subjects than religion. Alluding to Seneca (*De Clementia*, I. i. 9), Jonson argues that he who is religious must necessarily be just and merciful, and justice and mercy are strong ties on mankind. Where the Prince is good, Jonson contends, alluding to Euripides, God is a guest in a human body. See also POET; PRINCE.

Remigius. See Nicholas REMY.

Remus. Brother of Romulus, legendary founder of Rome. Amulius usurped the throne of his brother Numitor and forced Numitor's daughter Rhea Silvia to become a vestal virgin so she would have no children, but she bore the twin sons Romulus and Remus by the god Mars. Amulius imprisoned Rhea and set the twin boys adrift on the Tiber. Romulus and Remus floated safely ashore and were suckled by a she-wolf until they were found and reared by a royal shepherd, Faustulus. When the boys grew up, they killed Amulius and restored the throne to Numitor, after which they decided to establish a city on the spot where they were first rescued from the Tiber. When Romulus was selected by omen as the founder of the new city, a quarrel broke out between the two brothers, and Remus was slain. Romulus populated this new city with fugitives and led the rape of the Sabine women to get them wives. After a long reign Romulus disappeared in a thunderstorm and was worshipped as the god Quirinus.

Remy, Nicholas. Nicholas Remigius, author of *Daemonolatria* (1595), one of Jonson's authorities on witchcraft which he used in *The Masque of Queens*.

Reuben. The Reconciler in *The Sad Shepherd*. He is mentioned in the cast of characters, but the play is incomplete and he does not appear.

Revel. A symbolic character in *The Vision of Delight* who has no speaking part but accompanies Delight at the opening of the masque.

Rhadamanthus. Son of Zeus and Europa who became one of the judges of Hades who was famous for his justice.

Rhea. A Titan who was the wife and sister of Cronus. She bore Zeus, Poseidon, Hades, Hestia, Hera, and Demeter. She helped Zeus overthrow Cronus. She was known as the mother of the gods and in Rome was identified with Ops. The Greeks frequently identified her with Gaea and Cybele.

Rheese. A Welshman who appears in *For the Honor of Wales* and offers a song for the pleasure of the king.

rhetoric. See POET.

Rhodiginus (Richerius), Callius. Author of *Lectiones Antiquae* (1517), one of Jonson's authorities on archaeology.

Rich, Sir Henry. See Henry Rich, Earl of HOLLAND

Rich, Sir Robert (d. 1658). The eldest son of Robert, Lord Rich. He was made a knight of the Bath in 1603, was created Earl of Warwick in 1618, and succeeded to his father's title in 1619. In Charles I's reign he joined the Puritan party and became a prominent member, serving as Lord High Admiral in 1643–45 and 1648–49. He danced in *The Haddington Masque*. Jonson wrote a speech for him and his brother given at a tilting on March 24, 1613 ("Two noble knights, whom true desire and zeal").

Richard Crookback. A lost tragedy written by Jonson for Philip Henslowe in 1602.

Richard I (1157–1199). Became King of England, Count of Anjou, and Duke of Aquitaine and Normandy when his father, Henry II, died in 1189. Known as Richard the Lion-Hearted, he spent little time in England and was concerned with it primarily as a source of revenue, but his personal traits and military exploits have made him a central figure in English romance and chivalry, and he is so portrayed by Merlin in *The Speeches at Prince Henry's Barriers.*

Richard III (1452–1485) King of England 1483–1485. Formerly Duke of Gloucester. In Jonson's *The Devil Is an Ass* (II. iv), Fitzdottrel alludes to him as one fatally connected with Gloucester.

Ridley, Mark (1560–1624), published *The Navigator's Supply* (1597), which described the compass in the early chapters. Ridley claimed to have been physician to the Emperor of Russia. In 1613 he published *A Short Treatise of Magnetical Bodies and Motions.* He engaged in a scholarly debate in print about magnetism with William Barlow, Archdeacon of Salisbury (d. 1625). Both Ridley and Barlow are mentioned in *The Magnetic Lady* (I. iv).

Rimee (Rime, Rymer), James. Bookseller in London from 1599 to 1600 who had a shop in Blackfriars. He is mentioned in *Epig.* XCII.

Ripa, Cesare. Author of *Iconologia* (1593; 1603; 1605), one of Jonson's sources for *The King's Coronation Entertainment, The Masque of Beauty, Hymenaei, Lovers Made Men,* and the portrait of Fame in *The Masque of Queens.*

Ripley, Sir George (d. 1490), who popularized Raymond Lully's works, was canon of Bridlington and wrote *The Com-*

pound of Alchemie (1471) and *Medulla Alchemiae* (1476). In *The Alchemist* (II. v), Subtle asks Ananias if he is a follower of Ripley's.

Rivers. In *Chloridia*, symbolic characters who help to celebrate the glory of the spring and of Chloris.

Robert II King of Scots. A lost tragedy upon which Jonson collaborated with Thomas Dekker, Henry Chettle, and others in 1599.

Robin Hood. In *The Sad Shepherd*, Robin Hood lives with his lady, Marian, and his "family," or entourage, in Sherwood Forest. He welcomes the shepherds and shepherdesses to his feast and is grieved and gentle when he hears of Aeglamour's sadness. His and Marian's true love for each other is celebrated, so he is surprised and hurt when Maudlin, disguised as Marian, insults him. He is happy when he and Marian are reconciled. He sends out the witch-hunters. The second time Maudlin disguises herself as Marian, he is not fooled, and he steals her magic belt.

Robinson, Richard (d. 1648). An actor who, as one of the King's Men, performed in *Catiline* in 1611. In the same year he also acted in *The Second Maiden's Tragedy*. Apparently he was very adept in playing women's roles, for Jonson lauded him in this capacity in *The Devil Is an Ass* (II. viii; III. iv). Robinson acted in Shakespeare's plays and was a signatory to the dedication of the Beaumont and Fletcher Folio in 1647.

Roe (Rowe), Sir John (1581–?1606), the eldest son of William Roe, a London merchant, was an intimate friend of Jonson's. He died of the plague in Jonson's arms, probably about 1606. According to the *Conversations* (ll. 155–59), Jonson claimed Roe loved him and that when they were ushered from a masque by Lord Suffolk Roe wrote a moral epistle to him which stated that next to plays the Court and the State were best. Jonson said that Roe was a big spender, but when he died Jonson paid the funeral expenses, for which he was later reimbursed (ll. 184–87). Jonson wrote an inscription in Latin for Roe which he included in a gift copy of Casaubon's edition of Persius (1605). *Epig.* XXVII, XXXII, and XXXIII are meditations on the death of Sir John, who addressed two 1604 poems to Jonson: "The state and men's affairs are the best plays" and "If great men wrong me, I will spare myself" (both of which were first published in *Poems of John Donne* [1635]).

Roe, Sir Thomas (1581–1644), second son of William Roe, entered Magdalen College, Oxford, in 1593. He was knighted in 1605. In 1614 he was ambassador to the Great Mogul, and he was made Chancellor of the Garter in 1621. Jonson addressed *Epig.* XCVIII and XCIX to Sir Thomas. Roe may have been the "T. R." who prefixed verses to the 1605 quarto of *Sejanus* and to the 1607 quarto of *Volpone*.

Roe, William (1585–1667), third son of William Roe, was educated at Eton and entered King's College, Cambridge, as a scholar in 1604. In 1610 Jonson appeared as a witness for Roe in a lawsuit between Roe and Walter Garland. In *Epig.* LXX Jonson offered counsel to the young Roe, and in *Epig.* CXXVIII he wished him well on a journey.

Romano, Julio (1492?–1546). Italian painter, architect, and decorator. His real name was Giulio Pippi. He was Raphael's favorite pupil; after Raphael's death Romano completed the frescoes in the Vatican of the life of Constantine, begun by Raphael. In 1524 he entered the service of the Duke of Mantua, for whom he completed a number of painting, architectural, and engineering projects. Known as one of the creators of mannerism, Romano was appointed architect to St. Peter's in 1546, but he died later that year. Jonson mentions him in *Und.* LXXVII and in *Timber* (l. 1584). See also PAINTING.

Rome. A well-known puppet play about Julius Caesar mentioned in *Every Man out* (after the second sounding).

Romulus. See REMUS.

Ronsard, Pierre (1524?–1585). French poet, royal born, who became the leader of the Pléiade. He composed poems on a variety of themes including patriotism, love, and death. He wrote sonnets on Petrarch, Pindaric and Horatian odes, elegies, eclogues, and songs. He left unfinished his most ambitious project, an epic entitled *La Franciade* (1572). His most famous love poems were published in *Sonnets pour Hélène* (1578). Jonson mentions Ronsard's Cassandra in *Und.* XXVII. According to Drummond (l. 72), Jonson said that Ronsard's best pieces were his odes.

Rosin, Father. In *A Tale of a Tub*, a minstrel who is to perform with his boys at the wedding of Awdrey.

Rosinus, Johannes (1551–1626). German antiquarian and theologian. Author of *Romanae Antiquitates* (1583), one of Jonson's authorities for archaeology.

Rowe, Nicholas (1674–1718). English dramatist and editor who was made poet laureate in 1715. His best plays were *The Fair Penitent* (1703) and *Jane Shore* (1714), both tales of man's inhumanity to woman. In his well-known *The Works of Mr. William Shakespear* (1709), Rowe wrote that Jonson was certainly a good scholar and in that respect had a certain advantage over Shakespeare, although what books gave to Jonson was more than balanced out by what nature gave to Shakespeare. Rowe helped to preserve the tradition that Shakespeare intervened with his company to persuade them to produce Jonson's *Every Man in His Humour,* in which we know that Shakespeare did play a leading role.

Rowley, William (d. 1626). An actor who joined the King's Men in 1623. He played the part of the fat Bishop in Middleton's *A Game at Chess.* Rowley's death is alluded to in *The Staple of News* (III. ii).

Rudyerd, Sir Benjamin (1572–1658), was knighted and made Surveyor of the Court of Wards in 1618. He began a political career in 1620, advocating redress of grievances. He and the 3rd Earl of Pembroke were friends, and their poems were published together in 1660. Jonson praised Rudyerd in *Epig.* CXXI, CXXII, and CXXIII.

Rufus. One of the conspirators against Sabinus in *Sejanus.* He expresses hope that the trickery of his friends and himself will win one of them a consulship and gossips maliciously about Sabinus' ties to Agrippina. He hides while Latiaris tricks Sabinus into criticizing Tiberius, then rushes out and drags him away on a charge of treason.

Rumming, Elinor, ran an alehouse at Leatherhead near the royal palace of Nonsuch in the reign of Henry VIII. She was made famous by John Skelton's *The Tunnyng of Elynour Rumming,* about the drunken women who gathered at her place. Jonson mentions her in *A Tale of a Tub* (v. vii), and she appears in the antimasque of *The Fortunate Isles.*

Rut, Doctor. In *The Magnetic Lady,* the physician to Lady Loadstone.

Rutland, Elizabeth Sidney, Countess of (d. 1612). The daughter of Sir Philip Sidney and the wife of Roger Manners, 5th Earl of Rutland, whom she married in 1599. Jonson lauded her in *Epig.* LXXIX and *Forest* XII. According to the *Conversations* (l. 397), she was also a character in his lost play *The May Lord.* Jonson probably also addressed *Und.* L to her, but he suppressed her name. She danced in *Hymenaei* and died in 1612. In the *Conversations* (ll. 213–22), Jonson stated that the countess was not inferior in poetry to her father, that Sir Thomas Overbury was in love with her and asked Jonson to read Overbury's *The Wife* to her, and that Beaumont wrote an elegy on her death. Jonson also said that one day when he was eating with Lady Rutland her husband came in and accused her of keeping table to poets. She wrote Jonson about it, and he answered her, but his letter was intercepted by her husband; however, Lord Rutland apparently never challenged Jonson (ll. 357–60).

Rutter, Joseph, one of Jonson's literary sons, contributed an elegy ("Now thou art dead, and thy great wit and name") to *Jonsonus Virbius.* Jonson had prefixed a commendatory poem ("To My Dear Son, and Right-Learned Friend, Master Joseph Rutter") to Rutter's first play *The Shepherd's Holy-Day* (1635). Rutter's patron was Sir Kenelm Digby, Jonson's literary executor.

Rymer, Thomas (1643?–?1713). English critic and historiographer educated at Cambridge. In 1673, he refused a call to the bar and turned his efforts to criticism of drama. In 1677 he published *The Tragedies of the Last Age,* which included a hostile attack on contemporary dramatists. Made historiographer royal in 1692, Rymer began work on *Foedera,* a multivolume compilation of all public documents showing relations between England and other nations from 1101 to 1654. The last volume of *Foedera* was not published until 1735, twenty-two years after Rymer's death. In *A Short View of Tragedy* (1693), Rymer criticized Jonson's *Catiline* on several grounds. He considered the chorus unnecessary and ludicrous. He said too much of the play was word for word translation and that Jonson had included too much comedy and too many apocryphal matters in the history. "Where the poet has chosen a subject of importance sufficient and proper for tragedy, there is no room for this petty interlude in diversion."

S

Sabinus, Titius. A noble, high-minded Roman in *Sejanus,* friend to Germanicus and cousin to Latiaris. He and Silius meet at the beginning of the play and comment on how they are out of place at the corrupt Roman court. Sabinus speaks scornfully of Sejanus and his lackeys and Tiberius and highly praises Drusus senior and Germanicus. He is counted as a threat by Sejanus and Tiberius for his devotion to Agrippina. He is shocked and horrified by the charges against Silius, his death, and the burning of Cordus' books. Latiaris tricks Sabinus into speaking against Tiberius before witnesses; he is arrested and dragged away. Arruntius speaks almost immediately afterward of his death.

Sackville, Sir Edward. See Sir Edward Sackville, Earl of DORSET.

Sackville, Richard (1622–1677), Baron Buckhurst, succeeded his father Edward as 5th Earl of Dorset in 1652. He contributed an elegy ("If Romulus did promise in the fight") to *Jonsonus Virbius.*

Sad Shepherd, The.
Acted: The play is a fragment, but it seems to have been performed privately at some nobleman's house during the reign of Charles II.

Published: 1640 in folio by Thomas Walkley.

Printer: Unknown.

There have been two attempts to complete the play. F. G. Waldron published his continuation in 1783, and Alan Porter his in 1935.

Prologue. Jonson tells his audience that if they patiently attend his play, he will give them an English pastoral to rival those of other nations. He gives a short sketch of the setting of the story and the complication of Aeglamour's lost love. He then criticizes those who say that a pastoral cannot be happy, saying that this is its natural mood. He says that he will not heed the critics if they judge his play harshly or unfairly dislike it just because it does not fit current fashion, and he warns his audience against the "folly" of judging works this way.

Act I. Aeglamour, "the sad" shepherd, comes on stage and mourns for his love Earine, "the beautiful" shepherdess, who Maudlin, "the envious" of Papplewicke, has told him is drowned. Meanwhile, in Robin Hood's bower, Marian decides to pass the time until Robin returns by hunting a stag for food at the feast. Friar Tuck orders the details of setting for the feast with George-a-Green and Much, Robin Hood's porter and bailiff. Aeglamour enters and tells them why he is mourning and how he cannot be cheered; they fear that this will ruin the feast.

Robin welcomes the shepherds and shepherdesses to his feast. Clarion, "the rich" shepherd, criticizes those people who think they neglect their duties for merry making, and Tuck criticizes those greedy shepherds who really do abuse their own and their neighbors' flocks. They reminisce about the "happy age" when all the rural folk joined in celebrating spring. Aeglamour speaks of getting revenge on the river in which Earine was drowned; he refuses to be comforted. Karolin, "the kind" shepherd, Earine's brother, sings to try to console him but Aeglamour forces Amie, "the gentle" shepherdess, to kiss Karolin for his reward, then leaves. Clarion and the others speak of the sadness of love and of the perfect love of Robin and Marian. Marian enters and tells of catching the stag and of the Raven, which cried over it while they cut it up. They all decide that the Raven was probably Maudlin. Marian leaves to see to the stag; Maudlin comes on disguised as Marian. She offends Robin and his men, calling them rude names, and has the stag sent to her own house. Robin and his men are baffled at what they believe to be Marian's conduct.

Act II. Maudlin meets her daughter, Douce, "the proud," and joyfully tells her of the doubts and confusions she has sown. She tells Douce to dress in Earine's clothes and charm the shepherds, and she reveals that Earine is not drowned but locked up in a tree as the prisoner of her son, Lorel, "the rude" swineherd. Lorel tries to woo Earine by telling her of his wealth and offering her hedgehogs and badgers, but she is disdainful of him. Maudlin upbraids him for his awkwardness. She tells Douce that she may change her shape many times that day, but that her daughter may always recognize her by her magic belt, made one night at a witches' sabbath.

Back at Robin's bower, Amie is distressed and does not know why. Marian meets Robin, who is at first cold and distrusting. They realize that Maudlin deceived them by pretending to be Marian, and they are reconciled. Maudlin comes and ironically thanks Marian for the deer. While she is there, Robin's man Scathlock returns with the deer, which was reclaimed as soon as the misunderstanding was revealed. Maudlin flies into a fury and curses Robin's cook, who is suddenly stricken with a crippling disease. Amie reveals that she is lovesick for Karolin. Little John, Alken ("the wise" shepherd), Robin's man Scarlet, Scathlock, and George go to hunt Maudlin, and speak of the trickery they must use and of the horrors of the "Witches' Dell" where Maudlin lives.

Act III. Puck-Hairy enters and tells how he is Maudlin's devil and is bound to help her. Karolin meets Douce and speaks with her; Aeglamour comes in; Douce flees and Aeglamour thinks Douce was Earine's ghost. Clarion goes to find him. Lionel, "the courteous" shepherd, tells Karolin of Amie's love for him. Maudlin comes dressed as Marian and tries to keep them from going to cure Amie of her lovesickness; Robin enters, senses the deception, and steals Maudlin's belt. She flees in her own shape and goes to tell Puck her troubles. He tells her to "be wary." They meet Lorel, who is going to the tree to woo Earine.

Jonson's fragment ends here, but F. G. Waldron's continuation finishes the play as follows:

Lorel again tries to woo Earine, who still scorns him. Clarion happens along; Lorel shuts Earine back up in the tree and flees. Earine sings, charming Clarion and haunting Aeglamour, who wanders across the stage. Earine manages to put her hand through a crack in the tree; as Clarion runs toward it, Maudlin causes darkness suddenly to fall. Clarion suspects that Earine may be trapped in the tree by Maudlin's witchcraft. Douce enters, wondering at the change in how people treat her since she has been dressed in Earine's clothes. Maudlin enters, grumbling at Lorel. She tells her children to go gather weeds for her potions. Puck reveals that he has only a short time left to serve Maudlin, and then he can be a good fairy and torment her and her children. Robin brings Maudlin's belt to Marian; Lionel and Mellifleur, "the sweet" shepherdess, pair up; and Karolin kisses and sings away Amie's lovesickness. The scene switches to the

witch-hunters who, by their impatience, have just narrowly missed capturing Maudlin. Alken tells them that Puck tormented and frightened Lorel and Douce when they were in the swamp. The witch-hunters find Maudlin, working magic, in her dell; Douce and Lorel come to her with the herbs they have gathered; Lorel tells of being frightened in the woods. The witch hunters run to capture her, but Puck, performing his last service for her, helps her disappear and so to be saved from them.

Act IV. Robin and Marian reenter and congratulate Karolin and Amie on their love; they speak of the joys of living in Sherwood Forest. Robin encourages Lionel to kiss Mellifleur. The witch-hunters return with Earine, delighting all present. Alken tells of their battle with Lorel, whom Little John finally overcame and so saved Earine. He says that they came upon Maudlin as Puck was leaving her and fixed an amulet around her neck that renders her powerless and cannot be removed until she repents. Mellifleur returns and says that while she and Lionel were dallying by the river, they found that Aeglamour had drowned himself. The company mourns as Aeglamour's body is brought in; Clarion tells how he tried and failed to save him, and the company goes to the cell of Reuben, a devout hermit. Puck sees their sadness and resolves to do all he can, as a good fairy, to save Aeglamour. The scene shifts to Lorel's oak, where Lorel lies bleeding from the witch-hunters' attack. Douce resolves to reform, and Lorel decides that things cannot get worse for him, so he will at least go along with her. They meet Maudlin, who is nursing her pain. She quarrels with Lorel, and her children help her to Reuben's cell when she also decides to reform. Reuben enters near his cell and tells of the joys of his holy hermit's life. The procession of shepherds and Robin Hood's entourage bring Aeglamour in. Reuben instructs them to pray for Aeglamour and goes into his cell to do so himself. Tuck praises Reuben and God, Robin's entourage praises him for his clear reassurance, unlike the confused messages often given in churches. Douce and Lorel bring Maudlin in; she begs forgiveness from Tuck and is horrified to learn that she has been the cause of Aeglamour's drowning. Offering to help in what way she can to rescue Aeglamour, Maudlin goes with Tuck to see Reuben, as Douce and Lorel leave.

240

Act V. Earine sings, praising God in prayer and asking for Aeglamour to be returned to life. Maudlin and Douce enter, and Earine is frightened, but Douce assures her that they have both reformed. Clarion enters and says that Aeglamour is breathing, but is crazed and calling for Earine; she flies to him. Clarion is taken with Douce and pledges his love and riches. Douce cannot believe her good fortune. Maudlin approves gratefully of the match, and Clarion says that he will pay her "every filial duty and respect." Puck comes on and tells of his part in saving Earine; he taunts Lorel, who is still surly and vengeful toward Aeglamour. Lorel says that he wants to reform; Puck tells him to go to Reuben, then delights in being a good fairy. Earine, at Reuben's suggestion, holds Aeglamour's hand and sings to him. He recovers but at first cannot be convinced that he is not in heaven. Robin thanks Puck and Reuben. Aeglamour's senses clear, and he knows where he is. Maudlin asks everyone's pardon, and Douce and Lorel show that they have reformed. Clarion tells of his plan to marry Douce and make Lorel his herdsman. The amulet falls from Maudlin's neck, showing that she has truly reformed. Reuben asks all present to pardon her completely. Tuck agrees to marry the three couples—Lionel and Mellifleur, Karolin and Amie, Clarion and Douce—and the play ends with all the characters singing and joyfully going to Robin's feast.

Porter's continuation is as follows:

Lorel decides to use force on Earine and breaks open the tree, but she still resists him. Before he can follow through with his threats to her, he hears someone coming and hurriedly pushes her back into the tree. Clarion enters, exclaiming that he thought he had heard voices in strife. Earine begins to sing, and her singing not only moves Clarion but also draws in Aeglamour, who is nearby. They are both enthralled by the music, and Aeglamour, overcome by sadness, leaves. Clarion discovers Earine's hand protruding from the tree and desires to see the whole body of such a beautiful creature. He asks her to speak, and voices respond from the tree. Suddenly a mist descends, and Clarion rushes away in confusion and darkness, whereupon Maudlin, Lorel, and Douce appear. Maudlin tells Lorel to get on with the wooing of Earine, but he says he is not

interested in her anymore. Lorel goes to the tree and stuffs Earine completely inside as Maudlin curses Robin for stealing her girdle and vows revenge. She then instructs her children to go and gather materials for her cauldron. As they leave, Puck enters with everything she needs and chastises Maudlin for not calling upon him, reminding her that he is the source of her cunning, but she disagrees as they leave for her den. Friar Tuck, John, Scathlock, Scarlet, and George enter, hot on the trail of the witch. They are shortly drawn by Alken, who reports that he has seen Maudlin and Puck in her den. They all go to capture her there as Alken reminds them not to be too impatient. Maudlin is seen before her cauldron working a spell on Robin and conjuring up schemes. When the witch-hunters who are watching can endure no more, they charge Maudlin, and she escapes but not before they are able to land a few blows on her. The witch-hunters decide to return to Robin to report what has happened and to warn him of the witch's intended malice.

Act IV. Inspired by the happy effects upon Amie of Karolin's kiss, Lionel and Mellifleur renew their own affection in revisiting the scenes of their first falling in love. Meanwhile Amie and Karolin outvie each other in expressing the depth of their love. Robin, Friar Tuck, Little John, and George enter, discussing the encounter with Maudlin while Karolin and Amie wander off. Clarion in a pensive mood joins them, and they are interrupted by Much, who reports that Puck has caused the dishes for the feast to be ruined, but Clarion offers to replenish all from his own supply. As Robin, Tuck, and Little John leave to go to find Marian, Clarion is joined by Douce, who is well-dressed and who has been told by Maudlin to show herself among the shepherd folk. Clarion confesses to Douce that he is in love, and since she is taken with him and suspects that he loves Earine she tells him about the tree and agrees to help him find his lover in the forest. Meanwhile Tuck recovers Maudlin's girdle, and she plans further mischief, as Alken decides to take Aeglamour to the good hermit Reuben to see if he can comfort the sad shepherd. Douce leads Clarion to the tree and releases Earine, who is grateful but wants to see Aeglamour. Disappointed, Clarion agrees to take her to Robin's bower to rest. Maudlin discovers that Earine had been freed, and Puck tells her that Clarion set Earine free. Puck vows to have nothing more to do with helping Maudlin as she herself schemes new plots.

Act V. At Robin's bower, as Tuck and Much are busy preparing the feast, Clarion enters and reports that Earine has been found. When Tuck and Much leave, Maudlin, disguised as Earine, enters, feigns love to Clarion, and leaves. Robin and Marian come in and note joyfully Clarion's changed disposition. Lorel arrives and reports that Reuben has a message for Robin, and all depart to discover what it is. Meanwhile at the hermit's dell, Reuben instructs Aeglamour in courage. Robin, Marian, and Clarion arrive and announce that Earine lives. Reuben then delivers his message to Robin, which is that the king has pardoned Robin and made him keeper of Sherwood Forest and Earl of Huntingdon. Thereafter, still believing in the false Earine's protestation, Clarion falls into conflict with Aeglamour over Earine, but Reuben assures him that he is the victim of another of Maudlin's schemes. They vow vengeance upon her, but Reuben persuades them to have pity on the disenchanted old woman. At Robin's bower Maudlin again appears as Earine but is exposed and invited to the feast, but she storms away angry. Lorel and Douce arrive, and the true Earine and Aeglamour are reunited, and Clarion is comforted by Douce. Karolin and Amie, and Lionel and Mellifleur come in, and all dance a Morris, after which the friar offers thanks to God and Robin makes a speech lauding the pastoral life. Puck creeps up and snatches away Robin's plate as the feast finally begins.

Sailors. A group of "pickled sailors" from Neptune's fleet appears as the second antimasque in *Neptune's Triumphs for the Return of Albion.*

Saint-Amant, Gerard, Marc-Antoine, Sieur de. Included in *L'Albion Caprice Heroï-Comique* (1640), first printed in *Oeuvres Complètes de Saint-Amant* (1855), is a poem entitled "Le vain Anglois," one stanza of which exclaims:

Il a neanmois l'audace
De vanter ses rimailleurs;
A son goust ils sont meilleurs
Que Virgile ny qu'Horace.
Seneque au prix d'un Jonson
Pour la force et pour la son
N'est qu'un poete insipide,
Et le fameux Euripide
N'a ny grace ny façon.

Saint-Evremond, Charles de Saint-Denis, Seigneur de. In his *Oeuvres meslées* (1705) de Saint-Evremond in writing of the two playwrights as representative of their respective countries declares: "Notre Molière à qui les Anciens ont inspiré le bon espirit de la Comédie, égale leur Ben Johnson à bien représenter les diverses Humeurs & les differentes Manieres des hommes; l'un & l'autre conservant dans leur peintures un juste rapport avec le génie de leur Nation."

Salisbury, Sir Robert Cecil, Earl of (1563?–1612), son of William Cecil, Baron Burghley, was a sickly, deformed child. He was educated at home and at Cambridge. In 1588 he was a member of Lord Derby's mission to negotiate a peace with the Spanish Netherlands, and he later entered Parliament and gradually came to rank second only to his father as adviser to Queen Elizabeth, beginning about 1589 to perform the duties of secretary of state and being officially appointed to that position in 1596. The following year he was made chancellor of the duchy of Lancaster. Despite the rivalry of Sir Francis Bacon and the Earl of Essex, Cecil succeeded his father in 1598 as chief minister. When Essex was executed in 1601, the way was cleared for Cecil to secretly negotiate the accession of James VI of Scotland to the English throne as James I after the death of Elizabeth. After James's accession, Cecil was created Baron Cecil in 1603, Viscount Cranborne in 1604, and Earl of Salisbury in 1605. Cecil, unlike the Earl of Somerset and the Duke of Buckingham, who also had great influence with the king, was powerful because of his abilities. For the rest of his life nearly the entire administration of the government was in his care. In 1608 he was also made Lord Treasurer. Salisbury exhibited considerable financial skill, reducing the public debt and attempting to restrain James's extravagance. Salisbury greatly increased customs duties without the consent of Parliament, began the ruinous Stuart policy of attempting to circumvent Parliament in acquiring revenue, and failed to get acceptance for his proposed Great Contract with Parliament, whereby James would have received a settled income in return for abandoning his feudal revenues. In foreign affairs, Salisbury tried to maintain a balance of power between France and Spain although after 1604 he received a pension from Spain. His hope that England might become the leader of a Protestant alliance led him to support the marriage of James's daughter to the Elector Palatine. Before his death in 1612 Salisbury planned and had constructed the great Jacobean mansion known as Hatfield House, which remained in possession of the family. During his lifetime, Salisbury restrained James from serious error, but the earl's adherence to outmoded Elizabethan policies did not prepare James for the new problems facing him.

Jonson's relationship with Salisbury seems to have had its ups and downs. In 1597, as Sir Robert Cecil, Salisbury was a member of the Privy Council that found *The Isle of Dogs* offensive. When Jonson was imprisoned for his part in *Eastward Ho,* Salisbury was one of the powerful persons to whom Jonson appealed for help in gaining his freedom. Two days after the abortive Gunpowder Plot Salisbury commissioned Jonson to convey a promise of safe conduct to an unnamed priest who had offered to help the state, but Jonson was unable to locate the priest, as he reported in an extant letter to Salisbury. In the *Conversations* (ll. 317–21), Jonson told Drummond that when he was at the end of Salisbury's table with Inigo Jones and Salisbury asked him why he was not happy Jonson replied that the lord had said that he would dine with him, but that he did not because the poet could not eat from his lord's dish. Later in the *Conversations* (ll. 353–54), Jonson said that Salisbury never cared for any man longer than he could use him. Despite his ambivalent attitude toward Salisbury, Jonson did address three epigrams to him (*Epig.* XLIII, LXIII, LXIV) and he wrote the entertainments for the two kings and for the king and queen given by Salisbury at Theobalds, a Cecil family seat before it was transferred to James.

Sallust (86–?34 B.C.). Caius Sallustius Crispus, Roman historian, served as tribune of the people in 52 B.C. and as praetor in 46 B.C. He was ejected from the Senate in 50 B.C., ostensibly for adultery but probably because of his support of Caesar. After his praetorship, he served as Caesar's governor in Numidia, where he was accused of enriching himself from the province. His principal work is the *Bellum Catilinarium,* which Jonson had a copy of in his personal library and used as one of his main sources for *Catiline His Conspiracy.* Sallust's account of the Jugurthine War is of little value as history, his history of Rome probably covering 78 B.C. to 67 B.C. is extant only in fragments, and his two extant letters in highly rhetorical style are of dubious authenticity. As a historian Sallust was inaccurate and biased, but he was important as one of the first writers to produce historical monographs dealing with limited events and periods, and his style is direct and terse, his character sketches being particularly vivid.

Salomon. John Littlewit's servant in *Bartholomew Fair,* whose only action is going for Cokes's marriage license when Waspe comes to get it.

Salusbury, Sir Thomas (d. 1643). The grandson of Sir John Salusbury to whom Robert Chester dedicated *Love's Martyr.* In 1601, Sir Thomas wrote an elegy on the death of Jonson ("An Elegy Meant Upon the Death of Ben Jonson") which may have been meant for inclusion in *Jonsonus Virbius* but was not published until 1935, when Sir Israel Gollancz printed it in the *Times Literary Supplement,* October 8. In 1636 Sir Thomas published a poem entitled *The History of Joseph.*

Sandys, Sir Edwin (1561–1629). English statesman. A pupil of Richard Hooker's. He was a leading promoter of the colony in Virginia. Although he was knighted upon the accession of James I in 1603, he later denied the divine right of kings. In 1605 he published *A Relation of the State of Religion.* He is mentioned in *Timber* (l. 903) as a man excellent in both wit and language.

Sanga, Quintus Fabius. In *Catiline,* Cicero's emissary to the ambassadors from the Allobroges from whom he gets documentary evidence of Catiline's conspiracy for the Senate.

Sanquinius. A minor character in *Sejanus,* one of the Senators who blindly follows Sejanus in hope of gaining power for himself. He is only mentioned by name when Arruntius mocks him for hurrying, with "his slow belly, and his dropsie," to the Senate to acclaim Sejanus. His only lines involve his joining group opinion, first in praising, then deriding, Sejanus.

Sappho. Usually considered the greatest of the early Greek lyric poets, Sappho lived about 600 B.C. and was born on Lesbos although she lived much of her life in Sicily. She was married to Cerkylas and had a daughter named Cleis. One of her brothers was named Charaxus. Sappho headed a school or cult of young girls devoted to the study of poetry and music and to the worship of Aphrodite, goddess of beauty and love. Many of her poems were apparently written to young girls in this cult. The date or circumstances of Sappho's death are uncertain, but legend has it that she committed suicide by leaping from the Leucadian Rock, out of despair over her unrequited love for the youth Phaon. Sappho's poetry was greatly admired by the ancients, who often considered her the tenth Muse.

Saron. A little-known marine god sometimes considered the god of navigation, he appears as one of the characters in *Neptune's Triumph for the Return of Albion* who lauds Neptune and celebrates Albion's triumphant return. He also appears in a significant role in *The Fortunate Isles, and Their Union,* where he extols Neptune's glory.

Sartorio (del Sarto), Andrea (1486–1531). Florentine painter. He painted mostly religious subjects and was noted for his harmonious colors and consonance of figures and background. He is mentioned in *Timber* (l. 1585) as one of six famous Italian painters. See also PAINTING.

Satan. The great devil in Jonson's *The Devil Is an Ass.*

'Satires.' In the *Conversations* (l. 102), Drummond indicates that Jonson read to him a satire of his on a lady "come from the Bath" and another one (ll. 105–07) on "all the abuses in England and the world." Neither of these pieces has survived.

Satiro-Mastix, or The Untrussing of the Humorous Poet. See Thomas DEKKER.

Saturn. An agricultural god of Italy who was later identified with the Greek god Cronus. Saturn was the husband of Ops and the father of Jupiter, Juno, Neptune, Ceres, and Pluto. He became a legendary king of Rome and was praised for introducing agriculture and for helping to establish Roman civilization. His reign was considered a golden age. In celebration of this age, the Romans held a Saturnalia, a festival at the end of December at which time gifts were exchanged, schools and courts were closed, war was held off, and slaves and masters were allowed to eat at the same table.

Saturnalia. See SATURN.

Saturnius. Indicating a son of Saturn, particularly Jupiter, Pluto, or Neptune.

satyrs. Followers of Dionysus, satyrs were minor gods associated with the country and with fertility and nature. They were part human and part bestial creatures found in forests and mountains, usually represented as hairy, having the tails and ears of a horse, and the horns of a goat. A satyr was depicted as similar in appearance to the silenus and faun. Satyrs were represented in Greek literature as wild and licentious creatures who were always merrily drinking and dancing and engaging in mischief.

Savile, Sir Henry (1549–1622), was a Fellow of Merton College in 1565 and Warden in 1585. He became Provost of Eton College in 1596. At Oxford he founded chairs of geometry and astronomy. In 1591 he translated four books of the *Histories* of Tacitus, adding an original section, *The End of Nero and the Beginning of Galba.* His edition of Chrysostom was published in eight volumes from 1610 to 1613. One of the most learned men of his day, Sir Henry was lauded by Jonson in *Epig.* XCV and served as one of the translators of the Bible under King James.

Saviolina. In *Every Man out of His Humour,* a court lady who is dull-witted but is admired by Fastidious Brisk.

Savory, Abraham. Actor in the Duke of Lennox's company in 1605. He later became a conjurer and was implicated in the Overbury murder. In Jonson's *The Devil Is an Ass* (I. ii), Fitzdottrel alludes to him as one who is unable to show man the devil.

Scala, Flaminio. An actor professionally known as Flavio in the *commedia dell'arte* who published a collection of scenari in Venice in 1611. In *Volpone* (II. iii), Corvino calls the disguised Volpone by this name when he beats him away in the mountebank scene.

Scaliger, Joseph Justus (1540–1609), son of Julius Caesar Scaliger, was born in 1540 in France. Like his father, Joseph became a classical scholar. He became a Protestant in 1562, served as a companion to a Poitevin nobleman from 1563 to 1570, studied under Cujas at Valence from 1570 to 1572, and was appointed professor of philosophy at Geneva from 1572 to 1574. After 1593 he was a research professor at Leiden. A man of great erudition, Scaliger was learned in mathematics, philosophy, and many languages. He was a promoter of critical scientific methods of textual criticism and classical study. Scaliger surveyed all the ways known then of measuring time and established knowledge of ancient calendars on a scientific basis in *De emendatione temporum* (1583), restored the content of the lost original of Eusebius' chronicle (second book), and summarized the chronological basis for the modern study of ancient history in *Thesaurus temporum* (1606).

Scaliger's *Cyclometrica Elementa* (1594), a highly controversial work, is ridiculed in *The New Inn* (II. v). In the *Conversations* (ll. 517–19), Jonson said that Scaliger wrote an epitaph (in his *Opuscula* [1612] to Casaubon (actually Stephanus Ubertus) in which he scorned his speaking Latin, for he thought he had spoken English to him. Jonson's discussion of envy in *Timber* (ll. 258–305) is taken from Scaliger's *Opuscula*.

Scaliger, Julius Caesar (1484–1558). Italian philologist and physician. He studied medicine and settled as a physician in 1526 in Agen, where he became a naturalized French citizen. Very learned but vain and contentious, he quarreled with Erasmus and Jerome Cardan. He analyzed Cicero's style in his *De causis linguae Latinae* (1540) and pointed out over six hundred errors of his humanist predecessors. Scaliger also wrote medical and botanical commentaries on Hippocrates, Theophrastus, and Aristotle, and he called for an improved classification of plants on the basis of their unique characteristics. His famous *Poetice* (1561), in which he praised Virgil and Seneca, was particularly important in the establishment of neoclassical principles such as the so-called unities.

Jonson used Scaliger's *De causis linguae Latinae* as one of his authorities for the first book of *The English Grammar*, and he was familiar with Scaliger's *Poetice*, citing it as one of his authorities for the epithalamium in *Hymenaei*. In Chorus I of *The Magnetic Lady*, Jonson employed Scaliger's terminology in the *Poetice* for the parts of comedy. Jonson's annotations in his copy of Chapman's *The Whole Works of Homer, Prince of Poets* (1616) indicate that Jonson was critical of Chapman's harsh treatment of Scaliger in his commentary for the edition.

Scamander. A river near Troy which for fighting Achilles was attacked and burned by Vulcan.

Scapethrift. In *Eastward Ho,* an adventurer who plans to sail with Sir Petronel Flash to Virginia.

Scarlet. One of Robin Hood's huntsmen in *The Sad Shepherd,* brother to Scathlock. He goes with Marian to hunt the stag, and when the hunting party returns, tells of how he saw Maudlin sitting and broiling a bone. Scarlet is one of the witch-hunters and tells some witch-hunting lore he knows.

Scathlock. One of Robin Hood's huntsmen in *The Sad Shepherd,* brother to Scarlet. He is common and superstitious, but brave. He accompanies Marian on her stag hunt and tells how he thought the ominous crow which croaked when they killed the stag was Maudlin. After they realize that Maudlin fooled them by pretending to be Marian and ordering the stag sent to her, Scathlock goes and reclaims the stag from Lorel which he earlier took there. Marian gives him gold for his trouble. He is one of the witch-hunters who goes to catch Maudlin.

Scoto of Mantua. A professional actor, celebrated in England for his juggling and magic tricks. He was the leader of an Italian company licensed by the Duke of Mantua. His real name was Dionisio. In the mountebank scene (II), Volpone impersonates him.

Scriben, Diogenes. In *A Tale of a Tub,* a supposedly great writer who is a companion to Tobie Turfe.

Scrivener. A man who comes on stage before *Bartholomew Fair* and reads the terms of an "agreement" between Jonson and his audience.

Scriverius, Petrus (1576–1660). Dutch scholar and writer. Editor of *Martial* (1619). Jonson owned a copy of Scriverius' edition and heavily annotated it.

Sculpture. A symbolic character who appears in *Chloridia* and supports the efforts of Fame to immortalize great actions.

Scylla. A sea monster with six heads and twelve feet who lived on the rocks opposite the whirlpool Charybdis and seized sailors from passing ships. Odysseus and Jason and the Argonauts passed between

Charybdis and Scylla in their wanderings. In another version of the myth, Scylla was the daughter of Nisus, king of Megara, who because she was madly in love with Minos, an enemy of her father's, cut off her father's hair in which his strength had its source. Afterwards, when she sought Minos' love, he scorned her. Eventually Nisus was changed into a sea eagle and Scylla into a sea bird eternally pursued by him.

Seagull. In *Eastward Ho,* a sea captain who heads Sir Petronel Flash's ship to Virginia.

Sea-horses. See TRITONS.

Sebasis. A symbolic personage representing veneration and appearing in a scene in Jonson's part of the *King's Coronation Entertainment.*

Sebastian. Servant to Count Ferneze in *The Case Is Altered.* He greets Valentine and the other servants and jokes with them at the beginning of the play. He is one of the servants who exasperate Count Ferneze because they cannot find Paulo. He plays a minor role in the play, his only other appearance being to joke with the rest of the servants during Onion's fencing bout with Martino. He could be (although he is not named) among the servants who bring in Camillo at the end of the play.

Sebastian of Venice (1485?–1547). Sebastiano del Piombo, whose real name was Sebastiano Luciani. A painter of the Venetian school who was influenced by Michelangelo, Sebastiano is most famous for his portraits. In *Timber* (l. 1584), he is mentioned as one of six famous Italian painters.

Secundus, Satrius. In *Sejanus,* one who hopes to gain power by following Sejanus. He is mocked early in the play by the noble Romans and arranges to have Eudemus meet Sejanus. He acts as a spy for Sejanus and is the primary accuser of Cordus at the Senate. He brings Sejanus the news of the first ill omens against him and is present at Sejanus' sacrifice to Fortune. Acting as a messenger, he brings word that Macro has come, and he advises Sejanus on how to receive him.

Security. In *Eastward Ho,* an old usurer and panderer who agrees to finance Sir Petronel Flash's journey to Virginia in exchange for the land belonging to Sir Pet-

ronel's wife, Gertrude. When the expedition fails because of a shipwreck, Security is imprisoned and mortified, but he is finally released through the intercession of Golding.

Segar, Captain Francis. Brother of Sir William Segar, Garter Principal King of Arms, Captain Francis was rewarded for his service to King James I. The album of Captain Francis contains an inscription in Latin by Jonson.

Seile, Henry. Bookseller in London from 1622 to 1661 who published *Jonsonus Virbius* in 1638.

Sejanus, Aelius. Crafty, corrupt, ambitious adviser to Tiberius in *Sejanus.* Noble Romans deplore the dictatorial sway he holds over Rome and his selfish manipulation of the already corrupt Tiberius. When he first appears, he grants Eudemus' request for an interview, then with the offer of a powerful job bribes Eudemus into betraying Livia's confidence and arranging an interview between Livia and Sejanus. He flatters Tiberius, who announces that a statue of him will be set up in Pompey's theater. Drusus draws on Sejanus when he demands that Drusus give way before him—Sejanus vows a crafty vengeance. Sejanus plots with Livia and Eudemus to have Drusus poisoned. He counsels Tiberius to act mercilessly against Agrippina and her followers, playing on Tiberius' fears. He sends Posthumus to tell Tiberius' mother, of supposed plots on Tiberius' life, to feed Tiberius' fears to a greater extent. He plots the destruction of Silius and Cordus and is happy with the results. When he asks for Livia's hand in marriage, however, Tiberius begins to realize the extent of his ambition and to fear him. In soliloquy Sejanus boasts of his power and his disdain of Caesar. Tiberius sets Macro to watch Sejanus while he leaves Rome; Macro's desire to ruin Sejanus grows when the story of how Sejanus saved Tiberius' life comes to Rome. Sejanus has Nero, Agrippina, and Drusus junior taken prisoner. His pride grows with his success, but Sejanus begins to fear when bad omens appear for him, and he engages in a ceremony to Fortune. When Fortune's statue turns from him, however, he is so proud that he takes the movement as a good omen and speaks again of his defiance of the gods. He makes provisions to guard himself against Macro, when he hears that the Senate is meeting, but he is taken in by Macro's story that a great honor awaits him, and he dismisses his guards. At the Senate, a letter from Tiberius denouncing him is read, and Sejanus, taken by surprise, is arrested. News is soon brought of his death and subsequent dismemberment by the mob.

Sejanus, His Fall.

Acted: 1603 by the King's Men.

Published: 1605 in quarto by Thomas Thorp.

Printer: George Elde.

Sejanus was not popular when it was first performed; the dedication says it "suffer'd no less violence from our people here, than the subject of it did from the rage of the people of Rome." Moreover, according to the *Conversations* (ll. 325–27), Jonson was summoned before the Privy Council at the behest of his enemy the Earl of Northampton to answer for Popish and treasonable tendencies in the play. There is no other record of such a summons or the outcome of it. The groundlings may not have liked the play, but Jonson's friends did—eight of them wrote commendatory poems that were prefixed to the quarto.

Dedication: to Lord Aubigny. Jonson says that his play has suffered the same disgrace as its namesake but is again gaining repute, because of "the love of good men," especially Aubigny.

To the Readers. Jonson apologizes for transgressing the proper poetic form, especially in terms of time, in *Sejanus,* but says that he should be forgiven this because of the play's serious merit. He announces his intention to publish soon his translation of, and commentary on, Horace's *Art of Poetry,* in which he will speak further of how far it is possible to observe the classical laws and forms in making plays for the present time. He adds that he has included the many marginal citations of his sources "to shew my integrity in the Story," tells what edition of Tacitus he used, says the play has been revised (by substituting lines of his own for those of a collaborator) since first acted, and ends by asserting that he is not entrusting his "felicity" to public opinion of the play.

Act I. Sabinus and Silius, two Roman senators, meet at the court of Tiberius Caesar; they are surprised to see each other there since both abominate the court, which is full of intriguers. They spot Satrius and Natta, two lackeys of Tiberius' favorite, Sejanus, and discuss the crimes they have committed in Sejanus' service. Two senators, Cordus, who has just finished writing a history of Rome from Pompey's time down to the present, and Arruntius, join Sabinus and Silius. The four men deplore the lawlessness and viciousness of Sejanus and Tiberius and recall the days of the Republic and the noble men of the past. (Throughout the play these men, especially Arruntius, and their friends serve as a sort of chorus, as they observe the actions of evil men and privately remark on them.) Drusus senior, son of Tiberius, passes through the court, and the four men discuss him. Arruntius faults him for loose living, but Sabinus and Silius praise him for opposing Sejanus and for his kind behavior to his cousins, the children of the late Germanicus, whose recent death (by poison, given him, it is rumored, on Sejanus' orders) grieves the four senators. They talk of Germanicus and his virtues. Sejanus enters the court, and Satrius tells him that one Eudemus wants to buy a tribuneship. When Sejanus learns that Eudemus is the physician of Livia, wife of Drusus senior, he asks Satrius to bring Eudemus, with his money, to him. The four senators discuss how Sejanus, who rose from the lowliest origins, is now virtually as powerful as Tiberius and has recently further strengthened his position by gathering the many separate bands of the Praetorian guard under one command, his own. Arruntius points out that next in the line of succession after Drusus senior are the three children of Germanicus, surely "too many for [Sejanus] to have a plot upon?"

Sejanus and Eudemus meet. Sejanus cajoles Eudemus into betraying Livia's confidences and Eudemus promises to arrange a meeting between Livia and Sejanus.

Tiberius, Sejanus, and Drusus appear at court; Tiberius receives messages from the Senate, among them a request for permission to build a temple to Tiberius. He makes a great show of disliking flattery and adulation and refuses the request but approves the Senate's decree that a statue of Sejanus be set up in Pompey's theater.

Drusus senior is outraged at this new mark of favor to Sejanus and later confronts Sejanus in anger, drawing his sword. Sejanus privately plots revenge.

Act II. Sejanus, who has sent his wife, Apicata, away because he now intends to marry Livia, meets with Livia and Eudemus, and the three discuss how to go about poisoning Drusus. They decide to have Lygdus, Drusus' cup-bearer, administer the poison, and discuss how to secure his cooperation. Sejanus is called away; while he is gone Eudemus advises Livia on cosmetics and ways of making herself attractive to Sejanus. Sejanus returns to say he is called to attend Tiberius. Livia and Eudemus go out, and Sejanus soliloquizes, reveling in his own wickedness: "Adultery? it is the lightest ill, / I will commit."

Sejanus and Tiberius talk of Agrippina, Germanicus' widow, and her friends. Sejanus plays upon Tiberius' fears that she, her friends, and her sons pose a threat to Tiberius. Sejanus suggests that destroying some members of the circle is the best course. They plan to destroy Silius, his wife Sosia, and Cordus immediately, Sabinus later.

Posthumus, one of Sejanus' followers, tells Sejanus of a meeting at Agrippina's; Sejanus asks Posthumus to have his lover Mutilia Prisca tell Augusta, Tiberius' mother, that Agrippina and her friends are plotting against Tiberius. Sejanus hopes Augusta will tell her son what she has heard, thus increasing his paranoia.

Sejanus' spies loiter near Agrippina's house, and her friends warn her to say nothing that could be used against her, advice she proudly refuses to allow. Drusus junior brings the news that Drusus senior has been poisoned and is dying. The senators exit, to attend the Senate meeting called by Tiberius at Sejanus' instigation, leaving Sosia with Agrippina.

Act III. At the Senate before the meeting Sejanus arranges for the consul Varro to accuse Silius of treason. Just as Silius is charged, Tiberius enters, makes a great show of sorrow over Drusus' death and speaks fondly of Germanicus' sons Nero and Drusus junior, whom he calls into the Senate. He asks the Senate to be their guardians. Throughout, Arruntius makes asides that scorn Tiberius' hypocrisy. Sejanus and many senators flatter Tiberius. Varro and Afer question and accuse Silius. Silius answers nobly but is finally goaded into speaking out against the corrupt leaders of government. After an impassioned speech, he draws his sword and kills himself. Tiberius pretends that he had intended to be merciful to Silius; at Lepidus' urging (in an aside Arruntius praises Lepidus) most of Silius' estate is left to his children instead of being confiscated. Sosia is declared proscribed, and then Cordus is accused of treason by Satrius and Natta. He defends his history, saying that Julius Caesar and Augustus Caesar tolerated writings critical of them. It is decided to try Cordus at another time, but orders are given to burn his history. Arruntius, Sabinus, and Lepidus lament what has befallen.

In private Tiberius and Sejanus gloat over their triumph. Sejanus asks Tiberius for Livia's hand. Tiberius refuses; he speaks disdainfully of Sejanus' not being a patrician and says that the match is politically unwise.

Sejanus, in angry soliloquy, plans to lull Tiberius into total preoccupation with the satisfaction of his perverse lusts and increase his own control of the government.

Tiberius confides to a servant that he fears Sejanus is ambitious to become emperor. He decides to set Macro against Sejanus and sends for Macro. Tiberius tells Macro to watch Rome and Sejanus in Tiberius' absence. Macro soliloquizes, revealing his ambition and utter lack of scruple.

Act IV. Agrippina talks of her friends who have been destroyed by Tiberius and Sejanus and her fears. News comes that Sejanus has saved Tiberius from being crushed when a roof collapsed; Agrippina laments that the danger to her sons— Nero, Drusus junior, and Caligula— increases as Sejanus' power grows.

Macro, alarmed at the news that Sejanus has saved Tiberius, decides to move against Sejanus quickly.

Three of Sejanus' followers—Rufus, Opsius, and Latiaris (who is Sabinus' cousin)—plot to destroy Sabinus in order to gain favor with Sejanus. Refus and Opsius hide while Latiaris tricks Sabinus into speaking against Tiberius; then they rush out and arrest him.

Macro advises Caligula to go to Tiberius and beg for mercy and to tell Tiberius that Sejanus is plotting against him.

Arruntius and Lepidus lament the growth of Sejanus' power and the death of Sabinus. Laco and the Lictors bring Nero in, on his way to exile, and report that Drusus junior has been taken prisoner and Agrippina banished. Arruntius rails against Tiberius for the monstrous acts he commits in his seclusion at Capri—rapes, torture, and murders. A group of Sejanus' followers, overheard by Lepidus and Arruntius, worriedly discuss the possibility that Sejanus may be falling out of favor with Tiberius.

Act V. Sejanus' followers tell him of various ill omens and urge him to make sacrifices to the gods. Sejanus scorns their advice, saying that Fortune is the only deity he adores. He orders them to prepare a ceremony at her temple.

At the house of the consul Regulus, Macro, Regulus, and Laco make plans to arrest Sejanus at a special meeting of the Senate that Tiberius is ordering.

The statue of Fortune turns its back on Sejanus in the ceremony he ordered. Sejanus orders the Praetorian guard called up when he learns that Macro has been with Regulus and that a meeting of the Senate has been called without his knowledge. Macro comes to Sejanus and tells him that Tiberius has called the special meeting for the purpose of making Sejanus a tribune. Rumor of this spreads among Sejanus' followers. His fears lulled, Sejanus sends the Praetorian guard away.

At the Senate, Sejanus' lackeys praise him and fight to sit near him. A letter from Tiberius to the Senate is read. When it begins to denounce Sejanus, his followers quickly move away from him. Sejanus is accused of treason and led away; Latiaris and Natto are also named and taken prisoner. Macro tells the Senate that Tiberius has given him Sejanus' former powers. The Senators are quick to denounce Sejanus and praise Caesar.

Lepidus speaks of how Sejanus' fall was dramatically sudden; he and Arruntius speak of the fickleness of common men and of "chance," and Arruntius prophesies that Macro will soon be as corrupt and powerful as Sejanus. Terentius tells them that the mob has torn Sejanus apart. Nuntius brings word that Macro ordered the murder of Sejanus' two young children and that their mother, Apicata, has vowed to expose Livia, Lygdus, and Eudemus as the murderers of Drusus senior. He says that the mob is beginning foolishly to repent of their action and to grieve for Sejanus. Lepidus, Arruntius, and Terentius warn against excessive pride and trust in fortune, telling the man who decides to mock the gods and stand alone to be cautioned by Sejanus' fall.

Selden, John (1584–1654). English jurist and scholar. Educated at Oxford, called to the bar in 1612, and elected to Parliament in 1623. He supported the rights of Parliament in its struggle with the crown, was prominent in the trial of the Duke of Buckingham, and helped to draft the Petition of Rights in 1628. In 1629 he was imprisoned for his part in the recalcitrant Parliament, but he was released in 1631, and represented Oxford University in the Long Parliament from 1640 to 1649. One of the most learned men of his day, Selden published *England's Epinomis* and *Jani Anglorum* (1610), both of which established him as the father of legal antiquarianism. He made a lifelong study of the origins of British law and summarized much of his findings in the preface to his edition of the Fleta (1647). Selden had a reputation as an Orientalist after the publication of his *De Diis Syris* (1617), and he wrote several studies of rabbinical law. His *History of Tithes* (1618) proved controversial, and the work was suppressed by James's government. His *Mare Clausum* (1635), written in response to Hugo Grotius' *Mare Liberum*, was a defense of England's right of sovereignty over the seas between that country and the Continent. Selden is perhaps best remembered for the record of his conversations kept by his secretary, Richard Milward, and published as *Table Talk* (1689).

Apparently, Jonson and Selden had a very pleasant relationship and were on good terms, as can be seen from Jonson's *Underwood* XIV which was originally prefixed to Selden's *Titles of Honour*. In *Titles of Honour* Selden explains how he used Jonson's library and drew upon his knowledge to clear up a number of matters, and in the second edition of the same work (1631) Selden states that "your curious learning and judgement may correct where I have erred and adde where my notes and memory have left me short." Jonson also respected Selden's opinion greatly and in 1615 apparently asked Selden to compile for him from holy scripture the text usually brought against the counterfeiting of sexes by apparel. Jonson's interest in this topic is also evident in his use of the subject in *Bartholomew Fair* (v. v). Selden was one of the guests at the celebration after Jonson's deliverance from the

Eastward Ho difficulties, and in 1618 Jonson helped placate the anger of King James who was offended when Selden wrote his *History of Tithes* in the spirit of a scholar instead of a partisan. Selden prefixed a commendatory poem to the 1616 folio of Jonson's *Works,* and Jonson mentioned Selden in *Und.* XLIII.

In the *Conversations* (ll. 604–06), Jonson called Selden the law book of the judges of England and the bravest man in all languages. Jonson also said Selden's *Titles of Honour* was written to his chamber-fellow [Edward] Heyward, and he recommended to Drummond (ll. 143–45) for the study of antiquities Selden's *De Diis Syris* and the *Titles of Honour* both of which, together with *Jani Anglorum,* Jonson had copies of in his own personal library. In his *Table Talk* Selden asserted: "Ben Jonson satirically expressed the vain Disputes of Divines, by Inigo Lanthorn disputing with his puppet in a Bartholomew Fair."

Selman, John, was known as the Christmas cutpurse because he attempted to pick the purse of Leonard Barry, servant to Lord Harrington, in the King's Chapel on Christmas Day, 1611, Sir Francis Bacon pronounced judgment on Selman, and he was executed in 1612. Jonson alludes to him in *Bartholomew Fair* (III. v) and *Love Restored.*

Semiramis, daughter of the Syrian goddess Derceto, was abandoned at birth by her mother and left in the desert to die, but doves miraculously fed her. Semiramis married Onnes after whose suicide she became the queen of Ninus, king of Assyria. She bore Ninus a son and succeeded to the throne after the king's death, reigning for forty-two years. She was renowned in war and as a builder of Babylon. After a long and brilliant reign, she resigned the kingdom to her son, disappeared, and was transformed into a dove, which was held sacred.

Sempronia. In *Catiline,* the snobbish, intellectual, feminist wife of Decius Brutus, who supports Catiline in his conspiracy to seize power in Rome but escapes punishment because Cicero argues that a government should not show its anger against fools or women.

Seneca, Lucius Annaeus (3 B.C.?–A.D. 65), son of the rhetorician Marcus Annaeus,

was born in Córdoba. The younger Seneca gained fame as a philosopher, dramatist, and statesman. While a young man, he went to Rome, studied rhetoric and philosophy, and gained fame as an orator when still a youth. In A.D. 41 he was exiled by Claudius on the ostensible grounds of his intimacy with Julia, the daughter of Germanicus. In 49 he was recalled to tutor the young Nero, and during Nero's first years as emperor, Seneca, together with Afranius Burrus, was essentially the ruler of the empire. The ascendancy of Poppaea brought about the death of Burrus in 62, and Seneca, who had amassed a huge fortune, asked to retire. In 65 he was accused of conspiracy and Nero ordered him to commit suicide. He opened his veins. Seneca's death was considered remarkably noble by the Romans, and his writings reveal an unselfish, Stoic nobility.

His *Epistolae* are essays on ethics written for his friend Lucilius junior, to whom he also addressed his philosophical work on natural phenomena—*Quaestiones naturales.* The *Dialogi* include essays on anger, divine providence, Stoic impassivity, and peace of soul. Other moral essays deal with the duty of a ruler to be merciful and the award and reception of favors. The *Apocolocyntosis* is a satire on the apotheosis of Claudius. In European literature, Seneca's most influential works were his tragedies, written for recitation, not stage performance, and based on Greek models: *Hercules Furens, Medea, Troades, Phaedra, Agamemnon, Oedipus, Hercules Oetaeus, Phoenissae,* and *Thyestes.* Seneca strongly influenced Renaissance tragedy. His gloom, horrors, rhetoric, bombast, and Stoicism all contributed to the formation of Renaissance tragedy. The best known play greatly influenced by Seneca is Kyd's *The Spanish Tragedy.*

Jonson was also greatly indebted to Seneca, and echoes of Seneca are heard throughout Jonson's canon. Some of the most obvious of Jonson's borrowings from Seneca are listed below:

Hercules Oetaeus and *Medea* are cited in *The Masque of Queens,* and *Medea* is quoted from in *Every Man in* (1601 quarto version, v. iii).

De consolatione (ad Marciam) was one of the sources for *Sejanus,* and *Oedipus* is borrowed from in the second act of *Sejanus.*

Phaedra is used in *Catiline* (II), and

Thyestes is employed in both *Catiline* (II) and *Sejanus* (II; v).

The *Apocolocyntosis* is borrowed from in *Every Man out* (III. vi) and *The Haddington Masque.*

Consolatio ad Helviam is reflected in *Timber* (ll. 1–10), and *De Beneficiis* is used in *Poetaster* (Dedication), *Sejanus* (IV; v), *Und.* XIII, and *Timber* (ll. 446–78).

De Brevitate Vitae is borrowed from in *Epig.* LXX and *Timber* (l. 2580), and *De Clementia* in *Sejanus* (IV; v) and *Timber* (ll. 1165–96; 1202–04).

De Constantia Sapientis is used in *Poetaster* (Apologetical Dialogue), *Sejanus* (III), *Epig.* XXVI, and *Cynthia's Revels* (III. iii).

De Ira is employed in *Catiline* (II); *De Providentia* in *Sejanus* (IV); and *De Remediis Fortuitorum* in *Cynthia's Revels* (III. iii) and *The Staple of News* (I. iii).

De Tranquillitate Animi is one of the sources for *Sejanus*, is cited in *Timber* (ll. 2411–16), and is used in *Epig.* CII and *Timber* (ll. 10–11; 2414–34).

De Vita Beata and *Naturales Quaestiones* are used, respectively, in *Cynthia's Revels* (II. iii; I. v).

Jonson makes frequent use of the *Epistolae: Cynthia's Revels* (Dedication; I. v), *Poetaster* (Apologetical Dialogue), *Volpone* (I. i; iv), *Love Restored, Epig.* LXX, *Epig.* CII, *Und.* XIII, *Und.* XVIII, and *Timber* (ll. 45–47; 543–69; 695–709; 948–66; 1373–1479).

Octavia is one of the sources for the *King's Coronation Entertainment.*

Seneca, Marcus Annaeus. Rhetorician born in Córdoba about 55 B.C. Little is known of his life. He was probably in Rome both as a young man and after his marriage. He became wealthy and may have held some official position in Spain or engaged in trade. He had three sons—Annaeus Novatus, who was adopted by L. Junius Gallio and became governor of Achaea; L. Annaeus, the philosopher; and M. Annaeus Mela, the father of Lucan. He died sometime between A.D. 37 and 41. His historical work covering the period from the civil war to his own death has not survived. Addressed to his sons, the *Oratorum sententiae divisiones colores* consists of extracts, supplied by his exceptional memory, from the declaimers whom he had heard during his long life, interspersed with commentary and digressions of his own. The work comprised ten books devoted to

controversiae, only five of which are extant. Seneca's work is a valuable source for the literary history of the early empire.

In *Timber* (ll. 481–82), Jonson mentions Seneca as an example of a man with a great memory, and in the course of a discussion (ll. 2233–36) of the need for brevity in letter writing notes that he may possibly be guilty of verbosity at times in his writings. While discussing the need for the poet to have natural wit, Jonson alludes to Seneca's comment that, according to Anacreon, it is pleasant to be frenzied at times (ll. 2414–15). Elsewhere in *Timber* Jonson borrows extensively from the *controversiae:* ll. 405–12; 419–37; 479–507; 602–10; 658–68; 824–45; 846–61; 862–98; 917–22.

Serenitas. A figure in *The Masque of Beauty* who represents one of the elements of beauty.

Servi. Servants who appear in *Sejanus* in Sejanus' and Regulus' houses and at Tiberius' court.

Servius. Servius Sulpicius Galba, Roman emperor from A.D. 68–69. He had a long career as a praetor in service to serveral emperors, and was governor of Germany under Caligula. After Nero's death, the praetorians chose him as their leader, and he became emperor. He was a tyrannical ruler and very unpopular, since he cruelly punished those who resisted him, removed many traditional privileges, savagely punished innocent men, and protected his friends. The army and the praetorians revolted, and he was murdered in A.D. 69. In *Poetaster* (III. v), Horace cites him as one of the evidences of the present corruption of Rome.

Seven Wise Men of Greece. The seven most distinguished men living from approximately 620 to 550 B.C. Lists of who these men were differ greatly, but a typical one might include: Bias, Chilon, Cleobulus, Periander, Pittacus, Solon, and Thales.

Shaa, Robert. One of the actors imprisoned with Jonson in 1597 for their part in the seditious *The Isle of Dogs.*

Shackles. The keeper of Newgate prison in *The Devil Is an Ass.*

Shadwell, Thomas (1642?–1692). English dramatist and poet. He wrote in the tradition of Jonson's humor comedies; his plays — among others, *The Sullen Lovers* (1668), *Epsom Wells* (1672), and *The Squire of Alsatia* (1688) — depict London life realistically and are noted for witty dialogue. Shadwell's excessive devotion to Jonson and his dramatic principles led to his famous quarrel with John Dryden, whom Shadwell succeeded as poet laureate in 1689. During this feud Shadwell attacked Dryden in *The Medal of John Bayes* (1682) and elsewhere and was himself ridiculed in Dryden's *Absalom and Achitophel* and *MacFlecknoe*.

Shadwell's criticism on Jonson covers essentially three areas: the nature of comedy, humor comedy, and Jonson's wit and humor. In the preface to his *Psyche: A Tragedy* (1675), Shadwell proclaims that he had rather be the author of one scene of comedy like Jonson's than anything else because Jonson's comedy is good comedy, which requires much more wit and judgment in the playwright than any type of rhyming or unnatural plays do. In the preface to *The Sullen Lovers* (1668), Shadwell explains that he has tried to represent a variety of humors as was the practice of Ben Jonson, whom he claims all dramatic poets ought to imitate because he was the only person Shadwell knows who was able to make perfect representations of human life and because he is the playwright Shadwell most admires. Shadwell later reiterates this opinion in the poetic epilogue to *The Humorists* (1671) when he proclaims that "'twas he alone true Humors understood, / And with great Wit and Judgment made them good." In the preface to *The Humorists* Shadwell includes a long reply to Dryden, who had argued (Preface to *An Evening's Love, or The Mock-Astrologer* [1671]) that although Jonson's comedies are pleasant, they lack genuine wit or sharpness of conceit. Shadwell defends Jonson, claiming that "he had more true wit than any of his contemporaries; that other men had sometimes things that seemed more firey than his, was because they were placed with so many sordid and mean things about them, that they made a greater show." Furthermore, Shadwell claims, "nor can I think, to the writing of his humors (which were not only the follies, but vices and subtleties of men) that wit was not required, but judgment; where, by the way, they speak as if judgment were a less thing than wit. But certainly it was meant otherwise by nature, who subjected wit to the government of judgment, which is the nobelest faculty of the mind." Shadwell concludes his defense by explaining that he once heard a person who was one of the greatest wits of his age claim that *Bartholomew Fair* was one of the wittiest plays in the world.

Shakespeare, William. Although little is known of Shakespeare's life, the few details that we have suggest that Shakespeare and Jonson were close friends even though they often disagreed and were quite different in temperament and personality. In his *Worthies,* Fuller refers to the combats of wit that supposedly took place between Shakespeare and Jonson at the Mermaid Tavern, probably between 1602 and 1610. In his notes, Plume records that Shakespeare was godfather to one of Jonson's children and that Jonson claimed Shakespeare never studied for anything he ever wrote. Moreover, Plume reports that Shakespeare composed a witty epitaph for Jonson, when they were both merry at a tavern. Whether or not Shakespeare took part against Jonson in the stage quarrel (the poetomachia of 1599–1601) is uncertain although Shakespeare did allude to the effects of the quarrel on the adult acting companies in *Hamlet* (II. ii) and, according to some interpreters, may have given Jonson some kind of purge. Since his name appears on the lists of the actors, it seems certain that Shakespeare performed in *Every Man in* (probably playing Old Knowell) and *Sejanus*. According to a late tradition initiated by Rowe, Shakespeare was also responsible for the Chamberlain company's deciding to produce Jonson's first humor comedy in 1598. Although some have thought that Virgil in *Poetaster* was intended to represent Shakespeare and that Shakespeare may have had a hand in the writing of *Sejanus*, it seems more likely that Chapman was the party in both instances, even though it may be true that *Julius Caesar* inspired *Sejanus*.

Both playwrights seem to have been influenced by each other or at least to have been aware of each other's works. In *Cynthia's Revels* (III. v) Amorphus' instructing in the art of courtship is reminiscent of Rosalind and Orlando's courtship in *As You Like It,* and Moria, Philautia, and Phantaste's discussion of their wooers (IV. i) echoes *The Merchant of Venice* (II. i). The duel of Daw and La-Foole in *Epicoene* (IV. v) may have been influenced by that of Aguecheek and Viola in *Twelfth Night*. The witches in *The Masque of Queens* may have been inspired by the witches in *Macbeth*. Jonson alludes specifically to Shakespeare's plays on the Wars of Roses in the Prologue to *Every Man in* (1616 folio version) and to

Henry IV in *Every Man out* (v. ii) and *Epicoene* (II. v), and in the "Ode to Himself" appended to *The New Inn* he refers to *Pericles* unfavorably, as he does to *Titus Andronicus* in the Induction to *Bartholomew Fair*. In *As You Like It*, Jaques, who reminds us of Asper in *Every Man out*, is Shakespeare's only attempt to portray a Jonsonian humor character.

Sometimes Jonson was very critical of Shakespeare. In the *Conversations* (l. 50), Drummond records that Jonson claimed Shakespeare wanted art. Later he said that Shakespeare had brought in a number of men in one of his plays (*Winter's Tale*) who said they had been shipwrecked in Bohemia, where there is no sea within a hundred miles (ll. 208–10). In the Induction to *Bartholomew Fair* Jonson attacked Shakespeare's romantic comedies (*Winter's Tale* and *The Tempest*) for confusing two types of art since the works contain dancing, and in *Timber* (l. 650) he proclaimed that Shakespeare should have blotted a thousand lines.

Although he could criticize Shakespeare for a number of deficiencies, Jonson's final assessment of Shakespeare was highly laudatory. Jonson's famous eulogy on Shakespeare ("To the Memory of My Beloved, the Author, Mr. William Shakespeare") prefaced to the First Folio admirably combines reasoned criticism and deserved praise and reveals the genuinely high esteem Jonson had for his contemporary dramatist and friend. In *Timber* (ll. 646–68), in the same passage in which he criticizes Shakespeare for not blotting enough lines, Jonson lauds him for his honesty, openness, free nature, excellent fancy, brave notions, gentle expressions, and controlled wit (even though it sometimes caused him to say ridiculous things). Jonson concludes that Shakespeare redeemed his vices with his many virtues and that there was always more in him to praise than to pardon.

According to one popular tradition, it was after a particularly merry drinking bout with Jonson and others at a local tavern that Shakespeare caught a chill and died.

Sharkwell. A doorkeeper at Littlewit's puppet show in *Bartholomew Fair*.

Sharpham, Edward. Gentleman of the Middle Temple who published two plays in 1607: *Cupid's Whirligig* and *The Fleire*. In the *Conversations* (ll. 51–52), Drummond notes that Jonson considered Sharpham, Day, Dekker, and Minshew all to be rogues.

Shelton, Sir Ralph. Knighted in 1607 Sir Ralph apparently had a reputation as a kind of buffoon. Jonson addressed *Epig.* CXIX to him. Shelton also appears humorously in *Epig.* CXXXIII.

Shepherd. An unnamed old shepherd appears in *Pan's Anniversary*, chastises the fencer and his followers, and directs the Arcadians in their celebration of Pan's rites.

Sheppard, Samuel. An obscure poetaster who seemed to claim in 1646 (in *The Times Displayed*) that he had given Jonson aid in writing *Sejanus* and was thus the other hand in the play Jonson referred to in his address to the readers. The only scholar ever to have taken Sheppard seriously was Brinsley Nicholson in 1875. Sheppard wrote two poems that laud Jonson, "The Poets' Invitation to Ben Jonson's Ghost to Appear Again" and "Ben Jonson's Due Encomium," both of which were first published in *Epigrammes, Six Books* (1651).

Shift. In *Every Man out of His Humour*, a cheater and a braggart who makes friends with the fool Sogliardo but is eventually rejected by him.

Shirley, James (1596–1666). English dramatist born in London. Ordained in the Church of England but converted to Catholicism, Shirley became a schoolmaster, serving as master at St. Albans Grammar School. Soon after the success of his first play, *Love Tricks*, in 1625, he resigned this position. Shirley's works include the comedies, *Hyde Park* (1632) and *The Lady of Pleasure* (1635); the tragedies, *The Traitor* (1631), and *The Cardinal* (1641); the masques, *The Triumph of Peace* (1633) and *The Contention of Ajax and Ulysses* (1659). He also wrote *Love's Cruelty* (1640), in which he indicated that a masque was essentially a spectacle of beauty, and *The Way Made Plain to the Latin Tongue* (1649). About 1636 he went to Dublin to manage the Werburgh Street Theatre for which he edited plays, wrote new plays, and composed prologues and epilogues for the plays he revived. One of the plays he revived and wrote a prologue for was *The Alchemist*. In his *Triumph of Peace*, Fancy, the presenter, seems to have been modeled on Phantasy from Jonson's *Vision of Delight*.

Shoreditch, Duke of. One of the mock-titles of the Finsbury Archers, constituted by Henry VIII into a fraternity of St. George in 1539. The Duke is mentioned in *A Tale of a Tub* (III. vi) and *The Devil Is an Ass* (IV. vii).

Short Discourse of the English Stage, A. See Richard FLECKNOE.

Short, Peter. Printer in London from 1589 to 1603 who in 1600 probably printed the second quarto of *Every Man out of His Humour* for William Holme.

Shrewsbury, Lady Jane Ogle, Countess of. Eldest daughter and co-heir of Cuthbert, Lord Ogle, Lady Jane married Edward, 8th Earl of Shrewsbury. He died in 1618, and she survived until 1625. She was buried near her husband in St. Edmund's Chapel, Westminster Abbey. Jonson wrote an epitaph ("I could begin with that grave forme, *Here Lies*") for her, one of his uncollected poems, but it was not used on the monument.

Shunfield. In *The Staple of News,* a man of war who has become a sea captain and presents himself as one of the suitors to Lady Pecunia.

Sibbald, Sir Robert (1614–1722), was an Edingburgh physician and antiquary who made a transcript of Drummond's manuscript of his conversations with Jonson. Drummond's own manuscript of the conversations has not survived, but Sibbald's transcript was published by David Laing in 1833.

Sibyl. A maiden priestess of Apollo who delivered oracles at his shrines, the most famous of which was Cumae.

Sibylline Books. A collection of prophecies offered to Tarquinius Superbus by the Cumaean Sibyl who kept burning the books until he paid her the high price she demanded for them.

Sidney, Mistress Philip (Philippa) (1594–1620), was the daughter of Robert Sidney, 1st Earl of Leicester. She married Sir John Hobart. Jonson addressed *Epig.* CXIV to her.

Sidney, Sir Philip (1554–1586). Author and courtier. Educated at Oxford. One of the leading lights of Queen Elizabeth's court and a model of Renaissance chivalry, he served in several diplomatic missions on the Continent. He was fatally wounded at the battle of Zutphen in 1586. Although he lived a relatively short time, Sidney exerted a strong influence on English poetry as patron, critic, and writer. During his lifetime, his literary efforts circulated only in manuscript. His *Arcadia* (1590), a series of verse idylls connected by prose narrative, is the earliest renowned pastoral in English literature and was written for his sister Mary, Countess of Pembroke. His famous treatise on the nature of poetry, written in rebuttal to Stephen Gosson's *The School of Abuse,* appeared in two slightly different versions—*The Defense of Poesie* and *An Apology for Poetry* (both 1595). His *Astrophel and Stella* (1591) is considered one of the great sonnet sequences in English. Although this work was inspired by Sidney's love for Penelope Devereux, later Lady Rich, Sidney married Frances Walsingham in 1583.

In *Timber* (ll. 907–8), Jonson praised Sidney as a great master of wit and language and asserted (l. 1798) that Sidney, because of his clarity, should be read before Donne. According to the *Conversations* (ll. 213–14), Jonson thought Sidney's daughter, the Countess of Rutland, was not inferior to her father in poetry. Although Jonson was apparently not particularly attracted to the *Arcadia*, Sidney's *An Apology for Poetry* seems to have appealed to him strongly. Jonson did, however, mention the *Arcadia* in the *Conversations* (ll. 190–93), *Every Man out* (II. iii. Grex; III. v), and *Bartholomew Fair* (IV. iii), and he claimed in the Conversations (ll. 148–50) that there was no more fitting subject for heroic poetry than the Arthurian legend and that Sidney had intended to transform his *Arcadia* into stories about Arthur. Jonson alluded to *Astrophel and Stella* in *Cynthia's Revels* (IV. iii), *The New Inn* (III. ii), and *Und.* XXVII.

In the *Conversations* (ll. 17–19; 611–12), Drummond records that Jonson's censure of Sidney was that he did not maintain decorum in his pastorals in having everyone speak as well as himself. Later Jonson said that Sidney had translated some of the psalms which went abroad under the name of the Countess of Pembroke (ll. 204–5). Still later Jonson remarked that Sidney was not a man with a pleasant countenance, having pimples, and that the eldest son of the Earl of Worcester [should be Leicester] resembled Sidney (ll. 230–32). According to Jonson, Sidney's mother, after she had the smallpox, never showed herself in court without a mask (ll. 348–49). Jonson also claimed that the king said Sidney was no poet and that he had seen no verses in England better than those of the "Scullor" [John Taylor] (ll. 371–72). See also Elizabeth Sidney, Countess of RUTLAND.

Sidney, Sir Robert. Brother of Sir Philip, Robert was knighted for bravery at Zutphen in 1586; he became Baron Sidney of Penshurst, in 1605 Viscount Lisle, and in 1618 Earl of Leicester. He is alluded to as the great lord in *For.* II.

Sidney, Sir William, the son of Robert, Lord Sidney, was born at Flushing in 1590. He was knighted in 1611. In 1612 he died at Baynards Castle in London and was buried in the chancel at Penshurst. *For.* XIV is an ode addressed to Sir William on his birthday.

Silenus. The son of Hermes or Pan, Silenus was considered the oldest of the satyrs. He was represented as a creature of the forests, part bestial and part human. He was considered by some to be a prophet, but, according to others, he was so often befuddled by drink that he was unable to distinguish truth from falsehood. He is usually thought of as the companion and adviser of Dionysus.

Silius, Caius. A noble, high-minded Roman soldier in *Sejanus,* husband to Sosia, famous for his bravery under Germanicus in defeating Sacrovir. He and Sabinus meet at the beginning of the play and comment on how they are out of place at the corrupt Roman court. He speaks with scorn of Sejanus' lackeys and with disdain of the suspicions and accusations which flourish. He praises Drusus senior and Germanicus and is counted as a serious threat by Sejanus and Tiberius because of his popularity and his ties to Agrippina. He leaves his wife with Agrippina when he goes to the Senate. While there, he nobly answers the men who accuse him of treason, but he is driven to commit suicide, and his land and possessions are forfeited.

Silkworm, Sir Diaphanous. In *The Magnetic Lady,* a courtier who is one of the suitors to Lady Loadstone's niece.

Simmes, Valentine. Printer in London from about 1585 to 1622 who in 1604 printed in quarto for Edward Blount Jonson's part of the *King's Entertainment through the City of London,* together with the *Entertainment of the Queen and Prince at Althorp* and *A Panegyre.* In 1606 he printed *Hymenaei* in quarto for Thomas Thorpe.

Simois, a tributary of the Scamander, was the scene of many legendary events during the siege of Troy.

Simpson, Evelyn (1885–1962). Evelyn (Spearing) Simpson taught at Bedford College, was a Fellow at Newnham College, Oxford, and served as English Tutor at St. Hugh's College, Oxford. In 1924 she published *A Study of the Prose Works of John Donne,* and she collaborated with George Potter in editing Donne's *Sermons* (10 vols., 1953–62). After the death of C. H. Herford, she joined forces with her husband

Percy Simpson to complete the Oxford edition of Jonson's *Works,* co-editing with him vols. VI–XI (1938–52). She died less than a year after the death of her husband, who was twenty years her senior.

Simpson, Percy (1865–1962), was a critic, teacher, and editor who served in a number of academic posts between 1887 and 1951, the last as Honorary Fellow of Selwyn College, Cambridge. He published a number of critical studies on Elizabethan drama, masques, and Shakespeare, and he was co-editor, first with C. H. Herford and after Herford's death with his wife, Evelyn Simpson, of the Oxford edition of Jonson's *Works,* which is still considered the standard critical edition.

Simylus. Little known Greek writer of comedy who probably flourished in the fourth century B.C. In the *Discoveries* (ll. 2501–2), Jonson quotes Simylus (as reported by Stobaeus) on the relationship between nature and art. See also STOBAEUS.

Sindefy. In *Eastward Ho,* the mistress of Quicksilver, who serves as gentlewoman and confidante to Gertrude and finally becomes engaged to Quicksilver.

Sinon. Greek soldier who pretended to be a deserter from the armies besieging Troy. He told the Trojans a false tale of the building of the Trojan horse, released the Greek soldiers hidden inside it after the horse was inside the city walls, and joined in the attack on the city.

Sirens. Sea nymphs that lived on an island near Scylla and Charybdis. So charming was their song that all who heard them were drawn to the island and killed on the dangerous rocks surrounding it. To avoid this fate Jason and the Argonauts were saved from the Sirens by the music of Orpheus, and Odysseus escaped the Sirens by having himself tied to the mast of his ship and by plugging the ears of his men.

Sisyphus. Son of Aeolus and legendary founder and king of Corinth. Considered very cunning, Sisyphus attempted to escape death by having death chained; for his disrespect to Zeus he was condemned to eternal punishment in Hades: forever he must push a heavy stone up a hill and forever the stone would roll back down the hill just as he got it to the top.

Skelton, John (1460?–1529). English poet and humanist. Skelton became rector of Diss, Norfolk, around 1502 and began to call himself royal orator in 1512. The author of a long allegorical poem entitled

The Garland of Laurel (1523), he is best known for his satires on the court, the clergy, and Cardinal Wolsey—*The Bowge of Court* (1499); *Speak, Parrot* (1521); *Colin Clout* (1522); *Why Come Ye Not to Court?*—and the mock dirge "Philip Sparrow." Skelton often wrote in so-called Skeltonics—a kind of doggerel verse, often alliterative, with short lines and insistent rhymes, sometimes repeated through several sets of couplets.

A tutor to Prince Henry (later Henry VIII), Skelton is alluded to in *A Tale of a Tub* (v. vii). Conjured up by Johphiel, he appears as a character in *The Fortunate Isles* and, speaking in Skeltonic verse, suggests several interesting people who might appear for Merefool.

Skogan (Scogan). A character who appears along with Skelton in the antimasque of *The Fortunate Isles.* It is not entirely clear which Skogan Jonson intended the character to represent. John Scogan was court fool to Edward IV; his jests were published in 1556. Henslowe's *Diary* (1601) records the composition of a play about Scogan and Skelton written by Hathway and Rankins. Henry Scogan (1361?–1407), a friend of Chaucer's, was the author of *A Moral Ballad* . . . , a poem of twenty-one stanzas in which Chaucer's *Gentilesse* is inserted after stanza thirteen and which was printed in all the early editions of Chaucer.

Slander. The name of one of the witches making up the antimasque in *The Masque of Queens.*

Sledge. The constable in *The Devil Is an Ass.*

Slitgut. In *Eastward Ho,* a butcher's apprentice who happens to observe the boat wreck of Security on the tempestuous Thames and later of Winifred, Quicksilver, and Sir Petronel Flash.

Slug. A lighterman who appears in *The Masque of Augurs* and, together with his cohorts, wants to present a masque before the court.

Sly, William (d. 1608). An actor who, as a member of the Chamberlain's men, played in *Every Man in His Humour, Every Man out of His Humour, Sejanus,* and *Volpone.* He eventually became a housekeeper of both the Globe and Blackfriars Theaters, and he acted in Shakespeare's plays.

Smethwick (Smithwicke), John. Bookseller in London from 1597 to 1640. In the 1616 folio of Jonson's *Works* published by William Stansby, some copies of the title page have Smethwick's name on the imprint. Smethwick had acquired the copyright from Nicholas Ling in 1607.

Smith, Captain. A character in *Love's Welcome at Bolsover* who appears as a blacksmith in Colonel Vitruvius' dance of the mechanics.

Smith, John. Listed as one of the actors in the initial performance of *Epicoene,* but nothing is known of his life or career.

Smith, Sir Thomas (1513–1577). English scholar and statesman. He was the author of *De Republica Anglorum: the Maner of Governement or Policie of the Realme of England* (1583) and *De recta et emendata Linguae Anglicae Scriptione Dialogus* (1568), which Jonson freely used as one of his authorities, especially on the pronunciation of English, in his *English Grammar.* Smith is cited for his eloquence in *Timber* (ll. 902–4), and Smith refers to Jonson as "our Laureat worthy Benjamin" in his *Voiage and Entertainment in Rushia* (1605).

Snodham, Thomas. Printer in London from 1603 to 1625 who printed in 1612 *The Alchemist* in quarto for Walter Burre.

Snow. In *Chloridia,* seven symbolic characters who appear in the eighth entry of the antimasque.

Sogliardo. In *Every Man out of His Humour,* the brother of Sordido who wants to be a gentleman but is actually a buffoon.

Solinus, Gaius Julius. About A.D. 200 he wrote *Collectanea Rerum Memorabilium,* a geographical summary of parts of the known world. Jonson cites him as an authority in *The Masque of Queens.*

Solomon, King. Son and successor of David in the Bible. He was famous for his wealth, extravagance, and wisdom. In *The Alchemist* (II. i, ii), Solomon is said to have possessed the philosopher's stone and to have used it to make gold. The *Song of Solomon* was regarded by some interpreters as an alchemical allegory.

Solon (639?–559 B.C.). Athenian statesman and poet known as the founder of Athenian democracy. Some of his patriotic verse is still extant. He is also known as a giver of laws and a reformer. He became political leader of Athens at a time when conditions were critical and power was in the hands of the nobles while the peasants were rapidly losing their land and their freedom. Solon instituted a number of reforms including the annulment of all mortgages and debts, limitations on the amount of land anyone could add to his holdings, and the outlawing of contracts in which a person's liberty was pledged. As a result of his reforms, there was civil strife at first, but Solon's program remained the basis of the Athenian state from then on. As a poet Solon wrote mostly on political, social, and philosophical themes.

Somerset, Edward. See Edward Somerset, Earl of WORCESTER.

Somerset, Lady Frances Howard, Countess of (formerly Countess of Essex) (d. 1632), was the second daughter of Thomas, Earl of Suffolk. In *Hymenaei* Jonson celebrated her marriage in 1606 to Robert, Earl of Essex. In 1613 Frances divorced Essex and married her lover, Robert Carr, Earl of Somerset. The marriage was vehemently opposed by Sir Thomas Overbury, Carr's friend and adviser. So strong was his hostility that the Howards exerted enough pressure to get the king to imprison Overbury in the Tower, where he was poisoned. In 1616 Carr and Lady Somerset were tried and found guilty of Overbury's murder although Carr's guilt was never firmly established. The Somersets were pardoned but not released until 1622.

In the *Conversations* (l. 396), Jonson told Drummond that Lady Somerset was a character in his lost pastoral *The May Lord* and that (ll. 404–5) the untitled epithalamium in his printed works was written for Lady Frances's first marriage, to the Earl of Essex. For her marriage to the Earl of Somerset Jonson wrote *A Challenge at Tilt* and *The Irish Masque* although he suppressed reference to the occasion of the works in the folio text. Lady Frances danced in *The Masque of Queens*.

Somerset, Robert Carr (Ker), Earl of (1587?–1645), was born in Scotland. He spent time in France before he arrived at the court of James I, where he soon became James's favorite. He was knighted in 1607, and was granted lands in 1609 that had been forfeited by Sir Walter Raleigh. In 1611 he was created Viscount Rochester, became James's personal secretary, and was made Earl of Somerset in 1613. In the same year he married Frances Howard, the Countess of Essex, who had obtained a divorce from the Earl of Essex in a sensational case. Somerset's marriage was vehemently opposed by his friend and adviser, Sir Thomas Overbury, whose hostility was so great that Lady Somerset's family exerted sufficient pressure on the king so that Overbury was imprisoned in the

Tower, where he was poisoned. Somerset was named Lord Chamberlain in 1614 and became an important counselor to the king, but his arrogance and jealousy eventually alienated James. In 1616 Carr and his wife were tried and convicted of the murder of Overbury, although Carr's guilt was never definitely established. They were both pardoned but not released until 1622.

Jonson wrote a poem ("They are not those, are present with their face") in celebration of Somerset's marriage, and he contributed *A Challenge at Tilt* and *The Irish Masque* to the festivities in honor of the marriage at court although he suppressed any reference to the occasion of the works in the folio text.

sonnet. For the Elizabethans, sonnet and lyric were often synonymous, but sonnet has come to mean a poem of fourteen (occasionally twelve or sixteen) lines, usually in iambic pentameter (if in English) and employing one of the following rhyme schemes. The Petrarchian (or Italian) sonnet has two divisions: the octave (the first eight lines) and the sestet (the last six lines). The rhyme scheme is *abba abba cde cde;* the sestet is sometimes *cd cd cd,* or some variant. The English (or Shakespearian) sonnet is usually divided into three quatrains and a couplet, rhyming *abab cdcd efef gg.*

Jonson objected to the rigidity of the sonnet and in the *Conversations* (ll. 60–63) cursed Petrarch for redacting verses to sonnets. It is also worthy of note that in his tributes to Shakespeare and Drayton Jonson completely ignored their sonnets. Jonson wrote only six sonnets himself (three Petrarchian and three English), none of which is distinguished. The Petrarchian ones are: "A work not smelling of the lamp, tonight" (the court prologue to *The Staple of News*); *Und.* XXVIII; and "In picture, they which truly understand" (prefixed to Wright's *The Passions of the Mind in General* [1604]). The English ones are: *Epig.* LVI; *Und.* LXVIII; and "Thou, that wouldst find the habit of true passion" (dedication to Breton's *Melancholike Humours* [1600]).

Sons of Ben. See TRIBE OF BEN.

Sophocles (496?–406 B.C.). Younger than Aeschylus and older than Euripides, both of whom were his contemporaries, Sophocles was a general and a priest as well as a poet and playwright. Wealthy, charming, and brilliant, he was famous in his lifetime and worshipped as a hero after his death. When he was sixteen, he led the chorus in a paean on the victory of Salamis, and in 468 B.C. he won his first dramatic prize (over Aeschylus). He wrote more than 120 plays, of which only seven complete tragedies, part of a satyr play, and roughly 1000 fragments from the other plays have come down to us. He won first prize in the drama contests about twenty times and never finished lower than second. He made many important innovations in dramatic practice: he introduced scene painting, added a third actor, increased the size of the chorus, and abandoned the traditional trilogy of plays for the self-contained tragedy. His most famous play is *Oedipus Rex*, cited by Aristotle as a perfect example of tragedy. A sequel, *Oedipus at Colonus*, was written shortly before Sophocles' death and was produced by his son in 401. Generally, Sophocles' characters are governed more by their own faults than by actions of the gods. There is a tradition that Sophocles said that Aeschylus composed correctly without realizing it, that Euripides portrayed men as they were, and that he presented them as they ought to be.

In *Poetaster* (I. i) Ovid writes a poem in which he proclaims that Sophocles' fame will last as long as the sun and the moon, and Jonson mentions *Ajax* in *Timber* (ll. 2794-95).

Sordido. In *Every Man out of His Humour*, a wealthy farmer who attempts to hang himself out of despair but is rescued by some local rustics.

Sosia. Wife of Silius in *Sejanus*. She stays with Agrippina and speaks against Sejanus' spies; she remains there while Silius goes to the Senate, is accused of treason, and commits suicide. Soon afterward, Agrippina angrily lists her as one of the friends lately destroyed by Sejanus and his followers.

Soteria. A symbolic personage representing safety and appearing in a scene in Jonson's part of the *King's Coronation Entertainment*.

Southwell, Robert (1561?–1595). English Jesuit poet born in Norfolk who was venerated by Roman Catholics as a martyr. Reared as a Catholic and educated mainly at Douai, Southwell made his vows as a Jesuit in 1580. Desiring martyrdom, he asked to be sent to England in 1586 with Father Garnett to minister to the oppressed Catholics. After serving as a priest in the south of England for six years, he was arrested and imprisoned in 1592. Southwell was tortured and tried for treason, and upon admitting his priesthood he was brutally hanged in 1595. Deeply religious, his poetry extolls the beauty of the spiritual in contrast to the material. His major work is *St. Peter's Complaint* (1595), but he also wrote several fine short devotional poems, including "The Burning Babe," which Jonson greatly admired. He told Drummond in the *Conversations* (ll. 180–82) he would have destroyed many of his own poems if he could have written such a work.

sovereignty. In *Timber* (ll. 1139–57), Jonson, paraphrasing Machiavelli (*Il Principe*, ix. 2–7), records that *"There* is a great variation betweene him, that is rais'd to the *Soveraignity*, by favour of his Peeres; and him that comes to it by the suffrage of the people."* The former has difficulty because he was raised by many who consider themselves his equal. The latter has less difficulty because he was raised by those who sought to be defended from oppression. Moreover, he who was raised by the people has the masses as his friend and has less fear of the nobility, who are few in number. When a Prince governs the people so that they have genuine need of his administration, they will be faithful to him.

Spanish Tragedy, The. A tragedy in blank verse probably written around 1589 by Thomas Kyd. The play was first acted in 1592, registered in the same year by Abel Jeffes, and printed in 1594. It is important as a prototype of revenge tragedy and because of its popularity and influence upon succeeding drama. In 1601 and 1602, according to entries in Henslowe's diary, Henslowe paid Jonson to prepare additions to the play. However, these additions, some 320 lines, do not seem characteristic of Jonson's dramatic work, and most scholars have attributed them to some other playwright, usually John Webster. Some seventeenth-century booksellers ascribed the entire play to Shakespeare, but this ascription is not usually taken very seriously.

The victory of Spain over Portugal in 1580 forms the political background of the play. Horatio is the son of Hieronimo, marshal of Spain, and he and Lorenzo, son of the Duke of Castile, have captured in the war Balthazar, son of the viceroy of Portugal. Balthazar courts Bel-imperia, daughter of the Duke of Castile, and his suit is favored by her brother Lorenzo and the King of Spain for political reasons. However, when Lorenzo and Balthazar discover that Bel-imperia actually loves Horatio, they kill him and hang his body on a tree. When Hieronimo learns of the murder, he is mad with grief, finds out who the murderers are, and with Bel-imperia plots their destruction. Before the court, he engages the murderers to act with him and Bel-imperia a play that allows him to carry out his revengeful purpose. During the course of the action, Lorenzo and Balthazar are killed, Bel-imperia stabs herself, and Hieronimo commits suicide.

speech. In *Timber* (ll. 1881–2030), Jonson, adapting largely from Vives (*De Ratione Dicendi,* I) and Quintilian (*Instit. Orat.*), includes a long passage on the dignity of speech. He notes that speech is the only benefit man has to express his excellence of mind above other creatures: speech is the instrument of society. In speech, words and sense are as the body and the soul, and sense is as the life and soul of language, without which words are dead. Sense is made out of experience, knowledge of human life, and actions, or of the liberal arts. Words are peoples among which there is a choice to be made according to the persons we cause to speak or the things we speak about. The elegance and propriety of words are seen in their proper use, when we draw forth their strength and nature by way of metaphor.

Speeches at Prince Henry's Barriers, The.
Performed: January 6, 1610.
Published: 1616 in folio by William Stansby.
Printer: William Stansby.
These speeches were delivered in 1610 before and after the Barriers of Prince Henry who was not quite sixteen at the time. The speeches are the only examples of Jonson's attempts to make use of the Arthurian legend in his works.

The Lady of the Lake was discovered, and she proclaimed the glories of Britain under James but deplored the decay of the House of Chivalry. King Arthur was then discovered as a Star above, and he praised the virtues of James as brighter than his own, called for the appearance of the young knight who was to restore the lost glories of knighthood and chivalry, presented the Lady with a symbolic shield devised by the fates to honor the young knight's maiden valor, and urged the Lady to awaken Merlin. At her call Merlin arose from his tomb and called for the appearance of the young knight whose name was Meliadus. Meliadus and his six attendants entered, and Merlin and the Lady alternately praised their virtues, after which

Merlin explained the past glory of Britain and her heroes from Edward to James symbolized in the shield given to Meliadus to inspire his own valor and sense of honor and tradition. Afterwards, the Lady told Meliadus that he should learn especially to imitate James and that he should prepare to prove himself. Merlin called forth Chivalry from her cave, and she appeared and lauded Meliadus for reviving knighthood which had been dormant for so long. The Barriers then followed in which Prince Henry apparently performed quite well, after which Merlin reentered and exhorted the triumphant Meliadus to emulate the virtues of James—justice, fortitude, prudence, and love of peace—and reassured the king and queen that their young son had shown that he would ever bring more honor and glory to the state in the years to come.

Spencer, Gabriel. An actor of Henslowe's company who quarreled with Jonson, fought a duel with him, and was killed by him at Hoxton Fields on September 22, 1598. Spencer was buried two days later, and Jonson was arrested for felony. In October he was tried at the Old Bailey. Jonson confessed the indictment but escaped the gallows by pleading benefit of clergy. His goods were all confiscated, and a Tyburn brand was placed on his thumb. In the *Conversations* (ll. 246–49), Jonson told Drummond that Spencer's sword was ten inches longer than his and that Spencer had wounded him in the arm during their duel. We do not know what the quarrel between the two was all about.

Spencer, Sir Robert. Created Baron Spencer of Wormleighton in Warwickshire in 1603, Sir Robert was noted for his sheep breeding and was one of the wealthiest men in England. In 1603 he entertained Queen Anne and Prince Henry at Althorp as they progressed from Edinburgh to London. Jonson wrote *The Entertainment at Althorp* for the occasion. Sir Robert died on October 25, 1627.

Spendall. In *Eastward Ho,* an adventurer who plans to sail with Sir Petronel Flash to Virginia.

Spenser, Edmund (1552–1599), was born in London and educated at Merchant Taylor's School and Cambridge. He became the friend of men eminent in literature and at court, including Gabriel Harvey, Sir Philip Sidney, Sir Walter Raleigh, and Robert Sidney. After he had served as secretary to the Bishop of Rochester, Spenser was appointed in 1580 secretary to

Lord Grey, lord deputy of Ireland, after which Spenser lived in Ireland, where he held minor civil offices and received the lands and castle of Kilcolman, County Cork. Sponsored by Raleigh, Spenser went to London in 1589 to seek court preference and to arrange for the publication of the first three books of the *Faerie Queene.* Following the Tyrone rebellion of 1598, during which Kilcolman Castle was burned, Spenser returned to London, where he apparently died in poverty. He was buried in Westminster Abbey.

His contemporaries considered Spenser the foremost poet of his day—a master of meter and language and a profound moral poet. Patterning his literary career after that of Virgil, Spenser published twelve pastoral eclogues of *The Shepherd's Calendar* (1579), followed in 1591 by his *Complaints* and *Daphnaida,* an elegy on Douglas Howard. In 1595 appeared *Colin Clouts Come Home Again,* a pastoral allegory dealing with Spenser's first London journey and the vices of court life; *Astrophel,* his elegy on Sir Philip Sidney; *Amoretti,* a sonnet sequence commemorating Spenser's courtship of Elizabeth Boyle; and *Epithalamion,* a wedding poem in honor of his marriage in 1594. In 1596 he published *Four Hymns,* an explication of his Platonic and Christian views of love and beauty; *Prothalamion;* and the first six books of the *Faerie Queene,* his unfinished epic masterpiece. Spenser's only extended prose work, *A View of the Present State of Ireland,* was published posthumously in 1633.

Although Jonson was critical of Spenser, he seems to have respected him as a poet, and he borrowed from or was influenced by several of his works. In *Timber* (ll. 617–21), Jonson deplores his own speculation that many people would probably prefer the poetry of Taylor, the water poet, over that of Spenser, who is referred to in *The Masque of Queens* (l. 599) as "grave and diligent." In *The Golden Age Restored* Spenser is portrayed as one of the poets of the golden age, and in *Und.* LXXVIII (l. 24) the *Faerie Queene* is called "a noble book." In the *Conversations* (ll. 128–29) Drummond reports that Jonson knew by heart Cuddie's praise of wine in *The Shepherd's Calendar* (October, ll. 103–14). In *Timber* (ll. 1806–8), Jonson remarks that although in affecting the ancients Spenser wrote no language, he should still be read for his matter, as Virgil read Ennius.

In the *Conversations* (ll. 20–22), Drummond (not always an accurate recorder) notes that Jonson's censure of Spenser was that his stanzas did not please him, nor did his matter, the meaning of which allegory Spenser had explained in some papers delivered to Sir Walter Raleigh. Later (ll. 172–79), Jonson stated that the Irish robbed Spenser, burned his house and child, but he and his wife escaped. Spenser died poor and refused some money sent to him by Lord Essex. According to Jonson, in the papers Raleigh had on the allegory of the *Faerie Queene* it is explained that the Blatant Beast is supposed to stand for the Puritans and Duessa for the Queen of Scots.

As Spenser's contemporaries often did, Jonson compared Daniel and Spenser (*Epicoene* II. ii). Moreover, several of his masques are partially indebted to Spenser's works: *Hymenaei* to *Epithalamion; The Masque of Beauty* and *The Masque of Queens* to the *Four Hymns; For the Honor of Wales* to the *Faerie Queene* (III. iii); *Chloridia* to *The Shepherd's Calendar* (April, ll. 122–23); and the portrait of Bunduca in *The Masque of Queens* to her portrait in the *Ruins of Time.* Douce's impersonation of Earine in *The Sad Shepherd* was probably inspired by Duessa-Una of the *Faerie Queene. The Sad Shepherd* also reflects in I. v the influence of *Colin Clouts Come Home Again* (ll. 632–35) and in II. ii the influence of *The Shepherd's Calendar* (February, ll. 102–3, 109–10).

Spenser, John. Bookseller in London and Librarian of Sion College from 1617 to 1680 who in 1635 published the second quarto of *Catiline.*

Sphinx. 1. Mythical beast originally of ancient Egypt which was represented in various shapes and forms throughout the ancient Near East and Greece. In Greek mythology the Sphinx was a winged monster with the head and breasts of a woman and the body of a lion. In the Oedipus legend the Sphinx acts as a destructive agent of the gods, posing her famous riddle. She killed those who could not answer the riddle, but when Oedipus solved the riddle she killed herself.

2. A mythological character who appears in *Love Freed From Ignorance and Folly* and represents ignorance.

Spinola, Ambrogio (1569–1630). Spanish general born in Italy of a noble Genoese family. Philip III made him commander in the Netherlands in 1603, and Spinola took Ostend from Maurice of Nassau the following year. Spinola negotiated the twelve-year truce of 1609, but his most famous accomplishment was the capture of Breda in 1625. His conciliatory policy in the Netherlands lost him the favor of Philip IV, who appointed him governor of Milan in 1628. Spinola died in 1630 while trying to take Casale in the war for the succession to Montferrat. Spinola is mentioned in *Volpone* (II. i), *The Staple of News* (I. iv; III. ii), and *Und.* XLIV.

Splendor. A figure in *The Masque of Beauty* who represents one of the elements of beauty.

Sport. 1. A symbolic character in *The Vision of Delight* who has no speaking part but accompanies Delight at the opening of the masque.

2. A character who appears with Cupid in *Time Vindicated to Himself and His Honors* and helps to direct the dancing of the masquers and the audience.

Spring. A symbolic character in *Chloridia* who first appears with Zephyrus, then descends to earth, and helps to celebrate the glory of Chloris. See also FAVONIUS.

Sprint, John. Bookseller in London from 1698 to 1727 who was one of the publishers of the so-called Bookseller's Edition of Jonson's *Works* in 1716–17.

Squib, Arthur. A teller of the Exchequer who received his grant in 1616 and lived at Henley Park in Surrey. Jonson addressed *Underwood* XLV and LIV to him.

Squire, John. Author of *The Triumphs of Peace*, a pageant for the Lord Mayor of London's show of October 30, 1620, which is alluded to in *Und.* XLIII.

Stafford, Anthony (1587–?1645), was a writer of religious books, one of the most important of which was *The Female Glory* (1635), for which Jonson wrote a commendatory poem ("The Ghyrlond of the Blessed Virgin Mary").

Stagekeeper. A character who "sneaks" on stage before *Bartholomew Fair* and tells the audience that Jonson has not represented the fair accurately and has mocked him and cuffed him for giving advice.

Stanhope, Edward. Bishop of London's vicar-general and official in spirituals before whom Jonson's citations for recusancy were tried in 1606.

Stansby, William. A printer and bookseller in London from 1597 to 1639 who gained considerable position in the trade. Among the many works he produced were Sir Walter Raleigh's *History of the World*

(1614), Jonson's first folio in 1616, and the second quarto of *Epicoene* in 1620. When Stansby died sometime in 1638 or early 1639, his widow assigned her copyrights to George Bishop.

Staple of News, The.
Acted: 1626 at the Blackfriars by the King's Men.
Published: 1631 in folio by Robert Allot.
Printer: John Beale.

In the induction four gossips named Mirth, Tattle, Expectation, and Censure, all "lady-like attired," interrupt the prologue and take seats on the stage where they may better see and be seen. As the play proceeds, they comment upon the characters and the action following each act, criticizing the play because it has neither a fool nor a devil in it, ridiculing the news that is given out, and accusing the playwright of having a "decayed wit."

Act I. Pennyboy junior, a carefree prodigal, celebrates his coming of age. He is surrounded by his parasites: Leatherleg, his shoemaker; Fashioner, his tailor; Thomas, his barber; his linener; his haberdasher; and his spurrier. His father has died. He is 21, has received his considerable inheritance, and is totally free to do as he pleases. From Thomas, who has a talent for spreading gossip and is a master of arts, Pennyboy junior learns of the establishment in the same building where Pennyboy junior lives of a Staple of News, "where all the news of all sorts shall be brought and there be examined, and then registered, and so issued under the seal of the office of the Staple of News no other news be current." Promising to satisfy Thomas's desire for a clerkship in the new office, Pennyboy junior decides to visit the staple. He pays all his parasites' bills without even looking at them and departs with an old canter, or vagabond, whom Pennyboy junior fancifully refers to as his "-founder" since he was the first one who brought Pennyboy junior the news of his father's death. The canter, who decries Pennyboy junior's prodigal and carefree spending, is actually Pennyboy's father in disguise. At the staple, Cymbal, the staple master, Fitton, the court reporter or emissary, and Nathaniel, the chief clerk of the office, are all busy filing all sorts of news for future use, and Pennyboy junior is greatly impressed with their enterprise. He has no difficulty in negotiating with Cymbal for a clerkship for Thomas, but he shortly thereafter learns secretly from Picklock, his attorney who has purchased a post as emissary, that Cymbal has designs on a great woman once intended for Pennyboy himself. This woman is Lady Pecunia, who is the ward of Pennyboy junior's uncle Richer Pennyboy, or Pennyboy senior, and she has many suitors—Dr. Almanac, Captain Shunfield, Master Piedmantle, and Master Madrigal. Encouraged by Picklock, Pennyboy junior resolves to beat out all his rivals for her hand.

Act II. Pennyboy senior is a cantankerous old usurer who has been a strict guardian of Lady Pecunia, and now that he is aging he has prepared her for appropriate suitors. Pennyboy senior's wealth seems to attract gifts from those who would gain his favor, and he must instruct Lickfinger, his cook and an erstwhile poet, to dispose of the overabundance of food he has accumulated. Soon the suitors all begin to appear—Piedmantle, the heraldet; Almanac, the doctor; Fitton, the courtier; Shunfield, the man of war turned sea captain; and Madrigal, the poetaster. Richer Pennyboy contemptuously dismisses all of them even though they accuse him of being Pecunia's jailor, slave, and idolator. But when Pennyboy junior, the flourishing new heir, arrives, the old man welcomes him profusely. Attended by Broker, her secretary, Statute, her first woman, Band, her second woman, Wax, her chambermaid, and Mortgage, her nurse, Pecunia makes a grand entrance. Richer Pennyboy introduces her to Pennyboy junior. The great lady greets Pennyboy junior with hearty affection and agrees to accompany him to dine in the Apollo Room of the Devil Tavern and to visit the Staple of News.

Act III. Picklock, Pennyboy junior's two-faced attorney, quickly hastens to the staple to prepare Cymbal and his associates for the arrival of Pecunia and her party and urges all in the office to "make court unto her" so that she will be attracted to the staple and will quickly grow tired of Pennyboy junior. When Pecunia and Pennyboy junior enter the office, they see it bustling with activity, and when they demand news, they are inundated with news of all sorts. During the course of this business, Cymbal surreptitiously tries to win Pecunia away from Pennyboy junior while his associates work on her many attendants, but they are all unsuccessful in their attempts. The party soon departs for the Apollo, followed soon after by the rejected suitors, who, at least, hope for a good meal and an opportunity for some jeering at Lickfinger's establishment.

Meanwhile, Cymbal hurries to call upon Richer Pennyboy, offers himself as a suitor with an income of £6000 a year, and promises to give the old usurer half of his share of the staple profits if he will only let his ward sojourn at the office. During the discussion Pennyboy senior miraculously undergoes and recovers from several ailments but finally launches into a vehement tirade against the decay of honest trade and the folly and extravagance of the age. When Cymbal protests that the old man is trying to monopolize the conversation and is not seriously listening to the staple master's offer, the old usurer becomes enraged, and the interview abruptly terminates with each calling the other names.

Act IV. In the Apollo Room the jeerers decide to join the party of Pecunia and Pennyboy junior in spite of the mockery heaped upon them by the old canter. All of the men praise and court Pecunia; aware at last of her power and encouraged by Pennyboy junior, she flirts with and kisses them all. Madrigal composes verses in her honor, fiddlers and a singer are brought in, and the party is becoming quite riotous, as the old canter observes and deplores how Pecunia is being prostituted by Pennyboy junior. Shortly, disturbed by the long absence of his ward, Richer Pennyboy comes to the Apollo to get Pecunia and to take her home, but she refuses to leave Pennyboy junior and his companions and to return to what she now considers her prison. She exposes the old man's strict treatment of her, and in the end he is kicked and thrown out of doors. The fiddlers drown out the noise, and the riotous behavior continues. Finally, because he can endure the proceedings no longer, the old canter denounces the folly of all present, especially that of Pennyboy junior who has demonstrated his inability to take care of Pecunia and to treat her worthily. The old vagabond throws off his disguise, takes Pecunia under his own charge, vents his contempt upon his ignoble and wayward son and his friends, and the indignant father now bequeaths his ragged cloak to his prodigal son.

Act V. Abandoned and now penitent in his rags, Pennyboy junior hears from Thomas the news that the staple has gone bankrupt because Pecunia was unable to sojourn there. Although it is little consolation, the news that Picklock and his father have had a falling-out stirs Pennyboy from his self-pity. It seems that the two-faced attorney denies the feoffment and the trust of the estate Pennyboy junior's father made out to the lawyer to be administered for Pennyboy junior's benefit. Later, while feigning friendship and consoling Pennyboy junior, Picklock secretly plots to ruin both father and son, but the attorney unguardedly admits that such a deed does exist, and by a clever stratagem of his own Pennyboy junior is able to get possession of it. Meanwhile, because of the loss of Pecunia and other problems, Richer Pennyboy has gone mad and is arraigning his dogs for his misfortune, when he is set upon by the jeerers, who are now led by Cymbal, but the distressed old man holds his own against them and is finally rescued by Pennyboy junior and his father. The jeerers are dispersed, Richer Pennyboy recognizes his own folly, father and repentant son are reconciled, and the dishonest Picklock is set in the pillory. Out of gratitude to both brother and nephew, Richer Pennyboy makes Pennyboy junior his heir and gives him the hand of Pecunia in marriage.

Statilius. In *Catiline,* one of the conspirators who supports Catiline's abortive attempt to seize power in Rome.

Stationers' Register, The. In order to increase its power and influence over the book trade in London, the organization of booksellers, publishers, and printers known as the Stationers' Company sought and was granted in 1557 a royal charter of incorporation. Thereafter the company dominated and controlled the book trade in the city. The governance of the company itself was vested in a master and two wardens elected annually. Every member of the company was required to enter in *The Stationers' Register* the name of any work which he claimed as his property and desired to print, paying at the time of registration a fee for his entry. Although those who were not members of the company or who held privileges or monopolies did not have to enter their properties, *The Register* became in effect a fairly complete and reliable record of the major publishing activity for the period. Moreover, since the only form of copyright recognized at the time was entry of copy in *The Register* by a member of the company, the right to publish became vested in the Stationer who could establish the earliest entry for a work. Unless he held patents or monopolies (that is, exclusive rights granted by the government to publish and market the work), the author retained no right to print it.

Following is a chronological list of the earliest entry for each of Jonson's registered works. As can be seen, not all of his works were registered, and some of those that were entered were later transferred to another stationer before publication.

Work(s)	Date of entry	Registered by
Every Man out	April 8, 1600	William Holme
Every Man in	August 4, 1600	(Chamberlain's Men?)
Cynthia's Revels	May 23, 1601	Walter Burre
Poetaster	December 21, 1601	Matthew Lownes
King's Coronation Entertainment	March 19, 1604	Edward Blount
Sejanus	November 2, 1604	Edward Blount
Eastward Ho	September 4, 1605	William Aspley, Thomas Thorpe
Masques of Blackness and Beauty	April 21, 1608	Thomas Thorpe
The Case Is Altered	January 26, 1609	Richard Bonion, Henry Walley
The Masque of Queens	February 22, 1609	Richard Bonion, Henry Walley
Epicoene	September 20, 1610	John Browne, John Busby, Jr.
The Alchemist	October 3, 1610	Walter Burre
Volpone	October 3, 1610	Thomas Thorpe
Epigrams	May 15, 1612	John Stepneth
Certain Masques at Court Never Yet Printed [*Highgate,* two *Theobalds, Speeches at Prince Henry's Barriers, Oberon, Love Freed, Love Restored, A Challenge at*	January 20, 1615	William Stansby

263

Work(s)	Date of entry	Registered by
Tilt, Irish Masque, Mercury Vindicated, Golden Age Restored]		
The Staple of News	April 14, 1626	John Waterson
The New Inn	April 17, 1631	Thomas Alchorne
"Eupheme" [third and fourth poems of Und. LXXXIV]	November 4, 1639	John Benson
Execration Against Vulcan. With Divers Epigrams by the Same Author to Several Noble Personages in This Kingdom	December 16, 1639	John Benson
Ars Poetica	February 8, 1640	John Benson
The Gypsies Metamorphosed	February 20, 1640	John Benson
Masque of Augurs, Time Vindicated, Neptune's Triumph, Pan's Anniversary, Sundry Elegies, and Other Poems	March 20, 1640	Andrew Cooke, Richard Serger
"Third Volume" of the Second Folio [fifteen masques, Ars Poetica, English Grammar, Timber, Underwood, Magnetic Lady, Tale of a Tub, Sad Shepherd, Devil Is an Ass]	September 17, 1658	Thomas Walkley

Statius, Publius Papinius (A.D. 45?–?96). Latin poet born in Naples. Favored by the Emperor Domitian, he won the poetry prize at an annual festival under Domitian's auspices, but he was an unsuccessful competitor at the Capitoline contest in Rome. Statius spent his last years in Naples, esteemed as a poet in his own time and throughout the Middle Ages. His surviving works include two epics fashioned after Virgil—the *Thebaid*, on the Seven Against Thebes, and the *Achilleid* (unfinished), on the early life of Achilles—and the *Silvae*, a collection of pleasing occasional poems. Jonson's titles *Forest*, *Underwood*, and *Timber* are various translations of "silvae." In *Epicoene* (II), Daw dismissed Statius as worthless along with many other ancient writers, but Jonson used him as one of his sources for *The King's Coronation Entertainment*, *The Masque of Blackness*, *Hymenaei*, *The Masque of Augurs*, and *Neptune's Triumph*. The epigraph for *Und.* LXXXIV was taken from Statius. Jonson borrowed from the *Silvae* in *Forest* III and *Sejanus* (V) and from the *Thebaid* in *Catiline* (IV). In a discussion of imitation in *Timber* (ll. 2480–81), Jonson cited Virgil and Statius' imitation of Homer as one of his examples.

Statute. In *The Staple of News*, the first woman to Lady Pecunia.

Stentor. According to Homer, a man who could shout as loudly as fifty ordinary people.

Stephano (Stephen). A foolish young gallant, nephew to Lorenzo senior (Knowell) and cousin to Lorenzo junior (Edward) in the Q 1601 (F 1616) version of *Every Man in His Humour*. (Differing names and courses of action in the 1616 folio version are given here in parentheses.) Stephano's uncle despises not only his ignorant protestations that hunting and hawking are the most important arts for a fashionable young man to know but also his thoughtless conduct as evidenced in his artificial quarrel with Prospero's (Wellbred's) servant over an imagined insult. Stephano is self-conscious, afraid that Lorenzo junior is laughing at him when he is actually laughing at Prospero's letter, and he turns melancholy because he feels that it is the most fashionable way to be. He accompanies Lorenzo junior to Florence (London) and impulsively overpays for Musco's (Brainworm's) sword. Lorenzo junior and Prospero mock and bait him and the other two gulls. Stephano picks up Bobadilla's habit of swearing to great excess, and overdoes it even more than Bobadilla. He praises Matheo's (Matthew's) verse when Lorenzo junior encourages him to, and picks up Giuliano's (Downright's) cloak when it falls off in a fight. He stubbornly claims to have bought the cloak, but gives it back when Giuliano arrests him and brings him before Clement. Clement realizes that he is foolish, but invites him to his dinner with the others (and assigns him to eat with and to entertain Cob and Tib in the "butteries").

Stephanus, Henricus. See ESTIENNE FAMILY.

Stephen, Master. See STEPHANO.

Stephens, John. Dramatist who published anonymously in 1613 *Cynthia's Revenge,* for which Jonson wrote a commendatory poem ("Who takes thy volume to his virtuous hand").

Stepneth, John. Bookseller in London from 1609 to 1612 who, in partnership with Walter Burre, published *The Alchemist* in 1610. Stepneth entered Jonson's *Epigrams* in *The Stationers' Register* in 1612 but died before he could publish the book.

Steropes. One of the Cyclopes.

Stevinus, Simon (1540–1609), of Burges, was a distinguished mathematician, physicist, and inventor who was employed by Prince Maurice of Orange. One of Stevinus' best known inventions was a system of sluices for the defense of the Netherlands. Jonson alludes to him in *The New Inn* (II. v).

Stiles. City captain mentioned in *Und.* XLIV.

Stilo, Lucius Aelius. One of the earliest Roman grammarians. He instructed Varro in grammar and Cicero in rhetoric. In *Timber* (ll. 2549–54), Jonson cites Stilo's comment that if the muses had wanted to speak Latin they would have used the language of Plautus and Varro's pronouncement that Plautus was the prince of letters in the Roman language.

Stobaeus. Greek anthologist of the sixth century B.C. In *Timber* (ll. 2499–2502), Jonson alludes to a quote by Simylus taken from Stobaeus' *Florilegium,* II, indicating that nature is incomplete without art and vice versa.

Stone. A famous English fool whose death is discussed in *Volpone* (II. i).

Stone, George. A famous bear, killed at court in 1606. Mrs. Otter says in *Epicoene* (III. i) that before she married her husband, the only time lords and ladies saw him was when they looked out of banquet windows and saw him baiting this bear.

Stote. See FERRET.

Stow, John (1525?–1605). One of the most trustworthy of the sixteenth-century chroniclers. A tailor in his youth, he devoted himself after 1560 to the collection of historical documents and manuscripts. Stow's patron was Archbishop Matthew Parker, whose Society of Antiquaries Stow joined. Stow's edition of Chaucer was published in 1561, and in 1565 his *Summarie of Englyshe Chronicles* appeared. Since he was suspected of Roman Catholic inclinations, his work was periodically examined by the government. His *Chronicles of England* (1580) first appeared in 1592 under the title by which it is best known—*Annales of England.* He produced editions of the work of Holinshed and other English chroniclers. Stow published in 1598 his *Survey of London,* an invaluable account of the city in Elizabethan times.

In the *Conversations* (ll. 599–601), Jonson said that Stow was a tailor, that he had many monstrous observations in his chronicle, and that while walking with Jonson, Stow asked two cripples what they wanted to take him into their order. Stow's monstrous observations are alluded to by Sir Politic in *Volpone* (II. i). The main source for Jonson's *Mortimer His Fall* was Stow's *Annales of England.*

Strabo. Greek geographer and historian who was born about 63 B.C. and died sometime after A.D. 21. He studied in Asia Minor, Greece, Rome, and Alexandria and traveled in Europe, North Africa, and West Asia. He is best known for his *Geographica,* which is based on his own observations and the works of his predecessors, including Homer, Eratosthenes, Polybius, and Posidonius. The work contains historical material as well as descriptions of places and peoples and is a rich source of ancient knowledge about the world although the work is uneven—Strabo attributed to Homer an accurate knowledge of places and peoples mentioned in his epics and almost completely disregarded Herodotus' information, which was often firsthand. Although a Latin translation of the *Geographica* appeared in 1472, the first printed edition in the original Greek was the Aldine one of 1516.

Strabo was one of the sources for *The Masque of Augurs* and *Neptune's Triumph,* and Jonson borrowed from him in the Dedication to *Volpone.*

Strachey, William (1572–1621). English historian. His writings are important sources for the early history of Virginia. In 1609 Strachey sailed for Virginia with Sir Thomas Gates but was shipwrecked in the Bermudas, where the party remained for nearly a year. A letter written by Strachey describing this experience may have served as Shakespeare's inspiration for *The Tempest*. Strachey wrote a commendatory poem ("How high a poor man shows in low estate") for the 1605 quarto of Jonson's *Sejanus*.

Strode, William (1600–1645). English poet and playwright. His tragi-comedy *The Floating Island* was published posthumously in 1655. He translated into Latin Jonson's ode on himself affixed to the published version of *The New Inn*.

Stuart, Lady Arabella (1575–1615), was the only child of Charles Stuart, 5th Earl of Lennox. Because she was a cousin of King James's, restrictions were put on her marriage. In 1610 she married William Seymour, for which she was imprisoned, but in 1611 she escaped from the Bishop of York who had charge of her by playing an epicene part in boy's clothes, an episode which may have been alluded to in Jonson's *Epicoene* (v. i). She was recaptured and put in the Tower, where she died in 1615. She danced in *The Masque of Beauty*.

Stuart, Lady Frances (1617?–1694), was the daughter of Esmé, 3rd Duke of Lennox and Seigneur Aubigny. The Stuart family were kinsmen of James I. In 1632 Frances married Hierome Weston; the event was celebrated in Jonson's *Underwood* LXXV. Her marriage to Weston produced one son, Charles, who was killed in a naval battle with the Dutch in 1665.

Stuart, Sir Francis. Second son of James Stuart, husband of Elizabeth, Countess of Moray. Sir Francis was knighted in 1610. He was a sailor and a scholar and a companion of Jonson's at the Mermaid Club. Jonson dedicated *Epicoene* to Sir Francis.

Stuart, John (of Leith). Shipper with whom Jonson stayed at Leith in 1618 while on his famous walking tour to Scotland.

Stuart, Ludovic. See Ludovic Stuart, Duke of LENNOX.

Stub. A character in *The King's Entertainment at Welbeck* who is to be the bridegroom of Pem.

Stuckius, Johannes Gulielmus. Author of *Sacrorum, Sacrificiorumque Gentilium Descrip-*tio (1598), which Jonson used as one of his authorities on archaeology.

studies (liberal). In *Timber* (ll. 160–174), Jonson, borrowing partially from Juan Luis Vives (*De Causis Corruptarum Artium* [*Opera*, 1555, i. 326]), defends the supremacy of the liberal arts over the servile arts: "*Arts* that respect the mind, were ever reputed nobler, then those that serve the body: though wee lesse can bee without them."

Later in *Timber* (ll. 1636–96), Jonson includes a passage that is apparently part of a letter to a lord (probably the Earl of Newcastle) concerning the education of his sons. Relying heavily on Quintilian (*Instit. Orat.* I. i; ii; iii), Jonson stresses that in the education of children "the care must be the greater had of their beginnings, to know, examine, and weigh their natures: which though they bee proner in some children to some disciplines; yet are they naturally prompt to taste all by degrees, and with change. For change is a kind of refreshing in studies, and infuseth knowledge by way of recreation." A child should not be made to hate study before he knows why he should love it. Jonson advises in favor of public schooling instead of private: "to breed them at home, is to breed them in a shade; where in a schoole they have the light, and heate of the Sunne. They are us'd, and accustom'd to things, and men." He notes, too, that children should be sent to schools where their industry is increased by praise and kindled by emulation. And finally Jonson thinks children should be spared from the threat of the rod at school.

studies (servile). See STUDIES (LIBERAL).

Stuff, Nick. In *The New Inn*, a tailor to Lady Frampul.

Stuff, Pinnacia. In *The New Inn*, the wife of Lady Frampul's tailor.

style. In *Timber* (ll. 1541–48), Jonson, drawing in part on Pliny (*Epist.* III. xiii), argues that as in painting where light and shadow are required, so in style height and humbleness are required, but one's style should not be too humble, as Pliny observed about the writings of Regulus. Jonson notes that some writers because of their own obscene apprehensions refuse to use fit and proper words, "so the curious industry in some of having all alike good, hath come neerer a vice, then a vertue."

Later in *Timber* (ll. 1697–1754), he includes a short essay on style largely extracted from Quintilian (*Instit. Orat.*

II. vii, viii; x. iii). Jonson notes that there are three requirements for a man to write well: to read the best authors, to observe the best speakers, and to practice his own style. Concerning style in particular, Jonson states that the writer must consider "what ought to be written; and after what manner; Hee must first thinke, and excogitate his matter; then choose his words, and examine the weight of either. Then take care in placing, and ranking both matter, and words, that the composition be comely; and to doe this with diligence, and often. No matter how slow the style be at first, so it be labour'd, and accurate: seeke the best, and be not glad of the forward conceipts, or first words, that offer themselves to us, but judge of what wee invent; and order what wee approve." Finally, he argues that as in an instrument so in style there must be harmony and "concent of parts."

In the course of a discussion of teaching included in *Timber* (ll. 1772–77), Jonson notes that one's style should not be dry, empty, winding, or wanton with far-fetched description.

Again in *Timber* (ll. 1980–2030), he adapts from Vives (*De Ratione Dicendi,* I) some observations on style and figurative language, stressing clarity, grace, and directness in expression. Of hyperbole, he notes that it must be used with discrimination. One's metaphors should not be mixed, and an allegory should not be drawn out too long. In concluding the passage, he points out that one sometimes may have to depart from the natural ways of speech because of the necessity to avoid offending the listener, to avoid obsceneness, or to provide pleasure and variety.

Styx. River of Hades across which the souls of the dead had to go on their journey from the realm of the living. Since it was a sacred river, even the gods took their most solemn oath by its name. The river was personified as a nymph, who was the daughter of Oceanus and Tethys and the mother of Nike.

Subtle. In *The Alchemist,* a trickster who is taken into Lovewit's house by Face and who pretends to be an alchemist. With Dol, his female colleague, he cheats many people by promising them gold, including Mammon, Dapper, Drugger, Kastril, and Ananias. He sets Face up as his "lungs," or assistant. He is forced to escape without his booty when Lovewit returns home unexpectedly.

Suckling, Sir John (1609–1642). English Cavalier poet, one of the Sons of Ben. He was much given to the extravagances of the court of Charles I. He was renowned for his gambling, his wenching, and his scintillating wit. He is usually given credit for inventing the game of cribbage. An ardent royalist, he suffered a humiliating defeat in the Scottish campaign of 1639. In 1641 he participated in the unsuccessful plot to rescue Strafford, the king's impeached minister. After the plot failed, Suckling fled to France, where he died. It is usually speculated that being unable to face poverty, he was driven to suicide. *Fragmenta Aurea,* a collection of his poems, plays, letters, and tracts, was published in 1646. In 1659 Humphrey Moseley published *The Last Remains of Sir John Suckling.*

In his *A Session of the Poets,* Suckling gently ridicules Jonson's publication of his plays as works and his efforts to purge the stage, and he also expresses his high opinion of *Epicoene, Volpone,* and *The Alchemist.* In *The Last Remains,* Moseley justifies the publication of Suckling's fragment *The Sad One* by citing the precedent of Jonson's *The Sad Shepherd.* In *The Sad One* itself Suckling alludes (v. i) to Jonson as the poet laureate who has created a rare masque.

Suetonius (A.D. 69?–?140). Caius Suetonius Tranquillus, Roman biographer, was taken as a model by many later biographers. Little is known about his life except that he was briefly the private secretary of Emperor Hadrian. His *De vita Caesarum,* which was translated by Robert Graves as *The Twelve Caesars* (1957), has survived almost in its entirety. Also extant are fragments of a much larger collection of biographies entitled *De viris illustribus.* Since he assembled all sorts of anecdotes, Suetonius' biographies are lively and informative.

In the *Conversations* (l. 147), Jonson told Drummond that Suetonius had written about the secrets of the cabinet and the court, and in *Timber* (ll. 1673–75), he characterized Suetonius' style as a concise one "which expresseth not enough, but leaves somewhat to bee understood." Suetonius served as one of the sources for *Sejanus* and *Poetaster* (IV. v).

Suffolk, Thomas Howard, Earl of (1561–1626). Created Earl of Suffolk in 1603, he was Lord Chamberlain from 1603 to 1614, and Lord High Treasurer from 1614 to 1619. According to the *Conversations* (ll. 155–56), Suffolk ejected Jonson and John Roe from Sam Daniel's masque in 1604, but in 1605 he helped secure the release from prison of Jonson and George Chapman, who had been incarcerated for their part in *Eastward Ho*. Perhaps in gratitude Jonson praised Suffolk in *Epig*. LXVII and wrote *Hymenaei* for the marraige in 1606 of Suffolk's daughter, Frances, to the Earl of Essex.

Summer, Squire. A character in *Love's Welcome at Bolsover* who appears as a carpenter in Colonel Vitruvius' dance of the mechanics.

Surly, Pertinax. A gamester and friend of Mammon's in *The Alchemist*. He refuses to believe in Subtle and mocks all the devices of alchemy as being trickery. He disguises himself as a Spaniard and comes to Subtle in order to expose him; he is mistreated, then taken to see Dame Pliant. He tries to convince Pliant that she is being tricked and confronts Subtle, who sets Kastril to quarreling foolishly with him and Drugger and Ananias to abusing him. Surly leaves, but returns with Mammon. Finding the door locked since Lovewit has returned, Surly gets officers to break down the door. He leaves after he finds that Lovewit has married Pliant.

Suspicion. The name of one of the witches making up the antimasque in *The Masque of Queens*.

Sutton, Bartholomew. Bookseller in London who in 1609 published with William Barrenger *The Case Is Altered* in quarto.

Sutton, Christopher. Dr. Sutton was the author of a devotional book entitled *Disce Mori*. In 1629 he and several others gave a grant from the Dean and Chapter of Westminster to Jonson during his illness.

Swinburne, Algernon Charles (1837–1909). English poet. Attended Eton (1849–53) and Oxford (1856–60), after which he settled in London. His first published work, two blank-verse plays, *The Queen Mother* and *Rosamond* (both 1860), brought him little attention, but *Atalanta in Calydon* (1865), a poetic drama modeled on Greek tragedy, made him famous. His *Poems and Ballads* (1866) were attacked for their sensuality and anti-Christian attitude, but they were also praised for infusing vitality into Victorian poetry and for their technical facility. Swinburne's enthusiasm for the republican aspirations of Mazzini was reflected in *A Song of Italy* (1867) and in *Songs Before Sunrise* (1871). Dissipation and recurrent epileptic attacks brought Swinburne near death in 1878 and 1879, but he was restored to health under the supervision of Theodore Watts-Dunton, with whom he lived after 1879 until his death. He wrote three closet dramas on

Mary Queen of Scots—*Chastelard* (1865), *Bothwell* (1874), and *Mary Stuart* (1881). In 1882 he published *Tristram of Lyonesse*, an intensely passionate version of the medieval legend which is rich in imagery and eloquent verse and to which he appended a sonnet on Jonson ("Broad-based, broad-fronted, bounteous, multiform") and one on the tribe of Ben ("Sons born of many a loyal Muse to Ben"). Many of Swinburne's lyrics are weakened by verbosity and by excessive use of stylistic devices, and his critical studies are often marred by exaggerated vituperation and praise, by digressiveness, and by a frequently flamboyant and involved style, but he performed an important critical service in helping to stimulate an appreciation for William Blake and for older dramatists, such as Webster, Ford, Chapman, and Jonson. In 1889, Swinburne published his highly impressionistic but deeply appreciative critical study of Jonson, and this work is the one usually considered to have revived modern scholarly interest in Jonson.

Swynnerton, John, the son of Sir John Swinnerton, Lord Mayor (1612) of London, was a city captain. He is mentioned in *Und*. XLIV.

Syllanus. In *Catiline,* a senator who strongly favors death for the arrested conspirators.

Sylla's ghost. In *Catiline,* Sylla's ghost gives the prologue, describing Catiline's inhuman crimes and invoking on Rome terror comparable to that which Sylla himself had wrought.

Sylvan. Several of these characters appear as guards of the Fairy Prince in *Oberon, the Fairy Prince.*

Sylvanus. A goat-like man, comparable to Pan as a hunter, who was attended by sylvans.

Sylvester, Joshua (1563–1618), was the groom of Prince Henry's chamber and his first poet pensioner. Sylvester translated extensively from French and in 1605 published his edition of Guillaume du Bartas's *Divine Weeks*. Prefixed to it was *Epig*. CXXXII in which Jonson praised Sylvester's translation, but in the *Conversations* (ll. 29–31), he says that he changed his opinion after he had learned French.

Symancha. Didacus de Dimancus, a Spanish jurist, authority on canon and civil law, and bishop. He lived in the sixteenth century. After dismissing a long list of authors including Homer and Virgil as "not worthy to be nam'd for authors," John Daw claims highly to respect Symancha as an author in *Epicoene* (II).

Symmachus. Roman statesman, scholar, and famous orator of the fourth century A.D. His letters were collected and published after his death; his style was modeled on Pliny. In *Every Man in His Humour* (1616 folio version) Edward tells Wellbred that the letter Wellbred wrote him is better than any by Symmachus (III. i).

Symonds, John Addington (1840–1893). English author. Educated at Harrow and Oxford. Because of ill health, he spent the greater part of his life in Italy and Switzerland. A prolific writer, his many works include travel books (*Sketches in Italy and Greece* [1874] and *Italian Byways* [1883]), literary essays (*Introduction to the Study of Dante* [1872] and *Studies of Greek Poets* [1873–76]), biographies (Shelley [1878], Sir Philip Sidney [1886], Ben Jonson [1886], and Michelangelo [1893]), an excellent translation of the autobiography of Benvenuto Cellini [1888]), and several volumes of poems, including *Many Moods* (1878) and *Animi Figura* (1882). Symonds's major work is a collection of sketches in cultural history, *The Renaissance in Italy* (7 vols., 1875–86), but his study of Jonson was one of the most influential ones before Swinburne.

Symposius, Caelius Firmianus. Reputed author of an epigram entitled "De livore" which is quoted in *Every Man out of His Humour* (I. i). Symposius lived in the fourth or fifth century A.D.

Syrinx. An Arcadian nymph comparable to Diana in appearance who was wooed by Pan. To escape him she begged the earth and the river nymphs to give her another form. She was changed into the marsh reeds from which Pan made his pipe.

T

Tacitus (A.D. 55?–?117). Cornelius Tacitus, Roman historian. Little is known of his life. He was a friend of Pliny the Younger and married the daughter of C. Julius Agricola. In 97 he was substitute consul

under Nerva and later was proconsul of Asia. His first book was the *Dialogus*, an eloquent discussion of oratory after Cicero. He then published a biography of his father-in-law. One of his best known works is *De origine et situ Germanorum*. It and Julius Caesar's earlier writings on the subject are the principal accounts of the Germanic tribes. Tacitus' two long works, the *Histories* and the *Annals*, offer severe criticism of contemporary Rome fallen from the glory and virtue of the old republic. The extant books of the *Histories* cover only the reign of Galba and the beginning of Vespasian's reign but provide a vivid view of Roman life. The extant books of the *Annals* cover the reign of Tiberius, the last years of Claudius, and the first years of Nero. They provide incisive character sketches, ironic passages, and eloquent moral conclusions, all written in a polished and noble style.

Jonson greatly admired Tacitus, and in the *Conversations* (l. 138) told Drummond that Tacitus was one of those who spoke the best Latin and that he wrote the secrets of the Council and Senate (l. 146). Later (l. 602), Jonson said that he had translated an oration of Tacitus, whose style he described as strict and succinct (*Timber* [ll. 1970–72]) in *Sejanus*, the primary source for which was Tacitus. Jonson quoted Tacitus in the Fenchurch section of the *King's Coronation Entertainment* and used him as a source for *The Masque of Blackness* and for the portrait of Voadicea in *The Masque of Queens*. Daw, in *Epicoene* (II. iii), dismisses Tacitus as worthless, but later claims (IV. v) that he does intend to finish reading him. In the *Conversations* (l. 603), Jonson said that the first four books of Tacitus which had been translated in English (by R. Greneway in 1598) were ignorantly done. See also 2nd Earl of ESSEX.

Tagus. A river with golden sands mentioned by Ovid.

Tailbush, Lady. The lady projectress in *The Devil Is an Ass.*

Tailor. **1.** A craftsman called to take part in the courtship contest in *Cynthia's Revels.* He aids Amorphus and Mercury in their staged primping, and takes abuse from the latter.

2. An unnamed member of the boys of Boeotia who perform an antimasque in *Pan's Anniversary.*

Tale of a Tub, A.
    Acted: 1633 at the Cockpit by Queen Henrietta's Men.

Published: 1640 in folio by Thomas Walkley.

Printer: unknown.

The original version of this play was probably written about 1596–97 but for some reason was abandoned. In 1633 when Jonson was bedridden and his dramatic powers were weakened, he seems to have reworked the old version, adding new scenes and material, especially the caricature of Inigo Jones, who had become his enemy. In the first revision of the play, Jonson had included a much stronger attack on his old enemy, but Jones, using his influence as surveyor to the King's works, succeeded in getting the censor to require Jonson to strike completely the character of Vitruvius Hoop (Inigo Jones) and to eliminate the motion of the tub. In the final revision, which was licensed in 1633, Jonson seems to have saved what he could of Hoop in the character of In-and-In Medlay, and the masque in the last act of the play as we now have it was apparently in the first revision a much more caustic and effective attack on Jones and his work.

The last of Jonson's plays to be staged before his death, A Tale of a Tub has never been popular.

Act I. Early on Valentine's Day Sir Hugh, Vicar of Pancras, appears before Squire Tub's residence at Totten Court and arouses him from sleep to report that Awdrey, daughter of Tobias Turfe (high constable of Kentish-Town), has drawn as her valentine John Clay, a tile maker, and will marry him later that day. Since the Squire had hoped to have Awdrey for himself, he and Sir Hugh conspire to prevent the wedding by using Basket-Hilts, the Squire's governor. In the meantime, at Turfe's house the following characters are gathered: Clench, a farrier and petty constable; In-and-In Medlay, a cooper; Scriben, a writer; Pan, a tinker; Puppy, the high constable's man; and Turfe. They all discuss the approaching wedding and recall that only thirty years ago Turfe and his wife had each picked the other as valentine. Although Turfe had promised his daughter to Tub, he believes that the squire is too fine a man for his daughter and that he is too much influenced by his mother, Lady Tub. John Clay, the bridegroom, arrives, followed shortly by Father Rosin and his minstrels, who are to help celebrate the wedding, and they all prepare to leave for the church. Meanwhile, in Maribone at the residence of Justice Preamble (alias Bramble), Sir Hugh and the Justice also conspire to stop the marriage because Preamble would like Awdrey for himself. They intend to employ the Justice's clerk, Miles Metaphor, to secure the attire of a pursuivant to assist them in their plot. Back at Totten Court, Lady Tub arises and sends her usher, Pol-Martin, whom she has recently made a gentleman, to bring her son to her. Pol reports that the squire has already gone out, and Lady Tub sends her usher out to find him. After he leaves, Lady Tub and her woman, Dido Wispe, discuss the kind of man each hopes to get as her valentine.

Act II. In the fields near Pancras, the wedding party makes its way to church, but they are interrupted by Hilts, who is disguised. He asks for the high constable, identifies himself as one of Capt. Thums's men, reports that they have all been robbed that very morning, and demands that the constable raise hue and cry and catch the robbers immediately. When Turfe explains that he is on the way to his daughter's wedding and will pursue the robbers later, Hilts describes the leader of the band of thieves, and all recognize that the description fits John Clay. Hilts insists that Clay be arrested and taken by the constable to Paddington, there to confront Capt. Thums. Turfe reluctantly agrees and departs with Clay and the others, leaving Awdrey in the escort of Puppy. When everyone is gone, Puppy offers himself to Awdrey, but she thinks he is scorning her. Shortly, Hilts reenters, asks Puppy to take a message to the constable about where precisely Capt. Thums can be found in Paddington, and offers to escort Awdrey. Puppy leaves and Hilts prepares to take Awdrey to his master, but the squire himself enters, dismisses Hilts, and begins to woo Awdrey, who is not very receptive to his advances. Metaphor, disguised as a pursuivant, and Preamble overtake Tub and Awdrey, and Metaphor serves Tub a warrant requiring his personal appearance before the Council. Puzzled and reluctant, Tub and Hilts depart with Metaphor, leaving Awdrey in the company of Preamble to be escorted to her father. On the way, Hilts threatens Metaphor with his sword and gets him to admit who he really is, to confess that the warrant was a part of the plot for Preamble to have Awdrey, and to explain that Preamble is taking Awdrey to Pancridge, where the vicar is waiting to marry them. Hoping to stop the marriage, Tub rushes off to Paddington to find Turfe and tell him the news.

Act III. At Kentish-Town, not having been able to find Capt. Thums, Turfe bemoans the difficulties of being high constable. Dame Turfe and Puppy enter without Awdrey, and Puppy reports what happened, expressing his fear that Awdrey has now run off with Hilts—the serving man. During the course of this conversation, John Clay sneaks off and is not missed until later. Shortly after they discover that Clay has gone, Tub enters and reports Bramble's plot to marry Awdrey, and Turfe departs for Pancridge, vowing that he will stop the marriage and have his daughter married to Clay. Lady Tub, Pol-Martin, and Wispe then arrive before Turfe's house. The two women see Puppy and decide to share him for their valentine, but he is reluctant to be wooed by them and causes a commotion. Hearing the disturbance, Dame Turfe comes out and discovers Lady Tub, reports what has happened, and Lady Tub is curious about her son's involvement in the whole affair.

At Pancras, Awdrey, who has been rescued from Bramble by her father, bemoans the fact that she still does not have a husband although she has come close on three occasions, but Turfe advises her to relax and dream on proper men. In another part of Pancras, Preamble bemoans his bad luck in not being able to complete his marraige to Awdrey before her father interrupted and stopped the ceremony. Miles persuades Preamble with a bogus story that the squire was only able to escape because Miles was attacked and beaten by a group of ruffians and had to flee for his life. Although Preamble and Hugh still cannot figure out how the squire found out about their plot so quickly, they agree to come up with a new scheme to keep Awdrey from marrying Clay. At Turfe's house, Dame Turfe expresses her thanks to Lady Tub for the squire's saving of Awdrey, and Lady Tub learns that her son has often visited Awdrey in the past. Puppy is dispatched to find Clay; Lady Tub, Wispe, and Pol leave for home; and Dame Turfe and her company prepare to leave for church again. Disguised as Capt. Thums, Sir Hugh enters, asks for the high constable, and serves him a warrant requiring that he appear before Justice Preamble to explain why he has not raised hue and cry to find Clay. Puppy reports that Clay cannot be found, and Turfe goes with Hugh to appear before the justice.

Act IV. Before Justice Preamble, Capt Thums presses his case and further accuses Turfe of harboring Clay since he was to marry his daughter. Turfe attempts a defense by telling the truth, but Thums is not satisfied and charges Turfe with dereliction of duty, and seeks restitution of the money he lost in the theft plus punitive damages—some one hundred pounds total. To save face, Turfe agrees to pay the money to Sir Hugh at Capt. Thums's request, and sends Miles to the constable's house with a key to get the money. Before Miles leaves, Thums takes him aside and instructs him to bring Awdrey back with him so that Preamble can marry her. In a brief "scene interloping" located in the country near Maribone, Medlay, Clench, Pan, and Scriben engage in some witty dialogue about the implications of names.

Meanwhile in the country near Kentish-Town, Tub and Hilts commiserate over their failure to find Clay, Awdrey, Hugh, or Turfe. They come upon Miles, and when Hilts threatens him with a sword, Miles tells them all about the plot of Preamble and Hugh. For half of the money, Miles agrees to give them Awdrey after he has gotten her. When the squire has Awdrey in his possession, his mother and Pol overtake them, and Lady Tub demands that the Squire accompany her back home and that Pol take charge of escorting Awdrey to her father. When they are alone, Pol begins to woo Awdrey, and she responds favorably to his advances. At Kentish-Town, Lady Tub and the squire report to Dame Turfe that Awdrey is being escorted to her father at Pancridge to be married to John Clay. Puppy and the squire discover Clay hiding in the barn, and the squire, realizing that something is amiss, leaves immediately to find Awdrey. Fearing that Awdrey will be married to an undesirable, Dame Turfe calls everyone together to leave to find Awdrey while Lady Tub is apprehensive about the fate of her son.

Act V. In the fields near Kentish-Town, the squire overtakes Pol and Awdrey and instructs Pol to disguise Awdrey so that she cannot be recognized by Sir Hugh and to wait for his return. In town the squire makes arrangements for a lavish masque to be given at Totten Court. Shortly thereafter his mother finds him and Dame Turfe finds the high constable. Lady Tub realizes that something must be amiss when Dame Turfe reports that she gave both the money and Awdrey to Miles when he came to her with the key. Canon Hugh enters and reports that he has recently married a couple, and they turn out to be Awdrey and Pol. Thereafter the parties are reconciled, and Lady Tub invites them all to Totten Court for a merry celebration. As they all leave for Totten Court, Puppy and Wispe tarry behind, and Puppy proposes to her, and she accepts. At Totten

Court, Pol and Awdrey are congratulated as are also another new bride and groom — Puppy and Wispe. Clay is reported to have become a laughing stock in feeling overly sorry for himself, but everyone else enjoys a masque designed by In-and-In Medlay and entitled "Tale of a Tub," which presents symbolically the essential action that has taken place in the play.

Tamberlain (Tamerlane). Mongol conqueror who lived from 1336(?) until 1405 and who controlled land from the Euphrates to the Ganges Rivers during his lifetime. Christopher Marlowe wrote a play, *Tamburlaine*, acted around 1587, in which he was the central character and spoke with great emphasis and gesticulation. In *Every Man in His Humour* (1601 quarto version) Lorenzo junior says that Musco, because of his strutting and bearing, could be taken for "the Tamberlain . . . of the rout" when disguised as a soldier (III. ii). In *Timber* (ll. 775–79), Jonson cites *Tamburlaine* as an example of scenical strutting and furious vociferation. In Jonson's day the play and the character had become a byword for noise.

Tambarine. A zany in a troupe of Italian comedians that was headed by Zan Ganassa. The troup visited France in 1572; Tambarine supposedly took up residence there, and King Charles IX acted as godfather to his son. In the mountebank scene in *Volpone* (II), Volpone accuses his competitors of retelling Tambarine's "stale" tales instead of putting on a proper show.

Tamer-Chams. A lost play, probably modeled on Marlowe's *Tamburlaine*. Two parts of *Tamer-Chams* were acted by Henslowe's company in 1592 and 1596. In *Timber* (l. 777), Jonson alludes to the play.

Tamesis. A symbolic personage appearing in a scene in Jonson's part of the *King's Coronation Entertainment* and representing the Thames River. Tamesis makes a short speech in praise of James.

Tannenbaum, Samuel Aaron. Physician and writer born in Hungary in 1874. In 1886 he went to the United States. Editor of the *Shakespeare Association Bulletin* and an authority on Elizabethan handwriting and forgeries, Tannenbaum compiled and published a concise bibliography on Jonson in 1938 and together with Dorothy R. Tannenbaum published a supplement in 1947, one year before his death. These bibliographies became standard ones for Jonson.

Tantalus, king of Sipylos, was the son of Zeus and the father of Pelops and Niobe. He was admitted to the society of the gods but aroused their ire, and Zeus condemned him to suffer eternally at Tartarus. As punishment Tantalus had to hang from the bough of a fruit tree over a pool of water. When he bent to take a drink, the water would recede, and when he reached for a piece of fruit, the wind would blow it from his reach. Another account of his punishment is that above his head was suspended a great rock that might fall at any moment.

Tarache. A symbolic personage representing tumult and appearing in a scene in Jonson's part of the *King's Coronation Entertainment*.

Tarleton, Richard (d. 1588). Famous English actor and clown, who was a member of the Queen's Men. He was well known for his improvised jests, jigs, and doggerel. He is alluded to by the stage-keeper in the Induction to *Bartholomew Fair*.

Tarquin. Lucius Tarquinius Superbus, member of an Etruscan family that ruled Rome. Under his rule, the power of the monarchy was absolute, and he was despised by the people for his tyranny. He was deposed by the Senate in 510 B.C. In romantic tradition Tarquin was deposed because his son Sextus raped Lucretia (Lucrece), wife of Lucius Tarquinius Collatinus. Lucretia subsequently committed suicide.

In *Catiline* (III), Catiline plans to mercilessly kill all the Romans in the take-over "as Tarquine did the poppy heads."

Tartarus. The lowest region of the underworld where the wicked were sent for punishment.

Tasso, Torquato (1544–1595), was one of the great Italian poets of the Renaissance. Educated in Naples by the Jesuits and later at the University of Padua, he published *Rinaldo* in 1562 and gained a high reputation. After completing his studies at the University of Bologna, he was invited in 1565 to join the court of the Este at Ferrara, where he long remained and wrote his pastoral play *Aminta* (1573) and the first version (1575) of his masterpiece, *Jerusalem Delivered*, an epic of the exploits of Godfrey of Boulogne in the First Crusade. Suffering from recurring insanity, Tasso wandered restlessly through Italy, writing poems on religion and love. He died in Rome shortly before he was to have been made poet laureate. Byron, Goethe, and others have made him a romantic hero by writing about the legend of Tasso's doomed love for Leonora d'Este. *Jerusalem Delivered* is often considered the greatest poem of the Catholic Reformation.

Lady Politic in *Volpone* (III. iv) tries to impress Volpone by mentioning Tasso.

Tatius, Achilles. Alexandrian rhetorician of the 3rd century A.D., an imitator of Heliodorus. He wrote *The Loves of Leucippe and Cleitophon* in eight books (first English translation: Heidelberg, 1601). Latin translations of part of the work had appeared earlier. Jonson used Tatius as a source for *The Masque of Beauty* and mentioned him in *The New Inn* (III. ii) and *The Sad Shepherd* (I. v).

Tattle. A gossip who appears in the induction and intermeans of *The Staple of News*.

Taygete. One of the Pleiades.

Taylor, John (1580?–1653), the "Water Poet," was born in Gloucester. He sailed with Essex on the Cádiz raid and later became a Thames waterman. He celebrated his fantastic journeys, such as his attempted one to Queenborough in a paper boat, in verse and prose, and in 1630 published in folio his *Works*. In 1614 when there were no theaters open on the Bankside, to the great loss of the watermen, Taylor petitioned the King to prohibit theaters within four miles of the city on the north bank.

In the *Conversations* (l. 607), Jonson claimed that Taylor, who made a walking tour to Scotland at the same time that Jonson did, was sent to Scotland to scorn him, but Taylor in his *The Penniless Pilgrimage* (1618) denied that charge and described an amicable meeting between the two in Scotland. Also in the *Conversations* (ll. 371–72), Jonson told Drummond that King James liked Taylor's verses, which tend to be doggerel, and in *Timber* (ll. 612–17), he stated that Taylor's verses have their applause and that he thought most people would vote for Taylor's verses over Spenser's.

Taylor included a poem on Jonson ("Thou canst not die, for though the stroke of death") in his *The Sculler Rowing from Thames to Tiber* (1612), and he wrote a long elegy on the death of Jonson, whom he apparently admired and considered his friend: *A Funeral Elegy in Memory of the Rare, Famous, and Admired Poet Mr. Benjamin Jonson, Deceased.*

Taylor, Joseph (d. 1652). An actor who joined the Lady Elizabeth's Men in 1611 and who is referred to in *Bartholomew Fair* (v. iii). He played Truewit in *Epicoene*, Face in *The Alchemist*, and Mosca in *Volpone*. He also performed in Shakespeare's plays. In 1619 he joined the King's men after the death of Burbadge.

teaching. In *Timber* (ll. 1755–1820), Jonson includes a short essay on the modes of teaching, largely adapted from Quintilian (*Instit. Orat.* I. prooemium 26; I. i, ii, viii; II. iv, v). He stresses the importance of both precept and practice and argues that young writers should be given time to reach maturity and should be encouraged even though they make mistakes; "Therefore a Master should temper his owne powers, and descend to the others infirmity." In particular he argues that young students should be encouraged to read the best and clearest writers first: Livy before Sallust, Sidney before Donne. They should not try Gower and Chaucer too early, but when the students have developed firm judgment they should be allowed to read carefully both ancient and new writers. Spenser, although he "writ no language," should be read for his matter, but as Virgil read Ennius. As Quintilian recommended, Homer and Virgil should be studied for both their verse and their matter. Tragic, lyric, and comic poetry should also be read. In the Greek poets and Plautus, the student should discover the economy and disposition of poetry better observed than in Terence or many new poets.

Telia. A symbolic character who appears in *Hymenaei* as one of the powers of Juno.

Tempe. Celebrated valley between Mt. Olympus and Ossa in Thessaly. The region was much celebrated by ancient poets for its beauty. The Vale of Tempe was sacred to Apollo.

Temperies. A figure in *The Masque of Beauty* who represents one of the elements of beauty.

Tempest. 1. A nymph who dances with the four winds.

2. In *Chloridia*, a symbolic character who appears with four Winds in the fourth entry of the antimasque.

Tenedos. In several poems by Homer, Tenedos is an island in the Aegean Sea which served as a station for the Greek fleet in the Trojan War.

Tennyson, Alfred, Lord. English poet born in 1809 who wrote a prize-winning poem, *Timbuctoo* (1829), during his three years at Cambridge and developed a close friendship with Arthur Henry Hallam, whose death in 1833 overwhelmed Tennyson. His *Poems* (1842) expressed his philosophic doubts in a materialistic and scientific age. With this work he was acclaimed a major poet and in 1845 was given a government pension. In 1850 he published his masterpiece, *In Memoriam*, an elegy sequence recording his years of doubt and despair after Hallam's death and culminating in an acceptance of immortality. Also in 1850 he was appointed poet laureate and married Emily Sellwood. Occasional poems, such as *The Charge of the Light Brigade* (1855), were written as part of his official duties as laureate. In 1859 he published the first group of *The Idylls of the King*, which he expanded in 1869, 1872, and 1885, when he added the final poem. In the Arthurian legend, Tennyson reflected his view of the hollowness of his own civilization. After his death in 1892, he was momentarily neglected, but is now a significant poet and important spokesman for his times.

In *Alfred Lord Tennyson: A Memoir by his Son* (1897), Tennyson's son records that his father could not read Jonson's comedies and quoted him as saying, "To me he appears to move in a wide sea of glue."

Terence (c. 195–c. 159 B.C.). Publius Terentius Afer was born in Carthage. As a boy he was a slave of Terentius Lucanus, a Roman senator, who brought the young boy to Rome, educated him, and set him free. He became a Roman comic writer, and six of his plays have survived. All of them were adapted freely from Greek plays by Menander and others, and they reveal a polished and urbane style, present broad humor, and portray realistic characters.

Jonson admired Terence, and he had a fifteenth-century manuscript copy of Terence in his personal library. In *Timber* (ll. 2619–21), Jonson records that Horace highly esteemed Terence, ascribed the art of Roman comedy to him alone, and ranked him with Menander. Jonson used Terence as a source for *The Masque of Beauty* and *Hymenaei;* he quoted from him in the Induction to *The Magnetic Lady* and alluded to him later in the play (I. iii; II. vii, chorus) and also in *Every Man in* (1601 quarto version, III. i).

Terentianus Maurus. Second century Latin grammarian and author of *De Literis, Syllabis, Pedibus, Metris,* which Jonson relied

upon as one of his authorities in *The English Grammar.*

Terentius, Marcus. A follower of Sejanus in *Sejanus*. He enters with Sejanus the first time Sejanus appears, speaking and plotting with him. Toward the end of the play, he is given credit as a close friend of Sejanus' when the lackeys eagerly ask him for news and trust his word. He brings Sejanus the news of the smoke that billowed from the statue of Sejanus and fearfully begs Sejanus to do homage to the gods, listing all the ill omens that have occurred. He takes part in Sejanus' ceremony to Fortune, tells how more ill omens occurred, and goes to get more protection for his leader. He tells Sejanus of visitors. He bitterly recounts the details of Sejanus' execution by the mob to Arruntius and Lepidus, and shows that he is a thoughtful, high-minded man when he ends the play by commenting that Sejanus' fall should serve as a lesson to proud men who selfishly mock the gods.

Terrent, Thomas (d. 1661). Educated at Westminster and Christ Church, Oxford, Terrent took his B.A. in 1629 and was chaplain and took his M.A. in 1632. He contributed a Latin elegy ("In Obitum Ben: Ionsoni Poetarum Facile Principis") to *Jonsonus Virbius.*

Testament of Love. See Thomas Usk.

Tethys. Titan who was the daughter of Gaea and Uranus, the wife of Oceanus, and the mother of the Oceanids.

Teucer. 1. Eponymous king of the Trojans, who were also called the Teucri.
2. Teucer was the greatest archer in the Trojan War. When he returned home, he was banished by his father to Cyprus, where he founded the town of Salamis and ruled as king.

Thalassius. The name of a Sabine deity invoked during marriage processions. According to Livy and Plutarch, Thalassius was the name of one of the Romans who won a wife for himself during the rape of the Sabine women, and since his marriage proved happy the term was henceforth used in marriage processions.

Thalia. A symbolic character who appears as one of the Graces and as an attendant of Venus in *The Haddington Masque.*

Thamesis. A figure in *The Masque of Beauty* who receives the daughters of Niger and four other nymphs. The figure was impersonated by Thomas Giles, the choreographer for the masque.

Thauma. A mute nymph, said to be lovely and high-minded, who attends Cynthia in *Cynthia's Revels.*

Thayer, Calvin G. (1922–). American scholar who since 1967 has been Professor of English at Ohio University. Educated at Stanford and the University of California, Berkeley. Author of articles on Shakespeare and Elizabethan literature, Thayer published his major study of Jonson's plays in 1963.

Themis. Titan goddess of law, order, and justice. By Zeus she was the mother of Horae (the seasons) and Moerae (the Fates). She may also have been the mother of Prometheus by Iapetus.

Theobald, Lewis (1688–1744). English author and editor born in Kent. He was the third editor of Shakespeare and is best known for his *Shakespeare Restored* (1726), which exposed the inaccuracies of Pope's edition and prompted Pope to retaliate by making Theobald the hero of the 1728 *Dunciad.* Despite Pope's caustic satire of Theobald, which damaged his reputation, many of Theobald's emendations to Shakespeare's text are still generally accepted. Theobald also wrote poems and plays. In 1715 he published *Memorandums of the Immortal Ben,* purported to have been written by Jonson but actually by Theobald.

Theocritus. Greek idyllic poet, who lived in the third century B.C. He is credited with being the inventor of pastoral poetry, and his pastoral works are nostalgic, graceful, and realistic. His works included *Idylls* and "Dirge on Daphnis." Virgil was greatly influenced by him. In *Poetaster* (v. iii), Virgil includes Theocritus in the list of poets Crispinus should read with a tutor in order to develop literary taste and discretion. Theocritus is quoted in *The Masque of Queens,* and he seems to have inspired some parts of *The Sad Shepherd.*

Theophrastus. Greek philosopher who lived about 372 to 287 B.C. and was Aristotle's successor as head of the Peripatetics. He wrote on many subjects, but his best-known writings are on plants and his *Characters,* a series of sketches of various ethical types. His *Characters* anticipated the studies of Sir Thomas Overbury, John Earle, and La Bruyère and may have influenced Jonson's development of humor characters.

Theosophia. A symbolic personage representing divine wisdom appearing in a scene in Jonson's part of the *King's Coronation Entertainment.*

Thersites. In Book II of the *Iliad,* an ugly, lame man with a vicious tongue. In *Timber* (ll. 353–55) Jonson, while discussing the wise tongue, mentions Thersites as an example of a man speaking without "judgement, or measure."

Theseus. Hero of Athens who was the son of King Aegeus (in some versions he is the son of Poseidon). When Theseus was a young boy, his father's wife Medea tried to kill him, but his father discovered the plot and saved him and exiled Medea. His most famous adventure was against the Minotaur of King Minos of Crete. With the aid of Ariadne, daughter of King Minos, Theseus was able to kill the Minotaur, after which he left Crete with Ariadne, but later abandoned her at Naxos. After the death of his father Theseus became king of Athens and instituted a number of reforms. Most memorable was the federalization of the Attic communities. Later he traveled to the land of the Amazons, where he abducted Antiope. A son, Hippolytus, was born to the couple. A vengeful Amazon army invaded Athens, but Theseus was able to defeat them. For attempting to help Pirithous to kidnap Persephone, Theseus was held prisoner in Hades until he was rescued by Hercules. After Theseus returned to Athens, he found his once great kingdom in turmoil, so he sailed to Skyros, where he was eventually murdered by King Lycomedes. Theseus was also famous for his tragic marriage to Phaedra and for his responsibility for the death of his son Hippolytus.

Thespia. A town on the slopes of Helicon associated with the Muses.

Thetis. A Nereid who was beloved by both Zeus and Poseidon, but because of a prophecy that her son would be greater than his father, the gods bestowed upon her the mortal Peleus, to whom she bore the son Achilles.

Thisbe. According to Ovid, the most beautiful maiden in the East, who lived next door to Pyramus with whom she fell in love. Although they were forbidden to see each other, they spoke daily through a crack in the wall. Finally they agreed to meet at a spot marked by a white mulberry tree. When Thisbe arrived early and was surprised by a lioness, she fled, leaving her blood-stained cloak. When Pyramus came later and found the cloak and the tracks, he concluded that Thisbe had been killed, and he committed suicide by stabbing himself. Thisbe returned, found Pyramus dying, and likewise stabbed herself to death.

To commemorate their deaths, the mulberry tree became a dark red.

Thomas. In the *The Staple of News,* a barber who desires to have a position as a clerk in the Staple of News office.

Thomyris. According to Jonson, Queen of the Scythians who lived during the age of Cyrus, the great Persian monarch. She appears as one of the virtuous queens in *The Masque of Queens.*

Thorello (Kitely). A foolish, rich merchant, husband to Biancha (Dame Kitely) in the 1601 quarto version of *Every Man in His Humour.* (Differing names and courses of action in the 1616 folio version are given in parentheses.) Thorello (Kitely) is afraid that the young gallants who meet in his house with his brother-in-law Prospero (Wellbred) are trying to entice away his wife and her unmarried sister. Highly gullible, he becomes jealous after they accuse him of being jealous. He is a little afraid of Prospero (Wellbred) and his companions and tries to prevent Giuliano (Downright) from starting trouble with them. He begins to tell Pizo (Cash) an important secret but impulsively becomes suspicious and does not. Thorello (Kitely) goes out on business but returns as soon as he hears that Prospero (Wellbred) and his companions have entered his house. He becomes especially jealous of Lorenzo junior (Edward) when Hesperida (Bridget) and Biancha (Dame Kitely) praise him. Prospero (Wellbred) inadvertently makes him believe that his food and clothes are poisoned. When Musco (Brainworm), disguised as Clement's man, comes in and tells him that Clement wishes to see him, he rushes out, giving Prospero (Wellbred) an opportunity to make Biancha (Dame Kitely) think her husband is being unfaithful with Cob's wife. She leaves to seek him at Cob's house, he returns, and Prospero (Wellbred) makes him believe that Biancha (Dame Kitely) is being unfaithful to him at Cob's house. They meet, and he, in anger, takes his wife, Lorenzo senior (Knowell), and others before Clement. They learn of the deception and are reconciled. (Kitely, with good humor, quotes verses from a jealous man's part in a play.) They attend Clement's dinner with the rest of the company.

Thorpe, Thomas. Bookseller in London from 1603 to 1625 who published in quarto the following of Jonson's works: *Sejanus* in 1605; *Hymenaei* in 1606; *Volpone* in 1607; and *The Masques of Blackness and Beauty* and *The Haddington Masque* in 1608. Together with William Aspley he also entered *Eastward Ho* on the *Stationers' Register* in 1605, but only Aspley's name appeared on the imprint of the published work.

Thucydides (460?–400 B.C.). Athenian historian and soldier. As a general in the Peloponnesian War, he failed to prevent the surrender of the city of Amphipolis to a Spartan general, and he was exiled until the end of the war. He thus had opportunity to acquire firsthand knowledge of both the Athenians and the Spartans for his history of the Peloponnesian War, covering 431 to 411 B.C. Essentially a military history, this work chronicles events by the seasons and interprets events in terms of the nature and behavior of men, not fate or some influence outside of man. In order to display their motives and beliefs about war, Thucydides invents speeches for important persons, the most outstanding one of these being Pericles' funeral oration.

In *Epicoene* (II. iii), Daw dismisses Thucydides, considered to be one of the greatest of the ancient historians, as a worthless writer. In *Catiline* (IV), in order to show off her knowledge of Greek, Sempronia misquotes Thucydides on the relationship between spies and ambassadors.

Thumb, Tom. The hero in a number of works including *The History of Tom Thumbe the Little . . .* (1621), he appears as a character in the antimasque for *The Fortunate Isles, and Their Union.*

Thums, Captain. See Chanon HUGH.

Thunder. In *Chloridia,* a symbolic character who appears in the sixth entry of the antimasque.

Tib. Wife to Cob in *Every Man in His Humour.* Her name is the same in both the 1601 quarto and the 1616 folio versions of the play. (Differing names and courses of action in the 1616 folio version are given here in parentheses). Cob fears that she is being unfaithful to him, so he orders her to shut herself up in their house. Prospero (Wellbred) jokingly sends Thorello (Kitely) and Biancha (Dame Kitely), each of whom thinks that the other is being unfaithful, to Cob and Tib's house. Lorenzo senior (Knowell) is sent there by Musco (Brainworm). When Cob finds them all there, he beats Tib, thinking that she has been unfaithful to him. They are brought before Clement but have no speeches in the 1601 quarto version to show that they are happily reconciled. (In the F 1616 version, they speak of their reconciliation, Clement declares that night their bridal night since they are "married anew," and they eat with Stephen in the "butterie.")

Tiberius (42 B.C.–A.D. 37). Tiberius Julius Caesar Augustus was the second Roman emperor, A.D. 14–37. The son of Tiberius Claudius Nero and Livia Drusilla, Tiberius campaigned in 20 B.C. in Armenia, became governor of Transalpine Gaul the following year, and in 12 B.C. aided his brother Drusus on the Rhine and Danube. In the same year his stepfather Augustus forced him to divorce his wife Vipsania Agrippina and marry Julia, Agrippa's widow and Augustus' daughter. After the death of Drusus in 9 B.C., he campaigned in Germany, and in 7 B.C. he retired to Rhodes for seven years. Upon his return he was adopted as heir of the emperor and succeeded Augustus without difficulty. As emperor, he continued the policies of Augustus, but he drastically cut luxury expenses and reformed the tax situation in the provinces. This greatly improved the financial state of the government but made him very unpopular in Rome. For years he depended heavily upon his aide and confidant Sejanus. In A.D. 26 he retired to Capri and ruled thereafter by correspondence. His chief aide, Sejanus, who developed ambitions of his own, was killed in A.D. 31. Generally, modern historians have assessed Tiberius' administration more favorably than did Roman historians. Tiberius is mentioned in Luke 3:1.

Tiberius is a major character in *Sejanus* and is mentioned in *The Alchemist* (II. ii).

Tibicines. Flute-players. They appear in *Sejanus* during Sejanus' sacrifice to Fortune.

Tibullus. 1. A gallant in *Poetaster* who writes poetry and is a friend of Ovid's. Ovid senior calls him foolish for his devotion to poetry, but says that he can afford it, since he is a man of wealth. He visits Ovid while Ovid is attempting to study law and laughs at him for writing law in verse. He brings Ovid a note from Julia and says that he will accompany him to Albius' house and meet his mistress, Plautia. At Albius' he shows his common sense by mocking foolish Crispinus. He invites Chloe and Cytheris to Ovid's masquerade, where he plays Bacchus and realizes that the song Crispinus claims for his own is plagiarized from Horace. Caesar upbraids him along with the others when he interrupts the masquerade, but he is soon pardoned, since he is a gentleman. He praises

Virgil to Caesar, and listens gladly to Virgil's reading of the *Aeneid*. He is given permission by Caesar to participate in the trial and punishment of the poetasters, and reads the indictment against them and their verses. Unlike some of the other characters in *Poetaster,* he is not a caricature of one of Jonson's contemporaries.

2. Tibullus was a Roman elegiac poet who lived from about 54 B.C. to 19 B.C. He was famous for his descriptions of the pleasures of love and country life and for his graceful style. He left four books of verse, including poems to his mistress Delia.

In *Epicoene* (II. iii), Daw dismisses Tibullus as a worthless ancient poet.

Tigellius, Hermogenes. A singer and songwriter in *Poetaster;* Horace mentions a musician with this name who was a hostile critic of him. He comes with the courtiers to Albius' house and pouts coyly but finally sings after Crispinus is highly praised for his singing. After Tigellius receives praise, it is hard to keep him from singing. He plays Momus at Ovid's masquerade and complains about various others. He sings with Crispinus and is chided with the others when Caesar enters.

Tilly, Count (1559–1632). Johann Tzerclaes, Count Tilly, was a general of the army of the Catholic League during the Thirty Years War. He is mentioned in *Und.* XLIV and *The Staple of News* (III. ii).

tilt. A joust or military exercise on horseback in which two combatants charge each other with lances or other weapons and try to unhorse each other. Sometimes a tilt is a symbolic exercise between two conflicting forces or claims, as in Jonson's *A Challenge at Tilt.*

Timber, or Discoveries. A miscellaneous collection of notes, jottings, and miniature essays that were first published in the 1640 folio. These writings were probably put together and seen through the press by Sir Kenelm Digby, who made no attempt to organize them in any way. Commonplace books were fashionable in the seventeenth-century, and Jonson had planned to publish a selection from his notebooks. Although Jonson was unable to complete the task, the signs of editorial preparation are quite evident in the care with which the selected passages are translated, abridged, or adapted. Many of Jonson's notes are couched in the first person, but to read them as strictly autobiographical is to misunderstand Jonson's habit of mind. His guiding principle in his reading was to study the ancients critically with a view to extract from them anything that threw light on the life or art of his own day, and this principle is evident throughout *Timber*. Although its finest sayings do not relate to books or theories of art but rather deal with life and conduct, the most finished section is that which deals with literary criticism, and it is this section which later critics most appreciated. John Dryden was particularly impressed with the essay on the drama, the essay that ends the work. *Timber* was saved from oblivion in the eighteenth century by Joseph Warton, who added a selection from the work to his reprint of Sidney's *Apology* in 1757.

Entries on the most important subjects discussed in *Timber* are included throughout this *Companion*.

Time. A mute nymph who attends Cynthia in *Cynthia's Revels,* said to be very lovely and high-minded.

Time Vindicated to Himself and to his Honours.

Performed: January 19, 1623.

Published: in 1623 in quarto. No imprint. Reprinted in 1640 folio by Thomas Walkley in section of masques.

Printers: unknown.

Originally scheduled for presentation on Twelfth Night, this masque was not actually performed until January 19, 1623, because of problems with the various ambassadors to be invited. The antimasque was intended to ridicule George Wither for his attempts at satire, but Jonson himself was criticized for even broaching what had become a sensitive subject at Court. Inigo Jones produced the masque.

To the sound of a trumpet, Fame entered, followed by the Curious, the Eyed, the Eared, and the Nosed. Fame announced that all should hear what Time would proclaim, and all seemed eager to listen, inquiring of Fame from whence she had come. Fame indicated that she had come from Saturn or Time (by some called Kronos) and that Time had sent Fame to summon all worthy people to a great spectacle that Time would present with all solemnity that very night. With great excitement all awaited the anticipated spectacle and Saturnalia Chronomastix then entered and began to criticize Time, and when Fame asked who he was, Nose replied that the new character was Chronomastix, the brave and famous satyre. When Chronomastix noticed Fame, he lauded her as his mistress and the sole object of his life, but Fame scorned

Chronomastix as a vain impostor who served only infamy. Indignant, Chronomastix appealed to the Curious and the others, claiming that since his pen had scourged all sorts of vices he did not deserve such ridicule. To put down Fame, Chronomastix declared that he had his supporters and admirers, too, and he called them forth. The antimasquers, who were all mutes, came forward, and Eyes, Ears, and Nose introduced them to Fame, who exclaimed that they were merely a confederacy of folly. Afterwards all except Fame danced the first antimasque in adoration of Chronomastix. Following the dance, Eyes, Ears, and Nose challenged Fame, if she could, to bring forth more interesting or amusing sport from Time. Although she proclaimed that such a request was an abuse of Time, Fame promised to satisfy their whim, and a second antimasque of Jugglers, Tumblers, a Cat and a fiddle, and the Curious was performed until the performers were all driven away. Fame then proclaimed,

"Why, now thy are kindly us'd, like such spectators,
that know not what they would have. Commonly,
the curious are ill-natured, and like flies,
Seeke times corrupted parts to blow upon:
But may the sound ones live with fame, and honour,
Free from the molestation of these Insects:
Who being fled, Fame now persues her errand.

To the sound of loud music the scene opened, and Saturn sitting with Venus was discovered above with some Votaries who were coming forth below. Fame announced that Saturn, at the request of Venus, had decided that to adorn the age and fill the court with beauty he would rescue certain youthful glories of the times who had been observed in the distant darkness by Hecate, and Venus proclaimed that whatever was done for love would be to the honor of Time. The masquers, who were the glories of the times, were discovered and that which had obscured them vanished. While the masquers descended, the Votaries and chorus celebrated their beauty, after which the masquers danced their entrance, and Venus and Saturn decided to have Cupid and Sport appear before the court to provide further delight for the audience.

After the main dance which followed, Cupid and Sport entered and suggested that the masquers take a break while they addressed the audience. Cupid implored the king not to be offended that Love and Sport had entered his noble court, and he exhorted the lords to put off all sadness and thought of business, but Sport warned them all not to trust Cupid, for he had plots on them all and only wanted to prove that there was no business but to be in love. Cupid and Sport both praised the beauty of the ladies and proclaimed that Time and Love both desired that beauty and youth should join in dance. The revels followed, after which the whole scene changed to a wood and Diana appeared, descending to Hippolytus.

Diana declared that she had been wronged that night by Love's report to Time about her youthful beauties (the glories of the time) who had been obscured, but Hippolytus answered her that all things would turn out for the best. Saturn and Venus discovered Diana, and they thought she had probably missed her troop and had come for them. Hippolytus then explained to Venus and Saturn that Diana had not intended in any way to defraud Time of any of the glories that were rightfully his and that her only purpose had been to honor Time. Diana related how she had called the youths forth when they were in their prime and had trained them in the ancient arts, especially in the art of hunting, so that they could serve Time more effectively. Both Saturn and Venus recognized Diana's noble purpose and thanked her for her efforts. The masque concluded with the chorus delivering a long speech in praise of hunting as a noble exercise that makes men active and wise and enables them to fight the true enemy of mankind—vice.

Timon. An anonymous play with several striking parallels to some of Jonson's plays, but there is no evidence that the play was ever acted or that Jonson had any hand in writing it.

Tinder-box-man. An unnamed member of the boys of Boeotia who perform an antimasque in *Pan's Anniversary*.

Tintoretto (1518–1594). One of the greatest of the Venetian painters. His real name was Jacopo Robusti. He studied briefly under Titian and aspired to combine the drawing of Michelangelo with the color of Titian. He is mentioned in *Und.* LXXVII.

Tipto, Sir Glorious. In *The New Inn*, a knight and colonel who is a guest of Lady

Frampul at the Inn and who enjoys drinking and carousing with Fly and the so-called house militia.

Titan. One of the race of ancient giants who were vanquished by the Olympian gods. In *Catiline* (III), Catiline refers to Prometheus, a Titan who brought fire to man, and who molded man out of clay, when he tells Aurelia to win women to his cause by promising them "men, for lovers, made of better clay, / Then ever the old potter Titan made."

Tithonus, prince of Troy and son of Laomedon, was loved by the dawn goddess Eos, who bore him Memnon. When Eos asked Zeus for immortality for her lover, she forgot to ask the god to grant her lover eternal youth, so Tithonus grew older and older until Eos changed him into a grasshopper.

Titian (1490–1576). Venetian painter. His real name was Tiziano Vecellio. He studied with Gentile and Giovanni Bellini, after whose death he was recognized as the foremost painter in Venice. Throughout his long and prolific career, rulers and nobles throughout Europe showered him with commissions and honors, and he lived much of his life in princely splendor. As a painter, he explored many artistic problems but is probably most famous for his innovations in the handling of color. Titian is mentioned in *Und.* LXXVII and is listed in *Timber* (l. 1583) among the famous painters of Italy who imitated the ancients.

Tityus. A giant and a son of earth whom Odysseus saw in Hades covering nine acres of ground while two vultures pecked at his liver. This was Tityus' punishment for raping Latona. Tityus was killed by either Zeus, Apollo, or Artemis.

tobacco. Although Shakespeare never mentions it in his works, Jonson has much to say about the new habit of taking tobacco. Shift in *Every Man out* teaches the art, and Drugger sells tobacco in *The Alchemist*. Generally, Jonson presents the habit in an unfavorable light. For his references to tobacco, see *The Case Is Altered* (II. iii); *Every Man in* (1601 quarto, III. ii, iii; 1616 folio, III. v, vii); *Every Man out* (III. iii, vi, ix; IV. iii); *Cynthia's Revels* (Ind.); and *The Alchemist* (I. iii).

Tonson, Jacob. Bookseller in London from 1677 to 1720 who was one of the publishers of the so-called Booksellers' Edition of Jonson's *Works* in 1716–17.

Tooke, Benjamine. Printer in Dublin from 1669 to 1685(?) and celebrated bookseller in London from 1669 to 1716 who was one of the publishers of the so-called Booksellers' Edition of Jonson's *Works* in 1716–17.

Tooth-drawer. An unnamed member of the boys of Boeotia who perform an antimasque in *Pan's Anniversary.*

To-Pan. In *A Tale of a Tub,* a tinker of Belsie who assists Tobie Turfe in his efforts to find a band of robbers.

Topcliffe, Richard. Informer against Jonson and his fellow actors for their part in 1597 in *The Isle of Dogs,* which was adjudged seditious.

Tossanus, Daniel. See LEGES CONVIVALES.

Touchstone, Mistress. In *Eastward Ho,* the wife of the goldsmith Touchstone and the mother of Gertrude, who supports her daughter's unfortunate marriage to the adventurous Sir Petronel Flash.

Touchstone, William. In *Eastward Ho,* the wealthy London goldsmith who is the father of Gertrude and Mildred and the master of Quicksilver and Golding. He dismisses Quicksilver, offers Mildred's hand in marriage to Golding, and reluctantly sanctions Gertrude's marriage to Sir Petronel Flash. Eventually he has Sir Petronel and Quicksilver imprisoned, but when he is convinced of their genuine repentance, he forgives them and is finally reconciled with both them and Gertrude.

Tooley (Tooly), Nicholas (d. 1623). An actor who played in *The Alchemist* and *Catiline* as one of the King's Men. He also performed in Shakespeare's plays.

Townley, Zouch. Scholar and divine who was a friend of Jonson's. In response to Alexander Gill's attack on Jonson's *The Magnetic Lady,* Townley wrote a poem defending the play ("It cannot move thy friends from Ben, that he"), and he wrote a commendatory poem for Jonson's translation of Horace's *Art of Poetry* ("Ben, the world is much in debt, and though it may"). When Jonson was examined in 1629 about his knowledge of certain verses lauding the assassin of Buckingham, Jonson told the attorney general, Sir Robert Heath, that he had heard that they were written by Townley.

Townshead. One of the clowns who appears in *The Gypsies Metamorphosed* and discovers that the gypsies have picked his pockets.

Townshend, Aurelian. A third-rate court poet who succeeded Jonson as masque writer for the court about 1632. Townshend alluded favorably to Jonson's elegy on the death of Venetia Digby (*Und.* LXXXIV) in his own elegy on Venetia.

Townshend, Sir Robert. A patron of both Fletcher and Jonson with whom Jonson apparently lived during part of 1602 and 1603. In 1605 Jonson inscribed a copy of the quarto of *Sejanus* for Townshend.

Trains. The servant of and assistant to Meercraft in *The Devil Is an Ass.*

Trash, Joan. A gingerbread woman in *Bartholomew Fair,* who is often Leatherhead's companion, although Leatherhead accuses her of selling rotten wares. Cokes buys her shop along with Leatherhead's, and it is ruined by Cokes.

Trebatius. A minor character in *Poetaster* who, unlike several of the other characters in the play, does not represent one of Jonson's contemporaries. He appears only once and tries to talk Horace out of writing satiric verse, since he will be more secure socially by writing verse in praise of Caesar.

Trebatius Testa, A. A famous jurist who had a high reputation as a legal expert during the reign of Augustus, Testa was a friend of Cicero. He sided with Caesar during the Civil War. He appears as a character in *Poetaster* (III. v).

Trebellius Pollio. Author of *Triginta Tyranni,* one of Jonson's sources for the portrait of Zenobia who appears as one of the virtuous queens in *The Masque of Queens.*

Tribe of Ben (Sons of Ben). A contemporary nickname for the poets and dramatists of the seventeenth century who directly or indirectly acknowledged Ben Jonson as their literary master. The group was also known as the Sons of Ben. Although not all of the so-called Sons knew Jonson personally, those who did met regularly for conversation and refreshments with him in various taverns and lodgings but usually in the Apollo Room of the Devil Tavern in Fleet Street, London. Over the entrance to the Apollo Room were inscribed the following lines:

Welcome all who lead or follow
To the Oracle of Apollo.
Here he speaks out of his pottle
Or the tripos, his tower bottle;
All his answers are divine,
Truth itself doth flow in wine,
Hang up all the poor hop-drinkers,
Cries old Sim, the King is skinkers;
He, the half of life abuses,
That sits watering with the Muses.
Those dull girls no good can mean us;

Wine it is the milk of Venus,
And the poet's horse accounted:
Ply it, and you all are mounted.
'Tis the true Phoebian liquor;
Cheers the brains, makes wit the quicker,
Pays all debts, cures all diseases,
And at once three senses pleases.
Welcome all who lead or follow
To the Oracle of Apollo.

Though there was apparently no formal organization, the Apollo Club did have some "by-laws," which had been drawn up in Latin by Jonson himself and appropriately entitled *Leges Convivales*. These rules were later translated into English as follows by Alexander Brome, publisher of the plays of Richard Brome, one of Jonson's dramatic Sons:

Let none but Guests or Clubbers
    hither come,
Let Dunces, Fools, sad, sordid men
    keep home;
Let learned, civil, merry men
    b'invited,
Let modest too; nor the choice of
    Ladies slighted:
Let nothing in the treate offend the
    Guests,
More for the delight than cost prepare
    the feasts:
The Cook and Purvey'r must our
    palats know;
And none contend who shall sit high
    or low:
The waiters must quick-sighted be and
    dumb,
And let the drawers quickly hear and
    come:
Let not our wine be mixt, but brisk
    and neat,
Or else the drinkers may the Wintners
    beat.
And let our only emulation be,
Not drinking much, but talking wittily.
Let it be voted lawful to stir up
Each other with a moderate chirping
    cup.
Let none of us be must, or talk too
    much,
On serious things or sacred, let's not
    touch
With sated heads and bellies: Neither
    may
Fidlers unask'd obtrude themselves to
    play:
With laughing, leaping, dancing, jests
    and songs,
And what ere else to grateful mirth
    belongs;

Let's celebrate our feasts; And let us
    see
That all our jests without reflection be:
Insipid Poems let no man rehearse,
Nor any be compell'd to write a verse.
All noise of vain disputes must be for-
    borne,
And let no lover in a corner mourn:
To fight and brawl (like Hectors) let
    none dare,
Glasses or windowes break, or hang-
    ings tare.
Who ere shall publish what's here
    done or said,
From our Society must be banished.
Let none by drinking do or suffer
    harm,
And while we stay, let us be alwaies
    warm.

[*Songs and Other Poems*, 2nd ed., London, 1664, p. 325]

According to these rules and to Jonson's "Epistle Answering to One That Asked to be Sealed of the Tribe of Ben" (*Und.* XLIX), the group was not to be construed as a drinking club or a school for scandal, but a social and literary society and philosophical confraternity in which its participants could enjoy true friendship and stimulating conversation without becoming envious of each other or castigating one another or those outside of the club. Consequently, the Tribe of Ben was composed of a varied group of poets, playwrights, and conversational wits, ranging from valets to titled gentlemen, all of whom were either members of the intimate club that usually met in the Apollo Room or who recognized Jonson as their literary master if not their intimate associate.

In general, the one salient interest that bound Jonson and his followers together in their literary activity was their study and imitation of the classics, and, in this respect, their devotion to classical ideals of literary form and subject matter represented a departure from the Puritanism and Italian romanticism of someone like Spenser. At least nineteen persons have been connected with Jonson in such a literary filial relationship. These Sons may generally be divided into two groups—Jonson's lyric disciples and his dramatic disciples—although some fall into more than one of these groups and some do not fit neatly into either but were so friendly with Jonson as to deserve inclusion as Sons.

In her *Classical Influence Upon the Tribe of Ben: A Study of Classical Elements in the*

Non-Dramatic Poetry of Ben Jonson and His Circle (Cedar Rapids, Iowa, 1939), Kathryn A. McEuen points out that, although some of the poets of Jonson's circle may have found their inspiration not so much in the classical poets themselves as in Continental versions of the classics, they all tended to favor and be influenced particularly by the following: the *Epigrams* of Martial; the *Satires* of Juvenal and Persius; the *Satires, Epistles,* and *Odes* of Horace; the *Odes* of Pindar; the *Poems* of Catullus; the *Elegies* of Tibullus and Propertius; the *Amores, Heroides, Ars Amatoria,* and *Remedia Amoris* of Ovid; the *Idylls* of Theocritus; the *Eclogues* of Virgil; the *Anacreontea;* and the *Greek Anthology.* The writers she identifies as members of the Tribe include: Thomas Carew (c. 1598–?1639); William Cartwright (1611–1643); Richard Corbet(t) (1582–1635); Sir Kenelm Digby (1603–1665); Lucius Cary, Lord Falkland (1610?–1643); James Howell (1594?–1666); Richard Lovelace (1618–1658); Thomas Randolph (1605–1635); Sir John Suckling (1609–1642); and Robert Herrick (1591–1674).

In *The Sons of Ben: Jonsonian Comedy in Caroline England* (Detroit: Wayne State University Press, 1967), Joe Lee Davis lists the following playwrights as important Sons of Ben, who attempted, with varying degrees of success, to perpetuate the kind of "realistic," morally centered, and classically imitative comedy exemplified in Jonson's own works: Richard Brome (1590?–?1652); William Cartwright; William Cavendish (1593–1676); William Davenant (1606–1668); Henry Glapthorne (1610–?1643); Peter Hausted (c. 1605–1645); Thomas Killigrew (1612–1683); Shackerley Marmion (1603–1639); Jasper Mayne (1604–1672); Thomas Nabbes (c. 1605–1641); and Thomas Randolph.

Tribuni. Tribunes. In *Sejanus,* the tribunes loyal to Sejanus come to him when the ill omens against him begin to occur.

Trimpi, W. Wesley, Jr. (1928–). Born in 1928 and educated at Stanford and Harvard, Trimpi has been Professor of English at Stanford since 1968. He has published several studies of Renaissance literature and literary theory. He wrote *Ben Jonson's Poems: A Study of the Plain Style,* an important study, which appeared in 1963.

Trio, Fulcinius. A corrupt consul in *Sejanus* who hopes to gain power by backing Sejanus. He does not appear until late in the play, when Sejanus sends for him after he hears that Macro has arrived in Rome. He hears the rumor started by Macro that Sejanus is to receive high honors at the Senate and foolishly spreads it. At the Senate, he at first acclaims Sejanus whose name he enters on the invocation. After Sejanus is disgraced, Trio is quick to turn on him and order his statues pulled down.

Tripoly. See Squire TUB.

Tritons. Sons of Poseidon, the Tritons were mermen. They rode over the sea on seahorses and blew on their trumpets of conch shells.

Triumph. A dramatic form in which the splendor of the denouement suggests the victory of the hero. Jonson's *Mercury Vindicated From the Alchemists at Court* is an example of the form.

Trivia. A translation of the title for Hecate as goddess of crossroads. Since Hecate was often associated with Artemis and Selene, and Diana was frequently identified with Artemis, the epithet is often used in connection with Diana.

Trouble-All. A madman in *Bartholomew Fair,* who was formerly an officer in the Court of Pie-poulders but who, since he was fired by Justice Overdo, runs mad asking everyone for Overdo's warrant and refusing to do anything unless he is commanded to by Overdo. Quarlous borrows his costume and wins both Overdo's signature on a marriage license and Dame Purecraft for a wife.

Troy. Ancient city also called Ilium. At the time of the Trojan War, Troy was a Phrygian city and the center of a region known as Troas. Since they thought that they were themselves descendents of Aeneas and other Trojans, the Romans favored the city.

Truewit. A friend of Dauphine Eugenie's in *Epicoene.* He becomes alarmed at first when he hears of Morose's desire to disinherit Dauphine and tries to talk Morose out of marrying, but is drawn into Dauphine and Clerimont's plan to have Morose marry Epicoene when he realizes that it is a trick. He arranges the mock quarrel between John Daw and Amorous La-Foole to make them appear ridiculous and to impress the ladies with Dauphine's cleverness. He and Clerimont often discuss women.

Trundle. In *The New Inn,* a coachman.

Trundle, John. A publisher of ballads and light literature, and bookseller in London from 1603 to 1626. He also published the first quarto of *Hamlet* in 1603 with Nicholas Ling. In *Every Man in His Humour* (1616 folio version) Edward says that if his father read Wellbred's letter without being shocked, he will voluntarily advertise John Trundle's ballads by singing them in the streets (I. iii). Trundle printed a ballad about a Sussex serpent in 1614 which is alluded to in *News from the New World*. In his satirical verses on *The Magnetic Lady,* Alexander Gill advises Jonson to let Trundle publish the play if it must be published.

Trusty, Mistress. A loyal servant to Lady Haughty in *Epicoene.*

Truth. 1. A symbolic character who appears in the Barriers for *Hymenaei* and argues for the married state's being preferable to the virgin state.

2. In *Timber* (ll. 531–42), Jonson, borrowing primarily from Justus Lipsius (*Politica,* I. i), observes that *"Truth is mans proper good; and the onely immortall thing, was given to our mortality to use."* He goes on to say that without truth all actions of mankind are malice rather than wisdom, and cites Homer (*Iliad,* ix. 312–13) and Euripides in support of this view. Later in *Timber* (ll. 2090–2124), Jonson alludes to Bacon and extracts from his *Of the Advancement of Learning* (Bk. 1, ch. 4) on the subject of truth, noting that the study of words is the first distemper of learning, vain matter the second, and deceit the third. Arguing that nothing is more ridiculous than to make an author like Aristotle a dictator as the schools have done, Jonson contends that Aristotle and many other ancients should have their due, but we should not be afraid to make further discoveries of truth if we can. Above all, we must seek the consonancy and concatenation of truth.

Tub, Lady. In *A Tale of a Tub,* Squire Tub's mother who dominates her son and is opposed to her son's marrying beneath himself.

Tub, Squire. In *A Tale of a Tub,* the squire of Totten Court who is dominated by his mother and who tries unsuccessfully to marry Awdrey. Also called Tripoly.

Tubicines. Trumpeters. In *Sejanus,* they blow their horns during Sejanus' sacrifice to Fortune.

Tucca, Pantilius. A foolish, changeable military captain in *Poetaster,* similar to other bombastic, self-important soldiers in Jonson's works, like Bobadilla in *Every Man in His Humour.* He speaks indignantly of how players mock courtiers to Ovid senior and agrees with him in his low opinion of true poets, such as Homer. Tucca borrows six drachmas from Ovid senior and never pays him back. He discovers Crispinus being arrested by Minos and the Lictors and, without knowing the cause of the arrest, persuades them to free Crispinus. He changes his method of address several times, alternately mocking and praising Minos. He invites himself to dinner at Histrio's, and tells him that he hates satire. He commands his pages to perform and delights in their actions. At Ovid's masquerade of the gods, he praises Chloe, mocks Horace, and plays Mars. He sneaks away when Caesar invades the masquerade and blames Horace for the interruption. He vows to slander Horace to Caesar and goes with Lupus to accuse him of treason to Caesar. Caesar realizes that he is foolish; Tucca advises Crispinus and Demetrius during their trial, then helps convict them as part of their jury. Caesar has the Lictors fasten a pair of masks on him and carry him away.

Tuck, Friar. Robin Hood's chaplain and steward in *The Sad Shepherd.* He orders the feast, making all the arrangements, and is compassionate toward Aeglamour. He criticizes greedy shepherds who abuse their neighbors and their neighbor's flocks. He brings the news of the effects of Maudlin's curse on the Cook, and takes the Cook's place while the witch-hunters go to catch Maudlin.

Tully. See CICERO.

Tumblers. Performers in the second antimasque in *Time Vindicated to Himself and his Honors.*

Turberville, George (1540?–1610). Secretary to Sir Thomas Randolph, Queen Elizabeth's ambassador to Scotland and Russia. Turberville was also a translator and poet and author of works on falconry and hunting, one of which, *The Noble Arte of Venerie,* (1575) served as one of Jonson's authorities for *The Sad Shepherd.*

Turfe, Awdrey. In *A Tale of a Tub,* the daughter of Tobie and Sibil Turfe, who is supposed to marry John Clay but is desired by Squire Tub and Justice Preamble and who finally marries Pol Martin.

Turfe, Sibil. In *A Tale of a Tub,* Awdrey's mother who wants her daughter to marry John Clay.

Turfe, Tobie. In *A Tale of a Tub,* the high constable of Kentish-Town who is the

father of Awdrey and who tries unsuccessfully to have his daughter married to
John Clay.

Turnebus, Adrianus. Author of *Adversaria*
(1581), one of the books in Jonson's library
which he used as an authority for *Sejanus.*

Turner, Mistress. Notorious poisoner of
Sir Thomas Overbury, Mistress Turner
was the madame of a brothel; she established the fashion of wearing yellow starch
as a cosmetic. She is alluded to in *Und.*
XXXIV.

Turnus. A legendary king of the Rutulians. In the *Aeneid,* he was portrayed as a
spirited warrior. When Lavinia was given
to the Trojan Aeneas by her father, Turnus led a force of Latins and Rutulians
against the Trojans, but after several
bloody battles, he was killed by Aeneas.

Twirepipe. Famous taborer celebrated in
the anonymous tract *Old Meg of Hereford-
shire* (1609) and mentioned in *Eastward Ho*
(V. v).

Twybil. A character in *Love's Welcome at
Bolsover* who appears as a carpenter's apprentice in Colonel Vitruvius' dance of the
mechanics.

Tydides. Refers to Diomedes, son of
Tydeus.

Tyndarides. Refers to Castor and Pollux
who were sometimes thought to be the
sons of Tyndareus and Leda.

Typhoeus, son of Gaea and Tartarus, was
an infuriated monster with one hundred
snake heads and dragon tongues from
which came forth many different sounds.
He was the father of Echidna, Cerberus,
Hydra, the Sphinx, and the Chimera.
Typhoeus nearly defeated Zeus, who considered him so frightful that he set him
afire and buried him alive under Mt.
Aetna.

tyrants. In *Timber* (ll. 1213–33), Jonson
observes that for some princes nothing is
sacred but their majesty and nothing is
profane but what challenges their power,
and, consequently, it is dangerous to offend them, for they do not know how to
forgive, and they will do anything to maintain or enlarge their power. However,
princes who so abuse their office very
often attract to themselves a Sejanus, who
will attempt to get above them, for no man
hates an evil ruler more than one who
helped him to gain his power. "The same
path leads to ruine, which did to rule,
when men professe a *Licence* in governing.
A *good King* is a publike Servant."

Tytirus (Tyrtaeus). Greek elegiac poet of
Sparta, who lived in the seventh century
B.C. He wrote poems which supposedly inspired and cheered the Spartans to victory
over the Messenians after an earlier defeat.
In *Poetaster* (I. i), Ovid says that "Tytirus . . .
shall be read, / Whil'st Rome of all the
conquer'd world is head."

U

Ulen-Spiegle (Owlglass), Tyl. Also known
as Till Eulenspiegel. A peasant clown of
the fourteenth century in North Germany
who was made famous in chapbooks describing his jokes on clerics and townspeople. Although the first chapbook was
probably in Saxon, Eulenspiegel's story
spread all over Europe and Britain. Jonson
mentions him in *Poetaster* (III. iv), *The Alchemist* (II. iii), *The Sad Shepherd* (II. iii),
and *The Fortunate Isles.*

Ulysses. 1. A Latin name for Odysseus
who in Greek mythology was the son and
successor of King Laertes of Ithaca. In the
Iliad, he is a leader of the Greek forces of
the Trojan War, and he is noted for his
clever strategy and his wise counsel. In
post-Homeric legend, however, he is portrayed as a wily, lying, and vicious man,
who avoided service in the Trojan War by
pretending madness until he was exposed
by Palamedes, whom he later caused to be
executed. The legends of Odysseus' wanderings are recorded in *The Odyssey.*
2. In *Timber* (ll. 361–62), Jonson,
while discussing the wise tongue, notes
that, in Homer, Ulysses is made a "long-
thinking man, before hee speaks . . ." See
also FABLE.

uncollected verse. About fifty or so of
Jonson's poems were never collected for
publication until the Herford and Simpson
edition. When Jonson first published his
works in 1616, he presumably included all
the poetry written up to the time he prepared copy for the volume (1612 or 1613)
by which he wanted to be remembered.
For various reasons he apparently decided
to omit a number of his poems, including
most of the songs from the plays, four
poems contributed to the collection *Love's
Martyr* (1601), and several poems prefixed
to various books by other authors. The
omission of a large number of poems from
the second folio (1640–41) of Jonson's
Works probably resulted from Sir Kenelm

Digby's haphazard method of editing material for the collection. Digby made no effort to go beyond the manuscripts that came into his hands at Jonson's death, and he did not even have access to all the manuscripts. The considerable body of uncollected verse includes: songs from the plays, a political poem delivered upon King James's triumphal appearance in London in 1604, an epithalamium from *The Haddington Masque* (1616), various poems that had prefaced the works of other authors, religious poems, personal poems, three caustic satires on Inigo Jones, and several pieces which have survived only in manuscript. As might be expected, this heterogeneous group varies substantially in form and quality.

Underwood, John. An actor who performed in *Cynthia's Revels* as one of the Children of the Chapel. He later joined the King's Men and acted in *The Alchemist* and *Catiline*. He also performed in Shakespeare's plays, and eventually acquired shares in the Globe, Blackfriars, and Curtain Theatres. He died in 1624.

Underwood, The. A collection of ninety of Jonson's poems first published in the second folio of 1640–41. Sometime about 1631 Jonson apparently had planned to publish a collection of his works which would update the first folio of 1616. For the poems Jonson had written since 1613, when he completed the text for the first folio, he selected the title *The Underwood* and composed a brief preface indicating that he considered the new poems a sequel to his second collection of poems, *The Forest*. However, only eighteen of the poems were published in the quarto and duodecimo editions of the poems in 1640, which appeared before the second folio itself. When Jonson died in 1637, all of the manuscripts for the poems passed to his literary executor, Sir Kenelm Digby, who published them all together for the first time as *The Underwood* in the second folio. In many ways, *The Underwood* is Jonson's most mature collection of verse, showing greater variety and power than his earlier two collections—*Epigrams* and *The Forest*—published in the first folio.

The ninety poems in *The Underwood* cover several subjects and exhibit a variety of forms. The collection begins with three religious poems in meters which Jonson did not employ elsewhere. There follows a series of love poems beginning with a group addressed to Charis. Throughout the entire collection are found poems attacking social corruptions and individuals

in the vein of Roman satire. Included also are several funeral poems, the best of which is his Pindaric ode on Sir Lucius Cary and Sir Henry Morison—the first Pindaric ode in English. Several of the poems are about Jonson himself—his relations with others, his misfortunes, his illness, and his poverty. Some of the poems show the distinctive influence of John Donne, and some of the elegies, in particular, are written in a manner so like Donne's that they offer perplexing problems of authorship. Some scholars attribute the eightieth poem ("Fair Friend, 'tis true, your beauties move my heart to a respect.") to Sidney Godolphin, minor poet and cavalier who died in 1643. The eighty-ninth poem ("Liber, of all thy friends, thou sweetest care") is a translation from Martial's *Epigrames* (Book VII, no. 77).

unities. Jonson did not allow himself to be entirely limited by the so-called classical dramatic unities of action, time, and place. Erroneously attributed to Aristotle, who only enjoined the unity of action and loosely alluded to the unity of time, the classical unities, as formulated by later critics, came to mean that the action of a play should not involve a subplot and that tragic and comic elements should not be mixed; that the time covered in a play should not exceed twenty-four hours; and that the action should all be limited to one location. In Jonson's day, these principles were vigorously defended by Sidney in the *Apology for Poetry,* and we may say that generally Jonson followed them, particularly in *Every Man in, Volpone, Epicoene,* and *The Alchemist,* but he departed from them in his other works, and we have no record that he insisted upon adherence to the unities as essential to good drama.

unity of design (in plays). See John DRYDEN.

unity of place. See John DRYDEN.

unxia. A symbolic character who appears in *Hymenaei* as one of the powers of Juno.

Urson, John. A bear-ward who appears with his bears in *The Masque of Augurs* and sings a ballad about the good ale to be enjoyed at St. Katharine's.

Ursula. A fat, grotesque woman with many skin diseases on her legs who roasts pigs at the fair in *Bartholomew Fair*. She is eager to exploit her customers. Knockem, Whit, Mrs. Overdo, Waspe, and the others get drunk at her shop, and she outfits Mrs. Overdo to look like a prostitute.

Usk, Thomas. Author of *Testament of Love* who was executed in 1388. In Jonson's day, the *Testament* was incorrectly attributed to Chaucer. In *The New Inn* (IV. iv), Jonson alludes to the *Testament*.

Uvedale, Lady (Mistress Cary). Daughter of Sir Edward Carey and wife of Sir William Uvedale. Jonson addressed *Epig.* CXXVI to her.

Uvedale, Sir William. Knighted in 1613, Sir William was appointed Treasurer of the Chamber in 1618 and later Treasurer of the Army of the North. He lent the King money in 1641. Jonson addresssed *Epig.* CXXV to him.

V

Valasca. According to Jonson, a Bohemian queen known for her courage. She appears as one of the virtuous queens in *The Masque of Queens*.

Valentine. A servant to Francisco Colonnia in *The Case Is Altered*. He is a great favorite with Count Ferneze's servants, who are drawn by his quick wit and the tales of distant lands which he has recently visited with his master. He is enthusiastically greeted by the servants and is saddened to hear of the death of the Countess Ferneze. He greatly enjoys joking with Juniper; even steward Christophero greets him respectfully. He tells the servants about the queer customs of the theater in "Utopia," in a thinly disguised satire on the behavior of the English public toward plays, and watches the fencing bout between Onion and Martino. Onion speaks derisively of him when Valentine does not write him a song to help him woo Rachel, but Juniper defends him. He jokes when Onion and Juniper, after finding Jaques's gold, dress like "gentlemen" and get very drunk.

Valerius Maximus (c. 49 B.C.–c. 30 A.D.) Roman author whose most famous work was *Factorum ac dictorum memorabilium*, nine books of memorable deeds and sayings which were very popular as a source for writers and orators. Artemisia and Hypsicratea in *The Masque of Queens* are derivative from this work. Jonson quotes Valerius on Euripides in *Timber* (ll. 2453–63).

Vallensis, Robertus. Alchemist and author of *De Veritate et Antiquitate Artis Chemicae*, from which Jonson quotes in *The Alchemist* (II. i).

Valois, Henry of. Henry of Valois, Duke of Anjou and king of Poland. In *Volpone* (III), Volpone tells Celia that he joined in the entertainment planned by the Doge and senators of Venice in 1574, when Henry was returning to France to take the throne as Henry III of France.

valor. Jonson's major discussions of valor, by which he seems essentially to mean fortitude, are found primarily in *The New Inn* (IV. iv), *The Magnetic Lady* (III. vi), and *Und.* XII and LIX.

Vangoose. A "rare artist" appearing in *The Masque of Augurs*, who has devised a masque which he wants to present before the court.

Vapors. A character who appears as a ruffian in the antimasque of *The Fortunate Isles, and Their Union*.

Vargunteius. In *Catiline*, one of the conspirators who supports Catiline's abortive attempt to seize power in Rome.

Varius Rufus. Roman elegiac, epic, and tragic poet, who lived in the first century B.C. He was a friend of Virgil's and was assigned to edit and publish the *Aeneid* if anything happened to Virgil. His most famous work is *Thyestes*, a tragedy of which only a fragment remains. In *Poetaster*, Crispinus says that he is a superior poet to Varius (III. i).

Varro. A follower of Sejanus in *Sejanus*. He accuses and questions Silius, unfairly, since, as Consul, he can be both prosecutor and judge. After Silius is convicted and commits suicide, Varro does not appear again.

Varro, Marcus Terentius (82–c. 37 B.C.). Roman poet. He followed the Alexandrian school and wrote the epic *Argonautica*. He was known as the most prolific and erudite author of his day, his publications being estimated at over six hundred volumes on a variety of subjects. In *Poetaster*, Ovid says that everyone will be told of Varro's fame (I. i). Jonson also cites Varro as one of his authorities for *The King's Entertainment* and *Hymenaei*. See also Lucius Aelius STILO.

Varus, Publius Quintilius. Roman general who died in 9 A.D. when he committed suicide after leading three legions of Augustus' troops into a massacre.

Vatablus, François. François Vatable (d. 1547), noted professor at the Royal College of France, authority on Aristotle and Biblical commentator. After dismissing a long list of authors, including Homer and

Virgil, to be "not worthy to be nam'd for authors," John Daw in *Epicoene* (II) claims to respect Vatablus.

Vaughn, Robert. See PORTRAITS OF JONSON.

Vennar (Vennard), Richard. A popular rhymer and member of Balliol and Lincoln's Inn who fooled the public by announcing that a play called *England's Joy*, containing episodes of English history including Elizabeth's reign, would be staged in 1602 at the Swan Theatre. After taking the entrance money Vennar disappeared; he was later captured and brought before a judge, who treated the whole affair as a joke. The fraud was often alluded to. Jonson mentions Vennar in *The Devil Is an Ass* (I. i) and alludes to *England's Joy* in *Love Restored* and *The Masque of Augurs*. Vennar is sometimes listed as Fennor.

Venus 1. Originally an Italian goddess of spring who protected vines and gardens, Venus became the Roman goddess of love, identified with the Greek goddess Aphrodite. In imperial Rome she was worshipped as Venus Genetrix, mother of Aeneas; Venus Felix, bringer of good fortune; Venus Victrix, the bringer of victory; and Venus Verticordia, protector of feminine chastity.

2. The Roman goddess of love who appears as the discoverer of the glories of the time in *Time Vindicated to Himself and to his Honors*.

3. In *Love's Triumph Through Callipolis*, she appears in a cloud, descends to earth and is discovered sitting on a throne, after which, together with the chorus, she offers a song in praise of the beauty and love epitomized in the King and Queen.

4. The goddess of love appears as a symbolic character in *The Haddington Masque*. She is attended by the Graces and is seeking her runaway son, Cupid.

5. A character who appears as a deaf old woman in *Christmas, His Masque* and who insists that she be allowed to watch her son Cupid, an apprentice actor, perform before the King.

Venustas. A figure in *The Masque of Beauty* who represents one of the elements of beauty.

Vere, Sir Horace (1565–1635), one of the finest English soldiers of his day, fought at the battle of Mulheim in 1605, defended Mannheim in 1622, and staged a brilliant attack to relieve Breda in 1625. For this last exploit he was created Baron Vere of Tilbury. In *Epig.* XCI Jonson praised him for his valor, humanity, and piety.

Vere, Lady Susan de. See Susan, Countess of MONTGOMERY.

Vermin. See FERRETT.

Vernon, John. Son of Robert of Camberwell, Surrey, John Vernon was admitted to the Inner Temple in 1626 and was called to the bar in 1634. He contributed an elegy ("If souls departed lately hence do know") to *Jonsonus Virbius*.

Vertue, George. See PORTRAITS OF JONSON.

Vertumus. An Etruscan god who, in attempting to woo Pomona, Roman goddess of fruits, assumed numerous disguises to win audiences with her in her garden.

Vesper. Another name for Hesperus.

Vesta. Roman hearth goddess, especially of the flame, Vesta was highly honored in every household. Her public cult had a sacred building in which the Vestal Virgins attended the communal hearth and fire that was not allowed to be extinguished. Vesta was identified with the Greek goddess Hestia.

Vice. A comic figure in old plays whose typical dress is described in the second intermean after the second act in *The Staple of News*. Iniquity in *The Devil Is an Ass* is a vice figure. In the *Conversations* (ll. 409–13), Jonson explained to Drummond how he used the vice character in this play and how his use departed historically and traditionally from that in conventional old English comedy. See also John DRYDEN.

Villiers, George. See George Villiers, Duke of BUCKINGHAM.

Vincent, Augustin. Author of *A Discoverie of Errors in the First Edition of the Catalogue of Nobility, Published by Ralph Brooke, York Herald* (1622), a defense of William Camden, Jonson's teacher. Jonson alludes to the quarrel between Vincent and Brooke and to their books in *The New Inn* (II. vi).

Vincentio. A servant to Count Ferneze in *The Case Is Altered*. He has only one line to speak. He greets Valentine and he could possibly be in the group of servants who bring in Camillo at the end of the play, but he is not named.

Vincent of Beauvais. Author of *Speculum* (1591) which Jonson probably consulted for *An Entertainment at the Blackfriars*.

Virgil (Vergil) (70–19 B.C.). Publius Vergilius Moro, the famous Roman poet, was born on a farm. He studied in Milan, Naples, and Rome, but his life on the farm was an essential part of his education as well. After his formal education, Virgil probably returned to the farm to work and to write. After 41 B.C. he went to Rome and became part of the literary circle patronized by Maecenas and Augustus. In 37 B.C. he completed his *Eclogues,* poems in which he idealized rural life in the manner of Theocritus. His *Georgics* were finished by 30 B.C. and these poems provided a realistic and didactic portrait of the charm of life on the farm. These two works won Virgil recognition as the greatest pastoral poet of antiquity. The rest of his life Virgil worked on his *Aeneid,* a national epic narrating the adventures of Aeneas. This work is considered one of the greatest masterpieces of world literature. Because of illness Virgil was unable to give the work the final revision he thought necessary and wanted the manuscript destroyed. The manuscript was saved at the command of Augustus. Virgil is the dominant figure in Latin literature and despite his paganism his influence continued throughout the Middle Ages when Dante chose him as master. His influence in the Renaissance was pervasive, and Jonson, like many others, looked to him as a guide.

Jonson makes Virgil a central character in *Poetaster.* He closely resembles the historical figure, receives high praise from Caesar, and is selected to help conduct the trial of the poetasters. Virgil is also mentioned in *The New Inn* (I. vi), *Und.* XLII and LIII, and *Timber* (ll. 2249–53). Jonson frequently alludes to Virgil's works, especially the *Aeneid: King's Entertainment, Masque of Blackness, Hymenaei, Haddington Masque, Masque of Queens, Masque of Augurs, Every Man in* (1601 quarto, v. iii), *The Sad Shepherd* (I. i), "A Celebration of Charis" (*Unid.* II), *Und.* XXV, "Ode. αλληγορικ ή," and *Timber* (ll. 1944–45; 2005–7; 2359–62; 2772–79). Virgil's *Eclogues* are referred to in *Every Man in* (1601 quarto, v. iii), *Bartholomew Fair* (III. iii), *The Sad Shepherd* (title page), *King's Entertainment, Masque of Blackness, Oberon,* and the *Masque of Augurs.* The *Georgics* are alluded to in *Masque of Blackness, Masque of Beauty, Hymenaei, Masque of Queens, Epig.* LXX, *For.* III, *Und.* LXXIII, and "Ode. αλληγορικὴ."

In the *Conversations* (ll. 33–34), Drummond notes that Jonson said the translation of Virgil (apparently referring to that of Phaer and Twyne) in long Alexandrines was merely prose. Later he records (ll. 69–70) that Jonson told Cardinal Duperron that his translations of Virgil were "naught."

Virginia. Jonson's most extensive discussion of the settlement in the new world occurs in *Eastward Ho* (II. ii; III. i and iii), but Virginia is also mentioned by Morose in *Epicoene* (II. v) and the Stagekeeper in the Induction to *Bartholomew Fair.*

Virtue. 1. A symbolic character who does not speak but appears sitting with Pleasure at the foot of Atlas in *Pleasure Reconciled to Virtue.*

2:. In *Timber* (ll. 1292–97), Jonson records that "When a vertuous man is rais'd, it brings gladnesse to his friends: griefe to his enemies, and glory to his Posterity" because the virtuous man who is honored becomes an example to all. Jonson versified this idea in *Und.* LXXV. ll. 113–20. Later in *Timber* (ll. 1323–72), Jonson, drawing on Apuleius (*De Magia*), observes that "A *good man* will avoide the spot of any sinne. The very aspersion is grievous: which makes him choose his way in his life, as hee would in his journey." In a personal note Jonson indicates that "*An Innocent* man needs no *Eloquence:* his *Innocence* is in stead of it: else I had never come off so many times these *Precipices,* whether mens malice hath pursued me." In an autobiographical passage Jonson states that he himself had been accused of many offenses by many men who were ignorant and liars and were more guilty themselves of the very offenses with which they charged him. In particular he notes that his accusers have attempted to use his own works against him by quoting comments out of context, and they have also attacked his poverty, which, Jonson claims, has been his good counselor and has kept him from cruelty and pride. No great or memorable work came out of but "poore cradles." In conclusion, he argues that "It was the ancient poverty, that founded Commonweales; built Cities, invented Arts, made wholesome Lawes; armed men against vices; rewarded them with their owne vertues; and preserv'd the honour, and state of Nations, till they betray'd themselves to Riches."

Still later in *Timber* (ll. 1455–67), Jonson, building on Seneca (*Epist.* CXV), notes that there can be no more miserable creatures than those who labor under their own misery or others' envy. A man should rather not covet, not fear, not repent of what he is, but be secure of himself and all opinion, for the worst opinion gotten for doing well should delight us. Jonson concludes that the man who would have his virtue published is not the true servant of virtue, but of vainglory.

In a brief passage in *Timber* (ll. 1489–1501) Jonson notes that we tend to revere more those things remote than near to us, so that "Men, and almost all sort of creatures, have their reputation by distance." But, Jonson argues, a man should live as renowned at home in his own country as in the whole world, "For it is Vertue that gives glory: that will endenizon a man every where."

Vision of Delight, The.

Performed: January 6 and 19, 1617.

Published: 1640 in folio by Thomas Walkley in the section of masques.

Printer: uncertain.

First performed at court in 1617, this masque was reportedly attended by the Virginian Princess Pocahontas, who was on a visit to England at the time. The work has certain striking similarities to the *Note d'Amore,* a series of musical spectacles performed at Florence in 1608 at a ball held in the Palazzo Vecchio. On June 27, 1911, His Majesty's Theatre revived *The Vision* as part of a performance at the coronation festivities of King George V. King George and Queen Mary were present, and many of the leading actors and actresses of the day took part in the performance of the masque.

The scene was a street surrounded by impressive buildings. In the distance Delight was discovered approaching, accompanied by Grace, Love, Harmony, Revel, Sport, Laughter, and Wonder. Delight came forth and sang: "Let us play, / and dance, and Sing, / Let us now turne every sort / O' the pleasures of the Spring, / to the graces of a court." A She-monster delivered of six Burrantines and six Pantalones entered and danced the first antimasque, after which Delight announced that the sports to be enjoyed were servants not of the sullen day but of humorous night, who would help produce the delightful vision. Night then rose in her chariot bespangled with stars while Delight explained that night would awaken the phantoms to assist her. After night and moon had both risen, night, hovering over the place and singing, summoned Phant'sie forth from the cave of cloud and demanded that a waking dream be created.

The scene changed to cloud, and Phant'sie entered and, after cataloguing many possibilities, inquired what kind of dream would delight all those present. Afterwards a second antimasque of Phantasms came forth and danced, and Phant'sie, promising a change that would be more pleasing to all, called attention to the descending of the gold-haired Hour, the keeper of the gate of heaven, the turner of the year who "makes another face of things appeare." As Hour descended, the whole scene was transformed into the Bower of Zephyrus while Peace sang about the astonishment at the sudden change to spring, and the choir responded: "We see, we heare, we feele, we taste, / We smell the change in every flowre, / We onely wish that all could last, and be as new still as the houre." After the song, Wonder lavishly praised the glories of the new spring, and Phant'sie extolled the ability of Wonder to make all things better than they appear. To the accompaniment of loud music, the Bower opened, and the masquers were discovered as the glories of the spring, after which Wonder lauded their splendor and inquired what power was responsible for them. Phant'sie replied: "Behold a King / Whose presence maketh this perpetuall Spring grow in that Bower, / And are the marks and beauties of his power," and the choir reiterated Phant'sie's exclamation.

Afterwards three dances were performed, ending with a dance between the masquers and the ladies, followed by the revels. Night and moon having then descended, Aurora appeared and reminded all of the approach of day, to which the choir responded: "They yield to Time, and so must all. / As night to sport, Day doth to action call, / Which they the rather doe obey, / Because the Morne, with Roses strew's the way." The masquers exited, dancing.

Vitruvius. Marcus Vitruvius Pollio lived in the late first-century B.C. and early first-century A.D. He was an engineer and architect for Augustus. His *De architectura,* published in ten volumes, is valuable for its encyclopedic nature, and his theories were very influential on Renaissance architects. Jonson quotes Vitruvius on chimeras in *Timber* (ll. 1567–71). He ridicules Inigo Jones's misunderstanding of Vitruvius in "An Expostulation with Inigo Jones."

Vitruvius, Colonel. A character in *Love's Welcome at Bolsover* who is apparently a satirical portrait of Inigo Jones. He presents an oration on the dance of the mechanics.

Vives, Juan Luis (1492–1540). Spanish humanist and philosopher, a friend of Erasmus'. Upon invitation of Henry VIII, Vives went to England, lectured at Oxford, and served as tutor to Princess Mary. Opposed to Henry's divorce from Katharine of Aragon, he left England and went to Bruges, where he eventually died. Vives objected to the authority of Aristotle and the conventions of scholasticism and was the forerunner of Francis Bacon in insisting upon the application of induction to philosophical inquiry. Two of his most famous works are *De anima et vita* (1538), one of the first works of modern psychology, and *De disciplinis* (1531), an analysis of educational theory. Jonson, who had a copy of Vives's *Works* in his personal library, was very much influenced by Vives, particularly in *Timber*, where he borrowed from Vives on a number of subjects: on learning, counsel, nature, and the liberal arts (ll. 65–173); on speech (ll. 1881–1918); and on composition and style (ll. 1957–2030).

Voadicea. Also known as Boadicea, Boodicia, Bunduica, Bunduca. Queen of the Iceni during the time of Nero, she led a revolt against Roman rule. She was celebrated by Spenser. She is one of the virtuous queens in *The Masque of Queens*.

Volatees. Creatures resembling man but being a kind of fowl partly feathered who were born on the Island of the Epicoenes in the moon and who perform an antimasque in *News From the New World Discovered in the Moon*.

Volaterranus, Raphael (1450–1521). Raphael Maffei of Volterra, the author of *Commentarii Urbani Libri XLV*. Jonson's portrayal of Valasca in *The Masque of Queens* is indebted to Volaterranus.

Volpone. In *Volpone*, a rich Venetian magnifico who pretends to be very ill. Because he is childless, many greedy men attempt to gain his favor in order to be named his heir; with the help of his parasite, Mosca, Volpone exploits their foolishness for his own gain and entertainment. Volpone himself is later outwitted by Mosca and is forced to reveal his own double-dealing to the Avocatori.

Volpone, or The Fox.

Acted: 1606 at the Globe by the King's Men.

Published: 1607 in quarto by Thomas Thorpe.

Printer: unknown.

Dedication. The play is dedicated to ''the most noble and most equal sisters''—Oxford and Cambridge. In the Introduction, Jonson attacks the poetasters, who he says are causing poetry to be the most despised form of art with their ''prophaneness,'' ''un-washed baudr'y,'' and ''exploded follies.'' He thanks Oxford and Cambridge for giving his play such a favorable reception and claims that with their support he will make poetry back into the noble art it should be. In the Prologue, Jonson answers those who have attacked

him and his plays, arguing that audiences like his plays, that he makes his own material instead of stealing it, and that his comic action is natural, not forced. He concludes by hoping his play not only pleases and amuses the audience but also teaches them something about themselves.

Act I. Volpone, a rich Venetian without heirs, pretends to be very ill. With the aid of his parasite, Mosca, he tricks greedy men who hope to become his heir into adding to his wealth. Voltore, an advocate, brings Volpone a precious plate, and Mosca assures him that he has been named heir. Corbaccio, a foolish, deaf old man, comes, offering a bag of money, and is tricked into disinheriting his son, Bonario, in favor of Volpone. Corvino, a merchant, arrives, bringing a pearl. When Corvino leaves to attend to his wife, Celia, Mosca describes her to Volpone in such glowing terms that he longs to see her, and Mosca explains that she is always locked up by her jealous husband. Upon Volpone's insistence, Mosca finally suggests that Volpone may be able to see Celia if he disguises himself in some way.

Act II. Peregrine, a gentleman traveler, meets Sir Politic Would-Be and recognizes that Would-Be is a very foolish man. They observe Volpone, disguised as a mountebank, performing before Corvino's house in hopes of seeing Celia. Curious about the mountebank, Celia appears at her window and throws a handkerchief to Volpone, an act which later causes Corvino to become enraged and to accuse Celia of licentiousness. In the middle of this accusation, Mosca comes in and convinces Corvino that he can win favor by offering his wife to the ill Volpone as a kind of nurse. Celia is recalled, pacified, and commanded to visit Volpone.

Act III. Mosca meets Bonario and tells him of his father's plan. When Bonario expresses disbelief, Mosca offers to let him witness the disinheritance, and Bonario grimly follows Mosca to Volpone's. Lady Would-Be comes to see Volpone and overwhelms him with her constant empty chatter and her pretensions of sophistication. Mosca rescues Volpone by telling Lady Would-Be that he has seen her husband in a gondola with a courtesan, and she rushes off at the news. Corvino and Celia arrive unexpectedly early, and Mosca sends Bonario out of hearing. Corvino argues with the reluctant Celia, hypocritically ridiculing the honor of which he was previously so jealous. Mosca finally persuades Corvino to leave. After he does, Volpone leaps from his couch and begins to woo

Celia. She is horrified. Volpone threatens to take her by force, but is interrupted when Bonario, who has overheard the commotion, comes to her rescue and promises to expose Volpone. Mosca and Volpone despair, and then meet with Corvino, Corbaccio, and Voltore and plot to discredit Bonario and Celia and thus save themselves.

Act IV. To Peregrine, Sir Politic relates his secret, nonsensical plans for getting rich and reads him his diary. Lady Would-be bursts in, mistakes Peregrine for the courtesan in disguise, and loudly berates both of them. Mosca enters and informs her that Peregrine is actually a gentleman, and she apologizes profusely. Later, Voltore, Mosca, Corbaccio, Corvino, Bonario, and Celia come before the Avocatori. With various lies and slander, Voltore convinces the judges that Celia is lewd and that Bonario is vicious. Corvino and Lady Would-Be testify against Celia, and the case rests when Volpone, feigning grave illness, is brought in on his couch. The judges announce that punishment will be decided "'ere night," and Mosca satisfies the competitors for Volpone's wealth with various lies.

Act V. Mosca and Volpone exult over their triumph, and Volpone decides to carry the deception one step further and spread the news that he is dead, so that he can watch the reaction of his gulls. Drawn by the news, the legacy hunters soon arrive and are disappointed when they are informed that Mosca is the lawful heir. Disguised, Volpone speaks to some of the disappointed hopefuls and torments them further. Meanwhile, Peregrine, with the aid of some merchants, has made Sir Politic appear ridiculous and has forced him to leave Venice to save face. Volpone continues to torment Corbaccio, Corvino, and Voltore until they all return to court to hear the punishment decided for Celia and Bonario. At court, however, Voltore changes his testimony and begins to tell the truth until Volpone, still in disguise, convinces him that Volpone is yet alive. Voltore then disgraces himself by pretending to have been possessed. Mosca enters, dismisses Voltore, and refuses to substantiate the testimony that Volpone is still alive. Rather than be whipped for insolence and false testimony and let Mosca get his wealth, Volpone throws off his disguise, and the plotting is revealed. Volpone, Mosca, Corbaccio, Corvino, and Voltore are all appropriately and severely punished, and Celia and Bonario duly rewarded.

Voltore. The greedy advocate in *Volpone* who brings Volpone gifts in hope of inheriting his wealth. He slanders Celia and Bonario at the Senate and makes the Avocatori believe that they are corrupt and Corvino and Volpone innocent. Later, when he thinks that Volpone has died and left Mosca as his heir, he tells the truth about Celia and Bonario, but when he learns that Volpone is still alive, he disgraces himself completely by changing his testimony again and pretending to have been possessed by a devil.

Volturtius. In *Catiline*, the conspirator captured with the Allobroges who gives evidence to the Senate against the other conspirators.

Votaries. Characters who appear as the supporters of Saturn and Venus in *Time Vindicated to Himself and to his Honors.*

Vulcan. 1. A Roman fire god, chiefly of destructive fire, Vulcan probably originated as a god of volcanoes. Volcanalia, which was held on August 23, was his festival. Vulcan was later identified with the Greek Hephaestus.

2. The god presides over the Cyclopes and appears as a symbolic character in *The Haddington Masque* and as the maker of a model of the celestial sphere.

3. The fire god appears in *Mercury Vindicated From the Alchemists at Court* and lauds the power of alchemy.

Vulturnus. 1. An early Latin name for the southeast wind. This wind was more generally known by the Greek name Euros.

2. A character in *The Masque of Beauty* who appears as a warm, calm wind.

W

Wadlow, Simon. Innkeeper of the Devil Tavern and vintner. Married in 1608 to Margaret Blott and died in 1627. His son John, who succeeded him as innkeeper, was baptized in 1623. Wadlow was known as Old Sym. He is mentioned in *Staple of News* (II. v) and "Over the Door at the Entrance into the Apollo."

Waker, Pem. An alewife mentioned in *The King's Entertainment at Welbeck* and "A Song of the Moon" (an uncollected poem of Jonson's).

Walkley, Thomas. A bookseller who in 1630 published in quarto *Love's Triumph Through Callipolis*. In 1631 he published in quarto *Chloridia*, and in 1640 he published the second volume (excepting the first three plays in the volume) of the second folio of Jonson's works.

Waller, Edmund (1606–1687). English poet. Educated at Eton and Cambridge. At an early age, he became a prominent speaker in Parliament. His early poems were addressed to "Sacharissa," Lady Dorothy Sidney, who refused his suit. Originally an antiroyalist, he later supported Charles I against Parliament and for his part in the plot to secure the city of London for the king was fined and banished. Waller was pardoned in 1651 and returned to Parliament after the Restoration where he served until his death in 1687. His poetic works are noted for their smoothness and polish and for their contribution to the development of the heroic couplet. The first collection of his *Poems* was published in 1645.

Waller contributed "Upon Ben Jonson, The Most Excellent of Comick Poets" to *Jonsonus Virbius*.

Waller, Henry. City captain alluded to in *Und.* XLIV.

Walley, Henry. Bookseller in London who in 1609 published, together with Richard Bonion, the first quarto of Shakespeare's *Troilus and Cressida* and in the same year the quarto of Jonson's *Masque of Queens*.

Walsingham, Sir Francis (1532?–1590). In the *Conversations* (ll. 564–65), Jonson noted that Sir Francis, when he was Ambassador in Scotland, said of the King: *hic nunquam regnabit super nos.* Sir Francis was the father-in-law of Sir Philip Sidney and a notable English statesman who believed in militant Protestantism. He entered Parliament in 1559, and after 1573 he served as joint secretary of state, during which time he developed an elaborate and effective spy system which led to the eventual execution of Mary Queen of Scots and the defeat of the Spanish Armada. Sir Francis was knighted in 1577.

Walsingham, Our Lady of. A famous shrine of the Virgin at Walsingham in Norfolk. The chapel there dated back to the twelfth century and was supposedly an exact copy of the holy cottage at Nazareth. Jonson mentions the shrine in *A Tale of a Tub* (III. i).

Walthoe, John. Bookseller in London and Stafford from 1683 to 1733 who was one of the publishers of the so-called Booksellers' Edition of Jonson's *Works* in 1716–17.

Walton, Izaak (1593–1683). English writer, author of *The Compleat Angler* (1653), one of the most famous books in the English language, which was frequently reissued with additional material during Walton's lifetime. Walton also wrote biographies of his famous friends: John Donne (1640), Sir Henry Wotton (1651), and George Herbert (1670). In 1680 Walton sent notes to Aubrey on his recollections of Jonson.

Ward, John. A famous pirate who raided ships in the Mediterranean Sea. In *The Alchemist* (v. iv), Dol reveals, as part of the booty she and Subtle have collected, a whistle from a sailor's wife who came to inquire for her husband, who was "with Ward."

Waring, Robert. Educated at Westminster and Christ Church, Oxford, Waring took his B.A. in 1634 and his M.A. in 1637. He became Camden Professor of Ancient History in 1647. He contributed a Latin elegy ("Vatum Principi Ben: Ionsono Sacrum") to *Jonsonus Virbius*. He died in Lincoln's Inn Fields in 1658.

Warner, William (1558?–1609). English poet. He is known for *Albion's England*, a history in both prose and verse originally published in three sections: I (1586), II (1589), and III (1592). In the *Conversations* (ll. 41–42), Drummond records that Jonson said that Warner, since the King's coming to England, had marred all of his *Albion's England*.

War of the Theaters. In literary history, the name often given to the controversy in the period 1599 to 1602 when John Marston was primarily writing for the Paul's Children and Jonson for the Children of the Chapel at Blackfriars. Thomas Dekker referred to the same period as the poetomachia. During this controversy Jonson and his rivals satirized each other on the stage, and their works were performed mostly by rival children's companies. In his Apologetical Dialogue affixed to *Poetaster* (written about 1602), Jonson claimed that his enemies had provoked him on stage for three years, and in 1619 he told Drummond of Hawthornden that he had had many quarrels with Marston and that they had all resulted from Marston's representing him on the stage.

In 1599 Marston represented Jonson as the poet and philosopher Chrisoganus in his *Histrio-mastix*. Although the portrait was not offensive and was probably intended as a compliment, Jonson did not like it. Later in the year, apparently in retaliation, Jonson satirized Marston's turgid style in *Every Man out* through the language of Clove who speaks "fustian a little . . . as you may read in Plato's Histriomastix." In response, the following year Marston ridiculed Jonson as Brabant Senior, the cuckold, in *Jack Drum's Entertainment,* a Paul's play. When the Children of the Chapel played *Cynthia's Revels* in 1601, it seemed that Jonson was satirizing Marston as Hedon, "a light voluptuous reveller," and Dekker as Anaides, "a strange arrogating puff." Consequently, Marston derided Jonson as Lampatho Doria in *What You Will*, probably a Paul's play produced later in the year.

Jonson must have heard that Dekker was preparing an attack himself, and so Jonson got in the first blow in his *Poetaster* (1601), a Chapel play in which Dekker was portrayed as Demetrius the "playdresser and plagiary" and Marston as Crispinus the "poetaster and plagiary." During the course of the play, Horace, who represents Jonson, gives Crispinus a pill to purge him of his windy words. Dekker, probably aided by Marston, replied in *Satiromastix* (1601), a Chamberlain's and a Paul's play. Both Demetrius and Crispinus ridicule Horace the laborious poet in the work and seem to have had the last word in the quarrel, which apparently was made up by no later than 1604 when Marston dedicated *The Malcontent* to Jonson and somewhat shortly thereafter collaborated with Jonson and Chapman on *Eastward Ho.* But even this collaboration produced trouble since Jonson and Chapman were imprisoned because the play was considered offensive, and Marston, who was responsible for most of the problem passages, escaped confinement. Jonson's comments to Drummond about Marston many years after the controversy would seem to suggest that Jonson, who did not forgive and forget easily, still had some ill feelings toward Marston.

Shakespeare referred to the war of the theaters in *Hamlet* (II. ii), where the adult actors are described as having to travel in the provinces because of the popularity in the city of the children's companies, who presented most of the plays in the quarrel.

For a more detailed analysis of the controversy, see Penniman's *The War of the Theatres* (1897) and Small's *The Stage Quarrel Between Ben Jonson and the So-Called Poetasters* (1899).

Warwick, Robert Rich, Earl of. See Sir Robert RICH.

Waspe, Humphrey. Cokes's grumbling guardian-servant in *Bartholomew Fair,* given to fits of rage and abusive profanity. He despairs of preventing Cokes from acting foolishly and squandering his money, and he constantly gives Cokes advice. He verbally abuses Cokes and picks quarrels with everyone else in the play who annoys him. He is shown to be as foolish as his young master when he loses the marriage license to Edgeworth and when he is put in the stocks.

Wassall. A character who appears as one of the children of Christmas in *Christmas, His Masque.*

Watermen. A group of unnamed watermen appear at the end of *An Entertainment at the Blackfriars* and celebrate in song the new child being christened.

Waterson, John. Bookseller who entered *The Staple of News* in the *Stationers' Register* in 1626 and transferred it to Robert Allot in 1631.

Wax (Rose). In *The Staple of News,* the chambermaid to Lady Pecunia.

Webb, Joseph. Physician and grammarian, author of *Eritheatus Materialis primus* and *Usus et Authoritas . . .* (1626). In a 1628 letter to Jonson, Webb sought Jonson's opinion of both works.

Webb, William. See MUSICAL SETTINGS.

Webster, John (c. 1580–?1634). English dramatist. Born in London. c. 1580. His literary reputation rests upon *The White Devil* and *The Duchess of Malfi,* revenge tragedies that mark a great advance over the tragedies of Kyd and others in the late sixteenth century, although they do tend to degenerate into sensationalism. In the Prefatory Address to the Reader for *The White Devil* (1612), Webster refers to the "labored and understanding works of Master Jonson." In his *Monumental Column* (1613), Webster borrows from *The Masque of Queens.*

Weever, John. In his *Epigrammes in the oldest cut and newest fashion* (1599), Weever lauded Jonson and John Marston for their ability to write tragedy. Later in *The Whipping of the Satyre* (1601), Weever cited Jonson as a humorist who attempted to discover and lay open the infirmities of his countrymen and, addressing him specifically, proclaimed, "had you been but so mean a philosopher as to have known that *mores sequuntur humores* you would questionless have made better humors if it had been but to better our manners and not instead of a moral medicine to have given them a mortal poison. . . ." For Jonson's opinion of Weever, see *Epig.* XVIII.

Wellborn, Grace. Justice Overdo's pretty, sensible ward in *Bartholomew Fair.* She has been promised in marriage to Cokes but disdains him because of his foolishness and, at the first opportunity, deserts him for the company of Quarlous and Winwife. She decides to marry Winwife and has an approved license by the end of the play.

Wellbred. See PROSPERO.

Wellbred's servant. See PROSPERO'S SERVANT.

West, Richard (1614–1690), was educated at Westminster and Christ Church, Oxford, receiving his B.A. in 1636, his M.A. in 1639, and his D.D. in 1660. He contributed an elegy ("Poet of Princes, Prince of Poets") to *Jonsonus Virbius* and later contributed to the *Elegies* on Sir Horatio Vere (1642). At the time of his death he was rector of Durweston, Dorset.

Weston, Lord Hierome. See Hierome Weston, Earl of PORTLAND.

Weston, Richard. See Richard Weston, Earl of PORTLAND.

Wever, Robert. Author of *Lusty Juventus* (1565), a work describing the frailty of youth which may have influenced Jonson in *The Staple of News* and *The Devil Is an Ass.*

Whalley, Peter (1722–1791). Author and editor who published an edition of Jonson's *Works* in 1756 in seven volumes. His edition was the first to include *The Case Is Altered.* Whalley made preparations for a second edition of Jonson's *Works* which Francis Godolphin Waldron began publishing in numbers in 1792, but the issue terminated with the second number. Whalley's corrected copy came into the hands of William Gifford, who used it when he published his edition in 1816.

Wheeler, Charles Francis (1906–). American scholar educated at Xavier University (Ohio) and the University of Cincinnati. In 1970 he was Professor of English Emeritus at Xavier. In 1938 he published his valuable book on classical mythology in Jonson's plays, masques, and poems.

Whetstone, George (1551?–1587). English dramatist and poet. His most famous play *Promos and Cassandra* (1578) was important in the development of English domestic drama and served as a source for Shakespeare's *Measure for Measure.* His *Mirror for Magistrates of Cities* (1584) is alluded to in the Induction to *Bartholomew Fair.*

Whetstone's works are full of grave moral pronouncements and are of value to literary and social historians.

Whit, Captain. A bawd in *Bartholomew Fair.* He speaks in a dialect which was supposed to sound Irish. He accosts Quarlous and Winwife at the fair, offering to pimp for them, and does not leave until they pay him. He gets drunk at Ursula's and plays a major role in persuading Mrs. Overdo and Win to act like prostitutes. He attends the puppet show with them.

Whitting, Ned. A famous bear. In *Epicoene,* Mrs. Otter says that before she married her husband, the only time lords and ladies saw him was when they looked out of banquet windows and saw him baiting this bear (III).

Whittington, Richard (d. 1423). Mercer who was three times mayor of London. Considered the last of the great medieval mayors. He is alluded to in *Eastward Ho* (IV. ii).

Wholesome, Tribulation. A pastor of the Brethren of Amsterdam in *The Alchemist.* He and Ananias come to Subtle to win the philosopher's stone for their sect. He gives Subtle much gold in hope of winning the stone and warns Ananias against being skeptical of Subtle. Subtle involves him in a scheme to counterfeit Dutch money. When Lovewit returns, Tribulation comes to take back his money but is turned away.

Williams, John (1582–1650). Bishop of Lincoln in 1621, Lord Keeper of the Privy Seal from 1621 to 1628. In 1637 he was charged with betraying the king's secrets and was imprisoned until 1640. In 1642 he was made Archbishop of York. Williams's fortune as Lord Keeper is told in *Gypsies Metamorphosed.* Williams was apparently Jonson's friend, and *Und.* LXI may well have been written when the Lord Keepership was taken from Williams.

Wilson, Robert. English dramatist and contemporary of Jonson who apparently wrote a *Catiline* play with Henry Chettle. The play is lost and probably did not influence Jonson. The shoemaker in Wilson's *The Cobbler's Prophecy* may have had some influence on *The Case Is Altered,* and Wilson's *The Three Lords and The Three Ladies of London* probably affected the structure of *Cynthia's Revels.*

Winchester, Lady Jane Pawlet, Marchioness of. The eldest daughter of Thomas Viscount Savage, of Rock Savage in Cheshire, Lady Jane was baptized in 1607, married John, 5th Marquis of Winchester, in 1622, and died in 1631 while giving birth to her second son. Jonson commemorated her in *Und.* LXXXIII, and Milton included an epitaph on her in his *Poems* (1645).

Winds. In *Chloridia*, four symbolic characters who appear with Tempest in the fourth entry of the antimasque.

Winifred. In *Eastward Ho*, the young wife of the old usurer Security. She attempts to leave her husband by sailing for Virginia but is shipwrecked and finally reconciled to her husband.

Winwife. A clever gentleman in *Bartholomew Fair* who woos Dame Purecraft for her money. With his companion, Quarlous, he exposes the folly and corruption of many people with whom he comes into contact, including Littlewit, Waspe, Busy, and the rogues of the fair. His cleverness finally wins Grace, Justice Overdo's pretty sensible ward, for a wife.

wisdom. In *Timber* (ll. 84–92), Jonson, borrowing from Juan Luis Vives (*De Consultatione* [*Opera*, i. 169–71]), notes that wisdom is one of "the chiefe things that give[s] a man reputation in counsell." Later in *Timber* (ll. 1003–1019), drawing on Erasmus (*Institutio Principis Christiani*, 1540), Franciscus Patricius (*De Regno et Regis Institutione*, 1567), and H. Farnese (*Diphthera Ionis*, 1607), Jonson records that "*Wise* is rather the Attribute of a Prince, then *learned*, or *good!*" He stresses that prudence is the Prince's chief art and safety and that "*Wisdome* may accompany fortitude, or it leaves to be, and puts on the name of *Rashnesse.*"

Wiseman, Sir W. Knighted in 1604, Wiseman is mentioned in Aubrey's notes on Jonson. Apparently, Jonson attempted to keep James I from naming Wiseman sheriff.

Wispe, Dido. In *A Tale of a Tub*, Lady Tub's woman who eventually marries Puppy, Tobie Turfe's man.

wit. In *Timber* (ll. 570–86), Jonson, paraphrasing Quintilian (*Instit. Orat.* II. v. II), records that "Some men are not witty; because they are not every where witty; then which nothing is more foolish." Continuing, he notes that " . . . now nothing is good that is naturall: Right and naturall language seeme[s] to have least of the wit in it; that which is writh'd and tortur'd, is counted the more exquisite."

Later in *Timber* (ll. 669–800), Jonson includes a short essay on the difference of wits, worked out from hints in Quintilian (*Instit. Orat.*) and Seneca (*Epist.*). Noting that "There are no fewer formes of minds, then of bodies amongst us," Jonson contends that "There is no doctrine will doe good, where nature is wanting." In categorizing the variety of wits, he lists first those that are "forward, and bold," claiming that they never "performe much, but quickly." Some wits "labour onely to ostentation," and others are in composition "nothing, but what is rough, and broken." The wits that have no composition at all, but only "a kind of tuneing, and riming fall," Jonson calls "Womens-Poets." Those, like Montaigne, who "write out of what they presently find, or meet, without choice," Jonson claims, bring their wit to the "*Stake* raw, and undigested." But others "dare presently to faine whole bookes, and authors, and lye safely." The worst, however, are the "obstinate contemners of all helpes, and Arts . . . thinking that way to get off wittily, with their Ignorance." Finally, Jonson concludes, "The true Artificer will not run away from nature, as hee were afraid of her; or depart from life, and the likenesse of Truth; but speake to the capacity of his hearers."

witchcraft. Jonson knew the classical and contemporary literature of witchcraft—the practice of black magic, sorcery, secret divination, Satanism, and various occult arts intended to gain the assistance of the demonic and evil powers of nature—but he made only limited use of witchcraft in his works. In *Volpone* (v. xii), Voltore feigns demonic possession. Satan, in *The Devil Is an Ass*, rehearses for Pug (I. i) the typical practices of witches on earth, mentioning the famous Lancashire and Northumberland witches, and later (v. viii) Fitzdottrel feigns possession. Witches appear as characters in two works. Maudlin the witch causes trouble in *The Sad Shepherd*, and twelve witches constitute the antimasque in *The Masque of Queens*.

Witches. Twelve witches provide the antimasque for *The Masque of Queens*. They represent the opposites of true fame and virtue and are named: Ignorance, Suspicion, Credulity, Falsehood, Murmur, Malice, Impudence, Slander, Execration, Bitterness, Rage, and Mischief.

Wither, George (1588–1667). English poet born in Hampshire. He studied at Oxford. He was imprisoned for his satires *Abuses Stript and Whipt* and while in prison composed five pastorals entitled *The Shepherd's Hunting* (1615), probably his best known work. When he became a Puritan about 1620, his writings took on a religious tone. During the civil war he served the Commonwealth as a soldier and politician.

Jonson apparently had little respect for Wither. In *Abuses Stript and Whipt* (1613), Wither comments on a number of his contemporaries; he praises Jonson but refers to his "deep conceit." Wither ultimately asks to be received as a fellow and a friend among the poets he lauds. For his response to Wither's overture, see Jonson's *Time Vindicated*, where Wither is represented as Chronomastix. "Master Jonson's Answer to Master Withers," a poem sometimes ascribed to Jonson that appeared in *A Description of Love* (1625), was probably written by Richard Johnson, who was the editor of *A Crown Garland of Golden Roses* (1612).

Wittipol. A young gallant in *The Devil Is an Ass* who assists Mrs. Frances Fitzdottrel in escaping her tyrannical husband.

Wolf. In *Eastward Ho*, a jail keeper who reports to Touchstone that Sir Petronel, Quicksilver, and Security have become model repentant prisoners.

Wolfe, John. Printer in London from 1579 to 1601 who may have printed the 1609 quarto of *The Case Is Altered*.

Wolf (Wolfgang Rumler), John. In 1604 Wolf was appointed apothecary to the queen, the prince, and the royal children, and in 1607 he was made apothecary to the king. He is mentioned in *Gypsies Metamorphosed*.

Women (Welsh). Two unnamed Welsh women appear in *For the Honor of Wales* and offer praise of the king and his family.

Wonder. A symbolic character in *The Vision of Delight* who accompanies Delight at the opening of the masque and later delivers a speech in praise of the glories of the spring.

Wood, Antony à (1632–1695). English antiquary. His meticulous research into the history of Oxford produced the two works upon which his fame rests: *The History and Antiquities of the University of Oxford* (1674 in Latin) and *Athenae Oxoniensis* (1691–92), containing biographies of noted Oxford graduates. For statements about the first Earl of Clarendon in *Athenae*, Wood was expelled from Oxford. *The History* is one of the authorities for the fact that Jonson was probably born in Westminster. In *Athenae* Wood includes *Motives* (published 1622) in the list of Jonson's works. If *Motives* ever

existed, it is now lost. It was probably an explanation for Jonson's conversion from Catholicism in 1612.

Wood, George. Printer in London 1613(?) to 1624 who printed works for George Wither. Wood is alluded to in an unfavorable light in *Time Vindicated*.

Woodstocke, Thomas of (1355–1397), the youngest son of Edward III, was created Duke of Gloucester by his nephew, Richard II, in 1385. He was murdered in 1397. In Jonson's *The Devil Is an Ass* (II. iv), Fitzdottrel alludes to him as one of those who was fatally connected with Gloucester.

Worth, Lady Mary. See WROTH.

Wortley, Sir Francis (1591–1652). Poet. Educated at Magdalen College, Oxford. He was knighted in 1610 and became a baronet in 1611. He defended Wortley House in 1644. He was sent to the Tower but was finally released in 1649. He contributed a poem ("En / Ionsonus Noster") to *Jonsonus Virbius*, and in 1641 wrote a poem on the sorrows of Elizabeth of Bohemia. In 1646 he published *Characters and Elegies*, a record of royalists killed in the war. In 1647 appeared his long poem *Mercurius Britannicus His Welcome to Hell*.

Wotton, Sir Henry (1568–1639). English poet and diplomat born in Kent. Originally secretary to the Earl of Essex, Wotton was a favorite at court. James I knighted him and appointed him ambassador to Venice. From 1624 until his death Wotton was provost of Eton. His literary fame rests primarily upon two pieces: "Character of a Happy Life" and a tribute to Elizabeth, Queen of Bohemia. In the *Conversations* (ll. 123–24; 128–29), Drummond records that Jonson had memorized Wotton's verses on a happy life, some of Chapman's translation of the *Iliad*, and some verses from Spenser's *Shepherds Calendar*. Later in the *Conversations* (ll. 495–500), Jonson claimed that Wotton, being in disguise for diplomatic reasons at Leith, was having relations with a young lady while everyone else was at church when he was interrupted by a wench. When he cursed the wench for interrupting the procreation of a child, he betrayed himself. There is some evidence that *Und.* LXXXI was actually written by Wotton (two ms. copies of the poem in the Bodleian attribute it to Wotton, and there are phrasings in it characteristic of Wotton) but Jonson never attributed it to him.

Wotton, Matthew. Bookseller in London from 1687 to 1725(?) who in 1692 was one of the publishers of the third folio of Jonson's *Works* and of the so-called Booksellers' Edition of 1716–17.

Wotton, William. In his *Reflections upon Ancient and Modern Learning* (1694), while stressing the peculiar form of each individual language, Wotton stated that Ben Jonson was the first man to do any considerable work with English grammar but that Jonson's work was imperfect because he relied upon Lilly's Latin grammar for his model and thus attempted to draw an analogy between English and a dead language that was of quite a different kind.

Would-Be, Lady Politic. Politic Would-Be's wife in *Volpone*, who makes herself ridiculous with her constant, empty chatter, vain manner, and lack of understanding of Venetian society. She becomes one of the people trying to be Volpone's heir.

Would-Be, Sir Politic. A pompous English knight in *Volpone* who pretends to be a seasoned traveler and a man of the world but succeeds only in making himself ridiculous by his constant references to non-existent espionage plots and his gross misunderstandings of Venetian society.

Wright, Thomas (d. 1624). A native of Yorkshire and a Jesuit who studied at the English College at Rome and completed his studies at Milan, where he later became Professor of Hebrew. In 1577 he returned to Yorkshire and began an evangelistic mission, for which he was imprisoned and finally banished in 1585. He became Vice-President of the English College at Rheims and Dean of Courtrai. Wright may have been the priest who converted Jonson to Catholicism during his imprisonment in 1598. In 1604 Wright published the authorized edition of his *Passions of the Mind in General*, a study of the Renaissance theory of the passions. Jonson wrote some prefatory verses for the volume, lauding Wright's study. The verses are among Jonson's uncollected poetry ("In picture, they which truly understand").

Wriothesley, Henry. See Henry Wriothesley, Earl of SOUTHAMPTON.

Writh (Raith), James. An Edinburgh advocate to whom Jonson asked to be remembered in a 1619 letter to Drummond of Hawthornden written after Jonson's return to England from his visit to Scotland.

writing. In *Timber* (ll. 2125–60), Jonson, extracting from John Hoskyns (*Directions for Speech and Style*), records that the conceits of the mind are pictures of things to be interpreted by the tongue. Since the order of God's creatures is not only admirable and glorious but also eloquent, he who "could apprehend the consequence of things in their truth, and utter his apprehensions as truly, were the best Writer, or Speaker." Pointing out that Cicero was correct when he noted that no one can speak rightly unless he apprehends wisely, Jonson goes on to develop, by analogy, the implications of this concept for the effective writer. In *Timber* (ll. 2161–2289), Jonson, paraphrasing John Hoskyns, includes a long discourse on the elements of epistolary writing, emphasizing that in the writing of letters two considerations are of particular importance—invention and fashion. Invention is determined by the nature of one's business. Fashion consists of four elements which are all qualities of one's style—brevity, perspicuity, vigor, discernment. Essentially, all of the elements of fashion are included in discernment which proceeds from ripeness of judgment that is obtained by four means—God, nature, diligence, and conversation.

Wroth (Worth), Lady. Mary Sidney, eldest daughter of Robert, Lord Sidney, 1st Earl of Leicester, and niece of Sir Philip Sidney, married Sir Robert Wroth of Durrants in 1604. She was praised by Wither and Chapman, and Jonson lauded her in his dedication to *The Alchemist* and in *Epig.* CIII and CV and *Und.* XXVIII. She danced in *The Masque of Blackness*. On July 13, 1621 was licensed *The Countess of Montgomery's Urania* (a pastoral romance in imitation of the *Arcadia*) to which Lady Mary appended one hundred sonnets and twenty songs. In the *Conversations* (ll. 355–56), Jonson said Lady Wroth had been married to a jealous husband, but Jonson praised Sir Robert in *For.* III. Later in the *Conversations* (ll. 393–98), Jonson told Drummond that Lady Mary had been a character in his lost pastoral *The May Lord*.

Wroth (Worth), Sir Robert (1576–1614), was knighted in 1601, married Lady Mary Sidney in 1604, and succeeded to his father's estates in 1606. He was known as a keen sportsman. Jonson praised Wroth in *For.* III although he described him as a "jealous husband" in the *Conversations* (ll. 355–56).

Wyatt, Sir Thomas (1503–1542). English poet and statesman. Knighted in 1536. He was probably Anne Boleyn's lover before her marriage to Henry VIII. Greatly influenced by the works of the Italian love poets, he produced the first series of sonnets in English modeled chiefly on Petrarch. In addition to sonnets he wrote lyrics, rondeaus, satires, and a paraphrase of the penitential psalms. His son became a famous conspirator who was hanged as a traitor in 1554. In *Timber* (l. 902), Jonson cited Wyatt for his eloquence.

X

Xenophon (c. 430 B.C.–c. 355 B.C.). Greek historian. Born in Athens, he was a young disciple of Socrates'. He left Athens to form the Greek force known as the Ten Thousand that was in the service of Cyrus the Younger of Persia. When Cyrus was killed at the battle of Cunaxa, the Ten Thousand had to fight their way through an unknown land, and Xenophon served as one of the leaders of the heroic retreat, the story of which he tells in his most famous work the *Anabasis*. His other writings include works on Socrates, farming, despotism, education, hunting, horsemanship, the military, and government. Jonson mentions Xenophon in *The Alchemist* (I. ii) and alludes to him in *Pleasure Reconciled*.

Y

Yohan. Wigmaker mentioned in *Every Man out* (V. vi).

Youll, Henry. See MUSICAL SETTINGS.

Young, Sir John. Probably knighted in 1685(?), Young, according to Aubrey's notes, gave a man eighteen pence to cut the famous inscription "O Rare Ben Jonson" on Jonson's tomb in Westminster Abbey.

Young, Robert. London printer. Young is named as printer on the title page of *Poetaster* in the 1640 folio.

Z

Zan Fritada. A well known zany and traveling singer. In the mountebank scene in *Volpone* (II), Volpone calls Nano by this name.

Zeno. Greek philosopher and founder of Stoicism. In *Timber* (ll. 370–80), Jonson mentions an anecdote about Zeno (recorded in Plutarch, *De Garrulitate*, 4). When he remained silent at a feast and was asked what should be said to the princes about him, Zeno replied nothing but that "you found an old man in *Athens,* that knew to be silent amongst his cups."

Zenobia. According to Jonson, Queen of the Palmyrenes, known for her bravery. She is one of the virtuous queens in *The Masque of Queens.*

Zephyrus. The west wind and a son of Eos, goddess of dawn. Zephyrus was sometimes identified with Favonius.

Zetzner, Lazarus. Author of *Theatrum Chemicum* (1602; 1613; 1622), a collection of alchemical treatises which Jonson may have consulted for *The Alchemist.*

Zeuxis. Greek painter of the fifth century B.C. who contributed to the development of light and shadow, as Jonson notes in *Timber* (ll. 1537–40). Since none of his paintings survive, they are known only through ancient writings, particularly those of Pliny.

Zodiac. In *The Haddington Masque,* the twelve powers that preside at nuptials.

Zoroastres (Zoroaster). Religious teacher and prophet of ancient Persia, famous in classical antiquity as the founder of the wisdom of the magi. He is mentioned in *The Fortunate Isles.*

Zouche, Lord. Supposedly a good friend of Jonson's. On the Zouche family vault at Harringworth there is a poem sometimes attributed to Jonson, which was first published in John Bridges's *The History of Northamptonshire* (1791) with the title "On the Family Vault of Lord Zouche at Harringworth." The poem is not usually included in Jonson's canon.

Zulziman. A lost play on an Eastern theme for which Jonson apparently played the leading role at Paris Garden when he was a young actor. This role becomes one of the objects of Dekker's satire on Jonson in *Satiro-mastix* (1602).

Selected Bibliography

Only books, monographs, or essays in books are listed below. For articles on Jonson, see the annual *MLA International Bibliography*.

I. WORKS

A. Although there are numerous editions of Jonson's individual plays and several editions of his poetry and prose works, the standard critical edition of the complete works is:

Ben Jonson, ed. C. H. Herford, Percy and E. M. Simpson. 11 vols. Oxford: Clarendon Press, 1925–52.

B. Facsimile of First Folio:

Workes of Benjamin Jonson. London: William Stansby, 1616; reprinted in facsimile, with an introduction by D. Heyward Brock, London: Scolar, 1976.

II. BIBLIOGRAPHIES

A. The standard bibliographies are:

Tannenbaum, Samuel A. *Ben Jonson: A Concise Bibliography.* New York, 1938, reprinted in *Elizabethan Bibliographies,* vol. 4. Port Washington, N.Y.: Kennikat, 1967. Valuable but not always reliable. No annotations.
Tannenbaum, Samuel A. and Dorothy R. Tannenbaum. *Supplement to A Concise Bibliography of Ben Jonson.* New York, 1947. Again, valuable but untrustworthy and no annotations. Also reprinted in *Elizabethan Bibliographies.*
Brock, D. Heyward, and James M. Welsh. *Ben Jonson: A Quadricentennial Bibliography, 1947–1972.* Metuchen, N.J.: Scarecrow, 1974. Supplements the Tannenbaum bibliographies. Contains articles, books, dissertations, editions, and some reviews. Annotated. Subject index.

B. Useful additions are:

Judkins, David C. *The Non-Dramatic Works of Ben Jonson: A Reference Guide.* Boston: G. K. Hall, 1982.
Lehrman, Walter D., Dolores J. Sarafinski, and Elizabeth Savage. *The Plays of Ben Jonson: A Reference Guide.* Boston: G. K. Hall, 1980.
Recent Research on Ben Jonson. Salzburg, Austria: Institut für Englische Sprache und Literatur, 1978. Contains a brief survey by James Hogg of recent German scholarship on Jonson. Includes German dissertations.

299

III. CONCORDANCES

There are no published concordances to the plays or the prose works, but there are two for the poems:

A Concordance to the Poems of Ben Jonson, ed. Mario A. DiCesare and Ephim Fogel. Ithaca: Cornell University Press, 1978.

A Concordance to the Poems of Ben Jonson, ed. Steven L. Bates and Sidney D. Orr. Athens, Ohio University Press, 1978.

IV. LIFE

There is no standard critical biography, but there are some biographical studies. Vol. I of Herford and Simpson's edition of Jonson also contains a short critical biography.

Aubrey, J. *Lives of Eminent Persons.* Ed. A. Clark. Oxford, 1898.

Chetwood, W. R. *Memoirs of the Life and Writings of Ben Jonson.* Dublin, 1756. Not very reliable or accurate.

Chute, Marchette. *Ben Jonson of Westminster.* New York: E. P. Dutton & Co., 1953. Interesting but uncritical.

Coleridge, S. T. *Notes on Ben Jonson.* [In *Literary Remains,* vol. I, 1836.]

Fuller, T. *The History of the Worthies of England.* ["Westminster," p. 243] 1662; 1811, ed. J. Nicholas, vol. II, p. 112.

Schmidt, A. *Essay on the Life and Dramatic Writings of Ben Jonson.* Danzig, 1847.

Steel, Byron [Steegmüller, Francis]. *O Rare Ben Jonson.* New York: A. A. Knopf, 1927. More fiction than fact.

V. CRITICAL STUDIES

A. Background

Bentley, Gerald Eades. *The Seventeenth-Century Stage: A Collection of Critical Essays.* Chicago: Chicago University Press, 1968.

Boas, Frederick S. *An Introduction to Stuart Drama.* Oxford: Oxford University Press, 1946.

Brotanek, R. *Die englischen Maskenspiele.* Vienna-Leipzig, 1902. Discusses Tudor and Stuart developments of the masque.

Bush, Douglas. *English Literature in the Earlier Seventeenth Century, 1600–1660.* Oxford: Clarendon Press, 1945.

Campbell, L. B. *Scenes and Machines on the English Stage during the Renaissance.* Cambridge: Cambridge University Press, 1923. Discusses stagecraft and treats Inigo Jones extensively.

Chambers, Sir E. K. *The Elizabethan Stage.* 4 vols. Oxford: Clarendon Press, 1923, I, chaps, 5, 6. Discusses stage arrangement and setting of the masque.

Chambers, Sir E. K. *The Medieval Stage.* 2 vols. Oxford: Clarendon Press, 1903. Discusses origin of masque.

Cunningham, J. V. *Elizabethan and Early Stuart Drama.* Literature in Perspective. New York: Evans Bros., 1965.

Donaldson, Ian. *The World Upside-Down: Comedy from Jonson to Fielding.* Oxford: Clarendon Press, 1970.

Dunn, Esther C. *Ben Jonson's Art: Elizabethan Life and Literature as Reflected Therein.* Northampton, Mass.: Smith College, 1925.

Ellis-Fermor, Una M. *The Jacobean Drama.* 3rd ed. London: Methuen, 1953.

Graves, Thornton Shirley. *Jonson in the Jest Books.* 1923.

Hyde, Mary Crapo. *Playwriting for Elizabethans, 1600–1605*. New York: Columbia University Press and Oxford University Press, 1949. Attempts to determine what Jonson, Shakespeare, and other dramatists and their audiences looked for in structure, theme, and characterization.

Inglis, Fred. *The Elizabethan Poets: The Making of English Poetry from Wyatt to Ben Jonson*. London: Evans Brothers, 1969, pp. 127–56.

Levin, Harry. *Jonson, Stow, and Drummond*. 1938.

Nicoll, Allardyce. *Stuart Masques and the Renaissance Stage*. New York, 1938. Includes extensive treatment of Inigo Jones.

Orgel, Stephen, and Roy Strong, eds. *Inigo Jones: The Theatre of the Stuart Court*. 2 vols. London: Sotheby, Parke Bernet; Berkeley: University of California Press, 1973.

Reyher, Paul. *Les Masques anglais*. Paris: Hachette, 1909. Full survey of the development of the masque.

Simpson, Percy, and C. F. Bell, eds. *Designs by Inigo Jones for Masques and Plays at Court*. Oxford: Walpole and Malone Societies, 1924. A description of over four hundred drawings for scenery and costume contained in the Chatsworth collection.

Simpson, Percy. *Studies in Elizabethan Drama*. Oxford: Clarendon Press, 1955.

Soergel, O. A. *Die englischen Maskenspiele*. 1882. Discusses Tudor and Stuart developments of the masque.

Starnes, DeWitt T., and Ernest William Talbert. *Classical Myth and Legend in Renaissance Dictionaries: A Study of Renaissance Dictionaries in their Relation to the Classical Learning of Contemporary Writers*. Chapel Hill: University of North Carolina Press; Cambridge: Oxford University Press, 1955.

Sullivan, Mary A. *Court Masques of James I*. New York: G. P. Putnam's and Sons, 1913. Treats extensively the competition among foreign ambassadors to secure precedence at the performances of court masques.

Summers, Joseph H. *The Heirs of Donne and Jonson*. New York and London: Oxford University Press, 1970.

Wells, Stanley. *Literature and Drama With Special Reference to Shakespeare and His Contemporaries*. London: Routledge and Kegan Paul, 1970.

Welsford, Enid. *The Court Masque*. Cambridge: University Press, 1927. Discusses analogues and examples from Italy.

Whipple, Thomas King. *Martial and the English Epigram from Sir Thomas Wyatt to Ben Jonson*. Berkeley: University of California Press, 1925.

White, Harold Ogden. *Plagiarism and Imitation during the English Renaissance: A Study in Critical Distinctions*. Cambridge, Mass.: Harvard University Press, 1935.

Zwager, Nicolaas. *Glimpses of Ben Jonson's London*. 1926.

B. General

Aronstein, Phillipp. *Ben Jonson*. Berlin: E. Felber, 1906.

Bamborough, J. B. *Ben Jonson*. London: Hutchinson, 1970.

Barish, Jonas A., ed. *Ben Jonson. A Collection of Critical Essays*. Englewood Cliffs, N.J.: Prentice-Hall, 1963. Essays by T. S. Eliot, L. C. Knights, Harry Levin, Edmund Wilson, C. H. Herford, Jonas Barish, Paul Goodman, Edward B. Partridge, Ray L. Heffner, Jr., Joseph H. Bryant, Jr., Dolora Cunningham.

Blissett, William, Julian Patrick, R. W. Van Fossen, eds. *A Celebration of Ben Jonson*. Toronto: University of Toronto Press, 1973. Previously unpublished essays by Clifford Leech, Jonas Barish, George Hibbard, D. F. McKenzie, Hugh Maclean, L. C. Knights.

Castle, Edward J. *Shakespeare, Bacon, Jonson, and Greene: A Study*. London: Low, Marston, 1897.

Castelain, M. *Ben Jonson, l'Homme et l'Oeuvre.* Paris, 1907.

Eliot, T. S. *The Sacred Wood.* London: Methuen, 1920. Includes seminal essay on Jonson.

Grene, Nicholas. *Shakespeare, Jonson, Molière: The Comic Contract.* London: Macmillan, 1980.

Hibbard, G. R., ed. *The Elizabethan Theatre IV.* Hamden, Conn.: Macmillan Co. of Canada Ltd., 1974. Previously unpublished essays on Jonson by S. Schoenbaum, T. J. B. Spencer, William Blissett, Eugene M. Waith, S. P. Zitner, Edward B. Partridge.

Johnston, George Burke. *Ben Jonson: Poet.* Columbia University Studies in English and Comparative Literature, No. 162. New York: Columbia University Press, 1945. First major critical study of Jonson as a poet.

Kaufmann, R. J., ed. *Elizabethan Drama: Modern Essays in Criticism.* New York: Oxford University Press, 1961.

Keast, William R., ed. *Seventeenth-Century English Poetry: Modern Essays in Criticism.* Rev. ed. New York: Oxford University Press, 1971.

Klein, David. *The Elizabethan Dramatists as Critics.* New York: Philosophical Library, 1963.

Knights, L. C. "Ben Jonson, Dramatist," in *Guide to English Literature,* vol. II, ed. Boris Ford. Baltimore: Penguin Books, 1956. pp. 302–11.

Kronenberger, Louis. *The Thread of Laughter: Chapters on English Stage Comedy from Jonson to Maugham.* New York: Alfred A. Knopf, 1952.

Leggatt, Alexander. *Ben Jonson: His Vision and His Art.* London: Methuen, 1981.

McCollom, William G. *The Divine Average: A View of Comedy.* Cleveland: Case Western Reserve University Press, 1971. Contains a chapter on *Bartholomew Fair.*

Mason, H. A. *Humanism and Poetry in the Early Tudor Period.* London: Routledge and Kegan Paul, 1959. Focuses on the works of More, Wyatt, and Jonson.

Messiaen, Pierre. *Theatre Anglais, Moyen-Age et XVIe siècle: Anonymes, Marlowe, Dekker, Heywood, Ben Jonson, Webster, Tourneur. . . .* Nouvelle traduction française avec remarques et notes. Paris: Desclee de Brouwer, 1948.

Mézières, Alfred Jean François. *Prédécesseurs et Contemporains de Shakespeare.* 2nd ed. Paris: Charpentier Libraire-éditeur, 1863.

Miner, Earl. *The Cavalier Mode from Jonson to Cotton.* Princeton, N.J.: Princeton University Press, 1971.

Nicoll, Allardyce. "The Growth of Realistic Comedy: Ben Jonson," in *World Drama from Aeschylus to Anouilh.* New York: Harcourt-Brace, 1949, pp. 288–93.

Nicoll, Allardyce. *English Drama: A Modern Viewpoint.* New York: Barnes and Noble, 1968. Jonson is discussed in Chapter 5, on Jacobean realism and artificiality.

Orgel, Stephen. *The Illusion of Power: Political Theater in the English Renaissance.* Berkeley: University of California Press, 1975. Extensive discussion of Jonson's masques.

Ornstein, Robert. *The Moral Vision of Jacobean Tragedy.* Madison: Wisconsin University Press, 1960.

Palmer, John. *Ben Jonson.* New York: Viking, 1934.

Parfitt, A. *Ben Jonson: Public Poet and Private Man.* New York: Barnes and Noble, 1977.

[Quinn, Edward.] "Jonson, Ben[jamin] (1572–1637)," in *The Reader's Encyclopedia of World Drama,* ed. John Gassner. New York: Thomas Y. Crowell Company, 1969, pp. 494–96.

[Ribner, Irving.] "Jonson, Ben[jamin] (1572–1637)," in *The Reader's Encyclopedia of Shakespeare,* ed. Oscar James Campbell and Edward G. Quinn. New York: Thomas Y. Crowell Company, 1966, pp. 406–8.

Smith, G. Gregory. *Ben Jonson.* London: Macmillan, 1919.

Stoll, Elmer Edgar. *Poets and Playwrights: Shakespeare, Jonson, Spenser, Milton.* Minneapolis: University of Minnesota Press, 1930:.

Summers, Claude J., and Ted-Larry Pebworth. *Ben Jonson.* Boston: Twayne Publishers, 1979.

Swinburne, A. C. *A Study of Ben Jonson.* London: Chatto and Windus, 1889. Highly influential on modern criticism.

Symonds, J. A. *Ben Jonson.* London: Longmans, Green, 1888.

Thomas, Mary Olive, ed. "Ben Jonson: Quadricentennial Essays." A special issue of *Studies in the Literary Imagination,* 6, no. 1 (April 1973). Previously unpublished essays by Alvin B. Kernan, George A. E. Parfitt, Marvin L. Vawter, L. A. Beaurline, David McPherson, Richard Levin, M. C. Bradbrook, Ian Donaldson, Edward B. Partridge, William Kerrigan, Richard S. Peterson.

Upton, J. *Remarks on three Plays of Ben Jonson.* London, 1749. [*Volpone, Epicoene, Alchemist.*]

von Baudissin, W. *Ben Jonson und seine Schule.* 2 vols. Leipzig, 1836.

Wada, Yuichi. *Ben Jonson.* Tokyo: Kenkyusha, 1963.

Walton, Geoffrey. *Metaphysical to Augustan.* London: Bowes and Bowes, 1955. Contains a chapter on the tone of Jonson's poetry, showing he anticipated the Augustans.

C. Specialized

A Score for Lovers Made Men, ed. Andrew J. Sabol. Providence: Brown University Press, 1963.

Allen, Percy. *Shakespeare, Jonson, and Wilkins as Borrowers: A Study in Elizabethan Dramatic Origins and Imitations.* London: C. Palmer, 1928.

Arnold, Judd. *A Grace Peculiar: Ben Jonson's Cavalier Heroes.* Penn State University Studies No. 35. University Park, Penn., 1972.

Barish, Jonas A. *Ben Jonson and the Language of Prose Comedy.* Cambridge, Mass.: Harvard University Press, 1960.

Barish, Jonas A., ed. *Jonson: "Volpone"; a Casebook.* London: Macmillan, 1972.

Baskerville, C. R. *English Elements in Jonson's Early Comedy.* Texas University Bulletin, no. 178, 1911.

Baum, Helena Watts. *The Satiric and the Didactic in Ben Jonson's Comedies.* Chapel Hill: University of North Carolina Press, 1947.

Beaurline, L. A. *Jonson and Elizabethan Comedy: Essays in Dramatic Rhetoric.* San Marino, Cal.: Huntington Library, 1978.

Bentley, Gerald Eades. *Shakespeare and Jonson. Their Reputations in the Seventeenth Century Compared.* 2 vols. Chicago: University of Chicago Press, 1945.

Bentley, Gerald Eades. *The Swan of Avon and the Bricklayer of Westminster.* Inaugural lecture at Princeton University, March 15, 1946. Princeton University Press, 1948.

Berlin, Normand. *The Base String: The Underworld in Elizabethan Drama.* Rutherford, N.J.: Fairleigh Dickinson University Press, 1968. Chapter 4 deals with Jonson and his treatment of the thieves, rogues, and vagabonds that populated the "Elizabethan underworld."

Bevington, David. "Shakespeare vs. Jonson on Satire," in *Shakespeare 1971: Proceedings of the World Shakespeare Congress, Vancouver, August 1971,* ed. Clifford Leech and J. M. R. Margeson. Toronto: University of Toronto Press, 1972, pp. 107–122.

Birck, F. P. *Literarische Anspielungen in den Werken Ben Jonson's.* Strasburg, 1908.

Boughner, Daniel C. *The Devil's Disciple: Ben Jonson's Debt to Machiavelli.* New York: Philosophical Library, 1968.

Bradley, J. F., and Adams, J. Q. *The Jonson Allusion-Book, 1597–1700.* New Haven: Yale University Press, 1922.

Bryant, J. A., Jr. *The Compassionate Satirist: Ben Jonson and His Imperfect World.* Athens, Georgia: University of Georgia Press, 1972.

Capone, Giovanna. *Ben Jonson: L'iconologia verbale come strategia de commedia.* Bologna: Casa Editrice Patron, 1969.

[Cartwright, Robert.] *Shakespeare and Jonson: Dramatic versus Wit Combats.* London: J. R. Smith, 1864.

Chalfont, Fran C. *Ben Jonson's London: A Jacobean Placename Dictionary.* Athens: University of Georgia Press, 1978.

Champion, Larry S. *Ben Jonson's "Dotages": A Reconsideration of the Late Plays.* Lexington: University of Kentucky Press, 1967.

Chan, Mary. *Music in the Theatre of Ben Jonson.* Oxford: Clarendon Press, 1980.

Davis, Joe Lee. *The Sons of Ben: Jonsonian Comedy in Caroline England.* Detroit: Wayne State University Press, 1967.

DeLuna, Barbara Nielson. *Jonson's Romish Plot: A Study of "Catiline" and Its Historical Context.* Oxford: Clarendon Press, 1967.

Dessen, Alan C. *Jonson's Moral Comedy.* Evanston: Northwestern University Press, 1971.

deVocht, Henry. *Comments on the Text of Ben Jonson's Cynthias Revels; An Investigation into the Comparative Value of the 1601-Quarto and 1616-Folio. Materials for the Study of the Old English Drama,* N.S., V. 21. Louvain: Uystpruyst, 1950.

deVocht, Henry. *Studies on the Texts of Ben Jonson's Poetaster and Sejanus. Materials for the Study of Old English Drama,* N.S., V. 27. Louvain: Uystpruyst, 1958.

Dick, Aliki L. *Paedeia Through Laughter: Jonson's Aristophanic Appeal to Human Intelligence.* The Hague: Mouton, 1974.

Dryden, John. *Examen of the Silent Woman.* [In *An Essay of Dramatick Poesie,* 1668.] Very influential study.

Duncan, Douglas J. M. *Ben Jonson and the Lucianic Tradition.* Cambridge: Cambridge University Press, 1979.

Enck, John J. *Jonson and the Comic Truth.* Madison: University of Wisconsin Press, 1957.

Evans, Willa McClung. *Ben Jonson and Elizabethan Music.* Lancaster, Penn.: Lancaster Press, 1929.

Ferry, Anne. *All in War with Time: Love Poetry of Shakespeare, Donne, Jonson, Marvell.* Cambridge, Mass.: Harvard University Press, 1975.

Foard, James T. *The Dramatic Dissensions of Jonson, Marston, and Dekker.* 1897.

Ford, Herbert L. *Collation of the Ben Jonson Folios, 1616–31–1640.* Oxford: University Press, 1932.

Fricker, Franz. *Ben Jonson's Plays in Performance and the Jacobean Theatre.* Bern: A. Francke, 1972.

Furniss, W. Todd. "Ben Jonson's Masques," in *Three Studies in the Renaissance: Sidney, Jonson, Milton,* ed. B. C. Nangle. New Haven: Yale University Press, 1958, pp. 89–179.

Gardiner, Judith K. *Craftsmanship in Context: The Development of Ben Jonson's Poetry.* The Hague: Mouton, 1975.

Gibbons, Brian. *Jacobean City Comedy: A Study of Satiric Plays by Jonson, Marston, and Middleton.* Cambridge, Mass.: Harvard University Press, 1968; London: Hart-Davis, 1968.

Gilbert, Allan H. *The Symbolic Persons in the Masques of Ben Jonson.* Durham, N.C.: Duke University Press, 1948.

Gilchrist, O. G. *An Examination of the Charges of Ben Jonson's Enmity towards Shakespeare.* London: Taylor and Hessey, 1808.

Goldsworthy, William Landsown. *Ben Jonson and the First Folio.* London: C. Palmer, 1931.

Gottwald, Maria. *Satirical Elements in Ben Jonson's Comedy.* Travaux de la Société des Sciences et des Lettres de Wroclaw. Wroclaw, 1969.

Gray, Arthur. *How Shakespeare "Purged" Jonson.* Cambridge, England: W. Heffer, 1928.
Greenwood, Granville George. *Ben Jonson and Shakespeare.* London: C. Palmer, 1921.
Grossmann, H. *Ben Jonson als Kritker.* Berlin, 1898.
Gum, Colburn. *The Aristophanic Comedies of Ben Jonson: A Comparative Study of Jonson and Aristophanes.* The Hague: Mouton, 1969.
Hazlitt, W. *On Shakespeare and Ben Jonson.* [In *Lectures on the English Comic Writers*, 1819.]
Hinze, Otto. *Studien zu Ben Jonsons Namengebung in seinen Dramen.* Leipzig, 1919.
Hoffschulte, H. *Ueber Ben Jonson's ältere Lustspiele.* Münster, 1894.
Hofmiller, J. *Die ersten sechs Masken Ben Jonson's in ihren Verhätnis zur antiken Literatur.* Freising, 1902.
Hollstein, Ernst. *Verhältnis von Ben Jonson "The Devil is an Ass" und John Wilsons Belphegor . . . zu Machiavellis Novelle von Belfagor.* Halle, 1901.
Hyland, Peter. *Disguise and Role-Playing in Ben Jonson's Drama.* Salzburg: Austria: Institut für Englische Sprache und Literatur, 1977.
Jackson, Gabriele B. *Vision and Judgment in Ben Jonson's Drama.* New Haven: Yale University Press, 1968.
Johansson, Bertil. *Religion and Superstition in the Plays of Ben Jonson and Thomas Middleton.* Essays and Studies on English Language and Literature, 7. Upsala: A.-B. Lundequist; Cambridge, Mass.: Harvard University Press, 1950.
Johansson, Bertil. *Law and Lawyers in Elizabethan England, as Evidenced in the Plays of Ben Jonson and Thomas Middleton.* Stockholm Studies in English, 18. Stockholm: Almqvist and Wiksell, 1967.
Jones-Davies, Marie Thérèse. *Inigo Jones, Ben Jonson et le Masque.* Paris: Didier, 1967.
Jonson's Masque of Gipsies in the Burley, Belvoir and Windsor Versions: An Attempt at Reconstruction, ed. Sir W. W. Greg. London: Oxford University Press, 1952.
Kernan, Alvin B. *The Cankered Muse: Satire of the English Renaissance.* New Haven: Yale University Press, 1959. Discusses Jonson and most of his major plays.
Kernan, Alvin B. *The Plot of Satire.* New Haven: Yale University Press, 1965. General comments on Jonson throughout; chapter 9 provides an extensive analysis of *Volpone.*
Kernan, Alvin, ed. *Two Renaissance Mythmakers: Christopher Marlowe and Ben Jonson.* Selected Papers from the English Institute, 1975–76, N.S. 1. Baltimore and London: Johns Hopkins University Press, 1977. Previously unpublished essays on Jonson by Gabriele Bernhard Jackson, Ian Donaldson, Richard C. Newton.
Kerr, M. *The Influence of Ben Jonson on English Comedy.* Philadelphia: University of Pennsylvania Press, 1912.
King, Arthur Henry. *The Language of the Satirized Characters in Poetaster: a Socio-Stylistic Analysis, 1597–1602.* Lund Stud. in Eng.: C. W. K. Gleerup, 1941.
Kirsch, Arthur A. "Guarini and Jonson," in *Jacobean Dramatic Perspectives.* Charlottesville: University of Virginia Press, 1972, pp. 7–24.
Kirschbaum, Leo. "Jonson, Seneca, and *Mortimer,*" in *Studies in Honor of John Wilcox,* ed. A. Dayle Wallace and Woodburn O. Ross. Detroit: Wayne State University Press, 1958, pp. 9–22.
Knights, L. C. *Drama and Society in the Age of Jonson.* London: Chatto and Windus, 1937.
Knoll, Robert E. *Ben Jonson's Plays: An Introduction.* Lincoln: University of Nebraska Press, 1964.

Koeppel, Emil. *Ben Jonson's Wirkung auf zeitgenössiche Dramatiker. . . .* Heidelberg: C. Winter, 1906.

Koeppel, Emil. *Quellenstudien zu den Dramen Ben Jonson's, John Marston's, und Beaumont's und Fletcher's.* Erlangen, 1895.

Lever, J. W. *The Tragedy of State.* London: Methuen, 1971. *Sejanus.*

Linklater, Eric. *Ben Jonson and King James.* London: J. Cape, 1931.

Lumley, Eleanor Patience. *The Influence of Plautus on the Comedies of Ben Jonson.* New York: Knickerbocker Press, 1901.

McClung, William Alexander. *The Country House in English Renaissance Poetry.* Berkeley and Los Angeles: University of California Press, 1977.

McEuen, K. A. *Classical Influence upon the Tribe of Ben.* Cedar Rapids, Iowa, 1939.

McKennen, W. *Critical Theory and Poetic Practice in Jonson.* 1937.

Maclean, Hugh. "Ben Jonson's Poems: Notes on the Ordered Society," in *Essays in English Literature from the Renaissance to the Victorian Age. Presented to A. S. P. Woodhouse,* ed. Millar MacLure and F. W. Watt. Toronto: University of Toronto Press, 1964, pp. 43–68.

Meagher, John C. *Method and Meaning in Jonson's Masques.* Notre Dame, Indiana: University of Notre Dame Press, 1966.

Musgrove, Sydney. *Shakespeare and Jonson.* The MacMillan Brown Lectures. New Zealand: Auckland University College Bulletin, No. 51, English Series No. 9, 1957.

Nason, A. H. *Heralds and Heraldry in Ben Jonson's Plays.* New York, 1907.

Nichols, J. G. *The Poetry of Ben Jonson.* New York: Barnes and Noble, 1969.

Noyes, Robert Gale. *Ben Jonson on the English Stage, 1660–1776.* Cambridge, Mass.: Harvard University Press, 1935.

Orgel, Stephen. *The Jonsonian Masque.* Cambridge, Mass.: Harvard University Press, 1965.

Partridge, A. C. *The Accidence of Ben Jonson's Plays, Masques, and Entertainments. With an Appendix of Comparable Uses in Shakespeare.* Cambridge: Bowes and Bowes, 1953.

Partridge, A. C. *Studies in the Syntax of Ben Jonson's Plays.* Cambridge: Bowes and Bowes, 1953.

Partridge, Edward B. *The Broken Compass: A Study of the Major Comedies of Ben Jonson.* London: Chatto and Windus; Cambridge, Mass.: Harvard University Press, 1958.

Pennanen, Esko V. *Chapters on the Language of Ben Jonson's Dramatic Works.* Annales Universitatis Turkuensis, Series B., 39. Turku, 1951.

Penniman, Josiah Harmar. *The War of the Theatres.* Boston: Ginn and Co., 1897.

Peterson, Richard S. *Imitation and Praise in the Poems of Ben Jonson.* New Haven: Yale University Press, 1980.

Pfeffer, Karl. *Das elisabethanische in seiner Verwendung Sprichtwort bei Jonson.* Gissen, 1933.

Platz, Norbert H. *Ethik und Rhetorik in Ben Jonsons Dramen.* Heidelberg: Winter, 1976.

Platz-Waury, Elke. *Jonsons Komische Charaktere: Untersuchungen zum Verhältnis von Dichtungstheorie und Bühnenpraxis.* Nürnberg: Hans Carl, 1976.

Praz, M. *L'Italia di Jonson. Rivista italiana del dramma,* 1937. [Reprinted in his *Machiavelli in Inghilterra ed altri saggi,* Rome, 1942.]

Praz, Mario. "Ben Jonson's Italy," in *The Flaming Heart: Essays on Crashaw, Machiavelli, and Other Studies in the Relations Between Italian and English Literature from Chaucer to T. S. Eliot.* Gloucester, Mass.: P. Smith, 1958.

Proebstef, L. *The Progress in the Comedies of Jonson from Classicism to Pure Realism.* 1941.

Randall, Dale B. J. *Jonson's Gypsies Unmasked: Background and Theme of The Gypsies Metamorphos'd.* Durham, N.C.: Duke University Press, 1975.

Redwine, James D., Jr., ed. *Ben Jonson's Literary Criticism*. Regents Critics Series. Lincoln: University of Nebraska Press, 1970.

Reinsch, H. *Ben Jonsons Poetik und seine Beziehungen zu Horaz*. Naumburg, 1898.

Rendall, Gerald H. *Ben Jonson and the First Folio Edition of Shakespeare's Plays*. Colchester: Benham, 1939.

Sackton, A. H. *Rhetoric as a Dramatic Language in Jonson*. New York: Columbia University Press, 1948.

The Sad Shepherd, Completed by Alan Porter. New York, 1944.

Saegelken, C. *Ben Jonson's Römerdramen*. Bremen, 1880.

Savage, James E. *Ben Jonson's Basic Comic Characters and Other Essays*. University and College Press of Mississippi, 1973.

Schelling, F. E. *Ben Jonson and the Classical School*. Baltimore, 1898. Seminal essay.

Sisson, C. J. "A Topical Reference in *The Alchemist*," in *John Quincy Adams: Memorial Studies*. Washington, D.C.: Folger Shakespeare Library, 1948, pp. 739–41.

Small, R. A. *The Stage Quarrel Between Ben Jonson and the So-Called Poetasters*. Breslau, 1899.

Stagg, Louis C. *Index to the Figurative Language of Ben Jonson's Tragedies*. Charlottesville: Biblio. Society of the University of Virginia, 1967.

Stainer, C. L. *Jonson and Drummond, their Conversations. A Few Remarks on an 18th Century Forgery*. Oxford: B. Blackwell, 1925.

Sternfeld, Frederick W. "Song in Jonson's Comedy: A Gloss on *Volpone*." *Studies in the English Renaissance Drama*, ed. Josephine W. Bennett, Oscar Cargill and Vernon Hall, Jr. New York: New York University Press, 1959, pp. 310–21.

Sturmberger, Ingeborg Maria. *The Comic Elements in Ben Jonson's Drama*. 2 vols. Salzburg, Austria: Institut für Englische Sprache und Literatur, 1975.

Taylor, Dick, Jr. "Clarendon and Ben Jonson as Witnesses for the Earl of Pembroke's Character," in *Studies in the English Renaissance Drama*, ed. Josephine W. Bennett, Oscar Cargill, and Vernon Hall, Jr. New York: New York University Press, 1959, pp. 322–44.

Taylor, George C. "Did Shakespeare, Actor, Improvise in *Every Man In His Humour*?" in *John Quincy Adams Memorial Studies*, ed. J. G. McManaway, G. E. Dawson, and E. A. Willoughby. Washington, D.C.: The Folger Shakespeare Library, 1948.

Thayer, C. G. *Ben Jonson: Studies in the Plays*. Norman: University of Oklahoma Press, 1963.

Tiedje, Egon. *Die Tradition Ben Jonsons in der Restaurationskomodie*. Hamburg: Cram, de Gruyfer & Co., 1963.

Townsend, Freda L. *Apologie for Bartholomew Fayre: The Art of Jonson's Comedies*. New York: The Modern Language Association of America, 1947.

Trimpi, Wesley. *Ben Jonson's Poems: A Study of the Plain Style*. Palo Alto: Stanford University Press, 1963.

Ure, Peter. "Shakespeare and the Drama of his Time: Jonson and the Satirists," in *A New Companion to Shakespeare Studies*, ed. Kenneth Muir and S. Schoenbaum. Cambridge: Cambridge University Press, 1971, pp. 216–18.

Vogt, Adolf. *Ben Jonsons Tragödie Catiline his Conspiracy und ihre Quellen*. Halle, 1905.

Walton, Geoffrey, "The Tone of Ben Jonson's Poetry," in *Seventeenth-Century English Poetry: Modern Essays in Criticisms*, ed. William R. Keast. New York: Oxford University Press, 1962, pp. 193–214.

Wheeler, C. F. *Classical Mythology in the Plays, Masques, and Poems of Jonson*. Princeton, 1938.

Woodbridge, E. *Studies in Jonson's Comedy*. Boston: Lamson, Wolffe, 1898.